# Rick Steves

## BEST OF

# ENGLAND

# Contents

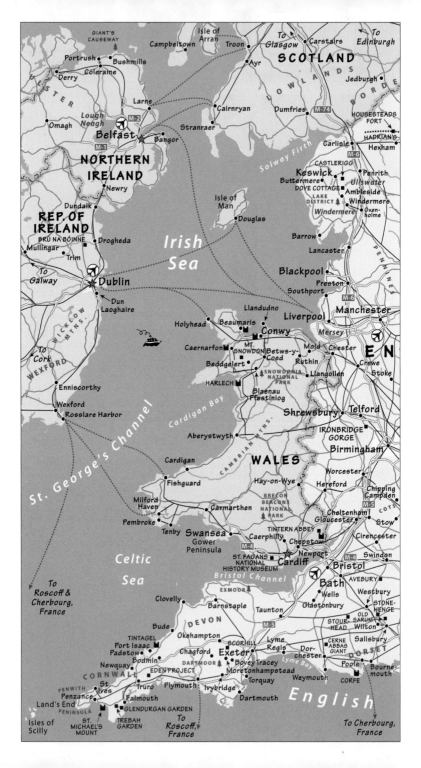

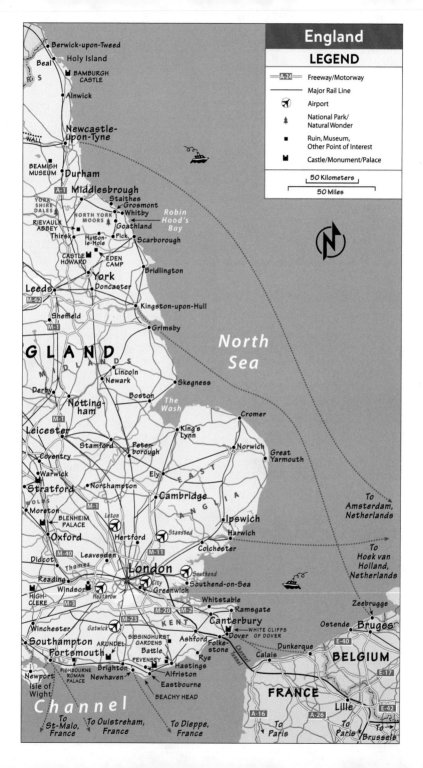

# Introduction

Climb the dome of St. Paul's Cathedral and marvel at the pageantry of the guards at Buckingham Palace. Strike up a conversation just to hear the Queen's English. Ponder an ancient stone circle and wander the windswept hills that inspired Wordsworth. See a Shakespeare play or the latest splashy West End musical. Bite into a scone smothered with clotted cream, sip a cup of tea, and wave your pinky as if it's a Union Jack. From some of the most appealing towns you'll ever experience to the grandeur of London, England delights.

England is the cultural heart of the United Kingdom and a touchstone for the almost one billion people who speak English. This ever-popular tourist destination has a strange influence and power over us. Regardless of the revolution we had a couple of centuries back, many American travelers feel that they "go home" when they visit England.

The English people have a worldwide reputation for being cheery, courteous, and well-mannered. When times get tough, they maintain a stiff upper lip ("Keep calm and carry on" is a now-famous English motto from pre-World War II).

Even as England races forward as a leading global player, it preserves its rich past. This means stone circles, ruined abbeys, cathedrals, castles, and palaces are still yours to explore.

Britannia rules—enjoy it royally.

## THE BEST OF ENGLAND

In this selective book, I recommend England's top destinations, offering a mix of exciting cities and irresistible villages.

London is one of the grandest cities in the world. The town of Bath has attracted visitors for centuries—back to the time of ancient Rome. Quaint Cotswolds towns offer an endearing contrast to the modern-day world. Literary Stratford spawned Shakespeare, while workaday Liverpool launched the Beatles. The serene Lake District—crisscrossed with trails, ridges,

and lakes—has enough pubs to keep hikers watered and fed. York, with its colorful old town and ghost walks, is a popular haunt for travelers.

Beyond the major destinations, I'll briefly cover the Best of the Rest—great destinations that don't quite make my top cut, but are worth seeing if you have more time or specific interests: historic Cambridge, stately Oxford, and small Durham with its huge cathedral.

To help you link the top sights, I've designed a two-week itinerary (see page 28) with tips to help you tailor it to your interests and time.

# THE BEST OF LONDON

This thriving, teeming metropolis packs in all things British with a cosmopolitan flair: royal palaces, soaring churches, world-class museums, captivating theater, and people-friendly parks. Come prepared to celebrate the tradition and fanfare of yesterday while catching the buzz of a city that's trumpeting its future.

❶ *London's many grand parks provide a peaceful respite from the big city.*

❷ *Plays at **Shakespeare's Globe** attract modern-day Juliets and Romeos.*

❸ *Spanning the Thames, the pedestrian-only **Millennium Bridge** connects St. Paul's Cathedral and Tate Modern.*

❹ *Fortunately, the pomp and pageantry of the **Changing of the Guard** never changes.*

❺ *It's easy to eat well and affordably in cosmopolitan London.*

❻ *A statue of Churchill overlooks historic **Parliament Square.***

❼ *The **London Eye** Ferris wheel, a fun addition to the cityscape, offers stunning views to riders.*

❽ *Street performers give London a lively vibe.*

# THE BEST OF BATH

This genteel Georgian showcase city, built around the remains of an ancient Roman bath, hosts an abbey, museums, a spa, walking tours, and graceful architecture that was part of Jane Austen's world.

Proud locals remind visitors that the town is routinely banned from the "Britain in Bloom" contest to give other towns a chance to win.

❶ Bath's glorious **abbey** takes center stage in town.

❷ **Jane Austen** lived—and set two of her novels—in Bath.

❸ The **baths** that gave the town its unusual name date to Roman times.

❹ The **Pump Room** has tea, goodies, and samples of "curative" spa water to drink.

❺ The fanciful **Parade Gardens,** worth a stroll, are near the shop-lined Pulteney Bridge.

❻ The **Bizarre Bath walking tour** makes any evening enjoyable.

❼ The **Thermae Bath Spa** taps the thermal springs burbling under Bath.

❽ The lawn in front of the **Royal Crescent** offers a royal place to relax.

# THE BEST OF THE COTSWOLDS

Scattered over this hilly countryside are fragrant fields, peaceful sheep, and dear villages. My favorites are cozy Chipping Campden and engaging Stow-on-the-Wold—each with pubs, hikes, and charm to spare. All the Cotswold towns run on slow clocks and yellowed calendars. If the 21st century has come, they don't care.

❶ *Lovely little **Chipping Campden** invites and rewards exploration.*

❷ *Sheep are as much a part of the Cotswolds as the people.*

❸ *Visitors cool off at **Bourton-on-the-Water.***

❹ *In the Cotswolds, the towns pose for pictures.*

❺ *In **Broadway,** as in other Cotswold towns, the buildings—made of local limestone—give off a warm glow.*

❻ *At **Cotswold Farm Park,** it's easy to make friends with a goat.*

❼ *Pubs throughout the Cotswolds provide an atmospheric destination for hikers, bikers, and drivers.*

# THE BEST OF STRATFORD-UPON-AVON

All the world's a stage, but if you want to see Shakespeare's work performed, his hometown is the top venue. Its half-timbered buildings, pleasant riverside setting, and above all, its wealth of Shakespeare sights—from the Bard's birthplace to his family home to his grave—have earned Stratford its popularity and place in history.

❶ *Shakespeare courted his wife at* **Anne Hathaway's Cottage,** *where she grew up.*

❷ *Through his work, Shakespeare explored the sweet sorrow of the human condition.*

❸ *The* **River Avon** *offers cruises, rental rowboats, and picnic perches.*

❹ **Mary Arden's Farm,** *where Shakespeare's mother grew up, recreates facets of 16th-century life like falconry.*

❺ *Stratford offers plays in several fine venues, including the* **Courtyard Theatre.**

❻ *The showpiece* **Royal Shakespeare Theatre,** *on the riverfront, hosts the Bard's plays.*

❼ *With its half-timbered buildings, Stratford seems a stage set for visitors.*

# THE BEST OF LIVERPOOL

A hit with Fab-Four fans, this rejuvenated port was the Beatles' hometown. Riffing off the success of this popular group, the town offers bus tours of Beatles sights by day and their catchy music played live every night. Beyond the Beatles, Liverpool provides an opportunity to sample the "real" England, with its maritime lore, dueling cathedrals, and lively nightlife.

❶ *John Lennon hangs out at the* **Cavern Club,** *named after the original club (now gone) where the Beatles played.*

❷ *Visitors can book a tour of both* **Paul McCartney's home** *(shown) and John Lennon's.*

❸ **Albert Dock** *is awash with attractions—museums, restaurants, and nighttime fun.*

❹ **Strawberry Field** *and* **Penny Lane** *are actual places that were woven into Beatles' tunes.*

❺ *The* **Museum of Liverpool** *engagingly tells the story of this salty port.*

❻ **Liverpool Cathedral** *is one of two cathedrals in the city. The other is the very modern Metropolitan.*

❼ *The most elegant pub in town is the* **Philharmonic Dining Rooms** *(which Lennon called the Phil).*

# THE BEST OF THE LAKE DISTRICT

The Lake District, about 30 miles long and 30 miles wide, is nature's lush, green playground. This idyllic region of rugged ridges and tranquil lakes offers scenic hikes, cruises, joyrides, timeless vistas, and William Wordsworth and Beatrix Potter sights, plus an ancient stone circle perfect for pondering it all.

**❶ Keswick,** *the best home base, has an appealing main square, fine eateries, and a lovely lake.*

**❷ Ullswater** *is one of the many lakes that give the district its name.*

**❸ At Dove Cottage,** *William Wordsworth wrote his finest poetry, inspired by the wonders of nature.*

**❹** *Visitors refuel and recharge at quaint pubs.*

**❺ Castlerigg Stone Circle,** *just outside Keswick, is 5,000 years old—as old as Stonehenge.*

**❻** *B&Bs provide a welcome home away from home for relaxation.*

**❼** *An easy loop trail around* **Buttermere Lake** *rewards hikers with serene views.*

# THE BEST OF YORK

Encircled by medieval walls, compact York has a glorious Gothic cathedral, a ruined abbey, modern museums (on Vikings and more), and an atmospheric old center called The Shambles. Founded in ancient Roman times, today's new York still knows how to draw a crowd.

❶ York's massive **Minster** offers up a divine evensong and magnificent, medieval stained glass.

❷ The **National Railway Museum**'s models range from early "stagecoaches on rails" to the sleek Eurostar.

❸ Marching past the Minster, British Army soldiers play bagpipes.

❹ A Viking amusement ride or a museum?

**Jorvik Viking Centre** is a bit of both.

❺ Breaking from the pope, Henry VIII closed all monasteries, leaving many—like **St. Mary's Abbey**—in ruins.

❻ Along the **Shambles** street, shops hang old-fashioned signs from old, tilting buildings.

❼ At **Bettys Café Tea Rooms,** window seats offer the best people-watching.

# THE BEST OF THE REST

With extra time, splice any of these destinations into your trip. **Cambridge,** a historic college town, has educated Newton, Darwin, and visitors who've taken its excellent walking tour. **Oxford** also shows off its impressive colleges, along with nearby **Blenheim Palace**—good enough for Churchill. **Durham,** known for its cavernous cathedral, has an open-air museum nearby and **Hadrian's Wall** beyond.

❶ *Durham's cathedral has Europe's tallest bell tower and memorials for saints, scholars, and coal miners.*

❷ *Durham's Castle offers tours of its great hall, chapel, and kitchens.*

❸ *Boasting 83 Nobel Prize winners, **Cambridge** is one of England's most successful college towns.*

❹ *In Cambridge and Oxford, rental punts await unsuspecting novices who think punting looks easy.*

❺ *The dining hall at **Oxford**'s Christ Church College puts most college cafeterias to shame.*

❻ *Near Oxford, **Blenheim Palace** attracts historians and garden lovers.*

❼ *Did **Newton's Tree** descend from the tree that inspired Newton to study gravity? Cambridge thinks so.*

❽ *Built by Romans, the now-ruined **Hadrian's Wall** blocked out invaders from what is now Scotland.*

# TRAVEL SMART

Approach England like a veteran traveler, even if it's your first trip. Design your itinerary thoughtfully, study up in advance to better understand your sightseeing, and follow the travel strategies here for the best possible experience.

## Designing an Itinerary

**Choose your top destinations.** My itinerary (on page 28) gives you an idea of how much you can reasonably see in 14 days, but you can adapt it to fit your own interests and timeframe.

London offers an amazing variety of sights, food, and the most entertainment. Historians can choose among sights prehistoric (Stonehenge), Roman (Bath), medieval (York), and royal (Tower of London, Windsor, Blenheim, and more). Nature lovers linger in the Lake District (with a range of easy-to-hard hikes in a lake-and-hills setting) and the Cotswolds (with easier hiking through villages and meadows). If you want to learn about historic colleges and enjoy the punting scene, try Cambridge or Oxford. Jesters and jousters enjoy Warwick Castle. Beatles fans from here, there, and everywhere head to Liverpool. Literary fans make a pilgrimage to Stratford (Shakespeare), Bath (Austen), and the Lake District (Wordsworth and Potter). Photographers want to go everywhere.

**Decide when to go.** July and August are peak season in England, with long days, the best weather, and a busy schedule of tourist fun. May and June can be lovely anywhere. Spring and fall have fewer crowds and decent weather.

Winter travelers encounter few crowds and soft room prices (except in London), but sightseeing hours are shorter and the weather is reliably bad. In the countryside, some attractions open only on weekends or close entirely (Nov-Feb). While rural charm falls with the leaves, city sightseeing is fine in winter.

**Connect the dots.** Link your destinations into a logical route. If your plans extend beyond England, determine which cities in Europe you'll fly into and out of (begin your search for transatlantic flights at Kayak.com).

Decide if you'll be traveling by car, public transportation, or a combination. A car is helpful for exploring the Cotswolds and the Lake District, where public transportation can be time-consuming, but is use-

less in cities (park it). You can rent a car for just a day or two (specifics are in pertinent chapters). If relying solely on trains, these cities are easy to visit: London, Bath, Oxford, Moreton-in-Marsh (Cotswolds), Stratford, Liverpool, and York. To reach Keswick in the Lake District, add a bus ride and it's yours. With more time, buses, and minibus tours, everything is workable without a car.

If your trip extends beyond England, look into budget flights (check Sky scanner.com for cheap flights within Europe).

**Fine-tune your itinerary.** Figure out how many destinations you can comfortably fit in the time you have. Don't overdo it—few travelers wish they'd hurried more. Allow enough days per destination. Check if any holidays or festivals will fall during your trip—these attract crowds and can close sights (for the latest, visit England's website, www.visitbritain.com).

Instead of spending the first few days of your trip in busy London, I'd recommend a gentler small-town start in Bath (the ideal jet-lag pillow), letting London be the finale of your trip. Going from Heathrow Airport to Bath takes just two hours by train. You'll be more rested and ready to tackle England's greatest city.

For detailed suggestions on how to spend your time, I've included day plans for destinations in the chapters that follow.

**Balance intense and relaxed days.** After a day of hectic sightseeing, plan for some downtime. Follow up big cities with laid-back towns. Minimize one-night stands to maximize rootedness; it's worth taking a drive (or bus ride) after dinner to get settled in a town for two nights. Staying in a home base (like London) and making day trips can be more time-efficient than changing locations and hotels.

**Give yourself some slack.** Every trip—and every traveler—needs slack time (laundry, picnics, people-watching, and so on). Many travelers greatly underestimate this. You can't see it all, so pace yourself. Assume you will return.

**Ready, set...** You've designed the perfect itinerary for the trip of a lifetime.

## Trip Costs per Person

Run a reality check on your dream trip. You'll have major transportation costs in addition to daily expenses.

**Flight:** A round-trip flight from the US to London costs about $1,000-2,000.

**Car Rental:** Figure on a minimum of $250 per week, not including tolls, gas, parking, and insurance. Weekly rentals and leases are cheapest if arranged from the US.

## ♫ Rick Steves Audio Europe

My free **Rick Steves Audio Europe app** makes it easy for you to download my **audio tours** of many of Europe's top

attractions. For this book, my audio tours cover these major sights and neighborhoods in London: Westminster Walk, British Museum, British Library, St. Paul's Cathedral, and the City of London (financial district). Sights covered by my audio tours are marked with this symbol: ♫. The app also offers a far-reaching library of insightful **travel interviews** from my public radio show with experts from around the globe—including many of the places in this book.

The Rick Steves Audio Europe app and all of its content are free. You can download it via Apple's App Store, Google Play, or the Amazon Appstore. For more info, see www.ricksteves.com/audioeurope.

# BEST OF ENGLAND IN 2 WEEKS

This unforgettable trip will show you the very best England has to offer. You can use public transit, rent a car, or use a combination. Renting a car for just a day or two is most fun in the Cotswolds and the Lake District.

| DAY | PLAN | SLEEP IN |
|---|---|---|
| | Arrive in London, head to Bath (2 hours by train from Heathrow, transfer at London's Paddington Station) | Bath |
| 1 | Bath | Bath |
| 2 | Bath | Bath |
| 3 | To Cotswolds (2 hours by train to Moreton-in-Marsh, then 45-minute bus ride) | Chipping Campden |
| 4 | Cotswolds | Chipping Campden |
| 5 | To Stratford (1 hour by bus) | Stratford-upon-Avon |
| 6 | To Liverpool (3 hours by train) | Liverpool |
| 7 | To Lake District (2.5 hours by train to Penrith, then 45 minutes by bus) | Keswick |
| 8 | Lake District | Keswick |
| 9 | To York (45 minutes by bus to Penrith, then 3.5 hours by train) | York |
| 10 | York | York |
| 11 | To London (2 hours by train) | London |
| 12 | London | London |
| 13 | London | London |
| 14 | London | London |
| | Fly home | |

If Shakespeare and the Beatles aren't your cup of tea, you could swap out Stratford or Liverpool for Oxford and/or Blenheim Palace.

If you start your trip in London (instead of Bath), keep in mind that you'll need to book another night in London at the end of your trip, so you'll be ready to fly home the next day. For a fun finale, book tickets for a musical for your last night in London.

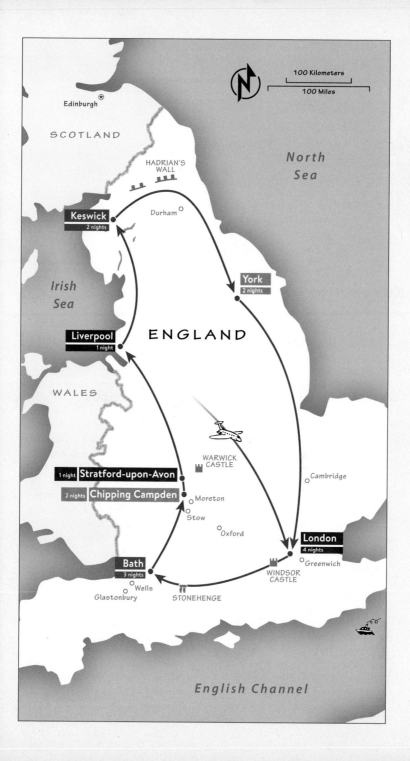

## Average Daily Expenses per Person: $160 in England ($200 in London)

| Cost | Category | Notes |
|---|---|---|
| $45 | Meals | $15 for lunch and $30 for dinner |
| $75 | Lodging | Based on two people splitting the cost of a $150 double room that includes breakfast (allow $180/double room in London); solo travelers pay about $100 per room |
| $30 | Sights and Entertainment | Figure $20-40 per major sight, $7 for minor ones, and $35-50 for splurges; figure an average of $30/day ($55/day for London) |
| $10 | City Transit | Tube or buses |
| $160 | **Total** | Figure on $200 in London |

**Public Transportation:** For a two-week trip, you'd spend about $600 to cover train and bus fares, including Tube fare in London. To reduce your train costs, you'll likely save money by getting a Brit-rail England Pass (8 days in a month, "standard" class cheaper than first class, buy in US); for specifics, see page 388. By purchasing individual train tickets online, you can get advance-purchase discounts, though you'll be locked into the travel time you choose; a rail pass gives you more flexibility if your plans change.

**Budget Tips:** It's easy to cut your daily expenses to about $100/day, particularly outside of London. Cultivate the art of picnicking, stay in hostels or cheap hotels, and see only the sights you most want to see. You could save money by limiting your time in pricey London, but even London offers some relief for budget travelers; seek out its free museums, concerts, and events (see page 56). When you splurge, save it for an experience you'll always remember (such as a walking tour, bus tour, concert, Shakespeare play, or a fun musical). Minimize souvenir shopping—how will you get it all home? Focus instead on collecting wonderful, lifelong memories.

## Travel Strategies on the Road

**Be your own tour guide.** As you travel, get up-to-date info on sights, reserve tickets and tours, reconfirm hotels and travel arrangements, and check transit connections. Upon arrival in a new town, lay the groundwork for a smooth departure; confirm the train, bus, or road you'll take when you leave. You can find out the latest by checking with tourist-information offices (TIs) and your hoteliers, and doing research on your own by phone or online.

**Join tours.** Your appreciation of a city and its history can increase dramatically if you join a tour in any big city (try London Walks) or at a museum (some offer live or audio tours), or even hire a private guide (some will drive you around). If you want to learn more about any aspect of England, you're in the right place with experts happy to teach you in a language you understand.

## *Before You Go*

❑ **Make sure your passport is valid.** If it's due to expire within six months of your ticketed date of return, renew it. Allow up to six weeks to get or renew a passport (www.travel.state.gov).

❑ **Book rooms well in advance,** especially if your trip falls during peak season (July-Aug) or any major holidays or festivals. For tips on making hotel reservations, see page 381.

❑ **Consider booking plays, sights, or tours in advance.** If there's a particular **play** you absolutely must see, you can buy tickets before you go (www.officiallondontheatre.co.uk; for Stratford, www.rsc.org.uk); otherwise get tickets on site. At **Stonehenge,** most are happy to view the stones from a distance, but if you want to go inside the circle, you'll need reservations (see www.english-heritage.uk/stonehenge). You can reserve a **tour** of the interior of Lennon and McCartney homes in Liverpool (see www.nationaltrust.org.uk/beatles).

❑ **Arrange your transportation.** Rent a car, or get a rail pass, or order train tickets for longer trips to get advance-purchase discounts. (You can wing it in Europe, but it may cost more.) If traveling to or from continental Europe on the Eurostar train, you can order a ticket in advance or buy it in Europe.

❑ **Consider travel insurance.** Compare the cost of the insurance to the cost of your potential loss. Check whether your existing insurance (health, homeowners, or renters) covers you and your posses-sions overseas. For tips, see www.ricksteves.com/insurance.

❑ **Call your bank.** Alert your bank that you'll be using your debit and credit cards in Europe; also ask about transaction fees, and get the PIN number for your credit card (see page 371). You won't need to bring along pounds for your trip—instead, withdraw currency from cash machines in England.

❑ **Bringing your phone?** Consider an international plan to reduce the cost of calls, texts, and data (or rely on Wi-Fi). See page 383 for different ways to stay connected in Europe.

❑ **Download apps** to your mobile device to use on the road, such as maps, transit schedules, and my free *Rick Steves Audio Europe* app (which has audio tours of London's top sights and most interesting neighborhoods).

❑ **Watt's up?** Bring an electrical adapter with three rectangular prongs (sold at travel stores in the US) to plug into England's outlets. You won't need a convertor because newer electronics—such as tablets, laptops, and battery chargers—are dual voltage and convert automat-ically to Europe's 220-volt system. Don't bring an old hair dryer or curler; buy a cheapie in Europe.

❑ **Pack light.** You'll walk with your luggage far more than you think (see packing list on page 401).

❑ **Refer to the Practicalities chapter,** where you'll find every-thing you need to know to travel smoothly in England.

❑ **Get updates** to this book at www.ricksteves.com/update.

**Take advantage of deals.** You'll find deals throughout England (and mentioned in this book). For example, early-bird dinners at nice restaurants are often a great value. City transit passes (for multiple rides or all-day usage) lessen your cost per ride. To take the financial bite out of sightseeing, consider combo-tickets and passes that cover multiple museums. Busy sightseers can get country-wide passes covering many sights (see page 42). Some accommodations give a discount for payment in cash and/or longer stays.

**Plan for rain.** No matter when you go, the weather can change several times in a day, but rarely is it extreme. Bring a jacket and dress in layers. Just keep traveling and enjoy the "bright spells." A bout of rain is the perfect excuse to go into a pub and make a new friend.

**Outsmart thieves.** Although theft isn't a major problem outside of London, it's still smart to wear a money belt. Tuck it under your clothes, and keep your cash, credit cards, and passport secure inside it. Carry only a day's spending money in your front pocket. In case of loss or theft, see page 369.

Be proactive to minimize the effects of potential loss: Keep your expensive gear to a minimum. Bring photocopies of important documents (passport and cards) to aid in replacement if they're lost or stolen. While traveling, back up your digital photos and files frequently.

**Guard your time, energy, and trip.** Taking a taxi can be a good value if it saves you a long wait for a cheap bus or an exhausting walk across town. To avoid long lines, take advantage of the crowd-beating tips in this book (such as visiting sights early or late). When problems arise (bad food, a late bus, or drizzly days), keep things in perspective. You're on vacation...and you're in England!

**Connect with the culture.** Enjoy the friendliness of the English people; most interactions come with an ample side-helping of fun banter. Ask questions—many locals are as interested in you as you are in them. Slow down, step out of your comfort zone, and be open to unexpected experiences. When an interesting opportunity pops up, say "yes."

Have a brilliant holiday!

*Rick Steves*

## Key to This Book

### Updates

This book is updated regularly—but things change. For the latest, visit www.ricksteves.com/update.

### Abbreviations and Times

I use the following symbols and abbreviations in this book:

Sights are rated:

▲▲▲ Don't miss

▲▲ Try hard to see

▲ Worthwhile if you can make it

**No rating** Worth knowing about

Tourist information offices are abbreviated as **TI,** and bathrooms are **WC**s. To categorize accommodations, I use a **Sleep Code** (described on page 379).

Like Europe, this book uses the **24-hour clock.** It's the same through 12:00 noon, and then keeps going: 13:00, 14:00, and so on. For anything over 12, subtract 12 and add p.m. (14:00 is 2:00 p.m.).

When giving **opening times,** I include both peak season and off-season hours if they differ. So, if a museum is listed as "May-Oct daily 9:00-16:00," it should be open from 9 a.m. until 4 p.m. from the first day of May until the last day of October (but expect exceptions).

For **transit** or **tour departures,** I first list the frequency, then the duration. So, a train connection listed as "2/hour, 1.5 hours" departs twice each hour, and the journey lasts an hour and a half.

## Map Legend

| | | |
|---|---|---|
| ⅄ Viewpoint | 🐂 Prehistoric Sight | )▭( Tunnel |
| ♠ Entrance | Ⓣ Taxi Stand | ------ Railway |
| ✪ Tourist Info | —🇹— Tram | ┅┅┅ Mtn. Rail |
| 🆆🅲 Restroom | Ⓑ Bus Stop | ·········· Ferry/Boat Route |
| ♜ Castle, Manor House | 🅿 Parking | ⊕ Airport |
| ⛪ Church | ⊖ Tube | ⅢⅢⅢ Stairs |
| ▪ Statue/Point of Interest | Pedestrian Zone | ····· Walk/Tour Route |
| ⚑ Pub | Park | ------ Trail |

# London

**A** longtime tourist destination, London seems perpetually at your service, with an impressive slate of sights and entertainment. Blow through this urban jungle on the open deck of a double-decker bus and take a pinch-me-I'm-here walk through the West End. Hear the chimes of Big Ben and ogle the crown jewels at the Tower of London. Cruise the Thames River and take a spin on the London Eye. Hobnob with poets' tombstones in Westminster Abbey and rummage through civilization's attic at the British Museum.

London is also more than its museums and landmarks, it's a living, breathing, thriving organism...a coral reef of humanity. The city has changed dramatically in recent years: Many visitors are surprised to find how diverse and cosmopolitan it is. Chinese takeouts outnumber fish-and-chips shops. Eastern Europeans pull pints in British pubs, and Italians express your espresso. Outlying suburbs are home to huge communities of Indians and Pakistanis. This city of eight million separate dreams is learning—sometimes fitfully—to live as a microcosm of its formerly vast empire.

## LONDON IN 4 DAYS

**Day 1:** Get oriented by taking my Westminster Walk from Big Ben to Trafalgar Square (stop in Westminster Abbey and the Churchill War Rooms on the way). Grab lunch near Trafalgar Square (maybe at the café at St. Martin-in-the-Fields Church), then visit the nearby National Gallery or National Portrait Gallery.

**On any evening:** Have an early-bird dinner and take in a play in the West End or at Shakespeare's Globe. Choose from a concert, walking tour, or nighttime bus tour. Extend your sightseeing into the evening hours; some attractions stay open late (see page 101). Settle in at a pub, or do some shopping at any of London's elegant department stores (generally open until 21:00). Stroll any of the main squares, fine parks, or the Jubilee Walkway for people-watching. Ride the London Eye Ferris wheel for grand city views.

**Day 2:** Take a double-decker hop-on, hop-off sightseeing bus tour from Victoria Station, and hop off for the Changing of the Guard at Buckingham Palace. After lunch, tour the British Museum and/or the nearby British Library.

**Day 3:** At the Tower of London, see the crown jewels and take the Beefeater tour. Then grab a picnic, catch a boat at Tower Pier, and have lunch on the Thames while cruising to Blackfriars Pier.

Tour St. Paul's Cathedral and climb its dome for views, then walk across Millen-

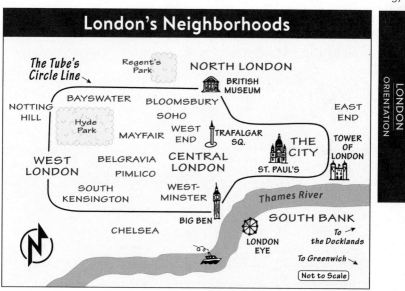

## London's Neighborhoods

The Tube's Circle Line

Regent's Park

NORTH LONDON

BRITISH MUSEUM

NOTTING HILL

BAYSWATER

Hyde Park

MAYFAIR

BLOOMSBURY

SOHO

WEST END

TRAFALGAR SQ.

EAST END

TOWER OF LONDON

WEST LONDON

BELGRAVIA

PIMLICO

CENTRAL LONDON

ST. PAUL'S

THE CITY

SOUTH KENSINGTON

WEST-MINSTER

Thames River

CHELSEA

BIG BEN

LONDON EYE

SOUTH BANK

To the Docklands

To Greenwich

Not to Scale

nium Bridge to the South Bank to visit the Tate Modern, tour Shakespeare's Globe, or stroll the Jubilee Walkway.

**Day 4:** Take your pick of the Victoria and Albert Museum, Tate Britain, Imperial War Museum, or Houses of Parliament. Hit one of London's many lively open-air markets. Or cruise to Kew Gardens or Greenwich.

# ORIENTATION

To make London more manageable, think of it as the old town in the city center without the modern, congested sprawl.

The Thames River (pronounced "tems") runs roughly west to east through the city, with most sights on the North Bank. Mentally, trim down your map to include only the area between the Tower of London (to the east), Hyde Park (west), Regent's Park (north), and the South Bank (south). This is roughly the area bordered by the Tube's Circle Line. This four-mile stretch between the Tower and Hyde Park (about a 1.5-hour walk), which looks like a milk bottle on its side, holds most of the sights mentioned in this chapter.

**Central London** contains **Westminster,** the location of Big Ben, Parliament, Westminster Abbey, Buckingham Palace, and Trafalgar Square, with its many major museums. It also includes the **West End,** the center of London's cultural life, where bustling Piccadilly Circus and Leicester Square host cinemas, tourist traps, and nighttime glitz. Soho and Covent Garden are thriving people zones with theaters, restaurants, pubs, and boutiques. And Regent and Oxford streets are the city's main shopping zones.

**North London** and its neighborhoods—including Bloomsbury, Fitzrovia, and Marylebone—contain such major sights as the British Museum and the overhyped Madame Tussauds Waxworks. Nearby, along busy Euston Road, is the British Library.

**"The City,"** which is today's modern financial district, was a walled town in Roman times. Gleaming skyscrapers are interspersed with historical landmarks such as St. Paul's Cathedral and the Museum of London. The Tower of London and Tower Bridge lie at The City's eastern border.

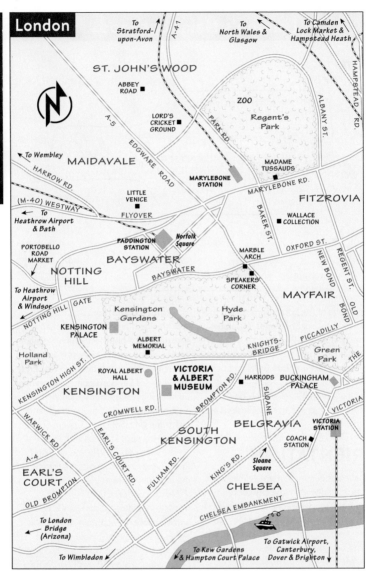

## London

To Stratford-upon-Avon
A-41
To North Wales & Glasgow
To Camden Lock Market & Hampstead Heath
HAMPSTEAD RD.

ST. JOHN'S WOOD
ABBEY ROAD
ZOO
Regent's Park
ALBANY ST.
LORD'S CRICKET GROUND
A-5
PARK RD.
EDGWARE ROAD
To Wembley
MAIDAVALE
HARROW RD.
MARYLEBONE STATION
MADAME TUSSAUDS
MARYLEBONE RD.
(M-40) WESTWAY
LITTLE VENICE
FITZROVIA
To Heathrow Airport & Bath
FLYOVER
BAKER ST.
WALLACE COLLECTION
PADDINGTON STATION
Norfolk Square
MARBLE ARCH
OXFORD ST.
NEW BOND ST.
REGENT ST.
PORTOBELLO ROAD MARKET
BAYSWATER
BAYSWATER
SPEAKERS' CORNER
MAYFAIR
OLD BOND
NOTTING HILL
To Heathrow Airport & Windsor
NOTTING HILL GATE
Kensington Gardens
Hyde Park
KENSINGTON PALACE
ALBERT MEMORIAL
KNIGHTS-BRIDGE
PICCADILLY
Green Park
THE
Holland Park
KENSINGTON HIGH ST.
ROYAL ALBERT HALL
VICTORIA & ALBERT MUSEUM
HARRODS
BUCKINGHAM PALACE
KENSINGTON
CROMWELL RD.
BROMPTON RD.
SLOANE
VICTORIA
WARWICK RD.
EARL'S COURT RD.
SOUTH KENSINGTON
BELGRAVIA
COACH STATION
VICTORIA STATION
A-4
FULHAM RD.
KING'S RD.
Sloane Square
EARL'S COURT
OLD BROMPTON
CHELSEA
To London Bridge (Arizona)
CHELSEA EMBANKMENT
To Wimbledon
To Kew Gardens & Hampton Court Palace
To Gatwick Airport, Canterbury, Dover & Brighton

The **East End** is the increasingly gentrified former stomping ground of Cockney ragamuffins and Jack the Ripper.

The **South Bank** of the Thames River offers major sights—Tate Modern, Shakespeare's Globe, and the London Eye—linked by a riverside walkway. Within this area, Southwark (SUTH-uck) stretches from the Tate Modern to London Bridge. Pedestrian bridges connect the South Bank with The City and Trafalgar Square.

**West London** contains neighborhoods such as Mayfair, Belgravia, Pimlico, Chelsea, South Kensington, and Notting Hill. It's home to London's wealthy and has many trendy shops and enticing restau-

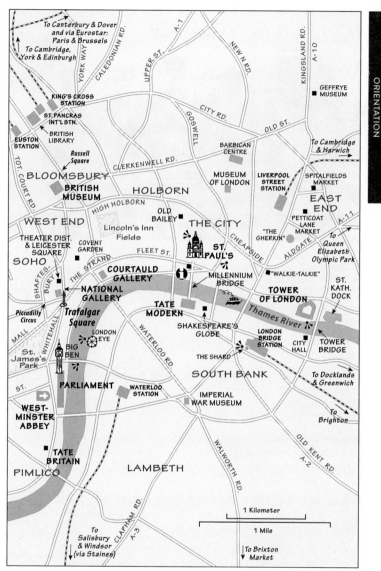

rants. Here you'll find the Victoria and Albert Museum, Tate Britain, and more museums, lively Victoria Station, and the vast green expanses of Hyde Park and Kensington Gardens.

Kew Gardens are outside the city center, southwest of London.

**Rick's Tip:** *Through an initiative called* **Legible London,** *the city has erected* **pedestrian-focused maps around town**—*especially handy when exiting* **Tube stations.** *In this sprawling city—where predictable grid-planned streets are relatively rare—it's smart to buy and use a good map.*

# LONDON AT A GLANCE

▲▲▲**Westminster Abbey** Britain's finest church and the site of royal coronations and burials since 1066. **Hours:** Mon-Fri 9:30-16:30, Wed until 19:00, Sat 9:30-14:30, closed Sun to sightseers except for worship. See page 49.

▲▲▲**Churchill War Rooms** Underground WWII headquarters of Churchill's war effort. **Hours:** Daily 9:30-18:00. See page 58.

▲▲▲**National Gallery** Remarkable collection of European paintings (1250-1900), including Leonardo, Botticelli, Velázquez, Rembrandt, Turner, Van Gogh, and the Impressionists. **Hours:** Daily 10:00-18:00, Fri until 21:00. See page 60.

▲▲▲**British Museum** The world's greatest collection of artifacts of Western civilization, including the Rosetta Stone and the Parthenon's Elgin Marbles. **Hours:** Daily 10:00-17:30, Fri until 20:30 (selected galleries only). See page 69.

▲▲▲**British Library** Fascinating collection of important literary treasures of the Western world. **Hours:** Mon-Fri 9:30-18:00, Tue until 20:00, Sat 9:30-17:00, Sun 11:00-17:00. See page 73.

▲▲▲**St. Paul's Cathedral** The main cathedral of the Anglican Church, designed by Christopher Wren, with a climbable dome and daily evensong services. **Hours:** Mon-Sat 8:30-16:30, closed Sun except for worship. See page 76.

▲▲▲**Tower of London** Historic castle, palace, and prison housing the crown jewels and a witty band of Beefeaters. **Hours:** Tue-Sat 9:00-17:30, Sun-Mon 10:00-17:30; Nov-Feb closes one hour earlier. See page 82.

▲▲▲**Victoria and Albert Museum** The best collection of decorative arts anywhere. **Hours:** Daily 10:00-17:45, Fri until 22:00 (selected galleries only). See page 95.

▲▲**Houses of Parliament** Landmark famous for Big Ben and occupied by the Houses of Lords and Commons. **Hours:** When Parliament is in session, generally open Mon-Thu, closed Fri-Sun and most of Aug-Sept. Guided tours offered year-round on Sat and most weekdays during Aug-Sept. See page 53.

▲▲**Trafalgar Square** The heart of London, where Westminster, The City, and the West End meet. **Hours:** Always open. See page 58.

▲▲**National Portrait Gallery** A who's who of British history, featuring portraits of this nation's most important historical figures. **Hours:** Daily 10:00-18:00, Thu-Fri until 21:00, first and second floors open Mon at 11:00. See page 63.

▲▲**Covent Garden** Vibrant people-watching zone with shops, cafés, street musicians, and an iron-and-glass arcade that once hosted a produce market. **Hours:** Always open. See page 64.

▲▲**Changing of the Guard at Buckingham Palace** Hour-long spectacle at Britain's royal residence. **Hours:** Generally May-July daily at 11:30, Aug-April every other day. See page 66.

▲▲**London Eye** Enormous observation wheel, dominating—and offering commanding views over—London's skyline. **Hours:** Daily 10:00-20:30, later in July and Aug. See page 87.

▲▲**Imperial War Museum** Exhibits examining the military history of the bloody 20th century. **Hours:** Daily 10:00-18:00. See page 88.

▲▲**Tate Modern** Works by Monet, Matisse, Dalí, Picasso, and Warhol displayed in a converted powerhouse. **Hours:** Daily 10:00-18:00, Fri-Sat until 22:00. See page 90.

▲▲**Shakespeare's Globe** Timbered, thatched-roofed reconstruction of the Bard's original "wooden O." **Hours:** Theater complex, museum, and actor-led tours generally daily 9:00-17:30; in summer, theater tours usually run only in morning. Plays are also staged here. See page 91.

▲▲**Tate Britain** Collection of British paintings from the 16th century through modern times, including works by William Blake, the Pre-Raphaelites, and J. M. W. Turner. **Hours:** Daily 10:00-18:00. See page 92.

## Tourist Information

It's hard to find unbiased sightseeing information in London. "Tourist Information" offices are advertised everywhere, but most are private agencies that sell tours and advance tickets for sights and the theater.

**The City of London Information Centre** next to St. Paul's Cathedral (just outside the church entrance) is the only publicly funded—and therefore impartial—TI. It sells Oyster cards, London Passes, and "Fast Track" sightseeing tickets. The TI gives out a free map of The City and sells several city-wide maps; ask if they have yet another free map with various coupons for discounts on sights (Mon-Sat 9:30-17:30, Sun 10:00-16:00; Tube: St. Paul's, tel. 020/7332-1456, www.visitthecity.co.uk).

**Visit London,** which serves the greater London area, doesn't have an office you can visit—but does have an information-packed website (www.visitlondon.com).

## Sightseeing Passes and Advance Tickets

To skip the ticket-buying queues at certain sights, you can buy **Fast Track tickets** (sometimes called "priority pass" tickets) in advance—and they can be cheaper than tickets sold right at the sight. They're smart for the Tower of London, London Eye, and Madame Tussauds Waxworks, which get busy in high season. They're available through various sales outlets around London (including the City of London TI, souvenir stands, and faux-TIs scattered throughout touristy areas).

The **London Pass** covers many big sights and lets you skip some lines. It's expensive but potentially worth the investment for extremely busy sightseers (£52/1 day, multiday options available; sold at City of London TI, major train stations, and airports; www.londonpass.com).

**Rick's Tip:** *The Artful Dodger is alive and well in London.* **Beware of pickpockets,** *particularly on public transportation, among tourist crowds, and at street markets.*

## Tours

🎧 To sightsee on your own, download my **free audio tours** for London's top sights and neighborhoods (see page 27 for details).

### ▲▲▲HOP-ON, HOP-OFF BUS TOURS

London is full of hop-on, hop-off bus companies, all competing for your tourist pound. To help narrow down your options, I've focused on the two companies I like the most: **Original** and **Big Bus.** Both offer essentially the same 2-to-3-hour, £32 tour of the city's sightseeing highlights, with nearly 30 stops on each route.

**Rick's Tip:** *For an efficient intro to London, catch an 8:30 departure of a* **hop-on, hop-off overview bus tour,** *riding 90 percent of the loop (which takes just over two hours, depending on traffic), and hopping off at Buckingham Palace in time to find a good spot to watch the* **Changing of the Guard** *ceremony at 11:30.*

Each company offers at least one route with live guides, and a second (sometimes slightly different route) that comes with recorded narration. Buses run daily about every 10-15 minutes in summer, every 10-20 minutes in winter. They start

## Daily Reminder

**SUNDAY:** The Tower of London and British Museum are both especially crowded today. Speakers' Corner in Hyde Park rants from early afternoon until early evening. The Houses of Parliament are closed. Westminster Abbey and St. Paul's are open during the day for worship but closed to sightseers. With all these closures, this morning is a good time to take a bus tour. Most big stores open late (around 11:30) and close early (18:00). Street markets flourish at Camden Lock, Spitalfields (at its best today), Petticoat Lane, and Brick Lane, but the Portobello Road market is closed. Because of all the market action, it's a good day to visit the East End. Most theaters are dark today.

**MONDAY:** Virtually all sights are open. The Houses of Parliament may be open as late as 22:30.

**TUESDAY:** Virtually all sights are open. The British Library is open until 20:00, and the Houses of Parliament may be open as late as 22:00.

**WEDNESDAY:** Virtually all sights are open. The Houses of Parliament may be open as late as 22:00.

**THURSDAY:** All sights are open, plus evening hours at the National Portrait Gallery (until 21:00).

**FRIDAY:** All sights are open, except the Houses of Parliament. Sights open late include the British Museum (selected galleries until 20:30), National Gallery (until 21:00), National Portrait Gallery (until 21:00), Victoria and Albert Museum (selected galleries until 22:00), and Tate Modern (until 22:00).

**SATURDAY:** Most sights are open, except legal ones (skip The City). The Houses of Parliament are open only with a tour. Tate Modern is open until 22:00. The Tower of London is especially crowded today. Today's the day to hit the Portobello Road street market; the Camden Lock and Greenwich markets are also good.

at about 8:00 or 8:30 and run until early evening in summer or late afternoon in winter. The last full loop usually leaves Victoria Station at about 20:00 in summer, and at about 17:00 in winter.

Sunday morning—when the traffic is light and many museums are closed—is a fine time for a tour. Traffic is at its peak around lunch and during the evening rush hour (around 17:00).

Buy tickets online in advance, or on the day of your trip from drivers or at street kiosks (credit cards accepted at kiosks at major stops such as Victoria Station, ticket good for 24 hours, or 48 hours in winter).

**Original:** £32, £4 discount with this book, limit four discounts per book, they'll rip off the corner of this page—raise bloody hell if the staff or driver won't honor this discount; also online deals, info center at 17 Cockspur Street, tel. 020/8877-1722, www.theoriginaltour.com.

**Big Bus:** £32, discount available online, tel. 020/7808-6753, www.bigbustours.com.

### NIGHT BUS TOURS

Various companies offer a lower-priced, after-hours sightseeing circuit (1-2 hours). The views at twilight are grand—though note that London just doesn't do floodlighting as well as, say, Paris. **See London By Night** buses offer live guides and frequent evening departures—starting from 19:30—from Green Park (£18, next

to Ritz Hotel, tel. 020/7183-4744, www.
seelondonbynight.com). The pricier
**Golden Tours** buses depart at 19:00 and
20:00 from the Golden Tours visitor center on Buckingham Palace Road (£27, tel.
020/7630-2028; www.goldentours.com).
For a memorable and economical evening, munch a scenic picnic dinner on the
top deck. (There are plenty of takeaway
options near the departure points.)

---

**Rick's Tip:** *If you're taking a bus tour mainly
to get oriented,* **save time and money by
taking a night tour.**

---

## ▲▲WALKING TOURS

Several times a day, top-notch local
guides lead groups through specific slices
of London's past. **London Walks** lists its
daily schedule on their amusing website and in brochures available at hotels
and in racks all over town. The two-hour
walks are led year-round by professional
guides (£10 cash only, private tours for
groups-£140, tel. 020/7624-3978, tel.
020/7624-9255 for a recording of today's
or tomorrow's walks and the Tube station
they depart from, www.walks.com).

London Walks also offers day trips
into the countryside (£18 plus £36-59 for
transportation and admission costs, cash
only: Stonehenge/Salisbury, Oxford/Cots-
wolds, Cambridge, Bath, and so on).

### PRIVATE GUIDES AND DRIVERS

Rates for London's registered Blue Badge
guides are standard (about £150-165
for four hours; £240 or more for nine
hours). I know and like **Sean Kelleher** (tel.
020/8673-1624, mobile 07764-612-770,
sean@seanlondonguide.com) and **Joel
Reid,** who specializes in off-the-beaten-
track London (mobile 07887-955-720,
joelyreid@gmail.com). Also, **London
Walks** has a huge selection of guides and
can book one for your particular interest
(£180/half-day).

Guides with cars or minivans offer
regional tours for about £550/day,

depending on the itinerary. Consider
**Janine Barton** (tel. 020/7402-4600,
http://seeitinstyle.synthasite.com, jbsiis@
aol.com) or cousins **Hugh Dickson** and
**Mike Dickson** (Hugh's mobile 07771-
602-069, hughdickson@hotmail.com;
Mike's mobile 07769-905-811, michael.
dickson5@btinternet.com).

## ▲▲CRUISE BOAT TOURS

Several companies offer tourist cruises,
most on slow-moving, open-top boats
accompanied by entertaining commentary. Take a **short city-center cruise** by
riding a boat 30 minutes from Westminster Pier to Tower Pier (particularly handy
if you're interested in visiting the Tower
of London anyway), or choose a **longer
cruise** that includes a peek at the East
End, riding from Westminster all the way
to Greenwich.

Each company runs cruises daily, about
twice hourly, from morning until dark;
many reduce frequency off-season. Boats
come and go from various docks in the
city center (see sidebar). The most popular places to embark are Westminster Pier
(at the base of Westminster Bridge across
the street from Big Ben) and Waterloo
Pier (at the London Eye, across the river
on the South Bank).

A one-way trip within the city center
costs about £10. A transit card (Oyster
card or Travelcard) can earn you a discount on some cruises (see page 117).

---

**Rick's Tip:** *Zipping through London every
20-30 minutes, the* **Thames Clippers are
designed for commuters.** *With no open
deck and no commentary, they're* **not the
best option for sightseeing.**

---

The three dominant companies are
**City Cruises** (handy 45-minute cruise
from Westminster Pier to Tower Pier;
www.citycruises.com), **Thames River
Services** (fewer stops, classic boats,
friendlier and more old-fashioned feel;
www.thamesriverservices.co.uk), and

# *Thames Boat Piers*

While Westminster Pier is the most popular, it's not the only dock in town. Consider all the options (listed from west to east, as the Thames flows):

**Millbank Pier** (North Bank): At the Tate Britain Museum, used primarily by the Tate Boat service (express connection to Tate Modern at Bankside Pier).

**Westminster Pier** (North Bank): Near the base of Big Ben, offers round-trip sightseeing cruises and lots of departures in both directions (though Thames Clippers commuter boats don't stop here). Parliament and Westminster Abbey are nearby.

**Waterloo Pier** (a.k.a. London Eye Pier, South Bank): At the base of the London Eye, a good, less-crowded alternative to Westminster, with many of the same cruise options (Waterloo Station is nearby).

**Embankment Pier** (North Bank): Near Covent Garden, Trafalgar Square, and Cleopatra's Needle (the obelisk on the Thames). This pier is used mostly for lunch and dinner cruises.

**Festival Pier** (South Bank): Next to the Royal Festival Hall, just downstream from the London Eye.

**Blackfriars Pier** (North Bank): In The City, not far from St. Paul's.

**Bankside Pier** (South Bank): Directly in front of the Tate Modern and Shakespeare's Globe.

**London Bridge Pier** (South Bank): Close to London Bridge.

**Tower Pier** (North Bank): At the Tower of London, at the east edge of The City and near the East End.

**St. Katharine's Pier** (North Bank): Just downstream from the Tower of London.

**Canary Wharf Pier** (North Bank): At the Docklands.

**Circular Cruise** (full cruise takes about an hour, operated by Crown River Services, www.crownrivercruise.co.uk).

**Cruising Downstream, to Greenwich:** Both **City Cruises** and **Thames River Services** head from Westminster Pier to Greenwich. To maximize both efficiency and sightseeing, take a narrated cruise to Greenwich one way, and go the other way on the DLR (Docklands Light Railway).

**Cruising Upstream, to Kew Gardens:** **Thames River Boats,** operated by the Westminster Passenger Service Association, leave for Kew Gardens from Westminster Pier (£13 one-way, £20 round-trip, cash only, discounts with Travelcard, 2-4/

day depending on season, 1.5 hours, boats sail April-Oct, www.wpsa.co.uk).

## Helpful Hints

**Medical Help:** Hospitals have 24-hour-a-day emergency care centers. St. Thomas' Hospital, immediately across the river from Big Ben, has a fine reputation.

**Wi-Fi:** Besides your hotel, many major museums, sights, and even entire neighborhoods offer free Wi-Fi. For easy access everywhere, sign up for a free account with **The Cloud,** a Wi-Fi service found in many convenient spots around London (www.thecloud.net/free-wifi, when you sign up, you'll have to enter a street address and postal code—use your hotel's, or the Queen's: Buckingham Palace, SW1A 1AA).

**Useful Apps:** Tube travelers may want to download Mapway's free **Tube Map London Underground** (www.mapway. com), which shows the easiest way to connect station A to station B. The **Citymapper** app for London covers every mode of public transit in the city. **City Maps 2Go** lets you download searchable offline maps; their London version is quite good. **Time Out** London's free app has reviews and listings for theater, museums, movies, and more (the "Make Your City Amazing" version is updated weekly).

**Maps:** Bensons *London Street Map,* sold at many newsstands and bookstores, is my favorite for efficient sightseeing and might be the best £3 you'll spend. I also like the *Handy London Map and Guide* version, which shows every little lane and all the sights, and comes with a transit map.

**Baggage Storage:** Train stations have replaced lockers with more secure left-luggage counters. Each bag must go through a scanner (just like at the airport). Expect long waits in the morning to check in (up to 45 minutes) and in the afternoon to pick up (most stations daily 7:00-23:00). You can also store bags at the airports (www.left-baggage.co.uk).

# WESTMINSTER WALK

Just about every visitor to London strolls along the historic Whitehall road from Big Ben to Trafalgar Square. This walk gives you a whirlwind tour as well as a practical orientation to London. Most of the sights you'll see are described in more detail later. (🎧 You can download a free, extended audio version of this walk to your mobile device; see page 27.)

---

**Rick's Tip: Cars drive on the left side of the road**—*as confusing for foreign pedestrians as for foreign drivers. Always look right, look left, then look right again just to be sure.* **Jaywalking is treacherous** *when you're disoriented about which direction traffic is coming from.*

---

## ❷ Self-Guided Walk

Start halfway across ❶ **Westminster Bridge** for that "Wow, I'm really in London!" feeling. Get a close-up view of the **Houses of Parliament** and **Big Ben.** Downstream you'll see the **London Eye,** the city's giant Ferris wheel. Down the

OXFORD CIRCUS STATION

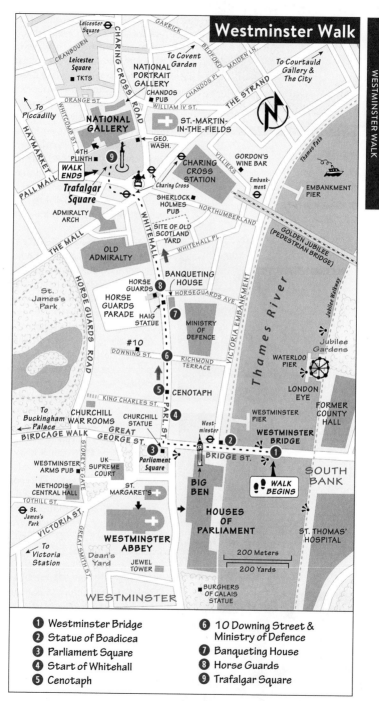

# Westminster Walk

Leicester
Square

Cranbourn

Leicester
Square
■ TKTS

GARRICK

CHARING CROSS ROAD

BEDFORD

MAIDEN LN.

To Covent
Garden

NATIONAL
PORTRAIT
GALLERY

CHANDOS
PUB

CHANDOS PL.

THE STRAND

To Courtauld
Gallery &
The City

ORANGE ST.

To
Piccadilly

WHITCOMB ST.

NATIONAL
GALLERY

WILLIAM IV ST.

ST.-MARTIN-
IN-THE-FIELDS

N

Thames Path

HAYMARKET

PALL MALL

4TH
PLINTH

GEO.
WASH.

❾

WALK
ENDS

Trafalgar
Square

CHARING
CROSS
STATION

VILLIERS

GORDON'S
WINE BAR

Charing Cross

Embank-
ment

EMBANKMENT
PIER

SHERLOCK
HOLMES
PUB

ADMIRALTY
ARCH

THE MALL

WHITEHALL

SITE OF OLD
SCOTLAND
YARD

NORTHUMBERLAND

WHITEHALL PL.

GOLDEN JUBILEE
(PEDESTRIAN BRIDGE)

OLD
ADMIRALTY

HORSE GUARDS ROAD

St.
James's
Park

BANQUETING
HOUSE

Horse
Guards

HORSE
GUARDS
PARADE

❽

HORSEGUARDS AVE.

❼

HAIG
STATUE

MINISTRY
OF
DEFENCE

VICTORIA EMBANKMENT

Thames River

Jubilee Walkway

#10

DOWNING ST.

❻

RICHMOND
TERRACE

WATERLOO
PIER

Jubilee
Gardens

❺

CENOTAPH

KING CHARLES ST.

LONDON
EYE

WESTMINSTER
PIER

FORMER
COUNTY
HALL

To
Buckingham
Palace

CHURCHILL
WAR ROOMS

GREAT
GEORGE ST.

CHURCHILL
STATUE

PARL. ST.

❹

West-
minster

❷

WESTMINSTER
BRIDGE

BIRDCAGE WALK

STOREY'S GATE

WESTMINSTER
ARMS PUB ■

UK
SUPREME
COURT

❸

Parliament
Square

BRIDGE ST.

❶

SOUTH
BANK

METHODIST
CENTRAL HALL

ST.
MARGARET'S

BIG
BEN

WALK
BEGINS

TOTHILL ST.

St.
James's
Park

VICTORIA ST.

GREAT SMITH ST.

HOUSES
OF
PARLIAMENT

ST. THOMAS'
HOSPITAL

To
Victoria
Station

WESTMINSTER
ABBEY

Dean's
Yard

JEWEL
TOWER

200 Meters

200 Yards

WESTMINSTER

■ BURGHERS
OF CALAIS
STATUE

❶ Westminster Bridge

❷ Statue of Boadicea

❸ Parliament Square

❹ Start of Whitehall

❺ Cenotaph

❻ 10 Downing Street &
Ministry of Defence

❼ Banqueting House

❽ Horse Guards

❾ Trafalgar Square

Ⓐ *Boadicea statue*
Ⓑ *Churchill statue in Parliament Square*
Ⓒ *Horse Guards*
Ⓓ *Banqueting House*

stairs to Westminster Pier are boats to the Tower of London and Greenwich (downstream) or Kew Gardens (upstream).

Near Westminster Pier is a big statue of a lady on a chariot. This is ❷ **Boadicea,** the Celtic queen who unsuccessfully resisted Roman invaders in A.D. 60. Julius Caesar was the first Roman general to cross the Channel, but even he was weirded out by the island's strange inhabitants, who worshipped trees, sacrificed virgins, and went to war painted blue. Later, Romans subdued and civilized them, building roads and making this spot on the Thames—"Londinium"—a major urban center.

For fun, call home from near Big Ben at about three minutes before the hour to let your loved one hear the bell ring. You'll find four red phone booths lining the north side of ❸ **Parliament Square** along Great George Street—also great for a phone-box-and-Big-Ben photo op.

Wave hello to Winston Churchill and Nelson Mandela in Parliament Square. To Churchill's right is the historic **Westminster Abbey,** with its two stubby, elegant towers. The white building (flying the Union Jack) at the far end of the square houses Britain's **Supreme Court.**

Head north up Parliament Street, which turns into ❹ **Whitehall,** and walk toward Trafalgar Square. In the middle of the boulevard you'll see the ❺ **Cenotaph** memorial, reminding passersby of the many Brits who died in the last century's world wars. To visit the **Churchill War Rooms,** take a left before the Cenotaph, on King Charles Street.

Continuing on Whitehall, stop at the barricaded and guarded ❻ **#10 Downing Street** to see the British "White House." This has been the traditional home of the prime minister since the position was created in the early 18th century. Break the bobby's boredom and ask him a question. The huge building across Whitehall from Downing Street is the **Ministry of Defence** (MOD), the "British Pentagon."

Nearing Trafalgar Square, look for the
❼ **Banqueting House** across the street.
England's first Renaissance building (1619-
1622) was designed by Inigo Jones, built
by King James I, and decorated by his son
Charles I. It's one of the few landmarks
spared by the fire that devastated London
in 1698. Today, you can enjoy its ceiling
paintings by Peter Paul Rubens—and the
exquisite hall itself (£6.60, daily 10:00-
17:00, may close for government functions, www.hrp.org.uk).

Also take a look at the ❽ **Horse
Guards** behind the gated fence. For 200
years, soldiers in cavalry uniforms have
guarded this arched entrance that leads
to Buckingham Palace. These elite troops
constitute the Queen's personal body-
guard. They change daily at 11:00 (10:00
on Sun), and a colorful dismounting ceremony takes place daily at 16:00.

❾ **Trafalgar Square,** London's central
meeting point, bustles around the world's
biggest Corinthian column, topped by
Admiral Horatio Nelson (he's celebrated
for defeating the once-invincible French
Napoleonic navy, off the coast of Spain's
Cape Trafalgar, in 1805). The stately
domed building on the far side of the
square is the **National Gallery,** filled with

the national collection of European paintings. To the right is the 1722 **St. Martin-in-
the-Fields Church.** Its steeple-over-the-
entrance style is the inspiration behind
many town churches in New England.

• *Our Westminster walk is over. But if you
want to keep going, walk up Cockspur Street
to Haymarket, then take a short left on
Coventry Street to colorful Piccadilly Circus.
Near here, you'll find a number of theaters
and Leicester Square, with its half-price
"TKTS" booth for plays (see page 100).
Covent Garden, with street musicians and
shops, is nearby.*

# SIGHTS

## Central London
### Westminster
These sights are listed in roughly geo-
graphical order from Westminster Abbey
to Trafalgar Square, and are linked in my
self-guided Westminster Walk, earlier,
and the ∩ free Westminster Walk audio
tour (see page 27 for details).

### ▲▲▲WESTMINSTER ABBEY
The greatest church in the English-
speaking world, Westminster Abbey
is where the nation's royalty has been
wedded, crowned, and buried since
1066. Indeed, the histories of Westminster Abbey and England are almost
the same. A thousand years of English
history—3,000 tombs, the remains of
29 kings and queens, and hundreds of
memorials to poets, politicians, scientists,
and warriors—lie within its stained-glass
splendor and under its stone slabs.

**Cost and Hours:** £20, £40 family ticket
(2 adults and 1 child), includes audioguide
and entry to cloisters; Mon-Fri 9:30-16:30,
Wed until 19:00 (main church only), Sat
9:30-14:30, last entry one hour before
closing, closed Sun to sightseers but open
for services; cloisters—daily 8:00-18:00;
no photos allowed, café in cellar, Tube:
Westminster or St. James's Park, tel. 020/
7222-5152, www.westminster-abbey.org.

*Trafalgar Square and St. Martin-in-the-Fields*

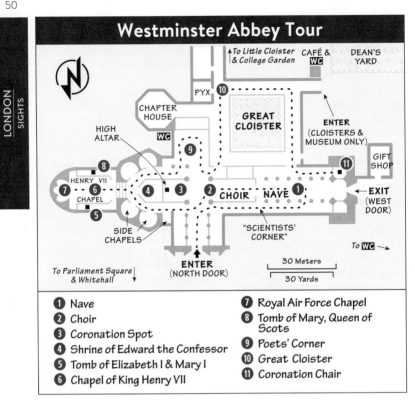

# Westminster Abbey Tour

▲To Little Cloister
& College Garden

CAFÉ &
**WC**

DEAN'S
YARD

PYX ⑩

CHAPTER
HOUSE

GREAT
CLOISTER

ENTER
(CLOISTERS &
MUSEUM ONLY)

HIGH
ALTAR

**WC**

⑨

GIFT
SHOP

⑧

HENRY VII

⑪

⑦ ⑥

④ ▪ ③ ② CHOIR NAVE ① ← EXIT
(WEST
DOOR)

CHAPEL

⑤

SIDE
CHAPELS

"SCIENTISTS'
CORNER"

To **WC** →

To Parliament Square
& Whitehall ↓

ENTER
(NORTH DOOR)

30 Meters

30 Yards

| | |
|---|---|
| ① Nave | ⑦ Royal Air Force Chapel |
| ② Choir | ⑧ Tomb of Mary, Queen of Scots |
| ③ Coronation Spot | |
| ④ Shrine of Edward the Confessor | ⑨ Poets' Corner |
| ⑤ Tomb of Elizabeth I & Mary I | ⑩ Great Cloister |
| ⑥ Chapel of King Henry VII | ⑪ Coronation Chair |

*The west facade of Westminster Abbey*

Rick's Tip: Westminster Abbey *is most crowded at midmorning and all day Saturday and Monday.* **Visit early, during lunch, or late.** *Weekdays after 14:30—especially Wednesday—are less congested; come after that time and stay for the 17:00 evensong. From April through September, you can bypass the long line at the main entrance by* **booking advance tickets online** *at www. westminster-abbey.org.*

It's free to enter just the cloisters (through Dean's Yard, around the right side as you face the main entrance), but if it's too crowded inside, the marshal at the cloister entrance may not let you in.

**Church Services and Music: Mon-Fri** at 7:30 (prayer), 8:00 (communion), 12:30 (communion), 17:00 evensong (except on Wed, when the evening service is generally spoken—not sung); **Sat** at 8:00 (communion), 9:00 (prayer), 15:00 (evensong; May-Aug it's at 17:00); **Sun** services generally come with more music: at 8:00 (communion), 10:00 (sung Matins), 11:15 (sung Eucharist), 15:00 (evensong), and 18:30 (evening service). Services are free to anyone. Free **organ recitals** are usually held Sun at 17:45 (30 minutes).

**Tours:** The included **audioguide** is excellent. To add to the experience, you can take an entertaining **guided tour** from a verger—the church equivalent of a museum docent (£5, schedule posted both outside and inside entry, up to 6/day in summer, 2-4/day in winter, 1.5 hours).

## ◑ SELF-GUIDED TOUR

You'll have no choice but to follow the steady flow of tourists through the church, along the route laid out for the audioguide. My tour covers the Abbey's top stops.

• *Walk straight through the north transept. Follow the crowd to the right and enter the spacious...*

**❶ Nave:** The Abbey's 10-story nave is the tallest in England. With saints in stained glass, heroes in carved stone, and the bodies of England's greatest citizens under the floor stones, Westminster Abbey is the religious heart of England.

Find Edward the Confessor, the king who built the Abbey, in the stained-glass windows on the left side of the nave (as you face the altar). He's in the third bay from the end (marked *S: Edwardus rex...*), with his crown, scepter, and ring.

On the floor near the west entrance of the Abbey is the flower-lined Grave of the Unknown Warrior, an ordinary WWI soldier buried in soil from France with lettering made from melted-down weapons from that war. Contemplate the million-man army from the British Empire and all those who gave their lives. Their memory is so revered that when Kate Middleton walked up the aisle on her wedding day, by tradition she had to step around the tomb (and her wedding bouquet was later placed atop this tomb, also in accordance with tradition).

• *Walk up the nave toward the altar. This is the same route every future monarch walks before being crowned. Midway up the nave, you pass through the colorful enclosure known as the...*

**❷ Choir:** These elaborately carved wood and gilded seats are where monks once chanted their services in the "quire"—as it's known in British church-speak. Today, it's where the Abbey boys' choir sings the evensong. You're approaching the center of a cross-shaped church. The "high" (main) altar, which usually has a cross and candlesticks atop it, sits on the platform up the five stairs in front of you.

• *It's on this platform that the monarch is crowned.*

**❸ Coronation Spot:** The area immediately before the high altar is where every English coronation since 1066 has taken place. Royalty are also given funerals here. Princess Diana's coffin was carried to this spot for her funeral service in 1997. The "Queen Mum" (mother of Elizabeth II) had her funeral here in 2002. This is also where most of the last century's royal weddings have taken place, including the unions of Queen Elizabeth II and Prince Philip (1947), Prince Andrew and Sarah Ferguson (1986), and Prince William and Kate Middleton (2011).

• *Veer left and follow the crowd. Pause at the wooden staircase on your right.*

**❹ Shrine of Edward the Confessor:** Step back and peek over the dark coffin of Edward I to see the tippy-top of the green-and-gold wedding-cake tomb of King Edward the Confessor—the man who built Westminster Abbey.

God had told pious Edward to visit St. Peter's Basilica in Rome. But with the Normans planning conquest, it was too dangerous for him to leave England. Instead, he built this grand church and dedicated it to St. Peter. It was finished just in time to bury Edward and to crown his foreign successor, William the Conqueror, in 1066. After Edward's death, people prayed at his tomb and got good results, so Pope Alexander III canonized

him. This elevated central tomb—which lost some of its luster when Henry VIII melted down the gold coffin-case—is surrounded by the tombs of eight kings and queens.

• *At the top of the stone staircase, veer left into the private burial chapel of Queen Elizabeth I.*

**❺ Tomb of Queens Elizabeth I and Mary I:** Although only one effigy is on the tomb (Elizabeth's), there are actually two queens buried beneath it, both daughters of Henry VIII (by different mothers). Bloody Mary—meek, pious, sickly, and Catholic—enforced Catholicism during her short reign (1553-1558) by burning "heretics" at the stake.

Elizabeth—strong, clever, and Protestant—steered England on an Anglican course. She holds a royal orb symbolizing that she's queen of the whole globe. When 26-year-old Elizabeth was crowned in the Abbey, her right to rule was questioned (especially by her Catholic subjects) because she was considered the bastard seed of Henry VIII's unsanctioned marriage to Anne Boleyn. But Elizabeth's long reign (1559-1603) was one of the greatest in English history, a time when England ruled the seas and Shakespeare explored human emotions. When she died, thousands turned out for her funeral in the Abbey. Elizabeth's face on the tomb, modeled after her death mask, is considered an accurate take on this hook-nosed, imperious "Virgin Queen" (she never married).

• *Continue into the ornate, flag-draped room up a few more stairs, directly behind the main altar.*

**❻ Chapel of King Henry VII** (The Lady Chapel): The colorful banners overhead and the elaborate tracery in stone, wood, and glass give this room the festive air of a medieval tournament. The prestigious Knights of the Bath meet here, under the magnificent ceiling studded with gold pendants. The ceiling—of carved stone (1519)—is the finest English

*Tomb of Elizabeth I (and Mary I)*

Perpendicular Gothic and fan vaulting you'll see (unless you're going to King's College Chapel in Cambridge). The ceiling was sculpted on the floor in pieces, then jigsaw-puzzled into place. It capped the Gothic period and signaled the vitality of the coming Renaissance.

• *Go to the far end of the chapel and stand at the banister in front of the modern set of stained-glass windows.*

**❼ Royal Air Force Chapel:** Saints in robes and halos mingle with pilots in parachutes and bomber jackets. This tribute to WWII flyers is for those who earned their angel wings in the Battle of Britain (July-Oct 1940). A bit of bomb damage has been preserved—look for the little glassed-over hole in the wall below the windows in the lower left-hand corner.

• *Exit the Chapel of Henry VII. Turn left into a side chapel with the tomb (the central one of three in the chapel).*

**❽ Tomb of Mary, Queen of Scots:** The beautiful, French-educated queen (1542-1587) was held under house arrest for 19 years by Queen Elizabeth I, who considered her a threat to her sovereignty. Elizabeth got wind of an assassination plot, suspected Mary was behind it, and had her first cousin (once removed) beheaded. When the childless Elizabeth died, Mary's son, James VI, King of Scots, also became King James I of England and Ireland. James buried his mum here (with her head sewn back on) in the Abbey's most sumptuous tomb.

• *Exit Mary's chapel. Continue on, until you*

*emerge in the south transept. You're in...*

**❾ Poets' Corner:** England's greatest artistic contributions are in the written word. Here the masters of arguably the world's most complex and expressive language are remembered: Geoffrey Chaucer *(Canterbury Tales)*, Lord Byron, Dylan Thomas, W. H. Auden, Lewis Carroll *(Alice's Adventures in Wonderland)*, T. S. Eliot *(The Waste Land)*, Alfred Tennyson, Robert Browning, and Charles Dickens. Many writers are honored with plaques and monuments; relatively few are actually buried here. Shakespeare is commemorated by a fine statue that stands near the end of the transept, overlooking the others.

• *Exit the church (temporarily) at the south door, which leads to the...*

**❿ Great Cloister:** The buildings that adjoin the church housed the monks. Cloistered courtyards gave them a place to meditate on God's creations. Monks had daily meetings in the **Chapter House,** which features fine architecture and stained glass, some faded but well-described medieval paintings and floor tiles, and—in the corridor—Britain's oldest door.

• *Go back into the church for the last stop.*

**⓫ Coronation Chair:** A gold-painted oak chair waits here under a regal canopy for the next coronation. For every English coronation since 1308 (except two), it's been moved to its spot before the high altar to receive the royal buttocks. The chair's legs rest on lions, England's symbol.

**▲▲HOUSES OF PARLIAMENT (PALACE OF WESTMINSTER)**

This Neo-Gothic icon of London, the site of the royal residence from 1042 to 1547, is now the meeting place of the legislative branch of government. Like the US Capitol in Washington, DC, the complex is open to visitors. You can view parliamentary sessions in either the bickering House of Commons or the sleepy House of Lords. Or you can simply wander on your own (through a few closely monitored

*Poets' Corner*

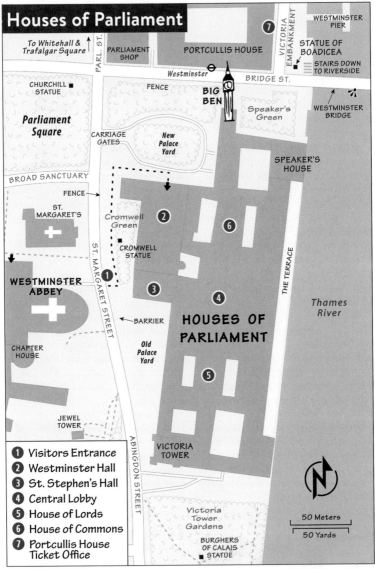

# Houses of Parliament

To Whitehall & Trafalgar Square

PARL. ST.

PARLIAMENT SHOP

PORTCULLIS HOUSE

❼

VICTORIA EMBANKMENT

WESTMINSTER PIER

STATUE OF BOADICEA

STAIRS DOWN TO RIVERSIDE

CHURCHILL STATUE

*Parliament Square*

Westminster

FENCE

BRIDGE ST.

BIG BEN

Speaker's Green

WESTMINSTER BRIDGE

CARRIAGE GATES

New Palace Yard

SPEAKER'S HOUSE

BROAD SANCTUARY

FENCE

ST. MARGARET'S

*Cromwell Green*

❷

❻

ST. MARGARET STREET

CROMWELL STATUE

❶

WESTMINSTER ABBEY

❸

❹

THE TERRACE

*Thames River*

BARRIER

HOUSES OF PARLIAMENT

CHAPTER HOUSE

*Old Palace Yard*

❺

JEWEL TOWER

ABINGDON STREET

VICTORIA TOWER

N

*Victoria Tower Gardens*

50 Meters
50 Yards

BURGHERS OF CALAIS STATUE

❶ Visitors Entrance
❷ Westminster Hall
❸ St. Stephen's Hall
❹ Central Lobby
❺ House of Lords
❻ House of Commons
❼ Portcullis House Ticket Office

rooms) to appreciate the historic building itself.

The Palace of Westminster has been the center of political power in England for nearly a thousand years. In 1834, a horrendous fire gutted the Palace. It was rebuilt in a retro, Neo-Gothic style that recalled England's medieval Christian roots—pointed arches, stained-glass windows, spires, and saint-like statues. At the same time, Britain was also retooling its government. Democracy was on the rise, the queen became a constitutional monarch, and Parliament emerged as the nation's ruling body. The Palace of Westminster became a kind of cathedral of democracy.

**Cost and Hours:** Free when Parliament is in session; paid audioguide or guided tour required at other times (see "Tours," below); House of Commons—Oct-late July Mon 14:30-22:30, Tue-Wed 11:30-19:30, Thu 9:30-17:30; House of Lords—Oct-late July Mon-Tue 14:30-22:00, Wed 15:00-22:00, Thu 11:00-19:30; last entry depends on the debates; get the exact schedule at www.parliament.uk.

**Tours:** On Saturdays and when Parliament is recessed, the only way to enter is by taking a 1.5-hour behind-the-scenes tour—with either an audioguide (£18.50) or a live guide (£25.50). Tours depart every 10 to 15 minutes on a timed-ticket system (Saturdays 9:00-16:30 and most weekdays during recess—days and times vary, so confirm schedule at www.parliament.uk). To guarantee a time slot, book ahead online or by calling 020/7219-4114—same-day tickets are not always available (ticket office open Mon-Fri 10:00-16:00, Sat 9:00-16:30, closed Sun, located in Portcullis House, entrance on Victoria Embankment). To clear security, arrive at the visitor entrance on Cromwell Green 30 minutes before your tour time.

**Rick's Tip:** *For the* **public galleries** *in either House,* **lines are longest** *at the start of each session, particularly on Wednesdays. For the shortest wait, show up* **later in the afternoon** *(but don't push it, as things sometimes close down early).*

**Choosing a House:** If you visit only one of the bicameral legislative bodies in session, choose the House of Lords. Though less important politically, the Lords meet in a more ornate room, and the wait time is shorter (likely less than 30 minutes). The House of Commons is where major policy is made, but the room is sparse and wait times are longer (30-60 minutes or more).

### ⊘ SELF-GUIDED TOUR

Enter midway along the west side of the building (across the street from Westminster Abbey), where a tourist ramp leads to the ❶ visitors entrance. Inside, you'll see all the public spaces described in this tour as you transit to the chamber you intend to visit.

• *First, take in the cavernous...*

❷ **Westminster Hall:** This vast hall—covering 16,000 square feet—survived the

*The history of the Houses of Parliament spans more than 900 years.*

## Affording London's Sights

London is one of Europe's most expensive cities. But with its many free museums and affordable plays, you can still enjoy the city without pinching pennies (or pounds).

**Free Museums:** Free sights include the British Museum, British Library, National Gallery, National Portrait Gallery, Tate Britain, Tate Modern, Imperial War Museum, Victoria and Albert Museum, and the Museum of London. Some museums request a donation of a few pounds, but whether you contribute is up to you.

**Free Churches:** Smaller churches let worshippers (and tourists) in free, although they may ask for a donation. The big sightseeing churches—Westminster Abbey and St. Paul's—charge admission fees, but offer free evensong services nearly daily (though you can't stick around afterward to sightsee). Westminster Abbey also offers free organ recitals most Sundays.

**Other Freebies:** London has plenty of free performances, such as lunch concerts at St. Martin-in-the-Fields (see page 63). For other freebies, check out www.whatsfreeinlondon.co.uk. There's no charge to enjoy the pageantry of the Changing of the Guard, rants at Speakers' Corner in Hyde Park (on Sun afternoon), displays at Harrods, the people-watching scene at Covent Garden, and the colorful streets of the East End. It's free to view the legislature at work in the Houses of Parliament. And you can see a bit of the Tower of London by attending Sunday services in its chapel.

**Good-Value Tours:** The London Walks tours with professional guides (£10) are one of the best deals going. Hop-on, hop-off big-bus tours, while expensive (£32), provide a great overview and include free boat tours as well as city walks. (Or, for the price of a transit ticket, you could get similar views—though no narration—from the top of a double-decker public bus.)

**Theater:** Compared with Broadway's prices, London's theater is a bargain. Seek out the freestanding TKTS booth at Leicester Square to get discounts from 25 to 30 percent on good seats (see page 100). A £5 "groundling" ticket for a play at Shakespeare's Globe is the best theater deal in town (see page 102).

1834 fire, and is one of the oldest and most important buildings in England. England's legal system was invented in this hall, as this was the major court of the land for 700 years. King Charles I was tried and sentenced to death here. Guy Fawkes was condemned for plotting to blow up the Halls of Parliament in 1605.

• *Walking through the hall and up the stairs, you'll enter the busy world of today's government. You soon reach...*

❸ **St. Stephen's Hall:** This long, beau-

tifully lit room was the original House of Commons for three centuries (from 1550 until the fire of 1834). Members of Parliament (MPs) sat in church pews—the ruling party on one side of the hall, the opposition on the other.

• *Next, you reach the...*

❹ **Central Lobby:** This ornate, octagonal, high-vaulted room is often called the "heart of British government," because it sits midway between the House of Commons (to the left) and House of Lords (right). Video monitors list the schedule of meetings and events in this 1,100-room governmental hive. Admire the Palace's carved wood, chandeliers, statues, and floor tiles.

• *This lobby marks the end of the public space where you can wander freely. To see the House of Lords or House of Commons you must wait in line and check your belongings.*

**❺ House of Lords:** When you're called, you'll walk to the Lords Chamber by way of the long Peers' Corridor—referring to the House's 800 unelected members, called "Peers." Paintings on the corridor walls depict the antiauthoritarian spirit brewing under the reign of Charles I. When you reach the House of Lords Chamber, you'll watch the proceedings from the upper-level visitors gallery. Debate may occur among the few Lords who show up at any given time, but these days the Peers' role is largely advisory—they have no real power to pass laws on their own.

The Lords Chamber is impressive, with stained glass and intricately carved walls. At the far end is the gilded throne where the Queen sits once a year to give a speech to open Parliament. In front of the throne sits the woolsack—a cushion stuffed with wool. Here the Lord Speaker presides, with a ceremonial mace behind the backrest. To the Lord Speaker's right are the members of the ruling party (a.k.a. "government"), and to his left are the members of the opposition (the Labour Party). Unaffiliated Crossbenchers sit in between.

**❻ House of Commons:** The Commons Chamber is less grandiose than the Lords', but this is where the sausage is made. The House of Commons is as powerful as the Lords, prime minister, and Queen combined.

Of today's 650-plus MPs, only 450 can sit—the rest have to stand at the ends. As in the House of Lords, the ruling party sits on the right of the Speaker (in his canopied Speaker's Chair), and opposition sits on the left. Keep an eye out for two red lines on the floor, which cannot be crossed when debating the other side. (They're supposedly two sword-lengths apart, to prevent a literal clashing of swords.) The clerks sit at a central table that holds the ceremonial mace, a symbol of the power given to Parliament by the monarch, who is not allowed in the Commons Chamber.

When the prime minister visits, his ministers (or cabinet) join him on the front bench, while lesser MPs (the "backbenchers") sit behind. The prime minister defends his policies while the opposition grumbles and harrumphs in displeasure. It's not unusual for MPs to get out of line and be escorted out by the Serjeant at Arms.

*Nearby:* Across the street from the Parliament building's St. Stephen's Gate, the **Jewel Tower** is a rare remnant of the old Palace of Westminster, used by kings until Henry VIII. The crude stone tower (1365-1366) contains a fine exhibit on the medieval Westminster Palace and the tower (£4.70, April-Sept daily 10:00-18:00; Oct until 17:00; Nov-March Sat-Sun 10:00-

*Big Ben*

16:00, closed Mon-Fri; tel. 020/7222-2219). Next to the tower (and free) is a quiet courtyard with picnic-friendly benches.

**Big Ben,** the 315-foot-high clock tower at the north end of the Palace of Westminster, is named for its 13-ton bell, Ben. The light above the clock is lit when Parliament is in session. The face of the clock is huge—you can actually see the minute hand moving. For a good view of it, walk halfway over Westminster Bridge.

### ▲▲▲CHURCHILL WAR ROOMS

Take a fascinating walk through the underground headquarters of the British government's WWII fight against the Nazis. It has two parts: the war rooms themselves, and a top-notch museum dedicated to Winston Churchill, who steered the war from here. Pick up the excellent audioguide at the entry, and dive in. The museum's gift shop is great for anyone nostalgic for the 1940s.

**Cost and Hours:** £19, includes audioguide, advance tickets available online; daily 9:30-18:00, last entry one hour before closing; get rations at the Switch Room café; on King Charles Street, 200 yards off Whitehall, follow the signs, Tube: Westminster, tel. 020/7930-6961, www.iwm.org.uk/churchill.

**Visiting the War Rooms and Museum:** The 27 **War Rooms,** the heavily fortified nerve center of the British war effort, were used from 1939 to 1945. Churchill's room, the map room, and other rooms are just as they were in 1945. As you fol-

low the one-way route, the audioguide explains each room and offers first-person accounts of wartime happenings here. While the rooms are spartan, you'll see how British gentility survived even as the city was bombarded—posted signs informed those working underground what the weather was like outside, and a cheery notice reminded them to turn off the light switch to conserve electricity.

The **Churchill Museum,** which occupies a large hall amid the war rooms, dissects every aspect of the man behind the famous cigar, bowler hat, and V-for-victory sign. Artifacts, quotes, political cartoons, clear explanations, and interactive exhibits bring the colorful statesman to life. You'll get a taste of Winston's wit, irascibility, work ethic, and drinking habits. The exhibit shows Winston's warts as well: It questions whether his party-switching was just political opportunism, examines the basis for his opposition to Indian self-rule, and reveals him to be an intense taskmaster who worked 18-hour days and was brutal to his staffers (who deeply respected him nevertheless).

Many of the items on display—such as a European map divvied up in permanent marker, which Churchill brought home from the postwar Potsdam Conference—drive home the remarkable span of history this man influenced.

***

**Rick's Tip:** *Some sights automatically add a* **"voluntary donation" of about 10 percent** *to their admission fees (those are the prices I give), and some free museums request donations. All such contributions are completely optional.*

***

## On Trafalgar Square

Trafalgar Square, London's central square (worth ▲▲), is at the intersection of Westminster, The City, and the West End. It's the climax of most marches and demonstrations and a thrilling place to simply hang out. At the top of the square

*Churchill War Rooms*

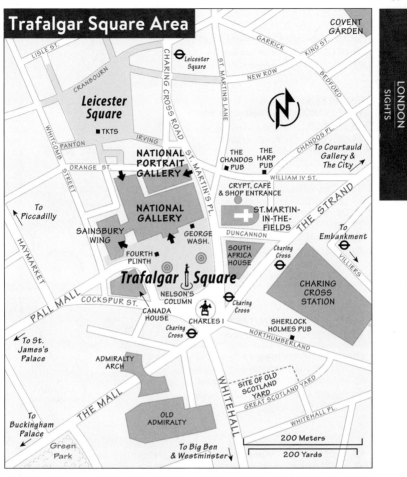

# Trafalgar Square Area

COVENT
GARDEN

GARRICK

KING ST.

BEDFORD

LISLE ST.

CRANBOURN

Leicester
Square

NEW ROW

ST. MARTINS LANE

CHARING CROSS ROAD

WHITCOMB

PANTON

Leicester
Square

■ TKTS

IRVING

ORANGE ST.

CHANDOS PL.

To Courtauld
Gallery &
The City

NATIONAL
PORTRAIT
GALLERY

THE
CHANDOS
PUB

THE
HARP
PUB

WILLIAM IV ST.

STREET

CRYPT, CAFÉ
& SHOP ENTRANCE

ST. MARTIN'S PL.

THE STRAND

To
Piccadilly

NATIONAL
GALLERY

ST. MARTIN-
IN-THE-
FIELDS

SAINSBURY
WING

GEORGE
WASH.

DUNCANNON

To
Embankment

FOURTH
PLINTH

SOUTH
AFRICA
HOUSE

Charing
Cross

VILLIERS

HAYMARKET

*Trafalgar ⚓ Square*

NELSON'S
COLUMN

Charing
Cross

CHARING
CROSS
STATION

PALL MALL

COCKSPUR ST.

CANADA
HOUSE

CHARLES I

Charing
Cross

SHERLOCK
HOLMES PUB

←To St.
James's
Palace

Charing
Cross

NORTHUMBERLAND

ADMIRALTY
ARCH

WHITEHALL

SITE OF OLD
SCOTLAND
YARD

GREAT SCOTLAND YARD

To
Buckingham
Palace

THE MALL

OLD
ADMIRALTY

WHITEHALL PL.

Green
Park

To Big Ben
& Westminster↓

200 Meters

200 Yards

*The massive National Gallery is one of the world's great art museums.*

## MEDIEVAL & EARLY RENAISSANCE

1 ANONYMOUS – The Wilton Diptych
2 UCCELLO – Battle of San Romano
3 VAN EYCK – The Arnolfini Portrait

## ITALIAN RENAISSANCE

4 LEONARDO – The Virgin of the Rocks
5 BOTTICELLI – Venus and Mars
6 CRIVELLI – The Annunciation,
   with Saint Emidius

## HIGH RENAISSANCE & MANNERISM

7 LEONARDO – Virgin and Child with
   St. Anne and St. John the Baptist
8 MICHELANGELO – The Entombment
9 RAPHAEL – Pope Julius II
10 BRONZINO – An Allegory with
   Venus and Cupid
11 TINTORETTO – The Origin of the
   Milky Way

## NORTHERN PROTESTANT ART

12 VERMEER – A Young Woman
   Standing at a Virginal
13 VAN HOOGSTRATEN – A Peepshow with
   Views of the Interior of a Dutch House
14 REMBRANDT – Belshazzar's Feast
15 REMBRANDT – Self-Portrait at the
   Age of 63

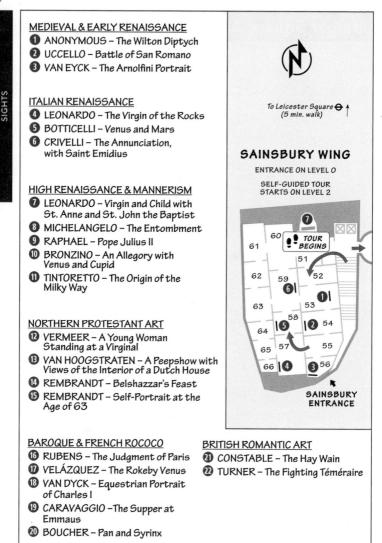

To Leicester Square ⊖ ↑
(5 min. walk)

**SAINSBURY WING**

ENTRANCE ON LEVEL 0

SELF-GUIDED TOUR
STARTS ON LEVEL 2

TOUR BEGINS

SAINSBURY
ENTRANCE

## BAROQUE & FRENCH ROCOCO

16 RUBENS – The Judgment of Paris
17 VELÁZQUEZ – The Rokeby Venus
18 VAN DYCK – Equestrian Portrait
   of Charles I
19 CARAVAGGIO – The Supper at
   Emmaus
20 BOUCHER – Pan and Syrinx

## BRITISH ROMANTIC ART

21 CONSTABLE – The Hay Wain
22 TURNER – The Fighting Téméraire

(north) sits the domed National Gallery with its grand staircase, and to the right, the steeple of St. Martin-in-the-Fields, built in 1722. In the center of the square, Lord Horatio Nelson stands atop a 185-foot-tall fluted granite column, gazing out toward Trafalgar, where he lost his life but defeated the French fleet. Part of this 1842 memorial is made from his victims' melt-ed-down cannons. He's surrounded by spraying fountains, giant lions, and hordes of people (Tube: Charing Cross).

▲▲▲NATIONAL GALLERY

Displaying an unsurpassed collection of European paintings from 1250 to 1900—including works by Leonardo, Botticelli, Velázquez, Rembrandt, Turner, Van Gogh, and the Impressionists—this is one of

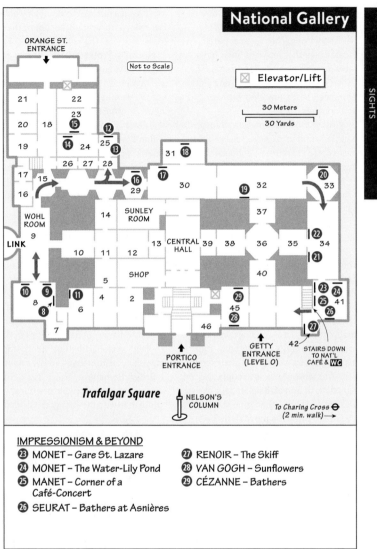

# National Gallery

⊠ Elevator/Lift

**IMPRESSIONISM & BEYOND**

㉓ MONET – Gare St. Lazare
㉔ MONET – The Water-Lily Pond
㉕ MANET – Corner of a Café-Concert
㉖ SEURAT – Bathers at Asnières
㉗ RENOIR – The Skiff
㉘ VAN GOGH – Sunflowers
㉙ CÉZANNE – Bathers

Europe's great galleries.

**Cost and Hours:** Free, but £20 suggested donation, special exhibits extra, daily 10:00–18:00, Fri until 21:00, last entry to special exhibits 45 minutes before closing, on Trafalgar Square, Tube: Charing Cross or Leicester Square, tel. 020/7747-2885, www.nationalgallery.org.uk.

**Tours:** Free one-hour overview tours leave from the Sainsbury Wing information desk daily at 11:30 and 14:30, plus Fri at 19:00. The £4 audioguides are excellent—choose from the one-hour highlights tour, several theme tours, or a tour option that lets you dial up any painting in the museum. You can get a helpful £1 floor plan from the info desk.

**Eating:** Consider splitting afternoon

tea at the excellent-but-pricey National Dining Rooms, on the first floor of the Sainsbury Wing. The National Café, located near the Getty Entrance, has a table-service restaurant and a café. The Espresso Bar, near the Portico and Getty entrances, has sandwiches, pastries, and soft couches.

**Visiting the Museum:** Go in through the Sainsbury Entrance (in the smaller building to the left of the main entrance), and approach the collection chronologically.

**Medieval and Early Renaissance:** In the first rooms, you see shiny paintings of saints, angels, Madonnas, and crucifixions floating in an ethereal gold never-never land.

After leaving this gold-leaf peace, you'll stumble into Uccello's *Battle of San Romano* and Van Eyck's *The Arnolfini Portrait,* called by some "The Shotgun Wedding." This painting—a masterpiece of down-to-earth details—was once thought to depict a wedding ceremony forced by the lady's swelling belly. Today it's understood as a portrait of a solemn, well-dressed, well-heeled couple, the Arnolfinis of Bruges, Belgium (she likely was not pregnant—the fashion of the day was to gather up the folds of one's extremely full-skirted dress).

**Italian Renaissance:** In painting, the Renaissance meant realism. Artists rediscovered the beauty of nature and the human body, expressing the optimism and confidence of this new age. Look for Botticelli's *Venus and Mars,* Michelangelo's *The Entombment,* and Raphael's *Pope Julius II.*

In Leonardo's *The Virgin of the Rocks,* Mary plays with her son Jesus and little Johnny the Baptist (with cross, at left) while an androgynous angel looks on. Leonardo brings this holy scene right down to earth by setting it among rocks, stalactites, water, and flowering plants.

In *The Origin of the Milky Way,* by Venetian Renaissance painter Tintoretto, the god Jupiter places his illegitimate son, baby Hercules, at his wife's breast. Juno says, "Wait a minute. That's not my baby!" Her milk spurts upward, becoming the Milky Way.

**Northern Protestant:** Greek gods and Virgin Marys are out, and hometown folks and hometown places are in. Highlights include Vermeer's *A Young Woman Standing at a Virginal* and Rembrandt's *Belshazzar's Feast.*

Rembrandt painted his *Self-Portrait at the Age of 63* in the year he would die. He was bankrupt, his mistress had just passed away, and he had also buried several of his children. We see a disillusioned, well-worn, but proud old genius.

**Baroque:** The museum's outstanding Baroque collection includes Van Dyck's *Equestrian Portrait of Charles I* and Caravaggio's *The Supper at Emmaus.* In Velázquez's *The Rokeby Venus,* Venus lounges diagonally across the canvas, admiring herself, with flaring red, white, and gray fabrics to highlight her rosy white skin and inflame our passion. This work by the king's personal court painter is a rare Spanish nude from that Catholic country.

**British Romantics:** The reserved British were more comfortable cavorting with nature than with the lofty gods, as seen in

*Van Eyck,* The Arnolfini Portrait

Constable's *The Hay Wain* and Turner's *The Fighting Téméraire.* Turner's messy, colorful style influenced the Impressionists and gives us our first glimpse into the modern art world.

**Impressionism:** At the end of the 19th century, a new breed of artists burst out of the stuffy confines of the studio. They set up their canvases in farmers' fields or carried their notebooks into crowded cafés, dashing off quick sketches in order to catch a momentary...impression. Check out works such as Monet's *Gare St. Lazare* and *The Water-Lily Pond,* Renoir's *The Skiff,* Seurat's *Bathers at Asnières,* and Van Gogh's *Sunflowers.*

Cézanne's *Bathers* are arranged in strict triangles. Cézanne uses the Impressionist technique of building a figure with dabs of paint (though his "dabs" are often larger-sized "cube" shapes) to make solid, 3-D geometrical figures in the style of the Renaissance. In the process, he helped inspire a radical new style—Cubism—bringing art into the 20th century.

▲▲NATIONAL PORTRAIT GALLERY
While some might consider this as interesting as someone else's yearbook, a selective walk through this 500-year-long *Who's Who* of British history is quick and free, and puts faces on the history of England. The collection is well-described, not huge, and in historical sequence, from the 16th century to today's royal family. Highlights include Henry VIII and wives; portraits of the "Virgin Queen" Elizabeth I, Sir Francis Drake, and Sir Walter Raleigh; the only real-life portrait of William Shakespeare; Oliver Cromwell and Charles I with his head on; Queen Victoria and her era; and the present royal family, including the late Princess Diana and the current Duchess of Cambridge, Kate.

**Cost and Hours:** Free, but £5 suggested donation, special exhibits extra; daily 10:00-18:00, Thu-Fri until 21:00, first and second floors open Mon at 11:00, last entry to special exhibits one hour before closing; audioguide-£3, no photos, basement café and top-floor view restaurant; entry 100 yards off Trafalgar Square (around the corner from National Gallery, opposite Church of St. Martin-in-the-Fields), Tube: Charing Cross or Leicester Square, tel. 020/7306-0055, recorded info tel. 020/7312-2463, www.npg.org.uk.

▲ST. MARTIN-IN-THE-FIELDS
The church, built in the 1720s with a Gothic spire atop a Greek-type temple, is an oasis of peace on noisy Trafalgar Square. St. Martin cared for the poor. "In the fields" was where the first church stood on this spot in the 13th century, between Westminster and The City. Inside, you still see the church's compassion for the needy. The modern east window—with grillwork bent into the shape of a warped cross—was installed in 2008 to replace one damaged in World War II.

A freestanding glass pavilion to the left of the church serves as the entrance to its underground areas. There you'll find the concert ticket office, a gift shop, a brass-rubbing center, and the recommended support-the-church Café in the Crypt.

**Cost and Hours:** Free, but donations

*Princess Diana's portrait at the National Portrait Gallery*

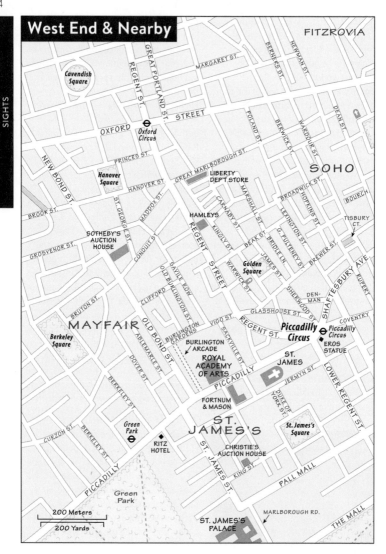

# West End & Nearby

FITZROVIA

Cavendish Square

OXFORD

Oxford Circus

PRINCES ST.

NEW BOND ST.

Hanover Square

HANOVER ST.

BROOK ST.

SOTHEBY'S AUCTION HOUSE

GROSVENOR ST.

CONDUIT ST.

MADDOX ST.

ST. GEORGE ST.

STREET

REGENT ST.

GREAT PORTLAND ST.

MARGARET ST.

POLAND ST.

BERNERS ST.

NEWMAN ST.

SOHO

GREAT MARLBOROUGH ST.

LIBERTY DEP'T STORE

HAMLEYS

CARNABY ST.

KINGLY ST.

WARWICK ST.

Golden Square

REGENT STREET

SAVILE ROW

MARSHALL ST.

BEAK ST.

BRIDLE LN.

LEXINGTON ST.

BROADWICK ST.

HOPKINS ST.

G. PULTENEY ST.

BREWER ST.

DENMAN

SHERWOOD ST.

GLASSHOUSE ST.

BERWICK ST.

WARDOUR ST.

DEAN ST.

BOURCH

TISBURY CT.

SHAFTESBURY AVE.

RUPERT

COVENTRY

MAYFAIR

Berkeley Square

BRUTON ST.

CLIFFORD ST.

OLD BURLINGTON ST.

BURLINGTON GARDENS

OLD BOND ST.

ALBEMARLE ST.

DOVER ST.

BERKELEY ST.

CURZON ST.

VIGO ST.

REGENT ST.

Piccadilly Circus

Piccadilly Circus

EROS STATUE

BURLINGTON ARCADE

ROYAL ACADEMY OF ARTS

SACKVILLE ST.

PICCADILLY

ST. JAMES

JERMYN ST.

DUKE OF YORK ST.

LOWER REGENT ST.

FORTNUM & MASON

Green Park

RITZ HOTEL

ST. JAMES'S

CHRISTIE'S AUCTION HOUSE

ST. JAMES'S ST.

KING ST.

St. James's Square

PALL MALL

PICCADILLY

Green Park

MARLBOROUGH RD.

THE MALL

ST. JAMES'S PALACE

200 Meters

200 Yards

---

welcome; hours vary but generally Mon-Fri 8:30-13:00 & 14:00-18:00, Sat 9:30-18:00, Sun 15:30-17:00; services listed at entrance; Tube: Charing Cross, tel. 020/7766-1100, www.smitf.org.

**Rick's Tip: St. Martin-in-the-Fields** *is famous for its* **concerts.** *Consider a free lunchtime concert (£3.50 suggested donation; Mon, Tue, and Fri at 13:00), an evening*

concert (£8-28, several weeknights at 19:30), or **Wednesday night jazz** (£5.50-12, Wed at 20:00). See www.smitf.org for the schedule.

## The West End and Nearby
### ▲▲COVENT GARDEN
This large square teems with people and street performers—jugglers, sword

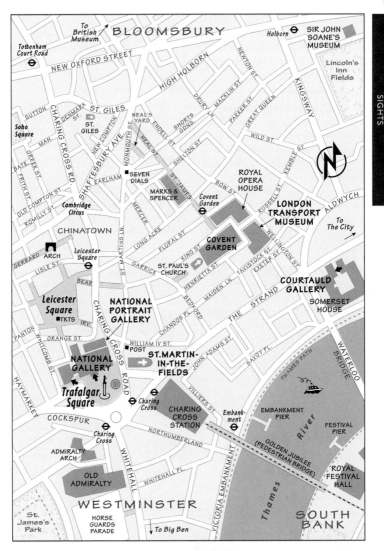

**BLOOMSBURY**

To British Museum

Tottenham Court Road

NEW OXFORD STREET

HIGH HOLBORN

Holborn

SIR JOHN SOANE'S MUSEUM

Lincoln's Inn Fields

NEWTON ST.

DRURY LN.

MACKLIN ST.

PARKER ST.

GREAT QUEEN

KINGSWAY

ST. GILES

SUTTON

DENMARK ST.

ST. GILES

NEAL'S YARD

SHORTS GDNS.

WILD ST.

KEMBLE ST.

Soho Square

CHARING CROSS RD.

NEW COMPTON

SHELTON ST.

NEAL ST.

MONMOUTH ST.

ENDELL ST.

ROYAL OPERA HOUSE

LONDON TRANSPORT MUSEUM

ALDWYCH

GREEK ST.

BATE ST.

FRITH ST.

ROMILLY ST.

OLD COMPTON ST.

MAN

SHAFTESBURY AVE.

EARLHAM

SEVEN DIALS

ST. JAMES

BOW ST.

RUSSELL ST.

WELLINGTON ST.

To The City

Cambridge Circus

MARKS & SPENCER

Covent Garden

MERCER

FLORAL ST.

COVENT GARDEN

CHINATOWN

LONG ACRE

KING ST.

TAVISTOCK ST.

EXETER ST.

COURTAULD GALLERY

ARCH

GERRARD

LISLE ST.

Leicester Square

ST. MARTIN'S LN.

GARRICK ST.

ST. PAUL'S CHURCH

HENRIETTA ST.

MAIDEN LN.

SOMERSET HOUSE

BEAR

**Leicester Square**

TKTS

IRV.

**NATIONAL PORTRAIT GALLERY**

CHARING CROSS ROAD

BEDFORD

CHANDOS PL.

THE STRAND

PANTON

ORANGE ST.

WHITCOMB ST.

WILLIAM IV ST.

POST

**ST. MARTIN-IN-THE-FIELDS**

JOHN ADAMS ST.

SAVOY PL.

THAMES PATH

WATERLOO BRIDGE

HAYMARKET

**NATIONAL GALLERY**

**Trafalgar Square**

Charing Cross

VILLIERS ST.

CHARING CROSS STATION

Embankment

EMBANKMENT PIER

River

FESTIVAL PIER

COCKSPUR

Charing Cross

NORTHUMBERLAND

GOLDEN JUBILEE (PEDESTRIAN BRIDGE)

ADMIRALTY ARCH

WHITEHALL

WHITEHALL PL.

VICTORIA EMBANKMENT

Thames

ROYAL FESTIVAL HALL

OLD ADMIRALTY

**WESTMINSTER**

St. James's Park

HORSE GUARDS PARADE

To Big Ben

**SOUTH BANK**

---

swallowers, and guitar players. London's buskers (including those in the Tube) are auditioned, licensed, and assigned times and places where they are allowed to perform.

The square's centerpiece is a covered marketplace. A market has been here since medieval times, when it was the "convent" garden owned by Westminster Abbey. Today's fine iron-and-glass struc-

*Covent Garden*

ture was built in 1830 to house the stalls of London's chief produce market. In 1973, its venerable arcades were converted to boutiques, cafés, and antique shops. A tourist market thrives here today.

---

**Rick's Tip: Beware of pickpockets.** *More than 7,500 purses are stolen annually at* **Covent Garden** *alone.*

---

Browse trendy crafts, boutique shops, market stalls, and food that's good for you (but not your wallet). For better Covent Garden lunch deals, walk a block or two away to check out the places north of the Tube station, along Endell and Neal streets.

### ▲PICCADILLY CIRCUS

Although this square is slathered with neon billboards and tacky attractions, the surrounding streets are swimming with youth and packed with great shopping opportunities. Nearby Shaftesbury Avenue and Leicester Square teem with fun-seekers, theaters, Chinese restaurants, and street singers. To the northeast is Chinatown and, beyond that, funky Soho. And curling to the northwest from Piccadilly Circus is genteel Regent Street, lined with exclusive shops.

### ▲SOHO

North of Piccadilly, seedy Soho has become trendy—with many restaurants—and is worth a gawk. It's the epicenter of London's colorful youth scene, a funky

*Sesame Street* of urban diversity.

Soho is also London's red light district (especially near Brewer and Berwick streets), where "friendly models" wait in tiny rooms up dreary stairways, voluptuous con artists sell strip shows, and eager male tourists are frequently ripped off. It's easy to avoid trouble if you're not looking for it. The sleazy joints share the block with respectable pubs and restaurants.

## Buckingham Palace Area

### ▲▲CHANGING OF THE GUARD AT BUCKINGHAM PALACE

Most visitors to London want to see this hour-long spectacle: stone-faced, red-coated (or, in winter, gray-coated), bearskin-hatted guards changing posts accompanied by a brass band. Everyone parades around, the guard passes the regimental flag (or "colour") with much shouting, the band plays a happy little concert, and then they march out. Most tourists just show up and get lost in the crowds, but those who anticipate the action and know where to perch will enjoy the event more. Follow the timeline in the sidebar on the next page.

**Cost and Hours:** Free, daily May-July at 11:30, every other day Aug-April, no ceremony in very wet weather; schedule subject to change—call 020/7766-7300 for the day's plan, or check www.royal.gov.uk; Buckingham Palace, Tube: Victoria, St. James's Park, or Green Park.

---

**Rick's Tip:** *Want to go inside* **Buckingham Palace?** *It's* **open to the public only in August and September,** *when the Queen is out of town (£22 for State Rooms; Aug-Sept daily from 9:15, last admission 17:15 in Aug and 16:15 in Sept; book timed-entry ticket in advance by phone, tel. 0303/123-7300, or online, www.royalcollection.org.uk).*

---

**Sightseeing Strategies:** The action takes place in stages over the course of

*Piccadilly Circus*

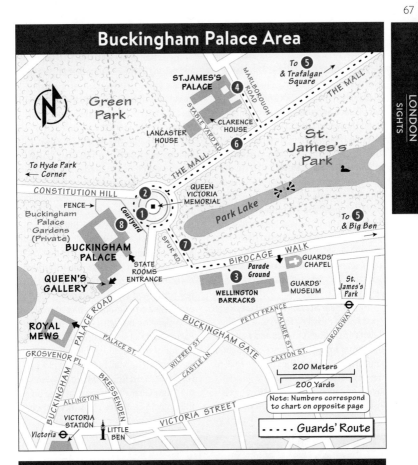

# Buckingham Palace Area

## Changing of the Guard Timeline

| 10:30 | Arrive now for a spot front and center by the ❶ fence outside Buckingham Palace. |
|---|---|
| 11:00-11:15 | ❷ Victoria Memorial gets crowded. "New Guard" gathers for inspection at ❸ Wellington Barracks. "Old Guard" gathers at ❹ St. James's Palace. |
| 11:00 (10:00 Sun) | Changing of the Horse Guard at ❺ Horse Guards Parade. |
| 11:00-11:30 | Tired St. James's Palace guards march down ❻ the Mall toward Buckingham Palace. Replacement troops head from Wellington Barracks down ❼ Spur Road to the palace. All guards gradually converge around the Victoria Memorial. |
| 11:30-12:00 | Changing of the Guard ceremony takes place inside ❽ the palace courtyard. |

an hour, at several different locations; see map on page 67. Here are a few options to consider:

**Watch near the Palace:** The main event is in the forecourt right in front of Buckingham Palace (between Buckingham Palace and the fence) from 11:30 to 12:00. Arrive no later than 10:30 to get a place front and center, next to the fence. Get right up front along the road or fence, or find some raised elevation to stand or sit on—a balustrade or a curb—so you can see over people's heads.

**Watch near the Victoria Memorial:** The high ground around the circular Victoria Memorial gives good (if more distant) views of the palace as well as the arriving and departing parades along The Mall and Spur Road. Come before 11:00 to get a place.

**Watch near St. James's Palace:** If you don't feel like jostling for a view, stroll down to St. James's Palace and wait near the corner for a great photo-op. At about 12:15, the parade marches up The Mall to the palace and performs a smaller changing ceremony—with almost no crowds.

**Follow the Procession:** You won't get the closest views, but you'll get something even better—the thrill of participating in the action. Start with the "Old Guard" mobilizing in the courtyard of St. James's Palace (11:00). Arrive early, and grab a spot just across the road (otherwise you'll be asked to move when the inspection begins). Just before they prepare to leave (at 11:13), march ahead of them down Marlborough Street to The Mall. Pause here to watch them parade past, band and all, on their way to the Palace, then cut through the park and head to the Wellington Barracks—where the "New Guard" is getting ready to leave for Buckingham (11:27). March along with full military band and fresh guards from the barracks to the Palace. At 11:30 the two guard groups meet in the courtyard, the band plays a few songs, and soldiers parade and finally exchange compliments before returning to Wellington Barracks and St. James's Palace (12:10). Use this time to snap a few photos of the guards before making your way across The Mall to Clarence House (on Stable Yard Road), where you'll see the "New Guard" pass one last time on their way to St. James's Palace. On their

*The Changing of the Guard is all about pomp and ceremony.*

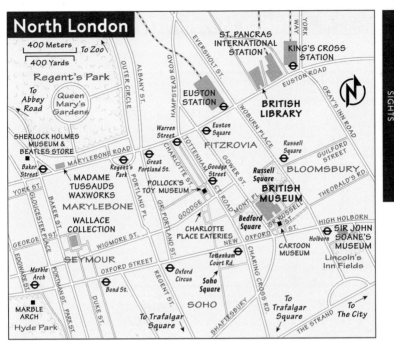

way, the final piece of ceremony takes place—one member of the "Old Guard" and one member of the first-relief "New Guard" change places here.

**Join a Tour:** Local tour companies such as **Fun London Tours** more or less follow the self-guided route above but add in history and facts about the guards, bands, and royal family to their already entertaining march (£15, tour starts at Piccadilly Circus at 10:00, must book online in advance, www.funlondontours.com).

## North London

### ▲▲▲BRITISH MUSEUM

This is the greatest chronicle of civilization...anywhere. A visit here is like taking a long hike through *Encyclopedia Britannica* National Park. The vast British Museum is wrapped around its huge entrance hall—the Great Court—with the most popular sections filling the ground floor: Egyptian, Assyrian, and ancient Greek, with the famous frieze sculptures from the Par-

thenon in Athens. The museum's stately Reading Room sometimes hosts special exhibits.

**Cost and Hours:** Free but £5 suggested donation, special exhibits usually extra; daily 10:00-17:30, Fri until 20:30 (selected galleries only), least crowded late on weekday afternoons; Great Russell Street, Tube: Tottenham Court Road, tel. 020/7323-8299, www.britishmuseum.org.

**Tours:** Free 30-minute **EyeOpener tours** are led by volunteers, who focus on select rooms (daily 11:00-15:45, generally

*British Museum*

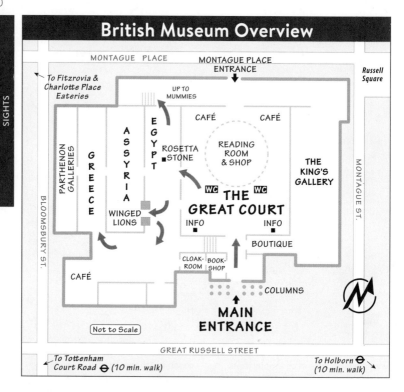

# British Museum Overview

MONTAGUE PLACE

MONTAGUE PLACE
ENTRANCE

Russell
Square

To Fitzrovia &
Charlotte Place
Eateries

UP TO
MUMMIES

CAFÉ          CAFÉ

**E
G
Y
P
T**

**A
S
S
Y
R
I
A**

ROSETTA
■STONE

READING
ROOM
& SHOP

**G
R
E
E
C
E**

**PARTHENON
GALLERIES**

**THE
KING'S
GALLERY**

MONTAGUE ST.

WC   WC

**THE
GREAT COURT**

WINGED
LIONS

INFO ■        ■ INFO

BLOOMSBURY ST.

BOUTIQUE

CLOAK-  BOOK-
ROOM   SHOP

CAFÉ

Not to Scale

●●●● ●●●●
●●●● ●●●●   COLUMNS

**MAIN
ENTRANCE**

GREAT RUSSELL STREET

To Tottenham
Court Road ⊖ (10 min. walk)

To Holborn ⊖
(10 min. walk)

every 15 minutes). Free 45-minute **gallery talks** on specific subjects are offered Tue-Sat at 13:15; a free 20-minute highlights tour is available on Friday evening. The £5 **multimedia guide** offers commentary on 200 objects, as well as several theme tours (must leave photo ID). There's also a fun children's multimedia guide. Or 🎧 download my free **audio tour**—see page 27.

### ❯ SELF-GUIDED TOUR

From the Great Court, doorways lead to all wings. To the left are the exhibits on Egypt, Assyria, and Greece—the highlights of your visit.

### EGYPT

Egypt was one of the world's first civilizations. The Egypt we think of—pyramids, pharaohs, and guys who walk funny—lasted from 3000 to 1000 B.C. with hardly any change in the government, religion, or arts. Imagine two millennia of Bush.

*A mummy case*

The first thing you'll see is the **Rosetta Stone.** When this black slab (dating from 196 B.C.) was unearthed in the Egyptian desert in 1799, it caused a sensation in Europe and led to a quantum leap in the study of ancient history. It contains a single inscription repeated in three languages. The bottom third is plain old Greek, while the middle is medieval Egyptian. By comparing the two known languages with the one they didn't know, translators figured out the hieroglyphics. Finally, Egyptian writing could be decoded.

Next, wander past the many **statues,** including a seven-ton Ramesses, with the traditional features of a pharaoh (goatee, cloth headdress, and cobra diadem on his forehead). When Moses told the king of Egypt "Let my people go!," this was the stony-faced look he got. You'll also see the Egyptian gods as animals—including Amun, king of the gods, as a ram, and Horus, the god of the living, as a falcon.

At the end of the hall, climb the stairs to **mummy** land (use the elevator if it's running). To mummify a body, you first disembowel it (but leave the heart inside), then pack the cavities with pitch, and dry it with natron, a natural form of sodium carbonate (and, I believe, the active ingredient in Twinkies). Then carefully bandage it head to toe with hundreds of yards of linen strips. Let it sit 2,000 years, and...*voilà!* The mummy was placed in a wooden coffin, which was put in a stone coffin, which was placed in a tomb. The result is that we now have Egyptian bodies that are as well preserved as Larry King. Many of the mummies here are from the time of the Roman occupation, when fine memorial portraits painted in wax became popular. X-ray photos in the display cases tell us more about these people. Don't miss the animal mummies. Cats were considered incarnations of the cat-headed goddess Bastet. Worshipped in life, preserved in death, and memorialized with statues, cats were given the adulation they've come to expect ever since.

## ASSYRIA

The British Museum's valuable collection of Assyrian artifacts has become even more priceless since the recent destruction of ancient sites in the Middle East by ISIS terrorists. Long before Saddam Hussein, Iraq was home to other palace-building, iron-fisted rulers—the Assyrians, who conquered their southern neighbors and dominated the Middle East for 300 years (c. 900-600 B.C.). Their strength came from a superb army (chariots, mounted cavalry, and siege engines), a policy of terrorism against enemies, ethnic cleansing, and efficient administration (roads and express postal service).

Standing guard over the exhibit halls are two human-headed **winged lions** from an Assyrian palace (11th-8th century B.C.). With the strength of a lion, the wings of an eagle, the brain of a man, and the beard of ZZ Top, they protected the king from evil spirits and scared the heck out of foreign ambassadors and left-wing journalists. (What has five legs and flies? Take a close look. These winged quintupeds, which appear complete from both the front and the side, could guard both directions at once.)

Carved into the stone between the bearded lions' loins, you can see one of

*Assyrian human-headed lions*

civilization's most impressive achieve-ments. This wedge-shaped **(cuneiform)** script is the world's first written language, invented 5,000 years ago by the Sume-rians and passed down to their less-civilized descendants, the Assyrians.

The **Nimrud Gallery** is a mini version of the throne room and royal apartments of King Ashurnasirpal II's Northwest Palace at Nimrud (9th century B.C.). It's filled with royal propaganda reliefs, 30-ton marble bulls, and panels depicting wounded lions (lion-hunting was Assyria's sport of kings).

## GREECE

During their civilization's Golden Age (500-430 B.C.), the ancient Greeks set the tone for all of Western civilization to follow. Democracy, theater, literature, mathematics, philosophy, science, gyros, art, and architecture, as we know them, were virtually all invented by a single generation of Greeks in a small town of maybe 80,000 citizens.

Your walk through Greek art history starts with pottery, usually painted red and black. The earliest featured geomet-ric patterns (eighth century B.C.), then a painted black silhouette on the natural orange clay, then a red figure on a black background. Later, painted vases show a culture really into partying.

The highlight is the **Parthenon Sculp-tures,** taken from the temple dedicated to Athena—the crowning glory of an enormous urban-renewal plan during Greece's Golden Age. The sculptures are also called the Elgin Marbles for the shrewd British ambassador who had his men hammer, chisel, and saw them off the Parthenon in the early 1800s. Though the Greek government complains about losing its marbles, the Brits feel they res-cued and preserved the sculptures. These much-wrangled-over bits of the Parthe-non (from about 450 B.C.) are indeed impressive. The marble panels lining the walls of this large hall are part of the frieze that originally ran around the exterior of the Parthenon, under the eaves. The statues at either end of the hall once filled the Parthenon's triangular-shaped ped-iments and showed the birth of Athena. Decorative relief panels tell the story of the struggle between the forces of human civilization and barbarism.

### THE REST OF THE MUSEUM

Venture upstairs to see artifacts from **Roman Britain** that surpass anything

*Admiring the ancient Greek Parthenon sculptures at the British Museum*

you'll see at Hadrian's Wall or elsewhere in the country. Also look for the Sutton Hoo Ship Burial artifacts from a seventh-century royal burial on the east coast of England (Room 41). A rare Michelangelo cartoon (preliminary sketch) is in Room 90 (level 4).

## ▲▲▲BRITISH LIBRARY

Here, in just two rooms, are the literary treasures of Western civilization, from early Bibles, to Shakespeare's *Hamlet,* to Lewis Carroll's *Alice's Adventures in Wonderland,* to the Magna Carta. You'll see the Lindisfarne Gospels transcribed on an illuminated manuscript, Beatles lyrics scrawled on the back of a greeting card, and Leonardo da Vinci's genius sketched into his notebooks. The British Empire built its greatest monuments out of paper.

**Cost and Hours:** Free, but £5 suggested donation, fee for some special exhibits; Mon-Fri 9:30-18:00, Tue until 20:00, Sat 9:30-17:00, Sun 11:00-17:00; 96 Euston Road, Tube: King's Cross St. Pancras or Euston, tel. 019/3754-6060 or 020/7412-7676, www.bl.uk.

**Tours:** There are no guided tours or audioguides for the permanent collection, but you can 🎧 download my free British Library **audio tour** (see page 27). There are guided tours of the building itself—the archives and reading rooms. Touchscreens in the permanent collection let you page virtually through some of the rare books.

## ⟳ SELF-GUIDED TOUR

Everything that matters for your visit is in the delightful Sir John Ritblat Gallery and an adjacent room. We'll concentrate on a handful of documents—literary and historical—that changed the course of history. Exhibits change often, and many of the museum's old, fragile manuscripts need to "rest" periodically in order to stay well preserved.

Start at the far side of the Ritblat Gallery and the display case of historic ❶ **maps** showing how humans' perspective of the world expanded over the centuries. Next, move into the area dedicated to ❷ **sacred texts and early Bibles** from several cultures. This section includes the oldest complete Bibles in existence. In the display cases called ❸ **Art of the Book,** you'll find illuminated Bibles from the early medieval period, including the Lindisfarne Gospels (A.D. 698). Look out

*The British Library is filled with treasures ranging from the Magna Carta to Beatles song sheets.*

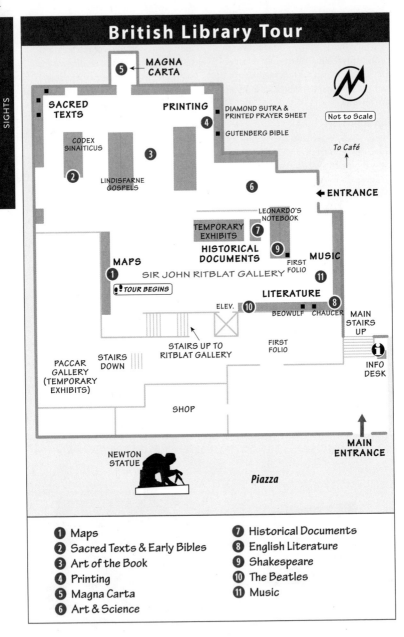

# British Library Tour

MAGNA CARTA — 5

SACRED TEXTS

PRINTING

DIAMOND SUTRA & PRINTED PRAYER SHEET

GUTENBERG BIBLE

Not to Scale

To Café

2 — CODEX SINAITICUS

3

LINDISFARNE GOSPELS

4

6

← ENTRANCE

LEONARDO'S NOTEBOOK

TEMPORARY EXHIBITS — 7

HISTORICAL DOCUMENTS

9

FIRST FOLIO

MUSIC

MAPS — 1

SIR JOHN RITBLAT GALLERY

11

TOUR BEGINS

LITERATURE

ELEV. — 10

BEOWULF    CHAUCER — 8

MAIN STAIRS UP

STAIRS UP TO RITBLAT GALLERY

FIRST FOLIO

INFO DESK

PACCAR GALLERY (TEMPORARY EXHIBITS)

STAIRS DOWN

SHOP

NEWTON STATUE

MAIN ENTRANCE

Piazza

1 Maps
2 Sacred Texts & Early Bibles
3 Art of the Book
4 Printing
5 Magna Carta
6 Art & Science
7 Historical Documents
8 English Literature
9 Shakespeare
10 The Beatles
11 Music

for some of the first-ever English translations of the Bible.

In the glass cases featuring early ❹ **printing,** you'll see the Diamond Sutra (c. 868), the world's earliest complete, printed book, and the Gutenberg Bible, the first book printed in Europe using movable type (c. 1455).

Through a nearby doorway is a small room that holds the ❺ **Magna Carta,** assuming it's not "resting." The basis for England's constitutional system of government, this "Great Charter" listing rules about mundane administrative issues was radical because of the simple fact that the king had agreed to abide by them as law.

Return to the main room to find display cases featuring ❻ **art and science.** Pages from Leonardo da Vinci's notebook show his powerful curiosity, his genius for invention, and his famous backward and inside-out handwriting. Nearby are many more ❼ **historical documents.** The displays change frequently, but you may see letters by Henry VIII, Queen Elizabeth I, Darwin, Freud, Gandhi, and others.

Next, trace the evolution of ❽ **English**

**literature.** Check out the A.D. 1000 manuscript of *Beowulf,* the first English literary masterpiece, and *The Canterbury Tales* (c. 1410), Geoffrey Chaucer's bawdy collection of stories. The Literature wall is often a greatest-hits sampling of literature in English, from Brontë to Kipling to Woolf to Joyce to Dickens. The most famous of England's writers—❾ **Shakespeare**—generally gets his own display case. Look for the First Folio—one of the 750 copies of the first nearly complete collection of his plays, printed in 1623.

Now fast-forward a few centuries to ❿ **The Beatles.** Find photos of John Lennon, Paul McCartney, George Harrison, and Ringo Starr before and after their fame, as well as manuscripts of song lyrics written by Lennon and McCartney. In the ⓫ **music** section, there are manuscripts by Mozart, Beethoven, Schubert, and others (kind of an anticlimax after the Fab Four, I know). George Frideric Handel's famous oratorio, the *Messiah* (1741), is often on display and marks the end of our tour. Hallelujah.

*Lewis Carroll's manuscript for* Alice's Adventures in Wonderland

*The only known manuscript of the epic saga* Beowulf

## ▲MADAME TUSSAUDS WAXWORKS

This waxtravaganza is gimmicky, crass, crowded, and crazily expensive, but dang fun. The original Madame Tussaud did wax casts of heads lopped off during the French Revolution (such as Marie Antoinette's) and took her show on the road before ending up in London in 1835. Today, a visit is all about photo-ops with eerily realistic wax dummies—squeezing Leonardo DiCaprio's bum, singing with Lady Gaga, and partying with Brangelina. You can also tour a hokey haunted-house exhibit; learn how they created this waxy army; cruise through a kid-pleasing "Spirit of London" time trip; and visit with Marvel superheroes. A nine-minute "4-D" show features a 3-D movie heightened by wind, "back ticklers," and other special effects.

**Rick's Tip:** *To* **skip Madame Tussauds' ticket-buying line** *(which can be an hour or more), purchase a Fast Track ticket (from souvenir stands, tourist shops, or the TI) or consider getting the pricey* **Priority Entrance** *ticket and reserving a time slot at least a day in advance. If you* **arrive after 15:00,** *the crowds—which can mob popular exhibits—thin out a bit.*

**Cost:** £34, kids-£29.80 (free for kids under 5), family passes available online; up to 25 percent discount and shorter lines if you buy tickets on their website (also consider a combo-deal with the London Eye).

**Hours:** Mid-June-Aug and school

*The Beatles at Madame Tussauds*

holidays daily 8:30-19:30, Sept-mid-June Mon-Fri 9:30-17:30, Sat-Sun 9:00-18:00, these are last entry times—closing is roughly two hours later; Marylebone Road, Tube: Baker Street, tel. 0871-894-3000, www.madametussauds.com.

# The City

When Londoners say "The City," they mean the one-square-mile business center in East London that 2,000 years ago was Roman Londinium. The outline of the Roman city walls can still be seen in the arc of roads from Blackfriars Bridge to Tower Bridge.

🎧 Download my free audio tour of The City, which peels back the many layers of history in this oldest part of London (see page 27).

## ▲▲▲ST. PAUL'S CATHEDRAL

There's been a church on this spot since 604. After the Great Fire of 1666 destroyed the old cathedral, Sir Christopher Wren replaced it with this Baroque masterpiece. Since World War II, St. Paul's has been Britain's symbol of resilience. Despite 57 nights of bombing, the Nazis failed to destroy the cathedral, thanks to volunteer fire watchmen who stayed on the dome.

Even now, as skyscrapers encroach, the 365-foot-high dome of St. Paul's rises majestically above the rooftops of the neighborhood. The tall dome is set on classical columns, capped with a lantern, topped by a six-foot ball, and iced with a cross. As the first Anglican cathedral built in London after the Reformation, it is Baroque: St. Peter's in Rome filtered through clear-eyed English reason. Though often the site of historic funerals (such as Queen Victoria's and Winston Churchill's), St. Paul's most famous recent ceremony was the wedding between Prince Charles and Lady Diana Spencer in 1981.

**Cost and Hours:** £18, £16 if purchased in advance online, includes church entry, dome climb, crypt, tour, and audioguide;

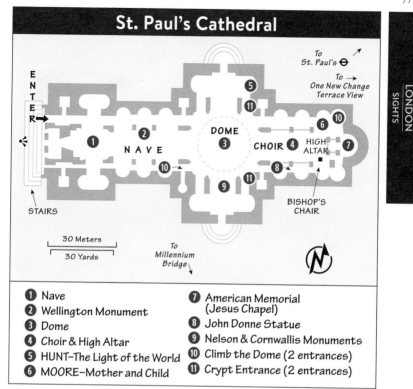

# St. Paul's Cathedral

ENTER

To
St. Paul's ⊖

To →
One New Change
Terrace View

**DOME**

**5**

**11**

**1**

**2**

**3**

**NAVE**

**CHOIR** **4** HIGH
ALTAR

**6** **10**

**7**

**10**

**9**

**11**

**8**

STAIRS

BISHOP'S
CHAIR

30 Meters

30 Yards

To
Millennium
Bridge ↓

**1** Nave
**2** Wellington Monument
**3** Dome
**4** Choir & High Altar
**5** HUNT–The Light of the World
**6** MOORE–Mother and Child

**7** American Memorial
(Jesus Chapel)
**8** John Donne Statue
**9** Nelson & Cornwallis Monuments
**10** Climb the Dome (2 entrances)
**11** Crypt Entrance (2 entrances)

*Majestic St. Paul's Cathedral is one of London's most iconic buildings.*

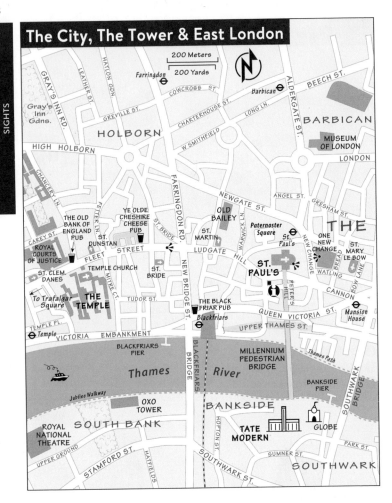

## The City, The Tower & East London

Mon-Sat 8:30-16:30 (dome opens at 9:30), closed Sun except for worship; book ahead online to skip the line or you might be waiting 15-30 minutes at busy times; Tube: St. Paul's, recorded info tel. 020/7246-8348, reception tel. 020/7246-8350, www.stpauls.co.uk.

**Church Services and Music:** Check the website for worship times the day of your visit. Communion is generally Mon-Sat at 8:00 and 12:30. On Sunday, services are held at 8:00, 10:15 (Matins), 11:30 (sung Eucharist), 15:15 (evensong), and 18:00. The rest of the week, evensong is at 17:00

Tue-Sat (not Mon). On some Sundays, there's a free organ recital at 16:45.

**Rick's Tip:** *If you come to St. Paul's 20 minutes* **early for evensong worship** *(under the dome), you may be able to grab a big wooden stall in the choir, next to the singers.*

**Tours:** Along with the **audioguide,** admission includes a 1.5-hour guided **tour** (Mon-Sat at 10:00, 11:00, 13:00, and 14:00); reserve a place at the guiding desk when you arrive. Free 20-minute **introductory talks** are offered throughout the day. You

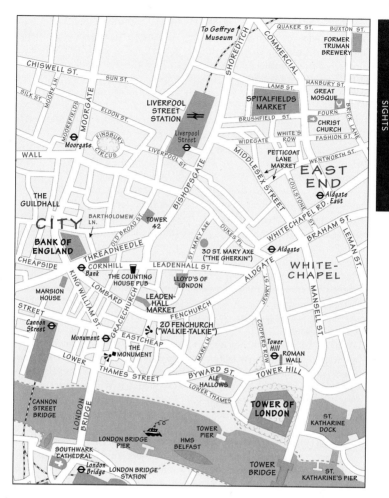

To Geffrye Museum

QUAKER ST.    BUXTON ST.

FORMER
TRUMAN
BREWERY

CHISWELL ST.

SUN ST.

SILK ST.

MOOR LN.

MOORGATE

MOOREFIELDS

ELDON ST.

LIVERPOOL
STREET
STATION

Liverpool
Street

LAMB ST.    HANBURY ST.

SPITALFIELDS
MARKET

GREAT
MOSQUE

BRUSHFIELD  ST.

FOURN.
CHRIST
CHURCH

COMMERCIAL

SHOREDITCH

BRICK LANE

FASHION ST.

FINSBURY
CIRCUS

Moorgate

WALL

Liverpool St.

WIDEGATE

WHITE'S
ROW

MIDDLESEX STREET

PETTICOAT
LANE
MARKET

WENTWORTH ST.

EAST
END

COULSTONE ST.

WHITECHAPEL RD.

Aldgate
East

THE
GUILDHALL

CITY

BARTHOLOMEW
LN.

OLD BROAD ST.

TOWER
42

BISHOPSGATE

ST. MARY AXE

DUKES PL.

BRAHAM ST.

LEMAN ST.

BANK OF
ENGLAND

THREADNEEDLE

CHEAPSIDE

CORNHILL

Bank

30 ST. MARY AXE
("THE GHERKIN")

Aldgate

WHITE-
CHAPEL

MANSION
HOUSE

STREET

KING WILLIAM ST.

LOMBARD

THE COUNTING
HOUSE PUB

LEADENHALL ST.

LLOYD'S OF
LONDON

ALDGATE

JEWRY ST.

MANSELL ST.

Cannon
Street

GRACECHURCH ST.

LEADEN-
HALL
MARKET

FENCHURCH

COOPER'S ROW

Monument

EASTCHEAP

20 FENCHURCH
("WALKIE-TALKIE")

MARK LN.

Tower
Hill

ROMAN
WALL

LOWER

THE
MONUMENT

THAMES STREET

BYWARD ST.

ALL
HALLOWS

TOWER HILL

LOWER THAMES

CANNON
STREET
BRIDGE

LONDON BRIDGE

SOUTHWARK
CATHEDRAL

LONDON BRIDGE
PIER

London
Bridge

LONDON BRIDGE
STATION

TOWER
PIER

HMS
BELFAST

TOWER OF
LONDON

ST.
KATHARINE
DOCK

TOWER
BRIDGE

ST.
KATHARINE'S PIER

---

can also 🎧 download my free St. Paul's Cathedral **audio tour** (see page 27).

### ⊖ SELF-GUIDED TOUR

Enter, buy your ticket, pick up the free visitor's map, and stand at the far back of the ❶ **nave,** behind the font. At 515 feet long and 250 feet wide, this is Europe's fourth largest church, after cathedrals in Rome (St. Peter's), Sevilla, and Milan. The spaciousness is accentuated by the relative lack of decoration. The simple, cream-colored ceiling and the clear glass in the windows light everything evenly. Wren wanted a simple, open church with

nothing to hide. Unfortunately, only this entrance area keeps his original vision—the rest was encrusted with 19th-century Victorian ornamentation.

Ahead and on the left is the towering, black-and-white ❷ **Wellington Monument.** Wren would have been appalled, but his church has become so central to England's soul that many national heroes are buried here (in the basement crypt).

The ❸ **dome** you see from here, painted with scenes from the life of St. Paul, is only the innermost of three. From the painted interior of the first dome, look up through the opening to see the light-filled lantern of the second dome. Finally, the whole thing is covered on the outside by the third and final dome, the shell of lead-covered wood that you see from the street. Wren's ingenious three-in-one design was psychological as well as functional—he wanted a low, shallow inner dome so worshippers wouldn't feel diminished. The ❹ **choir** area blocks your way, but you can see the **altar** at the far end under a golden canopy.

Do a quick clockwise spin around the church. In the north transept (to your left as you face the altar), find the big painting, ❺ *The Light of the World* (1904), by the Pre-Raphaelite William Holman Hunt. Inspired by Hunt's own experience of finding Christ during a moment of spiritual crisis, the crowd-pleasing work was criticized as "syrupy" and "simple"—even as it became the most famous painting in Victorian England.

Along the left side of the choir is the modern statue ❻ *Mother and Child,* by modern sculptor Henry Moore. This Mary and Baby Jesus—inspired by the sight of British moms nursing babies in WWII bomb shelters—renders a traditional subject in an abstract, minimalist way.

The area behind the altar, with three modern stained-glass windows, is the ❼ **American Memorial Chapel**—honoring the Americans who sacrificed their lives to save Britain in World War II. In colored panes that arch around the big windows, spot the American eagle (cen-ter window, to the left of Christ), George Washington (right window, upper-right corner), and symbols of all 50 states (find your state seal). In the carved wood beneath the windows, you'll see birds and foliage native to the US. The Roll of Honour (a 500-page book under glass, immediately behind the altar) lists the names of 28,000 US servicemen and women based in Britain who gave their lives during the war.

Around the other side of the choir is a shrouded statue honoring ❽ the great poet **John Donne** ("never wonder for whom the bell tolls—it tolls for thee"), who also served as a passionate preacher in old St. Paul's (1621-1631). In the south transept are monuments to military greats ❾ **Horatio Nelson,** who fought Napoleon, and **Charles Cornwallis,** who was finished off by George Washington at Yorktown.

❿ **Climbing the Dome:** During your visit, you can climb 528 steps to reach the dome and great city views. Along the way, have some fun in the Whispering Gallery (257 steps up). Whisper sweet nothings into the wall, and your partner (and anyone else) standing far away can hear you. For best effects, try whispering (not talking) with your mouth close to the wall, while your partner stands a few dozen yards away with his or her ear to the wall.

⓫ **Visiting the Crypt:** The crypt is a world of historic bones and interesting cathedral models. Many legends are buried here—Horatio Nelson, the Duke

*The cathedral's interior is dazzling.*

*The city views from St. Paul's dome are worth the climb.*

# London's Best Views

For some viewpoints, you need to pay admission. At the bars or restaurants, you'll need to buy a drink. The only truly free spots are One New Change Rooftop Terrace, 20 Fenchurch, and Primrose Hill.

**London Eye:** Ride the giant Ferris wheel for stunning London views. See page 87.

**St. Paul's Dome:** You'll earn a striking, unobstructed view by climbing hundreds of steps to the church's cupola. See page 76.

**One New Change Rooftop Terrace:** Get fine free views—nearly as good as those from St. Paul's Dome—from the rooftop terrace of the shopping mall just behind and east of the church.

**Tate Modern:** Take in a classic vista across the Thames from the restaurant/bar on the museum's sixth level. See page 90.

**20 Fenchurch** (a.k.a. "The Walkie-Talkie"): Get 360-degree views of London from the mostly enclosed Sky Garden, along with a garden, bar, restaurants, and lots of locals. It's free but you'll need to make reservations and bring a photo ID (Mon-Fri 10:00-18:00, Sat-Sun 11:00-21:00, 20 Fenchurch Street, Tube: Monument, www.skygarden.london).

**National Portrait Gallery:** A mod top-floor restaurant peers over Trafalgar Square and the Westminster neighborhood. See page 63.

**Waterstones Bookstore:** Its hip, low-key, top-floor café/bar has sweeping views of the London Eye, Big Ben, and the Houses of Parliament (www.5thview.co.uk).

**OXO Tower:** Perched high over the Thames River, the building's upscale restaurant/bar boasts views over London and St. Paul's, with al fresco dining in good weather (Barge House Street, Tube: Blackfriars or Southwark, tel. 020/7803-3888, www.harveynichols.com/restaurants/oxo-tower-london).

**London Hilton, Park Lane:** You'll spot Buckingham Palace, Hyde Park, and the London Eye from Galvin at Windows, its 28th-floor restaurant/bar (22 Park Lane, Tube: Hyde Park Corner, tel. 020/7208-4021, www.galvinatwindows.com).

**The Shard:** The observation decks that cap this 1,020-foot-tall skyscraper offer London's most commanding views, but at a high price (£25 if booked at least a day in advance, £30 for same-day reservations; daily 10:00-22:00, last entry slot at 21:00; Tube: London Bridge—use London Bridge exit and follow signs, tel. 0844-499-7111, www.theviewfromtheshard.com).

**Primrose Hill:** Get 360-degree views from this huge grassy expanse just north of Regent's Park (off Prince Albert Road, Tube: Chalk Farm or Camden Town, www.royalparks.org.uk/parks/the-regents-park).

of Wellington, and even Wren himself, whose tomb is marked by a simple black slab with no statue. Back up in the nave, on the floor directly under the dome, is Christopher Wren's name and epitaph (written in Latin): "Reader, if you seek his monument, look around you."

## ▲MUSEUM OF LONDON

This museum tells the fascinating story of London, taking you from its pre-Roman beginnings to the present and featuring distinguished citizens ranging from Neanderthals, to Romans, to Elizabethans, to Victorians, to Mods, to today. The displays are chronological, spacious, and informative. Scale models and costumes help you visualize everyday life in the city at different periods. In the last room, you'll see the museum's prized possession: the Lord Mayor's Coach, a golden carriage pulled by six white horses, looking as if it had pranced right out of the pages of *Cinderella*. There are enough whiz-bang multimedia displays (including for the Plague and the Great Fire) to spice up otherwise humdrum artifacts.

**Cost and Hours:** Free, daily 10:00-18:00, last admission an hour before closing, see the day's events board for special talks and tours, café, 150 London Wall at Aldersgate Street, Tube: Barbican or St. Paul's plus a five-minute walk, tel. 020/7001-9844, www.museumoflondon.org.uk.

## THE MONUMENT

Wren's recently restored 202-foot-tall tribute to London's 1666 Great Fire is at the junction of Monument Street and Fish Street Hill. Climb the 311 steps inside the column for a monumental view of The City (£4, £10.50 combo-ticket with Tower Bridge, cash only, daily 9:30-18:00, until 17:30 Oct-March, Tube: Monument).

## ▲▲▲TOWER OF LONDON

The Tower has served as a castle in wartime, a king's residence in peacetime, and, most notoriously, as the prison and exe-cution site of rebels. See the crown jewels, take a witty Beefeater tour, and ponder the executioner's block that dispensed with Anne Boleyn, Sir Thomas More, and troublesome heirs to the throne.

**Cost and Hours:** £15, family-£63, entry fee includes Beefeater tour (see later); Tue-Sat 9:00-17:30, Sun-Mon 10:00-17:30; Nov-Feb closes one hour earlier; skippable audioguide-£4; Tube: Tower Hill, tel. 0844-482-7788, www.hrp.org.uk.

**Advance Tickets:** To avoid the long ticket-buying lines at the Tower, buy your ticket at the Trader's Gate gift shop, located down the steps from the Tower Hill Tube stop (can be used any day). Tickets are also sold at various locations (such as travel agencies) throughout London. You can also try buying tickets, with credit card only, at the Tower Welcome Centre to the left of the normal ticket lines—though on busy days they may turn you away. It's easy to book online, but you must use your ticket within seven days from the date you select (www.hrp.org.uk, 10 percent discount).

---

**Rick's Tip:** *The* **Tower of London** *is most crowded in summer, on weekends (especially Sundays), and during school holidays. The line for the crown jewels can be just as long as the ticket line.* **Arrive before 10:00 and go straight for the jewels.** *Alternatively, arrive in the afternoon, tour the rest of the Tower first, and see the jewels an hour before closing time, when crowds die down.*

---

*Tower of London*

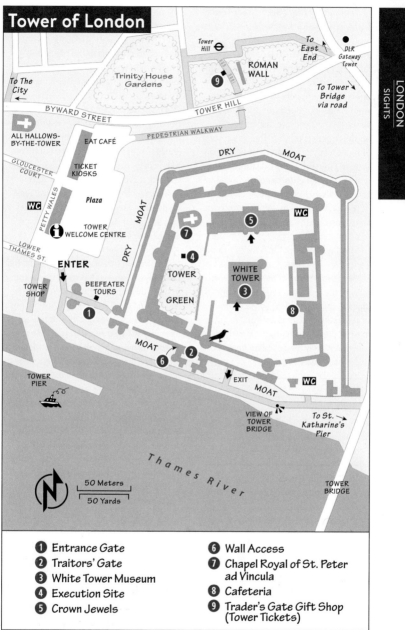

# Tower of London

- Tower Hill
- To East End
- DLR Gateway Tower
- Trinity House Gardens
- ROMAN WALL
- To The City ←
- To Tower Bridge via road
- BYWARD STREET
- TOWER HILL
- ALL HALLOWS-BY-THE-TOWER
- PEDESTRIAN WALKWAY
- EAT CAFÉ
- GLOUCESTER COURT
- TICKET KIOSKS
- Plaza
- DRY MOAT
- WC
- PETTY WALES
- TOWER WELCOME CENTRE
- LOWER THAMES ST.
- DRY MOAT
- WC
- ENTER
- BEEFEATER TOURS
- TOWER GREEN
- WHITE TOWER
- TOWER SHOP
- MOAT
- EXIT
- MOAT
- WC
- TOWER PIER
- VIEW OF TOWER BRIDGE
- To St. Katharine's Pier
- Thames River
- 50 Meters
- 50 Yards
- TOWER BRIDGE

1. Entrance Gate
2. Traitors' Gate
3. White Tower Museum
4. Execution Site
5. Crown Jewels
6. Wall Access
7. Chapel Royal of St. Peter ad Vincula
8. Cafeteria
9. Trader's Gate Gift Shop (Tower Tickets)

**Yeoman Warder (Beefeater) Tours:** Today, while the Tower's military purpose is history, it's still home to the Beefeaters—the 35 Yeoman Warders and their families. (The original duty of the Yeoman Warders was to guard the Tower, its prisoners, and the jewels.) The free, worthwhile, one-hour Beefeater tours leave every 30 minutes from just inside the entrance gate (first tour Tue-Sat at 10:00, Sun-Mon at 10:30, last one at 15:30—or 14:30 in Nov-Feb). The boisterous Beefeaters are great entertainers, whose historical talks include lots of bloody anecdotes and corny jokes. When groups are large, don't be shy about standing close to hear.

**Sunday Worship:** On Sunday morning, visitors are welcome for free to worship in the Chapel Royal of St. Peter ad Vincula on the grounds. You can see only the chapel—no sightseeing (9:15 communion or 11:00 service with fine choral music, meet at west gate 30 minutes early, dress for church, may be closed for ceremonies—call ahead).

---

**Rick's Tip:** *To scenically—though circuitously—connect the* **Tower of London** *with* **St. Paul's Cathedral,** *detour through Southwark on the South Bank (and stop by Borough Market for the fun food scene).*

---

**Visiting the Tower:** William the Conqueror, still getting used to his new title, built the stone "White Tower" (1077-1097) to keep Londoners in line, a gleaming reminder of the monarch's absolute power. You could be feasting on roast boar in the banqueting hall one night and chained to the walls of the prison the next. The Tower also served as an effective lookout for seeing invaders coming up the Thames.

This square, 90-foot-tall tower was the original structure that gave this castle complex of 20 towers its name. William's successors enlarged the complex to its present 18-acre size. Because of the security it provided, the Tower of London served over the centuries as a royal residence, the Royal Mint, the Royal Jewel House, and, most famously, as a prison and execution site.

You'll find more bloody history per square inch in this original tower of power than anywhere else in Britain. Inside the White Tower is a **museum** with exhibits re-creating medieval life and chronicling the torture and executions that took place here. In the Royal Armory, you'll see some suits of armor of Henry VIII—slender in his youth (c. 1515), heavyset by 1540—with his bigger-is-better codpiece. On the top floor, see the Tower's actual execution ax and chopping block. The **execution site,** however, in the middle of Tower Green, looks just like a lawn. Henry VIII axed a couple of his ex-wives here (divorced readers can insert their own joke), including Anne Boleyn and Catherine Howard.

The Tower's hard stone and glittering **crown jewels** represent the ultimate power of the monarch. The Sovereign's

*A Beefeater on duty*

*Execution ax and block*

# Henry VIII (1491-1547)

The notorious king who single-handedly transformed England was a true Renaissance Man—six feet tall, handsome, charismatic, well-educated, and brilliant. When 17-year-old Henry, the second monarch of the House of Tudor, was crowned king, all of England rejoiced.

Henry left affairs of state in the hands of others and filled his days with sports, war, the arts—and women. In 1529, Henry's personal life changed the course of history. Henry wanted a divorce, partly because his wife had become too old to bear him a son, and partly because he'd fallen in love with Anne Boleyn. Henry begged the pope for an annulment, but the pope refused. Henry divorced his wife anyway and was excommunicated.

Henry's rejection of papal authority sparked the English Reformation. He forced monasteries to close, sold off some church land, and confiscated everything else for himself and the Crown. Within a decade, centuries-old monastic institutions were left gutted. Meanwhile, the church was reorganized into the Anglican Church of England, with Henry as its head. Though Henry himself adhered to basic Catholic doctrine, he discouraged the veneration of saints and relics, and commissioned an English translation of the Bible.

Henry famously had six wives. The issue was not his love life, but the politics of royal succession. To guarantee the Tudor family's dominance, he needed a male heir born by a recognized queen. Henry's first marriage, to Catherine of Aragon, bore Henry a daughter, but no sons. Next came Anne Boleyn, who also gave birth to a daughter. After a turbulent few years with Anne and several miscarriages, a frustrated Henry had her beheaded. His next wife, Jane Seymour, finally had a son (but Jane died soon after giving birth). A blind marriage with Anne of Cleves ended quickly when she proved to be politically useless. His next bride, Catherine Howard, cheated on him, so she was executed. Henry finally found comfort—but no children—in his later years with his final wife, Catherine Parr.

Henry's last years were marked by paranoia and sudden rages. His perceived enemies were charged with treason and beheaded. Once-wealthy England was depleted, thanks to Henry's expensive habits, which included making war on France, building and acquiring 50 palaces, and collecting fine tapestries and archery bows.

Still, Henry forged a legacy. He expanded the power of the monarchy while simultaneously strengthening Parliament—largely because it agreed with his policies. He annexed Wales and imposed English rule on Ireland (provoking centuries of resentment). He expanded the navy, paving the way for Britannia to rule the waves. And England would forever be a Protestant nation.

Scepter is encrusted with the world's largest cut diamond—the 530-carat Star of Africa. The Crown of the Queen Mother (Elizabeth II's famous mum, who died in 2002) has the 106-carat Koh-I-Noor diamond glittering on the front (considered unlucky for male rulers, it only adorns the crown of the king's wife). The Imperial State Crown is what the Queen wears for official functions such as the State Opening of Parliament. Among its 3,733 jewels are Queen Elizabeth I's former earrings (the hanging pearls, top center), a stunning 13th-century ruby look-alike in the center, and Edward the Confessor's ring (the blue sapphire on top, in the center of the Maltese cross of diamonds).

The Tower was defended by state-of-the-art **walls** and fortifications in the 13th century. Walking along them offers fine views of the famous Tower Bridge, with its twin towers and blue spans.

## TOWER BRIDGE

The iconic Tower Bridge (often mistakenly called London Bridge) has been recently painted and restored. The hydraulically powered drawbridge was built in 1894 to accommodate the growing East End. While fully modern, its design has a retro Neo-Gothic look.

The drawbridge lifts to let ships pass a thousand times a year (best viewed from the Tower side of the Thames). For the bridge-lifting schedule, check the website or call.

You can tour the bridge at the **Tower Bridge Exhibition,** with a history display and a peek at the Victorian engine room that lifts the span. Included in your entrance is the chance to cross the bridge—138 feet above the road along a see-through glass walkway. The exhibit is overpriced, though the adrenaline rush and spectacular city views from the walkways might justify the cost.

**Cost and Hours:** £9, £10.50 combo-ticket with The Monument, daily 10:00-18:00 in summer, 9:30-17:30 in winter, enter at northwest tower, Tube: Tower Hill, tel. 020/7403-3761, www.towerbridge.org.uk.

## On the South Bank

The South Bank of the Thames is a thriving arts and cultural center, tied together by the riverfront Jubilee Walkway. Most of these sights are in Southwark (SUTH-uck), the core of the tourist's South Bank. Southwark was for centuries the place

*The Tower Bridge has spanned the Thames since 1894.*

Londoners would go to let their hair down. A run-down warehouse district through the 20th century, it's now been gentrified with classy restaurants, office parks, pedestrian promenades, and major sights.

### ▲JUBILEE WALKWAY

This riverside path is a popular, pub-crawling pedestrian promenade that stretches all along the South Bank, offering grand views of the Houses of Parliament and St. Paul's. On a sunny day, it's the place to see Londoners out strolling. The Walkway hugs the river except just east of London Bridge, where it cuts inland for a couple of blocks. It has been expanded into a 60-mile "Greenway" circling the city, including the 2012 Olympics site.

---

**Rick's Tip:** *If you're visiting London in summer,* **visit the South Bank after hours.** *Take a trip around the* **London Eye at sunset** *(the wheel spins until late—last ascent at 20:30, later in July-Aug). Then cap your night with a stroll along the* **Jubilee Walkway.**

---

### ▲▲LONDON EYE

This giant Ferris wheel, towering above London opposite Big Ben, is one of the world's highest observational wheels. Riding it is a memorable experience, even though London doesn't have much of a skyline, and the price is borderline outrageous. Whether you ride or not, the wheel is a sight to behold.

The experience starts with an engaging, four-minute show combining a 3-D movie with wind and water effects. Then it's time to spin around the Eye, designed like a giant bicycle wheel. It's "green," running extremely efficiently and virtually silently. Twenty-five people ride in each of its 32 air-conditioned capsules (representing the boroughs of London) for the 30-minute rotation (you go around only once). From the top of this 443-foot-high wheel—the second-highest public viewpoint in the city—even Big Ben looks small.

**Cost:** £24.95, about 10 percent cheaper if bought online, family deal (online only). Combo-tickets save money if you plan on visiting Madame Tussauds. Buy tickets in advance at www.londoneye.com, by calling 0870-500-0600, or in person at the box office (in the corner of the County

*The London Eye is one of the latest additions to London's skyline.*

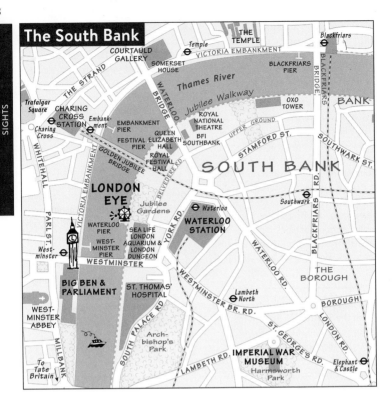

## The South Bank

Hall building nearest the Eye).

**Hours:** Daily 10:00-20:30, until 21:30 or later in July and August, check the website for latest schedule, these are last-ascent times, closed Dec 25 and a few days in Jan for annual maintenance, Tube: Waterloo or Westminster. Thames boats come and go from Waterloo Pier at the foot of the wheel.

**Rick's Tip:** *The* **London Eye** *is busiest between 11:00 and 17:00, especially on weekends and every day in July and August.* **Call ahead or go online to book your ticket;** *then you can print it at home, or retrieve it from an onsite ticket machine (bring your confirmation code and payment card), or stand in the "Ticket Collection" line. Even with a reservation, you'll still have to wait to board the wheel (but it's not worth paying an extra £8 for a Fast Track ticket).*

**By the Eye:** The area next to the London Eye has developed a cotton-candy ambience of kitschy, kid-friendly attractions. There's a game arcade, an aquarium, and the Shrek's Adventure amusement ride.

## ▲▲IMPERIAL WAR MUSEUM

This impressive museum covers the wars of the last century—from World War I

*Imperial War Museum*

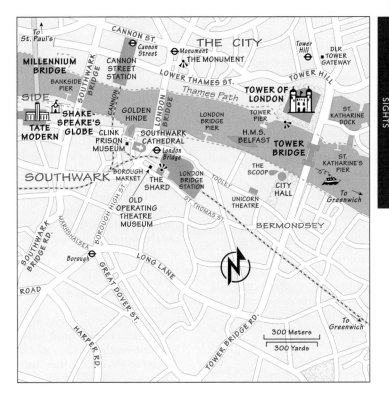

biplanes, to the rise of fascism, the Cold War, the Cuban Missile Crisis, the Troubles in Northern Ireland, the wars in Iraq and Afghanistan, and terrorism. Rather than glorify war, the museum encourages an understanding of the history of modern warfare and the wartime experience, including the effect it has on the everyday lives of people back home.

Highlights are the galleries devoted to World War I, World War II, the Secret War (espionage), and the Holocaust. War wonks love the place, as do history buffs who enjoy patiently reading displays. For the rest, there are enough interactive experiences and multimedia exhibits and submarines to keep it interesting.

The museum (which sits in an inviting park equipped with an equally inviting café) is housed in what had been the Royal Bethlam Hospital. Also known as "the Bedlam asylum," the place was so

wild that it gave the world a new word for chaos. Back in Victorian times, locals—without reality shows and YouTube—paid admission to visit the asylum on weekends for entertainment.

**Cost and Hours:** Free, £5 suggested donation, daily 10:00-18:00, special exhibits extra, various free audioguides may be available—ask at the info desk, Tube: Lambeth North or Elephant and Castle; buses #3, #12, and #159 come here from Westminster area; tel. 020/7416-5000, www.iwm.org.uk.

**◔ SELF-GUIDED TOUR**

Start with the atrium to grasp the massive scale of warfare as you wander among and under notable battle machines, then head directly for the museum's recently renovated **WWI galleries.** Firsthand accounts connect the blunt reality of a brutal war with the contributions, heartache, and efforts of a nation.

How different this museum would be if the war to end all wars had lived up to its name. Instead, the museum, much like history, builds on itself. Ascending to the first floor, you'll find the **Turning Points** galleries progressing up to and through World War II, including sections explaining Blitzkrieg and its effects (see an actual Nazi parachute bomb like the ones that devastated London). The **Family in Wartime** exhibit shows London through the eyes of an ordinary family.

The second floor houses the **Secret War** exhibit, which features actual surveillance equipment and peeks into the intrigues of espionage from World Wars I and II through present-day security. You'll learn about MI5 (Britain's domestic spy corps), MI6 (their international spies), and the Special Operations Executive (SOE), who led espionage efforts during World War II.

The third floor houses temporary art and film exhibits speckled with military-themed works, including **John Singer** Sargent's *Gassed* (1919), showing besieged troops in World War I.

The fourth-floor section on the **Holocaust,** one of the best on the subject anywhere, tells the story with powerful videos, artifacts, and fine explanations.

Crowning the museum on the fifth floor is the Lord Ashcroft Gallery and the **Extraordinary Heroes** display. More than 250 stories celebrate Britain's highest military award for bravery with the world's largest collection of Victoria Cross medals. Civilians who earned the George Cross medal for bravery are also honored.

## ▲▲TATE MODERN

Dedicated in the spring of 2000, this striking museum opened the new century with art from the previous one. Filling a derelict old power station across the river from St. Paul's, its powerhouse collection highlights international works of modern art since 1900. You'll see the heavy hitters, including pieces by Dalí, Picasso, Warhol, Beuys, and many more.

The Tate opened a new wing in 2016, doubling the museum's exhibition space and adding a panoramic roof terrace. The goal of the expansion—to foster interaction between art and community in the 21st century—is as modern as the collection itself.

**Cost and Hours:** Free, but £4 suggested donation, fee for special exhibitions; open daily 10:00-18:00, Fri-Sat until 22:00, last entry to special exhibits 45 minutes before closing, especially crowded on weekend days (crowds thin out on Fri and Sat evenings); multimedia guide-£4.50, free 45-minute guided tours are offered about four times daily (ask for schedule at info desk), view restaurant on top floor, no photos beyond entrance hall; tel. 020/7887-8888, www.tate.org.uk.

**Getting There:** Cross the Millennium Bridge from St. Paul's; take the Tube to Southwark, London Bridge, St. Paul's, Mansion House, or Blackfriars and walk 10 to 15 minutes; or catch Thames Clippers' Tate Boat ferry from the Tate Britain

*Imperial War Museum atrium*

*Tate Modern*

for a 15-minute crossing (£7.50 one-way, discount with Travelcard or Oyster card, departs every 40 minutes when galleries are open, www.tate.org.uk/visit/tate-boat).

**Visiting the Museum:** Artworks in the permanent collection are arranged according to theme—such as "Poetry and Dream"—not chronologically or by artist. Paintings by Picasso, for example, are scattered throughout the building. Don't expect to see just the Old Masters of Modernism; the museum's collection is ever-growing with new contemporary works.

Temporary exhibits are cutting-edge. Each year, the vast main hall features a different monumental installation by a prominent artist.

## ▲MILLENNIUM BRIDGE

The pedestrian bridge links St. Paul's Cathedral and the Tate Modern across the Thames. This is London's first new bridge in a century, nicknamed the "blade of light" for its sleek minimalist design (370 yards long, 4 yards wide, stainless steel with teak planks). Its clever aerodynamic handrails deflect wind over the heads of pedestrians.

## ▲▲SHAKESPEARE'S GLOBE

This replica of the original Globe Theatre was built as it was in Shakespeare's time—half-timbered and thatched (in fact, with the first thatched roof constructed in London since they were outlawed after the Great Fire of 1666). The original Globe opened in 1599, with its debut play, Shakespeare's *Julius Caesar*. It accommodated 2,200 seated and another 1,000 standing. Today's Globe, allowing space for reasonable aisles, is slightly smaller, holding 800 seated and 600 groundlings. The working theater hosts authentic performances of Shakespeare's plays with actors in period costumes, modern interpretations of his works, and some works by other playwrights. For details on attending a play, see page 102.

The Globe complex has four parts: the Globe theater itself, the box office, a museum (called the Exhibition), and the Sam Wanamaker Playhouse (an indoor Jacobean theater around back). The Playhouse, which hosts performances through the winter, is horseshoe-shaped, intimate (seating fewer than 350), and sometimes uses authentic candle lighting for period performances. The repertoire focuses less on Shakespeare and more on the work of his contemporaries (Jonson, Marlow, Fletcher), as well as concerts.

**Cost:** £13.50 ticket (good all day) includes Exhibition, audioguide, and 40-minute tour of the Globe; when theater is in use, you can tour the Exhibition only for £6.

**Hours:** The complex is open daily 9:00-17:30; tours start every 30 minutes. During the Globe theater season (late April-mid-Oct), it's safest to arrive for a tour before noon (last tour Tue-Sat at 12:30, Sun at 11:30, Mon at 17:00). Located on the South Bank over the Millennium

*Millennium Bridge*

*Shakespeare's Globe*

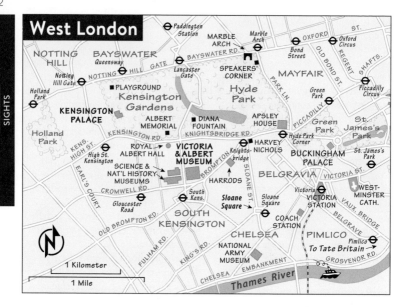

West London

Bridge from St. Paul's, Tube: Mansion House or London Bridge plus a 10-minute walk; tel. 020/7902-1400, box office tel. 020/7401-9919, www.shakespearesglobe.com.

**Visiting the Globe:** You browse on your own in the **Exhibition** (with the included audioguide) through displays of Elizabethan-era costumes and makeup, music, script-printing, and special effects (the displays change). There are early folios and objects that were dug up on site. Videos and scale models help put Shakespearean theater within the context of the times. You'll also learn how they built the replica in modern times, using Elizabethan materials and techniques.

You must **tour the theater** at the time stamped on your ticket, but you can come back to the Exhibition museum afterward. A guide (usually an actor) leads you into the theater to see the stage and the various seating areas for the different classes of people. Learn how the new Globe is similar to the old Globe (open-air performances, standing-room by the stage, no curtain) and how it's different (female actors, lights for night performances, con-

crete floor). It's not a backstage tour, but the guides bring the Elizabethan period to life.

**Eating:** The Swan at the Globe café offers a restaurant (for lunch and dinner, reservations recommended, tel. 020/7928-9444), a drinks-and-plates bar, and a sandwich-and-coffee cart (daily 9:00-closing, depending on performance times).

# West London
## ▲▲TATE BRITAIN

One of Europe's great art houses, Tate Britain specializes in British painting from the 16th century through modern times. This is people's art, with realistic paintings rooted in the people, landscape, and stories of the British Isles. The Tate shows off Hogarth's stage sets, Gainsborough's ladies, Blake's angels, Constable's clouds, Turner's tempests, the naturalistic realism of the Pre-Raphaelites, and the camera-eye portraits of Hockney and Freud.

**Cost and Hours:** Free but £4 suggested donation, admission fee for special exhibits; daily 10:00-18:00, last entry 45 minutes before closing; free tours generally daily (ask at the information desk or call ahead), or use the Tate's Wi-Fi to download their handy room-by-room app; café and restaurant, tel. 020/7887-8888, www.tate.org.uk.

**Getting There:** It's on the Thames River, south of Big Ben and north of Vauxhall Bridge. Tube to Pimlico, then walk seven minutes. Or hop on the Tate Boat museum ferry from Tate Modern (see page 124).

## ❍ SELF-GUIDED TOUR

Works from the early centuries are located in the west half of the building, 20th-century art is in the east half, and the works of J. M. W. Turner are in an adjacent wing (the Clore Gallery). Certain artists' work is placed in special rooms outside the chronological flow. Other rooms focus on a particular aspect of British art. The Tate's great strength is championing contemporary British art in special exhibitions—there are two exhibition spaces (one free, the other usually requiring separate admission).

• *From the main Millbank entrance, walk through the bright, white rotunda and down the long central hall. Near the far end, enter the rooms on the left, labeled* Walk Through British Art, *where you'll find the beginnings of British painting (as you enter each room, you'll see the year etched into the floor).*

**1540s-1650s—Portraits Rule:** Stuffy portraits of Lord and Lady Whoeverthe-yare try to turn crude country nobles into refined men and delicate women. Men in ruffled collars clutch symbols of power. Women in ruffled collars, puffy sleeves, and elaborately patterned dresses display their lily-white complexions, turning their pinkies out.

English country houses often had a long hall built specially to hang family portraits. You could stroll along and see your noble forebears looking down their noses at you.

**1700s—Art Blossoms:** With peace at home, a strong overseas economy, and a growing urban center in London, England's artistic life began to bloom. As the English grew more sophisticated, so did their portraits. Painters branched out into other subjects, capturing slices of everyday life (find William Hogarth, with his unflinchingly honest portraits, and Thomas Gainsborough's elegant, educated women). The Royal Academy added a veneer of classical Greece to even the simplest subjects.

**1800-1850—The Industrial Revolution:** Many artists rebelled against "progress" and the modern world. They escaped the dirty cities to commune with nature (Constable and the Romantics), found a new spirituality in intense human emotions (dramatic scenes from history or literature)—or they left the modern world altogether.

William Blake, whose work hangs in a darkened room to protect his watercolors from deterioration, painted angels, not the dull material world. Blake turned his gaze inward, illustrating the glorious visions of the soul. In visions of the Christian heaven or Dante's hell, his figures have superhero musculature. The colors are almost translucent.

**1837-1901—The Victorian Era:** In the world's wealthiest nation, the prosperous middle class dictated taste in art. They admired paintings that were realistic, depicting slices of everyday life. Some paintings tug at the heartstrings, with scenes of parting couples, the grief of death, or the joy of families reuniting.

*Victorian-era* Lady of Shalott

Overdosed with the gushy sentimentality of their day, the Pre-Raphaelites were a band of artists—including Sir John Everett Millais, Dante Gabriel Rossetti, and William Holman Hunt—who dedicated themselves to creating less saccharine art. Like the Impressionists who followed them, they left stuffy studios to set up outdoors, painting trees, streams, and people. They captured nature with such close-up clarity that it's downright unnatural.

**British Impressionism:** Realistic British art stood apart from the Modernist trends in France, but some influences drifted across the Channel. American-born John Singer Sargent studied with Parisian Impressionists, learning the thick, messy brushwork and play of light at twilight. James Tissot used Degas' snapshot technique to capture a crowded scene from an odd angle. And James McNeill Whistler (born in America, trained in Paris, lived in London) composed his paintings like music—see some of his paintings' titles.

**The Turner Collection:** Walking through J. M. W. Turner's life's work, you can trace his evolution from clear-eyed realism to hazy proto-Impressionism. You'll also see how Turner dabbled in different subjects: landscapes, seascapes, Roman ruins, snapshots of Venice, and so on.

The corner room of the Clore Gallery is dedicated to Turner's great rival and contemporary, John Constable, who painted the English landscape as it was—realistically, without idealizing it.

**1900-1950—World Wars:** As two world wars whittled down the powerful British Empire, it still remained a major cultural force. British art mirrored many of the trends pioneered in Paris: cubism like Picasso's, abstract art like Mondrian's, and so on.

Henry Moore's statues—mostly female, mostly reclining—catch the primitive power of carved stone. He captured the human body in a few simple curves, with minimal changes to the rock itself.

Britain survived the Blitz, World War II, and the loss of hundreds of thousands of men—but at war's end, the bottled-up horror came rushing out. Francis Bacon's deformed half-humans/half-animals express the existential human predicament of being caught in a world not of your making.

**1950-2000—Modern World:** No longer a world power, Britain in the Swinging '60s became a major exporter of pop culture. Look for works by David Hockney, Lucian Freud, Bridget Riley, and Gilbert and George.

▲HYDE PARK

London's "Central Park," originally Henry VIII's hunting grounds, has more than 600 acres of lush greenery, Santander Cycles rental stations, the huge man-made Serpentine Lake (with rental boats and a lakeside swimming pool), the royal Kensington Palace, and the ornate Neo-Gothic Albert Memorial across from the Royal Albert Hall. The western half of the park is known as Kensington Gardens. The park is huge—study a Tube map to choose the stop nearest to your destination (for more about the park, see www.royalparks.org.uk/parks/hyde-park).

On Sundays, from just after noon until early evening, **Speakers' Corner** offers soapbox oratory at its best. Characters climb their stepladders, wave their flags, pound emphatically on their sandwich boards, and share what they are convinced is their wisdom. Regulars have

*Hyde Park*

resident hecklers who know their lines and are always ready with a verbal jab or barb. "The grass roots of democracy" is actually a holdover from when the gallows stood here and the criminal was allowed to say just about anything he wanted to before he swung. Raise your voice and gather a crowd—it's easy to do (northeast corner of the park, Tube: Marble Arch).

The **Princess Diana Memorial Fountain** honors the "People's Princess," who once lived in nearby Kensington Palace. The low-key circular stream, great for cooling off your feet on a hot day, is in the south-central part of the park, near the Albert Memorial and Serpentine Gallery (Tube: Knightsbridge). A similarly named but different sight, the **Diana, Princess of Wales Memorial Playground,** in the park's northwest corner, is loads of fun for kids (Tube: Queensway).

### KENSINGTON PALACE

For nearly 150 years (1689-1837), Kensington was the royal residence, before Buckingham Palace became the official home of the monarch. Sitting primly on its pleasant parkside grounds, the palace gives a glimpse into royal life, especially that of Queen Victoria, who was born and raised here.

After Queen Victoria moved the monarchy to Buckingham Palace, lesser royals bedded down at Kensington. Princess Diana lived here both during and after her marriage to Prince Charles (1981-1997). More recently, Will and Kate moved into a thoroughly renovated Apartment 1A (the southern flank of the palace complex, with four stories and 20 rooms). And Prince Harry lives in their old digs, a "cottage" on the other side of the main building. However—as many disappointed visitors discover—none of these more recent apartments are open to the public.

The palace has three main exhibits. To see them chronologically, start with the **Queen's State Apartments** (with highly conceptual exhibits focusing on the later Stuart dynasty—William and Mary, and Mary's sister, Queen Anne). Then move on to the **King's State Apartments** (the grandest spaces, from Hanoverian times), and finish with the **Victoria Revealed** exhibit (telling the story, through quotes and artifacts, of Britain's longest-ruling monarch).

**Cost and Hours:** £18, daily 10:00-18:00, Nov-Feb until 17:00, last entry one hour before closing, booking online saves a few pounds; least crowded in mornings; friendly and knowledgeable "explainers" will answer questions for free; a long 10-minute stroll through Kensington Gardens from either High Street Kensington or Queensway Tube stations, tel. 0844-482-7788, www.hrp.org.uk.

*Nearby:* Garden enthusiasts enjoy popping into the secluded Sunken Garden, 50 yards from the exit. Consider afternoon tea at the nearby Orangery, built as a greenhouse for Queen Anne in 1704 (see page 108). On the south side of the palace are the golden gates that became famous in 1997 as the backdrop to the sea of flowers left here by Princess Diana's mourners.

### ▲▲▲VICTORIA AND ALBERT MUSEUM

You could spend days wandering "the V&A," which encompasses 2,000 years of decorative arts (ceramics, stained glass, fine furniture, clothing, jewelry, carpets, and more). There's much to see, including Raphael's tapestry cartoons, five of Leonardo da Vinci's notebooks, the huge

*Kensington Palace*

Islamic Ardabil Carpet (4,914 knots in every 10 square centimeters), a cast of Trajan's Column that depicts the emperor's conquests, and rock memorabilia, including the jumpsuit Mick Jagger wore for the Rolling Stones' 1972 world tour.

**Cost and Hours:** Free, but £5 suggested donation, extra for some special exhibits; daily 10:00-17:45, some galleries open Fri until 22:00; get the much-needed £1 museum map, free tours daily, on Cromwell Road in South Kensington, Tube: South Kensington, from the Tube station a long tunnel leads directly to museum, tel. 020/7942-2000, www.vam.ac.uk.

---

**Rick's Tip:** *The museum is huge and tricky to navigate. Spend £1 for the* **Greatest Treasures brochure** *available from the info desk. It describes—and tells you how to find—the museum's must-see objects.*

---

**Visiting the Museum:** In the Grand Entrance lobby, look up to see the colorful **chandelier/sculpture** by American artist Dale Chihuly. This elaborate piece epitomizes the spirit of the V&A's collection—beautiful manufactured objects that demonstrate technical skill and innovation, wedding the old with the new, and blurring the line between arts and crafts.

The V&A has arguably the best collection of **Italian Renaissance sculpture** outside Italy. One prime example is *Samson Slaying a Philistine,* by Giambologna (c. 1562), carved from a single block of marble. Its spiral-shaped pose is reminiscent of Michelangelo.

The museum's **Islamic art** reflects both religious influences and sophisticated secular culture. Notice floral patterns (twining vines, flowers, arabesques) and geometric designs (stars, diamonds). But the most common pattern is calligraphy—elaborate inscriptions in Arabic.

The **British Galleries** sweep through 400 years of British high-class living (1500-1900). Look for rare miniature portraits—a popular item of Queen Elizabeth I's day—including Hilliard's oft-reproduced *Young Man Among Roses* miniature. A room dedicated to Henry VIII has a portrait of him, his writing box, and a whole roomful of furniture, tapestries, jewelry, and dinnerware.

# Greater London
## ▲▲KEW GARDENS

This fine riverside park and its palatial greenhouse are every botanist's favorite escape. Wander among 33,000 different types of plants, spread across 300 acres. For a quick visit, spend a fragrant hour wandering through three buildings: the Palm House, a humid Victorian world of iron, glass, and tropical plants built in 1844; a Waterlily House that Monet would swim for; and the Princess of Wales Conservatory, a modern greenhouse with many different climate zones. With extra time, check out the Xstrata Treetop Walkway, a 200-yard-long scenic steel walkway that puts you in the canopy 60 feet above the

*Victoria and Albert Museum*

*Kew Gardens*

ground. Young kids will love the Climbers and Creepers indoor/outdoor playground and little zip line, as well as a slow and easy ride on the hop-on, hop-off Kew Explorer tram (adults-£4.50, kids-£1.50 for narrated 40-minute ride, departs Victoria Gate, ask for schedule when you enter).

**Cost and Hours:** £16.50, June-Aug £11 after 16:00, kids 4-16 £3.50, free for kids under 4; April-Aug Mon-Fri 10:00-18:30, Sat-Sun until 19:30, closes earlier Sept-March—check schedule online, free one-hour walking tours daily at 11:00 and 13:30, tel. 020/8332-5000, www.kew.org.

**Getting There:** If taking the Tube, ride to Kew Gardens; from the Tube station, cross the footbridge over the tracks, which drops you in a community of plant-and-herb shops, a two-block walk from Victoria Gate (the main garden entrance). Another option is to take a boat, which runs April-Oct between Kew Gardens and Westminster Pier (see page 45).

**Eating:** For lunch or a snack, walk 10 minutes from the Palm House to the Orangery Cafeteria (Mon-Fri 10:00-17:30, Sat-Sun 10:00-18:30, until 15:15 in winter, closes early for events).

# EXPERIENCES

## Shopping

Most stores are open Monday through Saturday from roughly 9:00 or 10:00 until 17:00 or 18:00, with a late night on Wednesday or Thursday (usually until 19:00 or 20:00). Many close on Sundays. Large department stores stay open later during the week (until about 21:00 Mon-Sat) and are open shorter hours on Sundays.

### Shopping Streets

London is famous for its shopping. The best and most convenient shopping streets are in the West End and West London (roughly between Soho and Hyde Park). You'll find midrange shops along **Oxford Street** (running east from Tube:

Marble Arch). Fancier shops line **Regent Street** (stretching south from Tube: Oxford Circus to Piccadilly Circus; funky Carnaby Street runs parallel a block east) and **Knightsbridge** (where you'll find Harrods and Harvey Nichols; Tube: Knightsbridge). Other streets are more specialized, such as **Charing Cross Road** for books, **Jermyn Street** for old-fashioned men's clothing (just south of Piccadilly Street), and **Floral Street** for fashion boutiques (connecting Leicester Square to Covent Garden).

### Department Stores in West London

**Harrods** is London's most famous and touristy department store, with more than four acres of retail space covering seven floors (Mon-Sat 10:00-21:00, Sun 11:30-18:00, Brompton Road, Tube: Knightsbridge, tel. 020/7730-1234, www.harrods.com).

**Harvey Nichols,** once Princess Diana's favorite, remains the department store *du jour* (Mon-Sat 10:00-20:00, Sun 11:30-18:00, near Harrods, 109 Knightsbridge, Tube: Knightsbridge, tel. 020/7235-5000, www.harveynichols.com).

**Rick's Tip:** *The fifth floor at* **Harvey Nichols** *is a* **veritable food fest,** *with a gourmet grocery store, a fancy restaurant, a sushi bar, and a café. Get takeaway food for a* **picnic in the Hyde Park rose garden,** *two blocks away.*

**Fortnum & Mason,** the official department store of the Queen, embodies British upper-class taste, with a storybook atmosphere (Mon-Sat 10:00-21:00, Sun 11:30-18:00, 181 Piccadilly, Tube: Green Park, tel. 020/7734-8040, www.fortnumandmason.com). Elegant tea is served in its Diamond Jubilee Tea Salon (see page 108).

**Liberty** is a still-thriving 19th-century institution known for its artful displays and interior, constructed of two decommissioned battleships (Mon-Sat 10:00-20:00, Sun 12:00-18:00, Great Marlborough Street, Tube: Oxford Circus, tel. 020/7734-1234, www.liberty.co.uk).

## Street Markets

Antiques buffs and people-watchers love London's street markets. The best, combining lively stalls and colorful neighborhoods with characteristic shops of their own, are Portobello Road and Camden Lock Market.

### IN NOTTING HILL

**Portobello Road** stretches for several blocks through the funky-but-quaint Notting Hill neighborhood. Already-charming streets lined with pastel-painted houses and offbeat antique shops are enlivened on Fridays and Saturdays with 2,000 additional stalls (9:00-19:00), plus food, live music, and more (Tube: Notting Hill Gate, near recommended accommodations, tel. 020/7727-7684, www.portobelloroad.co.uk).

**Rick's Tip:** *Browse* **Portabello Road on Friday.** *Most stalls are open, but you can expect half the crowds of Saturday.*

### IN CAMDEN TOWN

**Camden Lock Market** is a huge arts-and-crafts festival divided into three areas, each with its own vibe. The main market, set alongside the picturesque canal, sells boutique crafts and artisanal foods. The market on the opposite side of Chalk Farm Road has ethnic food stalls, punk crafts, and canalside seating. The Stables, a sprawling, incense-scented complex, is squeezed into tunnels under the old rail bridge just behind the main market (daily 10:00-18:00, busiest on weekends, tel. 020/3763-9999, www.camdenlockmarket.com).

### IN THE EAST END

**Spitalfields Market** combines old brick buildings and sleek modern ones, all covered by a giant glass roof. The shops, stalls, and a rainbow of restaurants are open every day (Mon-Fri 10:00-17:00, Sat 11:00-17:00, Sun 9:00-17:00, Tube: Liverpool Street; from the Tube stop, take Bishopsgate East exit, turn left, walk to Brushfield Street, and turn right; www.spitalfields.co.uk).

**Petticoat Lane Market,** just a block from Spitalfields Market, sits on the otherwise dull Middlesex Street; adjoining Wentworth Street is grungier and more characteristic (Sun 9:00-14:00, sometimes later; smaller market Mon-Fri on Wentworth Street only; closed Sat; Middlesex Street and Wentworth Street, Tube: Liverpool Street).

The **Truman Markets,** housed in a former brewery on Brick Lane, are gritty and avant-garde, selling handmade clothes, home decor, and ethnic street food in the heart of the "Banglatown" Bangladeshi community. The markets are in full swing on Sundays (roughly 10:00-17:00), though you'll see some action on Saturdays (11:00-18:00). Surrounding shops and eateries are open all week (Tube: Liverpool Street or Aldgate East, tel. 020/7770-6028, www.bricklanemarket.com).

**Brick Lane** is lined with Sunday market stalls all the way up to Bethnal Green Road, about a 10-minute walk (leading north out of the Truman Markets). Continuing straight (north) about five more minutes takes you to Columbia Road, a colorful shopping street made even more so on Sunday by the **Columbia Road Flower Market** (Sun 8:00-15:00, closed Mon-Sat, http://columbiaroad.info). Halfway up Columbia Road, little Ezra Street has characteristic eateries, boutiques, and antiques vendors.

### IN THE WEST END

The iron-and-glass **Covent Garden Market,** originally the garden of Westminster Abbey, is a mix of fun shops, eateries, and markets. Mondays are for antiques, while arts and crafts dominate the rest of the week. Produce stalls are open daily (10:30-18:00) and on Thursdays, a food market brightens up the square (Tube: Covent Garden, tel. 020/7395-1350, www.coventgardenlondonuk.com).

**Jubilee Hall Market,** on the south side of Covent Garden, features antiques on Mondays, a general market Tuesday through Friday, and arts and crafts on Saturdays and Sundays (Mon 5:00-17:00, Tue-Fri 10:30-19:00, Sat-Sun 10:00-18:00, tel. 020/7379-4242, www.jubileemarket.co.uk).

### IN SOUTH LONDON

**Borough Market** has been serving Southwark for over 800 years. These days, there are as many people taking photos as buying fruit, cheese, and beautiful breads, but it's still a fun carnival atmosphere with fantastic stall foods. For maximum market and minimum crowds, join the locals on Thursdays (full market open Wed-Thu 10:00-17:00, Fri 10:00-18:00, Sat 8:00-17:00, closed Sun; surrounding food stalls open daily; south of London Bridge, where Southwark Street meets Borough High Street; Tube: London Bridge, tel. 020/7407-1002, www.boroughmarket.org.uk).

# Theater (a.k.a. Theatre)

London's theater scene rivals Broadway's in quality and often beats it in price. Choose from 200 offerings—Shakespeare, musicals, comedies, thrillers, sex farces, cutting-edge fringe, revivals starring movie celebs, and more. London does it all well.

**Rick's Tip:** *For the best list of what's happening and a look at the* **latest London scene,** *check www.timeout.com/london.*

## West End Shows

Nearly all big-name shows are hosted in the theaters of the West End, clustering

around Soho (especially along Shaftes-bury Avenue) between Piccadilly and Covent Garden. With a centuries-old tra-dition of pleasing the masses, they present London theater at its grandest.

I prefer big, glitzy musicals over serious fare because London can deliver the mul-timedia spectacle I rarely get back home. If that's not to your taste, you might prefer revivals of classics or cutting-edge works by the hottest young playwrights. London is a magnet for movie stars who want to stretch their acting chops.

The free *Official London Theatre Guide*, updated weekly, is a handy tool (find it at hotels, box offices, the City of London TI, and online at www.officiallondontheatre.co.uk).

Most performances are nightly except Sunday, usually with two or three mati-nees a week. The few shows that run on Sundays are mostly family fare (*Matilda, The Lion King,* and so on). Tickets range from about £25 to £120. Matinees are gen-erally cheaper and rarely sell out.

**Rick's Tip:** *Just like at home, London's* **theaters sell seats in a range of levels**— *but the Brits use different terms: stalls (ground floor), dress circle (first balcony), upper circle (second balcony), balcony (sky-high third balcony), and slips (cheap seats on the fringes). Discounted tickets are called "concessions" (abbreviated as "conc" or "s").*

## TICKETS

Most shows have tickets available on short notice—likely at a discount. If your time in London is limited or you have your heart set on a particular show that's likely to sell out, you can buy peace of mind by booking your tickets from home. For floor plans of various theaters, see www.theatremonkey.com.

**Advance Tickets:** Buy your tickets directly from the theater, either through its website or by calling the box office. Often, a theater will reroute you to a third-party ticket vendor such as Ticket-master. You'll pay with a credit card, and generally be charged a per-ticket booking fee (around £3). You can have your tickets emailed to you or pick them up before show time at the theater's Will Call win-dow. Many third-party websites sell Lon-don theater tickets, but generally charge higher prices and fees.

**Discount Tickets:** The **TKTS Booth** at Leicester Square sells discounted tick-ets (25-30 percent off) for many shows, though they may not have the hottest shows in town. Buy in person at the kiosk. The best deals are same-day only (£3/ ticket service charge, open Mon-Sat 10:00-19:00, Sun 11:00-16:30).

**Rick's Tip:** *The* **real TKTS booth** *(with its prominent sign) is a freestanding kiosk at the south edge of Leicester Square. Several dis-honest outfits advertise "official half-price tickets"—avoid these, where you'll actually pay much closer to full price.*

The list of shows and prices is posted outside the booth and on the constantly refreshed website www.tkts.co.uk. Come early in the day—the line starts forming even before the booth opens, but moves quickly. Have a second-choice show in mind, in case your first choice is sold out. If TKTS runs out of its ticket allotment for a certain show, it doesn't necessarily mean

## Evening Sightseeing

To experience the sights with fewer crowds, go late. Some places offer evening hours.

**Westminster Abbey** (main church): Wed until 19:00

**Houses of Parliament:** House of Commons—Oct-late July Mon until 22:30, Tue-Wed until 19:30; House of Lords—Oct-late July Mon-Wed until 22:00, Thu until 19:30

**London Eye:** Last ascent daily at 20:30, at 21:30 or later July-Aug

**Madame Tussauds:** July-Aug daily until 19:30 (last entry time; stays open about 2 hours longer)

**British Museum** (some galleries): Fri until 20:30

**British Library:** Tue-Thu until 20:00

**National Gallery:** Fri until 21:00

**National Portrait Gallery:** Thu-Fri until 21:00

**Tate Modern:** Fri-Sat until 22:00

**Victoria and Albert Museum** (some galleries): Fri until 22:00

the show is sold out—you can still try the theater's box office.

**Theater Box Office:** Even if a show is "sold out," there's usually a way to get a seat. Many theaters offer various discounts or "concessions": same-day tickets, cheap returned tickets, standing-room, matinee, senior or student standby deals, and more. Start by checking the show's website, calling the box office, or simply dropping by (many theaters are right in the tourist zone).

Same-day tickets (called "day seats") are generally available only in person at the box office, starting at 10:00 (people start lining up well before then). These tickets (£20 or less) tend to be either in the nosebleed rows or have a restricted view (behind a pillar or extremely far to one side). For a helpful guide to "day seats," see www.theatremonkey.com/dayseatfinder.htm.

Another strategy is to show up at the box office shortly before show time (best on weekdays) and—before paying full price—ask about any cheaper options. Last-minute return tickets are often sold at great prices as curtain time approaches.

For more tips on getting cheap and last-minute tickets, visit www.londontheatretickets.org and www.timeout.com/london/theatre.

**Third-Party Agencies:** Although booking through a middleman such as your hotel or a ticket agency is quick and easy, prices are greatly inflated. Ticket agencies and third-party websites are often just scalpers with an address. If you do buy from an agency, choose a member of the Society of Ticket Agents and Retailers (look for the STAR logo—short for "secure tickets from authorized retailers"). These legitimate resellers normally add a maximum 25 percent booking fee to tickets.

**Scalpers (or "Touts"):** As at any event, you'll find scalpers hawking tickets outside theaters. And, just like at home, those people may either be honest folk whose date just happened to cancel at the last minute...or they may be unscrupulous thieves selling forgeries. London has many of the latter.

### Beyond the West End

Tickets for lesser-known shows tend to be cheaper (figure £15-30), in part because most of the smaller theaters are government-subsidized. Plays don't need a familiar title or famous actor to be a worthwhile experience—read up on the latest offerings online; Time Out's website is a great place to start.

# Evensong

Evensong is an evening worship service that is typically sung rather than spoken. It follows the traditional Anglican service in the Book of Common Prayer, including prayers, scripture readings, canticles (sung responses), and hymns that are appropriate for the early evening—traditionally the end of the working day and before the evening meal. In major churches with resident choirs, a singing or chanting priest leads the service, and a choir—usually made up of both men and boys—sings the responses. The choir sings a cappella or is accompanied by an organ. Visitors are welcome and are given an order of service or a prayer book to help them follow along. (If you're not familiar with the order of service, watch the congregation to know when to stand, sit, and kneel.)

Impressive places for evensong in London include Westminster Abbey and St. Paul's. Evensong typically takes place in the small choir area, which is far more intimate than the main nave. It generally occurs daily between 17:00 and 18:00 (often two hours earlier on Sundays); check with individual churches for specifics. At smaller churches, evensong is sometimes spoken, not sung.

Evensong is not a performance—it's a worship service. If you enjoy worshipping in different churches, attending evensong can be a highlight. But if church services aren't your thing, consider an organ or choral concert, offered in most major churches. Look for posted schedules or ask at the information desk or gift shop.

## MAJOR THEATERS

The **National Theatre** has a range of impressive options, often starring recognizable names. Deeply discounted tickets are commonly offered (looming on the South Bank by Waterloo Bridge, Tube: Waterloo, www.nationaltheatre.org.uk).

The **Barbican Centre** puts on high-quality, often experimental work (right by the Museum of London, just north of The City, Tube: Barbican, www.barbican.org.uk), as does the **Royal Court Theatre,** which has £10 tickets for its Monday shows (west of the West End in Sloane Square, Tube: Sloane Square, www.royalcourttheatre.com).

**Menier Chocolate Factory** in Southwark is gaining popularity for its impressive productions and intimate setting—a mix of plays, musicals, and even an occasional comedian (behind the Tate Modern at 56 Southwark Street, Tube: Southwark,

www.menierchocolatefactory.com).

The **Royal Shakespeare Company** performs at various theaters around London and in Stratford-upon-Avon year-round. To get a schedule, contact the RSC (Royal Shakespeare Theatre, Stratford-upon-Avon, tel. 0844-800-1110, www.rsc.org.uk).

## SHAKESPEARE'S GLOBE

To see Shakespeare in a replica of the theater for which he wrote his plays, attend a play at the Globe. In this round, thatch-roofed, open-air theater, the plays are performed much as Shakespeare intended—under the sky, with no amplification. I've never enjoyed Shakespeare as much as here, performed as it was meant to be in the "wooden O." If you can't attend a show, take a guided tour of the theater and museum by day (see page 91).

The play's the thing from late April through early October (usually Tue-Sat 14:00 and 19:30, Sun 13:00 and/or 18:30, tickets can be sold out months in advance). You'll pay £5 to stand and £17-43 to sit, usually on a backless bench. Because only a few rows and the pricier Gentlemen's Rooms have seats with backs, £1 cushions and £3 add-on backrests are a good investment. Dress for the weather.

The £5 "groundling" tickets—which are open to rain—are most fun. Scurry in early to stake out a spot on the stage's edge, where the most interaction with the actors occurs. You're a crude peasant. You can lean your elbows on the stage, munch a picnic dinner (yes, you can bring in food), or walk around.

The indoor Sam Wanamaker Playhouse allows Shakespearean-era plays and early-music concerts to be performed through the winter. Many of the productions in this intimate venue are one-offs and can be quite pricey.

For tickets, call or drop by the box office (Mon-Sat 10:00-18:00, Sun until 17:00, open one hour later on performance days, New Globe Walk entrance, tel. 020/7401-9919). You can also reserve online (www.shakespearesglobe.com, £2.50 booking fee). If tickets are sold out, don't despair; call around noon on the day of the performance to see if the box office expects any returned tickets. If so, show

up a little more than an hour before the show, when these tickets are sold (first-come, first-served).

The theater is on the South Bank, directly across the Thames over the Millennium Bridge from St. Paul's Cathedral (Tube: Mansion House or London Bridge).

# EATING

Eating out has become an essential part of the London experience. The sheer variety of foods—from every corner of its former empire and beyond—is astonishing. But the thought of a £50 meal in Britain generally ruins my appetite, so my London dining is limited mostly to easygoing, moderately priced options. Pub grub and ethnic restaurants (especially Indian and Chinese) are good low-cost options. Chain restaurants are affordable and popular (see page 109 for a rundown). Picnicking is the fastest, cheapest way to go. Good grocery stores and sandwich shops, fine park benches, and polite pigeons abound.

Most London restaurants generally open daily no later than noon and close sometime between 22:00 and midnight.

## Central London
### Soho
Foodies skip the touristy zones near Piccadilly and Trafalgar Square and head to Soho. These restaurants are scattered throughout a chic, creative, and borderline-seedy zone that teems with hipsters, theatergoers, and London's gay community. Even if you plan to have dinner elsewhere, it's a treat just to wander around Soho.

**Rick's Tip:** *While gentrification has mostly stripped this area of its former **"red light district"** vibe, a few pockets survive. Only fools fall for the "£5 drink and show" lure outside the strip clubs (especially on Great Windmill Street).*

*A performance at Shakespeare's Globe*

## ON AND NEAR WARDOUR STREET

Stroll up this street—particularly from Brewer Street northward—to take your pick from Thai, Indonesian, Vietnamese, Italian, French, and even...English.

**Princi** is a vast, bright, efficient deli/bakery with Milanese flair. Display cases offer a tempting array of pizza rustica, panini sandwiches, focaccia, a few pasta dishes, and desserts. Order your food at the counter, then find a space at a long shared table; or get it to go (£7-13 meals, daily 8:00-24:00, 135 Wardour Street, tel. 020/7478-8888).

**Bi Bim Bap** is a popular diner named for what it sells: Korean *bibimbap,* a steaming stone bowl of rice and thinly sliced veggies, topped with a fried egg. Other toppings—including chicken, beef strips, and mushrooms—are a few pounds extra (£7-10 meals, Mon-Sat 12:00-15:00 & 18:00-23:00, closed Sun, 11 Greek Street, second location near British Museum at 8 Charlotte Street, tel. 020/7287-3434).

**Bocca di Lupo** serves half and full portions of classic regional Italian food. Stylish but fun, it's a place where you're glad you made a reservation. The counter seating, on cushy stools with a view into the open kitchen, is particularly memorable, or you can take a table in the snug, casual back end (£12-20 dishes, daily 12:30-15:00 & 17:30-23:00, 12 Archer Street, tel. 020/7734-2223, www.boccadilupo.com).

**Gelupo,** Bocca di Lupo's sister *gelateria* across the street, has a wide array of ever-changing but delicious dessert favorites as well as espresso drinks (daily 11:00-23:00, 7 Archer Street, tel. 020/7287-5555).

**Chain Restaurants:** While I wouldn't waste a Soho meal on a **chain restaurant,** they're a convenient fallback—**Byron Hamburgers** (appealing industrial-mod branch at 97 Wardour Street, also near Golden Square at 16 Beak Street and at 1A St. Giles High Street), **Thai Square** (27 St. Anne's Court, also at 5 Princes Street on Hanover Square), **Wagamama** (42 Great Marlborough Street), **Masala Zone** (9 Marshall Street), **Yo! Sushi** (52 Poland Street), and **Côte** (124 Wardour Street and near Oxford Circus at 4 Great Portland Street).

## ON LEXINGTON STREET

**Andrew Edmunds Restaurant** is a tiny, candlelit space with a loyal clientele—it's the closest I've found to Parisian quality in London. The extensive wine list, modern European cooking, and creative seasonal menu are worth the splurge (£12-20 main dishes, Mon-Sat 12:00-15:30 & 17:30-22:45, Sun 13:00-16:00 & 18:00-22:30, these are last-order times, come early or call ahead, request ground floor rather than basement, 46 Lexington Street, tel. 020/7437-5708, www.andrewedmunds.com).

**Mildred's Vegetarian Restaurant,** across from Andrew Edmunds, has an enjoyable menu and a pleasant interior filled with happy eaters (£8-11 meals, small takeaway menu, Mon-Sat 12:00-23:00, closed Sun, vegan options, 45 Lexington Street, tel. 020/7494-1634).

## Near Trafalgar Square

**St. Martin-in-the-Fields Café in the Crypt** is just right for a tasty meal on a monk's budget—maybe even on a monk's tomb. Their enticing buffet line is kept stocked all day, serving breakfast, lunch, and dinner (£7-10 cafeteria plates, hearty traditional desserts). They also serve a restful cream tea (£6.50, daily 14:00-18:00). You'll find the café directly under the St. Martin-in-the-Fields Church, facing Trafalgar Square—enter through the glass pavilion next to the church (generally about 8:00-20:00 daily, Tube: Charing Cross, tel. 020/7766-1158 or 020/7766-1100). On Wednesday evenings you can dine to the music of a live jazz band at 20:00 (£5.50-12 tickets). While here, check out the concert schedule for the busy church upstairs (or visit www.smitf.org).

**The Chandos Pub's Opera Room** floats apart from the tacky tourism around Trafalgar Square. Look for it opposite the National Portrait Gallery (corner of William IV Street and St. Martin's Lane) and climb the stairs to the Opera Room. They serve sandwiches and traditional pub meals for under £10—meat pies and fish-and-chips are their specialty. The ground-floor pub offers snugs (private booths) and serious beer drinking; order upstairs and carry it down (kitchen open daily 11:30-21:00, Fri until 18:00, order and pay at the bar, 29 St. Martin's Lane, Tube: Leicester Square, tel. 020/7836-1401).

Convenient for sightseers, the **National Gallery** has three on-site eateries (page 60) and the **National Portrait Gallery** has two (page 63).

## Near Piccadilly

**The Wolseley** is in the grand 1920s showroom of a long-defunct British car. Today, this old-time bistro bustles with formal waiters serving traditional Austrian and French dishes in an elegant setting fit for its location next to the Ritz. Although the food can be unexceptional, prices are reasonable considering the grand presentation and setting. It's popular for its fancy cream or afternoon tea. Reservations are a must (£13-30 main courses; cheaper "café menu" available; daily 7:00-24:00, 160 Piccadilly, tel. 020/7499-6996, www. thewolseley.com).

**The Savini at the Criterion,** a palatial dining hall, offers Italian cuisine in a dreamy Neo-Byzantine setting from the 1870s. It's a deal for the visual experience during lunch, especially if you order the £20-25 fixed-price meal (except on Sun, when you must order from the expensive à la carte menu). Anyone can drop in for coffee or a drink (daily 12:00-14:30 & 17:30-23:30, 224 Piccadilly, tel. 020/7930-0488, www.saviniatcriterion.co.uk).

## Covent Garden

**Joe Allen,** tucked in a brick cellar a block away from the market, serves modern international and American cuisine with both style and hubbub. It's comfortably spacious and popular with the theater crowd (£11-30 main courses, specials at lunch and for early birds, open daily 12:00-24:00, piano music after 19:00, 13 Exeter Street, tel. 020/7836-0651).

**Union Jacks,** a venture of celebrity chef Jamie Oliver, uses traditional British ingredients to make inventive modern dishes. Wood-fired pizzas are topped not with cheese and tomatoes, but roast pig shoulder or oxtail and brisket (£12-14 pizzas, £15 classic British dishes, daily 12:00-23:00, right inside Covent Garden market hall, tel. 020/3640-7086).

## Near the British Museum

To avoid the tourist crush around the museum (and in Soho), Londoners head a few blocks west to the Fitzrovia area. Tiny Charlotte Place is lined with small eateries; nearby, much bigger Charlotte Street has several more options. This area is a short walk from the Goodge Street Tube station.

**Salumeria Dino** serves hearty sandwiches, pasta, and coffee in an Italian deli so authentic you'll walk out singing "O Sole Mio" (£4-5 sandwiches, Mon-Fri 9:00-18:00, closed Sat-Sun, 15 Charlotte Place, tel. 020/7580-3938).

**Lantana OUT,** next door to Salumeria Dino, is an Australian coffee shop that sells modern soups, sandwiches, and salads at their takeaway window (£3-8

# Central London Eateries

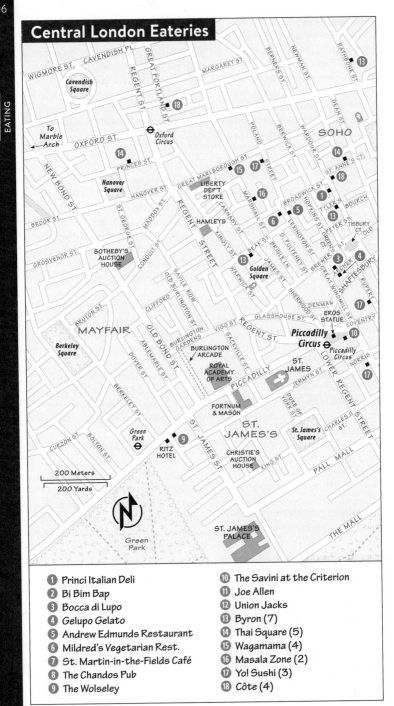

1. Princi Italian Deli
2. Bi Bim Bap
3. Bocca di Lupo
4. Gelupo Gelato
5. Andrew Edmunds Restaurant
6. Mildred's Vegetarian Rest.
7. St. Martin-in-the-Fields Café
8. The Chandos Pub
9. The Wolseley
10. The Savini at the Criterion
11. Joe Allen
12. Union Jacks
13. Byron (7)
14. Thai Square (5)
15. Wagamama (4)
16. Masala Zone (2)
17. Yo! Sushi (3)
18. Côte (4)

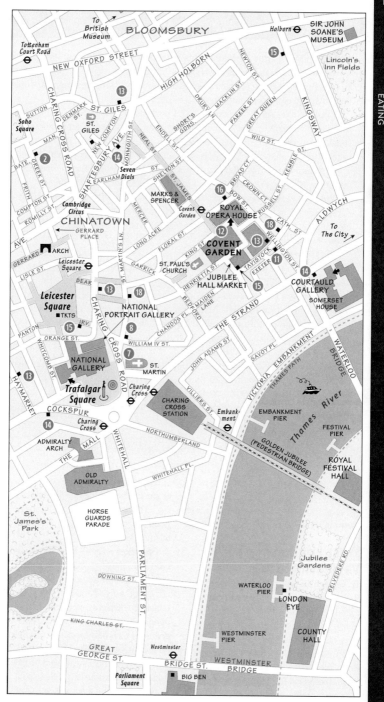

# Taking Tea

Many London visitors partake in this most British of traditions. While some tearooms—such as the finicky Fortnum & Mason—still require a jacket and tie, most happily welcome tourists in jeans and sneakers. Most tearooms are open for lunch and close at about 17:00.

Popular choices are a "cream tea," which consists of tea and a scone or two, or the pricier "afternoon tea," which comes with pastries and finger foods such as small, crust-less sandwiches (for more tea options, see page 377). Two people can order one afternoon tea and one cream tea and share the afternoon tea's goodies.

Many **museum cafés** offer a fine, inexpensive tea service. Try the restaurants inside the **National Gallery** or the **Victoria and Albert Museum.**

**The Wolseley** serves a good afternoon tea between their meal service. Split one with your companion and enjoy two light meals at a great price in classic elegance (£12 cream tea, £27 afternoon tea, £38 champagne tea, generally served 15:00-18:30 daily, see page 105).

**The Orangery at Kensington Palace** serves a £28 "Orangery tea" and a £34-38 champagne tea in its bright white hall. You can also order treats à la carte. The portions aren't huge, but who can argue with eating at a royal orangery or on the terrace? (Tea served 12:00-18:00, no reservations taken; a 10-minute walk through Kensington Gardens from either Queensway or High Street Kensington Tube stations to the orange brick building, about 100 yards from Kensington Palace; tel. 020/3166-6113, www.hrp.org.uk.)

The **Fortnum & Mason** department store offers tea at several different restaurants within its walls. Take tea in the Parlour (£24 including ice cream and scones; Mon-Sat 10:00-19:30, Sun 11:30-17:00) or in the Diamond Jubilee Tea Salon (£40-44, daily 12:00-19:00, Sun until 18:00, dress up—no shorts, "children must be behaved," 181 Piccadilly, reserve at least a week in advance, tel. 020/7734-8040, www.fortnumandmason.com).

meals, Mon-Fri 7:30-15:00, café also open Sat-Sun 9:00-17:00, 13 Charlotte Place, tel. 020/7637-3347). Pricier sit-down café **Lantana IN** serves £9-12 meals next door.

## West London
### Victoria Station Area
**St. George's Tavern** is the neighborhood's best pub for a full meal. Enjoy the same menu on the sidewalk, in the ground-floor pub, or in the downstairs dining room (£10-14 meals, food served daily 10:00-22:00, corner of Hugh Street and Belgrave Road, tel. 020/7630-1116).

**Seafresh Fish Restaurant** is the place for classic and creative fish-and-chips cuisine. Take out or eat in to enjoy the white-fish ambience (£5-8 meals to go, £13-17 to sit, Mon-Sat 12:00-15:00 & 17:00-22:30, closed Sun, 80 Wilton Road, tel. 020/7828-0747).

**Grumbles** brags it's been serving "good food and wine at nonscary prices since 1964." This unpretentious little place has cozy booths inside and four nice sidewalk tables (£11-18 plates, early-bird specials, open daily 12:00-14:30 & 18:00-23:00, reservations wise, half-block north of Belgrave Road at 35 Churton Street, tel. 020/7834-0149, www.grumblesrestaurant.co.uk).

**Chain Restaurants: Yo! Sushi** and **Wasabi** are in the main concourse of Victoria Station (another Wasabi is at 131 Victoria Street). You'll also find **Wagamama** (at Cardinal Place off Victoria Street) and an **Itsu** (163 Victoria Street). **Le Pain Quotidien** is a block east of the station (128 Wilton Road).

**Groceries:** A handy **M&S Simply Food** is inside Victoria Station (daily 7:00-24:00, near the front, by the bus terminus), along with a **Sainsbury's Local** (daily 6:00-23:00, at rear entrance, on Eccleston Street). A large **Sainsbury's Local** is a couple of blocks southeast of the station (Mon-Sat 7:00-23:00, Sun 11:00-17:00, on Wilton Road near Warwick Way).

## Bayswater and Notting Hill

**Geales** has been serving Notting Hill-billies fish-and-chips since 1939. Today, the menu is varied, but the emphasis is still on fish. The crispy cod that put them on the map is still the best around (lunch—£10 two-course express menu; dinner—£4-11 starters and salads, £14-23 main dishes; daily 12:00-15:00 & 18:00-22:30, reservations smart, 2 Farmer Street, just south of Notting Hill Gate Tube stop, tel. 020/7727-7528, www.geales.com).

**The Churchill Arms** pub and **Thai Kitchen** (same location) are local hangouts, with good beer and a thriving old-English ambience in front, and hearty £9 Thai plates in an enclosed patio in the back. The place is festooned with Churchill memorabilia and chamber pots. Arrive by 18:00 or after 21:00 to avoid a line. During busy times, diners are limited to an hour at the table (food served daily 12:00-22:00, 119 Kensington Church Street, tel. 020/7727-4242 for the pub or tel. 020/7792-1296 for restaurant reservations, www.churchillarmskensington.co.uk).

**Hereford Road,** a cozy, mod eatery tucked away on Leinster Square, serves English cuisine with modern panache. Cozy two-person booths face the open kitchen up top; the main dining room is down below (£14-17 main dishes, reserva-

tions smart, daily 12:00-15:00 & 18:00-22:00, 3 Hereford Road, tel. 020/7727-1144, www.herefordroad.org).

**The Prince Edward** serves good grub in a comfy, family-friendly, upscale-pub setting and at its sidewalk tables (£10-15 meals, daily 10:30-23:00, 2 blocks north of Bayswater Road at the corner of Dawson Place and Hereford Road, 73 Prince's Square, tel. 020/7727-2221).

**Chain Restaurants:** Choices are **Byron Hamburgers** (103 Westbourne Grove), **Masala Zone** (75 Bishop's Bridge Road), **Yo! Sushi** (Whiteleys Shopping Centre), **Itsu** (100 Notting Hill Gate), and **Côte** (98 Westbourne Grove). To the south, past Kensington Palace, is **Wagamama** (26 Kensington High Street).

# SLEEPING

I've focused my recommendations on good-value B&Bs that cluster near Victoria Station, and on a range of hotels found north of Kensington Gardens and near Paddington Station. Prices for London rooms often flex seasonally and/or with demand. Check online for specific rates and last-minute deals.

If you'd like to stay at a no-frills chain hotel with well-priced rooms, the following all have convenient London locations:

### Sleep Code

**Price Rankings for Double Rooms (Db)**

$$$ Most rooms £125 or more
$$ £75-125
$ £75 or less

**Abbreviations:** Db=Double with bathroom. D=Double with bathroom down the hall

**Notes:** Room prices change; verify rates online or by email. For the best prices, book direct with the hotel.

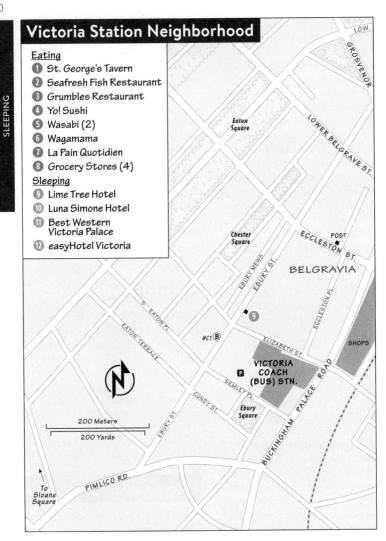

## Victoria Station Neighborhood

### Eating
1. St. George's Tavern
2. Seafresh Fish Restaurant
3. Grumbles Restaurant
4. Yo! Sushi
5. Wasabi (2)
6. Wagamama
7. La Pain Quotidien
8. Grocery Stores (4)

### Sleeping
9. Lime Tree Hotel
10. Luna Simone Hotel
11. Best Western Victoria Palace
12. easyHotel Victoria

**Premier Inn** (King's Cross-St. Pancras, Euston, and Victoria; www.premierinn. com), **Travelodge** (King's Cross, Euston, and Covent Garden; www.travelodge. co.uk); and **Ibis** (Euston-St. Pancras; www.ibishotel.com).

**EasyHotel,** another no-frills chain, offers tiny, efficient but thin-walled rooms that feel popped out of a plastic mold. Rates can be very low (with doubles as cheap as £30 for early booking), but extras are pricey, such as TV use, Wi-Fi, bag storage, fresh towels, and daily cleaning. Book far ahead and skip the extras for the best price (Victoria, South Kensington, Earl's Court, and Paddington; www.easyhotel. com).

Also consider these accommodation discount sites: www.londontown. com, athomeinlondon.co.uk and www. londonbb.com (both list central B&Bs), and www.visitlondon.com.

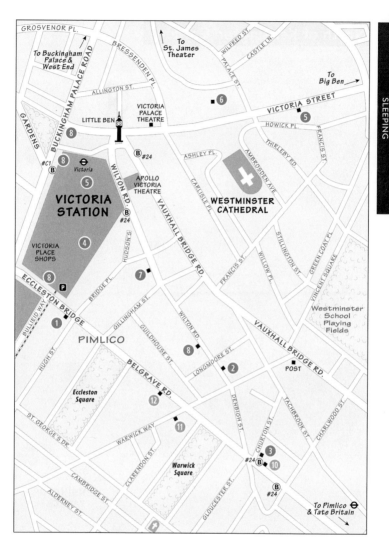

# Near Victoria Station

The safe, surprisingly tidy streets behind Victoria Station teem with moderately priced B&Bs.

**$$$ Lime Tree Hotel** is a gem with 25 spacious, stylish, comfortable rooms, a helpful staff, and a fun-loving breakfast room. It's two blocks over from Victoria Station, in Belgravia (Db-£175, usually cheaper Jan-Feb, small lounge opens onto quiet garden, 135 Ebury Street, tel. 020/7730-8191, www.limetreehotel.co.uk, info@limetreehotel.co.uk).

**$$ Luna Simone Hotel** rents 36 fresh, spacious, remodeled rooms with modern bathrooms in Pimlico (Db-£115-140, family rooms, ask about Rick Steves discount, at 47 Belgrave Road near the corner of Charlwood Street, handy bus #24 stops out front, tel. 020/7834-5897, www.lunasimonehotel.com, stay@ lunasimonehotel.com).

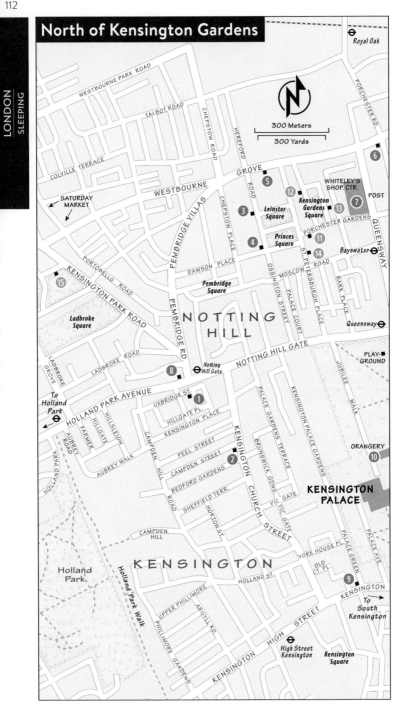

# North of Kensington Gardens

300 Meters

300 Yards

WESTBOURNE PARK ROAD

TALBOT ROAD

CHEPSTOW ROAD

HEREFORD ROAD

COLVILLE TERRACE

GROVE

WESTBOURNE

PEMBRIDGE VILLAS

CHEPSTOW PLACE

SATURDAY MARKET

PORTOBELLO ROAD

KENSINGTON PARK ROAD

DAWSON PLACE

**Pembridge Square**

**15**

**Ladbroke Square**

**NOTTING HILL**

PEMBRIDGE RD.

**5**

**3**  **Leinster Square**

**4**  **Princes Square**

**12**

WHITELEY'S SHOP. CTR.

**Kensington Gardens Square**  **13**

**7**  POST

PORCHESTER RD.

**6**

Royal Oak

QUEENSWAY

PORCHESTER GARDENS

**11**

**14**  Bayswater

MOSCOW ROAD

OSSINGTON STREET

PALACE COURT

ST PETERSBURGH PLACE

Queensway

PARK PLACE

LADBROKE ROAD

**Notting Hill Gate**  **8**  Notting Hill Gate

NOTTING HILL GATE

PLAY-GROUND

LADBROKE GROVE

To Holland Park

HOLLAND PARK AVENUE

UXBRIDGE ST.

HILLGATE PL.

**1**

KENSINGTON PLACE

HILLGATE

HILLSLEIGH ROAD

CAMPDEN HILL ROAD

AUBREY ROAD

FARMER

AUBREY WALK

PEEL STREET

CAMPDEN STREET

**2**

BEDFORD GARDENS

SHEFFIELD TERR.

HORTON ST.

CAMPDEN HILL

KENSINGTON CHURCH STREET

PALACE GARDENS TERRACE

BRUNSWICK GDNS.

VIC. GATE

VIC. GATE

KENSINGTON PALACE GARDENS

JUBILEE WALK

ORANGERY

**10**

**KENSINGTON PALACE**

**KENSINGTON**

Holland Park

Holland Park Walk

YORK HOUSE PL.

OLD CT. PL.

PALACE GREEN

PALACE AVE.

**9**

KENSINGTON

To South Kensington

UPPER PHILLIMORE GARDENS

ARGYLL RD.

HOLLAND ST.

PHILLIMORE GARDENS

KENSINGTON HIGH STREET

High Street Kensington

Kensington Square

Ladbroke Square

Pembridge Square

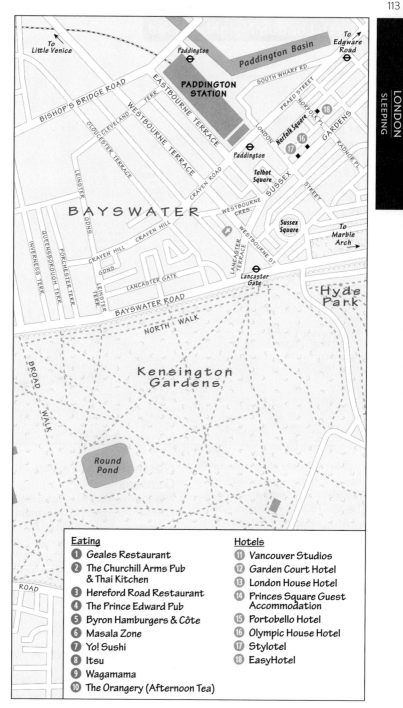

**Eating**
1. Geales Restaurant
2. The Churchill Arms Pub & Thai Kitchen
3. Hereford Road Restaurant
4. The Prince Edward Pub
5. Byron Hamburgers & Côte
6. Masala Zone
7. Yo! Sushi
8. Itsu
9. Wagamama
10. The Orangery (Afternoon Tea)

**Hotels**
11. Vancouver Studios
12. Garden Court Hotel
13. London House Hotel
14. Princes Square Guest Accommodation
15. Portobello Hotel
16. Olympic House Hotel
17. Stylotel
18. EasyHotel

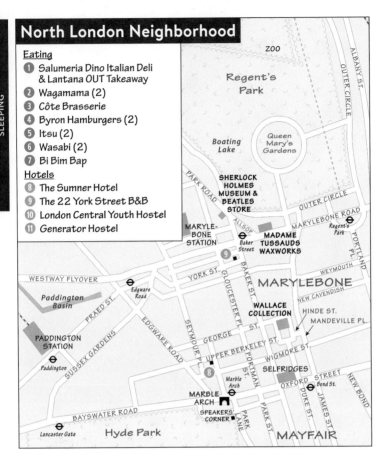

## North London Neighborhood

**Eating**

1. Salumeria Dino Italian Deli & Lantana OUT Takeaway
2. Wagamama (2)
3. Côte Brasserie
4. Byron Hamburgers (2)
5. Itsu (2)
6. Wasabi (2)
7. Bi Bim Bap

**Hotels**

8. The Sumner Hotel
9. The 22 York Street B&B
10. London Central Youth Hostel
11. Generator Hostel

---

**$$ Best Western Victoria Palace** offers modern business-class comfort. Choose from the 43 rooms in the main building (Db-about £120, sometimes includes breakfast, elevator, at 60 Warwick Way), or pay about 20 percent less for a nearly identical room in one of the annexes, each a half-block away (Db-£85-90, breakfast-£12.50, air-con, no elevator, 17 Belgrave Road and 1 Warwick Way, reception at main building; tel. 020/7821-7113, www.bestwesternvictoriapalace.co.uk, info@bestwesternvictoriapalace.co.uk).

**$ EasyHotel Victoria** is part of the budget chain described on page 110 (36 Belgrave Road).

## North of Kensington Gardens

From the core of the tourist's London, the vast Hyde Park spreads west, eventually becoming Kensington Gardens. Bayswater is along the northern edge of the park, and Notting Hill spreads out from the northwest tip of Kensington Gardens. Just east of Bayswater, the neighborhood around Paddington Station has less charm but is very convenient to the Heathrow Express airport train.

### Bayswater and Notting Hill

**$$$ Vancouver Studios** offers one of the best values in this neighborhood. Its 45 modern, tastefully furnished rooms

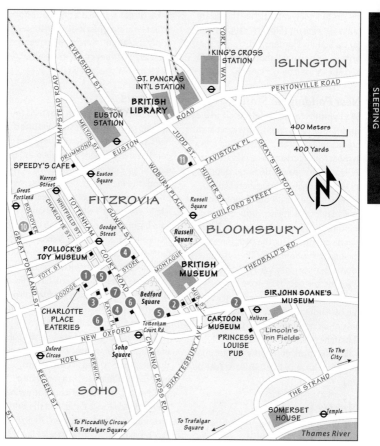

come with fully equipped kitchenettes (no breakfast). It has a welcoming lounge and its own tranquil garden patio out back, which is refreshing if you land a somewhat-smoky room (Db-£149, 30 Princes Square, tel. 020/7243-1270, www.vancouverstudios.co.uk, info@vancouverstudios.co.uk).

**$$$ Garden Court Hotel** is understated, with 40 simple, homey-but-tasteful rooms (Db-£129, family rooms, includes continental breakfast or pay £3.50 for English breakfast, elevator, 30 Kensington Gardens Square, tel. 020/7229-2553, www.gardencourthotel.co.uk, info@gardencourthotel.co.uk).

**$$$ London House Hotel** has 103

modern, cookie-cutter rooms on a tranquil, tidy park (generally Db-£105 weekdays and £130 on weekends, basement family rooms, continental breakfast-£7, elevator, 81 Kensington Gardens Square, tel. 020/7243-1810, www.londonhousehotels.com, reservations@londonhousehotels.com).

**$$ Princes Square Guest Accommodation** rents 50 crisp, businesslike rooms with pleasant, modern decor (generally Db-£100-160; elevator, 23 Princes Square, tel. 020/7229-9876, www.princessquarehotel.co.uk, info@princessquarehotel.co.uk).

**$$$ Portobello Hotel** is on a quiet residential street in the heart of Notting

Hill. Its 21 freshly refurbished rooms are funky yet elegant (Db-£175-315, elevator, 22 Stanley Gardens, tel. 020/7727-2777, www.portobellohotel.com, stay@portobellohotel.com, Hannah).

### Near Paddington Station

**$$ Olympic House Hotel** has clean public spaces and 38 business-class rooms with predictable comfort (Db-£105, air-con in most rooms costs extra, elevator, pay Wi-Fi, 138 Sussex Gardens, tel. 020/7723-5935, www.olympichousehotel.co.uk, olympichousehotel@btinternet.com).

**$$ Stylotel** is stylish, modern, and aluminum-clad, with 39 tidy rooms. Rooms can be cramped, but the beds have space for luggage underneath (Db-£95, family rooms, elevator, pay Wi-Fi, 160 Sussex Gardens, tel. 020/7723-1026, www.stylotel.com, info@stylotel.com, well-run by Andreas). There are eight fancier, air-conditioned suites across the street (kitchenettes, no breakfast).

**$ EasyHotel,** part of the budget chain, has a branch at 10 Norfolk Place (see page 110).

## North London

**$$$ The Sumner Hotel** rents 19 rooms in a 19th-century Georgian townhouse sporting large contemporary rooms. This swanky place packs in all the amenities and is conveniently located north of Hyde Park and near Oxford Street—it's close to Selfridges and a Marks & Spencer (Db-£193-£229, ask about Rick Steves rates, air-con, elevator, 54 Upper Berkeley Street, a block and a half off Edgware Road, Tube: Marble Arch, tel. 020/7723-2244, www.thesumner.com, reservations@thesumner.com).

**$$$ The 22 York Street B&B** offers a casual alternative in the city center, renting 10 traditional, hardwood, comfortable rooms, each named for a notable London landmark (Db-£150, inviting lounge; near Marylebone/Baker Street: from Baker Street Tube station, walk 2 blocks down

Baker Street and take a right to 22 York Street—no sign, just look for #22; tel. 020/7224-2990, www.22yorkstreet.co.uk, mc@22yorkstreet.co.uk, energetically run by Liz and Michael Callis).

## Hostels

**$ London Central Youth Hostel** is the flagship of London's hostels, with 300 beds and all the latest in security and comfortable efficiency. Families and travelers of any age will feel welcome in this wonderful facility. You'll pay the same price for any bed in a four- to eight-bed single-sex dorm—with or without private bathroom—so try to grab one with a bathroom (£18-34/bunk, twin D-£50-70, families welcome to book an entire room, members' kitchen, book long in advance, between Oxford Circus and Great Portland Street Tube stations at 104 Bolsover Street, tel. 0845-371-9154, www.yha.org.uk, londoncentral@yha.org.uk).

**$ Generator Hostel** is a brightly colored, hip hostel with a café, a DJ spinning the hits, and 870 beds in 220 rooms, including doubles. It's in a renovated building tucked behind a busy street halfway between Kings Cross and the British Museum (£18-34/bunk, twin Db-£70-120, breakfast-£5, 37 Tavistock Place, Tube: Russell Square, tel. 020/7388-7666, www.generatorhostels.com, london@generatorhostels.com).

# TRANSPORTATION

## Getting Around London

To travel smartly in a city this size, you must get comfortable with public transportation. London's excellent taxis, buses, and subway (Tube) system can take you anywhere you need to go—a blessing for travelers' precious vacation time, not to mention their feet. It's also the most expensive public transit in the world. While single-ride and paper tickets still exist, for most visitors the Oyster card is simply the only way to go—saving precious time and money.

For more information about public transit (bus and Tube), the best single source is the helpful *Hello London* brochure, which includes both a Tube map and a handy schematic map of the best bus routes (available free at TIs, museums, hotels, and at www.tfl.gov.uk). For specific directions on how to get from point A to point B on London's transit, detailed bus maps, updated prices, and general information, check www.tfl.gov.uk or call the automated info line at 0843-222-1234.

## Public Transit Tickets and Passes

While the transit system has six zones, almost all tourist sights are within Zones 1 and 2, so those are the prices I've listed (for all the prices, see www.tfl.gov.uk/tickets).

### INDIVIDUAL TICKETS

Individual paper tickets for the Tube are ridiculously expensive (£4.90 per Tube ride). Buy them at any Tube station, either at (often-crowded) ticket windows or at easy-to-use self-service machines. Tickets are valid only on the day of purchase. Unless you're taking only one Tube ride your entire visit, you'll save money (and time) by buying one of the following multiple-ride passes.

### TRANSIT CARDS

**Oyster Card:** A pay-as-you-go transit card, the Oyster card allows you to ride the Tube, buses, Docklands Light Railway (DLR), and Overground (mostly sub-

urban trains) for about half the rate of individual tickets. To use the card, simply touch it against the yellow card reader at the turnstile or entrance, the card reader flashes green, and the fare is automatically deducted. (You must also tap your card again to "touch out" as you exit.)

Buy the card at any Tube station ticket window, or look for nearby shops displaying the Oyster logo where you can purchase a card or add credit without the wait. You'll pay a £5 deposit up front, then load it with as much credit as you'll need. One ride in Zones 1 and 2 during peak time costs £2.90; off peak (after 9:30 on weekdays) is a little cheaper (£2.40 per ride). The system comes with an automatic price cap that guarantees you'll never pay more than £6.40 in one day for riding within Zones 1 and 2. If you think you'll take more than two rides in a day, £6.50 credit will cover you, but it's smart to add more if you expect to travel outside the city center. If you're staying five or more days, consider adding a 7-Day Travelcard to your Oyster card (details below).

Oyster cards are not shareable; each traveler will need his or her own. If your balance gets low, simply add credit—or "top up"—at a ticket window, machine, or shop. You can always see how much credit remains on your card by touching it to the pad at any ticket machine.

At the end of your trip, you can reclaim your deposit and unused balance (up to £10) by selecting "Pay as you go refund" on any ticket machine that gives change. This will deactivate your card. For balances of more than £10, you'll have to wait in line at a ticket window for your refund. If you don't deactivate your card, the credit never expires—you can use it again on your next trip.

**Visitor Oyster cards,** aimed specifically at tourists, function exactly the same as a regular Oyster card. But you must purchase it online in advance and have it delivered by mail before your trip, making it more expensive than a regular Oyster card.

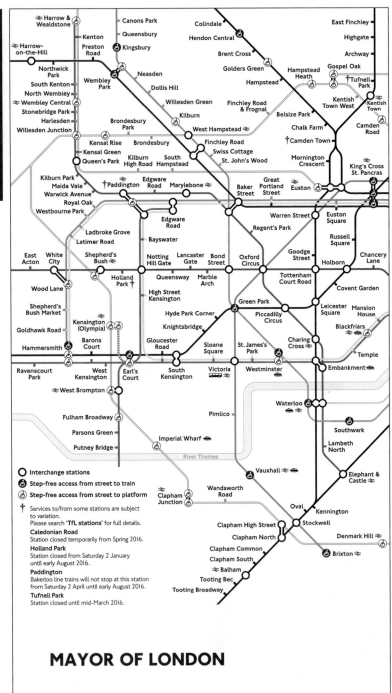

**MAYOR OF LONDON**

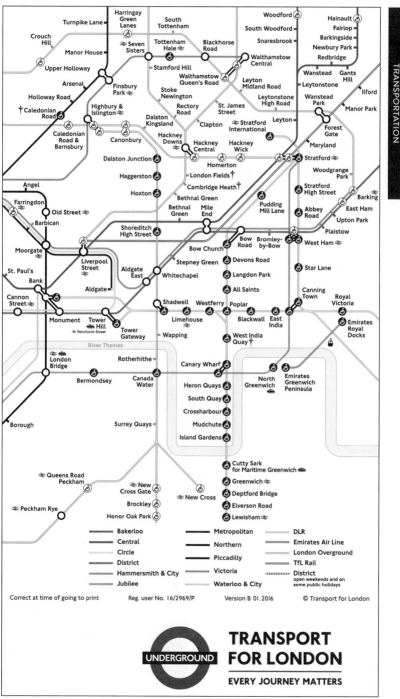

| Bakerloo | Metropolitan | DLR |
| Central | Northern | Emirates Air Line |
| Circle | Piccadilly | London Overground |
| District | Victoria | TfL Rail |
| Hammersmith & City | Waterloo & City | District |
| Jubilee | | open weekends and on some public holidays |

Correct at time of going to print     Reg. user No. 16/2969/P     Version B 01.2016     © Transport for London

**UNDERGROUND**

# TRANSPORT
# FOR LONDON

**EVERY JOURNEY MATTERS**

**Travelcards:** These paper tickets let you ride as many times as you want within a one- or a seven-day period for one fixed price, but are only a good deal in limited instances. Buy it at any Tube station ticket window or machine, then feed it into a turnstile (and retrieve it) to enter and exit the Tube. On a bus, just show it to the driver when you get on.

Your one-day options are the **Anytime Day Travelcard** (Zones 1-4, £12.10) or the **Off-Peak Day Travelcard** (Zones 1-6, covers one day of travel after 9:30 on weekdays, anytime on weekends, £12.10). However, an Oyster card with its daily cap is almost always a better deal.

The **7-Day Travelcard,** which comes in a paper version or can be added to an Oyster card, is the best option if you're staying five or more days and plan to use public transit a lot (£32.40 for Zones 1-2; £59.10 for Zones 1-6). For most travelers, the Zone 1-2 pass works best. (Heathrow Airport is in Zone 6, but you can pay a small supplement to cover the difference.)

**The Bottom Line:** Wondering which pass works best for your trip? On a short visit (three or fewer days), consider purchasing an Oyster card and adding £20-25 of credit (£6.50 daily cap times three days, plus extra for any rides outside Zones 1-2). If you'll be taking fewer rides, £15 will be enough (£2.90 per ride during peak time gets you 5 rides), and if not you can always top up. If you're in London for five days or longer, the 7-Day Travelcard will likely pay for itself.

### DISCOUNTS AND DEALS

**Families:** A paying adult can take up to four kids (ages 10 and under) for free on the Tube, Docklands Light Railway (DLR), Overground, and buses. Explore other child and student discounts at www.tfl.gov.uk/tickets or ask a clerk at a Tube ticket window which deal is best.

**River Cruises:** A Travelcard gives you a 33 percent discount on most Thames cruises (see page 44). The Oyster card gives you roughly a 10 percent discount on Thames Clippers, including the Tate Boat museum ferry.

## By Tube

London's subway system is called the Tube or Underground (but not "subway," which, in Britain, refers to a pedestrian underpass). The Tube is one of this planet's great people-movers and usually the fastest long-distance transport in town (runs Mon-Sat about 5:00-24:00, Sun about 7:00-23:00; Central, Jubilee, Northern, Piccadilly, and Victoria lines also run Fri-Sat 24 hours). Two other commuter rail lines are tied into the network and use the same tickets: the Docklands Light Railway (DLR) and the Overground.

Each line has a name (such as Circle, Northern, or Bakerloo) and two directions (indicated by the end-of-the-line stops). Find the line that will take you to your destination, and figure out roughly which direction (north, south, east, or west) you'll need to head to get there.

At the Tube station, there are two ways to pass through the turnstile. If using an Oyster card, touch it flat against the turnstile's yellow card reader, both when you enter and exit the station. With a paper ticket or Travelcard, you'll feed it into the turnstile, reclaim it, and hang on to it—you'll need it later.

Find your train by following signs to your line and the (general) direction it's

headed (such as Central Line: east). Since some tracks are shared by several lines, double-check before boarding a train— make sure your destination is one of the stops listed on the sign at the platform. Also, check the electronic signboards that announce which train is next, and make sure the destination (the end-of-the-line stop) is the direction you want. Some trains, particularly on the Circle and District lines, split off for other directions, but each train has its final destination marked above its windshield.

Trains run about every 3-10 minutes. For a rough idea of how long it takes to get from point A to point B by Tube, estimate five minutes per stop (which includes time to walk into and out of stations, and to change trains). So a destination six stops away will take you about 30 minutes.

When you leave the system, "touch out" with your Oyster card at the electronic reader on the turnstile, or feed your paper ticket into the turnstile (it will eat your now-expired ticket). With a Travelcard, it will spit out your still-valid card. When leaving a station, save walking time by choosing the best street exit—check the maps on the walls or ask any station personnel.

If you get confused, ask for advice from a local, a blue-vested staff person, or at the information window located before the turnstile entry. Online, get help from the "Plan a Journey" feature at www.tfl.gov.uk, which is accessible (via free Wi-Fi) on any mobile device within most Tube stations before you go underground.

**TUBE ETIQUETTE**
- When your train arrives, stand off to the side and let riders exit before you try to board.
- Avoid using the hinged seats near the doors of some trains when the car is jammed; they take up valuable standing space.
- If you're blocking the door when the train stops, step out of the car and off to the side, let others off, then get back on.
- On escalators, stand on the right and pass on the left. But note that in some passageways or stairways, you might be directed to walk on the left (the direction Brits go when behind the wheel).
- Discreet eating and drinking are fine (nothing smelly); drinking alcohol and smoking are not.

## By Bus

If you figure out the bus system, you'll swing like Tarzan through the urban jungle of London (see sidebar for a list of handy routes). Get in the habit of hopping buses for quick little straight shots, even just to get to a Tube stop. However, during bump-and-grind rush hours (8:00-10:00 and 16:00-19:00), you'll usually go faster by Tube.

You can't buy single-trip tickets for buses, and you can't use cash to pay for your fare when boarding. Instead, you must have an Oyster card, a Travelcard, or a one-day Bus & Tram Pass (£5, can buy on day of travel only—not beforehand, available from ticket machine or window in any Tube station). If you're using your Oyster card, any bus ride in downtown London costs £1.50 (with a cap of £4.40 per day).

When you're waiting at a stop, as your bus approaches, it's wise to hold your arm out to let the driver know you want on. Hop on and confirm your destination with the driver (often friendly and helpful).

As you board, touch your Oyster card to the card reader, or show your paper Travelcard or Bus & Tram Pass to the driver (there's no need to show or tap your card when you hop off). On the older heritage "Routemaster" buses without card readers (used on the #15 route), you simply take a seat, and the conductor comes around to check cards and passes.

To alert the driver that you want to get off, press one of the red buttons (on the poles between the seats) before your stop.

# Handy Bus Routes

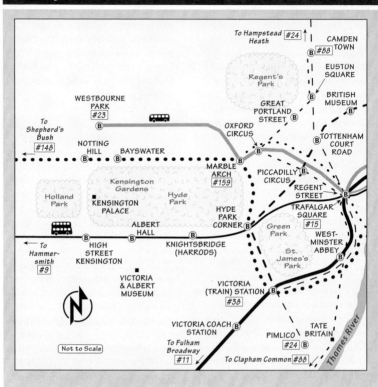

Ever since London instituted a congestion charge for cars, the bus system has gotten faster, easier, and cheaper. Tube-oriented travelers need to get over their tunnel vision, learn the bus system, and get around fast and easy. The best views are upstairs on a double-decker.

Here are some of the most useful routes:

**Route #9:** High Street Kensington to Knightsbridge (Harrods) to Hyde Park Corner to Trafalgar Square to Aldwych (Somerset House).

**Route #11:** Victoria Station to Westminster Abbey to Trafalgar Square to St. Paul's and Liverpool Street Station and the East End.

**Route #15:** Trafalgar Square to St. Paul's to Tower of London (sometimes with heritage "Routemaster" old-style double-decker buses).

**Routes #23 and #159:** Paddington Station (#159 begins at Marble Arch) to Oxford Circus to Piccadilly Circus to Trafalgar Square; from there, #23 heads east to St. Paul's and Liverpool Street Station, while #159 heads to Westminster and the Imperial War Museum. In addition, several buses (including #6, #13, and #139) also make the corridor run between Marble Arch, Oxford Circus, Piccadilly Circus, and Trafalgar Square.

**Route #24:** Pimlico to Victoria Station to Westminster Abbey to Trafalgar Square

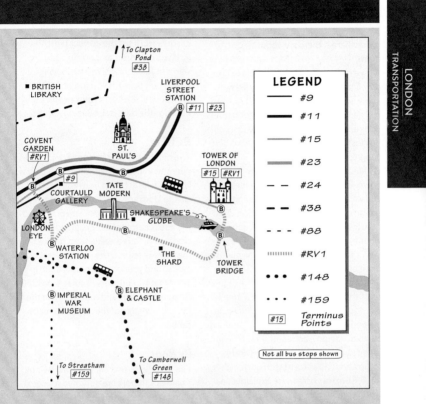

to Euston Square, then all the way north to Camden Town (Camden Lock Market).

**Route #38:** Victoria Station to Hyde Park Corner to Piccadilly Circus to British Museum.

**Route #88:** Tate Britain to Westminster Abbey to Trafalgar Square to Piccadilly Circus to Oxford Circus to Great Portland Street Station (Regent's Park), then north to Camden Town.

**Route #148:** Westminster Abbey to Victoria Station to Notting Hill and Bayswater (by way of the east end of Hyde Park and Marble Arch).

**Route #RV1** (a scenic South Bank joyride): Tower of London to Tower Bridge to Southwark Street (five-minute walk behind Tate Modern/Shakespeare's Globe) to London Eye/Waterloo Station, then over Waterloo Bridge to Aldwych and Covent Garden.

## By Taxi

London is the best taxi town in Europe. Big, black, carefully regulated cabs are everywhere—there are about 25,000 of them.

I've never met a crabby cabbie in London. They love to talk, and they know every nook and cranny in town. I ride in a taxi each day just to get my London questions answered. Drivers must pass a rigorous test on "The Knowledge" of London geography to earn their license.

If a cab's top light is on, just wave it down. Drivers flash lights when they see you wave. They have a tight turning radius, so you can hail cabs going in either direction. If waving doesn't work, ask someone where you can find a taxi stand. Telephoning a cab will get you one in a few minutes, but it costs a little more.

**Rates:** Rides start at £2.40. The regular tariff #1 covers most of the day (Mon-Fri 6:00-20:00), tariff #2 is during "unsociable hours" (Mon-Fri 20:00-22:00 and Sat-Sun 6:00-22:00), and tariff #3 is for nighttime (22:00-6:00) and holidays. Rates go up about 20 percent with each higher tariff. All extra charges are explained in writing on the cab wall. Tip a cabbie by rounding up (maximum 10 percent).

Connecting downtown sights is quick and easy, and will cost you about £8-10 (for example, St. Paul's to the Tower of London, or between the two Tate museums). All cabs can carry five passengers, and some take six, for the same cost as a single traveler.

Don't worry about meter cheating. Licensed British cab meters come with a sealed computer chip and clock that ensures you'll get the correct tariff.

If you overdrink and ride in a taxi, be warned: Taxis charge £40 for "soiling" (a.k.a., pub puke). If you forget this book in a taxi, call the Lost Property office and hope for the best (tel. 0845-330-9882).

## By Uber

The on-demand car hire service **Uber** operates in London with rates comparable to taxis. Like at home, you request a car via the Uber app on your mobile device (connected to Wi-Fi or a data plan), and the fare is automatically charged to your credit card. Cars aren't always marked, but the app will tell you the vehicle's make and model, and your driver's name. Keep in mind that Uber drivers often rely on GPS to route your trip, and may not have the same knowledge of the city as do many cabbies.

## By Boat

The sleek, 220-seat catamarans used by **Thames Clippers** are designed for commuters rather than sightseers. Think of the boats as express buses on the river— they zip through London every 20-30 minutes, stopping at most of the major docks en route. They're fast: roughly 20 minutes from Embankment to Tower, 10 more minutes to Docklands, and 10 more minutes to Greenwich. However, the only outside access is on a crowded deck at the exhaust-choked back of the boat, where you're jostling for space to take photos. Any one-way ride costs £7.50, and a River Roamer all-day ticket costs £17.35 (discounts with Travelcard and Oyster card, www.thamesclippers.com).

Thames Clippers also offers two express trips. The **Tate Boat** ferry service, which directly connects the Tate Britain (Millbank Pier) and the Tate Modern (Bankside Pier), is made for art lovers (£7.50 one way, covered by River Roamer day ticket; buy ticket at self-service machines before boarding or use Oyster Card; for frequency and times, see the Tate Britain and Tate Modern listings, earlier, or www.tate.org.uk/visit/tate-boat). The **O2 Express** runs only on nights when there are events at the O2 arena in Greenwich (departs from Waterloo Pier).

## By Bike

London operates a citywide bike-rental program similar to ones in other major European cities, and new bike lanes are still cropping up around town.

Still, London isn't (yet) ideal for biking. Although the streets are relatively uncongested, the network of designated bike lanes is far from complete, and the city's many one-way streets (not to mention the need to bike on the "wrong" side) can make biking challenging.

**Santander Cycles,** intended for quick point-to-point trips, are fairly easy to rent. Approximately 700 bike-rental stations are scattered throughout the city (£2/day access fee; first 30 minutes free; £2 for every additional 30-minute period).

You can hire bikes as often as you like (which will start your free 30-minute period over again), as long as you wait five minutes between each use. Pick up a map of the docking stations at any major Underground station. The same map is also available online at www.tfl.gov.uk (click on "Santander Cycles") and in a free app (http://cyclehireapp.com).

## By Car

If you have a car, stow it—you don't want to drive in London. A £10 **congestion charge** is levied on any private car entering the city center during peak hours (Mon-Fri 7:00-18:00, no charge Sat-Sun and holidays, fee payable at gas stations, convenience stores, and self-service machines at public parking lots, or online at www.cclondon.com). There are painfully stiff penalties for late payments.

# Arriving and Departing
## By Plane

London has six airports; I've focused my coverage on the two most widely used—Heathrow and Gatwick—with a few tips for using the others (Stansted, Luton, London City, and Southend).

### HEATHROW AIRPORT

For Heathrow's airport, flight, and transfer information, call the switchboard at 0844-335-1801, or visit the helpful website at www.heathrowairport.com (airport code: LHR).

Heathrow's terminals are numbered T-1 through T-5. Each terminal is served by different airlines and alliances; for example, T-5 is exclusively for British Air and Iberia Air flights, while T-2 serves mostly Star Alliance flights, such as United and Lufthansa. Screens posted throughout the airport identify which terminal each airline uses; this information should also be printed on your ticket or boarding pass.

To navigate, read signs and ask questions. You can walk between T-2 and T-3. From this central hub (called "Heathrow Central"), T-4 and T-5 split off in opposite directions (and are not walkable). The easiest way to travel between the T-2/T-3 cluster and either T-4 or T-5 is by Heathrow Express train (free, departs every 15-20 minutes). You can also take a shuttle bus (free, serves all terminals), or the Tube (requires a ticket, serves all terminals).

If you're flying out of Heathrow, it's critical to confirm which terminal your flight will use—if it's T-4 or T-5, allow extra time. Taxi drivers generally know which terminal you'll need based on the airline, but bus drivers may not.

**Services:** Each terminal has an airport information desk (open long hours daily), car-rental agencies, exchange bureaus, ATMs, a pharmacy, a VAT refund desk, room-booking services, and baggage storage (daily 5:00-23:00, www.left-baggage.co.uk). Heathrow offers free Wi-Fi and

# London's Airports

Luton

Luton

Stansted

Not to Scale

Reading

ST. PANCRAS

PADDINGTON

Windsor
#71 & #71

Rail Air Link

Tube

VICTORIA

LIVERPOOL STREET

Southend

D.L.R.

Southend

To Bath

Heathrow

VICTORIA COACH STN.

London City

Thames

London

Guildford

EUROSTAR

Gatwick

Ashford

To Paris

Rail
Eurostar Rail
Tube & D.L.R.
Bus

ALL BUSES ARE NATIONAL EXPRESS
UNLESS NOTED

To Brighton

English Channel

---

pay Internet access points (in each terminal, check map for locations). You'll find a post office on the first floor of T-3 (departures area). Each terminal also has cheap eateries.

Heathrow's small **"TI"** (tourist info shop) is worth a visit if you're nearby and want to pick up a simple map or the *London Planner* visitors guide (long hours daily, 5-minute walk from T-3 in Tube station, follow signs to Underground; bypass queue for transit info to reach window for London questions).

**Getting Between Heathrow and Downtown London:** You have five basic options for traveling the 14 miles between Heathrow Airport and downtown London: Tube, bus, direct shuttle bus, express train (with connecting Tube or taxi), or taxi. The one that works best for you will depend on your arrival terminal, your

destination in central London, and your budget.

**By Tube (Subway):** The Tube takes you from any Heathrow terminal to downtown London in 50-60 minutes on the Piccadilly Line (6/hour, buy ticket at Tube station ticket window or self-service machine). If you plan to use the Tube for transport in London, it makes sense to buy a pay-as-you-go Oyster card or Travelcard at the airport's Tube station ticket window. (For details on these passes, see page 117.) If your transit card covers only Zones 1-2, you'll need to pay a small supplement for the initial trip from Heathrow (Zone 6) to downtown.

If you're taking the Tube from downtown London *to* the airport, note that Piccadilly Line trains don't stop at every terminal. Trains either stop at T-4, then T-2/T-3 (also called Heathrow Central), in that order; or T-2/T-3, then T-5. When leaving central London on the Tube, allow extra time if going to T-4 or T-5, and check the reader board in the station before you board to make sure that the train goes to the right terminal.

**By Bus:** Most London-bound buses depart from the outdoor common area called the Central Bus Station, a five-minute walk from the T-2/T-3 complex. To connect between T-4 or T-5 and the Central Bus Station, ride the free Heathrow Express train or the shuttle buses.

**National Express** has regular service from Heathrow's Central Bus Station to Victoria Coach Station in downtown London, near several of my recommended hotels. While slow, the bus is affordable and convenient for those staying near Victoria Station (£6-9, 1-2/hour, less frequent from Victoria Station to Heathrow, 45-75 minutes depending on time of day, tel. 0871-781-8181, www.nationalexpress.com). A less-frequent National Express bus goes from T-5 directly to Victoria Coach Station.

**By Shuttle Bus: Heathrow Shuttle** is an economical shuttle-bus service that goes to/from your hotel and your terminal at Heathrow. You'll share a minivan with other travelers who are also being picked up or dropped off, so it's not much of a time-savings over taking the Tube (£20/person, progressive discounts for groups of two or more, 1 child under age 10 travels free with 2 adults, runs daily 4:00-18:00, book at least 24 hours in advance, tel. 020/309-2771, www.heathrowshuttle.com, info@heathrowshuttle.com). Another option is **Just Airports,** which offers a private car service between five London airports and the city center (from £32/car; see website for price quote, tel. 020/8900-1666, www.justairports.com).

**By Train:** Two different trains run between Heathrow Airport and London's Paddington Station. At Paddington Station, you're in the thick of the Tube system, with easy access to any of my recommended neighborhoods. The **Heathrow Connect** train is the slightly slower, much cheaper option, serving T-2/T-3 at a single station called Heathrow Central; use free transfers to get from either T-4 or T-5 to Heathrow Central (£10.20 one-way, £20.40 round-trip, 2/hour Mon-Sat, 1-2/hour Sun, 40 minutes, tel. 0345-604-1515, www.heathrowconnect.com).

The **Heathrow Express** train is fast and runs more frequently, but it's pricey (£22 one-way, £36 round-trip, £5 more if you buy your ticket on board, 4/hour; 15 minutes to downtown from Heathrow Central Station serving T-2/T-3, 21 minutes from T-5; for T-4 take free transfer to Heathrow Central; covered by BritRail pass, daily 5:10-23:48, tel. 0345-600-1515, www.heathrowexpress.co.uk).

**By Taxi:** Taxis from the airport cost £45-75 to west and central London (one hour). For four people traveling together, this can be a reasonable option. Hotels can often line up a cab back to the airport for about £50.

*Getting to Bath:* If you're going from the airport to Bath, the train via London will get you there fastest, and if you have a Britrail pass, your journey is covered (hourly, 2 hours). Otherwise, a train-and-bus combination via Reading is more affordable (allow 2.5 hours total). For details, see page 175.

## GATWICK AIRPORT

More and more flights land at Gatwick Airport, which is halfway between London and the south coast (airport code: LGW, tel. 0844-892-0322, www.gatwickairport.com). Gatwick has two terminals, North and South, which are easily connected by a free two-minute monorail ride. Boarding passes say "Gatwick N" or "Gatwick S" to indicate your terminal. British Airways flights generally use Gatwick North. The Gatwick Express trains (described next) stop only at Gatwick South.

**Getting Between Gatwick and Downtown London: Gatwick Express trains** are the best way into London from this airport. They shuttle conveniently between Gatwick South and London's Victoria Station (£20 one-way, £35 round-trip, cheaper if purchased online, Oyster cards accepted, 4/hour, 30 minutes, runs 5:00-24:00 daily, a few trains as early as 3:30, tel. 0845-850-1530, www.gatwickexpress.com). If going from Victoria Station *to* the airport, note that Gatwick Express has its own ticket windows right by the platform (tracks 13 and 14).

A train also runs between Gatwick South and **St. Pancras International Station**—useful for travelers taking the Eurostar train (to Paris or Brussels) or staying in the St. Pancras/King's Cross neighborhood (£10.30, 6/hour, 60 minutes, www.thetrainline.com).

Even slower, but cheap and handy to the Victoria Station neighborhood, you can take the **bus.** National Express runs a bus from Gatwick direct to Victoria Station (£8, at least hourly, 1.5 hours, tel. 0871-781-8181, www.nationalexpress.com).

### OTHER LONDON AIRPORTS

**Stansted Airport:** Airport code STN, tel. 0844-335-1803, www.stanstedairport.com. **Buses** run by National Express (£12, www.nationalexpress.com) and Terravision (£8-10, www.terravision.com) connect the airport and London's Victoria Station neighborhood in about 1.5-2 hours. Or you can take the faster Stansted Express train (£19, www.stanstedexpress.com). Stansted is expensive by **cab;** figure £100-120 one-way from central London.

**Luton Airport:** Airport code LTN, tel. 01582/405-100, www.london-luton.co.uk. The fastest way into London is by **train** to St. Pancras International Station (£10-14, 25-45 minutes, www.eastmidlandstrains.co.uk); catch the shuttle bus from outside the airport terminal to the Luton Airport Parkway Station. The National Express **bus** A1 runs from Luton to Victoria Coach Station (£7-11, 1-1.5 hours, www.nationalexpress.com). The Green Line express **bus** #757 runs to Bucking-ham Palace Road, just south of Victoria Station, and stops en route near the Baker Street Tube station (£10, 1-1.5 hours, www.greenline.co.uk).

**London City Airport:** Airport code LCY, tel. 020/7646-0088, www.londoncityairport.com. Take the Docklands Light Railway (DLR) to the Bank Tube station, which is one stop east of St. Paul's on the Central Line (£5, covered by Oyster card, 20 minutes, www.tfl.gov.uk/dlr).

**Southend Airport:** Airport code SEN, tel. 01702/538-500, www.southendairport.com. Trains connect this airport to London's Liverpool Street Station (£16.80, 55 minutes, www.abelliogreateranglia.co.uk).

## By Train

London, the country's major transportation hub, has a different train station for each region. There are nine main stations:

- **Euston:** Covers northwest England
- **St. Pancras International:** North and south England, plus the Eurostar to Paris or Brussels (for more on the Eurostar, see www.ricksteves.com/eurostar)
- **King's Cross:** Northeast England, including York
- **Liverpool Street:** East England
- **London Bridge:** South England
- **Waterloo:** South England
- **Victoria:** Canterbury, Oxford, and Bath, as well as Gatwick Airport
- **Paddington:** South and southwest England, including Heathrow Airport, Windsor, Bath, Oxford, and the Cotswolds

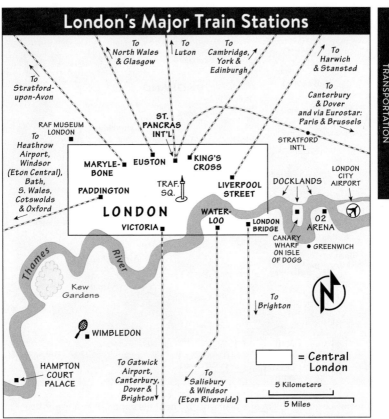

## London's Major Train Stations

Marylebone: Southwest and central England, including Stratford-upon-Avon

Any train station has schedule information, can make reservations, and can sell tickets for any destination. Most stations offer a baggage-storage service; because of long security lines, it can take a while to check or pick up your bag (www.left-baggage.co.uk). For details on the services offered at each station, see www.nationalrail.co.uk/stations.

UK **train and bus info** is available at www.traveline.org.uk. For information on tickets and rail passes, see page 387.

**TRAIN CONNECTIONS
FROM LONDON
From Paddington Station to Points
West: Windsor** (Windsor & Eton Central Station, 2-3/hour, 35 minutes, easy change at Slough; you can also reach Windsor from Waterloo Station—2/hour, 50 minutes—but get off at Windsor & Eton Riverside Station), **Bath** (2/hour, 1.5 hours), **Oxford** (2/hour direct, 1 hour, more with transfer), **Moreton-in-Marsh** (hourly, 1.5 hours).

**From King's Cross Station to Points North: York** (hourly, 2 hours), **Durham** (hourly, 3 hours), **Cambridge** (2/hour, 45 minutes).

**From Euston Station to Points North: Liverpool** (at least hourly, 2-2.5 hours, more with transfer), **Keswick** (hourly, 4 hours, transfer to bus at Penrith).

**From London's Other Stations to: Stratford-upon-Avon** from Marylebone (1-2/hour with transfers, 2 hours),

**Public Transportation near London**

To North England & Scotland

To York & Scotland

King's Lynn
Norwich

ENGLAND

Coventry

Stratford-upon-Avon
Warwick
Leam. Spa
Worcester
Moreton
Banbury

Long Buckby
Bedford
Hunt.
Ely

Cambridge

To Hoek van Holland

Stow
Cheltenham
COTSWOLDS
Blenheim
Swindon
Oxford
Didcot

Luton
Stansted
Harwich

To Cardiff
Avebury
Reading
Slough
London

London City
Southend

Bristol
Bath
Wells
Bedwyn
Windsor
Heathrow
EUROSTAR
Greenwich
Ramsgate

Canterbury
Dover

Glastonbury
Stonehenge
Gatwick
Ashford
(CHUNNEL)
Calais

Salisbury
South-ampton
Brighton
Rye

To Cornwall
Poole
Portsmouth
East-bourne
Hastings
Calais-Fréthun

Bournemouth
Isle of Wight
English Channel
To Paris

Weymouth

----- Rail
---- Bus
........ Boat

Note: Bus Lines Follow Most Rail Lines

30 Kilometers
30 Miles
(approx. scale)

FRANCE

**Greenwich** from the Bank or Monument Tube stop on the DLR—Docklands Light Railway (6/hour, 20 minutes).

## By Bus

Buses are slower but considerably cheaper than trains for reaching destinations around Britain and beyond. Most depart from **Victoria Coach Station,** which is one long block south of Victoria Station (Tube: Victoria). Inside the station, you'll find basic eateries, kiosks, and a helpful information desk.

Ideally you'll buy your tickets online (for tips on buying tickets and taking buses, see page 121). But if you must buy one at the station, try to arrive an hour before the bus departs, or drop by the day before. Ticketing machines are scattered around the station (separate machines for National Express/Eurolines and Megabus; you can buy either for today or for tomorrow); there's also a ticket counter near gate 21. For UK train and bus info, check www.traveline.org.uk.

**National Express buses** go to: **Bath** (nearly hourly, 3-3.5 hours), **Oxford** (2/hour, 2 hours), **Cambridge** (every 60-90 minutes, 2 hours), **Stratford-upon-Avon** (3/day, 3.5 hours), **Liverpool** (8/day direct, 5-6 hours, overnight available), **York** (4/day direct, 5.5 hours).

# NEAR LONDON

Greenwich, Windsor, and Stonehenge are three enjoyable day-trip possibilities near London.

Seafaring **Greenwich,** just east of downtown London, has the *Cutty Sark* tea clipper and the prime meridian. **Windsor Castle,** the primary residence of Her Majesty the Queen, is regally lived-in yet open to the public (23 miles west of London). **Stonehenge,** the world's most famous rock group, sits lonesome and adored in a mysterious field 90 miles southwest of the city.

*Rick's Tip: Take advantage of* **British Rail's "off-peak day return" ticket.** *This round-trip fare costs virtually the same as one-way, provided you depart London outside rush hour (usually after 9:30 on weekdays and anytime Sat-Sun). Ask for the "day return" ticket (round-trip within a single day) rather than the more expensive standard "return."*

# GREENWICH

Greenwich—England's maritime capital—feels like a small town all its own. Visitors come here for all things salty, including the *Cutty Sark* clipper, the area's premier attraction. Greenwich is synonymous with the prime meridian, timekeeping, and astronomy, and at the Royal Observatory, you can learn how those pursuits relate to seafaring. Since you can travel between central London and Greenwich on a cheap Tube ticket, it's a wonderful, inexpensive day out. And where else can you set your watch with such accuracy?

## Orientation

In this small town, located on the Thames, everything is walkable and mainly level, though the Royal Observatory is an uphill climb.

**Day Plan:** Head to Greenwich in the morning—some of the sights can get crowded with families and school groups, especially in summer and on weekends. Start at the *Cutty Sark,* forage for lunch at the food stalls at Greenwich Market, then head for the Royal Observatory. You can see these main sights in 2 to 3 hours. With more time, drop into the National Maritime Museum or stroll through the Old Royal Naval College.

*Rick's Tip: Be sure to browse the entertaining* **Greenwich Market,** *which hosts food stalls, a farmers market, and arts and crafts (Tue-Sun 10:00-17:30, closed Mon; also antiques on Tue, Thu, and Fri; www.greenwichmarketlondon.com). It's* **busiest on weekends** *with day-tripping Londoners.*

**Getting There:** It's a joy by boat or a snap by Docklands Light Railway (DLR). I enjoy a mix-and-match approach: Ride the boat to Greenwich for the scenery and commentary, and take the DLR back. On pleasant weekends, London-bound boats fill up quickly as everyone leaves around the same time (17:00-18:00)—another reason to boat here and take the DLR back to central London.

Various **tour boats**—with commentary and open-deck seating—leave from the piers at Westminster, Waterloo, and the Tower of London (2/hour, 30-75 minutes).

Greenwich

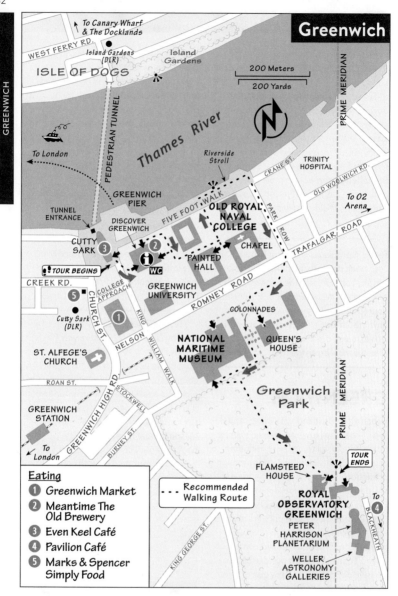

# Greenwich

To Canary Wharf & The Docklands

WEST FERRY RD.

Island Gardens (DLR)

Island Gardens

ISLE OF DOGS

200 Meters
200 Yards

PRIME MERIDIAN

Thames River

To London

PEDESTRIAN TUNNEL

GREENWICH PIER

Riverside Stroll

TRINITY HOSPITAL

CRANE ST.

OLD WOOLWICH RD.

To 02 Arena

TUNNEL ENTRANCE

FIVE FOOT WALK

OLD ROYAL NAVAL COLLEGE

PARK ROW

DISCOVER GREENWICH

CUTTY SARK ③

CHAPEL

TRAFALGAR ROAD

🛈②

WC

PAINTED HALL

TOUR BEGINS

CREEK RD.

COLLEGE APPROACH

GREENWICH UNIVERSITY

ROMNEY ROAD

⑤

CHURCH ST.

①

COLONNADES

Cutty Sark (DLR)

KING WILLIAM WALK

NELSON

NATIONAL MARITIME MUSEUM

QUEEN'S HOUSE

ST. ALFEGE'S CHURCH

ROAN ST.

GREENWICH HIGH RD

STOCKWELL

Greenwich Park

PRIME MERIDIAN

GREENWICH STATION

BURNEY ST.

To London

FLAMSTEED HOUSE

TOUR ENDS

## Eating

① Greenwich Market

② Meantime The Old Brewery

③ Even Keel Café

④ Pavilion Café

⑤ Marks & Spencer Simply Food

- - - Recommended Walking Route

ROYAL OBSERVATORY GREENWICH

To ④ BLACKHEATH

KING GEORGE ST.

PETER HARRISON PLANETARIUM

WELLER ASTRONOMY GALLERIES

---

Thames Clippers offers faster trips, with no commentary and only a small deck (2-3/hour, 20-45 minutes). See "Cruise Boat Tours," page 44.

The **DLR light rail** runs to Greenwich's Cutty Sark Station from London's Bank-Monument Station (6/hour, 20 minutes, covered by any Tube pass).

**Arrival in Greenwich:** By boat, you'll dock right in front of the *Cutty Sark*. By rail, exit the DLR station to the left, pass under the brick archway, and turn left; the

*Cutty Sark* is just ahead on your right.

**Tourist Information:** The TI is within the **Discover Greenwich visitors center,** inside the Old Royal Naval College gates (daily 10:00-17:00, Pepys House, 2 Cutty Sark Gardens, tel. 0870-608-2000, www. visitgreenwich.org.uk).

# Sights

### ▲▲*CUTTY SARK*

The Scottish-built *Cutty Sark* was the last of the great China tea clippers and the queen of the seas when launched in 1869. She was among the fastest clippers ever built: With 32,000 square feet of sail—and favorable winds—she could travel 300 miles in a day. But as a new century dawned, steamers began to outmatch sailing ships for speed, and by the mid-1920s the *Cutty Sark* was the world's last operating clipper ship.

You can stroll through the exhibit directly below the *Cutty Sark* (raised 11 feet above her dry dock) to view displays on the ship's 140-year history and the cargo she carried—everything from tea to wool to gunpowder—as she raced between London and ports all around the world. The Even Keel Café is also below deck, along with the WCs. You can walk on the deck, where the ship's rigging has been restored to original specifications. Outside the ship, street performers do shows in peak season for the public.

**Cost and Hours:** £13.50, family deals, Day Explorer combo-ticket with Royal Observatory-£18.50; daily 10:00-17:00; can reserve ahead by phone or online (a good idea for summer and weekends), reservation tel. 020/8312-6608, www.rmg. co.uk.

## ▲OLD ROYAL NAVAL COLLEGE

The former college, a complex of classical buildings overlooking a broad riverfront park, was originally a hospital founded by Queen Mary II and King William III in 1692 to care for naval officers. William and Mary spared no expense, hiring the great Christopher Wren to design the complex. After its days as a hospital ended, it served as a college for training naval officers. Now that the Royal Navy has moved out, the public is invited to view the college's elaborate Painted Hall (the Sistine Chapel of the UK) and the Neoclassical Chapel of Sts. Peter and Paul.

**Cost and Hours:** Free (£3 suggested donation), daily 10:00-17:00, www.ornc. org.

## ▲NATIONAL MARITIME MUSEUM

Great for anyone interested in the sea, this museum holds everything from a giant working paddlewheel to the uniform Admiral Horatio Nelson wore when he was killed at Trafalgar (look for the bullet hole in the left shoulder). A big glass roof tops three levels of slick, modern, kid-friendly exhibits about all things seafaring.

**Cost and Hours:** Free, daily 10:00-17:00, tel. 020/8858-4422, www.rmg.co.uk.

Cutty Sark

*Old Royal Naval College*

## ▲▲ROYAL OBSERVATORY GREENWICH

A visit here gives you a taste of the inter-related sciences of astronomy, timekeeping, and seafaring—as well as great views over Greenwich and the distant London skyline from the grounds.

The historic observatory, located on the prime meridian (0° longitude), is famous as the point from which all time is measured. It has several worthy exhibits, including one devoted to the early time-keepers that helped solve the problem of finding longitude at sea. Neighboring sights are the state-of-the-art Peter Harrison Planetarium and the free Weller Astronomy Galleries with interactive displays.

**Rick's Tip:** *If your only interest in the Royal Observatory is the famous* **prime meridian line,** *go through the unassuming iron gate just below the entrance for a free (and significantly less crowded) display of the prime meridian.*

**Cost and Hours:** Observatory—£9.50, includes audioguide, Day Explorer combo-ticket with *Cutty Sark*-£18.50, combo-ticket with planetarium-£12.50; Peter Harrison Planetarium—£7.50, 30-minute shows generally run every hour, see website for offerings and reservations (including family shows); entire complex open daily 10:00–17:00; tel. 020/8858-4422, www.rmg.co.uk. It's a 10-15 minute uphill walk from the Maritime Museum (take the tree-lined path behind the museum).

*Royal Observatory*

## Eating

The food stalls at the **Greenwich Market** offer an international variety of tasty options—from Yorkshire pudding to paella to Thai cuisine.

**Meantime The Old Brewery** is a gastropub decorated with beer memorabilia; an adjacent café serves cheap lunches (in the Discover Greenwich Center, with the TI).

Other good lunch options are the **Even Keel Café** (located directly beneath the shining copper hull of the *Cutty Sark*) and the elegant 1906 **Pavillion Café,** which offers counter-service (behind the planetarium in Greenwich Park).

The parks are picnic-perfect; pick up a ready-made lunch from **Marks & Spencer Simply Food** (55 Greenwich Church Street).

# WINDSOR CASTLE

Windsor Castle, rated ▲▲, has been the official home of the royal family—39 British monarchs—for almost a thousand years. It claims to be the largest and oldest continuously occupied castle in the world. William the Conqueror built the first fortified castle here; later kings added on to his early designs, rebuilding and expanding the castle and surrounding gardens.

The current Queen considers Windsor her primary residence, and generally hangs her crown here on weekends. Visitors see sprawling grounds, lavish staterooms, a crowd-pleasing dollhouse, a gallery of Michelangelo and Leonardo da Vinci drawings, and an exquisite Perpendicular Gothic chapel.

## Orientation

**Day Plan:** Follow my self-guided tour or the included audioguide through the grounds and castle. You could also take the free guided walk of the grounds. A typical castle visit lasts 2 to 3 hours.

**Getting There:** Windsor has two **train stations,** each a five-minute walk from

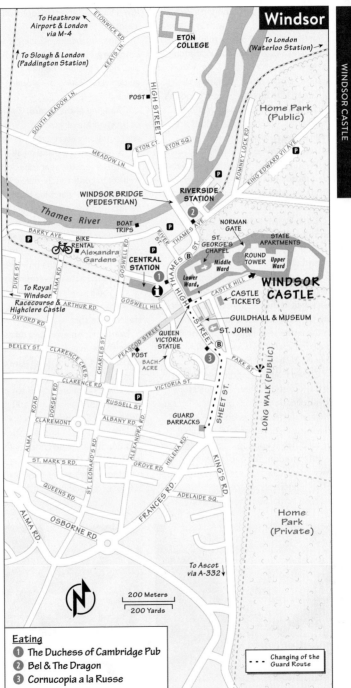

# Windsor

To Heathrow
Airport & London
via M-4

To Slough & London
(Paddington Station)

ETONWICK RD.

KEATS LN.

ETON COLLEGE

To London
(Waterloo Station)

POST

HIGH STREET

SOUTH MEADOW LN.

MEADOW LN.

ETON CT.

ETON SQ.

Home Park
(Public)

RONNEY LOCK RD.

KING EDWARD VII AVE.

WINDSOR BRIDGE
(PEDESTRIAN)

RIVERSIDE STATION

Thames River

BOAT TRIPS

RIVER ST.

THAMES AVE.

NORMAN GATE

STATE APARTMENTS

ST. GEORGE'S CHAPEL

BARRY AVE.

BIKE RENTAL

Alexandra Gardens

GOSWELL RD.

THAMES ST.

ROUND TOWER

Upper Ward

Middle Ward

WINDSOR CASTLE

CENTRAL STATION

Lower Ward

CASTLE HILL

DUKE ST.

ALMA RD.

GOSWELL HILL

CASTLE TICKETS

To Royal Windsor
Racecourse &
Highclere Castle

ARTHUR RD.

HIGH STREET

GUILDHALL & MUSEUM

ST. JOHN

OXFORD RD.

BEXLEY ST.

CLARENCE CRES.

CHARLES ST.

PEASCOD STREET

QUEEN VICTORIA STATUE

POST

PARK ST.

BACH ACRE

LONG WALK (PUBLIC)

CLARENCE RD.

DORSET RD.

VICTORIA ST.

SHEET ST.

RUSSELL ST.

CLAREMONT

ALBANY RD.

ALEXANDRA RD.

GUARD BARRACKS

ALMA ROAD

ST. MARK'S RD.

ST. LEONARD'S RD.

GROVE RD.

HELENA RD.

KING'S RD.

QUEENS RD.

FRANCES RD.

ADELAIDE SQ.

Home Park
(Private)

ALMA RD.

OSBORNE RD.

To Ascot
via A-332

200 Meters

200 Yards

## Eating
1. The Duchess of Cambridge Pub
2. Bel & The Dragon
3. Cornucopia a la Russe

- - - Changing of the
Guard Route

the castle. Trains from London's Paddington Station connect with Windsor & Eton Central (2-3/hour, 35 minutes, easy change at Slough); London Waterloo takes you to the Windsor & Eton Riverside station (2/hour direct, 55 minutes).

Green Line **buses** run from London's Victoria Colonnades coach station to the Parish Church stop on Windsor's High Street (1-2/hour, 1.5 hours, www. firstgroup.com).

Windsor is well-signposted from the **M-4 motorway.** Follow signs for pay-and-display parking in the center (there's no car lot at the castle).

**Cost:** £20 includes the castle grounds and all exhibits.

**Hours:** Grounds and most interiors open daily March-Oct 9:30-17:15, Nov-Feb 9:45-16:15, except St. George's Chapel, which is closed Sun (but open to worshippers; wait at the exit gate to be escorted in). On occasion, the State Apartments or the entire castle might close for royal business; check the website before you go (especially in mid-June).

**Crowd Control:** In summer, it's smart to buy tickets in advance online at www. royalcollection.org.uk (pick up tickets at prepaid ticket window on-site), or purchase in person at the Buckingham Palace ticket office in London.

**Information:** Tel. 020/7766-7324, www.royalcollection.org.uk. The Windsor TI is immediately adjacent to Windsor & Eton Central Station, in the Windsor Royal Shopping Centre (open daily, www. windsor.gov.uk).

**Tours:** An included audioguide covers both the grounds and interiors. For a good overview, consider the free 30-minute guided walk around the grounds (usually 2/hour).

**Changing of the Guard:** The ritual occurs nearly every morning in peak season (April-July Mon-Sat at 11:00, arrive by 10:30; never on Sun) and on alternating days the rest of the year (check Windsor website to confirm schedule). The fresh guards, led by a marching band, leave their barracks on Sheet Street, march up High Street, turn right at Victoria, and then left into the Lower Ward, arriving about 11:00. After about 45 minutes, the tired guards march back the way the new ones came. To watch the actual ceremony inside the castle, you'll need to have already bought your ticket, entered the grounds, and staked out a spot.

**Evensong:** An evensong takes place in the chapel nightly at 17:15 (free for worshippers, line up at exit gate to be admitted).

**Eating:** There are no real eateries at the castle (bring along a snack), but **The Duchess of Cambridge** serves up pub grub right across from the castle walls (3 Thames Street). Also consider the charming **Bel & The Dragon** (on Thames Street, near the bridge) or the cozy **Cornucopia a la Russe** (closed Sun, 6 High Street).

*Windsor Castle*

*Changing of the Guard at Windsor*

## ➲ Self-Guided Tour

**The Grounds:** The tower-topped, conical hill represents the historical core of the castle. William the Conqueror built this motte (artificial mound) and bailey (fortified stockade around it) in 1080—his first castle in England. Among the later monarchs who spiffed up Windsor were Edward III (flush with French war booty, he made it a palace fit for a 14th-century king), Charles II (determined to restore the monarchy properly in the 1660s), and George IV (Britain's "Bling King," who financed many such vanity projects in the 1820s).

The castle has three "baileys" (castle yards), which today make up Windsor's Upper Ward (where the Queen lives), Middle Ward (with St. George's Chapel), and Lower Ward (for castle workers). The Upper Ward's **Quadrangle** is surrounded by the State Apartments and the Queen's private apartments. The **Round Tower** sits atop the original motte. The red, yellow, and blue royal standard flies here when the Queen is in residence.

**Queen Mary's Dolls' House:** This palace in miniature (1:12 scale, from 1924) is "the most famous dollhouse in the world." It was a gift for Queen Mary (grandmother of the current Queen), who greatly enjoyed miniatures. It's basically one big, dimly lit room with the large dollhouse in the middle, executed with an astonishing level of detail. Each fork, knife, and spoon on the expertly set banquet table is perfect and made of real silver—and the tiny pipes of its plumbing system actually have running water.

**Drawings Gallery and China Museum:** This gallery displays a changing array of pieces from the Queen's enviable collection—which includes big names such as Michelangelo and Leonardo. The China Museum features items from the Queen's many exquisite table settings for royal shindigs.

**State Apartments:** Dripping with chandeliers, finely furnished, and strewn with history and the art of a long line of kings and queens, these royal rooms are the best I've seen in Britain. This is where Henry VIII and Charles I once lived, and where the current Queen wows visiting dignitaries.

You'll climb the Grand Staircase up to the **Grand Vestibule,** decorated with exotic items seized by British troops during their missions to colonize various corners of the world. (Ask a docent to help you find the bullet that killed Lord Nelson at Trafalgar.) The magnificent wood-ceilinged **Waterloo Chamber** is wallpapered with portraits of figures from the pan-European alliance that defeated Napoleon.

Many rooms are decorated with some of the finest works from the royal collection, including canvases by Rubens, Rembrandt, Van Dyck, and Holbein. **St. George's Hall** is decorated with emblems representing the knights of the prestigious chivalric Order of the Garter, established by Edward III in 1348. This hall is the site of elaborate royal banquets—imagine one long table stretching from one end of the room to the other, seating 160 VIPs.

You'll proceed into the rooms that were

*Round Tower*

restored after a fire in 1992, including the "Semi-State Apartments." The **Garter Throne Room** is where new members of the Order of the Garter are invested (ceremonially granted their titles).

**St. George's Chapel:** This church, which houses 10 royal tombs, is an exquisite example of the Perpendicular Gothic style from about 1500. It's also the spiritual home of the Order of the Garter.

Pick up a free map and circle the interior to view the highlights, including the burial spots of the current Queen's parents (King George VI and "Queen Mum" Elizabeth), Mad King George III (nemesis of American revolutionaries), Henry VIII, and Jane Seymour, Henry's favorite wife (perhaps because she was the only one who died before he could behead her). On your way out, pause at the door of the sumptuous 13th-century **Albert Memorial Chapel,** redecorated in 1861 after the death of Queen Victoria's husband, Prince Albert, and dedicated to his memory.

**Lower Ward:** This area is a living town where some 160 people who work for the Queen reside.

# STONEHENGE

As old as the pyramids, and older than the Acropolis and the Colosseum, this iconic stone circle amazed medieval Europeans, who figured it was built by a race of giants. And it still impresses visitors today. Stonehenge, worth ▲▲, retains an air of mystery and majesty (partly because cordons, which keep hordes of tourists from trampling all over it, foster the illusion that it stands alone in a field). Although some people are underwhelmed by Stonehenge, most of its almost one million annual visitors find that it's worth the trip.

## Orientation

**Day Plan:** Tour the visitors center, then head to Stonehenge by shuttle bus or on foot. Allow at least two hours to see everything.

**Getting There:** Several companies offer **big-bus day trips** to Stonehenge from London. These cover admission to Stonehenge, last 8-12 hours, and pack a 45-seat bus (**Evan Evans,** £45, www.eva-nevanstours.com; **Golden Tours,** £58-60, www.goldentours.com). **International Friends** runs smaller 16-person tours that include Windsor and Bath (£119, www.internationalfriends.co.uk).

**London Walks** offers a guided "Stonehenge and Salisbury Tour," but uses public train and bus connections (£79, cash only, May-Oct Tue 8:45, www.walks.com).

To go on your own on **public transport,** catch a train from London's Waterloo Station to Salisbury (around £39 for same-day return, 2/hour, 1.5 hours, www.nationalrail.co.uk). From Salisbury, you can get to Stonehenge by taxi (£40-50) or take the Stonehenge Tour bus (£14, £27 with Stonehenge admission; daily June-Aug 10:00-18:00, 2/hour, 30 minutes, fewer departures off-season, timetable at www.thestonehengetour.info).

**Cost:** £17.10, buy in advance online (see next), covered by English Heritage Pass (see page 374). In summer, there's a £5 refundable parking fee for drivers.

**Advance Tickets:** Booking a timed-entry ticket at least 24 hours in advance is the only way to assure you'll actually get into the site, which caps the number of visitors per day (www.english-heritage.org.uk/stonehenge). Either print your ticket to present at the site, or bring your booking reference number with you.

**Hours:** Daily June-Aug 9:00-20:00, mid-March-May and Sept-mid-Oct 9:30-19:00, mid-Oct-mid-March 9:30-17:00. Note that last entry is two hours before closing. Expect shorter hours and possible closures June 20-22 due to huge, raucous solstice crowds.

**Tours:** Audioguides are available behind the ticket counter; the same content can be downloaded to your mobile device from the English Heritage website using the visitors center's free Wi-Fi.

**Visiting the Inner Stones:** Special one-hour access to the stones' inner circle is available early in the morning or after closing. Only 26 people are allowed at a time, so reserve well in advance (£31.80, see website for details).

**Information:** Tel. 0870-333-1181, www.english-heritage.org.uk/stonehenge.

**Services:** The visitors center has WCs, a large gift shop, and free Wi-Fi. Services at the circle itself are limited to emergency WCs.

**Eating:** A large café is inside the visitors center.

---

**Rick's Tip:** *If you want to see a large* **Bronze Age burial mound,** *get off the shuttle bus at the Fargo Plantation. From there, you can walk the rest of the way to the stone circle in about 20 minutes. Some visitors prefer this more authentic approach.*

---

## ➲ Self-Guided Tour

Start by touring the exhibits at the visitors center, then take a shuttle (or walk) to the stone circle.

• *Collect your ticket (and rent or download the audioguide) before heading to the excellent exhibit space.*

### VISITORS CENTER

The **permanent exhibit** uses an artful combination of high-tech multimedia displays and prehistoric bones, tools, and pottery shards to explore the history of the people who built Stonehenge. Outside, visit the reconstructed **Neolithic huts,** modeled after the traces of a village discovered just northeast of Stonehenge.

• *Shuttle buses depart every 5-10 minutes from the platform behind the gift shop for the six-minute trip to the stone circle. Or you can walk 1.25 miles through the fields to the site.*

### STONE CIRCLE

As you approach the massive structure of Stonehenge, walk right up to the knee-high cordon and let your fellow 21st-century tourists melt away. It's just you and the druids...

England has hundreds of stone circles, but Stonehenge—which literally means "hanging stones"—is unique. It's the only one that has horizontal cross-pieces (lintels) spanning the vertical monoliths, and the only one with stones that have been made smooth and uniform. About half of the original structure remains—the rest was quarried centuries ago for other buildings.

*Stonehenge is the most famous of Britain's stone circles.*

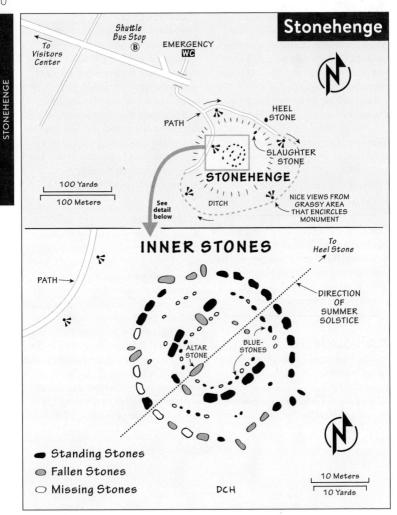

**Stonehenge**

*Shuttle Bus Stop* Ⓑ

EMERGENCY WC

To Visitors Center

PATH

HEEL STONE

SLAUGHTER STONE

STONEHENGE

DITCH

100 Yards
100 Meters

See detail below

NICE VIEWS FROM GRASSY AREA THAT ENCIRCLES MONUMENT

**INNER STONES**

To Heel Stone

PATH →

DIRECTION OF SUMMER SOLSTICE

ALTAR STONE

BLUE-STONES

● Standing Stones
● Fallen Stones
○ Missing Stones

DCH

10 Meters
10 Yards

Now do a slow **clockwise spin** around the monument. As you walk, mentally flesh out the missing pieces to re-erect the rubble.

It's now believed that Stonehenge, which was built in phases between 3000 and 1500 B.C., was originally used as a cremation **cemetery.** This was a hugely significant location to prehistoric peoples. There are several hundred burial mounds within a three-mile radius of Stonehenge—some likely belonging to

kings or chieftains. Some of the human remains are of people from far away, and others show signs of injuries—evidence that Stonehenge may have been used as a place of **medicine** or healing.

Whatever its original purpose, Stonehenge still functions as a celestial **calendar.** As the sun rises on the summer solstice (June 21), the **"heel stone"**—the one set apart from the rest, near the road—lines up with the sun and the altar at the center of the stone circle. A study of more than 300 similar circles in Britain found that each was designed to calculate the movement of the sun, moon, and stars, and to predict eclipses. That information helped early societies know when to plant, harvest, and party.

Some believe that Stonehenge is built at the precise point where six **"ley lines"** intersect. Ley lines are theoretical lines of magnetic or spiritual power that crisscross the globe. Belief in the power of these lines has gone in and out of fashion over time. They are believed to have been very important to prehistoric peoples, but then were largely ignored until the early 20th century, when the English writer Alfred Watkins popularized them (to the scorn of serious scientists). More recently, the concept was embraced by the New Age movement. Without realizing it, you follow these ley lines all the time: Many of England's modern highways follow prehistoric paths, and its churches are built over prehistoric monuments, themselves located where ley lines intersect.

Notice that two of the stones (facing the entry passageway) are blemished. At the base of one monolith, it looks like someone has pulled back the stone to reveal a concrete skeleton. This is a clumsy **repair job** to fix damage done long ago by souvenir seekers, who actually rented hammers and chisels to take home a piece of Stonehenge. Look to the right of the repaired stone: The back of another stone is missing the same thin layer of protective lichen that covers the others. The lichen—and some of the stone itself—was sandblasted off to remove graffiti. (No wonder they've got Stonehenge roped off now.)

Stonehenge's builders used two different types of stone. The tall, stout monoliths and lintels are sandstone blocks called **sarsen stones.** Most of the monoliths weigh about 25 tons (the largest is 45 tons), and the lintels are about 7 tons apiece. These sarsen stones were brought from "only" 20 miles away. The shorter stones in the middle, called **bluestones,** came from the south coast of Wales—240 miles away. Imagine the logistical puzzle of floating six-ton stones across Wales' Severn Estuary and up the River Avon, then rolling them on logs about 20 miles to this position—an impressive feat.

Why didn't the builders of Stonehenge use what seem like perfectly adequate stones nearby? This, like many other questions about Stonehenge, remains shrouded in mystery. Imagine congregations gathering here 5,000 years ago, raising thought levels, creating a powerful life force transmitted along the ley lines. Maybe a particular kind of stone was essential for maximum energy transmission. Maybe the stones were levitated here. Maybe psychics really do create powerful vibes. Maybe not. It's as unbelievable as electricity used to be.

# BEST OF THE REST

# CAMBRIDGE

This delightful town, 60 miles north of London, offers a mellow, fun-to-explore core and the big-league University of Cambridge. Wordsworth, Isaac Newton, Tennyson, Darwin, and Prince Charles are a few of its illustrious alumni. Cambridge is the epitome of a university town, with busy bikers, stately residence halls, and plenty of bookshops. Proud locals can point out where DNA was originally modeled, the atom first split, and electrons discovered.

In medieval Europe, higher education was the domain of the Church and was limited to ecclesiastical schools. Scholars lived in "halls" on campus. This academic

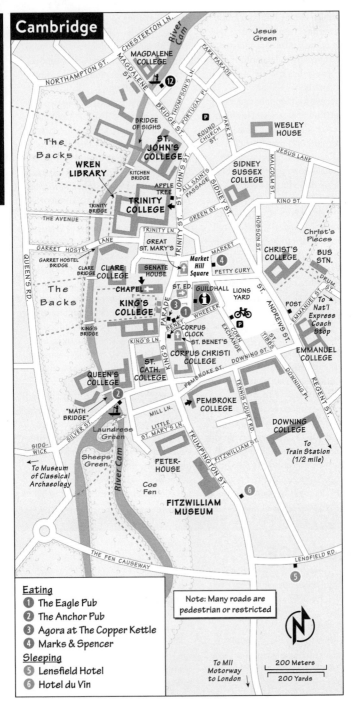

# Cambridge

**The Backs**

**The Backs**

CHESTERTON LN.

River Cam

Jesus Green

MAGDALENE COLLEGE

NORTHAMPTON ST.

MAGDALENE ST.

BRIDGE ST.

THOMPSON'S LN.

PORTUGAL ST.

Park Parade

PARK PARADE

ROUND CHURCH ST.

PARK ST.

P

WESLEY HOUSE

JESUS LANE

MALCOLM ST.

SIDNEY SUSSEX COLLEGE

KING ST.

BRIDGE OF SIGHS

ST. JOHN'S COLLEGE

WREN LIBRARY

KITCHEN BRIDGE

APPLE TREE

TRINITY BRIDGE

TRINITY COLLEGE

THE AVENUE

GARRET HOSTEL LANE

GARRET HOSTEL BRIDGE

CLARE BRIDGE

CLARE COLLEGE

CHAPEL

KING'S COLLEGE

KING'S BRIDGE

QUEEN'S RD.

ALL SAINTS PASSAGE

ST. JOHN'S ST.

TRINITY LN.

TRINITY ST.

GREEN ST.

SIDNEY ST.

MARKET

Market Hill Square

SENATE HOUSE

GREAT ST. MARY'S

KING'S PARADE

ST. ED.

**❹**

PETTY CURY

GUILDHALL

**ℹ**

LIONS YARD

HOBSON ST.

CHRIST'S COLLEGE

Christ's Pieces

BUS STN.

DRUMMER ST.

To Nat'l Express Coach Stop

POST

EMMANUEL ST.

ST. ANDREWS ST.

CHRIST'S COLLEGE

**❸ ❶**

BENE'T ST.

WHEELER

CORPUS CLOCK

ST. BENET'S

CORPUS CHRISTI COLLEGE

KING'S LN.

P

CORN EXCHANGE

DOWNING ST.

ST. TIBB'S

EMMANUEL COLLEGE

ST. CATH. COLLEGE

PEMBROKE ST.

TENNIS COURT RD.

DOWNING PL.

DOWNING ST.

REGENT ST.

QUEEN'S COLLEGE

**❷**

"MATH BRIDGE"

SILVER ST.

Laundress Green

MILL LN.

LITTLE ST. MARY'S LN.

PEMBROKE COLLEGE

DOWNING COLLEGE

SIDGWICK

Sheeps Green

River Cam

PETER-HOUSE

Coe Fen

TRUMPINGTON ST.

FITZWILLIAM ST.

To Train Station (1/2 mile)

To Museum of Classical Archaeology

FITZWILLIAM MUSEUM

**❻**

THE FEN CAUSEWAY

LENSFIELD RD.

**❺**

To M11 Motorway to London

N

Note: Many roads are pedestrian or restricted

## Eating
❶ The Eagle Pub
❷ The Anchor Pub
❸ Agora at The Copper Kettle
❹ Marks & Spencer

## Sleeping
❺ Lensfield Hotel
❻ Hotel du Vin

200 Meters

200 Yards

community of residential halls, chapels, and lecture halls connected by peaceful garden courtyards survives today in the 31 colleges that make up the University of Cambridge. These grand old halls in the town center date back centuries, with ornately decorated facades that try to one-up each other.

The university schedule has three terms: Lent (from mid-Jan to mid-March), Easter (from mid-April to mid-June), and Michaelmas (from early Oct to early Dec). During exams (roughly throughout May), the colleges are closed to visitors, which can impede access to some of the town's picturesque little corners. But the main sights—King's College Chapel and the Wren Library at Trinity College—stay open.

## Orientation

Cambridge is small. It has two main streets, separated from the Cam River by the most interesting colleges. The town center, brimming with tearooms, has a TI and a colorful open-air market square.

**Day Plan:** Cambridge can easily be seen as a day trip from London. A good plan is to take the TI's walking tour (includes King's College Chapel), see the Wren Library at Trinity College (open Mon-Sat only 12:00-14:00), tour the Fitzwilliam Museum if you enjoy art (closed Mon), and spend an hour on a punt ride. Music lovers stick around for the free evensong service at King's College Chapel (Mon-Sat 17:30, Sun 15:30).

*King's College Chapel*

**Getting There:** It's a quick, easy train trip from London's King's Cross Station (2/hour, 45 minutes, www.nationalrail.co.uk); note that for train travelers, Cambridge isn't conveniently on the way to anywhere, so day-tripping from London is the best way to go. Remember that you'll save money by getting an "off-peak day return" ticket (which means departing London after 9:30 on weekdays or anytime Sat-Sun, and returning the same day).

**Buses** run to Cambridge, but take longer than trains (every 60-90 minutes, 2 hours, departs London's Victoria Coach Station, arrives at Cambridge's Parkside stop, National Express X90, www.nationalexpress.co.uk).

**Arrival in Cambridge:** It's a mile from the train station to downtown Cambridge. You can walk (exit straight ahead on Station Road, bear right at the war memorial onto Hills Road, and follow it into town); take one of the frequent public **buses** (#1, #3, or #7); or pay about £6 for a **taxi.**

By **car,** follow signs from the M-11 motorway to any of the central short-stay parking lots, or alternatively, leave your car at a park-and-ride lot outside the city and ride a shuttle bus into town.

---

**Rick's Tip:** *Note that the TI's* **11:00 walking tour** *overlaps with the limited open time of the* **Wren Library** *(Mon-Sat 12:00-14:00); make a beeline to the library after the two-hour tour ends.*

---

**Tourist Information:** Cambridge's TI is just off Market Square in the town center (Mon-Sat 10:00-17:00, also Sun 11:00-15:00 in summer, Peas Hill, tel. 01223/791-500, www.visitcambridge.org). The TI offers **daily walking tours** of the colleges that include the King's College Chapel. Groups are limited to 20, so book online or call ahead to reserve a spot (£18, 2 hours, often Mon-Sat 11:00 and 13:00, Sun 13:00 and 14:00, additional times offered July-Aug, confirm schedule on website, tel. 01223/791-500, www.visitcambridge.org).

# Sights

## ▲▲KING'S COLLEGE CHAPEL

Built from 1446 to 1515 by Henrys VI through VIII, England's best example of Perpendicular Gothic architecture is the single most impressive building in Cambridge.

**Cost and Hours:** £9, generally Mon-Sat 9:30-15:30, Sun 13:15-14:30—hours shift with school term; confirm by calling recorded info tel. 01223/331-1212.

**Evensong:** When school's in session, you're welcome to enjoy an evensong service in this glorious space (free, Mon-Sat at 17:30, Sun at 15:30). To get prime seats in the choir, line up at the front entrance (on King's Parade) by 17:00.

**↪ Self-Guided Tour:** Stand inside, look up, and marvel, as Christopher Wren did, at what was then the largest single span of **vaulted roof** anywhere. Built between 1512 and 1515, its 2,000 tons of incredible fan vaulting—held in place by the force of gravity—are a careful balancing act resting delicately on the buttresses visible outside the building.

Lining the walls are giant **Tudor coats-of-arms.** The 26 **stained-glass windows** date from the 16th century. The lower panes show scenes from the New Testament, while the upper panes feature corresponding stories from the Old Testament.

Considering England's turbulent history, it's miraculous that these windows have survived for nearly half a millennium in such a pristine state. After Henry VIII separated from the Catholic Church in 1534, many such windows and other Catholic features around England were destroyed. But since Henry had just paid for these windows, he couldn't bear to destroy them. During World War II, the windows were taken out and hidden away for safekeeping, then painstakingly replaced after the war ended.

The **choir screen** that bisects the church was commissioned by Henry VIII to commemorate his marriage to Anne Boleyn. By the time it was finished, so was she (beheaded). But it was too late to remove her initials, which were carved into the screen (look for *R.A., Regina Anna*—"Queen Anne"). Behind the screen is the **choir** area, where the King's College Choir performs evensong.

Walk to the altar and admire Rubens' masterful Adoration of the Magi (1634).

*The prized stained-glass windows of King's College Chapel*

It's actually a family portrait: The admirer in the front (wearing red) is a self-portrait of Rubens, Mary looks an awful lot like his much younger wife, and Baby Jesus resembles their own newborn at the time. The chapel to the right of the altar is a moving memorial to those who died in the world wars.

Finally, check out the long and fascinating series of rooms that run the length of the nave on the left. It's the great little **Chapel Museum,** dedicated to the history and art of the church, and includes a model showing how the fan vaults were constructed.

## ▲▲TRINITY COLLEGE AND WREN LIBRARY

More than a third of Cambridge's 83 Nobel Prize winners have come from Trinity, the richest and biggest of the town's colleges, founded in 1546 by Henry VIII. The college has three sights to see: the entrance gate, the grounds, and the magnificent Wren Library.

**Cost and Hours:** Grounds—£3, daily 10:00-17:00; library—free, Mon-Fri 12:00-14:00, during full term also Sat 10:30-12:30, closed Sun year-round; only 20 people allowed in at a time, tel. 01223/338-400,

www.trin.cam.ac.uk. To see the Wren Library without paying for the grounds, access it from the riverside entrance (a long walk around the college via the Garret Hostel Bridge).

## ◐ SELF-GUIDED TOUR

**Trinity Gate:** You'll notice entrance gates like these in the facades of colleges around town. Above the door is a statue of **King Henry VIII,** who founded Trinity. His right hand is holding a chair leg instead of the traditional scepter with the crown jewels. This is courtesy of Cambridge's Night Climbers, who first replaced the scepter a century ago, and continue to periodically switch it out for other items. To the right of the entrance, notice the lone **apple tree.** Supposedly, this tree is a descendant of the very one that once stood in the garden of Sir Isaac Newton (who spent 30 years at Trinity). According to legend, Newton was inspired to investigate gravity when an apple fell from the tree onto his head.

**Trinity Grounds:** The grounds are enjoyable to explore. Inside the **Great Court,** the clock (on the tower on the right) double-rings at the top of each hour. It's a college tradition to take off

*Exploring the grounds at Trinity College*

running from the clock when the high noon bells begin, try to touch each of the four corners of the courtyard, then return to the clock before the ringing ends (takes 43 seconds to ring 24 times).

The **chapel** (right of the clock tower) feels like a shrine to thinking, with statues honoring great Trinity minds like Isaac Newton, Alfred Lord Tennyson, and Francis Bacon. Who's missing? The poet Lord Byron, who was such a hell-raiser during his time at Trinity that a statue of him was deemed unfit for Church property; his statue stands in the library instead.

**Wren Library:** Don't miss the 1695 Christopher Wren-designed library, with its wonderful decorative wood carving and fascinating rare manuscripts. Just outside the library entrance, Sir Isaac Newton clapped his hands and timed the echo to measure the speed of sound as it raced down the side of the cloister and back. In the library's 12 display cases (covered with cloth that you flip back), you'll see Newton's notebook and his annotated copy of *Principia Mathematica,* poems in Milton's hand, and A. A. Milne's original *Winnie the Pooh* (the real Christopher Robin attended Trinity College).

## ▲▲FITZWILLIAM MUSEUM

Britain's best museum of antiquities and art outside London is the Fitzwilliam. Housed in a grand Neoclassical building, a 10-minute walk south of the town center, it's a palatial celebration of beauty and humankind's ability to create it.

**Cost and Hours:** Free but £5 suggested donation, Tue-Sat 10:00-17:00, Sun 12:00-17:00, closed Mon, Trumpington Street, tel. 01223/332-900, www.fitzmuseum. cam.ac.uk.

**Visiting the Museum:** The Fitzwilliam's broad collection is like a mini-British Museum/National Gallery rolled into one; you're bound to find something you like. The ground floor features an extensive range of antiquities and applied arts—everything from Greek vases, Mesopotamian artifacts, and Egyptian sarcophagi to Roman statues, fine porcelain, and suits of armor.

Upstairs is the painting gallery, with works that span art history: Italian Venetian masters (Titian and Canaletto), a

*Wren Library*

*Fitzwilliam Museum*

*Punting is harder than it looks.*

worthy English section (Gainsborough, Reynolds, Hogarth, and others), and a notable array of French Impressionist art (Monet, Renoir, Pissarro, Degas, and Sisley).

### ▲PUNTING ON THE CAM

For a little exercise, try renting one of the traditional flat-bottom punts on the river and pole yourself up and down (or around and around, more likely—it's harder than it looks). Several companies rent punts and offer punting tours with entertaining narration. Try **Cambridge Chauffeur Punts** (www.punting-in-cambridge. co.uk) or the slightly pricier **Scudamore's** (www.scudamores.com). Both are located at Silver Street Bridge near Laundress Green (figure about £18 for 45-minute shared tour; £25/hour to rent).

## Eating

**The Eagle,** the oldest pub in town, is a Cambridge institution (8 Benet Street). In good weather, choose the riverside terrace at **The Anchor Pub** (Silver Street). **Agora at The Copper Kettle** is a popular place for Greek and Turkish *meze* (at 4 King's Parade, facing King's College).

Handy for picnickers, a **Marks & Spencer Simply Food** is at the train station (daily 7:00-23:00) and a larger **Marks & Spencer** is on Market Hill Square. A good picnic spot is Laundress Green, a grassy park on the river, where the punting companies are located. There are no benches, so bring something to sit on. Walking or picnicking on the grass at the colleges is generally not allowed.

## Sleeping

Cambridge makes a fine day trip from London, but if you'd rather stay the night, consider **$$$ Lensfield Hotel,** popular with visiting professors (53 Lensfield Road, www.lensfieldhotel.co.uk) , or the well-located **$$$ Hotel du Vin** (Trumpington Street 15, www.hotelduvin.com).

# Bath

**B**ath is within easy striking distance of London—just a 1.5-hour train ride away. Two hundred years ago, this city of 90,000 was the trendsetting Tinseltown of Britain. If ever a city enjoyed looking in the mirror, it's Bath. Built of creamy warm-tone limestone, it beams in its cover-girl complexion. It's a triumph of the Neoclassical style of the Georgian era (1714-1830) and—even with tourist crowds and high prices—a joy to visit.

Long before the Romans arrived in the first century, Bath was known for its healing hot springs. In 1687, Queen Mary, fighting infertility, bathed here. Within 10 months, she gave birth to a son...and Bath boomed as a spa resort, which was rebuilt in the 18th century as a "new Rome" in the Neoclassical style. It became a city of balls, gaming, and concerts—the place to see and be seen.

Today, tourism has stoked its economy, as has the fast morning train to London. Renewed access to Bath's soothing hot springs at the Thermae Bath Spa also attracts visitors in need of a cure or a soak.

## BATH IN 2 DAYS

**Day 1:** Take the City Sightseeing bus tour (the city tour—rather than the Skyline tour—offers the better city overview). Visit the abbey. Take the city walking tour at 14:00. Have afternoon tea and cakes in the Pump Room (or a cheaper tearoom). Stroll to Pulteney Bridge (visiting the Guildhall Market en route) and enjoy the gardens.

**On any evening:** Take a walking tour—the fun Bizarre Bath comedy walk (best choice), a ghost walk, or the free city walking tour. Visit the Roman Baths (open until 22:00 in July-Aug) or soak in the Thermae Bath Spa (both are also open during the day). Linger over dinner, enjoy a pub, or see a play in the classy theater. Just strolling in the evening is a pleasure given Bath's elegant architecture.

---

**Rick's Tip:** *Consider* **starting your trip in Bath** *(using it as your jet-lag recovery pillow), and then* **do London at the end of your trip.** *You can get from Heathrow Airport to Bath by train, bus, a bus/train combination, or a taxi service (offered by Celtic Horizons, page 156; for train and bus info,* *see page 175).*

---

**Day 2:** Tour the Roman Baths (buying a ticket at the TI saves you time in line). Then visit any of these sights, clustered in the neighborhood that features the Royal

Crescent and the Circus: No. 1 Royal Crescent Georgian house, Fashion Museum, or the Museum of Bath at Work.

**With extra time:** If you have another day, explore nearby sights—such as Stonehenge, Wells, and Glastonbury—by car, bus, or minibus tour.

# ORIENTATION

Bath's town square, three blocks in front of the bus and train station, is a cluster of tourist landmarks, including the abbey, Roman Baths, and the Pump Room. Bath is hilly. In general, you'll gain elevation as you head north from the town center.

## Tourist Information

The TI is in the abbey churchyard. It sells tickets for the Roman Baths, allowing you to skip the (often long) line, stocks visitor guides and maps (survey your options before buying one, £2), can suggest hikes, and posts event listings on the bulletin board (Mon-Sat 9:30-17:30, Sun 10:00-16:00, tel. 0844-847-5256, www.visitbath. co.uk).

## Tours

### ▲▲▲FREE CITY WALKING TOURS

Volunteers from **The Mayor's Corps of Honorary Guides** share their love of Bath during free two-hour tours. These chatty, historical, and gossip-filled walks are essential to understand the town and the Georgian social scene of its heyday. How else would you learn that the old "chair ho" call for your sedan chair evolved into today's "cheerio" farewell? Tours leave from outside the Pump Room in the abbey churchyard (free, no tips, year-round Sun-Fri at 10:30 and 14:00, Sat at 10:30 only; additional evening walks May-Sept Tue and Thu at 19:00; tel. 01225/477-411, www.bathguides.org.uk).

### ▲▲CITY BUS TOURS

**City Sightseeing's** hop-on, hop-off bus tours zip through Bath. Jump on a double-decker bus anytime at one of 17 sign-posted pickup points, pay the driver, climb upstairs, and hear recorded commentary about Bath. There are two 45-minute routes: a city tour and a "Skyline" route outside town (the city tour—rather than the Skyline tour—offers the better city overview). Try to get one with a live guide (June-Sept usually at :12 and :24 past the hour for the city tour, and on the hour for the Skyline route—confirm with driver). Otherwise, bring your own earphones if you've got 'em (the audio recording on the other buses is barely intelligible with the headsets provided). You could save money by taking the bus tour first—ticket stubs get you minor discounts at many sights (£14, ticket valid for 24 hours and both tour routes, generally 4/hour daily in summer 9:30-17:30, in winter 10:00-15:00, tel. 01225/330-444, www.city-sightseeing. com).

---

**Rick's Tip:** *Local* **taxis**, *driven by good talkers, go where big buses can't. A group of up to four can rent a cab for an hour (about £40; try to negotiate) and enjoy a fine, informative, and—with the right cabbie—entertaining private joyride. It's probably cheaper to let the meter run than to pay for an hourly rate, but ask the cabbie for advice.*

---

### TOURS TO NEARBY SIGHTS

Bath is a good launch pad for visiting nearby Wells, Avebury, Stonehenge, and more.

**Mad Max Minibus Tours** offers thoughtfully organized, informative tours led by entertaining guides and limited to 16 people per group. Check their website for the latest offerings and book ahead—as far ahead as possible in summer. The popular **Stonehenge, Avebury, and Villages** full-day tour covers 110 miles and visits Stonehenge; the Avebury Stone Circles; photogenic Lacock (LAY-cock); and Castle Combe, the southernmost Cotswold village (£38 plus Stonehenge entry fee, tours depart daily at 8:30 and

# BATH AT A GLANCE

▲▲▲**Free City Walking Tours** Top-notch tours that help you make the most of your visit, led by The Mayor's Corps of Honorary Guides. **Hours:** Sun-Fri at 10:30 and 14:00, Sat at 10:30 only; additional evening walks offered May-Sept Tue and Thu at 19:00. See page 151.

▲▲▲**Roman Baths** Ancient baths that gave the city its name, tourable with good audioguide. **Hours:** Daily July-Aug 9:00-22:00, March-June and Sept-Oct 9:00-18:00, Nov-Feb 9:30-17:30 except Sat until 18:00. See page 156.

▲▲**Bath Abbey** Five-hundred-year-old Perpendicular Gothic church, graced with beautiful fan vaulting and stained glass. **Hours:** Mon-Sat 9:00-18:00 except Nov-March until 16:30, Sun 13:00-14:30 & 16:30-17:30. See page 160.

▲▲**The Circus and the Royal Crescent** Stately Georgian buildings from Bath's 18th-century glory days. **Hours:** Always viewable. See page 161.

▲▲**No. 1 Royal Crescent** Your best look at the interior of one of Bath's high-rent Georgian beauties. **Hours:** Mon 12:00-17:30, Tue-Sun 10:30-17:30. See page 162.

▲**Pump Room** Swanky Georgian hall, ideal for a spot of tea or an unforgettable taste of "healthy" spa water. **Hours:** Daily 9:30-12:00 for coffee and breakfast, 12:00-14:30 for lunch, 14:30-17:00 for afternoon tea (dinner served July-Aug and Christmas holidays only). See page 159.

▲**Pulteney Bridge and Parade Gardens** Shop-strewn bridge and relaxing riverside gardens. **Hours:** Bridge—always open; gardens—Easter-Sept daily 10:00-17:00, shorter hours off-season. See page 161.

▲**Fashion Museum** Four hundred years of clothing under one roof, plus the opulent Assembly Rooms. **Hours:** Daily March-Oct 10:30-18:00, Nov-Feb 10:30-17:00. See page 162.

▲**Museum of Bath at Work** Gadget-ridden, circa-1900 engineer's shop, foundry, factory, and office. **Hours:** April-Oct daily 10:30-17:00, Nov and Jan-March weekends only, closed in Dec. See page 163.

▲**Thermae Bath Spa** Relaxation center that put the bath back in Bath. **Hours:** Daily 9:00-21:30. See page 164.

**Jane Austen Centre** Exhibit on 19th-century Bath-based novelist, best for her fans. **Hours:** April-Oct daily 9:45-17:30, July-Aug until 18:00; shorter hours and closed Sun off-season. See page 164.

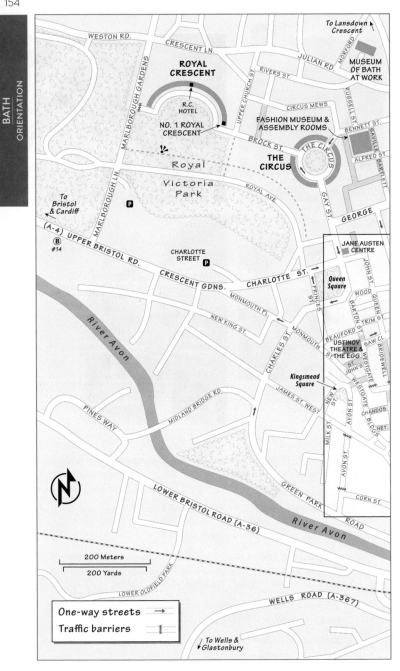

WESTON RD.

CRESCENT LN.

To Lansdown
Crescent

MORFORD

MUSEUM
OF BATH
AT WORK

JULIAN RD.

ROYAL
CRESCENT

RIVERS ST.

MARLBOROUGH GARDENS

UPPER CHURCH ST.

RUSSELL ST.

CIRCUS MEWS

R.C.
HOTEL

BENNETT ST.

SAVILLE ST.

FASHION MUSEUM &
ASSEMBLY ROOMS

NO. 1 ROYAL
CRESCENT

BROCK ST.

THE CIRCUS

ALFRED ST.

BARTLETT

THE
CIRCUS

Royal

GAY ST.

Victoria
Park

ROYAL AVE.

To
Bristol
& Cardiff

MARLBOROUGH LN.

P

GEORGE

(A-4)

UPPER BRISTOL RD.

B
#14

CHARLOTTE
STREET

P

JANE AUSTEN
CENTRE

CRESCENT GDNS.

CHARLOTTE    ST.

PRINCES ST.

Queen
Square

JOHN ST.

WOOD

QUEEN

MONMOUTH PL.

NEW KING ST.

CHARLES ST.

MONMOUTH ST.

BARTON ST.

TRIM ST.

BEAUFORD SQ.

SAW CL.

BRIDEWELL ST.

JOHN ST.

WESTGATE ST.

USTINOV
THEATRE &
THE EGG

River Avon

Kingsmead
Square

JAMES ST. WEST

NEW ST.

AVON ST.

WESTGATE
BLDGS.

CHANDOS

PINES WAY

MIDLAND BRIDGE RD.

MILK ST.

AVON ST.

HET.

CORN ST.

N

GREEN PARK

LOWER BRISTOL ROAD (A-36)

River Avon

200 Meters

200 Yards

LOWER OLDFIELD PARK

WELLS   ROAD (A-367)

One-way streets    →

Traffic barriers

To Wells &
Glastonbury

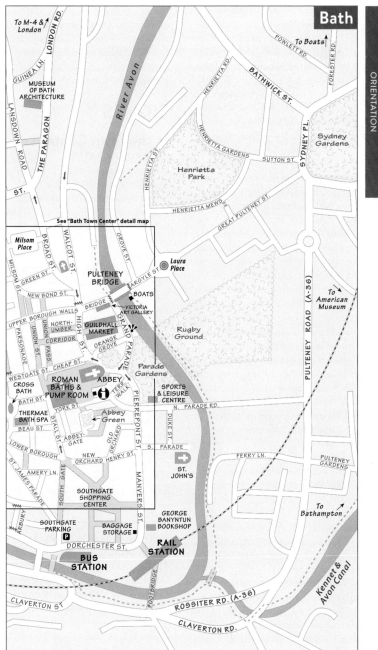

Bath

To M-4 &
London

GUINEA LN.
LONDON RD.

MUSEUM
OF BATH
ARCHITECTURE

River Avon

FOWLETT RD.
To Boats
FORESTER RD.

HENRIETTA RD.

BATHWICK ST.

SYDNEY PL.

Sydney
Gardens

LANSDOWN ROAD

THE PARAGON

ST.

HENRIETTA ST.

HENRIETTA GARDENS

SUTTON ST.

Henrietta
Park

HENRIETTA MEWS

GREAT PULTENEY ST.

See "Bath Town Center" detail map

Milsom
Place

BROAD ST.

WALCOT ST.

GROVE ST.

ARGYLE ST.

GREEN ST.

MILSOM ST.

NEW BOND ST.

PULTENEY
BRIDGE

Laura
Place

BRIDGE

BOATS

UPPER BOROUGH WALLS

UNION ST.

NORTH-
UMBER

HIGH ST.

VICTORIA
ART GALLERY

GUILDHALL
MARKET

GRAND PARADE

PARSONAGE

CORRIDOR

PASS.

ORANGE
GROVE

Rugby
Ground

WESTGATE ST.

CHEAP ST.

Parade
Gardens

PULTENEY ROAD (A-36)

To
American
Museum

CROSS
BATH

ROMAN
BATHS &
PUMP ROOM

ABBEY

FERRY WALK

SPORTS
& LEISURE
CENTRE

BATH ST.

THERMAE
BATH SPA

YORK ST.

STALL ST.

Abbey
Green

PIERREPONT ST.

N. PARADE RD.

DUKE ST.

BEAU ST.

LOWER BOROUGH

ABBEY
GATE

OLD
ORCHARD

S. PARADE

FERRY LN.

PULTENEY
GARDENS

ST. JAMES PARADE

SOUTH GATE

NEW
ORCHARD

HENRY ST.

MANVERS ST.

ST.
JOHN'S

AMERY LN.

SOUTHGATE
SHOPPING
CENTER

GEORGE
BANYNTUN
BOOKSHOP

To
Bathampton

ARBURY

SOUTHGATE
PARKING

P

BAGGAGE
STORAGE

RAIL
STATION

DORCHESTER ST.

BUS
STATION

FOOTBRIDGE

Kennet &
Avon Canal

CLAVERTON ST.

ROSSITER RD. (A-36)

CLAVERTON RD.

return at 17:30). They also offer several other all-day itineraries (one includes Wells and Glastonbury) a couple of times a week (info on website). All tours depart from outside the Abbey Hotel on Terrace Walk in Bath, a one-minute walk from the abbey. Arrive 15 minutes before your departure time and bring cash (or book online with a credit card at least 48 hours in advance, Rick Steves readers get £10 cash rebate from guide with online purchase of two full-day tours if requested at time of booking; mobile 07990-505-970, phone answered daily 8:00-18:00, www.madmaxtours.co.uk, maddy@madmaxtours.co.uk).

**Lion Tours** gets you to Stonehenge on their half-day **Stonehenge and Lacock** tour (£22 transportation only, £34 including Stonehenge entry fee; leaves daily at 12:15 and returns at 17:30, in summer this tour also leaves at 8:30 and returns at 12:00). They also run full-day tours, including one of the Cotswold Villages. You can bring your luggage along on the Cotswold tour and be dropped off in Stow or Moreton-in-Marsh for an additional charge; you must request this in advance. Lion's tours depart from the same stop as Mad Max Tours—see earlier (mobile 07769-668-668, book online at www.liontours.co.uk).

**Scarper Tours** runs four-hour, narrated minibus tours to Stonehenge, giving you two hours at the site (£19 transportation only, £32 including Stonehenge entry fee, daily mid-March-mid-Oct at 9:30 and 14:00, mid-Oct-mid-March at 13:00, departs from behind the abbey on Terrace Walk, tel. 07739/644-155, www.scarpertours.com).

**Celtic Horizons** offers tours from Bath to a variety of destinations, such as Stonehenge, Avebury, and Wells. They can provide a convenient transfer service (to or from London, Heathrow, Bristol Airport, the Cotswolds, and so on), with or without a tour itinerary en route. Allow about £35/hour for a group (comfortable minivans seat 4, 6, or 8 people) and £150 for Heathrow-Bath transfers (1-4 persons). Make arrangements and get pricing information by email at info@celtichorizons.com (tel. 01373/800-500, US tel. 855-895-0165, www.celtichorizons.com).

# SIGHTS

## In the Town Center
### ▲▲▲ROMAN BATHS

In ancient Roman times, high society enjoyed the mineral springs at Bath. Romans traveled from Londinium to Aquae Sulis, as the city was then called, to "take a bath" so often that it finally became known simply as Bath. Today, a fine museum surrounds the ancient bath. With the help of a great audioguide, you'll wander past well-documented displays, Roman artifacts, a temple pediment with an evocative bearded face, a bronze head of the goddess Sulis Minerva, excavated ancient foundations, and the actual mouth of the health-giving spring. At the end, you'll have a chance to walk around the big pool where Romans once splished and splashed.

**Cost and Hours:** £14, includes audioguide, £20 combo-ticket includes Fashion Museum, family ticket available, daily July-Aug 9:00-22:00, March-June and Sept-Oct 9:00-18:00, Nov-Feb 9:30-17:30 except Sat until 18:00, last entry one hour before closing, tel. 01225/477-785, www.romanbaths.co.uk.

---

**Rick's Tip:** *To* **avoid long lines at the Roman Baths, buy a ticket at the nearby TI.** *With voucher in hand, enter through the* **"fast track" lane,** *to the left of the general admission line.* **Visit early or late;** *peak time is between 13:00 and 15:00.*

---

**Tours:** Take advantage of the included essential **audioguide,** which makes your visit easy and informative. Look for posted numbers to key into your audioguide for

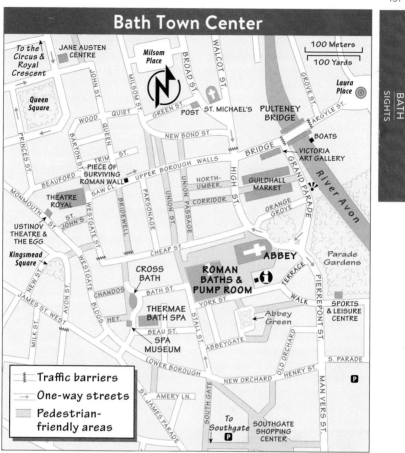

**Bath Town Center**

100 Meters
100 Yards

To the Circus & Royal Crescent

JANE AUSTEN CENTRE

Milsom Place

WALCOT ST.

BROAD ST.

GROVE ST.

Laura Place

Queen Square

JOHN ST.

MILSOM ST.

GREEN ST.

POST

ST. MICHAEL'S

PULTENEY BRIDGE

ARGYLE ST.

WOOD

QUIET

QUEEN ST.

NEW BOND ST.

BRIDGE

BOATS

VICTORIA ART GALLERY

PRINCES ST.

BARTON ST.

BEAUFORD

TRIM ST.

PIECE OF SURVIVING ROMAN WALL

UPPER BOROUGH WALLS

NORTH-UMBER.

HIGH ST.

GUILDHALL MARKET

GRAND PARADE

River Avon

MONMOUTH ST.

THEATRE ROYAL

SAW CL.

PARSONAGE

UNION ST.

UNION PASSAGE

CORRIDOR

ORANGE GROVE

ST. JOHN'S

BRIDEWELL

WESTGATE ST.

USTINOV THEATRE & THE EGG

Kingsmead Square

NEW ST.

WESTGATE BLDGS.

CHEAP ST.

ABBEY

Parade Gardens

TERRACE

PIERREPONT ST.

CROSS BATH

ROMAN BATHS & PUMP ROOM

JAMES ST. WEST

AVON ST.

CHANDOS

BATH ST.

WALK

SPORTS & LEISURE CENTRE

MILK ST.

HET.

THERMAE BATH SPA

YORK ST.

STALL ST.

Abbey Green

BEAU ST.

SPA MUSEUM

ABBEYGATE

OLD ORCHARD

S. PARADE

LOWER BOROUGH

NEW ORCHARD

HENRY ST.

MAN VERS ST.

P

ST. JAMES PARADE

AMERY LN.

SOUTH GATE

To Southgate

P

SOUTHGATE SHOPPING CENTER

**Legend:**
- Traffic barriers
- → One-way streets
- Pedestrian-friendly areas

specialty topics—including a kid-friendly tour and musings from American expat writer Bill Bryson. For those with a big appetite for Roman history, in-depth **guided tours** leave from the end of the museum at the edge of the actual bath (included with ticket, on the hour, a poolside clock is set for the next departure time, 20-40 minutes depending on the guide). You can revisit the museum after the tour.

⊙ **Self-Guided Tour:** Follow the one-way route through the bath and museum complex. This self-guided tour offers a basic overview; for more in-depth commentary, use the audioguide.

Begin by walking around the upper **terrace,** overlooking the Great Bath. This terrace—lined with sculptures of VIRs (Very Important Romans)—evokes ancient times but was built in the 1890s. The ruins of the bath complex sat undisturbed for centuries before finally being excavated and turned into a museum in the late 19th century.

Head inside to the **museum,** where exhibits explain the dual purpose of the buildings that stood here in Roman times: a bath complex, for relaxation and for healing; and a temple dedicated to the goddess Sulis Minerva, who was believed to be responsible for the mysterious and much-appreciated thermal springs. Cut-away diagrams and models resurrect both parts of this complex and help you get your bearings among the remaining fragments and foundations—including the original entrance (just off the main suspended walkway, on your right, as you pass through the temple courtyard and Minerva section).

Peer down into the **spring,** where air bubbles remind you that 240,000 gallons of water a day emerge from the earth—magically, it must have seemed to Romans—at a constant 115°F. The water you see now, heated more than a mile below the earth's surface, first fell to earth as rain onto nearby hills about 10,000 years ago...making the Romans seem relatively recent.

Go downstairs to get to know the Romans who built and enjoyed these baths. The fragments of the **temple pediment**—carved by indigenous Celtic craftsmen but with Roman themes—represent a remarkable cultural synthesis. Sit and watch for a while as a slide projection fills in historians' best guesses as to what once occupied the missing bits. The identity of the circular face in the middle puz-

zles researchers. (God? Santa Claus?) It could be the head of the Gorgon monster after it was slain by Perseus—are those snakes peeking through its hair and beard? And yet, the Gorgon was traditionally depicted as female. Perhaps instead it's Neptune, the god of the sea—appropriate for this aquatic site.

The next exhibits examine the importance of Aquae Sulis (the settlement here) in antiquity. This spot exerted a powerful pull on people from all over the realm, who were eager to partake in its healing waters. A display of the **Beau Street Hoard**—over 17,500 Roman coins dating from 32 B.C.-A.D. 274 that were found near the Baths—emphasizes just how well-visited this area was.

You'll also see some of the small but extremely heavy carved-stone tables that pilgrims hauled here as an offering to the gods. Take time to read some of the requests (inscribed on sheets of pewter or iron) that visitors made of the goddess. Many are comically spiteful and petty, offering a warts-and-all glimpse into day-to-day Roman culture.

As you walk through the temple's original foundations, keep an eye out for the

*The ancient Roman baths are surrounded by an excellent museum.*

sacrificial altar. The gilded-bronze head of the goddess **Sulis Minerva** (in the display case) once overlooked a flaming cauldron inside the temple, where only priests were allowed to enter. Similar to the Greek goddess Athena, Sulis Minerva was considered to be a life-giving mother goddess.

Engineers enjoy a close-up look at the spring overflow and the original **drain system**—built two millennia ago—that still carries excess water to the River Avon. Marvel at the cleverness and durability of Roman engineering. A nearby exhibit on pulleys and fasteners lets you play with these inventions.

Head outside to the **Great Bath** itself (where you can join one of the included guided tours for a much more extensive visit—look for the clock with the next start time). Take a slow lap (by foot) around the perimeter, imagining the frolicking Romans who once immersed themselves up to their necks in this five-foot-deep pool. The water is greenish because of algae; don't drink it. The best views are from the west end, looking back toward the abbey. Nearby is a giant chunk of roof span, from a time when this was a cavernous covered swimming hall. At the corner, you'll step over a small canal where hot water still trickles into the main pool. Nearby, find a length of original lead pipe, remarkably well preserved since antiquity.

Symmetrical bath complexes branch off at opposite ends of the Great Bath

*Sulis Minerva*

(perhaps dating from a conservative period when the Romans maintained separate facilities for men and women). The **East Baths** show off changing rooms and various bathing rooms, each one designed for a special therapy or recreational purpose (immersion therapy tub, sauna-like heated floor, and so on), as described in detail by the audioguide.

When you're ready to leave, head for the **West Baths** (including a sweat bath and a *frigidarium,* or "cold plunge" pool) and take another look at the spring and more foundations. After returning your audioguide, pop over to the fountain for a free taste of the spa water. Then pass through the gift shop, past the convenient public WCs (which use plain old tap water), and exit through the **Pump Room**—or stay for a spot of tea.

▲PUMP ROOM

For centuries, Bath was forgotten as a spa. Then, in 1687, the previously barren Queen Mary bathed here, became pregnant, and bore a male heir to the throne. A few years later, Queen Anne found the water eased her painful gout. Word of its miraculously curative waters spread, and Bath earned its way back on the aristocratic map. High society soon turned the place into a pleasure palace. The Pump Room, an elegant Georgian hall just above the Roman Baths, offers visitors their best chance to raise a pinky in Chippendale grandeur. Come for a light meal, or to try a famous (but forgettable) "Bath bun" with your spa water (the same water that's in the fountain at the end of the baths tour; also free in the Pump Rooms if you present your ticket). The spa water is served by an appropriately attired waiter, who will tell you the water is pumped up from nearly 100 yards deep and marinated in 43 wonderful minerals. Or for just the price of a coffee, drop in anytime (except during lunch) to enjoy live music and the atmosphere. Even if you don't eat here, you're welcome to enter the foyer for a view of the baths and dining room.

**Cost and Hours:** Daily 9:30-12:00 for coffee and £6-15 breakfast, 12:00-14:30 for £12-20 lunches, 14:30-17:00 for £21 traditional afternoon tea (last orders at 16:00), tea/coffee and pastries also available in the afternoons; open 18:00-21:00 for dinner July-Aug and Christmas holidays only; live music daily—string trio or piano, times vary; tel. 01225/444-477.

## ▲▲BATH ABBEY

The town of Bath wasn't much in the Middle Ages, but an important church has stood on this spot since Anglo-Saxon times. King Edgar I was crowned here in 973, when the church was much bigger (before the bishop packed up and moved to Wells). Dominating the town center, today's abbey—the last great church built in medieval England—is 500 years old and a fine example of the Late Perpendicular Gothic style, with breezy fan vaulting and enough stained glass to earn it the nickname "Lantern of the West."

**Cost and Hours:** £2.50 suggested donation; Mon-Sat 9:00-18:00 except Nov-March until 16:30, Sun 13:00-14:30 & 16:30-17:30, last entry 45 minutes

*Bath Abbey*

before closing; handy flier narrates a self-guided 19-stop tour, ask about schedule of events—including concerts, services, and evensong—also posted on the door and online, tel. 01225/422-462, www.bathabbey.org.

**Evensong:** A 20-minute evensong service is offered nightly at 17:30, but sung only on Sunday (Mon-Sat it's spoken).

**Visiting the Abbey:** Take a moment to appreciate the abbey's architecture from the square. The façade (c. 1500, but mostly restored) is interesting for some of its carvings. Look for the angels going down the ladder. The statue of Peter (to the left of the door) lost its head to mean-spirited iconoclasts; it was re-carved out of Peter's once supersized beard.

Going inside is worth the small suggested contribution. The glass, red-iron gas-powered lamps, and the heating grates on the floor are all remnants of the 19th century. The window behind the altar shows 52 scenes from the life of Christ. A window to the left of the altar shows Edgar's coronation. Note that a WWII bomb blast destroyed the medieval glass; what you see today is from the 1950s.

**Climbing the Tower:** You can reach the top of the tower only with a 50-minute guided (and worthwhile) tour. You'll hike up 212 steps for views across the rooftops of Bath and a peek down into the Roman Baths. In the rafters, you walk right up behind the clock face on the north transept, and get an inside-out look at the fan vaulting. Along the way, you'll hear a brief town history as you learn all about the tower's bells. If you've always wanted to clang a huge church bell for all the town to hear, this is your chance—it's oddly satisfying (£6, sporadic schedule but generally at the top of each hour when abbey is open, more often during busy times; Mon-Sat April-Oct 10:00-16:00, Nov-March 11:00-15:00, these are last tour-departure times; today's tour times usually posted outside abbey entrance, no tours Sun, buy tickets in abbey gift shop).

## ▲PULTENEY BRIDGE AND PARADE GARDENS

Bath is inclined to compare its shop-lined Pulteney Bridge with Florence's Ponte Vecchio. That's pushing it. But to best enjoy a sunny day, pack a picnic lunch and pay £1.50 to enter the Parade Gardens below the bridge (Easter-Sept daily 10:00-17:00, shorter hours off-season, includes deck chairs; ask about concerts held some Sun at 15:00 in summer; entrance a block south of bridge). Across the bridge at Pulteney Weir, tour boat companies run cruises.

Rick's Tip: *The frumpy little* **Guildhall Market,** *located across from Pulteney Bridge, is* **fun for browsing and picnic shopping.** *Its* **Market Café** *is a cheap place for a bite.*

# Northwest of the Town Center

Several worthwhile public spaces and museums can be found a slightly uphill 10-minute walk away.

### ▲▲THE CIRCUS AND THE ROYAL CRESCENT

If Bath is an architectural cancan, these are its knickers. These first Georgian "condos"—built in the mid-18th century by the father-and-son John Woods (the Circus by the Elder, the Royal Crescent by the Younger)—are well explained by the city walking tours. "Georgian" is British for

*Pulteney Bridge*

"Neoclassical." These two building complexes, conveniently located a block apart from each other, are quintessential Georgian and quintessential Bath.

**Circus:** True to its name, this is a circular housing complex. Picture it as a coliseum turned inside out. Its Doric, Ionic, and Corinthian capital decorations pay homage to its Greco-Roman origin, and are a reminder that Bath (with its seven hills) aspired to be "the Rome of England." The frieze above the first row of columns has hundreds of different panels representing the arts, sciences, and crafts. The ground-floor entrances were made large enough that aristocrats could be carried right through the door in their sedan chairs, and women could enter without disturbing their sky-high hairdos. The tiny round windows on the top floors were the servants' quarters. While the building fronts are uniform, the backs are higgledy-piggledy, infamous for their "hanging loos" (bathrooms added years later). Stand in the middle of the Circus among the grand plane trees, on the capped old well. Imagine the days when there was no indoor plumbing, and the servant girls gathered here to fetch water—this was gossip central. If you stand on the well, your clap echoes three times around the circle (try it).

**Royal Crescent:** A long, graceful arc of buildings—impossible to see in one glance unless you step way back to the edge of the big park in front—evokes the wealth and gentility of Bath's glory days. As you cruise the Crescent, pretend you're rich. Then pretend you're poor. Notice the "ha ha fence," a drop-off in the front yard that acted as a barrier, invisible from the windows, for keeping out sheep and peasants. The refined and stylish **Royal Crescent Hotel** sits virtually unmarked in the center of the Crescent (with the giant rhododendron growing over the door). You're welcome to (politely) drop in to explore its fine ground-floor public spaces and back garden, where a gracious and traditional tea is served (£14.50 cream tea, £32 afternoon tea, daily 13:30-17:00, sharing is OK, reserve a day in advance, tel. 01225/823-333, www.royalcrescent.co.uk).

### ▲▲NO. 1 ROYAL CRESCENT

This museum takes visitors behind one of those classy Georgian facades, offering your best look into a period house and how the wealthy lived in 18th-century Bath. Docents in each room hand out placards, but take the time to talk with them to learn many more fascinating details of Georgian life...such as how high-class women shaved their eyebrows and pasted on carefully trimmed strips of mouse fur in their place.

Start with the **parlor,** the main room of the house used for breakfast in the mornings, business affairs in the afternoon, and other activities throughout the evening. The bookcase was a status symbol of knowledge and literacy. In the **gentleman's retreat,** find a machine with a hand crank. This "modern" device was thought to cure ailments by shocking them out of you. Give it a spin and feel for yourself. Shops in town charged for these electrifying cures; only the wealthiest citizens had in-home shock machines. Upstairs in the **lady's bedroom** are trinkets befitting a Georgian socialite; look for a framed love letter, wig scratcher, and hidden doorway (next to the bed) providing direct access to the servants' staircase. The **gentleman's bedroom** upstairs is the masculine equivalent of the lady's room—rich colors, scenes of Bath, and manly decor. The back staircase leads directly to the **servants' hall.** Look up to find Fido, who spent his days on the treadmill powering the rotisserie.

Finally, you'll end in the **kitchen.** Notice the wooden rack hanging from the ceiling—it kept the bread, herbs, and ham away from the mice. The scattered tools here helped servants create the upper-crust lifestyle overhead.

**Cost and Hours:** £9, Mon 12:00-17:30, Tue-Sun 10:30-17:30, last entry at 16:30, corner of Brock Street and Royal Crescent, tel. 01225/428-126, www.bath-preservation-trust.org.uk.

### ▲FASHION MUSEUM

This museum displays four centuries of fashion on one floor. It's small, but the fact-filled, included audioguide can stretch a visit to an informative and enjoyable hour. Like fashion itself, the exhibits

*Bath's Royal Crescent is England's greatest example of Georgian architecture.*

change all the time. A major feature is the "Dress of the Year" display, for which a fashion expert anoints a new frock each year. Ongoing since 1963, it's a chance to view a half-century of fashion trends in one sweep of the head. You'll see how fashion evolved—just like architecture and other arts—from one historical period to the next: Georgian, Regency, Victorian, the Swinging '60s, and so on. If you're intrigued by all those historic garments, go ahead and lace up your own trainer corset (which looks more like a life jacket) and try on a hoop underdress.

Above the Fashion Museum, are the grand, empty **Assembly Rooms,** where card games, concerts, tea, and dances were held in the 18th century. Picture dashing young gentlemen and elegant ladies mingling in a Who's Who of high society. Although these rooms were gutted by WWII bombs, they have since been restored. Only the chandeliers are original.

**Cost and Hours:** £8.25, includes audioguide; £20 combo-ticket also covers Roman Baths, family ticket available; daily March-Oct 10:30-18:00, Nov-Feb 10:30-17:00, last entry one hour before closing, free 30-minute guided tour most days at 12:00 and 16:00; self-service café, Bennett Street, tel. 01225/477-789, www.fashionmuseum.co.uk.

**Rick's Tip:** *Notice the* **proximity of the Fashion Museum and the Museum of Bath at Work.** *While open-minded spouses appreciate both places, museum attendants tell me it's standard for husbands to visit the Museum of Bath at Work while their wives tour the Fashion Museum. Maybe it's time to divide and conquer?*

### ▲MUSEUM OF BATH AT WORK

This modest but lovable place explains the industrial history of Bath. The museum is a vivid reminder that there's always been a grimy, workaday side to this spa town. The core of the museum is the well-preserved, circa-1900 fizzy-drink business of one Mr. Bowler. It includes a Dickensian office, engineer's shop, brass foundry, essence room lined with bottled scents, and factory floor. It's just a pile of meaningless old gadgets—until the included audioguide resurrects Mr. Bowler's creative genius.

Upstairs are display cases featuring other Bath creations through the years, including a 1914 Horstmann car, wheeled sedan chairs (this *is* Bath, after all), and versatile plasticine (colorful proto-Play-Doh—still the preferred medium of Aardman Studios, creators of the stop-motion animated Wallace & Gromit movies). At the snack bar, you can buy your own historic fizzy drink (a descendant of the ones once made here). On your way out, don't miss the intriguing collection of small exhibits on the ground floor, featuring cabinetmaking, the traditional methods for cutting the local "Bath stone," a locally produced six-stroke engine, and more.

**Cost and Hours:** £5, includes audioguide, April-Oct daily 10:30-17:00, Nov and Jan-March weekends only, closed Dec, last entry one hour before closing,

*Museum of Bath at Work*

Julian Road, 2 steep blocks up Russell Street from Assembly Rooms, tel. 01225/318-348, www.bath-at-work.org.uk.

### JANE AUSTEN CENTRE

This exhibition focuses on Jane Austen's tumultuous five years in Bath (circa 1800, during which time her father died) and the influence the city had on her writing. There's little of historic substance here. Walk through a Georgian townhouse that she didn't live in (one of her real addresses in Bath was a few houses up the road, at 25 Gay Street). The exhibit describes various places from two novels set in Bath (*Persuasion* and *Northanger Abbey*). See reproductions of things associated with her writing as well as her waxwork likeness. It's overhyped, but that doesn't bother the happy Austen fans touring through the house.

Costumed guides give an intro talk (on the first floor, 15 minutes, 3/hour, on the hour and at :20 and :40 past the hour) about the romantic but down-to-earth Austen, who skewered the silly, shallow, and arrogant aristocrats' world, where "the doing of nothing all day prevents one from doing anything." They also show a 15-minute video; after that, you're free to wander through the rest of the exhibit. The gift shop is stocked with "I love Mr. Darcy" tote bags, teacups emblazoned with Colin Firth's visage, and more.

**Cost and Hours:** £9; April-Oct daily 9:45-17:30, July-Aug until 18:00; Nov-March Sun-Fri 11:00-16:30, Sat 9:45-17:30; last entry one hour before closing, between Queen's Square and the Circus at 40 Gay Street, tel. 01225/443-000, www.janeausten.co.uk.

**Tea:** Upstairs, the award-winning **Regency Tea Rooms** (open to the public) hits the spot for Austen-ites with costumed waitstaff and themed teas (most are £8-10); the all-out "Tea with Mr. Darcy" is £16.50 (£3 for just tea, opens at 11:00, closes same time as the center, last order taken one hour before closing).

# EXPERIENCES

## Thermal Baths

### ▲THERMAE BATH SPA

After simmering unused for a quarter-century, Bath's natural thermal springs once again offer R&R for the masses. The state-of-the-art spa is housed in a complex of three buildings that combine historic structures with new glass-and-steel architecture.

Is the Thermae Bath Spa worth the time and money? The experience is pretty pricey and humble compared to similar German and Hungarian spas. The tall, modern building in the city center lacks old-time elegance. Jets in the pools are very limited, and the only water toys are big foam noodles. There's no cold plunge—the only way to cool off between steam rooms is to step onto a small, unglamorous balcony. The Royal Bath's two pools are essentially the same, and the water isn't particularly hot in either—in fact, the main attraction is the rooftop view from the top one (best with a partner or as a social experience).

All that said, this is the only natural

*Jane Austen Centre*

thermal spa in the UK and your one chance to actually bathe in Bath. Bring your swimsuit and come for a couple of hours (Fri night and all day Sat-Sun are most crowded). Consider an evening visit, when—on a chilly day—Bath's twilight glows through the steam from the rooftop pool.

**Cost:** The cheapest spa pass is £32 for two hours (£35 on weekends), which includes a towel, robe, and slippers and gains you access to the Royal Bath's large, ground-floor "Minerva Bath"; four steam rooms and a waterfall shower; and the view-filled, open-air, rooftop thermal pool. Longer stays are £10 for each additional hour. If you arrived in Bath by train, your used rail ticket will score you a four-hour session for the price of two hours. The much-hyped £45 Twilight Package includes three hours and a meal (one plate, drink, robe, towel, and slippers). The appeal of this package is not the mediocre meal, but being on top of the building at a magical hour (which you can do for less money at the regular rate).

Thermae has all the "pamper thyself" extras: massages, mud wraps, and various healing-type treatments, including "watsu"—water shiatsu (£40-90 extra). Book treatments in advance by phone.

**Hours:** Daily 9:00-21:30, last entry at 19:00, pools close at 21:00. No kids under 16.

**Information:** It's 100 yards from the Roman Baths, on Beau Street (tel.

01225/331-234, www.thermaebathspa. com). There's a salad-and-smoothies café for guests.

**The Cross Bath:** Operated by Thermae Bath Spa, this renovated circular Georgian structure across the street from the main spa provides a simpler and less-expensive bathing option. It has a hot-water fountain that taps directly into the spring, making its water hotter than the spa's (£18-20/1.5 hours, daily 10:00-20:00, last entry at 18:00, check in at Thermae Bath Spa's main entrance across the street and you'll be escorted to the Cross Bath, changing rooms, no access to Royal Bath, no kids under 12).

**Spa Visitor Center:** Also across the street, in the Hetling Pump Room, this free one-room exhibit explains the story of the spa (Mon-Sat 10:00-17:00, Sun 11:00-16:00, audioguide-£2).

## Boating

The **Bath Boating Station,** in an old Victorian boathouse, rents rowboats, canoes, and punts (£7/person for first hour, then £4/hour; all day for £18; Easter-Sept daily 10:00-18:00, closed off-season, intersection of Forester and Rockcliffe roads, one mile northeast of center, tel. 01225/312-900, www.bathboating.co.uk).

## Swimming

The **Bath Sports and Leisure Centre** has a fine pool for laps as well as lots of waterslides. Kids will also enjoy the "Zany Zone" indoor playground (swimming-£4/adult, £3/kid, family discounts, Mon-Fri 6:30-22:00, Sat 10:30-19:00, Sun 8:00-20:00, kids' hours limited, call for open-swim times, just across the bridge on North Parade Road, tel. 01225/486-905, www. aquaterra.org).

## Evening Walks

For an entertaining walking-tour comedy act "with absolutely no history or culture," follow Toby or Noel on their creative and lively **Bizarre Bath** walk. This 1.5-hour

*Thermae Bath Spa*

"tour," which combines stand-up comedy with cleverly executed magic tricks, plays off unsuspecting passersby as well as tour members. Promising to insult all nationalities and sensitivities, it's sometimes racy but still good family fun (£10, £8 if you show this book, April-Oct nightly at 20:00, smaller groups Mon-Thu, leaves from The Huntsman Inn near the abbey, confirm at TI or call 01225/335-124, www.bizarrebath.co.uk).

**Ghost Walks** are another popular way to pass the after-dark hours—although you might save the supernatural for the city of York, which is said to be more haunted (£8, cash only, 1.5 hours, year-round Thu-Sat at 20:00, leave from The Garrick's Head pub—to the left and behind Theatre Royal as you face it, tel. 01225/350-512, www.ghostwalksofbath.co.uk).

---

**Rick's Tip:** *In* **July and August,** *the* **Roman Baths are open nightly until 22:00** *(last entry 21:00). The gas lamps flame and the baths are more romantic—and* **less crowded.** *To take a dip yourself, pop over to the Thermae Bath Spa (last entry at 19:00).*

---

## Theater

The 18th-century, 800-seat Theatre Royal, one of England's loveliest, offers a busy schedule of London West End–type plays, including many "pre-London" dress-rehearsal runs.

**Cost and Hours:** £20-40 plus small booking fee; shows generally start at 19:30 or 20:00, matinees at 14:30, box office open Mon-Sat 10:00-20:00, Sun 12:00-20:00 if there's a show, book in person, online, or by phone; on Saw Close, tel. 01225/448-844, www.theatreroyal.org.uk.

**Ticket Deals:** Same-day "standby" seats (actually 40 nosebleed spots on a bench) are sold daily except Sunday, starting at noon, for evening shows (£6, 2 tickets maximum). Or you can snatch up any "last minute" seats for £15-20 a half-hour before "curtain up" (cash only).

## Festivals and Events

The **Bath Literature Festival** is an open book in early March (www.bathlitfest.org.uk). The **Bath International Music Festival** bursts into song in late May (classical, folk, jazz, contemporary; www.bathmusicfest.org.uk), overlapped by the eclectic **Bath Fringe Festival** (theater, walks, talks, bus trips; generally similar dates to the Music Festival, www.bathfringe.co.uk). The **Jane Austen Festival** unfolds genteelly in late September (www.janeausten.co.uk/festivalhome). And for three weeks in December, the squares around the abbey are filled with a **Christmas market.**

Bath's festival **box office** sells tickets for most events (but not for those at the Theatre Royal), and can tell you exactly what's on tonight (housed inside the TI, tel. 01225/463-362, www.bathfestivals.org.uk). The city's weekly paper, the *Bath Chronicle,* publishes a "What's On" events listing each Thursday (www.thisisbath.com).

*Take a fun walking tour in Bath.*

*Theatre Royal*

# EATING

Bath has something for every appetite and budget—just stroll around the center of town. A picnic dinner of deli food or take-out fish-and-chips in the Royal Crescent Park or down by the river is ideal for aristocratic hoboes. The restaurants I recommend are small and popular—reserve a table for dinner—especially on Friday and Saturday. Most pricey little bistros offer big savings with their two- and three-course lunches and "pre-theatre" specials. Look for early-bird specials: As long as you order within the time window, you're in for a less-expensive meal.

## Romantic and Upscale

**Clayton's Kitchen** is fine for a modern English splurge in a woody, romantic, candlelit atmosphere. Michelin-star chef Rob Clayton offers affordable British cuisine without pretense (£15 two-course lunch deal, £10 starters, £20-30 main courses, daily from noon and from 18:00, a few outside tables, live jazz on Sundays, 15 George Street, tel. 01225/585-100, http://theporter.co.uk/claytons-kitchen).

**Casanis French Bistro-Restaurant** is an intimate place serving authentic Provençal cuisine (lunch and early dinner specials: £20 for two courses, £24 for three courses; open Tue-Sat 12:00-14:00 & 18:00-22:00, closed Sun-Mon, behind the Assembly Rooms at 4 Saville Row, tel. 01225/780-055, www.casanis.co.uk).

## Pubs

Bath is not a great pub-grub town, and with so many other tempting options, pub dining isn't as appealing as it is elsewhere.

**The Garrick's Head** is an elegantly simple gastropub around the corner from Theatre Royal, with a pricey restaurant on one side, a bar serving affordable pub classics on the other, and some tables outside (£7-12 pub grub, £14-18 main courses on the fancier menu; lunch and pre-theater specials: £17 for two courses, £20 for three courses; daily 12:00-14:30 & 17:30-21:00, 8 St. John's Place, tel. 01225/318-368).

**Crystal Palace,** a casual and inviting standby just a block from the abbey, faces the delightful little Abbey Green. It serves pub grub with a Continental flair in three different spaces, including an airy back patio (£12-20 meals, food served Mon-Fri 11:00-21:00, Sat 11:00-20:00, Sun 12:00-20:00, last drink orders at 22:45, 10 Abbey Green, tel. 01225/482-666).

**The Raven,** with a boisterous local crowd, is easygoing, serving up pints of real ale and a variety of meat pies (£10 pies; £3-9 sides, soups, and desserts; food served Mon-Fri 12:00-15:00 & 17:00-21:00, Sat-Sun 12:30-20:30, open longer for drinks; no kids under 14, 6 Queen Street, tel. 01225/425-045, www.theravenofbath.co.uk).

## Casual Alternatives

**Hall & Wood House Restaurant** has a ground-floor pub and a sprawling spiral staircase that leads to a woody restaurant and a roof terrace. With traditional English dishes, hamburgers, salads, and beers on tap, it's a hit with local students (£5 tapas, £10 main courses on bar menu; £12-15 main courses on fancier restaurant menu—but can order from either menu on either floor; daily, 1 Old King Street, tel. 01225/469-259).

**Loch Fyne Fish Restaurant,** a bright, youthful place with an open kitchen, serves fresh fish at reasonable prices

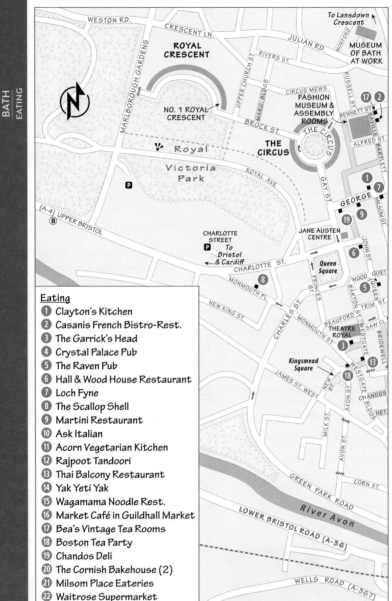

## Eating

1. Clayton's Kitchen
2. Casanis French Bistro-Rest.
3. The Garrick's Head
4. Crystal Palace Pub
5. The Raven Pub
6. Hall & Wood House Restaurant
7. Loch Fyne
8. The Scallop Shell
9. Martini Restaurant
10. Ask Italian
11. Acorn Vegetarian Kitchen
12. Rajpoot Tandoori
13. Thai Balcony Restaurant
14. Yak Yeti Yak
15. Wagamama Noodle Rest.
16. Market Café in Guildhall Market
17. Bea's Vintage Tea Rooms
18. Boston Tea Party
19. Chandos Deli
20. The Cornish Bakehouse (2)
21. Milsom Place Eateries
22. Waitrose Supermarket
23. M&S Kitchen & Café Revive
24. Sainsbury's Local

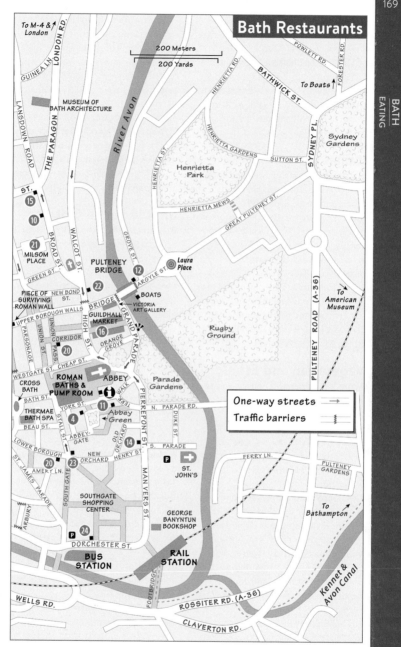

# Bath Restaurants

To M-4 & London

GUINEA LN.

LONDON RD.

MUSEUM OF BATH ARCHITECTURE

POWLETT RD.

FORESTER RD.

BATHWICK ST.

To Boats

LANSDOWN ROAD

THE PARAGON

River Avon

HENRIETTA RD.

SYDNEY PL.

Sydney Gardens

HENRIETTA GARDENS

SUTTON ST.

200 Meters

200 Yards

Henrietta Park

HENRIETTA ST.

ST.

BROAD ST.

WALCOT ST.

HENRIETTA MEWS

GREAT PULTENEY ST.

15

10

21

MILSOM PLACE

GREEN ST.

PULTENEY BRIDGE

22

GROVE ST.

Laura Place

ARGYLE ST.

12

PIECE OF SURVIVING ROMAN WALL

NEW BOND ST.

BRIDGE

BOATS

UPPER BOROUGH WALLS

UNION PASS.

UNION ST.

HIGH ST.

VICTORIA ART GALLERY

GUILDHALL MARKET

GRAND PARADE

Rugby Ground

To American Museum

PULTENEY ROAD (A-36)

PARSONAGE

CORRIDOR

16

ORANGE GROVE

20

WESTGATE ST.

CHEAP ST.

CROSS BATH

BATH ST.

ROMAN BATHS & PUMP ROOM

ABBEY

STALL WALK

Parade Gardens

THERMAE BATH SPA

YORK ST.

11

Abbey Green

PIERREPONT ST.

N. PARADE RD.

DUKE ST.

One-way streets

Traffic barriers

BEAU ST.

4

LOWER BOROUGH

STALL ST.

ABBEY-GATE

OLD ORCHARD

14

S. PARADE

ST. JAMES' PARADE

AMERY LN.

20

23

NEW ORCHARD

HENRY ST.

MANVERS ST.

P

ST. JOHN'S

FERRY LN.

PULTENEY GARDENS

To Bathampton

ARBURY

SOUTHGATE SHOPPING CENTER

SOUTH GATE

GEORGE BANYNTUN BOOKSHOP

P

24

DORCHESTER ST.

BUS STATION

RAIL STATION

WELLS RD.

FOOTBRIDGE

ROSSITER RD. (A-36)

CLAVERTON RD.

Kennet & Avon Canal

(£14-20 meals, £12 two-course special until 18:00, daily 12:00-22:00, 24 Milsom Street, tel. 01225/750-120).

**The Scallop Shell** is a trendy favorite for fish-and-chips. They have a modern restaurant with fancier fish dishes and a takeout counter (Mon-Sat 12:00-21:30, closed Sun, 27 Monmouth Street, tel. 01225/420-928).

## Italian

**Martini Restaurant** is classy and hopping (£11-13 pastas and pizzas, £17-23 meat and fish main courses, lunch and early dinner specials: £10 for two courses, £12 for three courses; open daily 12:00-14:30 & 18:00-22:30, veggie options, daily fish specials, extensive wine list, 9 George Street, tel. 01225/460-818).

**Ask Italian** is a bright chain dishing up reliable food in an inviting atmosphere (£8-13 pizzas and pastas, good salads, daily 11:30-23:00, entrance on Broad Street, tel. 01225/789-997).

## Vegetarian and Ethnic

**Acorn Vegetarian Kitchen** is highly rated for its understated interior and vegan vibe (£6-12 lunches, £8 starters and £17 main courses at dinner; lunch and early dinner specials: £17 for two courses, £20 for three courses; daily 12:00-15:00 & 17:30-21:30, 2 North Parade Passage, tel. 01225/446-059).

**Rajpoot Tandoori** serves award-winning Indian food in a plush atmosphere deep down in a sprawling cellar. The seating is tight and the ceilings low, but it's air-conditioned (£9 three-course lunch, £9-16 main courses; figure £20 per person with rice, naan, and drink; daily 12:00-14:30 & 18:00-23:00, 4 Argyle Street, tel. 01225/466-833, Ali).

**Thai Balcony Restaurant**'s elegant, spacious interior and fun atmosphere make for a memorable dinner (£10 two-course lunch special, £8-13 plates, daily 12:00-14:00 & 18:00-22:00, Saw Close, tel. 01225/444-450).

**Yak Yeti Yak** is a fun Nepalese restaurant with both Western and sit-on-the-floor seating. The menu includes plenty of vegetarian plates at prices that would delight a sherpa (£7-9 lunches, £7 veggie plates, £9 meat plates; daily 12:00-14:00 & 18:00-22:00; downstairs at 12 Pierrepont Street, tel. 01225/442-299).

**Wagamama Noodle Restaurant** is a sleek, pan-Asian slurp-a-thon with a modern flair (£10-13 meals, daily 11:30-23:00, 1 York Buildings, corner of George and Broad streets, tel. 01225/337-314).

## Simple Lunch Options

At **Market Café,** in the Guildhall Market across from Pulteney Bridge, you can dine cheaply surrounded by local old-timers (£3-6 traditional English meals, including fried breakfasts all day, Mon-Sat 8:00-17:00, closed Sun, tel. 01225/461-593 a block north of the abbey, on High Street).

**Bea's Vintage Tea Rooms,** just behind the Assembly Rooms and Fashion Museum, is a charming trip back to the 1940s, with light lunches, teas, and cakes (daily 10:00-17:00, 6 Saville Row, tel. 01225/464-552).

**Boston Tea Party** is the neighborhood coffeehouse and hangout, with outdoor seating overlooking a busy square. Its extensive breakfasts, light lunches, and salads are fresh and healthy (£4-7 breakfasts, £5-7 lunches, Mon-Sat 7:30-19:30, Sun 9:00-19:00, 19 Kingsmead Square, tel. 01225/319-901).

**Chandos Deli** has good coffee and breakfast pastries, as well as £3-5 gourmet sandwiches and wine for assembling a picnic (Mon-Fri 8:00-18:00, Sat 9:00-19:00, Sun 9:00-17:00, 12 George Street, tel. 01225/314-418).

**The Cornish Bakehouse** has freshly baked £3 takeaway pasties (Mon-Sat 8:30-17:30, Sun 10:00-17:00, kitty-corner from Marks & Spencer at 1 Lower Borough Walls, second location off High Street at 11A The Corridor, tel. 01225/426-635).

A pleasant hidden courtyard at **Milsom**

Place holds several dependable chain eateries: **Yo! Sushi, Jamie's Italian,** and **Côte Brasserie.**

**Supermarkets: Waitrose** is great for picnics and has a good salad bar (Mon-Sat 7:30-21:00, Sun 11:00-17:00, just west of Pulteney Bridge and across from post office on High Street). **Marks & Spencer,** near the bottom end of town, has a grocery at the back of its department store and two eateries: **M&S Kitchen** on the ground floor and **Café Revive** on the top floor (Mon-Sat 8:00-19:00, Sun 11:00-17:00, 16 Stall Street). **Sainsbury's Local,** across the street from the bus station, has the longest hours (daily 7:00-23:00, 2 Dorchester Street).

# SLEEPING

Bath is a busy tourist town. Reserve in advance. B&Bs favor those lingering longer; it's worth asking for a weekday, three-nights-in-a-row, or off-season deal. Friday and Saturday nights are tightest, especially if you're staying only one night (rates may go up 25 percent). If you're driving to Bath, stowing your car near the center will cost you—see "Parking" on page 176, or ask your hotelier.

## Near the Royal Crescent

These listings are all a 5- to 10-minute walk from the town center, and an easy 15-minute walk from the train station. With bags in tow you may want to either catch a taxi (£5-7) or (except for Brocks Guest House) hop on bus #14 or #14A (direction: Weston, catch bus inside bus station, pay driver £2.20, get off at the Comfortable Place stop—just after the car shop on the left, cross street and back-track 100 yards).

Marlborough, Brooks, and Cornerways all face a busy arterial street; those sensitive to traffic noise should request a rear- or side-facing room.

**$$$ Marlborough House** mixes modern style with antique furnishings and

features a welcoming breakfast room with an open kitchen. Each of the six rooms comes with a sip of sherry (Db-£105-155, rates vary with demand, must mention this book in your initial request for Rick Steves discount, £5 additional discount when you pay cash, air-con, minifridges, free parking, 1 Marlborough Lane, tel. 01225/318-175, www.marlborough-house.net, mars@manque.dircon.co.uk).

**$$$ Brooks Guesthouse** is the biggest and most polished of the bunch, albeit the least personal, with 22 modern rooms and classy public spaces (Db-£85-120, rates vary with room size and season/demand, shared guest fridge, limited parking-£8/day, 1 Crescent Gardens, Upper Bristol Road, tel. 01225/425-543, www.brooksguesthouse.com, info@brooksguesthouse.com).

**$$ Brocks Guest House** rents six rooms in a Georgian townhouse built by the great architect John Wood in 1765 and located between the Royal Crescent and the Circus (Db-£99, Db with fireplace-£109, larger Db-£119, Db suite-£129, little top-floor library, 32 Brock Street, tel. 01225/338-374, www.brocksguesthouse.co.uk, brocks@brocksguesthouse.co.uk).

**$$ Parkside Guest House** rents five large, thoughtfully appointed Edwardian

BATH
SLEEPING

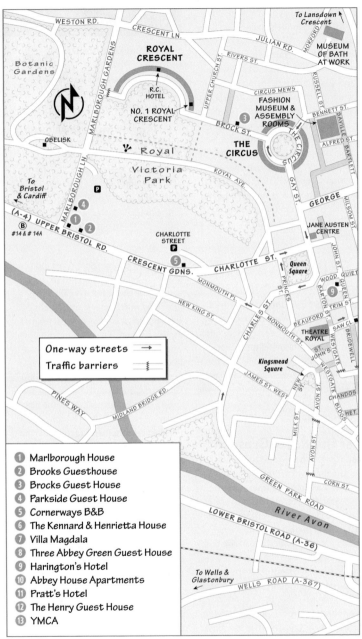

1 Marlborough House
2 Brooks Guesthouse
3 Brocks Guest House
4 Parkside Guest House
5 Cornerways B&B
6 The Kennard & Henrietta House
7 Villa Magdala
8 Three Abbey Green Guest House
9 Harington's Hotel
10 Abbey House Apartments
11 Pratt's Hotel
12 The Henry Guest House
13 YMCA

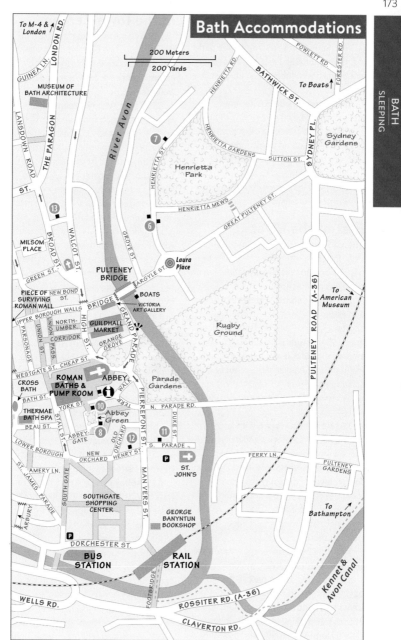

rooms. It's tidy, clean, homey, with a spacious back garden (Db-£90, these prices for Rick Steves readers, limited free parking, 11 Marlborough Lane, tel. 01225/429-444, www.parksidebandb.co.uk, post@parksidebandb.co.uk).

**$$ Cornerways B&B** is centrally located, simple, and pleasant, with three rooms and old-fashioned, homey touches (Db-£85, Tb-£98, 10 percent discount with this book and 3-night stay, DVD library, free parking, 47 Crescent Gardens, tel. 01225/422-382, www.cornerwaysbath.co.uk, info@cornerwaysbath.co.uk).

## East of the River

These listings are a 5- to 10-minute walk from the city center. From the train station, it's best to take a taxi, as there are no good bus connections.

**$$$ The Kennard,** with 12 colorfully and elaborately decorated rooms, is a short walk from Pulteney Bridge (prices are for Sun-Thu/Fri-Sat: Db-£115/£135, superior Db-£145/£165, free street parking permits, Georgian garden out back, 11 Henrietta Street, tel. 01225/310-472, www.kennard.co.uk, reception@kennard.co.uk).

**$$$ Henrietta House,** with large rooms, hardwood floors, and daily homemade biscuits and jam, is cloak-and-cravat cozy. Its name honors the mansion's former owner Lord Pulteney and his daughter (Db-£95-165, family suites, 33 Henrietta Street, tel. 01225/632-632, www.henriettahouse.co.uk, reception@henriettahouse.co.uk).

**$$$ Villa Magdala** rents 20 stately yet modern rooms in a freestanding Victorian townhouse opposite a park (Db-£150-225 depending on size, category, and demand, about £20 more Fri-Sun, family rooms, free parking for those booking direct, Henrietta Street, tel. 01225/466-329, www.villamagdala.co.uk, enquiries@villamagdala.co.uk).

## In the Town Center

You'll pay a premium to sleep right in the center. While Bath is so manageable by foot that a downtown location isn't essential, these options are particularly well-located.

**$$$ Three Abbey Green Guest House,** renting 10 spacious rooms, is bright, cheery, and located in a quiet, traffic-free courtyard only 50 yards from the abbey and the Roman Baths (Db-£100-160, four-poster Db-£140-200, family rooms, price depends on season and size of room, 2-night minimum on weekends, limited free parking, 2 ground-floor rooms work well for those with limited mobility, tel. 01225/428-558, www.threeabbeygreen.com, stay@threeabbeygreen.com). They also rent self-catering apartments (2-night minimum).

**$$$ Harington's Hotel** rents 13 stylish, modern rooms on a quiet street. It feels like a boutique hotel, but with a friendlier, laid-back vibe (Db-£98-170, large superior Db-£108-170, prices vary substantially with demand—always highest on weekends, ask for a Rick Steves discount, parking-£11/day, 8 Queen Street, tel. 01225/461-728, www.haringtonshotel.co.uk, post@haringtonshotel.co.uk). They also rent three self-catering apartments down the street (2-3 night minimum).

**$$$ Abbey House Apartments** rents flats on Abbey Green (with views of the abbey from well-equipped kitchens), including: Abbey Green (which comes with a washer and dryer), Abbey View, and Abbey Studio (Db-£100-175, price depends on size, 2-night minimum, rooms can sleep four with Murphy and sofa beds, Abbey Green, tel. 01225/464-238, www.laurastownhouseapartments.co.uk, bookings@laurastownhouseapartments.co.uk). They also rent other apartments scattered about town.

**$$$ Pratt's Hotel** rents 46 worn but comfy olde-English rooms. Since it's near a busy street, request a quiet room

(Db-£80-150, price depends on size and demand, breakfast-£10, check website for current rates and specials, children under 15 free with 2 adults, elevator, attached restaurant-bar, 4 South Parade, tel. 01225/460-441, www.sjhotels.co.uk/pratts, reservations.pratts@sjhotels.co.uk).

**$$ The Henry Guest House** is a simple, vertical place, renting seven clean rooms just two blocks from the train station (Db-£80-105, premier Db-£95-120, extra bed-£20, 2-night minimum on weekends, 6 Henry Street, tel. 01225/424-052, www.thehenry.com, stay@thehenry.com).

## Budget

**$** The **YMCA,** centrally located on a leafy square, has 210 beds in industrial-strength rooms—all with sinks and basic furnishings. Although it smells a little like a gym, it's safe, secure, quiet, and well-run (rates for Sun-Thu/Fri-Sat: twin D-£50/£60, D-£60/£64, dorm beds, family rooms, WCs and showers down the hall, includes small breakfast, free linens, rental towels, lockers, laundry facilities, down a tiny alley off Broad Street on Broad Street Place, tel. 01225/325-900, www.bathymca.co.uk, stay@bathymca.co.uk).

# TRANSPORTATION

## Arriving and Departing
### By Train

Bath's train station, called Bath Spa, has ticket machines and a staffed ticket desk (tel. 0345-748-4959). To get to the TI, exit straight out of the station and continue up Manvers Street for about five minutes, then turn left at the triangular "square" overlooking the riverfront park, following the small TI arrow on a signpost.

Directly in front of the train station is the SouthGate Bath **shopping center.** You can store bags at **The Luggage Store,** a half-block in front of the station (£4/bag/day, daily 8:00-22:00, 13 Manvers Street, tel. 01225/312-685).

**Train Connections to: Salisbury** (1-2/hour, 1 hour; from here, Stonehenge Tour buses run to Stonehenge), **Moreton-in-Marsh** (hourly, 2 hours, 1-2 transfers), **York** (hourly with transfer in Bristol, 4.5 hours), **Oxford** (hourly, 1.5 hours, transfer in Didcot).

**To/From London:** Trains connect Bath with London's Paddington Station (2/hour, 1.5 hours, best deals for travel after 9:30 and when purchased in advance, www.firstgreatwestern.co.uk).

**To/From Heathrow Airport:** It's fastest and most pleasant to take the **train via London;** if you have a Britrail pass, it's also the cheapest option, as the whole trip is covered. Without a rail pass, it's the most expensive way to go (£60 total for off-peak travel without rail pass, £10-20 cheaper bought in advance, up to £60 more for full-fare peak-time ticket; hourly, 2 hours, easy change between First Great Western train and Heathrow Express at London's Paddington Station).

If you don't have a rail pass, taking a **train-and-bus combination** via the town of Reading is cheaper than the train, more frequent, and faster than the direct bus— allow 2.5 hours total (RailAir Link shuttle bus from airport to Reading: 2-3/hour, 45 minutes; train from Reading to Bath: 2/hour, 1 hour; £31-41 for off-peak, non-refundable travel booked in advance— but up to double for peak-time trains; tel. 0118-957-9425, buy bus ticket from www.railair.com, train ticket from www.firstgreatwestern.co.uk).

### By Bus

The National Express **bus station** is immediately west of the train station, along Dorchester Street (bus info tel. 0871-781-8181, www.nationalexpress.com). For all public bus services in southwestern England, see www.travelinesw.com.

**Bus Connections to: Wells** (nearly hourly, less frequent on Sun, 1.5 hours, continuing to **Glastonbury,** add .5 hour)**, Salisbury** (hourly, 3 hours; or faster National Express #300 at 17:05, 1.5 hours; from Salisbury, buses run to Stonehenge), **Stratford-upon-Avon** (1/day, 4 hours, transfer in Bristol), and **Oxford** (3/day direct, 2 hours, more with transfer).

**To/From London:** The National Express bus is cheaper than the train but takes longer (direct buses nearly hourly, 3.5 hours, avoid those with layover in Bristol, one-way-£5-12, round-trip-£10-18, cheapest to purchase online several days in advance, www.nationalexpress.com). London's Coach Station is one block from Victoria (train) Station.

**To/From Heathrow Airport:** The National Express bus is direct and often much cheaper for those without a rail pass, but it's relatively infrequent and can take nearly twice as long as the train (nearly hourly, 3-3.5 hours, £24-40 one-way depending on time of day, tel. 0871-781-8181, www.nationalexpress.com). Also see the train-and-bus combination mentioned earlier in "By Train."

## By Plane

**Bristol Airport,** located about 20 miles west of Bath, is closer to Bath than Heathrow and has good connections by bus (Bristol Air Decker bus #A4, £14, 2/hour, 1.25 hours, www.airdecker.com). Otherwise, you can take a taxi (£40).

## By Car

**Parking:** As Bath becomes increasingly pedestrian-friendly, street parking in the city center is disappearing. **Park & Ride**

service is a stress-free, no-hassle option to save time and money. Shuttles from Newbridge, Lansdown, and Odd Down (all just outside of Bath) offer free parking and 10-minute shuttle buses into town (daily every 15 minutes, £3 round-trip). If you drive into town, try the **SouthGate Bath shopping center lot,** a five-minute walk from the abbey (£5/up to 3 hours, £14/24 hours, open 24/7, on the corner of Southgate and Dorchester streets). For more info on parking (including the Park & Ride service), visit the "Travel and Maps" section of http://visitbath.co.uk.

---

**Rick's Tip: Take the train or bus to Bath** *from London, and* **rent a car when you leave Bath.**

---

**Renting a Car: Enterprise** provides a pickup service for customers to and from their hotels (extra fee for one-way rentals, at Lower Bristol Road outside Bath, tel. 01225/443-311, www.enterprise.com). Other agencies include **Thrifty** (pickup service and one-way rentals available, in Burnett Business Park in Keynsham—between Bath and Bristol, tel. 01179/867-997, www.thrifty.co.uk), **Hertz** (one-way rentals possible, at Windsor Bridge, tel. 0843-309-3004, www.hertz.co.uk), and **National/Europcar** (one-way rentals available, £7 by taxi from the train station, at Brassmill Lane—go west on Upper Bristol Road, tel. 0871-384-9985, www.europcar.co.uk). Most offices close Saturday afternoon and all day Sunday, which complicates weekend pickups.

# NEAR BATH

Two towns near Bath are fun to visit if you have time: Glastonbury for its ruined abbey and hilltop tor, and Wells for its unique cathedral. Drivers can tour the towns easily in a same-day loop trip from Bath; visit Wells last to attend the afternoon evensong service if it's offered (Sept-June only, usually not July-Aug).

If you're in Bath without a car, you could take a Mad Max tour, which offers a twice-weekly minibus excursion to Glastonbury and Wells; see page 151. You can visit both towns by bus from Bath on your own, though it'd be challenging (involving at least four hours on the bus) to fit in both in one day; it's simpler to just visit the town that interests you more.

## GLASTONBURY

Marked by its hill, or "tor," and located on England's most powerful line of prehistoric sites, the town of Glastonbury gurgles with history and mystery. The extensive Glastonbury Abbey, laid waste by Henry VIII, is among England's oldest religious centers. It's the legendary resting place of the fifth-century King Arthur and his Queen Guinevere. Lore has it that the Holy Grail, the cup used by Christ at the Last Supper, is buried here, inducing a healing spring to flow (now known as the Chalice Well, located near Glastonbury Tor).

Today, Glastonbury and its tor are a center for "searchers"—just right for those looking for a place to recharge their crystals. Glastonbury is also synonymous with its music and arts festival, an annual long-hair-and-mud Woodstock re-creation.

## Orientation

**Day Plan:** Tour the abbey when you arrive in town, then ride the shuttle out to the base of the tor. Enjoy the views as you climb to the top of the tor, then stroll back to town (on the way, drop by the Chalice Well Gardens). You can picnic at the abbey or on the tor—pick something up from the shops on High Street.

**Getting There:** The nearest train station is in Bath. Buses run frequently

*Glastonbury*

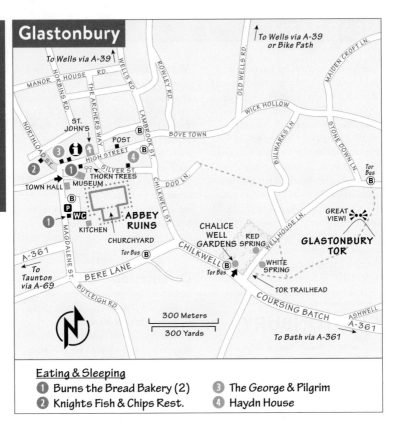

## Glastonbury

**Eating & Sleeping**
1 Burns the Bread Bakery (2)
2 Knights Fish & Chips Rest.
3 The George & Pilgrim
4 Haydn House

from Wells (3-4/hour, 25 minutes) and nearly hourly from Bath (2 hours, www.firstgroup.com).

**Arrival in Glastonbury:** The bus leaves you right in the town center, in sight of the abbey. Parking is immediately adjacent to the abbey.

*Rick's Tip: Nearly every summer around the June solstice, music fans and London's beautiful people make the trek to the **Glastonbury Festival** to see the hottest British and American bands (www.glastonburyfestivals. co.uk). Expect increased traffic and crowds.*

**Tourist Information:** The TI is on High Street in the 15th-century Tribunal townhouse (Mon-Sat 10:00-16:00, closed Sun, shorter hours off-season, 9 High Street,

tel. 01458/832-954, www.glastonburytic. co.uk).

## Sights

### ▲▲GLASTONBURY ABBEY

The massive and evocative ruins of the first Christian sanctuary in the British Isles stand mysteriously alive in a lush 36-acre park. Because it comes with a small museum, a dramatic history, and enthusiastic guides dressed in period costumes, this is one of the most engaging of England's many ruined abbeys.

The space that these ruins occupy has been sacred ground for centuries. The druids used it as a pagan holy site. In the 12th century—because of its legendary connection to King Arthur and the Holy Grail—Glastonbury was the leading Christian pilgrimage site in all of

Britain. The popular abbey grew powerful and very wealthy, employing a thousand people to serve the needs of the pilgrims. Then, in 1539, King Henry VIII ordered the abbey's destruction (as head of the new Church of England, he wanted to remove any reminders of the power of the Catholic Church).

**Cost and Hours:** £7.60, daily June-Aug 9:00-20:00, Sept-Nov and March-May until 18:00, Dec-Feb until 16:00, enter from Magdalene Street, tel. 01458/832-267, www.glastonburyabbey.com.

**Tours and Demonstrations:** Costumed guides offer 30-minute tours (generally daily March-Oct on the hour from 10:00).

→ **Self-Guided Tour:** Start by touring the informative **museum** at the entrance building. A model shows the abbey in its pre-Henry VIII splendor, and exhibits tell the story of a place "grandly constructed to entice the dullest minds to prayer."

Next, head out to explore the green park, dotted with bits of the **ruined abbey.** Before poking around the ruins, circle to the left behind the entrance building to find two **thorn trees.** According to legend, these trees are descended

from a thorn tree that sprouted when Joseph of Arimathea came here, climbed a nearby hill, and stuck his staff into the soil. (Joseph, a wealthy follower of Christ, is also credited in legend for bringing the Holy Grail to Glastonbury.) If the story seems far-fetched to you, don't tell the Queen—a blossom from the abbey's trees sits proudly on her breakfast table every Christmas morning.

Ahead and to the left of the trees, inside what was the north wall, look for two trap doors in the ground. Lift up the doors to see surviving fragments of the abbey's original tiled floor.

Now hike through the remains of the ruined complex to the far end of the abbey. From here, you can envision what had been the longest church nave in England. In this area, you'll find the tombstone (formerly in the floor of the church's choir) marking the spot where the supposed relics of **Arthur and Guinevere** were interred.

Continue around the far side of the abbey ruins, and head for the only surviving intact building on the grounds—the abbot's conical **kitchen,** with a humble exhibit about life in the abbey.

## ▲GLASTONBURY TOR

Seen by many as a Mother Goddess symbol, the Glastonbury Tor—a natural plug of sandstone on clay—has an undeniable geological charisma. A fine Somerset view rewards those who hike to its 520-foot summit. While you can hike up from either end of the tor, the trailhead near the Chalice Well Gardens is the gentler approach.

As you climb, survey the surrounding land—a former swamp. The ribbon-like man-made drainage canals that slice through the farmland are the work of Dutch engineers—Huguenot refugees imported centuries ago to turn the marsh into arable land.

The tor-top tower is the remnant of a chapel dedicated to St. Michael, the warrior angel that early Christians counted on

*Glastonbury Abbey*

for combatting pagan gods.

**Getting There:** From the town center, you can walk to the base of the tor in 20 minutes, take the tor shuttle bus (2/hour, departs from St. Dunstan's parking lot next to the abbey, doesn't run Oct-Easter), or take a taxi (about £5). There's no legal parking near the tor—it's best to leave a car in town and walk or bus from there.

### CHALICE WELL GARDENS

When Joseph of Arimathea brought the Holy Grail to Glastonbury, it supposedly ended up in the bottom of a well, which is now the centerpiece of the peaceful and inviting Chalice Well Gardens. Have a drink or take some of the precious water home—they sell empty bottles to fill.

**Cost and Hours:** £4, daily April-Oct 10:00-18:00, shorter hours off-season, on Chilkwell Street/A-361 near the tor shuttle bus stop, tel. 01458/831-154, www. chalicewell.org.uk.

## Eating and Sleeping

**Burns the Bread** makes hearty meat pies—great for a picnic (two branches—14 High Street and in the parking lot next to the abbey). The town's top chippy is **Knights Fish and Chips Restaurant** (closed Sun off-season, 5 Northload Street). For a vegetarian lunch, head to **Rainbow's End** (17 High Street).

**The George & Pilgrim Hotel** has a wonderfully Old World pub, and they rent rooms (1 High Street), as does **$ Haydn House** (13a Silver Street, www. hhglastonbury.com).

# WELLS

This small, well-preserved town (pop. just under 12,000) has one of the country's most interesting cathedrals, a wonderful evensong service (Sept-June), and medieval buildings still doing what they were originally built to do. You can still spot a number of the wells, water, and springs that helped give the town its name. Market day fills the town square on Wednesday (farmers market) and Saturday (general goods).

## Orientation

**Day Plan:** Little Wells is easy to handle in a half-day. You're here to see the cathedral (try to take in the evensong service, if it's offered and if timing allows). Save time to explore the quaint town, especially the

*Glastonbury Tor*

*Wells*

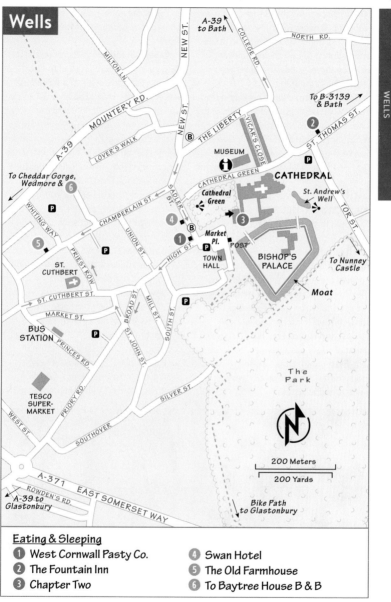

**Wells**

Eating & Sleeping
1 West Cornwall Pasty Co.
2 The Fountain Inn
3 Chapter Two
4 Swan Hotel
5 The Old Farmhouse
6 To Baytree House B & B

medieval, picturesque street called the Vicars' Close.

**Getting There:** There is no train station in Wells, but nearly hourly buses connect with **Bath** (1.5 hours, www.firstgroup.com) and frequent buses link **Glastonbury** (3-4/hour, fewer on Sun, 25 minutes). There's one direct bus daily from London's Victoria Coach Station (4 hours, www. nationalexpress.com).

**Arrival in Wells:** If you're coming by **bus,** get off in the city center at the Sadler

Street stop, around the corner from the cathedral. **Drivers** will find it easiest to park at the Princes Road lot (next to the bus station at the south end of town; enter on Priory Road) and walk five minutes to the cathedral.

**Tourist Information:** The TI is in the Wells Museum, across the green from the cathedral (April-Oct Mon-Sat 10:00-17:00, shorter hours off-season, closed Sun year-round, 8 Cathedral Green, tel. 01749/671-770, www.wellssomerset.com).

## Sights

### ▲▲WELLS CATHEDRAL

The city's highlight is England's first completely Gothic cathedral (dating from about 1200). Locals claim this church has the largest collection of medieval statuary north of the Alps. It certainly has one of the widest and most elaborate facades I've seen, and a unique figure-eight "scissor arch" that's unforgettable.

**Cost and Hours:** Free but £6 suggested donation, daily Easter-Sept 7:00-19:00, Oct-Easter until 18:00, £4 photography fee, tel. 01749/674-483, www.wellscathedral.org.uk.

**Tours:** Free one-hour tours run 4-5 times per day April-Oct Mon-Sat; fewer Nov-March.

⊙ **Self-Guided Tour:** Begin on the vast, inviting **green** in front of the cathedral. In the Middle Ages, the cathedral was enclosed within "The Liberty," an area free from civil jurisdiction until the 1800s. The Liberty included the green on the west side of the cathedral, which, from the 13th to the 17th century, was a burial place for common folk, including 17th-century plague victims. The green became a cricket pitch, then a field for grazing animals and picnicking people.

Today, it's the perfect spot to marvel at an impressive cathedral and its magnificent **facade.** The west front displays almost 300 original 13th-century carvings of kings and the Last Judgment.

Now head through the cloister and into the cathedral. At your first glance down the **nave,** you're immediately struck by the general sense of light and the unique "scissors" or hourglass-shaped **double arch** (added in 1338 to transfer weight away from the foundations sinking under the tower's weight). Until Henry VIII and

*Wells Cathedral*

*The nave culminates at the ingenious scissor arches.*

the Reformation, the interior was opulently painted in golds, reds, and greens. Later it was whitewashed. Then, in the 1840s, the church experienced the Victorian "great scrape," as locals peeled moldy whitewash off and revealed the bare stone we see today. The painted floral ceiling is based on the original medieval design.

Small, ornate 15th-century pavilion-like chapels flank the altar, carved in lacy Gothic for church VIPs. The **pulpit** features a post-Reformation, circa-1540 English script—rather than the standard Latin (see where the stonemason ran out of space when carving the inscription—we've all been there). Since this was not a monastery church, it escaped destruction in the Reformation.

In the apse you'll find the **Lady Chapel.** Examine the medieval stained-glass windows. Do they look jumbled? In the 17th century, Puritan troops trashed the precious original glass. Much was repaired, but many of the broken panes were like a puzzle that was never figured out. That's why today many of the windows are simply kaleidoscopes of colored glass.

As you walk, notice that many of the black **tombstones** set in the floor have decorative recesses that should be filled with brass. In the 16th century, the church was short on cash, so they sold the brass lettering to raise money for roof repairs.

In the south transept, you'll find several items of interest. The **old Saxon font** survives from a previous church (A.D. 705) and has been the site of Wells baptisms for more than a thousand years. (Its carved arches were added by Normans in the 12th century, and the cover is from the 17th century.) Nearby, notice the **carvings** in the capitals of the freestanding pillars, with whimsical depictions of medieval life (a man with a toothache; another with a thorn in his foot).

Also in the south transept, you'll find the entrance to the cathedral **Reading Room** (free). Housing a few old manuscripts, it offers a peek into a real 15th-century library.

**Rick's Tip:** *Lined with perfectly pickled 14th-century houses, **Vicars' Close** is the oldest continuously occupied complete street in Europe (since 1348). It's just a block north of the Wells cathedral—go under the big arch and look left.*

**▲▲CATHEDRAL EVENSONG SERVICE**
The cathedral choir takes full advantage of heavenly acoustics with a nightly 45-minute evensong service. You'll sit right in the old "quire" as you listen to a great pipe organ and the world-famous Wells Cathedral choir.

**Cost and Hours:** Free, Mon-Sat at 17:15, Sun at 15:00, but usually not in July-Aug—confirm times beforehand, tel. 01749/674-483 or www.wellscathedral. org.uk.

**Rick's Tip:** *If you attend evensong and **miss the last bus back to Bath,** here's what to do: Catch the bus to Bristol instead (hourly, one-hour trip), then take a 15-minute train ride to Bath.*

# Eating and Sleeping

**West Cornwall Pasty Company** sells good savory meat pies to eat in or take away (1a Sadler Street). For good pub grub, head to **The Fountain Inn** (no lunch on Mon, St. Thomas Street). **Chapter Two,** in the cathedral welcome center, offers a handy if not heavenly lunch.

The comfortable **$$ Swan Hotel** faces the cathedral; you can get a pub lunch in their garden with views over the green and cathedral (Sadler Street, www. swanhotelwells.co.uk). For a B&B, try **$$ The Old Farmhouse** (62 Chamberlain Street, www.wellssomerset.com) or **$ Baytree House B&B** (85 Portway, www. baytree-house.co.uk).

# The
# Cotswolds

The Cotswold Hills, a 25-by-90-mile chunk of Gloucestershire, are dotted with enchanting, time-passed villages. Enjoy a harmonious blend of man and nature: this almost pristine English countryside is decorated with rich wooden churches, tell-me-a-story stone fences, and "kissing gates" you wouldn't want to experience alone.

As with many fairy-tale regions of Europe, the present-day beauty of the Cotswolds was the result of an economic disaster. Wool was a huge industry in medieval England and Cotswold sheep grew the best wool. Wool money built fine towns, churches, and houses. With the rise of cotton and the Industrial Revolution, the woolen industry collapsed. Ba-a-a-ad news. The wealthy Cotswold towns fell into depression and the homes of impoverished nobility became gracefully dilapidated. Preserved as if by time warp, the Cotswolds are appreciated by 21st-century Romantics.

Two of the region's coziest towns and best home bases are Chipping Campden and Stow-on-the-Wold. Chipping Campden is prettier (with more thatched roofs), though Stow offers a wider range of restaurants and accommodations. The plain town of Moreton-in-Marsh, the nearest Cotswold town with a train station, is the simplest home base for nondrivers (though basing in Chipping Campden or Stow is possible—either town can be reached by bus from Moreton, except on Sunday, when bus service essentially stops).

Exploring the thatch-happiest villages and countryside of the Cotswolds is an absolute delight by car and, with a well-organized plan—and patience—is enjoyable even without one. Do your homework in advance; read this chapter carefully, though don't fret over the details. Then decide if you want to rent a car; rely on public transportation (budgeting for an inevitable taxi ride); or reserve a day with a tour company or private driver.

# THE COTSWOLDS IN 2 DAYS

Whether exploring by car or public transit, you can visit Chipping Campden (and nearby sights) on one day, and Stow-on-the-Wold (and nearby sights) on the other. If you love open-air markets and it's Tuesday, drop by the market in Moreton-in-Marsh.

Distances are short in the Cotswolds; you could visit Chipping Campden and Stow in a half-day (they're 10 miles apart, and respectively 8 and 4 miles away from Moreton-in-Marsh). But rushing the Cotswolds isn't experiencing them. Their charm has a softening effect on many uptight itineraries.

Keep in mind that you can rent a car for just a day or two; for rental agencies near Moreton-in-Marsh, see page 221 (and call in advance to reserve).

England's top countryside palace, Blenheim (see page 230), is at the eastern edge of the Cotswolds, between Moreton-in-Marsh and Oxford. You could easily visit Blenheim on your way into or out of the region (nondrivers catch a train to Oxford, then a bus to the palace).

## By Car

Use a good map and reshuffle this plan to fit your home base.

**Day 1:** Focus on Chipping Campden and the surrounding area. Browse through the town, following my self-guided walk. Heading south, you can take a loop drive, joyriding through Snowshill (lavender farm nearby), Stanway (Stanway House open Tue and Thu afternoon), and Stanton. If you're a garden lover, head north and sniff out Hidcote Manor Garden.

On any evening, you could have dinner at a pub; take a seat at the bar if you want to talk with locals. The long hours of sunlight in summer make an after-dinner stroll an appealing option.

**Day 2:** Focus on Stow-on-the-Wold and the surrounding area. Explore Stow and take my self-guided walk. Drive to the Slaughters, Bourton-on-the-Water, and Bibury. If you're up for a hike instead of a drive, walk from Stow to the Slaughters to Bourton-on-the-Water (about 3 hours at a relaxed pace), then catch the bus back to Stow.

---

**Rick's Tip:** *If you want to take in some* **Shakespeare,** *note that* **Stratford is only a 30-minute drive** *from Stow, Chipping Campden, and Moreton-in-Marsh. On the afternoon of your last day in the Cotswolds, you could drive to Stratford, set up in a hotel, and see a play that evening.*

---

## By Public Transportation

This plan is best for any day except Sunday—when virtually no buses run—and assumes you're home base is Moreton-in-Marsh.

**Day 1:** Take the morning bus to Chipping Campden to explore that town and take my self-guided walk. You could hike up Dover's Hill and back (about 1 hour round-trip). Eat lunch in Chipping Campden, then visit either Broad Campden or Broadway before returning directly from either town to Moreton-in-Marsh by bus. In the evening, have dinner at a pub and a stroll afterwards.

**Day 2:** Take a morning bus to Stow. After following my self-guided walk and poking around the town, hike from Stow through the Slaughters to Bourton-on-the-Water (a leisurely 3 hours),

# THE COTSWOLDS AT A GLANCE

## *Chipping Campden and Nearby*

▲▲**Chipping Campden** Picturesque market town with finest High Street in England, accented by a 17th-century Market Hall, wool-tycoon manors, and a characteristic Gothic church. See page 191.

▲▲**Stanway House** Grand, aristocratic home of the Earl of Wemyss, with the tallest fountain in Britain and a 14th-century tithe barn. **Hours:** June-Aug Tue and Thu only 14:00-17:00, closed Sept-May. See page 201.

▲**Stanton** Classic Cotswold village with flower-filled exteriors and 15th-century church. See page 202.

▲**Snowshill Manor** Eerie mansion packed to the rafters with eclectic curiosities collected over a lifetime. **Hours:** July-Aug Wed-Mon 11:30-16:30, closed Tue; April-June and Sept-Oct Wed-Sun 12:00-17:00, closed Mon-Tue; closed Nov-March. See page 203.

▲**Hidcote Manor Garden** Fragrant garden organized into color-themed "outdoor rooms" that set a trend in 20th-century garden design. **Hours:** March-Sept daily 10:00-18:00; Oct daily 10:00-17:00; Nov-Dec Sat-Sun 11:00-16:00, closed Mon-Fri; closed Jan-Feb. See page 204.

▲**Broad Campden, Blockley, and Bourton-on-the-Hill** Trio of villages with sweeping views and quaint homes, far from the madding crowds. See page 205.

## Stow-on-the-Wold and Nearby

▲▲**Stow-on-the-Wold** Convenient Cotswold home base with charming shops and pubs clustered around town square, plus popular day hikes. See page 205.

▲**Lower and Upper Slaughter** Inaptly named historic villages—home to a working waterwheel, peaceful churches, and a folksy museum. See page 212.

▲**Bourton-on-the-Water** The "Venice of the Cotswolds," touristy yet undeniably striking, with petite canals and impressive Motor Museum. See page 213.

▲**Cotswold Farm Park** Kid-friendly park with endangered breeds of native British animals, farm demonstrations, and tractor rides. **Hours:** Daily Feb-Oct 10:30-17:00, Nov-Dec 10:30-16:00, closed Jan. See page 214.

▲**Mechanical Music Museum** Tiny museum brimming with self-playing musical instruments, demonstrations, and Victorian music boxes. **Hours:** Daily 10:00-17:00. See page 214.

▲**Bibury** Village of antique weavers' cottages, ideal for outdoor activities like fishing and picnicking. See page 215.

▲**Cirencester** Ancient, 2,000-year-old city noteworthy for its crafts center and museum, showcasing artifacts from Roman and Saxon times. See page 215.

## Moreton-in-Marsh

▲**Moreton-in-Marsh** Relatively flat and functional home base with the best transportation links in the Cotswolds and a bustling Tuesday market. See page 216.

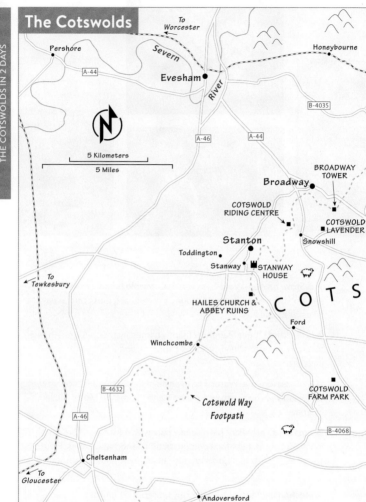

# The Cotswolds

To Worcester · Pershore · A-44 · Severn River · Evesham · Honeybourne · B-4035 · A-46 · A-44 · BROADWAY TOWER · Broadway · COTSWOLD RIDING CENTRE · COTSWOLD LAVENDER · Stanton · Snowshill · Toddington · Stanway · STANWAY HOUSE · To Tewkesbury · HAILES CHURCH & ABBEY RUINS · C O T S · Ford · Winchcombe · COTSWOLD FARM PARK · B-4632 · A-46 · *Cotswold Way Footpath* · B-4068 · Cheltenham · To Gloucester · Andoversford · A-436 · A-40 · To Bath · 5 Kilometers · 5 Miles

then return by bus or taxi to Moreton for dinner.

## Tourist Information

Local TIs stock a wide array of helpful resources and can tell you about any local events during your stay. Ask for the *Cotswold Lion,* the biannual newspaper, which includes suggestions for walks and hikes (spring/summer); bus schedules for the routes you'll be using; and the *Attractions and Events Guide* (with updated prices and hours for Cotswold sights). Each Cotswold village also has its own assortment of brochures, often for a small fee (£0.50-1) because the TIs have lost much of their funding and are struggling to make ends meet (some are run by volunteers).

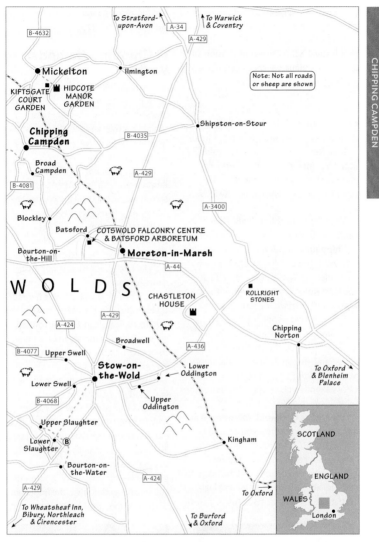

To Stratford-upon-Avon
A-34
To Warwick & Coventry
B-4632
A-429

Note: Not all roads or sheep are shown

Mickelton
Ilmington

KIFTSGATE COURT GARDEN
HIDCOTE MANOR GARDEN

Chipping Campden

Shipston-on-Stour

B-4035

Broad Campden
A-429

B-4081

Blockley

Batsford
COTSWOLD FALCONRY CENTRE & BATSFORD ARBORETUM

Bourton-on-the-Hill
Moreton-in-Marsh

A-44

W O L D S

CHASTLETON HOUSE
ROLLRIGHT STONES

A-3400

A-429
A-424

Broadwell
A-436
Chipping Norton

B-4077
Upper Swell

Stow-on-the-Wold
Lower Oddington
To Oxford & Blenheim Palace

Lower Swell
Upper Oddington

B-4068

Upper Slaughter

Lower Slaughter
B
Kingham

SCOTLAND

Bourton-on-the-Water
A-424
ENGLAND

A-429
To Oxford
WALES

To Wheatsheaf Inn, Bibury, Northleach & Cirencester
To Burford & Oxford
London

# CHIPPING CAMPDEN

Just touristy enough to be convenient, the north Cotswold town of Chipping Campden (CAM-den) is a ▲▲ sight. This market town, once the home of the richest Cotswold wool merchants, has some incredibly beautiful thatched roofs. Both the great British historian G. M. Trevelyan

and I call Chipping Campden's High Street the finest in England.

## Orientation

**Tourist Information:** The TI is tucked away in the old police station on High Street. Buy the town guide with map, or the local *Footpath Guide* (April-Oct daily 9:30-17:00; Nov-March Mon-Thu 9:30-13:00, Fri-Sun

9:30-16:00; tel. 01386/841-206, www. chippingcampdenonline.org).

**Festivals:** Chipping Campden's biggest festival is the **Cotswold Olimpicks,** a series of tongue-in-cheek countryside games, such as competitive shin-kicking (first Fri-Sat after Late May Bank Holiday, www.olimpickgames.co.uk). There's a **music festival** in May and an **open gardens festival** the third weekend in June.

**Bike Rental:** Call **Cycle Cotswolds,** at the Volunteer Inn pub (£12/day, daily 7:00-dusk, Lower High Street, mobile 07549-620-597, www.cyclecotswolds. co.uk).

**Taxi:** Try **Cotswold Private Hire** (mobile 07980-857-833), Barry Roberts at **Chipping Campden Private Hire** (also does tours, mobile 07774-224-684, www. cotswoldpersonaltours.com), or **Tour the Cotswolds** (mobile 07779-030-820, www.tourthecotswolds.co.uk).

**Parking:** Find a spot anywhere along High Street (or the street called Back Ends) and park for free with no time limit. A pay-and-display lot is on High Street, across from the TI (1.5-hour maximum). On weekends, you can park for free at the school (see map).

**Tours:** The **Cotswold Voluntary Wardens** are happy to show you around for a small donation to their conservation society (suggested donation-£3/person, 1-hour walk, walks June-Sept Tue at 14:30 and Thu at 10:00, meet at Market Hall). Tour guide and coordinator Ann Colcomb

can help arrange walks on other days as well (tel. 01386/832-131).

# ◗ Chipping Campden Walk

This self-guided stroll through "Campden" (as locals call their town) takes you from the Market Hall west to the old silk mill, and then back east the length of High Street to the church. It takes about an hour.

**Market Hall:** Begin at Campden's most famous monument—the Market Hall. It stands in front of the TI, marking the town center. The Market Hall was built in 1627 by the 17th-century Lord of the Manor, Sir Baptist Hicks. (Look for the Hicks family coat of arms on the east end of the building's facade.) Back then, it was an elegant—even over-the-top—shopping hall for the townsfolk who'd come here to buy their produce. In the 1940s, it was almost sold to an American, but the townspeople heroically raised money to buy it first, then gave it to the National Trust for its preservation.

The timbers inside are true to the original. Study the classic Cotswold stone roof, still held together with wooden pegs nailed in from underneath. (Tiles were cut and sold with peg holes, and stacked like waterproof scales.) Buildings all over the region still use these stone shingles. Today, the hall, which is rarely used, stands as a testimony to the importance of trade to medieval Campden.

*Quaint and cute Cotswolds*

*Chipping Campden Market Hall*

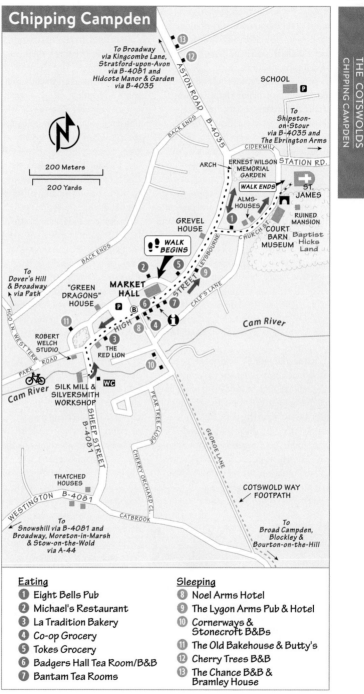

# Chipping Campden

To Broadway
via Kingcombe Lane,
Stratford-upon-Avon
via B-4081 and
Hidcote Manor & Garden
via B-4035

SCHOOL

To
Shipston-
on-Stour
via B-4035 and
The Ebrington Arms

CIDERMILL

N

200 Meters

200 Yards

ARCH

ERNEST WILSON STATION RD.
MEMORIAL
GARDEN

WALK ENDS

ST. JAMES

ALMS-
HOUSES

GREVEL
HOUSE

RUINED
MANSION

WALK BEGINS

COURT BARN MUSEUM

Baptist Hicks Land

To
Dover's Hill
& Broadway
via Path

"GREEN
DRAGONS"
HOUSE

MARKET
HALL

CHURCH ST.

CALF'S LANE

Cam River

ROBERT
WELCH
STUDIO

THE
RED LION

PARK
ROAD

Cam River

SILK MILL &
SILVERSMITH
WORKSHOP

WC

PEAR TREE CLOSE

GEORGE LANE

THATCHED
HOUSES

SHEEP STREET B-4081

CHERRY ORCHARD CL.

COTSWOLD WAY
FOOTPATH

WESTINGTON B-4081

CATBROOK

To
Snowshill via B-4081 and
Broadway, Moreton-in-Marsh
& Stow-on-the-Wold
via A-44

To
Broad Campden,
Blockley &
Bourton-on-the-Hill

## Eating
1. Eight Bells Pub
2. Michael's Restaurant
3. La Tradition Bakery
4. Co-op Grocery
5. Tokes Grocery
6. Badgers Hall Tea Room/B&B
7. Bantam Tea Rooms

## Sleeping
8. Noel Arms Hotel
9. The Lygon Arms Pub & Hotel
10. Cornerways & Stonecroft B&Bs
11. The Old Bakehouse & Butty's
12. Cherry Trees B&B
13. The Chance B&B & Bramley House

Adjacent to the Market Hall is the sober WWI monument—a reminder of the huge price paid by nearly every little town. Walk around it, noticing how 1918 brought the greatest losses.

Between the Market Hall and the WWI monument, you'll find a limestone disc embedded in the ground, marking the ceremonial start of the Cotswold Way (you'll find its partner in front of the abbey in Bath—100 miles away—marking the southern end).

The TI is just across the street, in the old police courthouse. If it's open, you're welcome to climb the stairs and peek into the **Magistrate's Court** (free, same hours as TI, ask at TI to go up). Under the open-beamed courtroom, you'll find a humble little exhibit on the town's history.

• *Walk west, passing the Town Hall and the parking lot that was originally the sheep market, until you reach the Red Lion Inn. Across High Street (and a bit to the right), look for the house with a sundial and sign over the door reading...*

**"Green Dragons":** The house's decorative black cast-iron fixtures (originally in the stables) once held hay and functioned much like salad bowls for horses. Fine-cut stones define the door, but "rubble stones" make up the rest of the wall. The pink stones are the same limestone but have been heated, and likely were scavenged from a house that burned down.

• *At the Red Lion, leave High Street and walk a block down Sheep Street. At the little creek*

*just past the public WC, a 30-yard-long lane on the right leads to an old Industrial-Age silk mill (and the Hart silversmith shop).*

**Silk Mill:** The tiny Cam River powered a mill here since about 1790. Today it houses the handicraft workers guild and some interesting history. In 1902, Charles Robert Ashbee (1863-1942) revitalized this sleepy hamlet of 2,500 by bringing a troupe of London artisans and their families (160 people in all) to town. Ashbee was a leader in the romantic Arts and Crafts movement—craftspeople repulsed by the Industrial Revolution who idealized the handmade crafts and preindustrial ways. Ashbee's idealistic craftsmen's guild lasted only until 1908, when most of his men grew bored with their small-town, back-to-nature ideals. Today, the only shop surviving from the originals is that of **silversmith David Hart.** His grandfather came to town with Ashbee, and the workshop (upstairs in the mill building) is an amazing time warp—little has changed since 1902. Hart is a gracious man as well as a fine silversmith, and he, his son William, and nephew Julian welcome browsers (Mon-Fri 9:00-17:00, Sat 9:00-12:00, closed Sun, tel. 01386/841-100). They're proud that everything they make is one of a kind. (While you could continue 200 yards farther to see some fine thatched houses, this walk doesn't.)

• *Return to High Street. On the corner is the studio shop of Robert Welsh, a local industrial designer who worked in the spirit of the Arts and Crafts movement. His son and daughter carry on his legacy in the fine shop (with a little museum case in the back). Turn right, and walk through town.*

**High Street:** Chipping Campden's High Street has changed little architecturally since 1840. (The town's street plan and property lines survive from the 12th century.) As you now walk the length of England's finest surviving High Street, study the skyline, see the dates on the buildings, and count the sundials. Notice the harmony of the long rows of buildings.

*On High Street*

While the street comprises different styles through the centuries, everything you see was made of the same Cotswold stone—the only stone allowed today.

To remain level, High Street arcs with the contour of the hillside. Because it's so wide, you know this was a market town. In past centuries, livestock and packhorses laden with piles of freshly shorn fleece would fill the streets. Campden was a sales and distribution center for the wool industry, and merchants from as far away as Italy would come here for the prized raw wool.

High Street has no house numbers: Locals know the houses by their names. In the distance, you'll see the town church (where this walk ends). Notice that the power lines are buried underground, making the scene wonderfully uncluttered.

As you stroll High Street, you'll find the finest houses on the uphill side—which gets more sun. Decorative features (like the Ionic capitals near the TI) are added for nonstructural touches of class. Most High Street buildings are half-timbered, but with cosmetic stone facades. You may see some exposed half-timbered walls. Study the crudely beautiful framing, made of hand-hewn oak (you can see the adze marks) and held together by wooden pegs.

Peeking down alleys, you'll notice how the lots are narrow but very deep. Called "burgage plots," this platting goes back to 1170. In medieval times, rooms were lined up long and skinny like train cars: Each building had a small storefront, followed by a workshop, living quarters, staff quarters, stables, and a garden at the very back. Now the private alleys that still define many of these old lots lead to comfy gardens. While some of today's buildings are wider, virtually all the widths are exact multiples of that basic first unit (for example, a modern building may be three times wider than its medieval counterpart).

• *Hike the length of High Street toward the church, to just before the first intersection, to find a house on the left with gargoyles hanging out above. This is the....*

**Grevel House:** In 1367, William Grevel built what's considered Campden's first stone house. Sheep tycoons had big

*Grevel House*

homes. Imagine back then, when this fine building was surrounded by humble wattle-and-daub huts. It had newfangled chimneys, rather than a crude hole in the roof. (No more rain inside!) Originally a "hall house" with just one big, tall room, it got its upper floor in the 16th century. The finely carved central bay window is a good early example of the Perpendicular Gothic style. The gargoyles scared away bad spirits—and served as rain spouts. The boot scrapers outside each door were fixtures in that muddy age—especially in market towns, where the streets were filled with animal dung.

• *Continue up High Street for about 100 yards. Go past Church Street (which we'll walk up later). On the right, at a big tree behind a low stone wall, you'll find a small Gothic arch leading into a garden.*

**Ernest Wilson Memorial Garden:** Once the church's vegetable patch, this small and secluded garden is a botanist's delight today. Pop inside if it's open. The garden is filled with well-labeled plants that the Victorian botanist Ernest Wilson brought back to England from his extensive travels in Asia. There's a complete history of the garden on the board to the left of the entry.

• *Backtrack to Church Street. Turn left, walk past the recommended Eight Bells pub, and hook left with the street. Along your right-hand side stretches...*

**Baptist Hicks Land:** Sprawling adjacent to the town church, the area known as Baptist Hicks Land held Hicks' huge estate and manor house. This influential Lord of the Manor was from "a family of substance," who were merchants of silk and fine clothing as well as moneylenders. Beyond the ornate gate (which you'll see ahead, near the church), only a few outbuildings and the charred corner of his **mansion** survive. The mansion was burned by royalists in 1645 during the Civil War—notice how Cotswold stone turns red when burned. Hicks housed the poor, making a show of his generosity, adding a long row of almshouses (with his family coat of arms) for neighbors to see as they walked to church. These almshouses (lining Church Street on the left) house pensioners today, as they have since the 17th century. Across the street is a ditch built as a "cart wash"—it was filled with water to soak old cart wheels so they'd swell up and stop rattling.

On the right, filling the old **Court Barn,** is a museum about crafts and designs from the Arts and Crafts movement, with works by Ashbee and his craftsmen (overpriced at £5, April-Sept Tue-Sun 10:00-17:00, Oct-March Tue-Sun 10:00-16:00, closed Mon year-round, tel. 01386/841-951, www.courtbarn.org.uk).

• *Next to the Hicks gate, a scenic, tree-lined lane leads to the front door of the church. On the way, notice the 12 lime trees, one for each of the apostles, that were planted in about 1760 (sorry, no limes).*

**St. James Church:** One of the finest churches in the Cotswolds, St. James Church graces one of its leading towns.

*Baptist Hicks Land*

*Tomb of Sir Baptist Hicks and his wife*

## Cotswold Appreciation 101

In the Cotswolds, a town's main street (called High Street) needed to be wide to accommodate the sheep and cattle being marched to market. Some of the most picturesque cottages were once weavers' cottages, usually located along a stream for their waterwheels (there are good examples in Bibury and Lower Slaughter). Walls and roofs are made of the local limestone; the tiles hang by pegs. To make the weight more bearable, smaller and lighter tiles are higher up. The decorative "toadstool" stones dotting front yards throughout the region are medieval staddle stones, which buildings were set upon to keep the rodents out. A strict building code keeps towns quaint.

In the morning, you'll hear sheep baa-ing. It costs more to shear a sheep than the 50 pence the wool will fetch, so the commercial wool industry is essentially dead. In the old days, sheep lived long lives, producing lots of wool. When they were finally slaughtered, the meat was tough and eaten as "mutton." Today, sheep are raised primarily for their meat, and slaughtered younger. When it comes to Cotswold sheep these days, it's lamb (not mutton) for dinner (not sweaters).

Towns are small: everyone knows everyone. The area is provincial yet polite. People rescue themselves from gossip by saying, "It's all very...mmm...yaaa." In contrast to the village ambience are the giant manors and mansions, now the country homes of celebrities like Madonna, Elizabeth Hurley, and Kate Moss.

Fields of yellow (rapeseed) and pale blue (linseed) separate pastures dotted with black and white sheep. This is walking country. The English vigorously defend their age-old right to free passage. Once a year the Ramblers, Britain's largest walking club, organizes a "Mass Trespass," when each of the country's 50,000 miles of public footpaths is walked. By assuring that each path is used at least once a year, they stop landlords from putting up fences. Any paths found blocked are unceremoniously unblocked.

Questions to ask locals: Do you think foxhunting should have been banned? Who are the Morris men? What's a kissing gate?

Both the town and the church were built by wool wealth. Go inside. The church is Perpendicular Gothic, with lots of light and strong verticality. Notice the fine vestments and altar hangings (intricate c. 1460 embroidery) behind protective blue curtains (near the back of the church). Tombstones pave the floor in the chancel (often under protective red carpeting)—memorializing great wool merchants through the ages.

At the altar is a brass relief of William Grevel, the first owner of the Grevel House (described earlier), and his wife. But it is Sir Baptist Hicks who dominates the church. His huge canopied tomb is the ornate final resting place for Hicks and his wife, Elizabeth. Study their faces, framed by fancy lace ruffs (trendy in the 1620s). Adjacent—as if in a closet—is a statue of their daughter, Lady Juliana, and her husband, Lutheran Yokels. Juliana commissioned the statue in 1642, when her husband died, but had it closed up until *she* died in 1680. Then, the doors were opened, revealing these two people holding hands and living happily ever after—at least in marble. The hinges were likely used only once.

As you leave the church, look

immediately around the corner to the right of the door. A small tombstone reads "Thank you Lord for Simon, a dearly loved cat who greeted everyone who entered this church. RIP 1980."

# Hiking

Since this is a particularly hilly area, long-distance hikes are challenging. The easiest and most rewarding stroll is to the thatchy, hobbit village of **Broad Campden** (about a mile, mostly level). From there, you can walk or take the bus (#22) back to Chipping Campden.

Or, if you have more energy, continue from Broad Campden up over the ridge and into picturesque **Blockley**—and, if your stamina holds out, all the way to **Bourton-on-the-Hill** (Blockley and Bourton-on-the-Hill are also connected by buses #21 and #22 to Chipping Campden and Moreton).

Alternatively, you can hike up to **Dover's Hill,** just north of the village. Ask locally about this easy, circular, one-hour walk that takes you on the first mile of the 100-mile-long Cotswold Way (which goes from here to Bath).

For more about hiking, see "Getting Around the Cotswolds—By Foot" on page 220.

# Eating

This town—filled with wealthy residents and tourists—comes with many choices. I've listed some local favorites below.

**Eight Bells** pub is a charming 14th-century inn on Leysbourne with a classy restaurant and a more rustic pub. The seasonal menu is as locally sourced as possible and includes a daily special and vegetarian dish. Reservations are smart (£8-12 lunches, £13-22 dinners, daily 12:00-14:00 & 18:30-21:00, tel. 01386/840-371, www.eightbellsinn.co.uk).

**The Lygon Arms** pub is cozy and inviting, with a good, basic bar menu. Order from the same menu in the colorful pub or the more elegant dining room across

the passage (£6-8 sandwiches, £8-15 meals, daily 11:30-14:30 & 18:00-22:00, tel. 01386/840-318).

**Michael's,** a fun Mediterranean restaurant on High Street, serves hearty portions and breaks plates at closing every Saturday night. The focus is Greek, with plenty of *mezes*—small dishes for £6-10 (also £15-21 larger dishes, £7 *meze* lunch platter, Tue-Sun 11:00-14:30 & 19:00-22:00, closed Mon, tel. 01386/840-826).

## Light Meals

If you want a quick takeaway sandwich, consider these options. Munch your lunch on the benches on the little green near the Market Hall.

**Butty's at the Old Bakehouse** offers tasty, inexpensive sandwiches and wraps made to order (Mon-Sat 7:30-14:30, closed Sun, free Wi-Fi, Lower High Street, tel. 01386/840-401).

**La Tradition** is a hardworking French bakery that serves sausage rolls, quiches, filled croissants, and Cornish pasties (takeaway only, Tue-Sat 8:30-17:00, closed Sun-Mon, 6 High Street, tel. 01386/840-766).

For **picnic supplies,** head to the **Co-op** grocery (Mon-Sat 7:00-22:00, Sun 8:00-22:00, next to TI on High Street). **Tokes,** on the opposite end of High Street, has a tempting selection of cheeses, meats, and wine (Mon-Fri 9:00-18:00, Sat 10:00-17:00, Sun 10:00-16:00, just past the Market Hall, tel. 01386/849-345).

## Tearooms

To visit a cute tearoom, try one of these places, located in the town center.

**Badgers Hall Tea Room** is pricey but good, with a wide selection of savory dishes and desserts. A tempting table of homemade cakes, crumbles, and scones lures passersby into its half-timbered dining room and a patio out back (£8-13 lunches, daily 10:00-16:30, possibly later in summer, £31 afternoon tea for two, 14:30-16:00, High Street).

**Bantam Tea Rooms,** near the Market Hall, is also a good value (£8 teas, £6 sandwiches, daily 10:00-16:00, High Street, tel. 01386/840-386).

# Sleeping

In Chipping Campden—as in any town in the Cotswolds—B&Bs offer a better value than hotels. Book well in advance, as rooms are snapped up early in the spring and summer. Rooms are tight on Saturdays (when many charge more and are reluctant to rent to one-nighters) and in September, another peak month. Parking is never a problem. Ask for a discount if staying longer than one or two nights.

## Sleep Code

**Price Rankings for Double Rooms (Db)**

$$$ Most rooms £100 or more
$$ £75-100
$ £75 or less

**Abbreviations:** Db=Double with bathroom. D=Double with bathroom down the hall.

**Notes:** Room prices change; verify rates online or by email. For the best prices, book direct with the hotel.

### On or near High Street

Located on the main street (or just off of it), these places couldn't be more central.

**$$$ Noel Arms Hotel,** the characteristic old hotel on the main square, has welcomed guests for 600 years. Its lobby was remodeled in a medieval-meets-modern style, and its 28 rooms are well-furnished with antiques (standard Db-£120, fancier Db-£140-180, some ground-floor doubles, attached restaurant/bar and café, free parking, High Street, tel. 01386/840-317, www.noelarmshotel.com, reception@noelarmshotel.com).

**$$$ The Lygon Arms Hotel** (pronounced "lig-un"), attached to the popular pub of the same name, has small public areas and 10 cheery, open-beamed rooms (huge "superior" Db-£120, lovely courtyard Db-£165, family deals, free parking, High Street, go through archway and look for hotel reception on the left, tel. 01386/840-318, www.lygonarms.co.uk, sandra@lygonarms.co.uk).

**$$ Cornerways B&B** is a bright, comfy home a block off High Street. The two huge, airy loft rooms are great for families. If you're happy to exchange breakfast for more space, ask about the cottage across the street (Db-£90, family rooms, 2-night minimum; cottage Db-£85, 3-night minimum; cash only, off-street parking, George Lane, just walk through the arch beside Noel Arms Hotel, tel. 01386/841-307, www.cornerways.info, carole@cornerways.info). For a fee, they can pick you up from the train station, or take you on village driving tours.

**$$ Stonecroft B&B,** next to Cornerways, has three polished, well-maintained rooms (one with low, slanted ceilings—unfriendly to tall people). The lovely garden with a patio and small stream is a tranquil place for meals or an early-evening drink (Db-£80, family rooms, no kids under 12, George Lane, tel. 01386/840-486, www.stonecroft-chippingcampden.co.uk, info@stonecroft-chippingcampden.co.uk).

**$$ The Old Bakehouse** rents two small but pleasant twin-bedded rooms in a 600-year-old home with exposed beams and cottage charm (Db-£85, cash only, Lower High Street, near intersection with Sheep Street, tel. 01386/840-979, mobile 07717/330-838, www.theoldbakehouse.org.uk, zoegabb@yahoo.co.uk).

### A Short Walk from Town on Aston Road

The B&Bs below are a 10-minute walk from Market Hall. They are listed in the order you would find them when strolling from town (if arriving by bus, ask to be dropped off at Aston Road).

**$$ Cherry Trees B&B,** set well off the road, is a spacious, modern home, with three king rooms and one superior king room with balcony (Db-£90-115, free parking, Aston Road, tel. 01386/840-873, www.cherrytreescampden.com, sclrksn7@tiscali.co.uk).

**$$$ The Chance B&B**—a modern home with Cotswold charm—has two tastefully decorated rooms with king beds (which can also be twins if requested) and a breakfast room that opens onto a patio. They also offer two self-catering cottages in town (Db-£100, call for cottage prices, cash only, free parking, 1 Aston Road, tel. 01386/849-079, www.the-chance.co.uk, enquiries@the-chance.co.uk).

**$$ Bramley House,** which backs up to a farm, has a spacious garden suite with a private outdoor patio and lounge area (bathroom downstairs from bedroom) and a superior king double. Crisp white linens and simple country decor give the place a light and airy feel (king Db-£90, garden suite Db-£97, 2-night minimum, homemade cake with tea or coffee on

arrival, locally sourced organic breakfast, 6 Aston Road, tel. 01386/840-066, www.bramleyhouse.co.uk, dppovey@btinternet.com).

# NEAR CHIPPING CAMPDEN

Because the countryside around Chipping Campden is particularly hilly, it's also especially scenic. This is a rewarding area to poke around and discover little thatched villages.

Due west of Chipping Campden lies the famous and touristy town of Broadway. Just south of that, you'll find my nominations for the cutest Cotswold villages. Like marshmallows in hot chocolate, Stanway, Stanton, and Snowshill nestle side by side, awaiting your arrival. (Note the Stanway House's limited hours—only Tue and Thu afternoons in summer—when planning your visit.)

Hidcote Manor Garden is just northeast of Chipping Campden, while Broad Campden, Blockley, and Bourton-on-the-Hill lie roughly between Chipping Campden and Stow (or Moreton)—handy if you're connecting those towns.

*The countryside around Chipping Campden is dotted with charming little villages.*

# Broadway

This postcard-pretty town, a couple of miles west of Chipping Campden, is filled with inviting shops and fancy teahouses. With a "broad way" indeed running through its middle, it's one of the bigger towns in the area. This means you'll likely pass through at some point if you're driving—but, since all the big bus tours seem to stop here, I usually give Broadway a miss. However, with a new road that allows traffic to skirt the town, Broadway has gotten cuter than ever. Broadway has good bus connections with Chipping Campden.

Just outside Broadway, on the road to Chipping Campden, you might spot signs for the **Broadway Tower,** which looks like a turreted castle fortification stranded in the countryside without a castle in sight. This 55-foot-tall observation tower is a "folly"—a uniquely English term for a quirky, outlandish novelty erected as a giant lawn ornament by some aristocrat with more money than taste. If you're also weighted down with too many pounds, you can relieve yourself of £5 to climb to its top for a view over the pastures. But the view from the tower's parklike perch is free, and almost as impressive (daily 10:00-17:00).

# Stanway

More of a humble crossroads community than a true village, sleepy Stanway is worth a visit mostly for its manor house, which offers an intriguing insight into the English aristocracy today. If you're in the area when it's open, it's well worth visiting.

## ▲▲STANWAY HOUSE

The Earl of Wemyss (pronounced "Weemz"), whose family tree charts relatives back to 1202, opens his melancholy home and grounds to visitors just two days a week in the summer. Walking through his house offers a unique glimpse into the lifestyles of England's eccentric and fading nobility.

**Cost and Hours:** £7 ticket covers house and fountain, £9 ticket also includes watermill; both tickets include a wonderful and intimate audioguide, narrated by the lordship himself; June-Aug Tue and Thu only 14:00-17:00, closed Sept-May, tel. 01386/584-469, www.stanwayfountain.co.uk.

**Getting There:** By car, leave the B-4077 at a statue of (the Christian) George slaying the dragon (of pagan superstition); you'll round the corner and see the manor's fine 17th-century Jacobean gatehouse. Park in the lot across the street. There's no public transportation to Stanway.

**Visiting the Manor:** The bitchin' **Tithe Barn** (near where you enter the grounds) dates to the 14th century, and predates the manor. It was originally where monks—in the days before money—would accept one-tenth of whatever the peasants produced. Peek inside: This is a great hall for village hoedowns. While the Tithe Barn is no longer used to greet motley peasants and collect their feudal

*Stanway House*

"rents," the lord still gets rent from his vast landholdings, and hosts community fêtes in his barn.

Stepping into the obviously very lived-in **manor,** you're free to wander around pretty much as you like, but keep in mind that a family does live here. His lordship is often roaming about as well. The place feels like a time warp. Ask a staff member to demonstrate the spinning rent-collection table. In the great hall, marvel at the one-piece oak shuffleboard table and the 1780 Chippendale exercise chair (half an hour of bouncing on this was considered good for the liver).

The manor dogs have their own cutely painted "family tree," but the Earl admits that his last dog, C. J., was "all character and no breeding." Poke into the office. You can psychoanalyze the lord by the books that fill his library, the DVDs stacked in front of his bed (with the mink bedspread), and whatever's next to his toilet.

The place has a story to tell. And so do the docents stationed in each room—modern-day peasants who, even without family trees, probably have relatives going back just as far in this village. Talk to these people. Probe. Learn what you can about this side of England.

Wandering through the expansive backyard you'll see the earl's pet project: restoring "the tallest **fountain** in Britain"—300 feet tall, gravity-powered, and running for 30 minutes at 14:45 and 16:00.

Signs lead to a working **watermill,**

which produces flour from wheat grown on the estate (about 100 yards from the house, requires higher-priced ticket to enter).

# From Stanway to Stanton

These towns are separated by a row of oak trees and grazing land, with parallel waves echoing the furrows plowed by medieval farmers. Centuries ago, farmers were allotted long strips of land called "furlongs." The idea was to dole out good and bad land equitably. (One square furlong equals 10 acres.) Over centuries of plowing these, furrows were formed. Let someone else drive, so you can hang out the window under a canopy of oaks, passing stone walls and sheep. Leaving Stanway on the road to Stanton, the first building you'll see (on the left, just outside Stanway) is a thatched cricket pavilion overlooking the village cricket green. Originally built for *Peter Pan* author J. M. Barrie, it dates from 1930 and is raised up (as medieval buildings were) on rodent-resistant staddle stones. Stanton is just ahead; follow the signs.

# Stanton

Pristine Cotswold charm cheers you as you head up the main street of the village of Stanton, worth ▲. Go on a photo safari for flower-bedecked doorways and windows. (A scant few buses serve Stanton.)

Stanton's **Church of St. Michael** (with the pointy spire) betrays a pagan past. It's safe to assume any church dedicated to St. Michael (the archangel who fought the devil) sits upon a sacred pagan site. Stanton is actually at the intersection of two ley lines (a line connecting prehistoric or ancient sights). You'll see St. Michael's well-worn figure (and, above that, a sundial) over the door as you enter. Inside, above the capitals in the nave, find the pagan symbols for the sun and the moon (see photo). While the church probably dates back to the ninth century, today's building is mostly from the 15th

*Pagan symbol in the Church of St. Michael*

century, with 13th-century transepts. On the north transept (far side from entry), medieval frescoes show faintly through the 17th-century whitewash. (Once upon a time, these frescoes were considered too "papist.") Imagine the church interior colorfully decorated throughout. Original medieval glass is behind the altar. The list of rectors (at the very back of the church, under the organ loft) goes back to 1269. Finger the grooves in the back pews, worn away by sheepdog leashes. (A man's sheepdog accompanied him everywhere.)

**Horse Riding:** Anyone can enjoy the Cotswolds from the saddle. Jill Carenza's **Cotswolds Riding Centre,** set just outside Stanton village, is in the most scenic corner of the region. The facility's horses can take anyone from rank beginners to more experienced riders on a scenic "hack" through the village and into the high country (per-hour prices: £30/person for a group hack, £40/person for a semi-private hack, £50 for a private one-person hack; lessons, longer rides, rides for experts, and pub tours available; tel. 01386/584-250, www.cotswoldsriding.co.uk, info@cotswoldsriding.co.uk). From Stanton, head toward Broadway and watch for the riding center on your right after about a third of a mile.

**Eating:** High on a hill at the far end of Stanton's main drag, nearest to Broadway, the aptly named **Mount Inn** serves upscale meals on its big, inviting terrace with grand views (£14-17 meals, food served daily 12:00-14:00 & 18:00-21:00, may be closed Mon off-season, Old Snowshill Road, tel. 01386/584-316).

**Sleeping: $$ The Vine B&B** has five rooms in a characteristic old Cotswold house near the center of town, next to the cricket pitch (Db-£85, tel. 01386/584-250, www.cotswoldsriding.co.uk, info@cotswoldsriding.co.uk).

# Snowshill

Another nearly edible little bundle of cuteness, the village of Snowshill (SNOWS-hill) has a photogenic triangular square with a characteristic pub at its base.

## ▲SNOWSHILL MANOR

Dark and mysterious, this old palace is filled with the lifetime collection of Charles Paget Wade. It's one big, musty celebration of craftsmanship, from finely carved spinning wheels to frightening samurai armor to tiny elaborate figurines carved by prisoners from the bones of meat served at dinner. Taking seriously his family motto, "Let Nothing Perish," Wade dedicated his life and fortune to preserving things finely crafted. The house (whose management made me promise not to promote it as an eccentric collector's pile of curiosities) really shows off Wade's ability to recognize and acquire fine examples of craftsmanship. It's all very...mmm...yaaa.

**Cost and Hours:** £11.30; manor house open July-Aug Wed-Mon 11:30-16:30, closed Tue; April-June and Sept-Oct Wed-Sun 12:00-17:00, closed Mon-Tue; closed Nov-March; gardens and ticket window open at 11:00, last entry one hour before closing, restaurant, tel. 01386/852-410, www.nationaltrust.org.uk/snowshillmanor.

**Getting There:** The manor overlooks the town square, but there's no direct access from the square; instead, the entrance and parking lot are about a half-mile up the road toward Broadway. Park there and follow the long walkway through the garden to get to the house. A golf-

*Snowshill Manor*

cart-type shuttle to the house is available for those who need assistance.

**Getting In:** This popular sight strictly limits the number of entering visitors by doling out entry times. No reservations are possible; to get a slot, you must report to the ticket desk. It can be up to an hour's wait—even more on busy days, especially weekends (when they can sell out for the day as early as 14:00). Tickets go on sale and the gardens open at 11:00. Therefore, a good strategy is to arrive close to the opening time, and if there's a wait, enjoy the gardens (it's a 10-minute walk to the manor). If you have more time to kill, head into the village of Snowshill itself (a half-mile away) to wander and explore—or get a time slot for later in the day, and return in the afternoon.

## Cotswold Lavender

In 2000, farmer Charlie Byrd realized that tourists love lavender. He planted his farm with 250,000 plants, and now visitors come to wander among his 53 acres, which burst with gorgeous lavender blossoms from mid-June through late August. His fragrant fantasy peaks late each July. Lavender—so famous in France's Provence—is not indigenous to this region, but it fits the climate and soil just fine. A free flier in the shop explains the variations of blooming flowers. Farmer Byrd produces lavender oil (an herbal product valued since ancient times for its healing, calming, and fragrant qualities)

and sells it in a lovely shop, along with many other lavender-themed items. In the café, enjoy a pot of lavender-flavored tea with a lavender scone.

**Cost and Hours:** Free to enter shop and café, £2.50 to walk through the fields and the distillery; generally open June-Aug daily 10:00-17:00; closed Sept-May; schedule changes annually depending on when the lavender blooms—call ahead or check their website, tel. 01386/854-821, www.cotswoldlavender.co.uk.

**Getting There:** It's a half-mile out of Snowshill on the road toward Chipping Campden (easy parking). Entering Snowshill from the road to the manor (described earlier), take the left fork, then turn left again at the end of the village.

## Hidcote Manor Garden

This is less "on the way" between towns than the other sights in this section—but the grounds around this manor house are well worth a detour if you like gardens. Worth ▲▲, Hidcote is where garden designers pioneered the notion of creating a series of outdoor "rooms," each with a unique theme (such as maple room, red room, and so on) and separated by a yew-tree hedge. The garden's design, inspired by the Arts and Crafts movement, is most formal near the house and becomes more pastoral as it approaches the countryside. Follow your nose through a clever series of small gardens that lead delightfully from one to the next. Among the best in

*Cotswold lavender*

*A "garden room" at Hidcote Manor*

England, Hidcote Gardens are at their fragrant peak from May through August. But don't expect much indoors—the manor house has only a few rooms open to the public.

**Cost and Hours:** £10.50; March-Sept daily 10:00-18:00; Oct daily 10:00-17:00; Nov-Dec Sat-Sun 11:00-16:00, closed Mon-Fri; closed Jan-Feb; last entry one hour before closing, café, restaurant, tel. 01386/438-333, www.nationaltrust.org.uk/hidcote.

**Getting There:** If you're driving, it's four miles northeast of Chipping Campden— roughly toward Ilmington. The gardens are accessible by bus and a 45-minute country walk. Buses #21 and #22 take you to Mickleton (one stop past Chipping Campden), where a footpath begins next to the churchyard. Continuing more or less straight, the path leads uphill through sheep pastures and ends at Hidcote's driveway.

## Broad Campden, Blockley, and Bourton-on-the-Hill

This trio of pleasant villages, worth ▲, lines up along an off-the-beaten-path road between Chipping Campden and Moreton or Stow. **Broad Campden,** just on the outskirts of Chipping Campden, has some of the cutest thatched-roof houses I've seen. **Blockley,** nestled higher in the picturesque hills, is a popular setting for films. The same road continues on to **Bourton-on-the-Hill,** with fine views looking down into a valley. All three of these towns are connected to Chipping Campden by bus #21 and #22, or you can walk (easy to Broad Campden, more challenging to the other two—see page 219).

# STOW-ON-THE-WOLD

Located 10 miles south of Chipping Campden, Stow-on-the-Wold—with a name that means "meeting place on the uplands"—is the highest point of the Cotswolds. Despite its crowds, it retains its charm and it merits ▲▲. Most of the tourists are day-trippers, so nights—even in the peak of summer—are peaceful. Stow has no real sights other than the town itself, some good pubs, antiques stores, and cute shops draped seductively around a big town square. Visit

*Stow-on-the-Wold*

the church, with its evocative old door guarded by ancient yew trees and the tombs of wool tycoons. A visit to Stow is not complete until you've locked your partner in the stocks on the village green.

## Orientation

**Tourist Information:** A small TI staffed by volunteers is run out of the library in St. Edwards Hall on the main square (hours erratic, generally Mon-Sat 10:00-14:00, sometimes as late as 17:00, closed Sun, tel. 08452-305-420). Don't expect much information—get serious questions answered in Moreton-in-Marsh instead (see page 216).

**Parking:** Park anywhere on Market Square free for two hours, and overnight between 18:00 and 9:00 (combining overnight plus daily 2-hour allowances means you can park free 16:00-11:00—they note your license, so you can't just move to another spot after your time is up; £50 tickets for offenders). You can also park for free on some streets farther from the center (such as Park Street and Well Lane) for an unlimited amount of time. Alternately, a convenient pay-and-display lot is at the bottom of town (toward the Oddingtons), and there's a free lot at Tesco Supermarket—an easy five-minute walk north of town (follow the signs).

## ◉ Stow-on-the-Wold Walk

This four-stop self-guided walk covers about 500 yards and takes about 45 minutes.

Start at the **stocks on the Market Square.** Imagine this village during the era when people were publicly ridiculed here as a punishment. Stow was born in pre-Roman times; it's where three trade routes crossed at a high point in the region (altitude: 800 feet). This square was the site of an Iron Age fort, and then a Roman garrison town. This main square hosted an international fair starting in 1107, and people came from as far away as Italy for the wool fleeces. This grand square was a vast,

grassy expanse. Picture it in the Middle Ages (before the buildings in the center were added): a public commons and grazing ground, paths worn through the grass, and no well. Until the late 1800s, Stow had no running water; women fetched water from the "Roman Well" a quarter-mile away.

With as many as 20,000 sheep sold in a single day, this square was a thriving scene. And Stow was filled with inns and pubs to keep everyone housed, fed, and watered. A thin skin of topsoil covers the Cotswold limestone, from which these buildings were made. **Stow Lodge** (next to the church) lies a little lower than the church; the lodge sits on the spot where locals quarried stones for the church. That building, originally the rectory, is now a hotel. The church (where we'll end this little walk) is made of Cotswold stone, and marks the summit of the hill upon which the town was built. The stocks are a great photo op (lock dad up for a great family Christmas card).

• Walk past The White Hart Inn to the market, and cross to the other part of the square. Notice how locals seem to be part of a tight-knit little community. Enjoy the stone work and the crazy rooflines. Note the cheap signage and think how shops have been coming and going for centuries in buildings that never change.

For 500 years, the **Market Cross** stood in the market, reminding all Christian merchants to "trade fairly under the sight

*The stocks on Market Square*

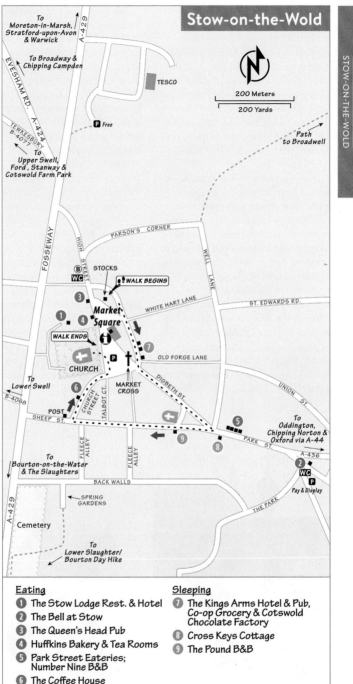

## Stow-on-the-Wold

To Moreton-in-Marsh, Stratford-upon-Avon & Warwick

EVESHAM RD. A-424

To Broadway & Chipping Campden

A-429

TESCO

200 Meters
200 Yards

TEWKESBURY B-4077

To Upper Swell, Ford, Stanway & Cotswold Farm Park

P Free

Path to Broadwell

FOSEWAY

HIGH STREET

PARSON'S CORNER

WELL LANE

STOCKS
B
WC
WALK BEGINS

WHITE HART LANE

ST. EDWARDS RD.

Market Square

WALK ENDS

To Lower Swell
B-4068

CHURCH

P

OLD FORGE LANE

UNION ST.

MARKET CROSS

DIGBETH ST.

CHURCH STREET

TALBOT CT.

POST

SHEEP ST.

To Oddington, Chipping Norton & Oxford via A-44

A-436

WC
P
Pay & Display

FLEECE ALLEY

FLEECE ALLEY

PARK ST.

To Bourton-on-the-Water & The Slaughters

A-429

BACK WALLS

SPRING GARDENS

THE PARK

Cemetery

To Lower Slaughter/ Bourton Day Hike

### Eating
1 The Stow Lodge Rest. & Hotel
2 The Bell at Stow
3 The Queen's Head Pub
4 Huffkins Bakery & Tea Rooms
5 Park Street Eateries; Number Nine B&B
6 The Coffee House

### Sleeping
7 The Kings Arms Hotel & Pub, Co-op Grocery & Cotswold Chocolate Factory
8 Cross Keys Cottage
9 The Pound B&B

of God." Notice the stubs of the iron fence in the concrete base—a reminder of how countless wrought-iron fences were cut down and given to the government to be melted down during World War II. (Recently, it's been disclosed that all that iron ended up in junk heaps—frantic patriotism just wasted.) The plaque on the cross honors the Lord of the Manor, who donated money back to his tenants, allowing the town to finally finance running water in 1878.

Scan the square for **The Kings Arms,** with its great gables and scary chimney. It was once where travelers parked their horses before spending the night. In the 1600s, this was considered the premium "posting house" between London and Birmingham. Today, The Kings Arms cooks up pub grub and rents rooms upstairs.

During the English Civil War, which pitted Parliamentarians against royalists, Stow-on-the-Wold remained staunchly loyal to the king. (Charles I is said to have eaten at The Kings Arms before a great battle.) Because of its allegiance, the town has an abundance of pubs with royal names (King's This and Queen's That).

The stately building in the center of the square with the wooden steeple is **St. Edward's Hall.** Back in the 1870s, a bank couldn't locate the owner of an account containing a small fortune, so it donated the funds to the town to build this civic center. It serves as a City Hall, library, TI, and meeting place. When it's open, you can wander around upstairs to see the largest collection of Civil War portrait paintings in England.

• *Walk past The Kings Arms down Digbeth Street. At the bottom of Digbeth you'll pass the traditional Lambournes butcher and a fragrant cheesemonger across the street. Digbeth ends at a little triangular park in front of the former Methodist Church and across from the Porch House Hotel. This hotel—along with about 20 others—claims to be the oldest in England, dating from 947.*

Just beyond the small grassy triangle with benches was the place where locals gathered for bloody cockfights and bearbaiting (watching packs of hungry dogs tear at bears). Today this is where—twice a year, in May and October—the Stow Horse Fair attracts nomadic Roma (Gypsies) and Irish Travellers from far and

*Market Cross*

*St. Edward's Hall*

wide. They congregate down the street on the Maugersbury Road. Locals paint a colorful picture of the Roma, Travellers, and horses inundating the town. The young women dress up because the fair also functions as a marriage market.

• *Hook right and hike up the wide street.*

As you head up **Sheep Street,** you'll pass a boutique-filled former brewery yard (on the left). Notice its fancy street-front office, with a striking flint facade. Sheep Street was originally not a street, but a staging place for medieval sheep markets. The sheep would be gathered here, then paraded into the Market Square down narrow alleys—just wide enough for a single file of sheep to walk down, making it easier to count them. You'll see several of these so-called "fleece alleys" as you walk up the street.

• *Walk a couple of blocks until about 50 yards before the streetlight and the highway, then make a right onto Church Street, which leads to the church.*

Before entering the **church,** circle it. On the back side, a door is flanked by two ancient yew trees. While many view it as the Christian "Behold, I stand at the door and knock" door, J. R. R. Tolkien fans see something quite different. Tolkien

*The door claimed by Tolkien fans as the portal to Middle Earth*

hiked the Cotswolds, and had a passion for sketching evocative trees such as this. *Lord of the Rings* enthusiasts are convinced this must be the inspiration for the door into Middle Earth.

While the church (open daily 9:00-18:00, except during services) dates from Saxon times, today's structure is from the 15th century. Its history is played up in leaflets and plaques just inside the door. The floor is paved with the tombs of big shots who made their money from wool and are still boastful in death. (Find the tombs crowned with the bales of wool.) Most of the windows are traditional Victorian (19th century) designs, but the two sets high up in the clerestory are from the dreamier Pre-Raphaelite school.

On the right wall as you approach the altar, a monument commemorates the many boys from this small town who were lost in World War I (50 out of a population of 2,000). There were far fewer in World War II. The biscuit-shaped plaque remembers an admiral from Stow who lost four sons defending the realm. It's sliced from an ancient fluted column (which locals believe is from Ephesus, Turkey).

During the English Civil War (1615), the church was ransacked, and more than 1,000 soldiers were imprisoned here. The tombstone in front of the altar remembers the royalist Captain Francis Keyt. His long hair, lace, and sash indicate he was a "cavalier," and true-blue to the king (Cromwellians were called "round heads"— named for their short hair). Study the crude provincial art—childlike skulls and (in the upper corners) symbols of his service to the king (armor, weapons).

Finally, don't miss the kneelers tucked in the pews. These are made by a committed band of women known as "the Kneeler Group." They meet most Tuesday mornings (except sometimes in summer) at 10:30 in the Church Room to needlepoint, sip coffee, and enjoy a good chat. (The vicar assured me that any tourist wanting to join them would be more than welcome. The help would be appreciated and the company would be excellent.) If you'd rather sing, the choir practices on the first and third Fridays of the month at 18:00, and visitors are encouraged to join in. And with Reverend Martin Short for the pastor, the services can be pretty lively.

# Hiking

Stow is made to order for day hikes. The most popular is the downhill stroll to **Lower Slaughter** (3 miles), then on to **Bourton-on-the-Water** (about 1.5 miles more). It's a two-hour walk if you keep up a brisk pace and don't stop, but dawdlers should allow three to four hours. At the end, from Bourton-on-the-Water, a bus can bring you back to Stow. While those with keen eyes can follow this walk by spotting trail signs, it can't hurt to bring a map (ask to borrow one at your B&B). These towns are described in more detail starting on page 212.

To reach the trail, find the cemetery (from the main square, head down Church Street, turn left on Sheep Street, right into Fleece Alley, right onto Back Walls, and left onto Spring Gardens). Walk past the community's big pea patch, then duck right through the cemetery to the far end. Here, go through the gate and walk down the footpath that runs alongside the big A-429 road for about 200 yards, then cross the road and catch the well-marked trail (gravel road with green sign noting *Public Footpath/Gloucestershire Way,* next to Quarwood Cottage). Follow this trail for a delightful hour across farms, through romantic gates, across a fancy driveway, and past Gainsborough-painting vistas. You'll enjoy an intimate backyard look at farm life. Although it seems like you might lose the trail, tiny easy-to-miss signs (yellow *Public Footpath* arrows—sometimes also marked *Gloucestershire Way* or *The Monarch's Way*—usually embedded in fence posts) keep you on target—watch for these very carefully to avoid getting lost. Finally, passing a cricket pitch, you reach **Lower Slaughter,** with its fine church and a mill creek leading up to its mill.

Hiking from Lower Slaughter up to **Upper Slaughter** is a worthwhile one-mile detour each way, if you have the time and energy.

*The old mill at Lower Slaughter*

From Lower Slaughter, it's a less-scenic 25-minute walk into the bigger town of **Bourton-on-the-Water.** Leave Lower Slaughter along its mill creek, then follow a bridle path back to A-429 and into Bourton. Walking through Bourton's burbs, you'll pass two different bus stops for the ride back to Stow; better yet, to enjoy some time in Bourton itself, continue all the way into town and—when ready—catch the bus from in front of the Edinburgh Woolen Mill (bus #801 departs roughly hourly, none on Sun except May-Aug when it runs about 2/day, 10-minute ride).

# Eating

These places are all within a five-minute walk of each other, either on the main square or downhill on Queen and Park streets.

## Restaurants and Pubs

**Stow Lodge** is the choice of the town's proper ladies. There are two parts: The formal but friendly bar serves fine pub grub (hearty £9-12 lunches and dinners, daily 12:00-14:00 & 19:00-20:30). The restaurant serves a popular £30 three-course dinner (nightly, veggie options, good wines, just off main square, tel. 01451/830-485). On a sunny day, the pub serves lunch in the well-manicured garden.

**The Bell at Stow,** on the edge of town at the end of Park Street, has a great scene and fun pub energy. They serve classic English dishes, sometimes with an Asian twist. Enjoy live music on Sunday evenings (£7-15 lunches, £12-15 dinners, veggies extra, daily 12:00-21:00, reservations recommended, tel. 01451/870-916, www.thebellatstow.com).

**The Queen's Head** faces the Market Square, near Stow Lodge. Join the local eccentrics to dine on pub grub and drink the local Cotswold brew, Donnington Ale. They have a meat pie of the day, good fish-and-chips, and live music on Saturdays (£5-7 sandwiches, £8-10

lunches, £9-13 dinners, daily 12:00-14:30 & 18:30-21:00, beer garden out back, tel. 01451/830-563).

**Huffkins Bakery and Tea Rooms** is an institution overlooking the center of the market square. Enjoy bakery-fresh meals—soups, sandwiches, all-day breakfast, tea and scones, and gluten-free options—in the well-worn tea room (£7-10 plates, daily 9:00-17:00, tel. 01451/832-870).

## Cheaper Options and Ethnic Food

Head to the grassy triangle where Digbeth hits Sheep Street to find takeout fish-and-chips, Chinese, and Indian food.

**Greedy's Fish and Chips,** on Park Street, is the go-to place for takeout. There's no seating, but they do have benches in front (£5 fish-and-chips, Mon-Sat 12:00-14:00 & 16:30-21:00, closed Sun, tel. 01451/870-821).

**Jade Garden Chinese Take-Away** is appreciated by locals who don't want to cook (£3-6 dishes, Wed-Mon 17:00-23:00, closed Tue, 15 Park Street, tel. 01451/870-288).

**The Prince of India** offers good Indian food to take out or eat in (£9-13 main dishes, nightly 18:00-23:30, 5 Park Street, tel. 01451/830-099).

**The Coffee House** provides a nice break from the horses-and-hounds cuisine found elsewhere, with pleasant garden seating out back (£5 soups, £9-10 salads and sandwiches, good coffee; April-Sept Mon-Sat 9:00-17:00, Sun 10:00-16:30; Church Street, tel. 01451/870-802).

---

**Rick's Tip:** *For* **dessert,** *munch a locally-made chocolate treat under the trees on the square's benches and watch the sky darken, the lamps come on, and visitors having their photo fun in the stocks.*

---

The **Cotswold Chocolate Factory** creates handmade chocolate bars, bon-bons, truffles, and more (daily 10:00-17:30, Digbeth Street, tel. 01451/798-082).

Small **grocery stores** face the main square (the **Co-op** is open daily 7:00-22:00; next to The Kings Arms), and a big **Tesco** supermarket is 400 yards north of town.

## Sleeping

**$$$ Stow Lodge Hotel** fills the historic church rectory with old English charm. Facing the town square, with its own sprawling and peaceful garden, this lavish old place offers 21 large, thoughtfully appointed rooms with soft beds, stately public spaces, and a cushy-chair lounge (slippery rates but generally Db-£130, £10 extra on Sat, cheaper Nov-April, closed Jan, free parking, The Square, tel. 01451/830-485, www.stowlodge.co.uk, enquiries@stowlodge.co.uk).

**$$$ The Kings Arms,** with 10 rooms above a pub, keeps its historic Cotswold character while feeling fresh and modern (standard Db-£100, superior Db-£120, steep stairs, three "cottages" out back, free parking, Market Square, tel. 01451/830-364, www.kingsarmsstow.co.uk, info@kingsarmsstow.co.uk).

**$$ Number Nine** has three large, bright, refurbished, and tastefully decorated rooms. This 200-year-old home comes with watch-your-head beamed ceilings and beautiful old wooden doors (Db-£80-85, 9 Park Street, tel. 01451/870-333, mobile 07779-006-539, www.number-nine.info, enquiries@number-nine.info).

**$$ Cross Keys Cottage** offers four smallish but smartly updated rooms—some bright and floral, others classy white—with modern bathrooms inside a 370-year-old beamed cottage (Db-£80-90, ask for Rick Steves cash discount, call ahead to confirm arrival time, Park Street, tel. 01451/831-128, www.crosskeyscottage.co.uk, rogxmag@hotmail.com).

**$ The Pound** is a cozy, 500-year-old, low-beamed home offering two bright,

inviting rooms and a classic old fireplace lounge (D-£70, family room, cash only, downtown on Sheep Street next to Grapevine Hotel, tel. 01451/830-229, patwhitehead1@live.co.uk).

# NEAR STOW-ON-THE-WOLD

These sights are all south of Stow: Some are within walking distance (the Slaughters and Bourton-on-the-Water), and one is 20 miles away (Cirencester). The Slaughters and Bourton are tied together by the countryside walk from Stow described on page 210.

## Lower and Upper Slaughter

"Slaughter" has nothing to do with lamb chops. It likely derives from an Old English word, perhaps meaning sloe tree (the one used to make sloe gin). These villages are worth ▲ and a quick stop.

**Lower Slaughter** is a classic village, with ducks, a charming little church, a working water mill, and usually an artist busy at her easel somewhere. The Old Mill Museum is a folksy ensemble with a tiny museum, shop, and café complete with a delightful terrace overlooking the mill pond, enthusiastically run by Gerald and his daughter Laura, who just can't resist giving generous tastes of their homemade ice cream (£2.50 for museum, March-Oct daily 10:00-18:00, Nov-Feb daily 10:00-dusk, tel. 01451/822-127, www.

*The church at Upper Slaughter*

oldmill-lowerslaughter.com). Just behind the Old Mill, two kissing gates lead to the path that goes to nearby Upper Slaughter, a 15-minute walk or 2-minute drive away (leaving the Old Mill, take two lefts, then follow the sign for *Wardens Way*). And if you follow the mill creek downstream, a bridle path leads to Bourton-on-the-Water (described next).

In **Upper Slaughter,** walk through the yew trees (sacred in pagan days) down a lane through the raised graveyard (a buildup of centuries of graves) to the peaceful church. In the back of the fine graveyard, the statue of a wistful woman looks over the tomb of an 18th-century rector (sculpted by his son). Notice the town is missing a war memorial—that's because every soldier who left Upper Slaughter for World War I and World War II survived the wars. As a so-called "Doubly Thankful Village" (one of only 13 in England and Wales), the town instead honors those who served in war with a simple wood plaque in the Town Hall.

**Getting There:** Though the stop is not listed on schedules, you should be able to reach these towns on bus #801 (from Moreton or Stow) by requesting the "Slaughter Pike" stop (along the main road, near the villages). Confirm with the driver before getting on. If driving, the small roads from Upper Slaughter to Ford and Kineton (and the Cotswold Farm Park, described later) are some of England's most scenic. Roll your window down and joyride slowly.

## Bourton-on-the-Water

Dubbed "the Venice of the Cotswolds" because of its quaint canals, this town is very pretty and worth ▲. But it can be mobbed with tour groups during the day. It's worth a short stop, especially if you can avoid the crowds. It's pleasantly empty in the early evening and after dark.

Bourton has a fine Motor Museum on High Street in the town center, plus a **leisure center** (big pool and sauna; Mon-Fri

6:30-22:00, Sat-Sun 8:00-20:00; shared with the school—which gets priority for use, a five-minute walk from town center off Station Road, tel. 01451/824-024).

**Getting There:** It's conveniently connected to Stow and Moreton by bus #801. It's also within walking distance of Stow (4 miles south) and Lower Slaughter (1 mile).

**Parking:** Drive into town and wait for a spot on High Street to open up (a long row of free two-hour spots is in front of the Edinburgh Woolen Mills Shop), or park in the pay-and-display parking lot a five-minute walk from the center.

**Tourist Information:** The TI is tucked across the stream a short block off the main drag, on Victoria Street, behind Village Hall (Mon-Fri 9:30-17:00, Sat 9:30-17:30, Sun 10:00-14:00 except closed Sun Oct-April, closes one hour earlier Nov-March, tel. 01451/820-211).

**Bike Rental: Hartwells** on High Street rents bikes by the hour or day and includes a helmet, map, and lock (£14/day, Mon-Sat 9:00-18:00, Sun opens at 10:00, tel. 01451/820-405, www.hartwells.supanet.com).

### ▲MOTOR MUSEUM
Lovingly presented, this good, jumbled museum shows off a lifetime's accumulation of vintage cars, old lacquered signs, threadbare toys, and prewar memorabilia. If you appreciate old cars, this is nirvana. Wander the car-and-driver displays, which range from the automobile's early days to the stylish James Bond era,

*Bourton-on-the-Water*

including period music to add mood. Talk to an elderly Brit who's touring the place for some personal memories.

**Cost and Hours:** £5.25, mid-Feb–early Dec daily 10:00–18:00, closed off-season, in the mill facing the town center, tel. 01451/821-255, www.cotswoldmotormuseum.co.uk.

## Cotswold Farm Park

Here's a delight for young and old alike. This park, worth ▲, is the private venture of the Henson family, who are passionate about preserving rare and endangered breeds of native British animals. While it feels like a kids' zone (with all the family-friendly facilities you can imagine), it's actually a fascinating chance for anyone to get up close to mostly cute animals, including the sheep that made this region famous—the big and woolly Cotswold Lion. The "listening posts" deliver audio information on each rare breed.

A busy schedule of demonstrations gives you a look at local farm life—check the events board as you enter for times for the milking, "farm safari," shearing, and well-done "sheep show." Join the included 20-minute tractor ride, with live narration. Buy a bag of seed upon arrival, or have your map eaten by munchy goats. Tykes love the little tractor rides, maze, and zip line, but the "touch barn" is where it's at for little kids.

**Cost and Hours:** £9.25, family deal, daily Feb-Oct 10:30–17:00, Nov-Dec

10:30–16:00, closed Jan, good guide-book (small fee), decent cafeteria, tel. 01451/850-307, www.cotswoldfarmpark.co.uk.

**Getting There:** It's well-signposted about halfway between Stow and Stanway (15 minutes from either), just off Tewkesbury Road (B-4077, toward Ford from Stow). A visit here makes sense if you're traveling between Stow and Chipping Campden.

## Northleach

One of the "untouched and untouristed" Cotswold villages, Northleach is worth a short stop. The town's impressive main square and church attest to its position as a major wool center in the Middle Ages. Park in the square called The Green or the adjoining Market Place. The town has no TI, but you can pick up a free town map and visitor guide at the Mechanical Music Museum or at the post office on the Market Place (Mon-Fri 9:00-13:00 & 14:00-17:30, Sat 9:00-12:30, closed Sun) and at other nearby shops. Information: www.northleach.gov.uk.

**Getting There:** Northleach is nine miles south of Stow, down the A-429. Bus #801 connects it to Stow and Moreton.

▲MECHANICAL MUSIC MUSEUM
This enjoyable little one-room place offers a unique opportunity to listen to 300 years of amazing self-playing musical instruments. It's run by people who are

*Motor Museum*

*Cotswold Farm Park*

passionate about their restoration work on these musical marvels. The curators delight in demonstrating about 20 of the museum's machines with each hour-long tour. You'll hear Victorian music boxes and the earliest polyphones (record players) playing cylinders and then discs—all from an age when music was made mechanically, without the help of electricity. The admission fee includes an essential hour-long tour.

**Cost and Hours:** £8, daily 10:00-17:00, last entry at 16:00, tours go constantly—join one in progress, High Street, Northleach, tel. 01451/860-181, www. mechanicalmusic.co.uk.

**Eating in Northleach:** Tucked along unassuming Northleach's main drag is a foodies' favorite, **The Wheatsheaf Inn.** With a pleasantly traditional dining room and a gorgeous sprawling garden, they serve up an intriguing eclectic menu of modern English cuisine. They pride themselves on offering a warm welcome, relaxed service, and a take-your-time approach to top-quality food. Reservations are smart (£17-22 meals, daily, on West End, tel. 01451/860-244, www. cotswoldswheatsheaf.com).

## Bibury

Six miles northeast of Cirencester, this ▲ village is a favorite with British picnickers fond of strolling and fishing. Bibury (BYE-bree) offers a row of very old weavers' cottages, a trout farm, a stream teeming with fat fish and proud ducks, and a church surrounded by rosebushes, each tended by a volunteer of the parish. A protected wetlands area on the far side of the stream hosts newts and water voles. Walk up the main street, then turn right along the old weavers' Arlington Row and back on the far side of the marsh, peeking into the rushes for wildlife.

For a closer look at the fish, cross the little bridge to the 15-acre **Trout Farm,** where you can feed them—or catch your own on weekends (£4 to walk the grounds, fish food-£0.50; daily April-Sept 8:00-18:00, Oct and March 8:00-17:00, Nov-Feb 8:00-16:00; catch-your-own only on weekends March-Oct 10:00-17:00, no fishing in winter, call or email to confirm fishing schedule, tel. 01285/740-215, www.biburytroutfarm.co.uk).

**Getting There:** Bus #855 goes direct from Moreton-in-Marsh and Stow to Bibury (3/day, 1 hour).

## Cirencester

Almost 2,000 years ago, Cirencester (SIGH-ren-ses-ter) was the ancient Roman city of Corinium. Worth ▲, it's 20 miles from Stow down A-429, which was called Fosse Way in Roman times. The **TI,** in the shop at the Corinium Museum, answers questions and sells a town map and a town walking-tour brochure (same hours as museum, tel. 01285/654-180).

**Getting There:** If traveling by bus, take #855 from Moreton-in-Marsh or Stow direct to Cirencester (3/day, 1.5 hours). Drivers follow *Town Centre* signs and find

*Bibury*

*Cirencester*

parking right on the market square; if parking is full, retreat to the Waterloo pay-and-display lot (a five-minute walk away).

**Sights:** Stop by the impressive **Corinium Museum** to find out why they say, "If you scratch Gloucestershire, you'll find Rome." The museum chronologically displays well-explained artifacts from the town's rich history, with a focus on Roman times—when Corinium was the second-biggest city in the British Isles (after Londinium). You'll see column capitals and fine mosaics before moving on to the Anglo-Saxon and Middle Ages exhibits (£5, Mon-Sat 10:00-17:00, Sun 14:00-17:00, Park Street, tel. 01285/655-611, www.coriniummuseum.org).

Cirencester's **church** is the largest of the Cotswold "wool" churches. The cutesy **New Brewery Arts** crafts center entertains visitors with traditional weaving and potting, workshops, an interesting gallery, and a good coffee shop (www.newbreweryarts.org.uk). Monday and Friday are general-**market** days, Friday features an antique market, and a crafts market is held on the second and fourth Saturdays of the month.

# MORETON-IN-MARSH

This workaday town—worth ▲—is like Stow or Chipping Campden without the touristy sugar. Rather than gift and antique shops, you'll find streets lined with real shops: ironmongers selling cottage nameplates and carpet shops strewn with the remarkable patterns that decorate B&B floors. A traditional market of 100-plus stalls fills High Street each Tuesday, as it has for the last 400 years; best if you go early (8:00-15:30, handicrafts, farm produce, clothing, books, and people-watching). The Cotswolds has an economy aside from tourism, and you'll feel it here.

## Orientation

Moreton has a tiny, sleepy train station two blocks from High Street, lots of bus connections, and the best **TI** in the region. The TI offers a room-booking service and discounted tickets for major sights (such as Blenheim Palace and Warwick Castle). Peruse the racks of fliers, confirm rail and bus schedules, and consider the inexpensive *Town Trail* self-guided walking tour leaflet (Mon 8:45-16:00, Tue-Thu 8:45-17:15, Fri 8:45-16:45, Sat 10:00-13:00, closed Sun, good public WC, tel. 01608/650-881).

**Baggage Storage:** While there is no formal baggage storage in town, the **Black Bear Inn** (next to the TI) might let you leave bags there—especially if you buy a drink.

**Parking:** It's easy—anywhere on High Street is fine any time, as long as you want, for free (though there is a 2-hour parking limit for the small lot in the middle of the street). On Tuesdays, when the market makes parking tricky, you can park at the **Budgens** supermarket for £3—refundable if you spend at least £5 in the store (2-hour limit).

*Moreton-in-Marsh*

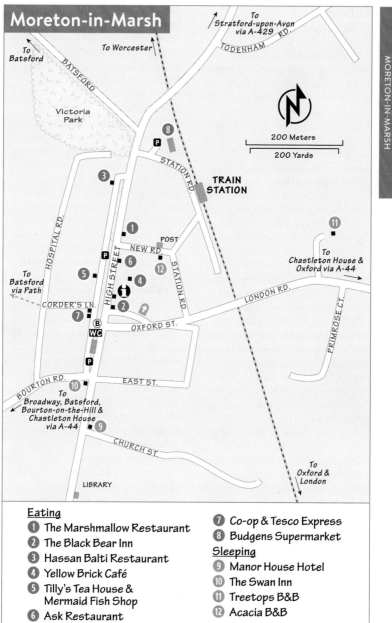

## Moreton-in-Marsh

### Eating
1. The Marshmallow Restaurant
2. The Black Bear Inn
3. Hassan Balti Restaurant
4. Yellow Brick Café
5. Tilly's Tea House & Mermaid Fish Shop
6. Ask Restaurant
7. Co-op & Tesco Express
8. Budgens Supermarket

### Sleeping
9. Manor House Hotel
10. The Swan Inn
11. Treetops B&B
12. Acacia B&B

# Eating

A stroll up and down High Street lets you survey your options.

**The Marshmallow** is relatively upscale but affordable, with a menu that includes traditional English dishes as well as lasagna and salads (£10-14 main courses, £13 afternoon tea, Mon 10:00-16:00, Tue-Sat 10:00-20:00, Sun 10:30-18:00, closed for dinner Jan, reservations smart, shady back garden for dining, tel. 01608/651-536, www.marshmallow-tea-restaurant.co.uk).

**The Black Bear Inn** offers traditional English food. Choose between the dining room on the left or the pub on the right (£10-15 meals and daily specials, restaurant: daily 12:00-14:00 & 18:30-21:00, pub: daily 10:30-23:30, tel. 01608/652-992).

**Hassan Balti,** with tasty Bangladeshi food, is a fine value for sit-down or takeout (£7-11 meals, daily 12:00-14:00 & 17:30-23:30, tel. 01608/650-798).

**Yellow Brick Café** has a delightful outdoor patio, cozy indoor seating, and a tempting display of homemade cakes. It's good for a late breakfast, midday lunch, or early dinner (£4-7 breakfasts, £6-8 sandwiches, £8-10 main courses, daily 9:00-17:00, 3 Old Market Way, tel. 01608/651-881).

**Tilly's Tea House** serves fresh soups, salads, sandwiches, and pastries for lunch in a cheerful spot on High Street across from the TI (£5-7 light meals, good cream tea-£5, Mon-Sat 9:00-17:00, Sun 10:00-16:00, tel. 01608/650-000).

**Ask** is a chain restaurant with decent pastas, pizzas, and salads, and a breezy, family-friendly atmosphere (£9-13 pizzas, daily 11:30-23:00, takeout available, tel. 01608/651-119).

**Mermaid** fish shop is popular for its takeout fish and tasty selection of traditional savory pies (£5.50 fish-and-chips, £2.50 pies, Mon-Sat 11:30-14:00 & 17:00-22:00, closed Sun, tel. 01608/651-391).

For **picnic supplies,** head to the small **Co-op** grocery on High Street (Mon-Sat 7:00-20:00, Sun 8:00-20:00) or the **Tesco Express** two doors down (daily 7:00-23:00). The big **Budgens** supermarket is indeed super (Mon-Sat 8:00-22:00, Sun 10:00-16:00, far end of High Street). You can picnic across the street in pleasant Victoria Park (with a playground).

# Sleeping

**$$$ Manor House Hotel** dates from 1545 but sports such modern amenities as toilets and electricity. Its 35 classy rooms and garden invite relaxation (standard Db-£170, superior Db-£200-230, family suites, £40 more for Sat night, rates are soft, elevator, log fire in winter, attached restaurants, free parking, on far end of High Street away from train station, tel. 01608/650-501, www.cotswold-inns-hotels.co.uk, info@manorhousehotel.info).

**$$ The Swan Inn,** perched on the main drag, has eight comfortable rooms with modern bathrooms, though the public halls look a bit worn and you enter through a bar/restaurant that's noisy on weekends. They offer transportation from the train station and to various destinations within 20 miles (standard Db-£70-115, four-poster Db-£105-130, free parking, restaurant gives guests 10 percent discount, High Street, tel. 01608/650-711, www.swanmoreton.co.uk, info@swanmoreton.co.uk).

**$ Treetops B&B** is plush, with seven spacious, attractive rooms, a sun lounge, and a three-quarter-acre backyard. There's a two-night minimum on weekends (large Db-£75, gigantic Db-£85, set far back from the busy road, London Road, tel. 01608/651-036, www.treetopscotswolds.co.uk, treetops1@talk21.com). It's an eight-minute walk from town and the train station (exit station, keep left, go left on bridge over train tracks, look for sign, then long driveway).

**$ Acacia B&B,** on the short road connecting the train station to the town center, is a convenient budget option. The public spaces are a bit tired, but the four rooms (one en suite, the other three share one bathroom) are bright and tidy, and most overlook a lovely garden (D-£60, Db-£65, tel. 01608/650-130, 2 New Road, www.acaciainthecotswolds.co.uk, acacia.guesthouse@tiscali.co.uk).

## Transportation

Moreton-in-Marsh, the only Cotswold town with a train station, is also the best base for exploring the region by bus (see "Getting Around the Cotswolds," below).

**Train Connections to: London**'s Paddington Station (every 1-2 hours, 1.5-2 hours), **Bath** (hourly, 2 hours, 1-2 transfers), **Oxford** (every 1-2 hours, 40 minutes), **Stratford-upon-Avon** (hourly, 1.5-3 hours, complicated with 3 transfers and expensive; better by bus). Train info: Tel. 0345-748-4950, www.nationalrail.co.uk.

**Bus Connections to: Chipping Campden** (hourly, 45 minutes, none on Sun), **Stow-on-the-Wold** (hourly, 20 minutes, none on Sun), **Stratford-upon-Avon** (hourly, 1.5 hours, none on Sun). Bus (and train) info: www.traveline.org.uk.

# TRANSPORTATION

## Getting Around the Cotswolds
### By Bus

The Cotswolds are so well-preserved, in part, because public transportation to and within this area has long been miserable. Fortunately, a few key buses connect the more interesting villages. Centrally located Moreton-in-Marsh is the region's transit hub—with the only train station and several bus lines.

To explore the towns, you can take buses that hop through the Cotswolds about every hour, lacing together main stops and ending at rail stations. In each case, the entire trip takes about an hour. Individual fares are around £4. If you plan on taking more than two rides in a day, consider the Cotswolds

Discoverer pass, which offers unlimited travel on most buses, including those listed below (£10/day, £25/3 days, www.escapetothecotswolds.org.uk/discoverer).

Unfortunately, the buses aren't particularly reliable—it's not uncommon for them to show up late, early, or not at all. The same journey can take, say, from 30 minutes up to 90 minutes, depending on the stops. Leave yourself a huge cushion of time if using buses to make another connection (such as a train to London), and always have a backup plan (such as the phone number for a few taxis/drivers or for your hotel, who can try calling someone for you). Bus service is essentially nonexistent on Sundays.

The TI hands out easy-to-read bus schedules for key lines (or check www.traveline.org.uk, or call the Traveline info line, tel. 0871-200-2233). Put together a one-way or return trip by public transportation, making for a fine Cotswold day. If you're traveling one-way through the Cotswolds, note that the villages lack official baggage-check services. You'll need to improvise; ask sweetly at the nearest TI or business.

No single bus connects the three major towns described in this chapter (Chipping Campden, Stow, and Moreton); to get between Chipping Campden and Stow, you'll have to change buses in Moreton. Since buses can be unreliable and connections aren't timed, it may be better to call a driver or taxi to get between Chipping Campden and Stow if you're in a hurry.

The following bus lines are operated by Johnsons Coaches (tel. 01564/797-070, www.johnsonscoaches.co.uk): **Buses #21** and **#22** run from Moreton-in-Marsh to Batsford to Bourton-on-the-Hill to Blockley, then either to Broadway or Broad Campden on their way to Chipping Campden, and pass through Mickleton before ending at Stratford-upon-Avon.

The following buses are operated by

Pulham & Sons Coaches (tel. 01451/820-369, www.pulhamscoaches.com): Bus **#801** goes hourly in both directions from Moreton-in-Marsh to Stow-on-the-Wold to Bourton-on-the-Water; most continue on to Northleach and Cheltenham. Bus **#855** goes from Moreton-in-Marsh and Stow to Northleach to Bibury to Cirencester.

## By Bike

Despite narrow roads, high hedgerows (blocking some views), and even higher hills, bikers enjoy the Cotswolds free from the constraints of bus schedules. For each area, TIs have fine route planners that indicate which peaceful, paved lanes are particularly scenic for biking. In summer, it's smart to book your rental bike a couple of days ahead—but note that only Chipping Campden and Bourton-on-the-Water have shops that rent out bikes.

In **Chipping Campden** your only choice is **Cycle Cotswolds,** at the Volunteer Inn pub (£12/day, daily 7:00-dusk, Lower High Street, mobile 07549-620-597, www.cyclecotswolds.co.uk). If you make it to **Bourton-on-the-Water,** you can rent bicycles through **Hartwells** (£14/

day, Mon-Sat 9:00-18:00, Sun 10:00-18:00, on High Street, tel. 01451/820-405, www.hartwells.supanet.com).

If you're interested in a biking vacation, **Cotswold Country Cycles** offers self-led bike tours of the Cotswolds and surrounding areas (tours last 2-7 days and include accommodations and luggage transfer, www.cotswoldcountrycycles.com).

## By Foot

Consider venturing across the pretty hills and meadows of the Cotswolds. Walking guidebooks and leaflets abound, giving you a world of choices for each of my recommended stops (choose a book with clear maps). If you're doing any hiking, get the excellent Ordnance Survey Explorer OL #45 map, which shows every road, trail, and ridgeline (£8 at local TIs). Nearly every hotel and B&B has a box or shelf of local walking guides and maps, including Ordnance Survey #45. Don't hesitate to ask for a loaner. For a quick circular hike from a particular village, peruse the books and brochures offered by that village's TI. Villages are generally no more than three miles apart, and most have pubs that would love your business.

Each of the home-base villages I recommend has hiking opportunities. Stow-on-the-Wold, immersed in pleasant but not-too-hilly terrain, is within easy walking distance of several interesting spots and is probably the best starting point. Chipping Campden sits along a ridge, which means that hikes from there are extremely scenic, but also more strenuous. Moreton-in-Marsh—true to its name—sits on a marsh, offering flatter and less picturesque hikes.

Here are three hikes to consider, in order of difficulty, with the easiest listed first. I've selected these for their convenience to the home-base towns and because the start and/or end points are on bus lines, allowing you to hitch a ride back to where you started (or on to the next town) rather than backtracking by foot.

• **Stow, the Slaughters, and Bourton-on-the-Water:** Walk from Stow to Upper and Lower Slaughter, then on to Bourton-on-the-Water (which has bus service back to Stow on #801). One big advantage of this walk is that it's mostly downhill (4.5 miles, allow 2 hours one-way, more for dawdling). For details, see page 210.

• **Chipping Campden, Broad Campden, Blockley, and Bourton-on-the-Hill:** From Chipping Campden, it's an easy mile walk into charming Broad Campden, and from there, a more strenuous hike to Blockley and Bourton-on-the-Hill (which are both connected by buses #21 and #22 to Chipping Campden and Moreton). For more details, see page 205.

• **Broadway to Chipping Campden:** This hardy hike takes you along the Cotswold Ridge; attempt it only if you're a serious hiker (5.5 miles).

If you'd prefer to take a **guided walk,** ask at any TI for the free *Cotswold Lion* newspaper. The walks range from 2 to 12 miles, and often involve a stop at a pub or tearoom (*Lion* newspaper also online at www.cotswoldsaonb.org.uk—click on "Publications").

Or leave the planning to a company such as **Cotswold Walking Holidays,** which can help you design a walking vacation, provide route instructions and maps, transfer your bags, and even arrange lodging. They also offer five- to six-night walking tours that come with a local guide. Walking through the towns allows you to slow down and enjoy the Cotswolds at their very best—experiencing open fields during the day and arriving into towns just as the day-trippers depart (www.cotswoldwalks.com).

## By Car

Joyriding here truly is a joy. Winding country roads seem designed to spring bucolic village-and-countryside scenes on the driver at every turn. Distances here are wonderfully short—but only if you invest in a good map. The £8 Ordnance Survey Explorer OL #45 map sold at TIs and newsstands is excellent but almost too detailed for drivers; a £5 tour map covers a wider area in less detail. Here are driving distances from Moreton: **Stow-on-the-Wold** (4 miles), **Chipping Campden** (8 miles), **Broadway** (10 miles), **Stratford-upon-Avon** (17 miles), **Warwick** (23 miles), **Blenheim Palace** (20 miles).

Car hiking is great. In this chapter, I cover the postcard-perfect (but discovered) villages. With a car and the local Ordnance Survey map, you can easily ramble about and find your own gems. The problem with having a car is that you are less likely to walk. Consider taking a taxi or bus somewhere, so that you can walk back to your car and enjoy the scenery.

**Car Rental:** Two places near Moreton-in-Marsh rent cars by the day—reserve yours in advance. **Value Self Drive,** based in Shipston-on-Stour (about six miles north of Moreton) and run by Steve Bradley, has affordable rates (£32-49/day plus tax, includes insurance, discount rates available for longer rentals; open Mon-Sat 8:15-17:30, Sun by appointment only; call ahead to arrange, mobile 07974-805-485, stevebradleycars@aol.com). Conveniently,

Steve will pick you up in Moreton (£18) or Stratford-upon-Avon (£20), and bring you back to Shipston to get your car. **Robinson Goss Self Drive,** also six miles north of Moreton-in-Marsh, is a bit more expensive and won't bring the car to you in Moreton (£31-61/day plus extras like navigation and gas, Mon-Fri 8:30-17:00, Sat 8:30-12:00, closed Sun, tel. 01608/663-322, www.robgos.co.uk).

## By Taxi or Private Driver

Two or three town-to-town taxi trips can make more sense than renting a car. While taking a cab seems extravagant, the distances are short (Stow to Moreton is 4 miles, Stow to Chipping Campden is 10), and one-way walks are lovely. If you call a cab, confirm that the meter will start only when you are actually picked up. Consider hiring a private driver at the hourly "touring rate" (generally around £35), rather than the meter rate. For a few more bucks than taking a taxi, you can have a joyride peppered with commentary. Whether you book a taxi or a private driver, expect to pay about £25 between Chipping Campden and Stow and about £20 between Chipping Campden and Moreton.

Note that the drivers listed here are not typical city taxi services (with many drivers on call), but are mostly individuals—it's smart to call ahead if you're arriving in high season, since they can be booked in advance on weekends.

**Moreton:** Try Stuart and Stephen at **ETC,** "Everything Taken Care of" (tel. 01608/650-343 or toll-free 0800/955-8584, cotswoldtravel.co.uk) or **Iain Taxis** (mobile 07836-374-491, iaintaxis@btinternet.com). See also the taxi phone numbers posted outside the Moreton train station office.

**Stow:** Try Iain (above) or **Tony Knight** (mobile 07887-714-047, anthonyknight205@btinternet.com).

**Chipping Campden:** Call Iain (earlier), Paul at **Cotswold Private Hire** (mobile 07980-857-833), Barry Roberts at **Chipping Campden Private Hire** (also does tours, mobile 07774-224-684, www.cotswoldpersonaltours.com), or **Les Proctor,** who offers village tours and station pick-ups (mobile 07580-993-492, Les also co-runs Cornerways B&B).

**Tours:** Tim Harrison at **Tour the Cotswolds** specializes in tours of the Cotswolds and its gardens, but will also do tours outside the area (mobile 07779-030-820, www.tourthecotswolds.co.uk).

## By Tour

**Departing from Bath: Lion Tours** offers a Cotswold Discovery full-day bus tour. If you request it in advance, you can also use the tour as transportation to the Cotswolds; you can pay extra to be dropped off with your luggage in Stow or Moreton. Or, if you want to head to London in time for a show, ask to be let off at Kemble Station (www.liontours.co.uk; also see page 156 of the Bath chapter).

**Departing from Moreton-in-Marsh: Cotswold Tour** offers a smartly arranged day of sightseeing for people with limited time and transportation. Reserve your spot online, then meet Becky at Moreton-in-Marsh's train station at 10:15 (10:30 on Sundays). Her minivan tour follows a set route that includes a buffet lunch and cream tea served in her cottage and returns to the station by 16:30—good timing for day-trippers returning to London for the evening. This tour is also a fine option if you're staying in Moreton without a car (£85/person, Mon-Sat departs Moreton-in-Marsh station at 10:15, Sun at 10:30, must reserve ahead online, no luggage allowed—if you're traveling with bags you'll have to find somewhere in Moreton to store them for the day, tel. 01608/674-700, www.cotswoldtourismtours.co.uk).

# BEST OF THE REST

## OXFORD

Oxford, founded in the seventh century and home to the oldest university in the English-speaking world, originated as a simple trade crossroads. Ever since the first homework was assigned in 1167, the University of Oxford's stellar graduates have influenced Western civilization; its alumni include 26 British prime ministers, more than 60 Nobel Prize winners, and even 11 saints.

For Oxford's many tourists, it's all about its historic colleges, grassy quads, and literary connections. But that doesn't mean Oxford is stodgy. This is a fun college town, filled with rollicking pubs.

Oxford is a convenient stop for people visiting the Cotswolds, the magnificent Blenheim Palace (just outside town), Stratford-upon-Avon, and Bath. Because of Oxford's proximity to other worthwhile destinations (and the relative economy of sleeping in a smaller town B&B), a stop here on the way to somewhere else is ideal.

## Orientation

While a typical American-style university has one campus, Oxford (like Cambridge) has colleges scattered throughout town. But the sightseers' Oxford is walkable and compact. Many of the streets in the center are pedestrian-only during the day.

**Day Plan:** You could spend a lot of time going from college to college here—but they all have similar features, so I'd focus on just a few. My top choice is the historically important Christ Church College. Then take a spin through the free Ashmolean Museum, and leave time to sample a pint of local ale at one of the many pubs that dot the town.

To include Blenheim Palace on this day, arrive in Oxford in the morning, head to Blenheim first (by bus), then on your

*The spires of All Souls College, Oxford*

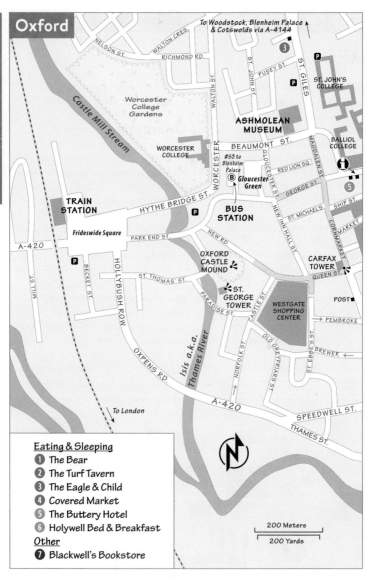

**Oxford**

To Woodstock, Blenheim Palace & Cotswolds via A-4144

Worcester College Gardens

WORCESTER COLLEGE

ASHMOLEAN MUSEUM

ST. JOHN'S COLLEGE

BALLIOL COLLEGE

BEAUMONT ST.

#53 to Blenheim Palace

Gloucester Green

RED LION SQ.

TRAIN STATION

HYTHE BRIDGE ST.

BUS STATION

Frideswide Square

PARK END ST.

NEW RD.

OXFORD CASTLE MOUND

CARFAX TOWER

QUEEN ST.

ST. THOMAS' ST.

ST. GEORGE TOWER

WESTGATE SHOPPING CENTER

POST

PEMBROKE

Isis a.k.a. Thames River

OXPENS RD.

To London

A-420

SPEEDWELL ST.

THAMES ST.

Eating & Sleeping
1. The Bear
2. The Turf Tavern
3. The Eagle & Child
4. Covered Market
5. The Buttery Hotel
6. Holywell Bed & Breakfast
Other
7. Blackwell's Bookstore

200 Meters
200 Yards

return, visit Oxford. Drivers can visit Blenheim on the way in or out of Oxford.

**Getting There:** Oxford is linked by **train** with London (Paddington Station, 2/hour direct, 1 hour), Bath (hourly, 1.25 hours), and Moreton-in-Marsh (every 1-2 hours, 40 minutes). Competing **bus** companies run frequently from London to Oxford's Gloucester Green bus station (2 hours, www.oxfordtube.com or www.oxfordbus.co.uk).

**Arrival in Oxford:** From the **train** station, the city center is a 10-minute walk or a £5 taxi ride; the **bus** station is just 5 minutes from town. **Drivers** day-tripping into Oxford should use one of the outlying

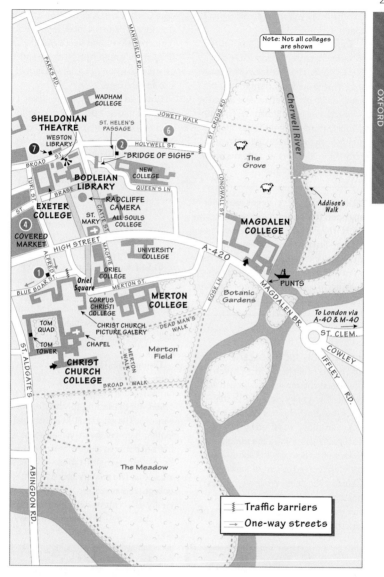

Note: Not all colleges are shown

MANSFIELD RD.

PARKS RD.

WADHAM COLLEGE

SHELDONIAN THEATRE

ST. HELEN'S PASSAGE

WESTON LIBRARY

JOWETT WALK

ST. CROSS RD.

**6**

**7**

BROAD ST.

**2**

HOLYWELL ST.

"BRIDGE OF SIGHS"

The Grove

Cherwell River

BODLEIAN LIBRARY

NEW COLLEGE

QUEEN'S LN.

Addison's Walk

TURL ST.

BRASE ST.

EXETER COLLEGE

RADCLIFFE CAMERA

ST. MARY

ALL SOULS COLLEGE

LONGWALL ST.

MAGDALEN COLLEGE

CATTE ST.

**4**

COVERED MARKET

HIGH STREET

MAGPIE ST.

UNIVERSITY COLLEGE

A-420

ALFRED ST.

**1**

BLUE BOAR ST.

Oriel Square

ORIEL COLLEGE

MERTON ST.

ROSE LN.

PUNTS

MAGDALEN BR.

To London via A-40 & M-40

ST. CLEM.

CORPUS CHRISTI COLLEGE

MERTON COLLEGE

Botanic Gardens

COWLEY RD.

IFFLEY RD.

ST. ALDGATE'S

TOM QUAD

CHRIST CHURCH PICTURE GALERY

DEAD MAN'S WALK

TOM TOWER

CHAPEL

MERTON WALK

Merton Field

CHRIST CHURCH COLLEGE

BROAD WALK

ABINGDON RD.

The Meadow

Traffic barriers
→ One-way streets

park-and-ride lots and take a 10-minute shuttle bus to the center. There's also time-limited pay-and-display street parking north of the Ashmolean Museum, on St. Giles Street.

**Tourist Information:** The TI offers daily "City and University" walking tours (£9, 2 hours), as well as various themed tours—book ahead on summer weekends. If you're headed to **Blenheim Palace,** you can buy tickets here at a discount (Mon-Sat 9:30-17:00, Sun 10:00-15:00, 15 Broad Street, tel. 01865/686-430, www.experienceoxfordshire.org).

**Private Guide:** William Underhill is a good Oxford-educated guide (£45/hour,

£150/half-day, williamunderhill@gmail.com).

**Tours: Blackwell's Walking Tours** focus on literary and historic Oxford (£8, 1.5 hours, check Blackwell's bookstore or website for current tours and times, 48 Broad Street, reserve ahead at www.blackwell.co.uk/oxford). The more casual **Oxford Walking Tours** depart hourly from the Trinity College gates across from the TI (£10, 1.5 hours, www.oxfordwalkingtours.com).

---

Rick's Tip: *Oxford's* **colleges are generally open to visitors,** *but each has its own hours. The entrance to each college is easy to spot—just look for a doorway with crests and a flagpole on the top. Each entry has an office with a porter who can tell you which buildings are open to visitors and if any special events are scheduled.*

---

# Sights

## ▲CHRIST CHURCH COLLEGE

Of Oxford's colleges, Christ Church is the largest and most prestigious. It was founded in 1524 by Henry VIII's chancellor, Cardinal Thomas Wolsey, on the site of an abbey dissolved by the king. The buildings survived the tumult of the Reformation because the abbey and its cathedral served as part of the king's new Church of England. While all colleges boast of their esteemed alumni, none can match Christ Church College: 13 of 26 Oxford-educated prime ministers were Christ Church alums. William Penn (founder of Pennsylvania), John Wesley (influential Methodist leader), John Locke (English Enlightenment thinker), and Charles Dodgson (a.k.a. Lewis Carroll) also studied here.

**Cost and Hours:** £9, family ticket-£16, Mon-Sat 10:00-17:00, Sun 14:00-17:00, last entry 45 minutes before closing, tel. 01865/276-492, located on St. Aldate's. To confirm opening times, call ahead or check the website (www.chch.ox.ac.uk).

**Evensong:** Most evenings in Christ Church Cathedral, an excellent choir service is open to anyone (free, Tue-Sun at 18:00, arrive 15-20 minutes early, Monday service is spoken rather than sung, enter at Tom Tower).

**◑ Self-Guided Tour:** Gentlemen wearing bowler hats, called custodians, are posted around the college to answer questions. You'll be routed along a one-way course with these main stops: dining hall, quadrangle, cathedral, and picture gallery.

**Dining Hall:** There's a Harry Potter commotion as you near the college's famous dining hall (which was the inspiration, not the setting, for the Hogwarts' version). The grand hall—with its splendid Gothic, hammer-beam ceiling and portraits of honored alumni looking down on its oh-so-old-English tables—is an amazing scene. The primary sponsor of the college is centered above the high table: Henry VIII in his younger, slimmer days.

Notice the Alice in Wonderland win-

*Christ Church College*

*Christ Church dining hall*

# Literary Oxford

Oxford has an impressive list of literary alumni:

**J. R. R. Tolkien** (1892-1973), author of *The Hobbit* and *The Lord of the Rings* series, graduated from the university and taught English literature here.

**C. S. Lewis** (1898-1963), best known for *The Chronicles of Narnia*, was an Oxford fellow and Tolkien's friend. Lewis was also the ringleader of the Inklings, a writing society that met at The Eagle and Child pub.

Poet **W. H. Auden** (1907-1973) was another friend of Tolkien's and one of the first critics to praise *The Lord of the Rings*.

Charles Lutwidge Dodgson, better known by his pen name **Lewis Carroll** (1832-1898), taught mathematics at Oxford, where he met young Alice Liddell, the dean's daughter and the inspiration for *Alice's Adventures in Wonderland*.

Literary great **Virginia Woolf** (1882-1941) was banned from using Oxford's library because she was a woman (Oxford didn't begin admitting women until 1920, though they could attend some classes before that). In her essay "A Room of One's Own," she parodied the university she nicknamed "Oxbridge."

**Oscar Wilde** (1854-1900) became famous for his novels (*The Picture of Dorian Gray*), plays (*The Importance of Being Earnest*), homosexuality (his famous trial sent him to jail), and wit.

Oxford's other notable literary stars include poet **Percy Bysshe Shelley, Jonathan Swift** (*Gulliver's Travels*), **T. S. Eliot** (*The Waste Land*), **Aldous Huxley** (*Brave New World*), **John le Carré** (*The Spy Who Came in from the Cold*), **Philip Pullman** (*The Golden Compass*), **Martin Amis** (*Time's Arrow*), **Helen Fielding** (*Bridget Jones's Diary*), and Theodor Seuss Geisel (a.k.a. **Dr. Seuss**).

dow (above the fireplace, on the left), rich with symbolic references to that book. In the upper half (left, in the yellow circle) is the real Alice (Alice Liddell), and opposite (right, in a similar circle) is Lewis Carroll, who was a math professor in the college.

**Quadrangle:** Now enter Tom Quad, a grassy field surrounded by college buildings. In the middle is a small fishpond with a statue of Mercury.

The tall tower, designed by Christopher Wren, holds a seven-ton bell called **Great Tom.** According to tradition, every night at 21:05 the bell clangs out 101 times—each chime calling the curfew for the 101 students who first boarded here. This gives the students 4.5 minutes to get from the pub through the gate by the last ring.

**Cathedral:** The college's 800-year-old chapel also serves as Christ Church Cathedral (the seat of an Anglican bishop). Built in the 12th century, it's one of oldest buildings in Oxford and one of England's smallest cathedrals. For 400 years, this was a monastery church, and it's one of the few to survive the Reformation. Bishop Berkeley (who inspired the founding of a great university in California) and John Wesley (who founded the Methodist Church) both preached from the pulpit here. Vibrant Pre-Raphaelite windows from 1858 by Edward Burne-Jones tell the story of St. Frideswide, an obscure local saint. A 1320 stained-glass window shows the martyrdom of Thomas Becket.

As you exit, you'll be steered around the church cloister, back through the Tom Quad again, and through Peckwater Quad. Note the graffiti on the walls there. This is the only allowable graffiti in Oxford: When rowing teams win, they can chalk their victory on the wall for all to see.

**Picture Gallery:** The sleepy Christ Church Picture Gallery has a good collection that houses a rotating exhibition of drawings and sketches by Albrecht Dürer, Michelangelo, Leonardo da Vinci, Raphael, and other Old Masters. There's also a permanent collection of oil paintings by the likes of Tintoretto, Veronese, Van Dyck, and Frans Hals (£4, £2 if you paid to enter the college; generally open Mon & Wed-Sat 10:30-17:00, Sun 14:00-17:00, closed Tue; if visiting without touring the campus, enter at Canterbury Gate, off Oriel Square).

---

Rick's Tip: *For* **great views** *of Oxford's many spires and colleges, climb the 127 narrow, twisting stairs of the bell tower of the* **University Church of St. Mary the Virgin** *(£4, High Street) or the 99 steps of* **Carfax Tower** *(£2.50, intersection of High and Cornmarket streets).*

---

### ▲▲BODLEIAN LIBRARY

The complex of buildings dominated by the Bodleian Library is where the

*Bodleian Library*

university was born—and where it's run from today. With some 11 million books and more than 100 miles of shelving in its underground stacks, "the Bod" is one of the world's largest and most famous libraries.

Guided tours allow visitors inside some of the Bodleian's historic rooms. Among the highlights is the **Divinity School**—rated ▲▲—the university's first purpose-built classroom, constructed with a magnificent Gothic ceiling in the 15th century, and used for teaching theology. **Duke Humfrey's Library** is a world of creaky old shelves of ancient-looking books, stacked neatly under a beautifully painted wooden ceiling (£6 for 30-minute tour, £8 for 1 hour, best to use Catte Street entrance via the Great Gate, tel. 01865/287-400, www.bodleian.ox.ac.uk/whatson/visit).

### OTHER COLLEGES

For locations of these colleges, see the map on page 224.

**Exeter College** is next to the Bodleian Library, free to visit, and worth a peek. The highlight is its jewel-like Neo-Gothic chapel—oh-so Victorian from the 1860s and inspired by Paris' Sainte-Chapelle. It features William Morris' *The Adoration of the Magi* tapestry (on the right). A bust of J. R. R. Tolkien, who studied here, is in the back (www.exeter.ox.ac.uk).

**All Souls College,** named for the dead of the Hundred Years' War, is notorious for having the toughest entrance exam. Famous alums at this research institution include Lawrence of Arabia and Christopher Wren. Looking through its gate on High Street, you'll see twin spires that resemble Westminster Abbey's (because they were designed by the same man) and, on the far left, an ornate sundial by Christopher Wren (www.asc.ox.ac.uk).

**Balliol College** is one of the oldest (founded 1263), most charming (fine grounds, chapel, and dining hall), and cheapest (£2 admission) of the Oxford colleges. While you'll see better in Oxford, this is a delightful little side-trip if you'd like to pop in (www.balliol.ox.ac.uk).

**Magdalen College** (pronounced "maudlin"), sitting on the upper edge of town, gets my vote for the prettiest in Oxford. Magdalen has the largest grounds of any of the Oxford colleges—big enough to include its own deer park. A relaxing café overlooks the river and lively punting scene. Evensong services take place in the exquisite chapel (Tue-Sun at 18:00 except July-Sept; www.magd.ox.ac.uk).

### ▲▲ASHMOLEAN MUSEUM OF ART AND ARCHAEOLOGY

In 1683, celebrated antiquary Elias Ashmole insisted his collection of curiosities deserved its own building. Half of his trove originated with an even-more-eccentric royal gardener, John Tradescant, who loved to seek out interesting items while traveling in search of plants. Since its founding, this eclectic museum has expanded its reach across art forms, cultures, and centuries. The vast and exceptionally well-presented collection features everything from antiquities to fine porcelain to paintings by some of the Old Masters.

**Cost and Hours:** Free but £4 suggested donation, Tue-Sun 10:00-18:00, closed Mon, audioguide-£3, rooftop café, Beaumont Street, tel. 01865/278-000, www.ashmolean.org.

### PUNTING

Long, flat boats can be rented for punting (pushing with a long pole) along the River Cherwell. Chauffeurs are available, but the do-it-yourself crowd has more fun...even if they get a little wet. Punting looks easier than it is, and you'll likely see first-timers creating log jams of incompetence. The guided ride includes a short lesson so you can actually learn how to do it right.

Cost and Hours: £20/hour per boat, £30 deposit, chauffeured punts-£25 per boat for 30 minutes and up to four people, rowboats and paddle boats available for the less adventurous, cash only, daily Feb-Nov 9:30-dusk, closed Dec-Jan, Magdalen Bridge Boathouse, tel. 01865/202-643).

## Eating and Sleeping

**The Bear,** close to the Christ Church Picture Gallery, is one of Oxford's most charming pubs (corner of Alfred and Blue Boar streets). The big and boisterous **Turf Tavern** is popular for its solid grub and outdoor beer garden (4 Bath Place). **The Eagle and Child** was the gathering place for the likes of J. R. R. Tolkien and C. S. Lewis (49 St. Giles Street). The **Covered Market**—a farmers market maze of shops and stands—has fine selections for lunch or a picnic (between Market and High streets, near Carfax Tower).

If staying the night, **$$$ The Buttery Hotel** has good-value rooms (11 Broad Street, www.thebutteryhotel.co.uk), and the **$$ Holywell Bed & Breakfast** is a real gem, hidden away in an ancient row house (14 Holywell Street, www.holywellbedandbreakfast.com).

*Magdalen College*          *The Bear Pub*

# BEST OF THE REST

## BLENHEIM PALACE

Just 30 minutes' drive from Oxford (and convenient to combine with a drive through the Cotswolds), Blenheim is one of England's best palaces—worth ▲▲▲. The 2,000-acre yard, designed by Lancelot "Capability" Brown, is as majestic to some as the palace itself.

John Churchill, first duke of Marlborough, defeated Louis XIV's French forces at the Battle of Blenheim in 1704. This pivotal event marked a turning point in the centuries-long struggle between the English and the French, and some historians claim that if not for his victory, we'd all be speaking French today. A thankful Queen Anne rewarded Churchill by building him this nice home, perhaps the finest Baroque building in England. Eleven dukes of Marlborough later, the palace is as impressive as ever. In 1874, a later John Churchill's American daughter-in-law, Jennie Jerome, gave birth at Blenheim to another historic baby in that line...and named him Winston.

Rick's Tip: *Americans who call the palace "blen-HEIM" are the butt of jokes.* **It's pronounced "BLEN-em."**

## Orientation

**Day Plan:** Start with the included state rooms tour and Winston Churchill Exhibition (allow 90 minutes to see both). From there, head to the delightful gardens. If you're into all things palatial, add on the private apartment tour (requires a special ticket). If you have limited time, skip the "Untold Story" exhibit. Give the "Churchills' Destiny" a 15-minute walk-through. Late in the afternoon, the palace is relaxed and quiet, even on the busiest of days.

**Getting There:** Blenheim Palace sits at the edge of the cute cobbled town of Woodstock. The train station nearest the palace (Hanborough, 1.5 miles away) has no taxi or bus service.

From **Oxford,** take bus #S3 from the Gloucester Green bus station (2/hour, 30 minutes, www.stagecoachbus.com). It goes to the Blenheim Palace Gates stop, about a half-mile from the palace, and the Woodstock/Marlborough Arms stop, in the heart of Woodstock; this adds a few more minutes' walking than the other bus stop but offers a spectacular approach to the palace and lake.

If you're coming from the **Cotswolds,** your easiest train connection is from Moreton-in-Marsh to Oxford, where you can catch the bus to Blenheim.

**Drivers** should simply head for Woodstock; the palace is well-signposted once in town. Parking is available near the palace.

**Cost and Hours:** £22.50, park and gardens only-£14; family deals; open mid-Feb-Oct daily 10:30-17:30; Nov-mid-Dec Wed-Sun 10:30-17:30. Palace doors close at 16:45, it's "everyone out" at 17:30, and the park closes at 18:00. Recorded info toll-free tel. 0800-849-6500, www.blenheimpalace.com.

Rick's Tip: *You can get* **discounted tickets** *for Blenheim Palace at the TIs in neighboring towns, including Oxford and Moreton-in-Marsh, and even on the #S3 bus from Oxford.*

**Tours:** Guided tours of the state rooms are included with your admission (2/hour, 45 minutes, daily except Sun); free walking tours also run daily in the gardens (11:30, 1 hour, book a spot when you arrive). From Feb-Sept, you can book a tour of the private apartments as well as "Upstairs" and "Downstairs" tours (£6, offered regularly throughout the day, reserve a spot when you arrive or in advance online).

**Eating:** The lovely Water Terraces Café sits at the garden exit for basic lunch and teatime treats.

## ➔ Self-Guided Tour

### STATE ROOMS

Your visit begins in the truly great Great Hall. While you can go "free flow" (reading info plaques and talking with docents in each room), it's better to take the included guided tour of the state rooms.

These most sumptuous rooms in the palace are ornamented with fine porcelain, gilded ceilings, portraits of past dukes, photos of the present duke's family, and "chaperone" sofas designed to give courting couples just enough privacy...but not *too* much.

Enjoy the series of 10 Brussels tapestries that commemorate military victories of the First Duke of Marlborough, including the Battle of Blenheim. After winning that pivotal conflict, he scrawled a quick note on the back of a tavern bill notifying the queen of his victory (you'll see a replica). Finish with the remarkable "long library"—with its tiers of books and stuccoed ceilings.

### WINSTON CHURCHILL EXHIBITION

This is a fascinating display of letters, paintings, and other artifacts of the great statesman, who was born here. Along with lots of intimate artifacts from his life, you'll see the bed in which Sir Winston was born in 1874.

### PRIVATE APARTMENTS

For a behind-the-scenes peek at the palace (book a spot as soon as you arrive), take a 30-minute guided walk through the private apartments of the duke. Tours leave frequently throughout the day—when His Grace is not in.

You'll see a chummy billiards room, luxurious china, servants quarters with 47 call bells (one for each room), private rooms, 18th-century Flemish tapestries, family photos, and more.

### CHURCHILLS' DESTINY

This exhibit in the "stables block" traces the military leadership of two great men who shared the name Churchill: John, who defeated Louis XIV at the Battle of Blenheim in the 18th century, and in whose honor this palace was built; and Winston, who was born in this palace and who won the Battle of Britain and helped defeat Hitler in the 20th century. It's remarkable that two of the most important military victories in the nation's history were overseen by these distant cousins.

### GARDENS

The palace's expansive gardens stretch nearly as far as the eye can see in every direction. From the main courtyard you'll emerge into the **Water Terraces;** from there, you can loop around to the left, behind the palace, to see (but not enter) the Italian Garden. Or, head down to the lake to walk along the waterfront trail; going left takes you to the rose gardens and arboretum, while turning right brings you to the Grand Bridge. You can explore on your own (using the map and good signposting), or join a free tour.

*Blenheim Palace*

# Stratford-upon-Avon

Stratford is Shakespeare's hometown. To see or not to see? Stratford is a must for every big bus tour in England and one of the most popular side-trips from London. English majors and actors are in seventh heaven here. Sure, it's touristy, and nonliterary types might think it's much ado about nothing. But nobody back home would understand if you skipped Shakespeare's house.

Shakespeare connection aside, the town's riverside and half-timbered charm, coupled with its hardworking tourist industry, make Stratford a fun stop. But the play's the thing to bring the Bard to life—and you can see the Royal Shakespeare Company making the most of their state-of-the-art theater complex. Even people who flunked English lit can enjoy a Shakespeare performance here.

Stratford is easy to reach by car—it's made to order for drivers connecting the Cotswolds with points north (Warwick Castle, Liverpool, or the Lake District). Stratford is also well-connected by train or bus to London, Oxford, Warwick, Moreton-in-Marsh, and more.

## STRATFORD IN 1 DAY

Stroll the charming core, and take the 11:00 daily walking tour; you can use the ticket stub to get discounts on attractions (including the combo-ticket for Shakespeare sights) and more.

Visit your choice of Shakespeare sights—Shakespeare's Birthplace is best and easiest. If you want to see all the five main Shakespeare sights, take the hop-on, hop-off bus for the narration and transportation to the outlying sights. (The bus-tour ticket is good for 24 hours; if you start the tour at 14:00 one day, it's good until 14:00 the next day, allowing you to spread out your sightseeing over two days, if you like.)

Walk along the riverfront and feed the swans. You can also rent a boat or a punt, or take a cruise.

Have an early-bird dinner and see a play at night. If you arrive in Stratford one night, spend the day and then stay over a second night, you could see a play both nights.

**With more time:** On your way to or from Stratford, whether you're traveling by car or public transit, Warwick Castle makes an easy and rewarding stop (see page 254).

## STRATFORD AT A GLANCE

### Sights from Shakespeare's Life
Most sights are in Stratford, but Mary Arden's Farm and Anne Hathaway's Cottage are outside of town.

▲▲**Shakespeare's Birthplace** Multimedia presentation on the life of the Bard, including a visit to his family home. **Hours:** Daily April-Oct 9:00-17:00, July-Aug until 18:00, Nov-March 10:00-16:00. See page 241.

▲▲**Mary Arden's Farm** Childhood home of Shakespeare's mother, now an open-air museum on 16th-century farm life, with an enjoyable falconry demonstration. **Hours:** Daily mid-March-Oct 10:00-17:00, visitors must leave by 17:30, closed Nov-mid-March. See page 243.

▲**Anne Hathaway's Cottage** Childhood home of Shakespeare's wife, with a cute cottage and interesting gardens. **Hours:** Daily mid-March-Oct 9:00-17:00, Nov-mid-March 10:00-16:00. See page 244.

**New Place & Nash's House** Garden and foundations of Shakespeare's last home, next door to Nash's House, which hosts exhibits on the Bard. **Hours:** Daily April-Oct 10:00-17:00, Nov-March 11:00-16:00. See page 241.

**Hall's Croft** Upscale home of Shakespeare's eldest daughter, who married a doctor, with displays on 17th-century medicine. **Hours:** Daily April-Oct 10:00-17:00, Nov-March 11:00-16:00. See page 242.

**Shakespeare's Grave** The playwright's tomb, inside a church. **Hours:** April-Sept Mon-Sat 8:30-17:40, Sun 12:30-16:40; Oct-March until 16:40 or 15:40. See page 242.

### More Sights
▲▲**The Royal Shakespeare Theatre** Fascinating venue for seeing Shakespeare's plays (a ▲▲▲ experience), with public areas, theater-history exhibits, backstage tours, eateries, and a tower view. **Hours:** Mon-Sat 10:00-23:00, Sun 10:00-17:00. See page 247.

▲**MAD Museum** Mechanical design museum with interactive machines and displays. **Hours:** Daily 10:30-17:30, off-season until 17:00. See page 250.

**Avon Riverfront** People-friendly setting, with a park, swans, trails, chain ferry, canal boats, cruises, and rentable punts and rowboats. See page 249.

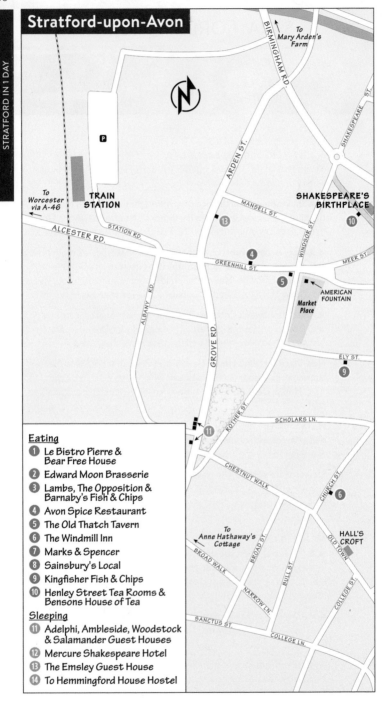

# Stratford-upon-Avon

To Mary Arden's Farm

BIRMINGHAM RD.

SHAKESPEARE ST.

ARDEN ST.

SHAKESPEARE'S BIRTHPLACE

**10**

MANSELL ST.

**13**

WINDSOR ST.

MEER ST.

TRAIN STATION

To Worcester via A-46

ALCESTER RD.

STATION RD.

GREENHILL ST.

**4**

**5**

AMERICAN FOUNTAIN

Market Place

ALBANY RD.

GROVE RD.

ELY ST.

**9**

ROTHER ST.

SCHOLARS LN.

**11**

CHESTNUT WALK

CHURCH ST.

**6**

To Anne Hathaway's Cottage

BROAD WALK

BROAD ST.

BULL ST.

HALL'S CROFT

OLD TOWN

COLLEGE ST.

NARROW LN.

SANCTUS ST.

COLLEGE LN.

## Eating

1. Le Bistro Pierre & Bear Free House
2. Edward Moon Brasserie
3. Lambs, The Opposition & Barnaby's Fish & Chips
4. Avon Spice Restaurant
5. The Old Thatch Tavern
6. The Windmill Inn
7. Marks & Spencer
8. Sainsbury's Local
9. Kingfisher Fish & Chips
10. Henley Street Tea Rooms & Bensons House of Tea

## Sleeping

11. Adelphi, Ambleside, Woodstock & Salamander Guest Houses
12. Mercure Shakespeare Hotel
13. The Emsley Guest House
14. To Hemmingford House Hostel

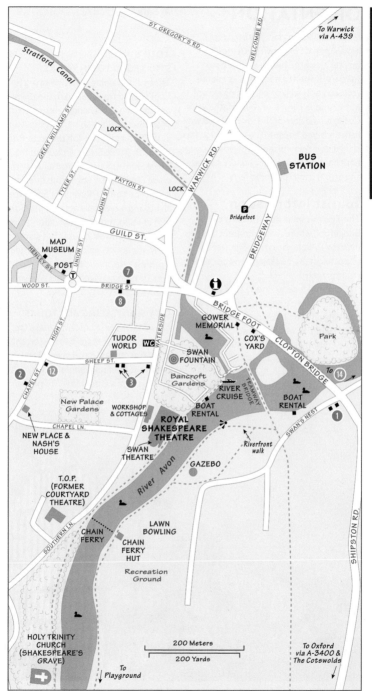

# ORIENTATION

Stratford, with around 30,000 people, has a compact old town, with the TI and theater along the riverbank, and Shakespeare's Birthplace a few blocks inland; you can easily walk to everything except Mary Arden's Farm and Anne Hathaway's Cottage. The core of the town is lined with half-timbered houses. The River Avon has an idyllic yet playful feel, with a park along both banks, paddleboats, hungry swans, and an old crank-powered ferry.

## Tourist Information

The TI is in a small brick building on Bridgefoot, where the main street hits the river (Mon-Sat 9:00-17:30, Sun 10:00-16:00, tel. 01789/264-293, www.discover-stratford.com).

**Combo-Tickets:** The TI sells a discounted "Town, Cottage, and Farm Pass," covering all five Shakespeare Birthplace Trust sights, as well as a special any-three combo-ticket, which gives you entry into your pick of three of the five sights: Shakespeare's Birthplace, Hall's Croft, New Place & Nash's House, Mary Arden's Farm, and Anne Hathaway's Cottage.

## Tours

### STRATFORD TOWN WALKS

These entertaining, award-winning two-hour walks introduce you to the town and its famous playwright. Tours run daily year-round, rain or shine. Just show up at the Swan fountain (on the waterfront, opposite Sheep Street) in front of the Royal Shakespeare Theatre and pay the guide (£6, kids-£3, ticket stub offers discounts on combo-tickets for Shakespeare sights and more, daily at 11:00, Sat-Sun also at 14:00, mobile 07855/760-377, www.stratfordtownwalk.co.uk). The same company offers an evening **ghost walk,** led by a professional magician (£6, kids-£4, Mon and Thu-Sat at 19:30, 1.5 hours, must book in advance).

### CITY SIGHTSEEING BUS TOURS

Open-top buses constantly make the rounds, allowing visitors to hop on and hop off at all the Shakespeare sights. Given the far-flung nature of two of the Shakespeare sights (Mary Arden's Farm

*Stratford-upon-Avon is notable for its half-timbered architecture.*

# William Shakespeare (1564-1616)

To many, William Shakespeare is the greatest author, in any language, period. In one fell swoop, he expanded and helped define modern English—the unrefined tongue of everyday people—and granted it a beauty and legitimacy that put it on par with Latin. In the process, he gave us phrases like "one fell swoop," which we quote without knowing that no one ever said it before Shakespeare wrote it.

Shakespeare was born in Stratford-upon-Avon in 1564 to John Shakespeare and Mary Arden. Though his parents were probably illiterate, Shakespeare is thought to have attended Stratford's grammar school, finishing his education at age 14. When he was 18, he married 26-year-old Anne Hathaway (who was three months pregnant with their daughter Susanna).

The beginning of Shakespeare's writing career is shrouded in mystery. We only know that seven years after his marriage, Shakespeare was living in London as a budding poet, playwright, and actor. He hit the big time, writing and performing for royalty, founding the Globe Theatre (a functioning replica now stands along the Thames' South Bank in London), and raking in enough dough to buy New Place, a mansion back in his hometown. Around 1611, he retired from the theater, moving back to Stratford, where he died at the age of 52.

Using borrowed plots, outrageous puns, and poetic language, Shakespeare wrote comedies (c. 1590—*Taming of the Shrew, As You Like It*), tragedies (c. 1600—*Hamlet, Othello, Macbeth, King Lear*), and fanciful combinations (c. 1610—*The Tempest*), exploring the full range of human emotions and reinventing the English language. Think of his stock of great characters and great lines: Hamlet ("To be or not to be, that is the question"), Othello and his jealousy ("It is the green-eyed monster"), ambitious Mark Antony ("Friends, Romans, countrymen, lend me your ears"), rowdy Falstaff ("The better part of valor is discretion"), and the star-crossed lovers Romeo and Juliet ("But soft, what light through yonder window breaks"). Even today, his characters strike a familiar chord.

His brilliant work, his humble beginnings, and the fact that no original Shakespeare manuscripts survive raise a few scholarly eyebrows. How could a journeyman actor with little education have written so many masterpieces? Perhaps he had help. He was surrounded by other great writers, such as his friend Ben Jonson. Most modern scholars, though, agree that Shakespeare did indeed write the plays and sonnets attributed to him.

His contemporaries had no doubts about Shakespeare—or his legacy. As Jonson wrote in the preface to the First Folio, "He was not of an age, but for all time!"

and Anne Hathaway's Cottage) and the fun and informative commentary, this tour makes the town more manageable. The full 11-stop circuit takes about an hour. Buses alternate between recorded commentary and live guides—for the best tour, wait for a live guide (£13.50, discount with town walk ticket stub, buy tickets on bus or as you board, ticket good for 24 hours, buses leave from the TI every 20 minutes in high season from about 9:30-17:00, every 30 minutes and shorter hours off-season; tel. 01789/412-680, www.citysightseeing-stratford.com).

## Helpful Hints

**Market Days:** A **crafts and food market** runs along the park between the Royal Shakespeare Theater and Bridge Street on Sundays (9:00-16:00).

**Baggage Storage: Mailboxes Etc.,** a 5-minute walk from the train station, can store luggage for day-trippers (Mon-Fri 9:00-17:30, Sat 9:00-16:00, closed Sun, 12a Greenhill Street, tel. 01789/294-968).

**Taxis:** Try **007 Taxis** (tel. 01789/414-007) or the taxi stand on Woodbridge, near the intersection with High Street. To arrange for a private car and driver, contact **Platinum Cars** (£40/hour, tel. 01789/264-626, www.platinum-cars.co.uk).

# SIGHTS

Stratford's five biggest sights are run by the same organization, the Shakespeare Birthplace Trust (www.shakespeare.org.uk). While they are designed to be crowd-pleasers rather than to tickle academics, they're well-run and genuinely interesting. Shakespeare's Birthplace, New Place & Nash's House, and Hall's Croft are in town; Mary Arden's Farm and Anne Hathaway's Cottage are just outside Stratford. Each has a tranquil garden and helpful, eager docents who love to tell a story; and yet, each is quite different, so visiting all five gives you a well-rounded look at the Bard.

If you're here for Shakespeare sightseeing—and have time to venture to the countryside sights—buy the Town, Cottage, and Farm Pass combo-ticket and drop into them all. If your time is more limited, visit only Shakespeare's Birthplace, which is the most convenient (right in the town center) and offers the best historical introduction to the playwright.

**Combo-Tickets:** Admission to the three Shakespeare Birthplace Trust sights in town—Shakespeare's Birthplace, Hall's Croft, and New Place & Nash's House—requires a combo-ticket; no individual tickets are sold. To visit only these three sights, get the £17.50 **Town Houses Pass,** which is sold at the participating sights. To add Anne Hathaway's Cottage and Mary Arden's Farm, you can buy the £26.25 **Town, Cottage, and Farm Pass** (sold at participating sights, good for one year; also available at a discount at the TI); this ticket also includes Holy Trinity Church, with Shakespeare's grave, which usually requests a £3 donation. You can buy individual tickets for Anne Hathaway's Cottage and Mary Arden's Farm (see "Just Outside Stratford," later).

Another option is the £15.50 **any-three combo-ticket,** sold only at the TI. This ticket lets you choose which trio of sights you want to see—for instance, the birthplace, Anne Hathaway's Cottage, and Mary Arden's Farm (buy at TI; you'll get a receipt, then show it at the first sight you visit to receive your three-sight card).

**Discounts:** If you've taken a Stratford town walk (described under "Tours," earlier), show your ticket stub to receive a 30 percent discount off any combo-ticket you buy at the sights. Also, ask your B&B owner if they have any discount vouchers—they often do.

**Closing Times:** What the Shakespeare sights list as their "closing time" is actually their last-entry time. If you show up at the closing time I've noted below, you'll still be able to get in, but with limited time to enjoy the sight.

# In Stratford

▲▲SHAKESPEARE'S BIRTHPLACE

Touring this sight, you'll experience a modern exhibit before seeing Shakespeare's actual place of birth. While the birthplace itself is underwhelming, the exhibit, helpful docents, and sense that Shakespeare's ghost still haunts these halls make it a good introduction to the Bard.

**Cost and Hours:** Covered by combo-tickets, daily April-Oct 9:00-17:00, July-Aug until 18:00, Nov-March 10:00-16:00, café, in town center on Henley Street, tel. 01789/204-016.

**Visiting Shakespeare's Birthplace:** Begin by touring an exhibit that provides an entertaining and easily digestible overview of what made the Bard so great. The exhibit includes a timeline of his plays, movie clips of his works, and information about his upbringing in Stratford, his family life, and his career in London. Historical artifacts, including an original 1623 First Folio of Shakespeare's work, are also on display.

Exit the exhibit into the garden, where you can follow signs to the **birthplace,** a half-timbered Elizabethan building where young William grew up. I find the old house disappointing, as if millions of visitors have rubbed it clean of anything authentic. It was restored in the 1800s, and, while the furnishings seem tacky and modern, they're supposed to be true to 1575, when William was 11. Chat up the well-versed, often-costumed atten-

dants posted in many of the rooms; they are eager to answer questions. You'll be greeted by a guide who offers an introductory talk, then set free to explore on your own. Look for the window etched with the names of decades of important visitors, from Walter Scott to actor Henry Irving.

Shakespeare's father, John—who came from humble beginnings, but bettered himself by pursuing a career in glovemaking (you'll see the window where he sold them to customers on the street)—provided his family with a comfortable, upper-middle-class existence. The guest bed in the parlor was a major status symbol: They must have been rich to afford such a nice bed that wasn't even used every day. This is also the house where Shakespeare and his bride, Anne Hathaway, began their married life together. Upstairs are the rooms where young Will, his siblings, and his parents slept (along with their servants). After Shakespeare's father died and William inherited the building, the thrifty playwright converted it into a pub to make a little money.

Exit into the fine **garden** where Shakespearean **actors** often perform brief scenes (they may even take requests). Pull up a bench and listen, imagining the playwright as a young boy stretching his imagination in this very place.

---

**Rick's Tip:** *Every year on the weekend nearest to* **Shakespeare's birthday** *(traditionally considered to be* **April 23**—*also the day he died), Stratford celebrates. The town hosts free events, including activities for children.*

---

NEW PLACE & NASH'S HOUSE

New Place & Nash's House provide an atmospheric stop on a tour of the Bard's life. About 400 years after his death, visitors can stroll the former foundation and gardens of the mansion Shakespeare called home after he made it big. While nothing remains of the house purchased

*Shakespeare's Birthplace*

in 1597 (it was demolished in the 18th century), the grounds still manage to seduce many visitors. At the least, they have nostalgic value—especially for fans who can picture him writing *The Tempest* on this very spot. Next door, Nash's House (Nash was the first husband of Shakespeare's granddaughter...not exactly a close connection) features items related to its recent excavation and Shakespeare's 19 years living in New Place before he died there in 1616.

**Cost and Hours:** Covered by combo-tickets; daily April-Oct 10:00-17:00, Nov-March 11:00-16:00; Chapel Street, tel. 01789/292-325.

### HALL'S CROFT

This former home of Shakespeare's eldest daughter, Susanna, is in Stratford town center. A fine old Jacobean house, it's the fanciest of the group. Since she married a doctor, the exhibits here are focused on 17th-century medicine. If you have time to spare and one of the combo-tickets, it's worth a quick pop-in. To make the exhibits interesting, ask the docent for the 15- to 20-minute introduction, or follow one of the large laminated self-guides, both of which help bring the plague—and some of the bizarre remedies of the time—to life.

**Cost and Hours:** Covered by combo-tickets, same hours as New Place & Nash's House, on-site tearoom, between Church Street and the river on Old Town Street, tel. 01789/338-533.

### SHAKESPEARE'S GRAVE

To see his final resting place, head to the riverside Holy Trinity Church. Shakespeare was a rector for this church when he died. While the church is surrounded by an evocative graveyard, the Bard is entombed in a place of honor, right in front of the altar inside. The church marks the ninth-century birthplace of the town, which was once a religious settlement.

**Cost and Hours:** £3 suggested donation; covered by Town, Cottage, and Farm Pass; April-Sept Mon-Sat 8:30-17:40, Sun 12:30-16:40; Oct-March until 16:40 or 15:40, 10-minute walk past the theater—see its graceful spire as you gaze down the river, tel. 01789/266-316, www.stratford-upon-avon.org.

## Just Outside Stratford

To reach Mary Arden's Farm or Anne Hathaway's Cottage, either drive or take the hop-on, hop-off bus (see "Tours," earlier)—unless you're staying at one of the Grove Road B&Bs, an easy 20-minute walk from Anne Hathaway's Cottage. Both sights are well-signposted (with brown signs) from major streets and ring roads around Stratford. If driving between

*Nash's House*

*Shakespeare's grave*

the sights, ask for directions at the sight you're leaving.

### ▲▲MARY ARDEN'S FARM

Along with Shakespeare's Birthplace, this is my favorite of the Shakespearean sights. Famous as the girlhood home of William's mom, this homestead is in Wilmcote (about three miles from Stratford). Built around two historic farmhouses, it's an open-air folk museum depicting 16th-century farm life...which happens to have ties to Shakespeare. The Bard is basically an afterthought here.

**Cost and Hours:** £13.25, covered by combo-ticket, daily mid-March–Oct 10:00-17:00, visitors must leave by 17:30, closed Nov-mid-March, tel. 01789/293-455.

**Visiting Mary Arden's Farm:** The museum hosts many special **events,** including the falconry show described below. The day's events are listed on a chalkboard by the entry, or you can call ahead to find out what's on. There are always plenty of activities to engage kids: It's an active, hands-on place.

Pick up a map at the entrance and wander from building to building, through farmhouses with good displays about farm life. Throughout the complex, you'll see period interpreters in Tudor costumes. They'll likely be going through the day's chores as people back then would have done—activities such as milking the sheep and cutting wood to do repairs on the house. They're happy to answer questions and provide fun, gossipy insight into

## Stratford Thanks America

Residents of Stratford are thankful for the many contributions Americans have made to their city and its heritage. Along with pumping up the economy day in and day out with tourist visits, Americans paid for half the rebuilding of the Royal Shakespeare Theatre after it burned down in 1926. The Swan Theatre renovation was funded entirely by American aid. Harvard University inherited—you guessed it—the Harvard House, and it maintains the house today. London's much-loved theater, Shakespeare's Globe, was the dream (and gift) of an American. And there's even an odd but prominent "American Fountain" overlooking Stratford's market square on Rother Street, which was given in 1887 to celebrate the Golden Jubilee of the rule of Queen Victoria.

what life was like at the time.

The first building, **Palmer's farm** (mistaken for Mary Arden's home for hundreds of years, and correctly identified in 2000), is furnished as it would have been in Shakespeare's day. Step into the kitchen to see food being prepared over an open fire—at 13:00 each day the "servants"

*Mary Arden's Farm*

*Falconry demonstration*

(employees) sit down in the adjacent dining room for a traditional dinner.

Mary Arden actually lived in the neighboring **farmhouse,** covered in brick facade and seemingly less impressive. The house is filled with kid-oriented activities, including period dress-up clothes, board games from Shakespeare's day, and a Tudor alphabet so kids can write their names in fancy lettering.

Of the many events here, the most enjoyable is the **falconry demonstration,** with lots of mean-footed birds (daily, usually at 11:15, 12:15, 13:00 and 16:00). Chat with the falconers about their methods for earning the birds' trust. The birds' hunger sets them to flight (a round-trip earns the bird a bit of food; the birds fly when hungry—but don't have the energy if they're *too* hungry). If things are slow, ask if you can feed one.

▲**ANNE HATHAWAY'S COTTAGE**
Located 1.5 miles out of Stratford (in Shottery), this home is a 12-room farmhouse where the Bard's wife grew up. William courted Anne here—she was 26,

he was only 18—and his tactics proved successful. (Maybe a little too much, as she was several months pregnant at their wedding.) Their 34-year marriage produced two more children, and lasted until his death in 1616 at age 52. The Hathaway family lived here for 400 years, until 1911, and much of the family's 92-acre farm remains part of the sight.

**Cost and Hours:** £10.25, covered by combo-ticket, daily mid-March-Oct 9:00-17:00, Nov-mid-March 10:00-16:00, tel. 01789/338-532.

**Getting There:** It's a 30-minute walk from central Stratford (20 minutes from the Grove Road B&Bs), a stop on the hop-on, hop-off tour bus, or a quick taxi ride from downtown Stratford (around £5). Drivers will find it well-signposted entering Stratford from any direction, with easy £1 parking.

**Visiting Anne Hathaway's Cottage:** After buying your ticket, turn right and head down through the garden to the thatch-roofed **cottage,** which looks cute enough to eat. The house offers an intimate peek at life in Shakespeare's day. In

*Anne Hathaway's Cottage*

## The Look of Stratford

Take time to appreciate the look of the town of Stratford itself. While the main street goes back to Roman times, the key date for the city was 1196, when the king gave the town "market privileges." Stratford was shaped by its marketplace years. The market's many "departments" were located on logically named streets: Sheep Street, Corn Street, and so on. Today's street plan—and even the 57' 9" width of the lots—survives from the 12th century. (Some of the modern storefronts in the town center are still that exact width.)

Starting in about 1600, three great fires gutted the town, leaving few buildings older than that era. After those fires, tinderbox thatch roofs were prohibited—the Old Thatch Tavern on Greenhill Street predates the law and is the only remaining thatch roof in town.

Bridge Street, the oldest street in town, looks the youngest. Its buildings retain the 19th-century Regency style—a result of a rough little middle row of wattle-and-daub houses being torn down in the 1820s to double the street's width.

Throughout Stratford, you'll see striking black-and-white half-timbered buildings, as well as half-timbered structures that were partially plastered over and covered up in the 19th century. During Victorian times, the half-timbered style was considered low-class, but in the 20th century—just as tourists came, preferring ye olde style—timbers came back into vogue, and the plaster was removed. Any black and white you see is likely to be modern paint. The original coloring was "biscuit yellow" and brown.

some ways, it feels even more authentic than his birthplace, and it's fun to imagine the writer of some of the world's greatest romances wooing his favorite girl right here during his formative years. Docents are posted in the first and last rooms to provide meaning and answer questions; while most tourists just stampede through, you'll have a more informative visit if you pause to listen to their introduction in the parlor and commentary throughout the house. (If the place shakes, a tourist has thunked his or her head on the low beams.)

Maybe even more interesting than the cottage are the **gardens,** which have several parts (including a prizewinning "traditional cottage garden"). Follow the signs to the "Woodland Walk" (look for the Singing Tree on your way), along with a fun sculpture garden littered with modern interpretations of Shakespearean characters (such as Falstaff's mead gut, and a great photo-op statue of the British Isles sliced out of steel). From April through June, the gardens are at their best, with birds chirping, bulbs in bloom, and a large sweet-pea display. You'll also find a music trail, a butterfly trail, and—likely—rotating exhibits, generally on a gardening theme.

## The Royal Shakespeare Company

The Royal Shakespeare Company (RSC), undoubtedly the best Shakespeare company on earth, performs year-round in Stratford and in London. Seeing a play here in the Bard's birthplace is a must for Shakespeare fans, and a memorable experience for anybody. Between its excellent acting and remarkable staging, the RSC makes Shakespeare as accessible and enjoyable as it gets.

The RSC makes it easy to take in a play, thanks to their very user-friendly website, painless ticket-booking system, and chock-a-block schedule that fills the summer with mostly big-name Shakespeare plays (plus a few more obscure titles to please the die-hard aficionados). Except in January and February, there's almost always something playing.

The RSC is enjoying renewed popularity this decade after the 2011 opening of its cutting-edge Royal Shakespeare Theatre. Even if you're not seeing a play, exploring this cleverly designed theater building is well worth your time. The smaller attached Swan Theatre hosts plays on a more intimate scale, with only about 400 seats.

### ▲▲▲Seeing a Play

Performances take place most days (Mon-Sat generally at 19:15 at the Royal Shakespeare Theatre or 19:30 at the Swan, matinees around 13:15 at the RST or 13:30 at the Swan, sporadic Sun shows). Shows generally last three hours or more, with one intermission; for an evening show, don't count on getting back to your B&B much before 23:00. There's no strict dress code—and people dress casually (nice jeans and short-sleeve shirts are fine)—but shorts are discouraged. You can buy a program for £4. If you're feeling bold, buy a £5 standing ticket and then slip into an open seat as the lights dim—if nothing is available during the play's first half, something might open up after intermission.

**Getting Tickets:** Tickets range from £5 (standing) to £60, with most around £40. Saturday evening shows—the most popular—are most expensive. You can book tickets as you like it: online (www.rsc.org.uk), by phone (tel. 01789/403-493), or in person at the box office (Mon-Sat 10:00-20:00, Sun 10:00-17:00). Pay by credit card, get a confirmation number, then pick up your tickets at the theater 30 minutes before "curtain up." Because it's so easy to get tickets online or by phone, it makes absolutely no sense to pay extra to book tickets through any other source.

Tickets go on sale months in advance. Saturdays and very famous plays (such as *Romeo and Juliet* or *Hamlet*)—or any play with a well-known actor—sell out the fastest; the earlier in the week the performance is, the longer it takes to sell out (Thursdays sell out faster than Mondays, for example). Before your trip, check the schedule on their website, and consider buying tickets if something strikes your fancy. But demand is difficult to predict, and some tickets do go unsold. On a past visit, on a sunny Friday in June, the riverbank was crawling with tourists. I stepped into the RSC on a lark to see if they had any tickets. An hour later, I was watching King Lear lose his marbles.

Even if there aren't any seats available, you may be able to buy a returned ticket on the same day of an otherwise sold-out show. Also, the few standing-room tickets in the main theater are sold only on the day of the show. While you can check at the box office anytime during the day, it's best to go either when it opens at 10:00 (daily) or between 17:30 and 18:00 (Mon-Sat). Be prepared to wait.

## Visiting the Theaters
### ▲▲THE ROYAL SHAKESPEARE THEATRE

The RSC's main venue reopened in 2011 after it was updated head to toe, with both a respect for tradition and a sensitivity to the needs of contemporary theatergoers. You need to take a guided tour (explained later) to see the backstage areas, but you're welcome to wander the theater's public areas anytime the building is open. Interesting tidbits of theater history and easy-to-miss special exhibits make this one of Stratford's most fascinating sights. If you're seeing a play here, come early to poke around the building. Even if you're not, step inside and explore.

**Cost and Hours:** Free entry, Mon-Sat 10:00-23:00, Sun 10:00-17:00.

**Guided Tours:** Well-informed RSC volunteers lead entertaining, one-hour building tours. Some cover the main theater while others take you into behind-the-scenes spaces, such as the space-age control room (try for a £8.50 behind-the-scenes tour, but if those aren't running, consider a £6.50 front-of-the-house tour—which skips the backstage areas; tour schedule varies by day, depending on performances, but there's often one at 9:15—call, check online, or go to box office to confirm schedule; best to book ahead, tel. 01789/403-493, www.rsc.org.uk).

**Background:** The flagship theater of the RSC has an interesting past. The original Victorian-style theater was built in 1879 to honor the Bard, but it burned down in 1926. The big Art Deco-style building you see today was erected in 1932 and outfitted with a stodgy Edwardian "picture frame"-style stage, even though a more dynamic "thrust"-style stage—better for engaging the audience—was the actors' choice. (It would also have been closer in design to Shakespeare's original Globe stage, which jutted into the crowd.)

The latest renovation addressed this ill-conceived design, adding an updated thrust-style stage. They've left the shell of the 1930s theater, but given it an unconventional deconstructed-industrial style, with the seats stacked at an extreme vertical pitch. Though smaller, the redesigned theater can seat about the same size audience as before (1,048 seats), and now there's not a bad seat in the house—no matter what, you're no more than 50 feet from the stage (the cheapest "gallery"

*The Royal Shakespeare Theatre*

seats look down right onto Othello's bald spot). Productions are staged to play to all the seats throughout the show. Those sitting up high appreciate different details from those at stage level, and vice versa.

**Visiting the Theater:** From the main lobby and box office/gift shop area, there's plenty to see. First head left. In the circular **atrium** between the brick wall of the modern theater and fragments of the previous theater, notice the ratty old floorboards. These were pried up from the 1932 stage and laid down here—so as you wait for your play, you're treading on theater history. Upstairs on level 2, find the **Paccar Room,** with generally excellent temporary exhibits assembled from the RSC's substantial collection of historic costumes, props, manuscripts, and other theater memorabilia. Continue upstairs to level 3 to the Rooftop Restaurant (described later). High on the partition that runs through the restaurant, facing the brick theater wall, notice the four **chairs** affixed to the wall. These are original seats from the earlier theater, situated where the back row used to be (90 feet from the stage)—illustrating how much more audience-friendly the new design is.

Back downstairs, pass through the box office/gift shop area to find the **Swan Gallery**—an old, Gothic-style Victorian space that survives from the original 1879 Memorial Theatre and hosts rotating exhibitions.

Back outside, across the street from the theater, notice the building with the steep gable and huge door (marked *CFE 1887*). This was built as a **workshop** for building sets, which could be moved in large pieces to the main theater. To this day, all the sets, costumes, and props are made here in Stratford. The row of **cottages** to the right is housing for actors. The RSC's reputation exerts enough pull to attract serious actors from all over the UK and beyond, who live here for the entire season. The RSC uses a repertory company approach, where the same actors

appear in multiple shows concurrently. Today's Lady Macbeth may be tomorrow's Rosalind.

**Tower View:** For a God's-eye view of all of Shakespeare's houses, ride the elevator to the top of the RSC's **tower** (£2.50, buy ticket at box office, closes 30 minutes before the theater). Aside from a few sparse exhibits, the main attraction here is the 360-degree view over the theater building, the Avon, and the lanes of Stratford.

**The Food's the Thing:** The main theater has a casual café with a terrace overlooking the river (£3-5 sandwiches, daily 10:00-21:00), as well as the fancier Rooftop Restaurant, which counts the Queen as a patron (£5-15 lunch menu; dinner-£20 two-course meal, £24 three-course meal; Mon-Sat 11:30 until late, Sun 12:00-18:00, dinner reservations smart, tel. 01789/403-449, www.rsc-rooftop-restaurant.co.uk).

### THE SWAN THEATRE

Adjacent to the RSC Theatre is the smaller (about 400 seats), Elizabethan-style Swan Theatre, named not for the birds that fill the park out front, but for the Bard's nickname—the "sweet swan of Avon." This galleried playhouse opened in 1986, thanks to an extremely generous donation from an American theater lover. It has a vertical layout and a thrust stage similar to the RSC Theatre, but its wood trim and railings give it a cozier, more traditional feel. The Swan is used for lesser-known Shakespeare plays and alternative works. Occasionally, the lowest level of seats is removed to accommodate "groundling" (standing-only) tickets, much like Shakespeare's Globe in London.

### TOP (FORMER COURTYARD THEATRE)

A two-minute walk down Southern Lane from the original Royal Shakespeare Theatre, the Courtyard Theatre (affectionately called the "rusty shed" by locals) was built as a replacement venue while the RSC was being renovated. It was used as a prototype for the main theater—a testing ground for the lights, seats, and structure of its big brother. Now it's being converted into an alternative, studio theater-type venue called The Other Place (TOP), which will showcase new writing and experimental works. Part of the building is also used for rehearsal space and a costume shop. The theater should be open by the time you visit, with plays, tours, and yet another opportunity to appreciate the legacy of Stratford's most famous native son.

## Other Sights

### AVON RIVERFRONT

The River Avon is a playground of swans and canal boats. The swans have been the mascots of Stratford since 1623, when, seven years after the Bard's death, Ben Jonson's poem in the First Folio dubbed him "the sweet swan of Avon." Join in the bird-scene fun and buy **swan food** to feed swans and ducks (sold at the TI for £1, and possibly by other vendors—ask around). Don't feed the Canada geese, which locals disdain (they say the geese are vicious and have been messing up the eco-balance since they were imported by a king in 1665).

For a nice **riverfront walk,** consider crossing over the Tramway Footbridge and following the trail to the right (west) along the south bank of the Avon. From here, you'll get a great view of the Royal Shakespeare Theatre across the river. Continuing down the path, you'll pass the lawn bowling club (guest players welcome, £3, Tue and Thu 14:00-16:00) and Lucy's Mill Weir, an area popular with fishers and kayakers, where you can turn around. On the way back, cross the river by chain ferry (£0.50) and return to the town center via the north bank for a full loop.

In the water you'll see colorful **canal boats.** These boats saw their workhorse days during the short window of time between the start of the Industrial Revolution and the establishment of the railways. Today, they're mostly pleasure boats. The boats are long and narrow, so two can pass in the slim canals. There are 2,000 miles of canals in England's Midlands, built to connect centers of industry with seaports and provide vital transportation during the early days of the Industrial Revolution. Stratford was as far inland as you could sail on natural rivers from Bristol; it was the terminus of

*Swans and canal boats populate the River Avon.*

the man-made Birmingham Canal, built in 1816. Even today you can motor your canal boat all the way to London from here. Along the embankment, look for the signs indicating how many hours it'll take—and how many locks you'll traverse—to go by boat to various English cities.

For a little bit of mellow river action, **rent a rowboat** (£5/hour per person) or, for more of a challenge, pole yourself around on a Cambridge-style **punt** (canal is poleable—only 4 or 5 feet deep; same price as the rowboat and more memorable/embarrassing if you do the punting—don't pay £10/30 minutes per person for a waterman to do the punting for you). You can rent these boats at the Swan's Nest Boathouse across the Tramway Footbridge; another rental station, along the river, next to the theater, has higher prices but is more conveniently located.

You can also try a sleepy 40-minute **river cruise** (£5.50, includes commentary, Avon Boating, board boat in Bancroft Gardens near the RSC theater, tel. 01789/267-073, www.avon-boating. co.uk), or jump on the oldest surviving **chain ferry** (c. 1937) in Britain, which shuttles people across the river just beyond the theater (£0.50).

The old **Cox's Yard,** a riverside timber yard until the 1990s, is a rare physical remnant of the days when Stratford was an industrial port. Today, Cox's has been taken over by a pricey, sprawling restaurant complex, with a steakhouse, a burger stand, a milkshake shop, lots of outdoor seating, and occasional live music. Upstairs is the Attic Theatre, which puts on fringe theater acts (www. treadtheboardstheatre.co.uk).

In the riverfront park, roughly between Cox's Yard and the TI, the **Gower Memorial** honors the Bard and his creations. Named for Lord Ronald Gower, the man who paid for and sculpted the memorial, this 1888 work shows Shakespeare up top ringed by four of his most indelible creations, each representing a human pursuit: Hamlet (philosophy), Lady Macbeth (tragedy), Falstaff (comedy), and Prince Hal (history). Originally located next to the theater, it was moved here after the 1932 fire.

### ▲MAD MUSEUM

A refreshing change of pace in Bard-bonkers Stratford, this museum's name stands for "Mechanical Art and Design." It celebrates machines as art, showcasing a changing collection of skillfully constructed robots, gizmos, and Rube-Goldberg machines that spring to entertaining life with the push of a button. Engaging for kids, riveting for engineers, and enjoyable to anybody, it's pricey but conveniently located near Shakespeare's Birthplace.

**Cost and Hours:** £6.80, daily 10:30-17:30, off-season until 17:00, last entry 45 minutes before closing, 45 Hanley Street, tel. 01789/269-356, www. themadmuseum.co.uk.

# EATING

## Restaurants

Stratford's numerous restaurants vie for your pre-theater business, with special hours and meal deals. Most offer light two- and three-course menus before 19:00. You'll find many hardworking places on Sheep Street and Waterside.

**Le Bistro Pierre,** across the river near the boating station, is an impressive French eatery with indoor or outdoor seating and slow service (£11 two-course lunches; £15 two-course meals before

18:45, otherwise £13-17 main courses; Mon-Fri 12:00-15:00 & 17:00-22:30, Sat 12:00-16:00 & 17:00-23:00, Sun 12:30-16:30 & 18:00-22:00, Swan's Nest, Bridge-foot, tel. 01789/264-804). The pub next door, **Bear Free House,** shares the same kitchen, but offers a different menu.

**Edward Moon** is an upscale English brasserie serving signature dishes like steak-and-ale pies and roasted lamb shank in a setting reminiscent of *Casablanca* (£6-7 starters, £12-18 main courses, Mon-Thu 12:00-14:30 & 17:00-21:30, Fri 12:00-15:00 & 17:00-20:00, Sun 12:00-15:00 & 17:00-21:00, closed Sat, 9 Chapel Street, tel. 01789/267-069, www.moonsrestaurants.com).

The next three places, part of the same chain, line up along **Sheep Street,** offering trendy ambience and modern English cuisine at relatively high prices (all three have pre-theater menus before 19:00—£14 two-course meal, £18 for three courses). **Lambs** is intimate and serves meat, fish, and veggie dishes with panache. The upstairs feels dressy, under low half-timbered beams (£13-20 main courses, Mon-Fri 17:00-21:00, Sat 16:30-21:30, Sun 18:00-21:00, lunch served Tue-Sun, 12 Sheep Street, tel. 01789/292-554). **The Opposition,** next door, has a less formal bistro ambience (£9-11 light meals, £14-20 main courses; Mon-Sat 12:00-14:00 & 17:00-21:00, Fri-Sat until 22:30, closed Sun; book in advance if you want to have a post-theater dinner here on Fri or Sat, tel. 01789/269-980). **The Vintner,** just up the street, has the best reputation and feels even trendier than its siblings. It's known for its £12 burgers (£9-11 light meals, £12-18 main courses, daily 9:30-22:00, until 21:30 Sun, 4 Sheep Street, tel. 01789/297-259).

**Avon Spice** has a good reputation for Indian food at good prices (£7-10 main courses, daily 17:00-23:30, until later Fri-Sat, 7 Greenhill Street, tel. 01789/267-067).

# Pubs

**The Old Thatch Tavern** serves up London-based Fuller's brews. The atmosphere is cozy, and the food is a cut above what you'll get in the other pubs; enjoy it either in the bar, in the tight, candlelit restaurant, or on the quiet patio (£10-12 main courses, food served Mon-Sat 12:00-21:00, Sun 12:00-15:00 & 17:00-21:00, on Greenhill Street overlooking the market square, tel. 01789/295-216).

**The Windmill Inn** serves decent, modestly-priced fare in a 17th-century inn. It's a few steps beyond the heart of the tourist zone, so it attracts locals as well. Order drinks and food at the bar, settle into a comfy chair, or head to the half-timbered courtyard (£8-10 pub grub, food served daily 11:00-22:00, Church Street, tel. 01789/297-687).

# Picnics

A picnic at Stratford's inviting riverfront park is a fine way to spend a midsummer night's eve. For groceries or prepared foods, find **Marks & Spencer** on Bridge Street (Mon-Sat 8:00-18:00, Sun 10:30-16:30, small coffee-and-sandwiches café upstairs, tel. 01789/292-430). Across the street, **Sainsbury's Local** stays open later than other supermarkets in town (daily 7:00-22:00).

**Barnaby's** is a greasy fast-food joint near the waterfront—but it's convenient if you want to get takeout for the riverside park just across the street (£5-8 fish-and-chips, daily 11:00-19:30, at Sheep Street and Waterside). For better food (but a less convenient location closer to my recommended B&Bs than to the park), queue up with the locals at **Kingfisher** for the freshly battered haddock (£6-7 fish-and-chips, Mon-Sat 11:30-13:45 & 17:00-22:00, closed Sun, a long block up at 13 Ely Street, tel. 01789/292-513).

# Tearoom

**Henley Street Tea Rooms,** across the street from Shakespeare's Birthplace, has indoor seating, outdoor tables, and friendly service (£4.50 cream tea, £13 afternoon tea, teas available all day, daily 9:00-17:30, Sept-March until 17:00, 40 Henley Street, tel. 01789/415-572). The same people run **Bensons House of Tea & Gift Shop,** just down the street (at #33).

# SLEEPING

Ye olde timbered hotels are scattered throughout the city center. Most B&Bs are a short walk away on the fringes of town, on the busy ring roads that route traffic away from the center. (The recommended places below generally have double-paned windows for rooms in the front, but still get some traffic noise.)

Fridays and Saturdays are busy throughout the season, but the weekend on or near Shakespeare's birthday (April 23) is particularly tight.

## On Grove Road

At the edge of town on busy Grove Road, across from a grassy square, these accommodations come with free parking when booked in advance. From here, it's about a 10-minute walk either to the town center or to the train station (opposite directions).

**$$$ Adelphi Guest House** provides a warm welcome, homemade gingerbread, and original art in every room (Db-£85-100, family rooms, 2 percent surcharge on credit cards, 10 percent discount if you stay at least 2 nights—mention this book when you reserve, 39 Grove Road, tel. 01789/204-469, www.adelphi-guesthouse.com, info@adelphi-guesthouse.com).

**$$ Ambleside Guest House** is run with quiet efficiency and attentiveness. Each of the seven rooms has been completely renovated, including the small but tidy bathrooms (Db-£60-80, family rooms, ground-floor rooms, 41 Grove Road, tel. 01789/297-239, www.

> ### Sleep Code
>
> **Price Rankings for Double Rooms (Db)**
>
> $$$ Most rooms £90 or more
> $$ £60-90
> $ £60 or less
>
> **Abbreviations:** Db=Double with bathroom. D=Double with bathroom down the hall.
>
> **Notes**: Room prices change; verify rates online or by email. For the best prices, book direct with the hotel.

amblesideguesthouse.com, peter@amblesideguesthouse.com—include your phone number in your request, since they like to call you back to confirm).

**$$ Woodstock Guest House** is a friendly, frilly, family-run, place with five comfortable rooms (Db-£60-85, family rooms, ground-floor room, get Rick Steves discount if you stay 2 or more nights—mention this book when you reserve, 5 percent surcharge on credit cards, 30 Grove Road, tel. 01789/299-881, www.woodstock-house.co.uk, jackie@woodstock-house.co.uk).

**$ Salamander Guest House** rents eight simple rooms a bit cheaper than their neighbors (Db-£50-65, family rooms, suite, 40 Grove Road, tel. 01789/205-728, www.salamanderguesthouse.co.uk, p.delin@btinternet.com).

## Elsewhere in Stratford and Beyond

**$$$ Mercure Shakespeare Hotel,** centrally located in a black-and-white building just up the street from New Place & Nash's House, has 78 business-class rooms, each named for a Shakespearean play or character. Some of the rooms are old-style Elizabethan with modern finishes, while others are contemporary (standard Db-£110-140, deluxe Db-£140-170, prices soft depending on demand, breakfast extra, pay parking, Chapel Street, tel. 01789/294-997, www.mercure.com, h6630-re@accor.com).

**$$ The Emsley Guest House** holds five bright modern rooms in a homey and inviting atmosphere (Db-£70-90, family rooms, no kids under 5, free off-street parking, 5 minutes from station at 4 Arden Street, tel. 01789/299-557, www.theemsley.co.uk, mel@theemsley.co.uk).

**$ Hemmingford House,** a hostel with 134 beds and some double rooms, is a 10-minute bus ride from town (dorm bed-£17-28, breakfast extra; take bus #15, #18, or #18A two miles to Alveston; tel. 01789/297-093, www.yha.org.uk/hostel/stratford-upon-avon, stratford@yha.org.uk).

# TRANSPORTATION

## Arriving and Departing
### By Train
Get off at the Stratford-upon-Avon station (not the Stratford Parkway station). Exit straight ahead from the train station, bear right up the stairs, then turn left and follow the main drag straight to the river. (For the Grove Road B&Bs, turn right at the first big intersection.) Train info: tel. 0345-748-4950, www.nationalrail.co.uk.

---

**Rick's Tip:** *If you're coming by train or bus, be sure to* **request a ticket for "Stratford-upon-Avon,"** *not just "Stratford" (to avoid a mix-up with Stratford Langthorne, near London, which hosted the 2012 Olympics and now boasts a huge park where the games were held).*

---

**Train Connections to: London** (3/day direct, more with transfers, 2-2.5 hours, to Marylebone Station), **Liverpool** (2/hour, 3 hours), **Warwick** (8/day, 30 minutes, more with transfer in Birmingham), **Oxford** (every 2 hours, 1.5 hours, change in Leamington Spa or Banbury), **Moreton-in-Marsh** (hourly, 1.5-3 hours, complicated with 3 transfers and expensive; better by bus).

### By Bus
Most intercity buses stop on Stratford's Bridge Street (a block up from the TI). For bus info that covers all the region's companies, call Traveline at tel. 0871-200-2233 (www.travelinemidlands.co.uk).

**Bus Connections to: Cotswolds** towns (bus #21 or #22, Mon-Sat 8/day, none on Sun, 35 minutes to **Chipping Campden,** 1-1.5 hours to **Moreton-in-Marsh;** Johnsons Coaches, tel. 01564/797-070, www.johnsonscoaches.co.uk), **Warwick** (#X16 is fastest, hourly, 30 minutes, also slower #X15/#X18, tel. 01788/535-555, www.stagecoachbus.com).

### By Car
If you're sleeping in Stratford, ask your B&B about **parking** (many have a few free parking spaces, but it's best to reserve ahead). If you're just here for the day, you'll find plenty of lots scattered around town, such as the Bridgefoot garage—big, easy, cheap, and a block from the TI.

Before or after seeing Stratford, **Warwick** makes a fine stop; it's only eight miles away (the castle is just south of town).

To head north to **Liverpool** or **Keswick** (the Lake District), you'll end up on the M-6. The highway divides into the free M-6 and an "M-6 Toll" road, designed to help drivers cut through the Birmingham traffic chaos. Take the toll road—it's a small price to pay to avoid the traffic (www.m6toll.co.uk). Stay relentlessly on the M-6 (direction: North West); exits for Liverpool and Keswick are clearly signed.

# NEAR STRATFORD-UPON-AVON

# WARWICK CASTLE

Just north of Stratford, you'll find England's single most spectacular medieval castle: Warwick (WAR-ick). This masterpiece, which has been turned into a virtual theme park, is extremely touristy—but it's also historic and fun, and may well be Britain's most kid-friendly experience. With a lush, grassy moat and fairy-tale fortifications, Warwick Castle will entertain you from dungeon to lookout.

The town of Warwick, huddled protectively against the castle walls, is a half-timbered delight. Warwick is an ideal on-the-way destination—lash it onto your itinerary as you head north from Stratford.

## Orientation

Warwick is small and manageable. The castle and old town center sit side by side, with the train station about a mile to the north. From the castle's main gate, a lane leads into the old town center a block away, where you'll find the TI and plenty of eateries.

**Day Plan:** Warwick Castle deserves at least three hours, but it can be an all-day outing for families. You can tour the sumptuous staterooms, climb the towers and ramparts for the views, stroll through themed exhibits populated by aristocratic wax figures, explore the sprawling grounds and gardens, and—best of all—interact with costumed docents who explain the place and perform fantastic demonstrations of medieval weapons and other skills.

**Getting There:** Warwick is easy for **drivers**—the main Stratford-Coventry road cuts right through Warwick. If you're coming from Stratford (8 miles to the south), you'll hit the castle parking lots first (£6-10, buy token from machines at the castle entrance). Plenty of other less-expensive lots are scattered throughout Warwick.

From Stratford-upon-Avon, choose between hourly **buses** (30 minutes, bus #X16, www.stagecoachbus.com) or frequent **trains** (8/day, 30 minutes). Direct trains from London's Marylebone Station take 1.5 hours (1-2/hour direct).

Warwick has two train stations—you want the one called "Warwick" (Warwick Parkway Station is farther from the castle). To reach the castle or town center from the station, take a **taxi** (£5) or **walk** (1 mile).

**Cost:** £24.60 entry fee, £21.60 for kids

*Warwick Castle is a great family destination.*

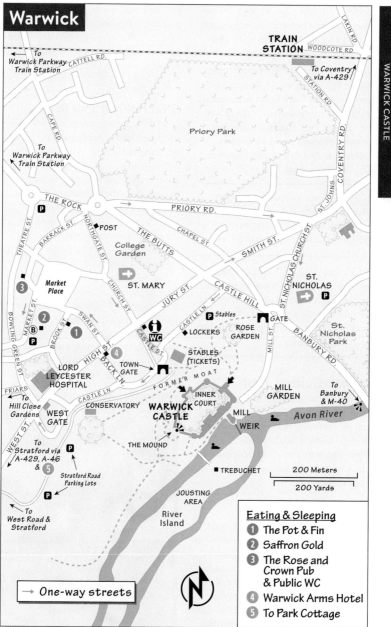

# Warwick

To Warwick Parkway Train Station

CATTELL RD.

TRAIN STATION

WOODCOTE RD.

LAKIN RD.

To Coventry via A-429

STATION RD.

CAPE RD.

To Warwick Parkway Train Station

Priory Park

ST. JOHN'S

COVENTRY RD.

THE ROCK

PRIORY RD.

NORTHGATE ST.

BARRACK ST.

POST

THE BUTTS

CHAPEL ST.

SMITH ST.

THEATRE ST.

College Garden

CHURCH ST.

ST. MARY

JURY ST.

CASTLE HILL

ST. NICHOLAS CHURCH ST.

ST. NICHOLAS

St. Nicholas Park

Market Place

**3**

MARKET ST.

**2**

B

**1**

BROOK ST.

SWAN ST.

HIGH ST.

BACK LN.

CASTLE ST.

WC

LOCKERS

CASTLE LN.

Stables

ROSE GARDEN

GATE

MILL ST.

BANBURY RD.

BOWLING GREEN ST.

**4**

TOWN GATE

STABLES (TICKETS)

FRIARS

LORD LEYCESTER HOSPITAL

To Hill Close Gardens

CASTLE LN.

CONSERVATORY

WEST GATE

FORMER MOAT

INNER COURT

WARWICK CASTLE

MILL GARDEN

To Banbury & M-40

MILL

WEIR

Avon River

WEST ST.

To Stratford via A-429, A-46 & 

**5**

Stratford Road Parking Lots

THE MOUND

TREBUCHET

200 Meters

200 Yards

To West Road & Stratford

JOUSTING AREA

River Island

→ One-way streets

N

## Eating & Sleeping

**1** The Pot & Fin

**2** Saffron Gold

**3** The Rose and Crown Pub & Public WC

**4** Warwick Arms Hotel

**5** To Park Cottage

under 12, £17.40 for seniors, includes gardens and most castle attractions except for the gory, skippable Castle Dungeon (£9 as an add-on); dry audioguide-£1.

**Rick's Tip:** *Warwick's TI sells discounted same-day* **Fast Track ticket vouchers** *to the castle (daily in season but closed Sun Jan-March, The Court House, Jury Street, www.visitwarwick.co.uk). Or* **book in advance online** *for a similar discount and line-skipping privileges.*

**Hours:** Open daily July-Sept 10:00-18:00, Oct-June until 17:00.

**Information:** Recorded info tel. 0871-265-2000, www.warwick-castle.com.

**Rick's Tip:** *When you buy your castle ticket,* **pick up the daily events flier.** *Plan your visit around these worthwhile events, which may include* **jousting competitions, archery demos, sword fights, jester acts,** *and* **falconry shows.**

## ● Self-Guided Tour

Buy your ticket and head through the turnstile into the moat area, where you'll get your first view of the dramatic castle. In good weather, this lawn-like zone is filled with tents populated by costumed docents demonstrating everyday medieval lifestyles.

### Inner Courtyard

From the moat, two different entrance gateways lead to the castle's **inner courtyard.** The bulge of land at the far right end of the courtyard, called **The Mound,** is where the original Norman castle of 1068 stood. Under this "motte," the wooden stockade (the "bailey") defined the courtyard in the way the castle walls do today. You can climb up to the top for a view down into the castle courtyard.

The main attractions are in the largest buildings along the side of the courtyard:

the Great Hall, five lavish staterooms, and the chapel. Progressing through these rooms, you'll see how the castle complex evolved over the centuries, from a formidable defensive fortress to a genteel manor home.

### Great Hall and State Rooms

Enter through the cavernous **Great Hall,** decorated with suits of equestrian armor. Adjoining the Great Hall is the state dining room, with portraits of English kings and princes. Then follow the one-way route through the **staterooms,** keeping ever more esteemed company as you go—the rooms closest to the center of the complex were the most exclusive, reserved only for those especially close to the Earl of Warwick.

You'll pass through three drawing rooms: first, one decorated in a deep burgundy; then the cedar drawing room, with intricately carved wood paneling, a Waterford crystal chandelier, and a Carrara marble fireplace; and finally the green drawing room, with a beautiful painted coffered ceiling and wax figures of Henry

*A Warwick state room*

VIII and his six wives. The sumptuous Queen Anne Room was decorated in preparation for a planned 1704 visit by the monarch. Finally comes the blue boudoir, an oversized closet decorated in blue silk wallpaper. The portrait of Henry VIII over the fireplace faces a clock once owned by Marie-Antoinette.

On your way out, you'll pass the earl's private **chapel.** The earl's family worshipped in the pews in front of the stone screen, while the servants would stand behind it.

## Other Exhibits

Back out in the courtyard are the entrances to other, less impressive exhibits. The **Kingmaker** exhibit (set in 1471) uses mannequins, sound effects, and smells to show how medieval townsfolk prepared for battle.

The **Secrets and Scandals of the Royal Weekend Party** exhibit lets you explore staterooms staged as they appeared in 1898, but with an added narrative: The philandering Daisy Maynard Greville, Countess of Warwick—considered the most beautiful woman in Victorian England—is throwing a party, and gossipy "servants" clue you in on who's flirting with whom.

The **Castle Dungeon,** a tacky knockoff of the tacky London Dungeon, is a pricey add-on attraction that features a series of costumed hosts who entertain and spook visitors on a 45-minute tour.

## Ramparts and Towers

You can climb up onto the ramparts and the tallest tower, leaving you at a fun perch from which to fire your imaginary longbow. The halls and stairs can be very crowded with young kids, and—as the signs warn—it takes 530 steep steps (both up and down) to follow the whole route.

The **Princess Tower** offers children (ages 3-8) the chance to dress up as princesses and princes for a photo op (included in castle ticket, but sign up at the information tent in the courtyard).

## Castle Grounds

Surrounding everything is a lush, peacock-patrolled, picnic-perfect park, complete with a Victorian rose garden. The castle grounds are often enlivened by a knight in shining armor on a horse or a merry band of musical jesters. The grassy moat area is typically filled with costumed characters and demonstrations, including archery and falconry. Near the entrance to the complex is the **Pageant Playground,** with medieval-themed slides and climbing areas for kids. Down by the river is a bridge across to **River Island** and the jousting area.

# Eating and Sleeping

Consider bringing a picnic to enjoy on the gorgeous grounds (otherwise you'll be left with the overpriced food stands). It's worth the 100-yard walk from the castle turnstiles to Warwick town's Market Place, with several lunch options on or near the square: **The Pot & Fin** (excellent fish-and-chips, closed Sun-Mon), **Saffron Gold** (tasty Indian food), or **The Rose and Crown** (pub classics).

If you want to overnight in Warwick, try the charming **$$$ Warwick Arms Hotel** (17 High Street, www.warwickarmshotel. com) or half-timbered **$$ Park Cottage** (113 West Street/A-429, www.park cottagewarwick.co.uk).

*A young knight*

Liverpool

**B**eatles fans flock to Liverpool to learn about the Fab Four's early days, but the city has much more to offer: a wealth of free and good museums, a pair of striking cathedrals, a dramatic skyline mingling old red-brick maritime buildings and glassy new skyscrapers, and—most of all—the charm of the Liverpudlians. It provides the best experience of urban England outside London.

Sitting at the mouth of the River Mersey, Liverpool has long been a major shipping center. Its physical devastation during World War II, followed by the advent of container shipping in the 1960s, led to economic decline through the 1970s and 1980s. But today, things are looking up. The city's status as the 2008 European Capital of Culture spurred gentrification and a cultural renaissance. The 50,000 students attending three universities in town keep Liverpool youthful, with a pub or nightclub on every corner.

## LIVERPOOL IN 1 DAY

Spend the morning at the Albert Dock, home to The Beatles Story, Merseyside Maritime Museum, and Museum of Liverpool—choose what interests you. When you're done with the dock, it's easy to take a Beatles bus tour (2 hours, departs from Albert Dock).

Mid-afternoon, visit the two cathedrals. Ramble down Hope Street, which connects the cathedrals and hosts recommended eateries and pubs, offering lots of good choices for dinner. Try to make time to stroll the downtown pedestrian core between Queen Square and the Liverpool One mall. Enjoy the lively nightlife scene.

If you're in town only to binge on the Beatles, you can easily fill a day with Fab Four sights: Tour the interior of John's and Paul's homes in the morning (smart to reserve in advance), then return to the Albert Dock to visit The Beatles Story. Take an afternoon Beatles bus tour from the Albert Dock to see the other Beatles sights in town, winding up at the Cavern Quarter to enjoy a Beatles cover band in the reconstructed Cavern Club.

International Beatles Week, celebrated in late August, is a very busy time in Liverpool, with lots of live musical performances.

## ORIENTATION

With nearly half a million people, Liverpool is Britain's fifth-biggest city. But most points of interest are concentrated in the pedestrian-friendly downtown. Interesting sights and colorful neighborhoods are scattered throughout this area, so it's enjoyable to connect your sightseeing on

▲▲**Museum of Liverpool** Three floors of intriguing exhibits, historical artifacts, and fun interactive displays tracing the port city's history, culture, and contributions to the world. **Hours:** Daily 10:00-17:00. See page 270.

▲▲**Liverpool Cathedral** Huge Anglican house of worship—the largest cathedral in Great Britain—with cavernous interior and tower climb. **Hours:** Daily 8:00-18:00; tower Mon-Fri 10:00-16:30 (last ascent), Thu until sunset March-Oct, Sat 9:00-16:30, Sun 12:00-15:30. See page 273.

▲**The Beatles Story** Well-done if overpriced exhibit about the Fab Four, with a great audioguide narrated by John Lennon's sister, Julia Baird. **Hours:** Daily May-Sept 9:00-19:00, Oct-April 10:00-18:00. See page 265.

▲**Merseyside Maritime Museum and International Slavery Museum** Duo of thought-provoking museums exploring Liverpool's seafaring heritage and the city's role in the African slave trade. **Hours:** Daily 10:00-17:00. See page 268.

▲**Metropolitan Cathedral of Christ the King** Striking, daringly modern Catholic cathedral with a story as interesting as the building itself. **Hours:** Daily 7:30-18:00, until 17:00 on Sun in winter; after 17:15 (during Mass), you can't walk around; crypt Mon-Sat 10:00-16:00, closed Sun, last entry 45 minutes before closing. See page 272.

▲**Inside the Lennon and McCartney Homes** The 1950s boyhood homes of Beatles John Lennon and Paul McCartney, with restored interiors viewable on a National Trust minibus tour (worth ▲▲▲ for diehard fans). Advance reservations recommended. **Hours:** Tours run mid-March-Oct daily 4/day, mid-Feb-mid-March and Nov Wed-Sun 3/day. See page 275.

**Tate Gallery Liverpool** Modern-art gallery with 20th-century statues and paintings. **Hours:** Daily 10:00-18:00. See page 270.

**Liverpool 360 Ferris Wheel** Offering sky-high views on the waterfront. **Hours:** Daily 10:00-21:00, until 23:00 Fri-Sat. See page 270.

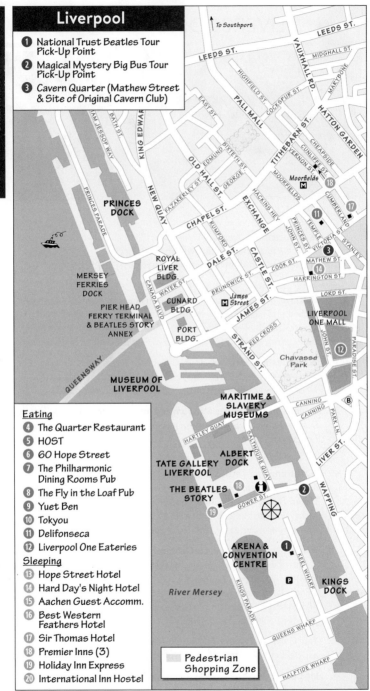

## Liverpool

1 National Trust Beatles Tour Pick-Up Point
2 Magical Mystery Big Bus Tour Pick-Up Point
3 Cavern Quarter (Mathew Street & Site of Original Cavern Club)

### Eating
4 The Quarter Restaurant
5 HOST
6 60 Hope Street
7 The Philharmonic Dining Rooms Pub
8 The Fly in the Loaf Pub
9 Yuet Ben
10 Tokyou
11 Delifonseca
12 Liverpool One Eateries

### Sleeping
13 Hope Street Hotel
14 Hard Day's Night Hotel
15 Aachen Guest Accomm.
16 Best Western Feathers Hotel
17 Sir Thomas Hotel
18 Premier Inns (3)
19 Holiday Inn Express
20 International Inn Hostel

Pedestrian Shopping Zone

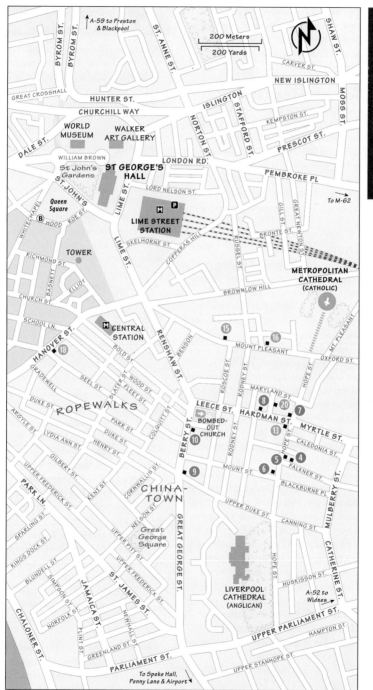

foot. You can walk from one end of this zone to the other in about 25 minutes. Beatles sights, however, are spread far and wide—it's much easier to connect them with a tour.

## Tourist Information

Liverpool's TI is at the **Albert Dock.** Pick up the free, good city map and the comprehensive *Liverpool Visitor Guide,* crammed with updated lists of museums, hotels, restaurants, shops, and more (daily April-Oct 10:00-17:30, Nov-March 10:00-17:00, just inland from The Beatles Story, tel. 0151/707-0729, www.visitliverpool.com).

## Tours

If you want to see as many Beatles-related sights as possible in a short time, these tours are the way to go. Each drives by the houses where the Fab Four grew up (exteriors only), places they performed, and spots made famous by their lyrics ("Penny Lane," "Strawberry Fields," the Eleanor Rigby graveyard, and so on). Even lukewarm fans will enjoy the narration and seeing the shelter on the roundabout, the barber who shaves another customer, and the banker who never wears a mack in the pouring rain. (Very strange.)

**Magical Mystery Big Bus Tours** offer enthusiastic live commentary and Beatles tunes cued to famous landmarks. Fans hop onto an old, psychedelically-painted bus for a spin past Liverpool's main Beatles landmarks, with photo ops along the way. As these tours often fill up, book at least a day ahead by phone or online (£17, 5-7/day, fewer on Sun and in off-season, 2 hours, buses depart from Albert Dock near The Beatles Story and TI, tel. 0151/703-9100, www.cavernclub.org).

**Phil Hughes Minibus Beatles and Liverpool Tours** are more extensive, fun, and intimate. These four-hour tours include information on historic Liverpool and a couple of *Titanic* and *Lusitania* sights, along with the Beatles stuff (£22/

## On the Scouse

Nicknamed "Scousers" (after a traditional local stew, originally brought here by Norwegian immigrants), the people of Liverpool have a reputation for being relaxed, easygoing, and welcoming to visitors. The Scouse dialect comes with a distinctive lilt and quick wit—the latter likely a means of coping with long-term hardship. Think of the Beatles' familiar accents and their sarcastic off-the-cuff remarks. Many Liverpudlians attribute these qualities to the Celtic influence here: Liverpool is a melting pot of not only English culture, but also of Irish and Welsh, as well as arrivals from all over Europe and beyond (Liverpool's diverse population includes many of African descent). Liverpudlians are also passionate about football (i.e., soccer). Locals will be quick to tell you that the Liverpool FC team is one of England's best.

person, private group tour with 5-person minimum, can coordinate tour to include pickup from end of National Trust tour of Lennon and McCartney homes or drop-off for late-day tour starting at Speke Hall, also does door-to-door service from your hotel or train station, 8-seat minibus, tel. 0151/228-4565, mobile 07961-511-223, www.tourliverpool.co.uk, tourliverpool@hotmail.com).

**Jackie Spencer Private Tours** tailor visits to your schedule and interests (up to 5 people in her chauffeur-driven minivan-£210, 3 hours, longer tours available, will pick you up at hotel or train station, mobile 0799-076-1478, www.beatleguides.com, jackie@beatleguides.com).

Two different hop-on, hop-off bus tours cruise around town, offering a quick overview that links the major sights. The options are **City Explorer** (£9, buy ticket from driver, valid 24 hours, live guides, 13 stops; April-Aug daily 10:00-16:30, 2/hour; Sept-March generally daily 10:00 until 15:00 or 16:00, 1-2/hour; tel. 0151/933-2324, www.cityexplorerliverpool.co.uk) and **Liverpool City Tours** (£10, buy ticket from driver, valid 24 hours, recorded commentary, 16 stops, April-Oct Mon-Sat 10:00-17:00, 3/hour, less frequent Sun and Nov-March, tel. 0151/298-1253, www.sightseeingliverpool.co.uk).

# SIGHTS

## On the Waterfront

In its day, Liverpool was England's greatest seaport, but trade declined after 1890, as the port wasn't deep enough for the big new ships. The advent of mega container ships in the 1960s put the final nail in the port's coffin, and by 1972 it was closed entirely.

Over the last couple of decades, this formerly derelict area has been the focus of the city's rejuvenation efforts. The waterfront is now a venue for some of the city's top attractions. The red-brick Albert Dock complex has museums, restaurants, and nightlife; nearby, to the south, is the Ferris wheel and futuristic arena. To the north, Pier Head hosts the Museum of Liverpool.

### At the Albert Dock

Opened in 1852 by Prince Albert and enclosing seven acres of water, the Albert Dock is surrounded by five-story brick warehouses. A half-dozen busy eateries are lined up here, protected from the rain by arcades. There's plenty of pay parking.

**Rick's Tip:** *The* **eateries at the Albert Dock** *aren't high cuisine, but they're handy to your sightseeing. Some come alive with club energy at night, but are sedate and pleasant in the afternoon and early evening. For an inexpensive lunch at the dock, try the café in* **Tate Gallery Liverpool** *(daily 10:00-16:30, open to public).*

▲**THE BEATLES STORY**

It seems almost wrong to bottle up the Beatles in a museum, but the exhibit—while overpriced and a bit small—is well done. The story is a fascinating one, and even an avid fan will pick up some new information. The Beatles Story has two

*Liverpool's rejuvenated waterfront*

## Meet the Beatles

Liverpool has become a pilgrimage site for Beatlemaniacs. Most Beatles sights focus on their early days, before the psychedelia, transcendental meditation, and Yoko. Because these sights are so spread out, the easiest way to connect all of them in one go is by tour (see "Tours").

All four Beatles were born here, spending their formative years amid the city's WWII-era bombed-out shell. Any tour glides by the **home** most identified with each one's childhood: John Lennon at "Mendips," Paul McCartney at 20 Forthlin Road, George Harrison at 12 Arnold Grove, and Ringo Starr (a.k.a. Richard Starkey) at 10 Admiral Grove.

Behind John's house at Mendips is a wooded area called **Strawberry Field** (he added the "s" for the song). This surrounds a Victorian mansion that was, at various times, a Salvation Army home and an orphanage. John enjoyed sneaking into the trees around the mansion to play. Today, visitors pose in front of Strawberry Field's red gate (a replica of the original).

In the mid-1950s, John formed a band called the Quarrymen. Paul met John when he saw the Quarrymen on July 6, 1957, at **St. Peter's Church** in Woolton. After the show, in the social hall across the street, Paul noted that John played only banjo chords (his mother had taught him to play on a banjo—he didn't even know how to tune a guitar). John, two years older, was a better improviser than a musician, so he was impressed when Paul played a note-perfect rendition of Eddie Cochran's "Twenty Flight Rock." Before long, Paul had joined the band.

In the St. Peter's Church graveyard is a headstone for a woman named **Eleanor Rigby.** But to this day, Paul swears that he never saw it, and made up the name for that famous song. Either he's lying, the name crept into his subconscious, or it's a truly remarkable coincidence.

The boys went to school on **Mount Street** in the center of Liverpool (near Hope Street, between the two cathedrals). John and his friend Stuart Sutcliffe

parts: the original, main exhibit at the south end of the Albert Dock; and a much smaller branch in the Pier Head ferry terminal, near the Museum of Liverpool, just to the north. A free shuttle runs between the two locations every 30 minutes.

**Cost and Hours:** £15 covers both parts, tickets good for 48 hours, includes audioguide, daily May-Sept 9:00-19:00, Oct-April 10:00-18:00, last entry one hour before closing, tel. 0151/709-1963, www.beatlesstory.com.

**Visiting the Museum:** Start in the **main exhibit** with a chronological stroll through the evolution of the Beatles, focusing on their Liverpool years: meeting as schoolboys, performing at (and helping decorate) the Casbah Coffee Club, making a name for themselves in Hamburg's red light district, meeting their

attended the Liverpool College of Art. Paul and his pal George Harrison went to Liverpool Institute High School for Boys. (When Paul suggested George as a possible new member for the band, John dismissed him as too young...until he heard George play.) Paul later bought his old school building and turned it into the Liverpool Institute for Performing Arts (LIPA).

As young men, the boys waited at a bus stop in the **Penny Lane** neighborhood. Later they wrote a nostalgic song about the things they observed there: the shelter by the roundabout, the barbershop, and so on. (While they also sing about the fireman with the clean machine, the firehouse itself is not actually on Penny Lane, but around the corner.)

After some shuffles in lineup, by 1960 the group had officially become The Beatles: John Lennon, Paul McCartney, George Harrison, and...Pete Best and Stu Sutcliffe. The quintet built a name in Liverpool's "Merseybeat" club scene. While the famous **Cavern Club** is gone (the one you see advertised is a reconstruction), the original **Casbah Coffee Club** is open for tours (3.5 miles northwest of downtown, prebook by calling the TI at tel. 0151/707-0729 or online at www.petebest.com).

The group went to Hamburg, Germany, to cut their teeth in its thriving music scene and performed as the backing band for Tony Sheridan's single "My Bonny." When this caught on back in Liverpool, promoter Brian Epstein took note, and signed the act. His shrewd management would eventually propel the Beatles to superstardom.

Many different people could be considered the "Fifth Beatle." John's friend Stu, who performed with the group in Hamburg, left to pursue his own artistic interests. Pete Best was the band's original drummer, but he was replaced with Ringo Starr (John later said, "Pete Best was a great drummer, but Ringo was a Beatle.") Manager Brian Epstein is another candidate. But it's hard to ignore the case for George Martin, who produced all the Beatles' albums except *Let It Be,* and was instrumental in both forging and developing their sound.

By early 1964, the Beatles were world-famous, but—as evidenced by their songs about Penny Lane and Strawberry Fields—they never forgot their Merseyside home.

manager Brian Epstein, and the advent of worldwide Beatlemania (with some help from Ed Sullivan). There are many actual artifacts (from George Harrison's first boyhood guitar to John Lennon's orange-tinted "Imagine" glasses), as well as large dioramas celebrating landmarks in Beatles lore (a reconstruction of the Cavern Club, a life-size re-creation of the *Sgt. Pepper* album cover, and a walk-through yellow submarine). The last rooms trace the members' solo careers, and the final few steps are reserved for reverence about John's peace work, including a replica of the white room he used while writing "Imagine." Rounding out the exhibits are a "Discovery Zone" for kids and (of course) the "Fab 4 Store," with an impressive pile of Beatles buyables.

The great audioguide, narrated by Julia Baird (John Lennon's little sister), captures the Beatles' charm and cheekiness in a way the stiff wax mannequins can't. You'll hear clips of interviews from the actual participants in the Beatles' story—their families, friends, and collaborators. Cynthia Lennon, John's first wife, still marvels at the manic power of Beatlemania, while producer George Martin explains why he wanted their original drummer dumped for Ringo.

While this is a fairly sanitized look at the Fab Four (LSD and Yoko-related conflicts are glossed over), the exhibits remind listeners of all that made the group earth-shattering—and even a little edgy—at the time. For example, performing before the Queen Mother, John Lennon famously quips: "Will the people in the cheaper seats clap your hands? And the rest of you, if you'll just rattle your jewelry." Surprisingly, there are no clips from Beatles movies or performances—not even the epic *Ed Sullivan Show* broadcast. You'll find that it's strong on Beatles' history, but you'll have to go elsewhere to understand why Beatlemania happened.

*Cavern Club replica*

The **Pier Head exhibit** is less interesting, but since it's included with the ticket, it's worth dropping into if you have the time. You'll find it upstairs in the Pier Head ferry terminal—10-minute walk north (at the opposite end of the Albert Dock, then another 5-minute walk across the bridge and past the Museum of Liverpool). The main attraction here is a corny "Fab 4D Experience," an animated movie that strings together Beatles tunes into something resembling a plot while mainly offering an excuse to play around with 3-D effects and other surprises (such as the smell of strawberries when you hear "Strawberry Fields Forever"). There are also rotating temporary exhibits here.

## ▲MERSEYSIDE MARITIME MUSEUM AND INTERNATIONAL SLAVERY MUSEUM

These museums tell the story of Liverpool, once the second city of the British Empire. The third floor covers slavery, while the first, second, and basement handle other maritime topics.

**Cost and Hours:** Free, donations accepted, daily 10:00-17:00, café, tel. 0151/478-4499, www.liverpoolmuseums.org.uk.

**Background:** Liverpool's port prospered in the 18th century as one corner of a commerce triangle with Africa and America. British shippers profited greatly through exploitation: About 1.5 million enslaved African people were taken to the Americas on Liverpool's ships (that's 10 percent of all African slaves). From Liverpool, the British exported manufactured goods to Africa in exchange for enslaved Africans; the slaves were then shipped to the Americas, where they were traded for raw material (cotton, sugar, and tobacco); and the goods were then brought back to Britain. While the merchants on all three sides made money, the big profit came home to England (which enjoyed substantial income from customs, duties, and a thriving smugglers' market). As Britain's economy boomed, so did Liverpool's.

After participation in the slave trade was outlawed in Britain in the early 1800s, Liverpool kept its port busy as a transfer point for emigrants. If your ancestors came from Scandinavia, Ukraine, or Ireland, they likely left Europe from this port. Between 1830 and 1930, nine million emigrants sailed from Liverpool to find their dreams in the New World.

**Visiting the Museums:** Begin by riding the elevator up to floor 3—we'll work our way back down.

On floor 3, three galleries make up the **International Slavery Museum.** First is a description of life in West Africa, which re-creates traditional domestic architecture and displays actual artifacts. Then comes a harrowing exhibit about enslavement and the Middle Passage. The tools of the enslavers—chains, muzzles, and a branding iron—and the intense film about the Middle Passage sea voyage to the Americas drive home the horrifying experience of being abducted from your home and taken in life-threatening conditions thousands of miles away to toil for a wealthy stranger. The exhibits don't shy away from how Liverpool profited from slavery; you can turn local street signs around to find out how they were named after slave traders—even Penny Lane has slavery connections. Finally, the museum examines the legacy of slavery—both the persistence of racism in contemporary society and the substantial positive impact that people of African descent have had on European and American cultures. Walls of photos celebrate important people of African descent, and a music station lets you sample songs from a variety of African-influenced genres.

Continue down the stairs to the **Maritime Museum,** on floor 2. This celebrates Liverpool's shipbuilding heritage and displays actual ship components, model boats, and a gallery of nautical paintings. Part of that heritage is covered in an extensive exhibit on the *Titanic.* The shipping line and its captain were based in Liverpool, and 89 of the crew members who died were from the city. The informative panels allow you to follow real people as they set off on the voyage and debunk many *Titanic* myths (no one ever said it was unsinkable).

Floor 1 shows footage and artifacts from another maritime disaster—the 1915 sinking of the Lusitania, which was torpedoed by a German U-boat. She sank off the coast of Ireland in under 20 minutes; 1,191 people died in the tragedy, including 405 crew members from Liverpool. The attack on an unarmed passenger ship sparked riots in Liverpool and almost thrust the US into the war. Also on this floor, an extensive exhibit traces the **Battle of the Atlantic** (during World War II, Nazi U-boats attacked merchant ships bringing supplies to Britain, in an attempt to cripple this island nation). You'll see how crew members lived aboard merchant ships. The **Hello Sailor!** exhibit explains how gay culture flourished at sea at a time when it was taboo in almost every other walk of British life.

Make your way to the basement, where exhibits describe the tremendous wave of **emigration** through Liverpool's port. And the **Seized!** exhibit looks at the legal and illegal movement of goods through that same port, including thought-provoking displays on customs, taxation, and smuggling.

*Merseyside Maritime Museum*

## TATE GALLERY LIVERPOOL

This prestigious gallery of modern art is near the Maritime Museum. It won't entertain you as well as its London sister, the Tate Modern, but if you're into modern art, any Tate is great. Its two airy floors dedicated to the rotating collection of statues and paintings from the 20th century are free; the top and ground floors are devoted to special exhibits. The Tate also has a fine, inexpensive café.

**Cost and Hours:** Free, donations accepted, £7-13 for special exhibits, daily 10:00-18:00, tel. 0151/702-7400, www.tate. org.uk/visit/tate-liverpool.

## LIVERPOOL 360 FERRIS WHEEL

You can take a spin for panoramic views on a Ferris wheel with 42 enclosed capsules (£9, family deals, daily 10:00-21:00, until 23:00 Fri-Sat, near Albert Dock—can't miss it, www.liverpool-360.co.uk).

## Pier Head

A five-minute walk across the bridge north of the Albert Dock takes you to the Pier Head area.

## ▲▲MUSEUM OF LIVERPOOL

This museum, which opened in 2011 in the blocky white building just across the bridge north of the Albert Dock, does a good job of fulfilling its goal to "capture Liverpool's vibrant character and demonstrate the city's unique contribution to the world." The museum is full of interesting items, fun interactive displays (great for kids), and intriguing facts that bring a whole new depth to your Liverpool experience.

**Cost and Hours:** Free, donations accepted, daily 10:00-17:00, guidebook-£1, café, Mann Island, Pier Head, tel. 0151/478-4545, www.liverpoolmuseums. org.uk/mol.

**Visiting the Museum:** If you're short on time, spend most of it on the second floor. First, stop by the information desk to check on the show times for the museum's various videos. If you have kids age six and under, you can get a free timed-entry ticket for the hands-on Little Liverpool exhibit on the ground floor.

**Ground Floor:** On this level, **The Great Port** details the story of Liverpool's defining industry and how it developed through

*The revitalized Pier Head area and the Museum of Liverpool*

the Industrial Revolution. On display is an 1838 steam locomotive that was originally built for the Liverpool and Manchester Railway. The **Global City** exhibit focuses on how Liverpool's status as a major British shipping center made it the gateway to a global empire and features a 20-minute video, *Power and the Glory,* about Liverpool's role within the British Empire.

**First Floor:** Don't miss the **Liverpool Overhead Railway** exhibit, which features the only surviving car from this 19th-century elevated railway. You can actually jump aboard and take a seat to watch 1897 movie footage shot from the train line. A huge interactive model shows the railway's route. Also on this floor is the **History Detectives** exhibit, which covers Liverpool's history and archaeology.

**Second Floor:** The **People's Republic** exhibit examines what it means to be a Liverpudlian (a.k.a. "Scouser") and covers everything from housing and health issues to military and religious topics. As industrialized Liverpool has long been a hotbed of the labor movement, exhibits here also detail the political side of the city, including child labor issues and women's suffrage.

One compelling display is the recreation of Liverpool's 19th-century court housing, which consisted of a series of tiny dwellings bunched around a narrow courtyard. With more than 60 people sharing two toilets, this was some of the most overcrowded and unsanitary housing in Britain at the time.

Next, the exhibit skips to religion and the centerpiece of this room: a 10-foot-tall model of Liverpool's Catholic cathedral that was never built. In 1932, Archbishop Richard Downey and architect Sir Edwin Lutyens commissioned this model to showcase their grandiose plans for constructing the world's second-largest cathedral. Their vision never came to fruition, and the Metropolitan Cathedral was built instead (for more on what happened, see page 272).

On the other side of the floor, the **Wondrous Place** exhibit celebrates the arts, cultural, and sporting side of Liverpool. An exhibit on the city's famous passion for soccer features memorabilia and the 17-minute video *Kicking and Screaming,* about the rivalry between the Everton and Liverpool football teams and the sometimes tragic history of the sport (such as when 96 fans were crushed to death at a Liverpool match).

Music is the other big focus here, with plenty of fun interactive stops that include music quizzes, a karaoke booth, and listening stations featuring artists with ties to Liverpool (from Elvis Costello to Echo & the Bunnymen). And of course you'll see plenty of Beatles mania, including their famous suits, the original stage from St. Peter's Church (where John Lennon was performing the first time Paul McCartney laid eyes on him; located in the theater), and an eight-minute film on the band.

Finally, in the **Skylight Gallery,** look for Ben Johnson's painting *The Liverpool Cityscape, 2008,* a remarkable and fun-to-examine melding of old and new art styles. At first glance, it's a typical skyline painting, but Johnson used computer models to create perfect depictions of each building before he put brush to canvas. This method allows for a photorealistic, highly detailed, but completely sanitized portrait of a city. Notice there are no cars or people.

## Cathedrals

Liverpool has not one but two notable cathedrals—one Anglican, the other Catholic. (As the Spinners song puts it, "If you want a cathedral, we've got one to spare.") Both are huge, architecturally significant, and well worth visiting. Near the eastern edge of downtown, they're connected by a 10-minute, half-mile walk on pleasant Hope Street, which is lined with theaters and good restaurants (see "Eating," later).

Liverpudlians enjoy pointing out that they have not only the world's only Catholic cathedral designed by a Protestant architect, but also the only Protestant one designed by a Catholic. With its large Irish-immigrant population, Liverpool suffered from tension between its Catholic and Protestant communities for much of its history. But during the city's darkest stretch of the depressed 1970s, the bishops of each church—Anglican Bishop David Sheppard and Catholic Archbishop Derek Worlock—came together and worked hard to reconcile the two communities for the betterment of Liverpool. (Liverpudlians nicknamed this dynamic duo "fish-and-chips" because they were "always together, and always in the newspaper.") It worked: Liverpool is a bold new cultural center, and relations between the two faiths remain healthy here. Join in this ecumenical spirit by visiting both of their main churches.

## ▲ METROPOLITAN CATHEDRAL OF CHRIST THE KING

This daringly modern building, a cone topped with a crowned cylinder, seems almost out of place in its workaday Liverpool neighborhood. The structure you see today bears no resemblance to Sir Edwin Lutyens' original 1930s plans for a stately Neo-Byzantine Catholic cathedral, which was to take 200 years to build and rival St. Peter's Basilica in Vatican City. (Lutyens was desperate to one-up the grandiose plans of Sir Giles Gilbert Scott, who was building the Anglican cathedral down the street.) The crypt for the ambitious church was excavated in the 1930s, but World War II (during which the crypt was used as an air-raid shelter) stalled progress for decades. In the 1960s, the plans were scaled back, and this smaller (but still impressive) house of worship was completed in 1967.

**Cost and Hours:** Cathedral—free entry but donations accepted, daily 7:30-18:00 (until 17:00 on Sun in winter)—but after 17:15 (during Mass), you won't be able to walk around; crypt—£3, Mon-Sat 10:00-16:00, closed Sun, last entry 45 minutes before closing, enter from inside church near organ; visitors center and café, Mount Pleasant, tel. 0151/709-9222, www.liverpoolmetrocathedral.org.uk.

**Visiting the Cathedral:** On the stepped plaza in front of the church,

*Metropolitan Cathedral of Christ the King*

you'll see the entrance to the cathedral's visitors center and café (on your right). You're standing on a big concrete slab that provides a roof to the humongous Lutyens Crypt, underfoot. The existing cathedral occupies only a small part of the would-be cathedral's footprint. Imagine what might have been—"the greatest building never built." Because of the cathedral's tent-like appearance and ties to the local Irish community, some Liverpudlians dubbed it "Paddy's Wigwam."

Climb up the stairs to the main doors, step inside, and let your eyes adjust to this magnificent dimly-lit space. Unlike a typical nave-plus-transept cross-shaped church, this cathedral has a round foot-print, with seating for a congregation of 3,000 fully surrounding the white marble altar. Like a theater in the round, it was designed to involve worshippers in the service. Suspended above the altar is a stylized crown of thorns.

Spinning off from the round central sanctuary are 13 smaller chapels, many of them representing different stages of Jesus' life. Each chapel is different. Explore, tuning into the symbolic details in each one. Also keep an eye out for the 14 exquisite bronze stations of the cross by local artist Sean Rice (on the wall).

The massive **Lutyens Crypt** (named for the ambitious original architect)—the only part of the originally planned cathedral to be completed has huge vaults and vast halls lined with six million bricks. The crypt contains a chapel—with windows by Lutyens—that's still used for Sunday Mass, the tombs of three archbishops, a treasury, and an exhibit about the cathedral's construction.

## HOPE STREET

The street connecting the cathedrals is the main artery of Liverpool's "uptown," a lively district loaded with dining and entertainment options. In addition to well-respected theaters, this street is home to the Philharmonic and its name-sake pub (see "Eating," later). At the inter-section with Mount Street is a monument consisting of concrete suitcases; just down this street are the high schools that Paul, George, and John attended.

## ▲▲LIVERPOOL CATHEDRAL

The largest cathedral in Great Britain, this gigantic Anglican house of worship hovers at the south end of downtown. Tour its vast interior and consider scaling its tower.

**Cost and Hours:** Free, £3 suggested donation, daily 8:00-18:00; £5 ticket includes tower climb (2 elevators and 108 steps), audioguide, and 10-minute *Great Space* film; tower—Mon-Fri 10:00-16:30 (last ascent), Thu until sunset March-Oct, Sat 9:00-16:30, Sun 12:00-15:30 (changes possible depending on bell-ringing schedule); St. James Mount, tel. 0151/709-6271, www.liverpoolcathedral.org.uk.

**Visiting the Cathedral:** Over the main door is a modern *Risen Christ* statue by Elisabeth Frink. Liverpudlians, not thrilled with the featureless statue and always quick with a joke, have dubbed it **"Frinkenstein."**

Stepping inside, pick up a floor plan at the information desk, go into the main hall, and take in the size of the place. When Liverpool was officially designated a "city" (seat of a bishop), they wanted to build a huge house of worship as a symbol of Liverpudlian pride. Built in bold Neo-Gothic style (like London's Parliament), it seems to trumpet with modern bombast the importance of this city on the Mersey. Begun in 1904, the cathedral's

*Liverpool Cathedral*

construction was interrupted by the tumultuous events of the 20th century and not completed until 1973.

Go to the big circular tile in the very center of the cathedral, under the highest tower. This is a plaque for the building's architect, **Sir Giles Gilbert Scott** (1880-1960). While the church you're surrounded by may seem like his biggest legacy, he also designed an icon that's synonymous with Britain: the classic red telephone box. Flanking this aisle, notice the highly detailed sandstone carvings.

Take a counterclockwise spin around the church interior. Head up the right aisle until you find the **model** of the original plan for the cathedral (press the button to light it up). Scott was a very young architect and received the commission with the agreement that he work closely under the wing of his more established mentor, George Bodley. These two architects' visions clashed, and Bodley usually won... until he died early in the planning stages, leaving Scott to pursue his own muse. If

Bodley had survived, the cathedral would probably look more like this model. As it was, only one corner of the complex (the Lady Chapel, which we're about to see) was completed before Giles changed plans to create the version you see today.

Nearby, the **"whispering arch"** spanning the sarcophagus has remarkable acoustics, carrying voices from one end to the other. Try it.

Continuing down the church, notice the colorful, modern painting *The Good Samaritan* (by Adrian Wiszniewski, 1995), high above on the right. The naked crime victim (who has been stabbed in his side, like the Crucifixion wound of Jesus) has been ignored by the well-dressed yuppies in the foreground, but the female Samaritan is finally taking notice. The canvas is packed with symbolism (for example, the Swiss Army knife, in a pool of blood in the left foreground, is open in the 3 o'clock position—the time that Jesus was crucified). This contemporary work of art demonstrates that this is a new, living church. But the congregation has its limits. This painting used to hang closer to the front of the church, but now they've moved it here, out of sight.

Proceeding to the corner, you'll reach the entrance to the oldest part of the church (1910): the **Lady Chapel,** with stained-glass windows celebrating important women. (Sadly, the original windows were destroyed in World War II; these are replicas.)

Back up in the main part of the church, continue behind the main altar to the **Education Centre,** with a fun, sped-up video showing all the daily work it takes to make this cathedral run.

Circling around the far corner of the church, you'll pass the children's chapel and chapterhouse, and then pass under another modern Wiszniewski painting (*The House Built on Rock*). Across from that painting, go into the choir to get a good look at the Last Supper altarpiece above the **main altar.**

*Cathedral nave*

Continuing back up the aisle, you'll come to the **war chapel.** At its entrance is a book listing Liverpudlians lost in war. Battle flags fly high on the wall above.

You'll wind up at the gift shop, where you can buy a ticket to climb up to the top of the tower. The cathedral's café is up the stairs, above the gift shop.

### Cavern Quarter: Beatles Sights

The narrow, bar-lined Mathew Street, right in the heart of downtown, is ground zero for Beatles fans. The Beatles frequently performed in their early days together at the original Cavern Club, deep in a cellar along this street. While that's long gone, a mock-up of the historic nightspot (built with many of the original bricks) lives on a few doors down. Still billed as "the **Cavern Club,"** this is worth a visit to see the reconstructed cellar that's often filled by Beatles cover bands. While touristy, dropping by in the afternoon or evening for a live Beatles tribute act in the Cavern Club somehow just feels right. You'll have Beatles songs stuck in your head all day anyway, so you might as well see a wannabe John and Paul strumming and harmonizing a close approximation of the original (daily 10:00-24:00; live music daily from 14:00, Sat from 13:00, cover charge Thu-Fri after 20:00 and Sat-Sun after 14:00, tel. 0151/236-9091, www.cavernclub.org).

Across the street and run by the same owners, the **Cavern Pub** lacks its sibling's

troglodyte aura, but makes up for it with walls lined with old photos and memorabilia from the Beatles and other bands who've performed here. Like the Cavern Club, the pub features frequent performances by Beatles cover bands and other acts (no cover, Mon-Wed 11:00-24:00, later Thu-Sun, tel. 0151/236-4041).

Out front is the Cavern's **Wall of Fame,** with a too-cool-for-school bronze John Lennon leaning up against a wall of bricks engraved with the names of musical acts that have graced the Cavern stage.

At the corner is the recommended **Hard Day's Night Hotel,** decorated inside and out to honor the Fab Four. Notice the statues of John, Paul, George, and Ringo on the second-story corners.

## Away from the Center
### ▲INSIDE THE LENNON AND MCCARTNEY HOMES

John's and Paul's boyhood homes are now owned by the National Trust and have both been restored to how they looked during the lads' 1950s childhoods. While some Beatles bus tours stop here for photo ops, only the National Trust minibus tour gets you inside the homes. This isn't Graceland—you won't find an over-the-top rock-and-roll extravaganza here. If you don't know the difference between John and Paul, you'll likely be bored. But for die-hard Beatles fans who want to get a glimpse into the time and place that created these musical masterminds, the National Trust tour is worth ▲▲▲.

Famous musicians who perform in Liverpool often make the pilgrimage to these homes—Bob Dylan turned up on one tour disguised in a hoodie—and Paul himself occasionally drops by. Ask the guides about recent memorable visitors.

Because the houses are in residential neighborhoods—and still share walls with neighbors—the National Trust runs only a few tours per day, limited to 15 or so Beatlemaniacs each.

**Cost and Reservations:** Tickets are

£23. Because so few people are allowed on each tour, it's strongly advised to make a reservation ahead of time, especially in summer and on weekends or holidays. It's a good idea to book as soon as you know your Liverpool plans (or at least two weeks ahead)—though at times, you may be able to get tickets a couple of days in advance. (On the flip side, tours can be booked up months in advance, such as during Beatles week in late August.) You can reserve online (www.nationaltrust.org.uk/beatles) or by calling 0151/427-7231. If you haven't reserved ahead, you can try to book a same-day tour (for the morning tours, call 0151/707-0729). The last tour is less likely to be full because it takes 30 minutes (by car or taxi) to reach the tour's starting point from central Liverpool—see below.

**Tour Options:** A minibus takes you to the homes of John and Paul, with about 45 minutes inside each. From mid-March–Oct, tours run daily from the Albert Dock at 10:00, 11:00, and 14:15; mid-Feb–mid-March and Nov Wed-Sun only (no tours Dec–mid-Feb). They depart from the Jurys Inn (south across the bridge from The Beatles Story, near the Ferris wheel) and follow a route that includes a quick pass by Penny Lane.

From mid-March–Oct, an additional tour leaves at 15:00 from Speke Hall, an out-of-the-way National Trust property located eight miles southeast of Liverpool. Drivers should allow 30 minutes from the city center to Speke Hall—follow the brown *Speke Hall* signs through dozens of roundabouts, heading in the general direction of the airport. If you don't have a car, hop in a taxi.

From either starting point, the entire visit takes about 2.5 hours. No photos are allowed inside either home.

**Visiting the Homes:** Each home has a caretaker who acts as your guide. These folks give an entertaining, insightful-to-fans 20- to 30-minute talk. You then have about 10-15 minutes to wander through the house on your own. Ask lots of questions if their spiel peters out early—these docents are a wealth of information.

**Mendips (John Lennon's Home):** Even though he sang about being a working-class hero, John grew up in the suburbs of Liverpool, surrounded by doctors, lawyers, and—beyond the back fence—Strawberry Field.

This was the home of John's Aunt Mimi, who raised him in this house from

*John Lennon's home*

*Paul McCartney's home*

the time he was five years old and once told him, "A guitar's all right, John, but you'll never earn a living by it." (John later bought Mimi a country cottage with those fateful words etched over the fireplace.) John moved out at age 23, but his first wife, Cynthia, bunked here for a while when John made his famous first trip to America. Yoko Ono bought the house in 2002 and gave it as a gift to the National Trust (generating controversy among the neighbors). The house's stewards make this place come to life.

On the surface, it's just a 1930s house carefully restored to how it would have been in the past. But delve deeper. It's been lovingly cared for—restored to be the tidy, well-kept place Mimi would have recognized (down to dishtowels hanging in the kitchen). It's a lucky quirk of fate that the house's interior remained mostly unchanged after the Lennons left: The bachelor who owned it decades after them didn't upgrade much, so even the light switches are true to the time.

If you're a John Lennon fan, it's fun to picture him as a young boy drawing and imagining at his dining room table. His bedroom, with an Elvis poster and his favorite boyhood books, offers tantalizing hints at his later musical genius. Sing a song to yourself in the enclosed porch—John and Paul did this when they wanted an echo-chamber effect.

**20 Forthlin Road (Paul McCartney's Home):** In comparison to Aunt Mimi's house, the home where Paul grew up is simpler, much less "posh," and even a little ratty around the edges. Michael, Paul's brother, wanted it that way—their mother, Mary (famously mentioned in "Let It Be"), died when the boys were young, and it never had the tidiness of a woman's touch. It's been intentionally scuffed up around the edges to preserve the historical accuracy. Notice the differences—Paul has said that John's house was vastly different and more clearly middle class. At Mendips, there were books on the bookshelves, but Paul's father had an upright piano. He also rigged up wires and headphones that connected the boys' bedrooms to the living-room radio so they could listen to rock 'n' roll on Radio Luxembourg.

More than a hundred Beatles songs were written in this house (including "I Saw Her Standing There") during days Paul and John spent skipping school. The photos from Michael, taken in this house, help make the scene of what's mostly a barren interior much more interesting. Ask your guide how Paul would sneak into the house late at night without waking up his dad.

# EXPERIENCES

## Nightlife

Liverpool hops after hours, especially on weekends.

**Ropewalks,** the area just east of the downtown shopping district and Albert Dock, is filled with lively pubs, nightclubs, and lounges—some are divey, some are stylish. While this area is aimed primarily at the college-age crowd, it's still worth a stroll, and has a few eateries worth considering.

The following pubs in the city center are best for serious drinkers and beer aficionados—the food is an afterthought. **The Ship and Mitre,** at the edge of downtown, has 30-plus selections of beer on tap and gets crowded (133 Dale Street, tel. 0151/236-0859, see festival schedule at www.theshipandmitre.com). **Thomas**

**Rigby's** has hard-used wooden floors that spill out into a rollicking garden court-yard (21 Dale Street). Around the corner and much more sedate, **Ye Hole in Ye Wall** brags that it's Liverpool's oldest pub, from 1726 (just off Dale Street on Hackins Hey).

# EATING

As a rollicking, youthful city, Liverpool is a magnet for creative chefs as well as upscale chain restaurants. Consider my suggestions, but also browse the surrounding streets. Finding a restaurant here is a joy, not a chore.

## On and near Hope Street

Hope Street, which connects the two cathedrals, is home to some excellent restaurants.

**The Quarter** dishes up Mediterranean food at rustic tables that sprawl through several connected houses. They also serve breakfast and have an attached deli (£4-7 starters, £8-11 pizzas and pastas, chalkboard specials, daily 9:00-23:00, 7 Falkner Street, tel. 0151/707-1965).

**HOST** (short for "Hope Street") features Asian fusion dishes in a casual, colorful, modern atmosphere. There are gluten-free and vegan options (£4-6 small plates, £10-13 big plates, daily 11:00-23:00, 31 Hope Street, tel. 0151/708-5831).

**60 Hope Street** offers English cuisine made with "as locally sourced as possible" ingredients in an upscale atmosphere. While the prices are high (£9-11 starters, £19-30 main dishes), the fixed-price meals are a good deal (£20/two courses, £25/three courses, £15 afternoon tea, open Mon-Sat 12:00-14:30 & 17:00-22:30, Sun 12:00-20:00, reservations smart—especially on weekends, 60 Hope Street, tel. 0151/707-6060, www.60hopestreet.com).

**The Philharmonic Dining Rooms,** kitty-corner from the actual Philharmonic, is actually a pub—but what a pub! John Lennon once said that his biggest

regret about fame was "not being able to go to the Phil for a drink." The bar is a work of art, the marble urinals are down-right genteel, and the three sitting areas on the ground floor (including the giant hall) are an enticing place to sip a pint. Food is usually served in the less-atmospheric upstairs (£8-15 pub grub, food served daily 11:00-22:00, bar open until late, corner of Hope and Hardman streets, tel. 0151/707-2837).

**The Fly in the Loaf** has a classic pub exterior and interior, with efficient service, eight hand pulls for real ales, and good food (£3-5 sandwiches, £7-9 meals, food served daily 12:00-18:45, bar open until late, 13 Hardman Street, tel. 0151/708-0817).

**Chinatown:** A few blocks southwest of Hope Street is Liverpool's thriving Chinatown, with the world's biggest Chinese arch. Restaurants line up along Berry Street in front of the arch and Cornwallis Street behind it. Among these, **Yuet Ben** is the most established (Tue-Sun 17:00-23:00, closed Mon, facing the arch at 1 Upper Duke Street, tel. 0151/709-5772). **Tokyou** features tasty £5 noodle and rice dishes with service that's fast and furious (daily 12:30-23:30, 7 Berry Street, tel. 0151/445-1023).

## Downtown

**Delifonseca** is a trendy eatery with two parts. In the cellar is a small deli counter and large bar, with prepared salads and made-to-order £3 sandwiches. Upstairs

is a casual bistro serving British, Mediterranean, and international cuisine. While not cheap, the food is high quality (£7-10 sandwiches and salads, £10-16 main dishes, food served Tue-Sat 12:00-21:00, bar open until late, closed Sun-Mon, 12 Stanley Street, tel. 0151/255-0808).

The **Liverpool One** shopping center, in the heart of town, is nirvana for chain restaurants. The upper Leisure Terrace has a row of popular chains, including **Café Rouge** (French), **Wagamama Noodle Bar, Gourmet Burger Company, Pizza Express**—all with outdoor seating.

# SLEEPING

Your best budget options are the central chain hotels—though I've listed several other options as well. Many hotels charge more on weekends (particularly Sat), especially when the Liverpool FC soccer team plays a home game. Rates shoot up even higher two weekends a year: during the Grand National horse race (long weekend in April) and during Beatles Week in late August. Prices drop on Sunday nights.

**$$$ Hope Street Hotel** is a class act located across from the Philharmonic on Hope Street (midway between the cathedrals, in an enticing dining neighborhood). This contemporary hotel has 89 luxurious rooms with lots of hardwood, exposed brick, and elegant extras (standard Db-officially £200, but often £120-160 Fri-Sat and £90-120 Sun-Thu; fancier and pricier deluxe rooms and suites available, breakfast-£12.50 if you prebook, elevator, some rooms handicap accessible, parking-£10, 40 Hope Street, tel. 0151/709-3000, www.hopestreethotel.co.uk, sleep@hopestreethotel.co.uk).

**$$$ Hard Day's Night Hotel** is the splurge for Beatles pilgrims. Located in a restored building in the heart of the Cavern Quarter, the decor is purely Beatles: What could have been tacky is instead tasteful, with subtle nods to the Fab

Four throughout its 110 rooms and public spaces. There's often live music in the afternoons in the lobby bar—and it's not all Beatles covers (standard Db-£90-150, deluxe Db-£20 more, prices can spike dramatically during peak times, especially busy for Sat weddings, breakfast-£16 but £10 if you prebook, air-con, elevator, Internet-enabled TVs with music playlists, parking-£10.50/day, Central Building, North John Street, tel. 0151/236-1964, www.harddaysnighthotel.com, enquiries@harddaysnighthotel.com).

**$$ Aachen Guest Accommodations** has 15 modern rooms in an old Georgian townhouse on a pleasant street just uphill from the heart of downtown (D-£49-85, Db-£59-95, rates depend on demand—higher price is usually for weekends, includes breakfast, 89-91 Mount Pleasant, tel. 0151/709-3477, www.aachenhotel.co.uk, enquiries@aachenhotel.co.uk).

**$$ Best Western Feathers Hotel** has tight hallways and 82 small rooms with mod decor and amenities (Db-generally around £69-79 Sun-Thu, £99-109 Fri, £149-159 Sat, breakfast-£10 if you prebook, no elevator and six floors, pay parking, 115 Mount Pleasant, tel. 0151/709-9655, www.feathers.uk.com, feathersreception@feathers.uk.com).

**$$ Sir Thomas Hotel** is centrally located and was once a bank. The lobby has been redone in a trendy style, and the 39 rooms are comfortable. As windows are thin and it's a busy neighborhood, ask for a quieter room (Db-£69-85 Sun-Thu, £91-151 Fri-Sat, little difference between "standard" and "superior" rooms, some rates include breakfast—otherwise £10, elevator, parking-£8.50/day, 10-minute walk from station, 24 Sir Thomas Street at the corner of Victoria Street, tel. 0151/236-1366, www.sirthomashotel.co.uk, reservations@sirthomashotel.co.uk).

**$$ Premier Inn** has 186 pleasant rooms inside the giant converted warehouses on the Albert Dock (Db-£68-140, averages £70-80 on weekdays, check website for specific rates and special deals, breakfast-£8.75, elevator, pay Wi-Fi, discounted parking in nearby garage, next to The Beatles Story, tel. 0151/702-6320, www.premierinn.com).

**$$ Holiday Inn Express** has a branch at the Albert Dock, next door and nearly identical to the Premier Inn described above (Db-generally around £70-100 Sun-Thu, £125-135 Fri-Sat, includes buffet breakfast, pay parking nearby, beyond The Beatles Story, tel. 0844-875-7575, www.holidayinnexpressliverpool.com, enquiries@exliverpool.com).

**$ International Inn Hostel,** run by the daughter of the Beatles' first manager, rents 100 budget beds in a former Victorian warehouse (Db-£38-47, dorm bed-£17-22, includes sheets, all rooms have bathrooms, guest kitchen with free toast and tea/coffee available 24 hours, laundry room, game room/TV lounge, video library, 24-hour reception, 4 South Hunter Street, tel. 0151/709-8135, www.internationalinn.co.uk, info@internationalinn.co.uk). From the Lime Street Station, the hostel is an easy 15-minute walk; if taking a taxi, tell them it's on South Hunter Street near Hardman Street.

# TRANSPORTATION

## Getting Around Liverpool

The city is walkable and fun to explore, so you may not need to take advantage of the local bus network. But if you're near the Lime Street Station and Queen Square Centre bus hub and need to get to the Cavern sights, Liverpool One mall, or the Albert Dock, you can take public bus #C5 (#C4 visits the same stops in the opposite direction). For more public-transit info, visit a Merseytravel center—there's one at the main bus hub on Queen Square Centre and another at the Liverpool One bus station (1 Canning Place), across the busy street from the Albert Dock (Mon-Sat 8:30-18:00, Sun 10:00-17:00, except Liverpool One closed Sun; tel. 0871-200-2233, www.merseytravel.gov.uk).

## Arriving and Departing
### By Train

Most trains use the main **Lime Street train station.** The station has eateries, shops, and baggage storage (tel. 0151/909-3697, www.left-baggage.co.uk; most bus tours and private minivan/car tours are able to accommodate day-trippers with luggage). Note that regional trains also arrive at the much smaller, confusingly-named **Central Station,** located just a few blocks south.

**Getting to the Albert Dock:** From Lime Street Station to the Albert Dock is about a 20-minute walk or a quick trip by bus, subway, or taxi.

To **walk,** exit straight out the front door. On your right, you'll see the giant Neoclassical St. George's Hall. To reach the Albert Dock, go straight ahead across the street, then head down the hill between St. George's Hall (on your right) and the big blob-shaped mall (on your left). This brings you to Queen Square Centre, a hub for buses. (The round pavilion with the "i" symbol is a transit info center—see "Getting Around Liverpool," earlier.) From here, you can continue by bus (see below) or take a pleasant walk through Liverpool's spiffed-up central core: Head around the right side of the transit-info pavilion, then turn left onto Whitechapel Street, which soon becomes a slick pedestrian zone lined with shopping malls. Follow this all the way down to the waterfront, where you'll see the big red-brick warehouses of the Albert Dock.

To ride the **bus,** walk to Queen Square Centre (see walking directions earlier); for the most direct route to the Albert Dock, take bus #C5 from stall 9 (2/hour—see schedule posted next to stall, bus prices vary—from about £2.20/ride, £3.90 for all-day ticket). To get back to the station from the Albert Dock, take bus #C4.

Alternatively, you can take a **subway** from Lime Street Station to James Street Station, then walk about five minutes to the Albert Dock (about £2.20, also covered by BritRail pass). Note that some regional trains may pass through James Street Station before reaching Lime Street Station; if so, you can hop out here rather than riding to Lime Street.

A **taxi** from Lime Street Station to the Albert Dock costs about £5. Taxis wait outside either of the side doors of the station.

**Train Connections to: Keswick/Lake District** (train to Penrith—roughly hourly with change in Wigan and possibly elsewhere, 2.5 hours; then 45-minute bus to Keswick), **Stratford** (2/hour, 3 hours), **York** (at least hourly, 2-2.5 hours, more with transfer), **London**'s Euston Station (at least hourly, 2-2.5 hours, more with changes). Note that many connections from Liverpool transfer at the Wigan North Western Station, which is on a major north-south train line. Train info: Tel. 0345-748-4950, www.nationalrail.co.uk.

## By Car

Drivers approaching Liverpool first follow signs to *City Centre* and *Waterfront,* then brown signs to *Albert Dock,* where there's a huge pay parking lot at the dock.

## By Plane

Liverpool John Lennon Airport is about eight miles southeast of downtown, along the river (tel. 0871-521-8484, www.liverpoolairport.com, airport code: LPL). Buses into town depart regularly from the bus stalls just outside the main terminal doors. Bus #500 to the city center is quickest, stopping at Queen Square Centre, Liverpool One bus hub, and Lime Street Station (2/hour, 35 minutes, about £3, covered by all-day ticket). Buses #80A, #82A, and #86A also go from the airport to the Liverpool One bus hub, but these take a bit longer.

# The Lake District

**W**illiam Wordsworth's poems still shiver in trees and ripple on ponds in the pristine playgrounds of the Lake District. Nature rules this land, and people keep a wide-eyed but low profile. It's a place to relax, recharge, and renew your poetic license.

There's a walking-stick charm about the way nature and culture mix here. Cruising a lake, walking along a windblown ridge, or climbing over a rock fence to look into the eyes of a ragamuffin sheep, even tenderfeet get a chance to feel outdoorsy.

The tradition of staying close to the land remains true—albeit in an updated form—in the 21st century; restaurants serve organic food and windows host stickers advocating environmental causes.

Expect rain mixed with brilliant "bright spells." Drizzly days can be followed by sunny evenings, so dress in layers. Pubs offer atmospheric shelter at every turn. Enjoy the long days. At this latitude it's light until 22:00 in midsummer.

Plan to spend the majority of your time in the unspoiled North Lake District. Make your home base in Keswick, near the lake called Derwentwater. The North Lake District works great by car or by bus (with easy train access via Penrith), delights nature lovers, and has good accommodations to boot. The South Lake District—slightly closer to London—is famous primarily for its Wordsworth and Beatrix Potter sights, and gets the promotion, the tour crowds, and the tackiness that comes with them. Buck the trend and focus on the north.

A visit here is only worthwhile if you make time to head up into the hills or out on the water at least once. And if great scenery is commonplace in your life, the Lake District can be more soothing (and rainy) than exciting.

# THE LAKE DISTRICT IN 2 DAYS

Nearly all the activities on Day 1 can be enjoyed without a car.

**Day 1:** Spend the morning (3-4 hours) combining a Derwentwater lake cruise with a hike: take the boat partway around the lake, get off at one of the stops to do either the Catbells high-ridge hike or the easier lakeside walk, then hop back on the boat at a later stop to finish the cruise.

For the afternoon, choose among hiking to Castlerigg Stone Circle (one-mile hike from Keswick, or three-mile drive), taking the Walla Crag hike (allow two hours), and visiting the Pencil Museum. Drivers could take the Latrigg Peak hike (trailhead is just outside Keswick).

**On any evening:** Enjoy a pub dinner and stroll through Keswick. Take a hike or evening cruise (or rent a rowboat), play pitch-and-putt golf, or see a play. Hike to the ancient stone circle—if you haven't yet—to toast the sunset (BYOT).

**Day 2: Drivers** have these options:

• Take the scenic loop drive from Keswick through the Newlands Valley, Buttermere, Honister Pass, and Borrowdale. Allow two hours for the drive; by adding stops for the Buttermere hike (an easy four miles) and the slate-mine tour at Honister Pass (last tour at 15:30), you'll have a full, fun day.

• Drive to Glenridding for a cruise and seven-mile hike along Ullswater (allow a day). For a shorter Ullswater experience, hike up to the Aira Force waterfall (1 hour) or up and around Lanty's Tarn (2-2.5 hours).

• You could day-trip into the South Lake District, though it only makes sense if you're interested in the Wordsworth and Beatrix Potter sights. Visiting the sights also works well en route if you're driving between Keswick and points south.

**Nondrivers** have these options:

• Take bus #77 or #77A, the Honister Rambler, which makes a lovely loop from Keswick around Derwentwater, over Honister Pass, through Buttermere, and down the Whinlatter Valley. You could get out at Buttermere to take the four-mile hike. Another good bus option is taking #78, the Borrowdale Rambler, which does another scenic loop from Keswick. See

*The Lake District is arguably the most scenic district in all of England.*

# THE LAKE DISTRICT AT A GLANCE

### North Lake District
### In Keswick
▲▲**Theatre by the Lake** Top-notch theater, a pleasant stroll from Keswick's main square. **Hours:** Shows generally at 20:00 in summer, possibly earlier fall through spring; box office open daily 9:30-20:00. See page 301.

▲**Derwentwater** Lake immediately south of Keswick, with good boat service and trails. See page 291.

▲**Pencil Museum** Paean to graphite-filled wooden sticks. **Hours:** Daily 9:30-17:00. See page 296.

▲**Pitch and Putt Golf** Cheap, easygoing course in Hope Park. **Hours:** Daily from 10:00, last start at 18:00, but possibly later in summer, closed Nov-Feb. See page 301.

### Near Keswick
▲▲▲**Scenic Loop Drive South of Keswick** Two-hour drive through the best of the Lake District's scenery, with plenty of fun stops (including the fascinating Honister Slate Mine) and short side-trip options. See page 298.

▲▲**Castlerigg Stone Circle** Evocative ring of Neolithic stones. See page 296.

▲▲**Catbells High Ridge Hike** Two-hour hike along dramatic ridge southwest of Keswick. See page 297.

▲▲**Buttermere Hike** Four-mile, low-impact lakeside loop in a gorgeous setting. See page 298.

▲**Honister Slate Mine** A 1.5-hour guided hike through a 19th-century mine at the top of Honister Pass. **Hours:** Daily at 10:30, 12:30, and 15:30; also at 14:00 in summer; Dec-Jan 12:30 tour only. See page 299.

## Ullswater Lake Area

▲▲**Ullswater Hike and Boat Ride** Long lake best enjoyed via steamer boat and seven-mile walk. **Hours:** Boats generally depart daily 9:45-16:45, 6-9/day April-Oct, fewer off-season. See page 305.

▲▲**Lanty's Tarn and Keldas Hill** Moderately challenging 2.5-mile loop hike from Glenridding with sweeping views of Ullswater. See page 305.

▲**Aira Force Waterfall** Easy, short uphill hike to thundering waterfall. See page 306.

## South Lake District

▲▲**Dove Cottage and Wordsworth Museum** The poet's humble home, with a museum that tells the story of his remarkable life. **Hours:** Daily March-Oct 9:30-17:30, Nov-Feb 9:30-16:30 except closed Jan. See page 306.

▲**Rydal Mount** Wordsworth's later, more upscale home. **Hours:** March-Oct daily 9:30-17:00; Nov-Dec and Feb Wed-Sun 11:00-16:00, closed Mon-Tue; closed Jan. See page 309.

▲**Hill Top Farm** Beatrix Potter's painstakingly preserved cottage. **Hours:** June-Aug Sat-Thu 10:00-17:30, April-May and Sept-Oct Sat-Thu 10:30-16:30, mid-Feb-March Sat-Thu 10:30-15:30, closed Nov-mid-Feb and Fri year-round. See page 309.

▲**Beatrix Potter Gallery** Collection of artwork by and background on the creator of Peter Rabbit. **Hours:** April-Oct Sat-Thu 10:30-17:00, mid-Feb-March Sat-Thu 10:30-15:30, closed Fri (except possibly in summer) and Nov-mid-Feb. See page 311.

# The Lake District

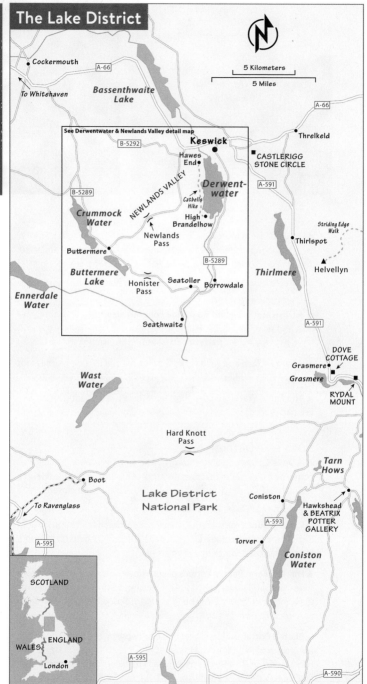

N

5 Kilometers

5 Miles

Cockermouth

To Whitehaven

A-66

Bassenthwaite
Lake

A-66

Threlkeld

See Derwentwater & Newlands Valley detail map

B-5292

Keswick

Hawes
End

CASTLERIGG
STONE CIRCLE

B-5289

Derwent-
water

A-591

NEWLANDS VALLEY

Crummock
Water

Catbells
Hike

High
Brandelhow

Striding Edge
Walk

Thirlspot

Newlands
Pass

Buttermere

B-5289

Helvellyn

Buttermere
Lake

Honister
Pass

Seatoller

Borrowdale

Thirlmere

Ennerdale
Water

Seathwaite

A-591

DOVE
COTTAGE

Grasmere

Grasmere

RYDAL
MOUNT

Wast
Water

Hard Knott
Pass

Tarn
Hows

Boot

To Ravenglass

A-595

Lake District
National Park

Coniston

Hawkshead
& BEATRIX
POTTER
GALLERY

A-593

Torver

Coniston
Water

SCOTLAND

WALES

ENGLAND

London

A-595

A-590

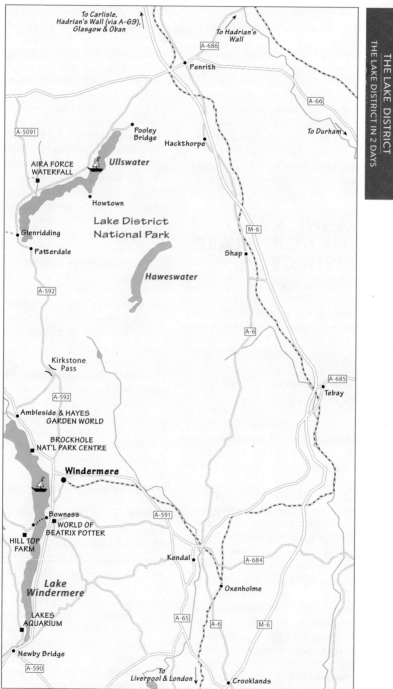

To Carlisle,
Hadrian's Wall (via A-69),
Glasgow & Oban

To Hadrian's
Wall

A-686

Penrith

A-66

To Durham

A-5091

Pooley
Bridge

Hackthorpe

AIRA FORCE
WATERFALL

*Ullswater*

Howtown

Lake District
National Park

M-6

Glenridding

Patterdale

Shap

*Haweswater*

A-592

Kirkstone
Pass

A-685

A-592

Tebay

Ambleside & HAYES
GARDEN WORLD

A-6

BROCKHOLE
NAT'L PARK CENTRE

**Windermere**

Bowness
WORLD OF
BEATRIX POTTER

A-591

HILL TOP
FARM

Kendal

A-684

*Lake
Windermere*

Oxenholme

LAKES
AQUARIUM

A-65

A-6

M-6

Newby Bridge

A-590

To
Liverpool & London

Crooklands

page 312 for bus specifics.
• Take a minibus tour (see "Tours," later).
• Rent a bike in Keswick and make a three-hour loop along the old railway track (now a bike path) and return via the stone circle. See page 313.

**Rainy Day Activities:** Take a hike anyway and wear rain gear; the weather could improve (or not). Visit the Pencil Museum, go swimming at the indoor pool, take a lake cruise (boats have a covered section), tour the slate mine, or relax at a pub or your B&B.

# KESWICK AND THE NORTH LAKE DISTRICT

Keswick (KEZ-ick, population 5,000) is far more enjoyable than other touristy Lake District towns. An important mining center for slate, copper, and lead through the Middle Ages, Keswick became a resort in the 19th century. Its fine Victorian buildings recall those Romantic days when city slickers first learned about "communing with nature."

Today, the compact town is lined with tearooms, pubs, gift shops, and hiking-gear shops. The lake called Derwentwater is a pleasant 10-minute walk from the town center.

## Orientation

Keswick is an ideal home base, with plenty of good B&Bs, an easy bus connection to the nearest train station at Penrith, and a prime location near the best lake in the area, Derwentwater. In Keswick, everything is within a 10-minute walk of everything else: the pedestrian-only town square, the TI, recommended B&Bs, grocery stores, the main bus stop, a lakeside boat dock, and a central parking lot.

Located on the main square is the town centerpiece, Moot Hall (meaning "meeting hall"), which once had a 16th-

century copper warehouse upstairs with an arcade below. The square is lively every day throughout the summer, especially on market days—Thursdays and Saturdays.

Keswick is popular with English holidaymakers who prefer to bring their dogs with them on vacation. The town square in Keswick can look like the Westminster Dog Show.

**Tourist Information:** The National Park Visitors Centre/TI is in Moot Hall on the town square. Staffers are pros at advising you about hiking routes. They can also help you figure out public transportation to outlying sights and tell you about the region's various adventure activities (daily Easter-Oct 9:30-17:30, Nov-Easter 9:30-16:30, tel. 017687/72645, www.lakedistrict.gov.uk and www.keswick.org).

The TI sells theater tickets, Keswick Launch tickets (at a £1 discount), fishing licenses, and brochures and maps that outline nearby hikes (£1-2, including a simple and driver-friendly *Lap Map* featuring sights, walks, and a mileage chart). The TI also has books and maps for hikers, cyclists, and drivers (more books are sold at shops all over town).

Check the boards inside the TI's foyer for information about walks, talks, and entertainment. You can also pick up the *Events and Guided Walks* guide. The daily weather forecast is posted just outside the front door (weather tel. 0844-846-2444).

## Tours
### Hikes

**KR Guided Walks** offers private guided hikes of varying levels of difficulty. The guides also provide transportation from Keswick to the trailhead (£80/day, Easter-Oct, wear suitable clothing and footwear, bring lunch and water, must book in advance, tel. 017687/71302, mobile 0709-176-5860, www.keswickrambles.org.uk, booking@keswickrambles.org.uk).

**Free walks** are offered several times a month in summer by TIs throughout the region. They're led by "Voluntary Rangers" (depart from Keswick TI; check schedule in the *Events and Guided Walks* guide, optional contribution welcome at end of walk).

## Bus Tours

Bus tours are great for people with bucks who'd like to wring maximum experience out of their limited time and see the area without lots of hiking or messing with public transport. (For a cheaper alternative, take public buses.) **Mountain Goat Tours** is the region's dominant tour company. Unfortunately, they run their minibus tours out of Windermere, though a few of their tours offer pickups on certain days in Keswick. If you head to Windermere to join a tour, add about an extra hour round-trip for the drive or bus ride (tours run daily, £28/half-day, £40-50/day, year-round if there are sufficient sign-ups, minimum 4 people to a maximum of 16 per bus, book in advance by calling 015394/45161, www.mountain-goat.com, enquiries@mountain-goat.

com). **Show Me Cumbria Private Tours** runs personalized tours all around the Lake District, and can pick you up in Keswick and other locations. Andy charges per hour, not per person, so his tours are a fine value for small groups (£30/hour, 1-6 people per tour, room for 2 small children in built-in child seats, based in Penrith, tel. 01768/864-825, mobile 0780-902-6357, www.showmecumbria.co.uk, andy@showmecumbria.co.uk).

## Sights

### ▲DERWENTWATER

One of Cumbria's most photographed and popular lakes, Derwentwater has four islands, good circular boat service, and plenty of trails. The pleasant town of Keswick is a short stroll from the shore, near the lake's north end. The roadside views aren't much, and while you can walk around the lake (fine trail, floods in heavy rains, 9 miles, 4 hours), much of the walk is boring. You're better off mixing a hike and boat ride, or simply enjoying the circular boat tour of the lake.

*Derwentwater is just a 10-minute walk from the ideal home-base town of Keswick.*

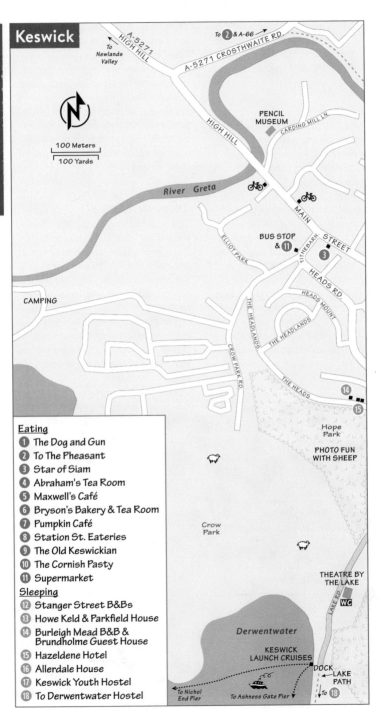

# Keswick

To Newlands Valley

A-5271 HIGH HILL

To **2** & A-66

A-5271 CROSTHWAITE RD.

HIGH HILL

PENCIL MUSEUM

CARDING MILL LN.

100 Meters
100 Yards

River Greta

MAIN STREET

BUS STOP & **11**

TITHEBARN ST.

**3**

ELLIOT PARK

HEADS RD.

HEADS MOUNT

CAMPING

THE HEADLANDS

THE HEADLANDS

CROW PARK RD.

THE HEADS

**14**

**15**

Hope Park

PHOTO FUN WITH SHEEP

Crow Park

THEATRE BY THE LAKE

WC

LAKE RD.

Derwentwater

KESWICK LAUNCH CRUISES

DOCK

LAKE PATH

To Nichol End Pier

To Ashness Gate Pier

To **18**

## Eating
1. The Dog and Gun
2. To The Pheasant
3. Star of Siam
4. Abraham's Tea Room
5. Maxwell's Café
6. Bryson's Bakery & Tea Room
7. Pumpkin Café
8. Station St. Eateries
9. The Old Keswickian
10. The Cornish Pasty
11. Supermarket

## Sleeping
12. Stanger Street B&Bs
13. Howe Keld & Parkfield House
14. Burleigh Mead B&B & Brundholme Guest House
15. Hazeldene Hotel
16. Allerdale House
17. Keswick Youth Hostel
18. To Derwentwater Hostel

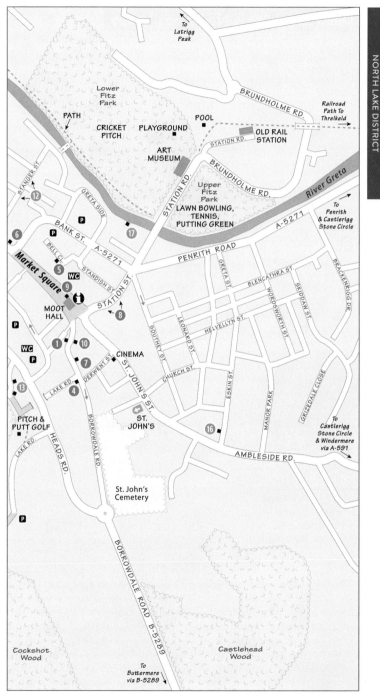

To
Latrigg
Peak

BRUNDHOLME RD.

Railroad
Path To
Threlkeld

Lower
Fitz
Park

PATH

POOL

Station Rd.

OLD RAIL
STATION

CRICKET
PITCH

PLAYGROUND

ART
MUSEUM

BRUNDHOLME RD.

River Greta

Upper
Fitz
Park
LAWN BOWLING,
TENNIS,
PUTTING GREEN

STATION RD.

A-5271

To
Penrith
& Castlerigg
Stone Circle

STANGER ST.

12

GRETA SIDE

P

17

PENRITH ROAD

GRETA ST.

BLENCATHRA ST.

SKIDDAW ST.

BRACKENRIGG DR.

6

BANK ST.

A-5271

P

BELL'S C.

5

STANDISH ST.

WC

9

STATION ST.

8

MOOT
HALL

i

SOUTHEY ST.

LEONARD ST.

HELVELLYN ST.

MORGROVE ST.

P

WC

P

1

10

7

CINEMA

DERWENT ST.

ST. JOHN'S ST.

CHURCH ST.

ESKIN ST.

MANOR PARK

GRIZEDALE CLOSE

13

4

LAKE RD.

PITCH &
PUTT GOLF

BORROWDALE RD.

ST.
JOHN'S

16

To
Castlerigg
Stone Circle
& Windermere
via A-591

LAKE RD.

HEADS RD.

AMBLESIDE RD.

P

St. John's
Cemetery

BORROWDALE ROAD  B-5289

Cockshot
Wood

Castlehead
Wood

To
Buttermere
via B-5289

Market Square

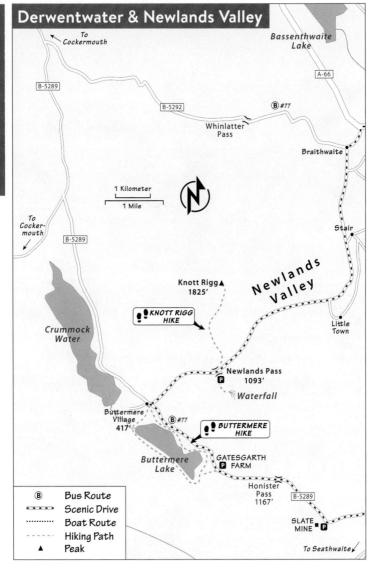

# Derwentwater & Newlands Valley

**Boating on Derwentwater:** Keswick Launch runs two **cruises** an hour, alternating clockwise and "anticlockwise" (boats depart on the half-hour, daily 10:00-16:30, July-Aug until 17:30, in winter 5-6/day generally weekends and holidays only, at end of Lake Road, tel. 017687/72263, www.keswick-launch.

co.uk). Boats make seven stops on each 50-minute round-trip (may skip some stops or not run at all if the water level is high—such as after a heavy rain). The boat trip costs about £2 per segment (cheaper the more segments you buy) or £10 per circle (£1 less if you book through TI) with free stopovers; you can get on

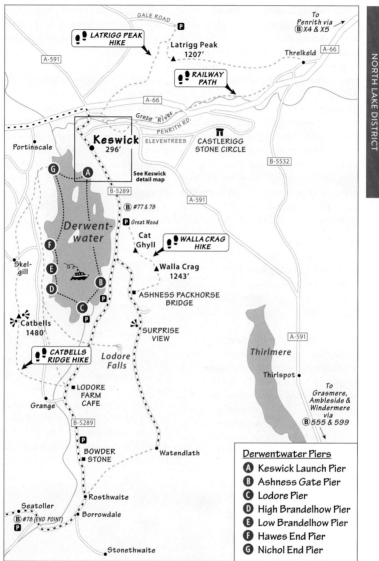

and off all you want, but tickets are collected on the boat's last leg to Keswick, marking the end of your ride. If you want to hop on a #77/#77A bus and also cruise Derwentwater, the £13 Derwentwater Bus & Boat all-day pass covers both. To be picked up at a certain stop, stand at the end of the pier, or the boat may not stop.

See the map for an overview of all the boat stops.

Keswick Launch also has a delightful **evening cruise** (see page 302) and rents **rowboats** for up to three people (£8/30 minutes, £12/hour, open Easter-Oct, larger rowboats and motor boats available).

**Combining Boating and Hiking:** You have two great options for taking the boat to reach a trail, hiking scenically to another dock, then getting back on a later boat to finish the cruise. I like the two-hour **Catbells High Ridge Hike** (get off the boat at Hawes End, hike up and along the ridge, then catch a later boat at High Brandelhow; see next page for specifics). An easier option, using the same stops, is the **Derwentwater Lakeside Walk**. The trail runs all along the lake, but you can stroll just the best stretch—a 1.5-mile level trail through peaceful trees—between the docks at High Brandelhow and Hawes End (start from either dock).

## ▲ PENCIL MUSEUM

Graphite was first discovered centuries ago in Keswick. A hunk of the stuff proved great for marking sheep in the 15th century. In 1832, the first crude Keswick pencil factory opened, and the rest is history (which is what you'll learn about here). While you can't actually tour the 150-year-old factory where the famous Derwent pencils were made, you can enjoy the smell of thousands of pencils getting sharpened for the first time. The adjacent charming and kid-friendly museum is a good way to pass a rainy hour; you may even catch an artist's demonstration. Take a look at the exhibit on "war pencils," which were made for WWII bomber crews (filled with tiny maps and compasses). Relax in the theater with a 10-minute video on the pencil-manufacturing process, followed by a sleepy animated-snowman short (drawn with Rexel Cumberland pencils).

**Cost and Hours:** £4.75, daily 9:30-17:00, last entry one hour before closing, humble café, 3-minute walk from town center, signposted off Main Street, tel. 017687/73626, www.pencilmuseum.co.uk.

## Near Keswick
### ▲▲ CASTLERIGG STONE CIRCLE

For some reason, 70 percent of England's stone circles are here in Cumbria. Castlerigg is one of the best and oldest in Britain, and an easy stop for drivers. The circle—90 feet across and 5,000 years old—has 38 stones mysteriously laid out on a line between the two tallest peaks on the horizon. They served as a celestial calendar for ritual celebrations. Imagine the ambience here, as ancient people filled this clearing in spring to celebrate fertility, in late summer to commemorate the harvest, and in the winter to celebrate the winter solstice and the coming renewal of light. Festival dates were dictated by how the sun rose and set in relation to the stones. The more that modern academics study this circle, the more meaning they

*Castlerigg Stone Circle*

find in the placement of the stones. The two front stones face due north, toward a cut in the mountains. The rare-for-stone-circles "sanctuary" lines up with its center stone to mark where the sun rises on May Day. (Party!) For maximum "goose pimples" (as they say here), show up at sunset (free, open all the time, 1-mile hike from town; by car it's a 3-mile drive east of Keswick—follow brown signs, 3 minutes off the A-66, easy parking; see map on page 294).

## Experiences
### Hikes and Drives

For an easy, flat stroll, consider the trail that runs alongside Derwentwater (see "Derwentwater Lakeside Walk," earlier). Longer options are described below. For tips on hiking, see "Getting Around the Lake District—By Foot" on page 312.

---

Rick's Tip: *Tiny* **biting insects called midges**—*similar to no-see-ums—might bug you in this region from late May through September, particularly at dawn and dusk.* **Insect repellant** *fends them off: Ask the locals what works if you'll be hiking.*

---

#### ▲▲CATBELLS HIGH RIDGE HIKE

Catbells is probably the most dramatic family walk in the area. From Keswick and the lake, you'll see silhouetted hikers—looking like stick figures—on the ridge. If you go, wear sturdy shoes, bring a raincoat, and watch your footing. You'll be rewarded with a great "king of the mountain" feeling, 360-degree views, and a close-up look at the weather blowing over the ridge.

You'll hike above Derwentwater about two hours from Hawes End up along the ridge to Catbells (1,480 feet) and down to High Brandelhow. Because the mountaintop is basically treeless, you're treated to striking panoramas the entire way up. From High Brandelhow, you can catch the boat back to Keswick or take the easy

path along the shore of Derwentwater to your Hawes End starting point. (Extending the hike farther around the lake to Lodore takes you to a waterfall, a fine café, and another boat dock for a convenient return to Keswick.) Note: When the water level is high (for example, after a heavy rain), boats can't stop at Hawes End—ask at the TI or boat dock before setting out.

**Getting There:** To reach the trailhead from Keswick, catch the "anticlockwise" boat (see "Boating on Derwentwater," earlier) and ride for 10 minutes to the second stop, Hawes End. (You can also ride to High Brandelhow and take this walk in the other direction, but I don't recommend it—two rocky scrambles along the way are easier and safer to navigate going uphill from Hawes End.) Note the schedule for your return boat ride. Drivers can park free at Hawes End, but parking is limited and the road can be hard to find—get clear directions in town before heading out. (Hardcore hikers can walk to the foot of Catbells from Keswick via Portinscale, which takes about 40 minutes—ask your B&B or the TI for directions.) The Keswick TI sells a *Catbells* brochure about the hike (£1).

**The Route:** The path is not signposted, but it's easy to follow, and you'll see plenty of other walkers. From Hawes End, walk away from the lake through a kissing gate to the turn just before the parking lot. Then turn left and go up, up, up. After about 20 minutes, you'll hit the first of two short scrambles (where the trail vanishes

*Catbells High Ridge*

into a cluster of steep rocks), which leads to a bluff. From the first little summit (great for a picnic break), and then along the ridge, you'll enjoy sweeping views of the lake on one side and of Newlands Valley on the other. The bald peak in the distance is Catbells. Broken stones crunch under each step, wind buffets your ears, clouds prowl overhead, and the sheep baa comically. Just below the summit, the trail disintegrates into another short, steep scramble. Your reward is just beyond: a magnificent hilltop perch.

After the Catbells summit, descend along the ridge to a saddle ahead. The ridge continues much higher, and while it may look like your only option, at its base a small unmarked lane with comfortable steps leads left. Take this path down to the lake. To get to High Brandelhow Pier, take the first left fork you come across down through a forest to the lake. When you reach Abbot's Bay, go left through a swinging gate, following a lakeside trail around a gravelly bluff, to the idyllic High Brandelhow Pier, a peaceful place to wait for your boat back to Keswick. (You can pay your fare when you board.)

### ▲▲BUTTERMERE HIKE

Outside Keswick, this ideal little lake with a lovely circular four-mile stroll offers nonstop, no-sweat Lake District beauty. If you're not a hiker (but kind of wish you were), take this walk. If you're short on time, at least stop here and get your shoes dirty.

Buttermere is connected with Borrow-

dale and Derwentwater by a great road that runs over the rugged Honister Pass. Buses #77/#77A make a 1.5-hour round-trip loop between Keswick and Buttermere that includes a trip over this pass. The two-pub hamlet of Buttermere has a pay-and-display parking lot, but many drivers park for free along the side of the road. The Syke Farm in Buttermere is popular for its homemade ice cream (tel. 017687/70277).

Another pay parking lot is at the Honister Pass end of the lake (at Gatesgarth Farm).

### ▲▲▲SCENIC LOOP DRIVE

This two-hour-long drive south of Keswick, which includes Newlands Valley, Buttermere, Honister Pass, and Borrowdale, gives you the best scenery you'll find in the North Lake District. (To do a similar route without a car from Keswick, take loop bus #77/#77A.) Distances are short, roads are quite narrow but have turnouts, and views are rewarding. Get a good map and ask your B&B host for advice. (For an overview of the route, see the map on page 294.)

From Keswick, leave town on Crosthwaite Road, then, at the roundabout, head west on Cockermouth Road (A-66, following *Cockermouth* and *Workington* signs). Don't take the first Newlands Valley exit, but do take the second one (through Braithwaite), and follow signs up the majestic Newlands Valley (also signed for *Buttermere*).

If the **Newlands Valley** had a lake, it would be packed with tourists. But it doesn't—and it isn't. The valley is dotted with 500-year-old family-owned farms. Shearing day is a reason to rush home from school. Sons get school out of the way ASAP and follow their dads into the family business. Neighbor girls marry those sons and move in.

Grandparents retire to the cottage next door. With the price of wool depressed, most of the wives supplement the family income by running B&Bs (virtually every

*Buttermere hike*

farm in the valley rents rooms). The road has one lane, with turnouts for passing. From the Newlands Pass summit, notice the glacial-shaped wilds, once forested, now not.

From the parking lot at **Newlands Pass,** at the top of Newlands Valley (unmarked, but you'll see a waterfall on the left), an easy 300-yard hike leads to a little waterfall. On the other side of the road, an easy one-mile hike climbs up to **Knott Rigg,** which probably offers more TPCB (thrills per calorie burned) than any walk in the region.

After Newlands Pass, descend to **Buttermere** (scenic lake, tiny hamlet with pubs and an ice-cream store—see "Buttermere Hike," earlier), turn left, drive the length of the lake, and climb over rugged **Honister Pass**—strewn with glacial debris, remnants from the old slate mines, and curious shaggy Swaledale sheep (looking more like goats with their curly horns). The U-shaped valleys you'll see are textbook examples of those carved out by glaciers. Look high on the hillsides for "hanging valleys"—small glacial-shaped scoops cut off by the huge flow of the biggest glacier, which swept down the main valley.

The **Honister Slate Mine,** England's last still-functioning slate mine (and worth ▲), stands at the summit of Honister Pass. The hostel next to it was originally built to house miners in the 1920s. The mine offers worthwhile tours (perfect for when it's pouring outside): You'll put on a hard hat, load onto a bus for a short climb, then hike into a shaft to learn about the region's slate industry. It's a long, stooped hike into the mountain, made interesting by the guide and punctuated by the sound of your helmet scraping against low bits of the shaft. Standing deep in the mountain, surrounded by slate scrap and the beams of 30 headlamps fluttering around like fireflies, you'll learn of the hardships of miners' lives and how "green gold" is trendy once again, making the mine viable. Even if you don't have time to take the tour, stop here for its slate-filled shop (£12.50, 1.5-hour tour; departs daily at 10:30, 12:30, and 15:30; additional tour at 14:00 in summer; Dec-Jan 12:30 tour only; call ahead to confirm times and to book a spot, helmets and lamps provided, wear good walking shoes and bring warm clothing even in summer,

*You'll find scenic vistas everywhere you venture in the Lake District.*

café and nice WCs, tel. 017687/77230, www.honister.com).

After stark and lonely Honister Pass, drop into sweet and homey **Borrowdale,** with a few lonely hamlets and fine hikes from Seathwaite. Circling back to Keswick past Borrowdale, the B-5289 (a.k.a. the Borrowdale Valley Road) takes you past the following popular attractions.

A set of stairs leads to the top of the house-size **Bowder Stone** (signposted, a few minutes' walk off the main road). For a great lunch or snack, including tea and homemade quiche and cakes, drop into the much-loved **High Lodore Farm Café** (Easter-Oct daily 9:00-18:00, closed Nov-Easter, short drive uphill from the main road and over a tiny bridge, tel. 017687/77221). Farther along, **Lodore Falls** is a short walk from the road, behind Lodore Hotel (a nice place to stop for tea and beautiful views). **Shepherds Crag,** a cliff overlooking Lodore, was made famous by pioneer rock climbers. This is risky climbing, with several fatalities a year.

A very hard right off the B-5289 (signposted *Ashness Bridge, Watendlath*) and a steep half-mile climb on a narrow lane takes you to the postcard-pretty **Ashness**

**Packhorse Bridge,** a quintessential Lake District scene (parking lot just above on right). A half-mile farther up, park the car and hop out (parking lot on left, no sign). You'll be startled by the "surprise view" of Derwentwater—great for a lakes photo op. Continuing from here, the road gets extremely narrow en route to the hamlet of **Watendlath,** which has a tiny lake and lazy farm animals.

Return to the B-5289 and head back to Keswick. If you have yet to see it, cap your drive with a short detour from Keswick to the Castlerigg Stone Circle.

## LATRIGG PEAK

For the easiest mountain-climbing sensation around, take the short drive to the Latrigg Peak parking lot just north of Keswick, and hike 15 minutes to the top of the 1,200-foot-high hill, where you'll be rewarded with a commanding view of the town, lake, and valley, all the way to the next lake over (Bassenthwaite). At the traffic circle just outside Keswick, take the A-591 Carlisle exit, then an immediate right (direction: Ormathwaite/Underscar). Take the next right, a hard right, at the *Skiddaw* sign, where a long, steep, one-lane road leads to the Latrigg parking lot at

*Watendlath's little lake*

the end of the lane. With more time, you can walk all the way from your Keswick B&B to Latrigg and back (it's a popular evening walk for locals).

## WALLA CRAG

From your Keswick B&B, a fine two-hour walk to Walla Crag offers great fell (mountain) walking and a ridge-walk experience without the necessity of a bus or car. Start by strolling along the lake to the Great Wood parking lot (or drive to this lot), and head up Cat Ghyl (where "fell runners"—trail-running enthusiasts—practice) to Walla Crag. You'll be treated to great panoramic views over Derwentwater and surrounding peaks.

## RAILWAY PATH

Right from downtown Keswick, this flat, easy, four-mile trail follows an old train track and the river to the village of Threlkeld (with two pubs). You can either walk back along the same path, or loop back via the Castlerigg Stone Circle (described earlier, roughly seven miles total). The Railway Path starts behind the leisure center (as you face the center, head right and around back; pick up £1 map/guide from TI).

## ▲Golf

A lush nine-hole pitch-and-putt golf course near the gardens in Hope Park separates the town from the lake and offers a classy, cheap, and convenient chance to golf near the birthplace of the sport.

This is a fun, inexpensive experience—just right after a day of touring and before dinner (choose pitch-and-putt, putting, or 18 tame holes of "obstacle golf," daily from 10:00, last round starts around 18:00, possibly later in summer, closed Nov-Feb, café, tel. 017687/73445).

## Swimming

While the leisure center doesn't have a serious adult pool, it does have an indoor pool kids love, with a huge waterslide and wave machine (swim times vary by day and by season—call or check website, no towels or suits for rent, lockers-£1 deposit, 10-minute walk from town center, follow Station Road past Fitz Park and veer left, tel. 017687/72760, www.carlisleleisure.com).

---

**Rick's Tip: Keswick Street Theatre,** *a walk through the town and its history, takes place on* **Tuesday evenings in summer** *(£3, 1.5 hours, usually starts at 19:30, weekly late May-early July, details at TI).*

---

## Nightlife
### ▲▲THEATRE BY THE LAKE

Keswickians brag that they enjoy "London theater quality at Keswick prices." Their theater offers events year-round and a wonderful rotation of six plays from late May through October (plays vary throughout the week, with music concerts on Sun in summer). There are two stages: The main one seats 400, and the smaller "studio" theater seats 100 (and features edgier plays that may involve rough language and/or nudity). Attending a play here is a fine opportunity to enjoy a classy night out.

**Cost and Hours:** £10-32, discounts for old and young, shows generally at 20:00, possibly earlier fall through spring, café, restaurant (pre-theater dinners start at 17:30 and must be booked 24 hours ahead by calling 017687/81102), parking at the adjacent lot is free after 19:00. It's smart to buy tickets in advance—book at box office (daily 9:30-20:00), by phone (tel. 017687/74411), at TI, or at www.theatrebythelake.com.

## EVENING CRUISE

In Hope Park, Keswick Launch's **evening lake cruise** comes with a glass of wine and a mid-lake stop for a short commentary. You're welcome to bring a picnic dinner and munch scenically as you cruise (£10.50, £24 family ticket, 1 hour, daily mid-July-Aug at 18:30 and 19:30—weather permitting and if enough people show up).

# Eating

Keswick has a huge variety of eateries catering to visitors, but I've found nothing enticing at the top end. The places listed here are just good, basic values. Most stop serving by 21:00.

**The Dog and Gun** has good pub food and great pub ambience. Muscle up to the bar to order; then snag a table. Mind your head and tread carefully: Low ceilings and wooden beams loom overhead, while paws poke out from under tables below, as canines wait patiently for their masters (£6-10 meals, food served daily 12:00-21:00, famous goulash, dog treats, 2 Lake Road, tel. 017687/73463). To socialize with locals, drop by on **quiz night,** where tourists are welcomed (£1, proceeds go to Keswick's Mountain Rescue team, 21:30 on most Thu).

**The Pheasant** is a walk outside town, but the food is worth the trek. The menu offers pub standards (fish pie, Cumbrian sausage, guinea fowl), as well as more inventive choices (£10-15 meals, kitchen open daily 12:00-14:00 & 18:00-21:00, bar open until 23:00, Crosthwaite Road, tel. 017687/72219). From the town square, walk past the Pencil Museum, hang a right onto Crosthwaite Road, and walk 10 minutes. For a more scenic route, cross the river into Fitz Park, go left along the riverside path until it ends at the gate to Crosthwaite Road, turn right, and walk five minutes.

**Star of Siam** serves authentic Thai dishes in a tasteful dining room (£8-11 plates, £10 lunch specials, daily 12:00-14:30 & 17:30-22:30, 89 Main Street, tel. 017687/71444).

**Abraham's Tea Room,** tucked away on the upper floor of the giant George Fisher outdoor store, is a fine value for lunch (£5-9 soups, salads, and sandwiches, gluten-free options; Mon-Sat 10:00-17:00, Sun 10:30-16:30, on the corner where Lake Road turns right, tel. 017687/71811).

**Maxwell's Café** serves burgers, tapas, and sandwiches during the day and cocktails in the evening. Outside tables face a big parking lot (£8 meals, Hendersons Yard, find the narrow walkway off Market Street between pink Johnson's sweet shop and The Golden Lion, tel. 017687/74492).

**Bryson's Bakery and Tea Room** has an inviting ground-floor bakery, serving light lunches and sandwiches (a bit cheaper if you get it to go). Upstairs is a popular tearoom. Their £22.50 two-person Cumberland Cream Tea is like afternoon tea in London, but less expensive and made with local products (£4-8 meals, daily 9:00-17:00, 42 Main Street, tel. 017687/72257).

**Pumpkin** has a small café space but a huge following. Stop by for homemade muffins, espresso, or a hot salmon salad (prices higher if you eat in, daily 9:00-16:30, 19 Lake Road, tel. 017687/75973).

**Casa Bella** is family-friendly, Italian, and popular—reserve ahead (£8-11 pizzas and pastas, daily 12:00-15:30 & 17:00-21:00, 24 Station Street, tel. 017687/75575, www.casabellakeswick.co.uk).

**Lakes Bar & Bistro,** across the street, offers burgers, meat pies, and good fixed-price meal deals (£4-7 starters, £10-13 main dishes, £14 two-course and £17 three-course meals, daily 10:00-23:00, 25 Station Street, tel. 017687/74088).

**The Old Keswickian,** on the town square, serves up old-fashioned fish-and-chips to go (Sun-Thu 11:00-22:30, Fri-Sat 11:00-23:30, closes earlier in winter).

**The Cornish Pasty,** just off the town square, offers an appealing variety of fresh meat pies to go (£3-4 pies, daily 9:00-17:00 or until the pasties are all gone, across from The Dog and Gun on Borrowdale Road, tel. 017687/72205).

For **picnic supplies,** try **Booths supermarket,** right where all the buses arrive (Mon-Sat 8:00-21:00, Sun 9:30-16:00, The Headlands).

Rick's Tip: *Advertised throughout this area,* **Kendal mint cakes** *are a local candy—big, flat, mint-flavored sugar cubes worth a try.*

# Sleeping

Reserve your room in advance in high season. From November through March, you should have no trouble finding a room. But to get a particular place (especially on Saturdays), call ahead. Also book ahead for the summer, when festivals and conventions draw crowds and accommodations fill up. Please honor your bookings—the B&B proprietors lose out on much-needed business if you don't show up.

Many of these listings charge extra for a one-night stay. Most won't book one-night stays on weekends (but if you show up and they have a bed free, it's yours). None of these listings have elevators and all have lots of stairs—ask for a ground-floor room if steps are a problem. Most listings don't welcome young children (generally under ages 8-12). If you have trouble finding a room that accepts small children, try searching online at www.keswick.org.

Most accommodations have inviting lounges with libraries of books on the region and loaner maps. Take advantage of these lounges to transform your tight B&B room into a suite. Expect huge breakfasts and shower systems that might need to be switched on to get hot water.

Parking is easy (each place has a line on parking).

## On Stanger Street

This street, quiet but just a block from Keswick's town center, is lined with moderate B&Bs situated in Victorian slate townhouses. Each of these places is small and family-run. They all offer comfortably sized rooms, free parking, and a friendly welcome.

**$$ Ellergill Guest House** has four spic-and-span rooms with an airy, contemporary feel—several with views (Db-£70-90 depending on room size, 2 percent surcharge for credit cards, 2-night minimum, no children under age 10, 22 Stanger Street, tel. 017687/73347, www.ellergill.co.uk, stay@ellergill.co.uk).

**$$ Badgers Wood B&B,** at the top of the street, has six modern, bright, unfrilly view rooms (Db-£78-83, 3 percent surcharge for credit cards, 2-night minimum, no children under age 10, special diets accommodated, 30 Stanger Street, tel. 017687/72621, www.badgers-wood.co.uk, enquiries@badgers-wood.co.uk).

**$$ Abacourt House,** with a daisy-fresh breakfast room, has five pleasant doubles (Db-£76-84, 3 percent surcharge for credit cards, no children, £5 sack lunches available, 26 Stanger Street, tel. 017687/72967, www.abacourt.co.uk, abacourt.keswick@btinternet.com).

**$$ Dunsford Guest House** rents four recently updated rooms at bargain prices. Stained glass and wooden pews give the breakfast room a country-chapel vibe (Db-£70, cash only, mention this book when reserving, 16 Stanger Street, tel. 017687/75059, www.dunsford.net, enquiries@dunsford.net).

## On The Heads

The Heads is a classy area lined with grand Victorian homes, close to the lake and theater, with great views overlooking the golf course and out into the hilly distance. A single yellow line on the curb means you're allowed to park there for free, but only overnight (16:00-10:00).

**$$$ Howe Keld** has the polished feel of a boutique hotel with all the friendliness of a B&B. Its 12 posh rooms are spacious and tastefully decked out. The breakfast is one of the best I've had in England (standard Db-£100-110, superior Db-£110-120, cash and 2-night minimum preferred, discount for 2 or more nights, family deals, tel. 017687/72417 or toll-free 0800-783-0212, www.howekeld.co.uk, david@howekeld.co.uk).

**$$$ Parkfield House** is a big, thoughtfully run Victorian house with a homey lounge. Its six rooms, some with fine views, are bright and attractive (Db-£85, superior king Db-£115, ask for discount with this book but you must reserve direct, 2-night minimum, no children under age 16, free parking, tel. 017687/72328, www.parkfield-keswick.co.uk, parkfieldkeswick@hotmail.co.uk).

**$$$ Burleigh Mead B&B** offers seven lovely rooms and a friendly welcome in a slate mansion from 1892 (north-facing Db with lesser views-£80-90, south-facing Db with grander views-£84-94, Db suite-£100-110, cash only, no children under age 8, tel. 017687/75935, www.burleighmead.co.uk, info@burleighmead.co.uk).

**$$$ Hazeldene Hotel,** on the corner of The Heads, rents 10 spacious rooms, many with commanding views (Db-£75-100 depending on view, one ground-floor unit available, free parking, tel. 017687/72106, www.hazeldene-hotel.co.uk, info@hazeldene-hotel.co.uk).

**$$ Brundholme Guest House** has four bright and comfy rooms, most with sweeping views at no extra charge (Db-£80, mini fridge, free parking, tel. 017687/73305, mobile 0773-943-5401, www.brundholme.co.uk, bazaly@hotmail.co.uk).

## On Eskin Street

**$$ Allerdale House,** a classy stone mansion just southeast of the town center, holds six rooms. It's within easy walking distance of downtown and the lake (standard Db-£80, superior Db-£94, mention this book when reserving, 3 percent surcharge for credit cards, free parking, 1 Eskin Street, tel. 017687/73891, www.allerdale-house.co.uk, reception@allerdale-house.co.uk).

## Hostels

These inexpensive hostels are handy sources of information and social fun.

**$ Keswick Youth Hostel,** with 85 beds in a converted old mill overlooking the river, has a big lounge and great riverside balcony. Travelers of all ages feel at home here, but book ahead for July through September—especially for family rooms (dorm bed-£13-30, members pay £3 less, breakfast extra, includes sheets, pay guest computer, free Wi-Fi, kitchen, laundry, café, bar, office open 7:00-23:00, center of town just off Station Road before river, tel. 017687/72484, www.yha.org.uk, keswick@yha.org.uk).

**$ Derwentwater Hostel** is a 220-year-old mansion on the shore of Derwentwater, two miles south of Keswick. It has 88 beds (dorm bed-£19-22, family rooms, breakfast extra, kitchen, laundry, 23:00 curfew; follow the B-5289 from Keswick—

entrance is 2 miles along the Borrowdale Valley Road about 150 yards after Ashness exit—look for cottage and bus stop at bottom of the drive; tel. 017687/77246, www.derwentwater.org, contact@derwentwater.org).

# ULLSWATER LAKE AREA

For advice on the Ullswater area, visit the **TI** at the pay parking lot in the heart of the lakefront village of Glenridding (daily 9:30-17:30, tel. 017684/82414, www.visiteden.co.uk). This stop is easy for drivers. If busing from Keswick, you'd transfer in Penrith to bus #508 for Glenridding.

### ▲▲ULLSWATER HIKE AND BOAT RIDE

Long, narrow Ullswater, which some consider the loveliest lake in the area, offers diverse and grand Lake District scenery. While you can drive or cruise its nine-mile length, I'd ride the steamer boat from Glenridding halfway up the lake to Howtown (which is nothing more than a dock) and hike back. Or walk first, then enjoy an easy ride back.

The old-fashioned **steamer boat** (actually diesel-powered) leaves Glenridding regularly for Howtown (departs daily generally 9:45-16:45, 6-9/day April-Oct, fewer off-season, 40-minute trip, £6.40 one-way, £10.20 round-trip, £13.60 round-the-lake ticket lets you hop on and off, covered by £15 Ullswater Bus & Boat day pass, family rates, café at dock, £4 walk-

ing route map, tel. 017684/82229, www.ullswater-steamers.co.uk).

From Howtown, spend three to four hours hiking and dawdling along the well-marked path by the lake south to Patterdale, and then along the road back to Glenridding. This is a serious seven-mile walk with good views, varied terrain, and a few bridges and farms along the way. For a shorter hike from Howtown Pier, consider a three-mile loop around Hallin Fell. A rainy-day plan is to ride the covered boat up the lake to Pooley Bridge at the northern tip of the lake, then back to Glenridding (£13.60, 2 hours). Boats don't run in really bad weather—call ahead if it looks iffy.

### ▲▲LANTY'S TARN AND KELDAS HILL

If you like the idea of an Ullswater-area hike, but aren't up for the long huff from Howtown, consider this shorter loop that starts at the TI's pay parking lot in Glenridding. It's 2.5 miles, moderately challenging, and plenty scenic; before embarking, buy the TI's well-described leaflet for this walk (allow 2-2.5 hours).

From the parking lot, head to the main road, turn right to cross the river, then turn right again immediately and follow the river up into the hills. After passing a row of cottages, turn left, cross the wooden bridge, and proceed up the hill through the swing gate. Just before the next swing gate, turn left (following *Grisedale* signs) and head to yet another gate. From here you can see the small lake called Lanty's Tarn.

*Ullswater steamer boat*

*Hike the Keldas Hill for a great view.*

While you'll eventually go through this gate and walk along the lake to finish the loop, first you can detour to the top of the adjacent hill, called Keldas, for sweeping views over the near side of Ullswater (to reach the summit, climb over the step gate and follow the faint path up the hill). Returning to—and passing through— the swing gate, you'll walk along Lanty's Tarn, then begin your slow, steep, and scenic descent into the Grisedale Valley. Reaching the valley floor (and passing a noisy dog breeder's farm), cross the stone bridge, then turn left and follow the road all the way back to the lakefront, where a left turn returns you to Glenridding.

### ▲AIRA FORCE WATERFALL

Wordsworth was inspired to write three poems at this powerful 60-foot-tall waterfall...and after taking this short walk, you'll know why.

Park at the pay-and-display lot, just where the Troutbeck road from the A-66 hits the lake, on the A-592 between Pooley Bridge and Glenridding. There's a delightful little park, a ranger trailer, and easy trails leading a half-mile uphill to the waterfall.

# SOUTH LAKE DISTRICT

The South Lake District has a cheesiness that's similar to other popular English resort destinations. Here, piles of low-end vacationers suffer through terrible traffic, slurp ice cream, and get candy floss caught in their hair.

The area around Windermere is worth a drive-through if you're a fan of Wordsworth or Beatrix Potter, but you'll still want to spend the majority of your Lake District time (and book your accommodations) up north.

Without a car, I'd skip the South Lake District entirely. But diehard Wordsworth fans could take bus #555 from Keswick to Windermere, then catch the hop-on, hop-off Lakeland Experience bus #599, which stops at the Wordsworth sights (3/ hour Easter-late Sept, 2/hour late Sept-Oct, 50 minutes each way, £8 Central Lakes Dayrider all-day pass).

## Sights
### Wordsworth Sights

William Wordsworth was one of the first writers to reject fast-paced city life. During England's Industrial Age, hearts were muzzled and brains ruled. Science was in, machines were taming nature, and factory hours were taming humans. In reaction to these brainy ideals, a rare few—dubbed Romantics—began to embrace untamed nature and undomesticated emotions.

Back then, nobody climbed a mountain just because it was there—but Wordsworth did. He'd "wander lonely as a cloud" through the countryside, finding inspiration in "plain living and high thinking." He soon attracted a circle of like-minded creative friends.

The emotional highs the Romantics felt weren't all natural. Wordsworth and his poet friends Samuel Taylor Coleridge and Thomas de Quincey got stoned on opium and wrote poetry (Coleridge's opium scale is on view in Dove Cottage). Today, opium is out of vogue, but the Romantic movement thrives as visitors continue to inundate the region.

### ▲▲DOVE COTTAGE AND WORDSWORTH MUSEUM

For poets, this two-part visit is the top sight of the Lake District. Take a short tour of William Wordsworth's humble cottage, and get inspired in its excellent museum, which displays original writings, sketches, personal items, and fine paintings.

The poet whose appreciation of nature and back-to-basics lifestyle put this area on the map spent his most productive years (1799-1808) in this well-preserved stone cottage on the edge of Grasmere. After functioning as the Dove and Olive

# Wordsworth at Dove Cottage

Lake District homeboy William Wordsworth (1770-1850) was born in Cockermouth and schooled in Hawkshead. But the 30-year-old man who moved into Dove Cottage in 1799 was not the carefree lad who'd once roamed the district's lakes and fields.

At the University of Cambridge, he'd been a C student, graduating with no job skills and no interest in a career. Instead, he hiked through Europe, where he had an epiphany of the "sublime" atop Switzerland's Alps. He lived a year in France during its Revolution, which stirred his soul. He fell in love with a Frenchwoman who bore his daughter, Caroline. But lack of money forced him to return to England, and the outbreak of war with France kept them apart.

Pining away in London, William hung out in the pubs and coffeehouses with fellow radicals; this is where he met poet Samuel Taylor Coleridge. They inspired each other to write, edited each other's work, and jointly published a groundbreaking book of poetry.

In 1799, his head buzzing with words and ideas, William and his sister (and soul mate) Dorothy moved into the former inn now known as Dove Cottage. He came into a small inheritance and dedicated himself to poetry full time. In 1802, with the war temporarily over, William returned to France to finally meet his daughter. He wrote of the rich experience: "It is a beauteous evening, calm and free... / Dear child! Dear Girl! that walkest with me here, / If thou appear untouched by solemn thought, / Thy nature is not therefore less divine."

Having achieved closure, Wordsworth returned home to marry a former kindergarten classmate, Mary. She moved into Dove Cottage, along with an initially jealous Dorothy. Three of their five children were born here, and the cottage was also home to Mary's sister, family dog Pepper (a gift from Sir Walter Scott), and frequent houseguests Scott, Coleridge, and Thomas de Quincey.

At Dove Cottage, Wordsworth penned his masterpieces. But after almost nine years, his family and social status had outgrown the humble cottage. They moved first to a house in Grasmere before settling down in Rydal Hall. After the Dove years, Wordsworth wrote less, settled into a regular job, drifted to the right politically, and was branded a sellout by some old friends. Still, his poetry became increasingly famous and he died as England's Poet Laureate. He is buried in St. Oswald's churchyard in Grasmere.

*Dove Cottage*

Bow pub for almost 200 years, it was bought by his family. This is where Wordsworth got married, had kids, and wrote much of his best poetry. Still owned by the Wordsworth family, the furniture was his, and the place comes with some amazing artifacts, including the poet's passport and suitcase (he packed light). Even during his lifetime, Wordsworth was famous, and Dove Cottage was turned into a museum

## Wordsworth's Poetry

At Dove Cottage, Wordsworth was immersed in the beauty of nature. The following are select lines from two well-known poems from this fertile time.

### Ode: Intimations of Immortality

There was a time when meadow, grove, and stream,
The earth, and every common sight
To me did seem
Apparelled in celestial light,
The glory and the freshness of a dream.
It is not now as it hath been of yore;
Turn wheresoe'er I may,
By night or day,
The things which I have seen I now can see no more.

### The Daffodils

I wandered lonely as a cloud
That floats on high o'er vales and hills,
When all at once I saw a crowd,
 A host, of golden daffodils;
Beside the lake, beneath the trees,
Fluttering and dancing in the breeze.

. . . . . . . . . . . . . . . . . . .

For oft, when on my couch I lie
 In vacant or in pensive mood,
They flash upon that inward eye
 Which is the bliss of solitude;
And then my heart with pleasure fills,
And dances with the daffodils.

in 1891—it's now protected by the Wordsworth Trust.

**Cost and Hours:** £7.75, daily March-Oct 9:30-17:30, Nov-Feb 9:30-16:30 except closed Jan, café, bus #555 from Keswick, bus #555 or #599 from Windermere, tel. 015394/35544, www.wordsworth.org.uk. Parking costs £1 in the Dove Cottage lot off the main road (A-591), 50 yards from the site.

**Visiting the Cottage and Museum:** Even if you're not a fan, Wordsworth's appreciation of nature, his Romanticism, and the ways his friends unleashed their creative talents with such abandon are appealing. The 25-minute cottage tour (which departs regularly—you shouldn't

*At the Wordsworth Museum*

have to wait more than 30 minutes) and adjoining museum, with lots of actual manuscripts handwritten by Wordsworth and his illustrious friends, are both terrific. In dry weather, the garden where the poet was much inspired is worth a wander. (Visit this after leaving the cottage tour and pick up the description at the back door. The garden is closed when wet.) Allow 1.5 hours for this visit.

#### ▲RYDAL MOUNT

Located just down the road from Dove Cottage, this sight is worthwhile for Wordsworth fans. The poet's final, higher-class home, with a lovely garden and view, lacks the humble charm of Dove Cottage, but still evokes the time and creative spirit of the literary giant who lived here for 37 years. His family repurchased it in 1969 (after a 100-year gap), and his great-great-great-granddaughter still calls it home on occasion, as shown by recent family photos sprinkled throughout the house. After a short intro by the attendant, you'll be given an explanatory flier and are welcome to roam. Wander through the garden William himself designed, which has changed little since then. Surrounded by his nature, you can imagine the poet enjoying it with you. "O happy garden! Whose seclusion deep hath been so friendly to industrious hours; and to soft slumbers, that did gently steep our spirits, carrying with them dreams of flowers, and wild notes warbled among leafy bowers."

**Cost and Hours:** £7.25; March-Oct daily 9:30-17:00; Nov-Dec and Feb Wed-Sun 11:00-16:00, closed Mon-Tue; closed Jan, occasionally closed for private functions—check website, tearoom, 1.5 miles north of Ambleside, well-signed, free and easy parking, bus #555 from Keswick, tel. 015394/33002, www.rydalmount.co.uk.

### Beatrix Potter Sights

Of the many Beatrix Potter commercial ventures in the Lake District, there are two serious sights: her home at Hill Top Farm and her husband's former office, which is now the Beatrix Potter Gallery, filled with her sketches and paintings. The sights are two miles apart, in or near Hawkshead, a 20-minute drive south of Ambleside. The Hawkshead TI is inside the Ooh-La-La gift shop across from the parking lot (tel. 015394/36946). Note that both of the major sights are closed on Friday (though the Beatrix Potter Gallery may be open on Fridays in summer—call ahead).

On busy summer days, the wait to get into Hill Top Farm can last several hours (only 8 people are allowed in every 5 minutes, and the timed-entry tickets must be bought in person). If you like cutesy tourist towns (Hawkshead), this can be a blessing. Otherwise, you'll wish you were wandering in the woods with Wordsworth.

#### ▲HILL TOP FARM

A hit with Beatrix Potter fans (and skippable for others), this dark and intimate cottage, swallowed up in the inspirational and

*Rydal Mount*

*Hill Top Farm*

## Beatrix Potter (1866-1943)

As a girl growing up in London, Beatrix Potter vacationed in the Lake District, where she was inspired to write her popular children's books. Unable to get a publisher, she self-published the first two editions of *The Tale of Peter Rabbit* in 1901 and 1902. When she finally landed a publisher, sales of her books were phenomenal. With the money she made, she bought Hill Top Farm, a 17th-century cottage, and fixed it up, living there sporadically from 1905 until she married in 1913. Potter was more than a children's book writer; she was a fine artist, an avid gardener, and a successful farmer. She married a lawyer and put her knack for business to use, amassing a 4,000-acre estate. An early conservationist, she used the garden-cradled cottage as a place to study nature. She willed it—along with the rest of her vast estate—to the National Trust, which she enthusiastically supported.

rough nature around it, provides an enjoyable if quick experience. The six-room farm was left just as it was when she died in 1943. At her request, the house is set as if she had just stepped out—flowers on the tables, fire on, low lights. While there's no printed information here, guides in each room are eager to explain things. Fans of her classic *The Tale of Samuel Whiskers* will recognize the home's rooms, furniture, and views—the book and its illustrations were inspired by an invasion of rats when she bought this place.

**Cost and Hours:** Farmhouse-£9.50, tickets often sell out by 14:00 or even earlier during busy times; gardens-free; June-Aug Sat-Thu 10:00-17:30, April-May and Sept-Oct Sat-Thu 10:30-16:30, mid-Feb-March Sat-Thu 10:30-15:30, closed Nov-mid-Feb and Fri year-round, tel. 015394/36269, www.nationaltrust.org.uk/hill-top.

*Hill Top Farm, Beatrix Potter's home*

**Avoiding Crowds:** You must buy tickets in person. To beat the lines, get to the ticket office when it opens—15 minutes before Hill Top starts its first tour. If you can't make it early, call the farm for the current wait times (if no one answers, leave a message for the administrator; someone will call you back).

**Getting There:** The farm is located in Near Sawrey, a village two miles south of Hawkshead. Drivers can take the B-5286 and B-5285 from Ambleside or the B-5285 from Coniston—be prepared for extremely narrow roads with no shoulders that are often lined with stone walls. Park and buy tickets 150 yards down the road, and walk back to tour the place.

▲**BEATRIX POTTER GALLERY**

Located in the cute but extremely touristy town of Hawkshead, this gallery fills Beatrix's husband's former law office with the wonderful, intimate drawings and watercolors that she did to illustrate her books. Each year, the museum highlights a new theme and brings out a different set of her paintings, drawings, and other items. Unlike Hill Top, the gallery has plenty of explanation about her life and work, including touchscreen displays and information panels. Even non-Potter fans will find this museum rather charming and her art surprisingly interesting.

**Cost and Hours:** £5.50, April-Oct Sat-Thu 10:30-17:00, mid-Feb-March Sat-Thu 10:30-15:30, closed Fri except possibly in summer (June-Aug; call or check online), closed Nov-mid-Feb, Main Street, drivers

use the nearby pay-and-display lot and walk 200 yards to the town center, tel. 015394/36355, www.nationaltrust.org.uk/beatrix-potter-gallery.

# TRANSPORTATION

## Getting Around the Lake District
### By Car

Nothing is very far from Keswick and Derwentwater. Pick up a good map (any hotel can loan you one), get off the big roads, and leave the car, at least occasionally, for some walking. In summer, the Keswick-Ambleside-Windermere-Bowness corridor (A-591, connecting the North and South Lake District) suffers from congestion. Back lanes are far less trampled and lead you through forgotten villages, where sheep outnumber people and stone churchyards are filled with happily permanent residents.

To **rent a car** here, try Enterprise in Penrith, and reserve at least a day in advance. You can pick up the car in Penrith upon arrival in the Lake District. But they'll even pick you up in Keswick and drive you back to their office to get the car, and also drive you back to Keswick after you've dropped it off (Mon-Fri 8:00-18:00, Sat 9:00-12:00, closed Sun, requires driver's license and second form of ID, located at David Hayton Peugeot dealer, Haweswater Road, tel. 01768/893-840). Larger outfits are more likely to have a branch in Carlisle, which is a bit to the north but well-served by train (on the same Glasgow-Birmingham line as Penrith) and only a few minutes farther from the Keswick area.

**Parking** is tight throughout the region. It's easiest to park in the pay-and-display lots (generally about £3/2-3 hours, £5/4-5 hours, and £7/12 hours; have coins on hand, as most machines don't make change or won't take credit cards without a chip). If you're parking for free on the roadside,

*Beatrix Potter Gallery*

never park on double yellow lines.

If you want a break from driving, consider parking your car at your B&B and using buses to get to sights and trailheads.

## By Bus

Those based in Keswick without a car manage fine. Because of the region's efforts to "green up" travel and cut down on car traffic, the bus service is efficient for hiking and sightseeing.

Keswick has no real bus station; buses stop at a turnout in front of the Booths supermarket. Local buses take you quickly and easily (if not always frequently) to all nearby points of interest. Check the schedule carefully to make sure you can catch the last bus home. Most bus routes run less frequently on Sundays.

The *Lakes Connection* booklet explains the schedules (available at TIs or on any bus; another resource is www.traveline. org.uk). On board, you can purchase an Explorer pass that lets you ride any Stagecoach bus throughout the area (£10.80/1 day, £24.70/3 days), or you can get one-day passes for certain routes (described below). The £13 Derwentwater Bus & Boat all-day pass covers the #77/#77A bus and a boat cruise on Derwentwater.

Buses **#X4** and **#X5** connect the Penrith train station to Keswick (hourly Mon-Sat, every 2 hours Sun, 45 minutes).

Bus **#77/#77A,** the Honister Rambler, makes the gorgeous circle from Keswick around Derwentwater, over Honister Pass, through Buttermere, and down the Whinlatter Valley (6/day clockwise, 5/day "anticlockwise," daily Easter-Oct, 1.5-hour loop). Bus **#78,** the Borrowdale Rambler, goes topless in the summer, affording a wonderful sightseeing experience in and of itself, heading from Keswick to Lodore Hotel, Grange, Rosthwaite, and Seatoller at the base of Honister Pass (nearly hourly, daily Easter-Oct, more frequent late July-Aug, 30 minutes each way). Both of these routes are covered by the £8 Keswick and Honister Dayrider all-day pass.

Bus **#508,** the Kirkstone Rambler, runs between Penrith and Glenridding (near the bottom of Ullswater), stopping in Pooley Bridge (5/day, 45 minutes). The £15 Ullswater Bus & Boat all-day pass covers bus #508 as well as steamers on Ullswater.

Bus **#505,** the Coniston Rambler, connects Windermere with Hawkshead (about hourly, daily Easter-Oct, 35 minutes).

Bus **#555** connects Keswick with the south (hourly, more frequent in summer, one hour to Windermere).

Bus **#599,** the open-top Lakeland Experience, runs along the main Windermere corridor, connecting the big tourist attractions in the south: Grasmere and Dove Cottage, Rydal Mount, Ambleside, Brockhole, Windermere, and Bowness Pier (3/hour Easter-late Sept, 2/hour late Sept-Oct, 50 minutes each way, £8 Central Lakes Dayrider all-day pass).

## By Boat

Boats cruise the larger lakes, stopping at docks along the way, allowing hikers to easily put together a fun cruise-hike-cruise combination. For example, a circular boat service glides you around Derwentwater (see page 294) and a steamer boat takes you up and down Ullswater (see page 305).

## By Foot

Hiking information is available everywhere. Don't hike without a good, detailed map; there's a wide selection at the Keswick TI and the many outdoor gear stores, or you can borrow one from your B&B. Helpful fliers at TIs and B&Bs describe the most popular routes. For an up-to-date weather report, ask at a TI or call 0844-846-2444. Wear suitable clothing and footwear (you can rent boots in town; B&Bs can likely loan you a good coat or an umbrella if weather looks threatening). Plan for rain. Watch your footing; injuries are common. Every year, several people die while hiking in the area (some from overexertion; others are blown off ridges).

### By Bike

Keswick works well as a springboard for bike rides; consider a three-hour loop trip up Newlands Valley, following the Railway Path along a former train track (now a biking path), and returning via the Castlerigg Stone Circle.

Several shops in Keswick rent road bikes and mountain bikes. Bikes come with helmets and advice for good trips. Try **Whinlatter Bikes** (£15/half-day, £20/day, Mon-Sat 10:00-17:00, Sun until 16:00, free touring maps, 82 Main Street, tel. 017687/73940, www.whinlatterbikes.com) or **Keswick Bikes** (£20/half-day, £25/day, daily 9:00-17:30, 133 Main Street, tel. 017687/73355, www.keswickbikes.co.uk).

## Arriving and Departing

If you're relying on public transportation to get to Keswick (which lacks a train station), you'll take the train to Penrith, then a bus to Keswick (see specifics later). For train and bus info, check at a TI, visit www.traveline.org.uk, or call 0345-748-4950 (train only).

### By Train

The nearest train station to Keswick is in Penrith (no lockers).

**Train Connections from Penrith to: Liverpool** (nearly hourly, 2.5 hours, change in Wigan or Preston), **Durham** (hourly, 3 hours, change in Carlisle and Newcastle), **York** (2/hour, 3.5 hours, 1-2 transfers), London's Euston Station (hourly, 4 hours), **Edinburgh** (9/day direct, 2 hours).

### By Bus

Buses link **Penrith** and **Keswick** (Stagecoach bus #X4 or #X5, hourly Mon-Sat, every 2 hours Sun, 45 minutes). Penrith's bus stop is just outside the train station (bus schedules posted inside and outside station). Keswick doesn't have an actual bus station either; buses stop at a turnout in front of the Booths supermarket.

### By Car

Leave the M-6 at Penrith and take the A-66 motorway for 16 miles to Keswick.

# York

After London, historic York is the best sightseeing city in England. Marvel at the York Minster, England's finest Gothic church. Ramble The Shambles, the preserved medieval quarter. Hop a train at one of the world's greatest railway museums. Travel to the 1800s in the York Castle Museum, head back 1,000 years to Viking times at the Jorvik Viking Centre, and dig into the city's buried past at the Yorkshire Museum.

York's rich history begins in A.D. 71, when it was Eboracum, the northernmost city in the Roman Empire. Constantine was proclaimed emperor here in A.D. 306. In the fifth century, after the empire fell, York—now called Eoforwic—became the capital of the Anglo-Saxon kingdom of Northumbria. The Vikings later took the town, and from the 9th through the 11th century, it was a Danish trading center called Jorvik. The invading and conquering Normans destroyed, then rebuilt the city, fortifying it with a castle and the walls you see today.

Medieval York, with 9,000 inhabitants, grew rich on the wool trade and became England's second city. Henry VIII used the city's fine Minster as the northern capital of his Anglican Church.

In the Industrial Age, York was the railway hub of northern England. When it was built, York's train station was the world's largest. During World War II, Hitler chose to bomb York by picking the city out of a travel guidebook (not this one).

Today, York's leading industry is tourism. Everything that's great about Britain finds its best expression here. With its strollable cobbles and half-timbered buildings, grand cathedral and excellent museums, thriving restaurant scene and welcoming locals, York delights.

# YORK AT A GLANCE

▲▲▲**Walking Tours** Variety of guided town walks and evening ghost walks covering York's history. **Hours:** Various times daily. See page 318.

▲▲▲**York Minster** York's pride and joy, and one of England's finest churches, with stunning stained-glass windows, textbook Decorated Gothic design, and glorious evensong services. **Hours:** Mon-Sat 9:00-18:30, Sun 12:30-18:30; shorter hours for tower and undercroft; evensong services Tue-Sat and some Mon at 17:15, Sun at 16:00. See page 326.

▲▲**Yorkshire Museum** Sophisticated archaeology and natural history museum with York's best Viking exhibit, plus Roman, Saxon, Norman, and Gothic artifacts. **Hours:** Daily 10:00-17:00. See page 332.

▲▲**Jorvik Viking Centre** Entertaining and informative Disney-style exhibit/ride exploring Viking lifestyles and artifacts. **Hours:** Daily April-Oct 10:00-17:00, Nov-March until 16:00. See page 333.

▲▲**York Castle Museum** Far-ranging collection displaying everyday objects from Victorian times to the present. **Hours:** Daily 9:30-17:00. See page 334.

▲▲**National Railway Museum** Train buff's nirvana, tracing the history of all manner of rail-bound transport. **Hours:** Daily 10:00-18:00. See page 336.

▲**The Shambles** Atmospheric old butchers' quarter, with colorful, tipsy medieval buildings. **Hours:** Always open. See page 325.

▲**Fairfax House** Glimpse into an 18th-century Georgian family house, with enjoyably chatty docents. **Hours:** Tue-Sat 10:00-16:30, Sun 11:00-15:30, Mon by tour only at 11:00 and 14:00, closed Jan-mid-Feb. See page 334.

▲**York Brewery** Honest, casual tour through an award-winning micro-brewery with the guy who makes the beer. **Hours:** Mon-Sat at 12:30, 14:00, 15:30, and 17:00. See page 337.

# YORK IN 2 DAYS

**Day 1:** Tour the Yorkshire Museum, then take my self-guided York Walk, which starts at the museum's garden. Have lunch along the way; explore The Shambles if it appeals.

Mid-afternoon, tour the massive Minster (includes guided tour and museum). Attend its evensong service (Tue-Sat and some Mon at 17:15, Sun at 16:00).

**On any evening:** Splurge on dinner at one of the city's bistros (cheaper if you go before 19:00). Enjoy the ghost walk of your choice (they depart at different times between 18:45 and 20:00). Or you could take the free city walking tour at 18:45 (evening tours offered June-Aug only), if you'd rather keep your day free to focus on museums. Stroll or bike along the riverside path, or settle in at a pub.

**Day 2:** Take the city walking tour in the morning (also offered mid-afternoon). Tour any of these fine museums: York Castle Museum, National Railway Museum, or the Fairfax House.

If you want to visit the popular Jorvik Viking Centre, you'll minimize your time in line if you go early, late, or pay a bit extra for a timed-entry ticket.

Have afternoon tea at an elegant tearoom (such as Bettys Café or Grays Court). Or go for a tasting at the York Brewery (afternoon tours Mon-Sat).

# ORIENTATION

There are roughly 200,000 people in York and its surrounding area; about 1 in 10 is a student. But despite the city's size, the sightseer's York is small. Virtually everything is within a few minutes' walk: sights, train station, TI, and B&Bs. The longest walk a visitor might take (from a B&B across the old town to the York Castle Museum) is about 25 minutes.

Bootham Bar, a gate in the medieval town wall, is the hub of your York visit. (In York, a "bar" is a gate and a "gate" is a

street. Blame the Vikings.) At Bootham Bar and on Exhibition Square, you'll find the starting points for most walking tours and bus tours, handy access to the medieval town wall, a public WC, and Bootham Street (which leads to my recommended B&Bs). To find your way around York, use the Minster's towers as a navigational landmark, or follow the strategically-placed signposts, which point out all places of interest to tourists.

## Tourist Information

York's TI, a block in front of the Minster, sells a £1 *York Map and Guide.* Ask for the free monthly *What's On* guide and the *York MiniGuide,* which includes a map. A screen lists upcoming events (Mon-Sat 9:00-17:00, Sun 10:00-16:00, pay Internet terminal, 1 Museum Street, tel. 01904/550-099, www.visityork.org).

---

Rick's Tip: *The TI sells a* **pricey sightseeing pass** *that doesn't cover the Yorkshire Museum or York Castle Museum.* **It isn't worth it** *for most people (£36/1 day, £48/2 days, £58/3 days, www.yorkpass.com).*

---

## Tours
### ▲▲▲ *Walking Tours*
**Free two-hour walks** are offered by charming local volunteers who are energetic and entertaining. These tours often go long because the guides love to tell stories. You're welcome to cut out early—but let them know, or they'll worry, thinking

*Take a walking tour in York.*

they've lost you (April-Oct daily at 10:15 and 14:15, June-Aug also at 18:15; Nov-March daily at 10:15 and also at 13:15 on weekends; depart from Exhibition Square in front of the art gallery, tel. 01904/550-098, www.avgyork.co.uk).

**Yorkwalk Tours** are serious 1.5- to 2-hour walks with a history focus. Choose from four different walks—Essential York, Roman York, Secret York, and The Snickelways of York—as well as a variety of "special walks" on more specific topics. Tours go rain or shine, with as few as two participants (£6, Feb-Nov daily at 10:30 and 14:15, Dec-Jan weekends only, depart from Museum Gardens Gate, just show up, tel. 01904/622-303, www.yorkwalk.co.uk—check website, ask TI, or call for schedule).

---

**Rick's Tip:** Hop-on, hop-off buses *circle York, taking tourists past secondary sights on the mundane perimeter of town. For most visitors,* **walking tours are a better choice.**

---

### Ghost Walks

Each evening, the old center of York is crawling with creepy ghost walks. These are generally 1.5 hours long, cost £5, and go every evening, regardless of the weather. There are no reservations (just show up) and no tickets (just pay at the start). At the advertised time and place, your black-clad guide appears, humorously collects the "toll," and you're off.

Companies come and go, but I find there are three general styles of walks: historic, street theater, and storytelling. Here are three reliable walks, one for each style. Each gives a £1 discount (limit two "victims" per book) off full price for Rick Steves readers with this book:

The **Terror Trail Walk** is historic, intellectual, and "all true" (18:45, meet at The Golden Fleece at bottom of The Shambles, www.yorkterrortrail.co.uk).

The **Ghost Hunt** is comedic street theater produced and usually performed

by Andy Dextrous, who introduces himself by saying, "My name is...unimportant" (19:30, meet at the bottom of The Shambles, www.ghosthunt.co.uk).

The **Original Ghost Walk** dates back to the 1970s. It's more classic spooky storytelling than comedy (20:00, meet at The Kings Arms at Ouse Bridge, www.theoriginalghostwalkofyork.co.uk).

# YORK WALK

Get a taste of Roman and medieval York on this easy stroll, which starts just in front of the Yorkshire Museum, covers a stretch of the medieval city walls, and then cuts through the middle of the old town.

Note that it's convenient to tour the worthwhile Yorkshire Museum before you begin the walk (though you can also easily return to visit the museum later).

## ⊙ Self-Guided Walk

Begin in the gardens just in front of the Yorkshire Museum, where you'll see the ruins of...

**St. Mary's Abbey:** This abbey dates to the age of William the Conqueror—whose harsh policies (called the "Harrowing of the North") consisted of massacres and destruction, including the burning of York's main church. His son Rufus, who tried to improve relations in the 11th century, established a great church here. The church became an abbey that thrived from the 13th century until the Dissolution of the Monasteries in the 16th century.

*St. Mary's Abbey*

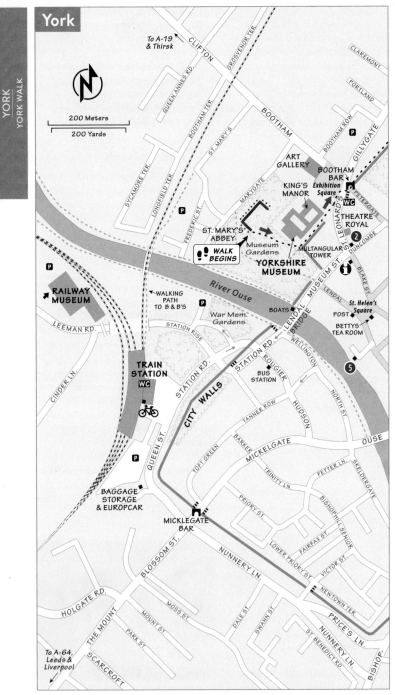

# York

N

200 Meters

200 Yards

To A-19 & Thirsk

CLIFTON

GROSVENOR TER.

CLAREMONT

PORTLAND

QUEEN ANNES RD.

BOOTHAM

BOOTHAM ROW

GILLYGATE

SYCAMORE TER.

LONGFIELD TER.

BOOTHAM TER.

ST. MARY'S

MARYGATE

FREDERIC ST.

ART GALLERY

KING'S MANOR

Exhibition Square

BOOTHAM BAR

WC

ST. LEONARD'S

PETERGATE

THEATRE ROYAL

2

DUNCOMBE

ST. MARY'S ABBEY

WALK BEGINS

Museum Gardens

MULTANGULAR TOWER

YORKSHIRE MUSEUM

MUSEUM ST.

LENDAL

BLAKE ST.

1

River Ouse

P

RAILWAY MUSEUM

WALKING PATH TO B & B'S

P

War Mem. Gardens

BOATS

LENDAL BRIDGE

St. Helen's Square

POST

BETTYS TEA ROOM

LEEMAN RD.

STATION RISE

STATION RD.

WELLINGTON

5

CINDER LN.

TRAIN STATION

WC

STATION RD.

ROUGIER

BUS STATION

CITY WALLS

TANNER ROW

HUDSON

NORTH ST.

OUSE

QUEEN ST.

BARKER

MICKELGATE

FETTER LN.

SKELDERGATE

P

TOFT GREEN

TRINITY LN.

PRIORY ST.

BISHOPHILL SENIOR

BAGGAGE STORAGE & EUROPCAR

MICKLEGATE BAR

FAIRFAX ST.

LOWER PRIORY ST.

VICTOR ST.

BLOSSOM ST.

NUNNERY LN.

NEWTOWN TER.

HOLGATE RD.

THE MOUNT

MOSS ST.

MOUNT ST.

DALE ST.

SWANN ST.

PRICE'S LN.

NUNNERY LN.

ST. BENEDICT RD.

BISHOP.

PARK ST.

To A-64, Leeds & Liverpool

SCARCROFT

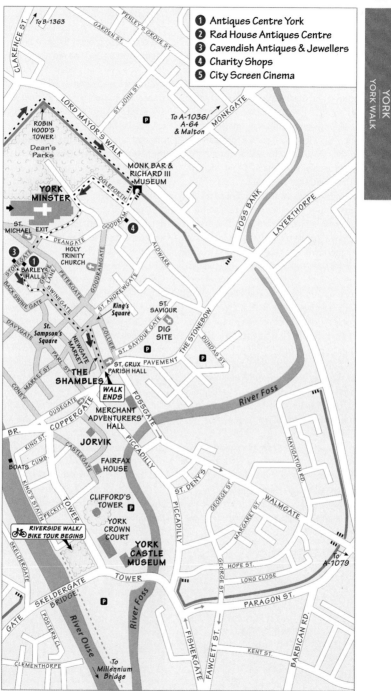

1 Antiques Centre York
2 Red House Antiques Centre
3 Cavendish Antiques & Jewellers
4 Charity Shops
5 City Screen Cinema

The Dissolution, which accompanied the Protestant Reformation and break with Rome, was a power play by Henry VIII. The king wanted much more than just a divorce: He wanted the land and riches of the monasteries. Upset with the pope, he demanded that his subjects pay him taxes rather than give the Church tithes.

As you gaze at this ruin, imagine magnificent abbeys like this scattered throughout the realm. Henry VIII destroyed most of them, taking the lead from their roofs and leaving the stones to scavenging townsfolk. Scant as they are today, these ruins still evoke a time of immense monastic power. The one surviving wall was the west half of a long, skinny nave. The tall arch marked the start of the transept. Stand on the plaque that reads *Crossing beneath central tower,* and look up at the air that now fills the space where a huge tower once stood. (Fine carved stonework from the ruined abbey is on display in a basement room of the adjacent Yorkshire Museum.)

Beyond the abbey, laid out like a dozen stone eggs, are 12 ancient **Roman sarcophagi** that were excavated at the train station. You'll also see a bowling green and the abbey's original wall (not part of the city walls).

• *With your back to the abbey, see the fine Neoclassical building housing the* **Yorkshire Museum.** *Walk past this about 30 yards to a corner of the city's* **Roman wall.** *A tiny lane through the garden (past a yew tree) leads through a small gated arch (may be locked), giving a peek into the ruined tower.*

**Multangular Tower:** This 12-sided tower (c. A.D. 300) was likely a catapult station built to protect the town from enemy river traffic. The red ribbon of bricks was a Roman trademark—both structural and decorative. The lower stones are Roman, while the upper (and bigger) stones are medieval. After Rome fell, York suffered through two centuries of a dark age. Then, in the ninth century, the Vikings ruled. Because they built with wood, almost nothing from that period remains. The Normans came in 1066 and built in stone, generally atop Roman structures (like this wall). The wall that defined the ancient Roman garrison town worked for the Norman town, too. But after the English Civil War in the 1600s and Jacobite rebellions in the 1700s, fortified walls were no longer needed in England's interior.

• *Now, return 10 steps down the lane and turn right, walking between the museum and the Roman wall. Continuing straight, the lane goes between the abbot's palace and the town wall. This is a "snickelway"—a small, characteristic York lane or footpath. The snickelway pops out on...*

**Exhibition Square:** With Henry VIII's Dissolution of the Monasteries, the abbey was destroyed and the Abbot's Palace became the **King's Manor** (from the snickelway, make a U-turn to the left and through the gate). Enter the building under the coat of arms of Charles I, who stayed here during the English Civil War in the 1640s. Today, the building is part of the University of York. Because the north-

*Multangular Tower*

*Bootham Bar*

erners were slow to embrace the king's reforms, Henry VIII came here to enforce the Dissolution. He stayed 17 days in this mansion and brought along 1,000 troops to make his determination clear. You can wander into the grounds and building. The Refectory Café serves cheap cakes, soup, and sandwiches to students, professors, and visitors like you (Mon-Fri 9:30-15:00, closed Sat-Sun).

Exhibition Square is the departure point for various walking and bus tours. You can see the towers of the Minster in the distance. Travelers in the Middle Ages could see the Minster from miles away as they approached the city. Across the street is a pay WC and **Bootham Bar**—one of the fourth-century Roman gates in York's wall—with access to the best part of the city walls (free, walls open 8:00-dusk).

• *Climb up the bar.*

**Walk the Wall:** Hike along the top of the wall behind the Minster to the first corner. Just because you see a padlock on an entry gate, don't think it's locked—give it a push, and you'll probably find it's open.

York's 13th-century walls are three miles long. This stretch follows the original Roman wall. Norman kings built the walls to assert control over northern England. Notice the pivots in the crenellations (square notches at the top of a medieval wall), which once held wooden hatches to provide cover for archers. The wall was extensively renovated in the 19th century (Victorians added Romantic arrow slits).

At the corner with the benches— **Robin Hood's Tower**—you can lean out and see the moat outside. This was originally the Roman ditch that surrounded the fortified garrison town. Continue walking for a fine view of the Minster, with its truncated main tower and the pointy rooftop of its chapter house.

Continue on to the next gate, **Monk Bar:** This fine medieval gatehouse is the home of the overly-slick Richard III Museum.

• *Descend the wall at Monk Bar, and step past the portcullis (last lowered in 1953 for the Queen's coronation) to emerge outside the city's protective wall. Take 10 paces and gaze up at the tower. Imagine 10 archers*

*City walls*

*Monk Bar*

A *York's Old Town*
B *Constantine statue*
C *Snickelways*
D *The Shambles*

behind the arrow slits. Keep an eye on the 17th-century guards, with their stones raised and primed to protect the town.

Return through the city wall. After a short block, turn right on Ogleforth. ("Ogle" is the Norse word for owl, hence our word "ogle"—to look at something fiercely.)

**York's Old Town:** Walking down Ogleforth, ogle (on your left) a charming little brick house from the 17th century called the **Dutch House.** It was designed by an apprentice architect who was trying to show off for his master, and was the first entirely brick house in town—a sign of opulence. Next, also of brick, is a former brewery with a 19th-century industrial feel.

Ogleforth jogs left and becomes **Chapter House Street,** passing the Treasurer's House to the back side of the Minster. Circle around the left side of the church, past the stonemasons' lodge (where craftsmen are chiseling local limestone for the church, as has been done here since the 13th century), to the statue of Roman Emperor Constantine and an ancient Roman column.

Step up to lounging **Constantine.** Five emperors visited York when it was the Roman city of Eboracum. Constantine was here when his father died. The troops declared him the Roman emperor in A.D. 306 at this site, and six years later, he went to Rome to claim his throne. In A.D. 312, Constantine legalized Christianity, and in A.D. 314, York got its first bishop. The thought-provoking plaque reads: "His recognition of the civil liberty of his Christian subjects and his personal conversion established the religious foundation of Western Christendom."

The **ancient column,** across the street from Constantine, is a reminder that the Minster sits upon the site of the Roman headquarters, or *principia.* The city placed this column here in 1971, just before celebrating the 1,900th anniversary of the founding of Eboracum—a.k.a. York.
• If you want to visit the **York Minster**

*now, find the entrance on its west side (see description on page 326). Otherwise, head into the town center. From opposite the Minster's south transept door (by Constantine), take a narrow pedestrian walkway—which becomes Stonegate—into the tangled commercial center of medieval York. Walk straight down Stonegate, a street lined with fun and inviting cafés, pubs, and restaurants. Just before the Ye Old Starre Inne banner hanging over the street, turn left down the snickelway called Coffee Yard. (It's marked by a red devil.) Enjoy strolling York's...*

**"Snickelways":** This is a made-up York word combining "snicket" (a passageway between walls or fences), "ginnel" (a narrow passageway between buildings), and "alleyway" (any narrow passage)—snickelway. York—with its population packed densely inside its protective walls—has about 50 of these public passages. In general, when exploring the city, you should duck into these—both for the adventure and to take a shortcut. While some of York's history has been bulldozed by modernity, bits of it hide and survive in the snickelways.

Coffee Yard leads past Barley Hall, popping out at the corner of Grape Lane and Swinegate. Medieval towns named streets for the business done there. Swinegate, a lane of pig farmers, leads to the market. Grape Lane is a polite version of that street's original crude name, Gropec*nt Lane. If you were here a thousand years ago, you'd find it lined by brothels. Throughout England, streets for prostitutes were called by this graphic name. Today, if you see a street named Grape Lane, that's usually its heritage.

Skip Grape Lane and turn right down Swinegate to a market (which you can see in the distance). The frumpy **Newgate Market,** popular for cheap produce and clothing, was created in the 1960s with the demolition of a bunch of colorful medieval lanes.

• *In the center of the market, tiny "Little Shambles" lane (on the left) dead-ends into*

*the most famous lane in York.*

**The Shambles:** This colorful old street, rated ▲, was once the "street of the butchers." The name is derived from "shammell"—a butcher's bench upon which he'd cut and display his meat. In the 16th century, this lane was dripping with red meat. Look for the hooks under the eaves; these were once used to hang rabbit, pheasant, beef, lamb, and pigs' heads. Fresh slabs were displayed on the fat sills, while people lived above the shops. All the garbage and sewage flushed down the street to a mucky pond at the end—a favorite hangout for the town's cats and dogs. Tourist shops now fill these fine, half-timbered Tudor buildings. Look above the modern crowds and storefronts to appreciate the classic old English architecture. Unfortunately, the soil here isn't great for building; notice how the structures have settled in the absence of a solid foundation.

Turn right and slalom down The Shambles. At the Mr. Sandwich shop, pop into the snickelway and look for old **woodwork.** Study the 16th-century carpentry—mortise-and-tenon joints with wooden plugs rather than nails.

Next door (on The Shambles) is the **shrine of St. Margaret Clitherow,** a 16th-century Catholic crushed by Protestants under her own door (as was the humiliating custom when a city wanted to teach someone a lesson). She was killed for hiding priests in her home here. Step into the tiny shrine for a peaceful moment to ponder Margaret, who in 1970 was sainted for her faith.

At the bottom of The Shambles is the cute, tiny, recommended **St. Crux Parish Hall,** which charities use to raise funds by selling light meals. Take some time to chat with the volunteers.

With blood and guts from The Shambles' 20 butchers all draining down the lane, it's no wonder The Golden Fleece, just below, is considered the most haunted pub in town.

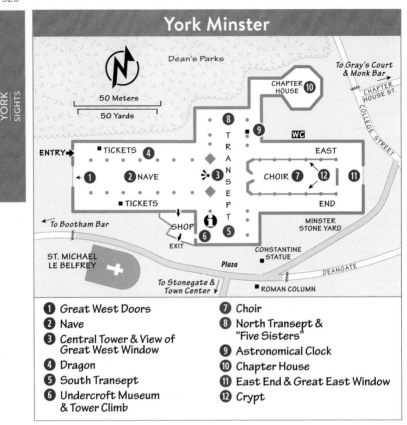

# York Minster

**1** Great West Doors
**2** Nave
**3** Central Tower & View of Great West Window
**4** Dragon
**5** South Transept
**6** Undercroft Museum & Tower Climb
**7** Choir
**8** North Transept & "Five Sisters"
**9** Astronomical Clock
**10** Chapter House
**11** East End & Great East Window
**12** Crypt

• *Your town walk is finished. From here, you're just a few minutes from plenty of fun: street entertainment and lots of cheap eating options on King's Square, good restaurants on Fossgate, and the York Castle Museum (a few blocks farther downhill, and the starting point for the Riverside Walk on page 338).*

# SIGHTS

## Inside York's Walls

### ▲▲▲YORK MINSTER

The pride of York, this largest Gothic church north of the Alps (540 feet long, 200 feet tall) brilliantly shows that the High Middle Ages were far from dark. The word "minster" means an important church chartered with a mission to evangelize. As it's the seat of a bishop, York Minster is also a cathedral. While Henry VIII destroyed England's great abbeys, this was not part of a monastery and was therefore left standing. It seats 2,000 comfortably; on Christmas and Easter, at least 4,000 worshippers pack the place. Today, more than 250 employees and 500 volunteers work to preserve its heritage and welcome 1.3 million visitors each year.

**Cost:** Cathedral-£10, includes guided tour, undercroft museum, and crypt; free for kids under age 16; tower climb-£5.

**Hours:** The cathedral is open for sightseeing Mon-Sat 9:00-18:30, Sun 12:30-18:30. It opens for worship daily at 7:30. Closing time flexes with activities, but last entry is generally at 17:30—call or look online to confirm. Sights within the Minster have shorter hours (listed below). The Minster may close for special events (check calendar on website).

**Information:** You'll get a free map with your ticket. For more information, pick up the *York Minster Short Guide* for £2.50. Helpful Minster guides stationed throughout are happy to answer your questions. Tel. 01904/557-217 or 0844-393-0011, www.yorkminster.org.

**Tower Climb:** It costs £5 for 30 minutes of exercise (275 steps) and forgettable views. The tower opens at 10:00 (later on Sun), with ascents every 45 minutes; the last ascent is generally at 17:30—later in peak season and earlier in winter (no children under 8, not good for acrophobes, closes in extreme weather). Be sure to get your ticket upon arrival, as only 50 visitors are allowed up at once; you'll be assigned an entry time. It's a tight, spiraling, claustrophobic staircase with an iron handrail. You'll climb about 150 steps to the top of the transept, step outside to cross a narrow walkway, then go back inside for more than 100 steps to the top of the central

tower. From here (while caged in), you can enjoy views of rooftops and the flat countryside.

**Undercroft Museum:** This museum focuses on the history of the site and its origins as a Roman fortress (Mon-Sat 10:00-17:00, Sun 12:30-16:00).

**Tours:** Free guided tours depart from the ticket desk every hour on the hour (Mon-Sat 10:00-15:00, can be more frequent during busy times, none on Sun, one hour, they go even with just one or two people). You can join a tour in progress, or if none is scheduled, request a departure.

**Evensong:** To experience the cathedral in musical and spiritual action, attend an evensong (Tue-Sat at 17:15, Sun at 16:00). On Mondays, visiting choirs fill in about half the time (otherwise it's a spoken service, also at 17:15). Visiting choirs also perform when the Minster's choir is on summer break (mid-July-Aug, confirm at church or TI). Arrive 15 minutes early and wait just outside the choir in the center of the church. You'll be ushered in and can sit in one of the big wooden stalls. As evensong is a worship service, attendees enter the church free of charge. For more on evensong, see page 102.

**Church Bells:** If you're a fan of church bells, you'll experience ding-dong ecstasy Sunday morning at about 10:00 and during the Tuesday practice session between 19:00 and 22:00. These performances are especially impressive, as the church holds a full carillon of 35 bells (it's the only English cathedral to have such a range). Stand in front of the church's west portal and imagine the gang pulling on a dozen ropes (halfway up the right tower—you can actually see the ropes through a little window) while one talented carillonneur plays 22 more bells with a keyboard and foot pedals.

## ● SELF-GUIDED TOUR

Enter the great church through the west portal (under the twin towers). Upon entering, decide if you're climbing the

*York Minster, south transept*

tower. If so, get a ticket (with an assigned time). Also consider visiting the Undercroft Museum (described later) if you want to get a comprehensive history and overview of the Minster before touring the church.

• *Entering the church, turn 180 degrees and look back at the...*

**❶ Great West Doors:** These are used only on special occasions. Flanking the doors is a list of archbishops (and other church officials) that goes unbroken back to the 600s. The statue of Peter with the key and Bible is a reminder that the church is dedicated to St. Peter, and the key to heaven is found through the word of God. While the Minster sits on the remains of a Romanesque church (c. 1100), today's church was begun in 1220 and took 250 years to complete. Up above, look for the female, headless "semaphore saints," using semaphore flag code to spell out a message with golden discs: "Christ is here."

• *Grab a chair and enjoy the view down the...*

**❷ Nave:** Your first impression might be of its spaciousness and brightness. One of the widest Gothic naves in Europe, it was built between 1280 and 1360—the middle period of the Gothic style, called "Decorated Gothic." Rather than risk a stone roof, builders spanned the space with wood. Colorful shields on the arcades are the coats of arms of nobles who helped tall and formidable Edward I, known as "Longshanks," fight the Scots in the 13th century.

The coats of arms in the clerestory (upper-level) glass represent the nobles who helped his son, Edward II, in the same fight. There's more medieval glass in this building than in the rest of England combined. This precious glass survived World War II—hidden in stately homes throughout Yorkshire.

Walk to the very center of the church, under the **❸ central tower.** Look up. An exhibit in the undercroft explains how gifts and skill saved this 197-foot tower from collapse. Use the neck-saving mirror to marvel at it.

Look back at the west end to marvel at the **Great West Window,** especially the stone tracery. While its nickname is the "Heart of Yorkshire," it represents the sacred heart of Christ, meant to remind people of his love for the world.

Find the **❹ dragon** on the right of the

*Choir screen with carvings of English monarchs*

nave (two-thirds of the way up the wall). While no one is sure of its purpose, it pivots and has a hole through its neck—so it was likely a mechanism designed to raise a lid on a baptismal font.

• *Facing the altar, turn right and head into the...*

**❺ South Transept:** Look up. The new "bosses" (carved medallions decorating the point where the ribs meet on the ceiling) are a reminder that the roof of this wing of the church was destroyed by fire in 1984, caused when lightning hit an electricity box. Some believe the lightning was God's angry response to a new bishop, David Jenkins, who questioned the literal truth of Jesus' miracles. (Jenkins had been interviewed at a nearby TV studio the night before, leading locals to joke that the lightning occurred "12 hours too late, and 17 miles off-target.") Regardless, the entire country came to York's aid. *Blue Peter* (England's top kids' show) conducted a competition among their young viewers to design new bosses. Out of 30,000 entries, there were six winners (the blue ones—e.g., man on the moon, feed the children, save the whales).

Two other sights can be accessed through the south transept: the **❻ Undercroft Museum** (explained later) and the **tower climb** (explained earlier). But for now, stick with this tour; we'll circle back to the south transept at the end, before exiting the church.

• *Head back into the middle of the nave and face the front of the church. You're looking at the...*

**❼ Choir:** Examine the choir screen—the ornate wall of carvings separating the nave from the choir. It's lined with all the English kings from William I (the Conqueror) to Henry VI (during whose reign it was carved, in 1461). Numbers indicate the years each reigned. It is indeed "slathered in gold leaf," which sounds impressive, but the gold is thin...a nugget the size of a sugar cube is pounded into a sheet the size of a driveway.

Step into the choir, where a service is held daily. All the carving was redone after an 1829 fire, but its tradition of glorious evensong services (sung by choristers from the Minster School) goes all the way back to the eighth century.

• *To the left as you face the choir is the...*

**❽ North Transept:** In this transept, the grisaille windows—dubbed the **"Five Sisters"**—are dedicated to British servicewomen who died in wars. Made in 1260, before colored glass was produced in England, these contain more than 100,000 pieces of glass.

The 18th-century **❾ astronomical clock** is worth a look (the sign helps you make sense of it). It's dedicated to the heroic Allied aircrews from bases here in northern England who died in World War II (as Britain kept the Nazis from invading in its "darkest hour"). The Book of Remembrance below the clock contains 18,000 names.

• *A corridor leads to the Gothic, octagonal...*

**❿ Chapter House:** This was the traditional meeting place of the governing

*Chapter House*

## The Church of England

The Anglican Church (a.k.a. the Church of England) came into existence in 1534 when Henry VIII declared that he, and not Pope Clement VII, was the head of England's Catholics. The pope had refused to allow Henry to divorce his wife to marry his mistress Anne Boleyn (which Henry did anyway, resulting in the birth of Elizabeth I). Still, Henry regarded himself as a faithful Catholic—just not a *Roman* Catholic—and made relatively few changes in how and what Anglicans worshipped.

Henry's son, Edward VI, later instituted many of the changes that Reformation Protestants were bringing about in continental Europe: an emphasis on preaching, people in the pews actually reading the Bible, clergy being allowed to marry, and a more "Protestant" liturgy in English from the revised Book of Common Prayer (1549). The next monarch, Edward's sister Mary I, returned England to the Roman Catholic Church (1553), earning the nickname "Bloody Mary" for her brutal suppression of Protestant elements. In 1558, Elizabeth I succeeded Mary and broke from Rome again. Today, many regard the Anglican Church as a compromise between the Catholic and Protestant traditions. In the US, Anglicans split off from the Church in England after the American Revolution, creating the Episcopal Church that still thrives today.

Ever since Henry VIII's time, the York Minster has held a special status within the Anglican hierarchy. After a long feud over which was the leading church, the archbishops of Canterbury and York agreed that York's bishop would have the title "Primate of England" and Canterbury's would be the "Primate of All England," directing Anglicans on the national level.

body (or chapter) of the Minster. On the pillar in the middle of the doorway, the Virgin holds Baby Jesus while standing on the devilish serpent. The Chapter House, without an interior support, is remarkable (almost frightening) for its breadth. The fanciful carvings decorating the canopies above the stalls date from 1280 (80 percent are originals) and are some of the Minster's finest. Stroll slowly around the entire room and imagine that the tiny sculpted heads are a 14th-century parade—a fun glimpse of medieval society. Grates still send hot air up robes of attendees on cold winter mornings. A model of the wooden construction illustrates the remarkable 1285 engineering.

The Chapter House was the site of an important moment in England's parliamentary history. Fighting the Scots in 1295,

Edward I (nicknamed "Longshanks") convened the "Model Parliament" here, rather than down south in London. (The Model Parliament is the name for its early version, back before the legislature was split into the Houses of Commons and Lords.) The government met here through the 20-year reign of Edward II, before moving to London during Edward III's rule in the 14th century.

• *Go back out into the main part of the church, turn left, and continue all the way down the nave (behind the choir) to the...*

**⓫ East End:** This part of the church is square, lacking a semicircular apse, typical of England's Perpendicular Gothic style (15th century). Monuments (almost no graves) were once strewn throughout the church, but in the Victorian Age, they were gathered into the east end, where you see them today.

The **Great East Window,** the size of a tennis court, is currently under restoration. Under it, two exhibits—"Stone by Stone" and "Let There Be Light"—give an intimate look at Gothic stone and glasswork. Curators hope that this grand window will finally come out from its scaffolding within a year or two.

"Let There Be Light" explains the significance of the window and the scope of the conservation project. It illustrates the painstaking process of removing, dismantling, cleaning, and restoring each of the 311 panels. Interactive computers let you zoom in on each panel, read about the stories depicted in them, and explore the codes and symbols that are hidden in the window.

Because of the Great East Window's immense size, the east end has an extra layer of supportive stonework, parts of it wide enough to walk along. In fact, for special occasions, the choir has been known to actually sing from the walkway halfway up the window. But just as the window has deteriorated over time, so too has the stone. Nearly 3,500 stones need to be replaced or restored (as explained in the "Stone by Stone" exhibit). On some days, you may even see masons in action in the stone yard behind the Minster.

• *Below the choir (on either side), steps lead down to the...*

❷ **Crypt:** Here you can view the boundary of the much smaller, but still huge, Norman church from 1100 that stood on this spot (look for the red dots, marking where the Norman church ended, and note how thick the wall was). You can also see some of the old columns and additional remains from the Roman fortress that once stood here, the tomb of St. William of York (actually a Roman sarcophagus that was reused), and the modern concrete save-the-church foundations (much of this church history is covered in the undercroft museum).

• *You'll exit the church through the gift shop*

*in the south transept. If you've yet to climb the tower, the entrance is in the south transept before the exit. Also before leaving, look for the entrance to the...*

**Undercroft Museum:** Well-described exhibits follow the history of the site from its origins as a Roman fortress to the founding of an Anglo-Saxon/Viking church, the shift to a Norman place of worship, and finally the construction of the Gothic structure that stands today. Videos re-create how the fortress and Norman structure would have been laid out, and various artifacts and remains provide an insight into each period. The museum fills a space that was excavated following the near collapse of the central tower in 1967.

Highlights include the actual remains of the Roman fort's basilica, which are viewable through a see-through floor. There are also patches of Roman frescoes from what was the basilica's anteroom. One remarkable artifact is the Horn of Ulf, an intricately carved elephant's tusk presented to the Minster in 1030 by Ulf, a Viking nobleman, as a symbol that he was dedicating his land to God and the Church. Also on view is the York Gospels manuscript, a thousand-year-old text containing the four gospels. Made by Anglo-Saxon monks at Canterbury, it's the only book in the Minster's collection that dates prior to the Norman Conquest. It is still used to this day to swear in archbishops. Your last stop in the undercroft is a small and comfortable theater where you can enjoy three short videos (10 minutes total) showing the Minster in action. One is about Roman Emperor Constantine and the rise of Christianity, another covers a day in the life of the cathedral (skippable), and the final video explores hidden treasures of the Minster.

• *This finishes your visit. Before leaving, take a moment to just be in this amazing building. Then, go in peace.*

**Nearby:** As you leave through the south transept, notice the people-friendly plaza created here and how effectively it ties the church in with the city that stretches before you. To your left are the Roman column from the ancient headquarters, which stood where the Minster stands today (and from where Rome administered the northern reaches of Britannia 1,800 years ago); a statue of Emperor Constantine (for more details, see page 324); and the covered York Minster Stone Yard, where masons are chiseling stone—as they have for centuries—to keep the religious pride and joy of York looking good.

## ▲▲YORKSHIRE MUSEUM

Located in a lush, picnic-perfect park next to the stately ruins of St. Mary's Abbey (described in my "York Walk," earlier), the Yorkshire Museum is the city's serious "archaeology of York" museum. You can't dig a hole in York without hitting some remnant of the city's long past, and most of what's found ends up here. While the hordes line up at the Jorvik Viking Centre, this museum has no crowds and provides a broader historical context, with more real artifacts. The three main collections—Roman, medieval, and natural history—are well described, bright, and kid-friendly.

**Cost and Hours:** £7.50, kids under 16 free with paying adult, daily 10:00-17:00, within Museum Gardens, tel. 01904/687-687, www.yorkshiremuseum.org.uk.

**Visiting the Museum:** At the entrance, you're greeted by an original, early fourth-century A.D. Roman statue of the god Mars. If he could talk, he'd say, "Hear me, mortals. There are three sections here: Roman (on this floor), medieval (downstairs), and natural history (a kid-friendly wing on this floor). Start first with the 10-minute video for a sweeping history of the city."

The **Roman** collection surrounds a large map of the Roman Empire, set on the floor. You'll see slice-of-life exhibits about Roman baths, a huge floor mosaic, and skulls accompanied by artists' renderings of how the people originally looked. (One man was apparently killed by a sword blow to the head—making it graphically clear that the struggle between Romans and barbarians was a violent one.) These artifacts are particularly interesting when you consider that you're standing in one of the farthest reaches of the Roman Empire.

The **medieval** collection is in the basement. During the Middle Ages, York was England's second city. One large room is dominated by ruins of the St. Mary's Abbey complex (described on page 319; one wall still stands just out front—be sure to see it before leaving). You'll also see old weapons, glazed vessels, and a well-preserved 13th-century leather box.

*Yorkshire Museum*

*8th-century helmet*

The museum's prized pieces are in this section: a helmet and a pendant. The eighth-century Anglo-Saxon helmet (known as the York Helmet or the Coppergate Helmet) shows a bit of barbarian refinement. Examine the delicate carving on its brass trim. The exquisitely etched 15th-century pendant—called the Middleham Jewel—is considered the finest piece of Gothic jewelry in Britain. The noble lady who wore this on a necklace believed that it helped her worship and protected her from illness. The back of the pendant, which rested near her heart, shows the Nativity. The front shows the Holy Trinity crowned by a sapphire (which people believed put their prayers at the top of God's to-do list).

In addition to the Anglo-Saxon pieces, the Viking collection is one of the best in England. Looking over the artifacts, you'll find that the Vikings (who conquered most of the Anglo-Saxon lands) wore some pretty decent shoes and actually combed their hair. The Cawood Sword, nearly 1,000 years old, is one of the finest surviving swords from that era.

The **natural history** exhibit (titled Extinct) is back upstairs, showing off skeletons of the extinct dodo and ostrich-like moa birds, as well as an ichthyosaurus.

Rick's Tip: *Lively* **King's Square,** *with its inviting benches, is great for* **people-watching**—*and prime real estate for buskers and street performers. Just beyond is the most characteristic street in old York: The Shambles.*

### ▲▲JORVIK VIKING CENTRE

Take the "Pirates of the Caribbean," sail them northeast and back in time 1,000 years, sprinkle in some real artifacts, and you get Jorvik (YOR-vik)—as much a ride as a museum. Between 1976 and 1981, more than 40,000 artifacts were dug out of the peat bog right here in downtown York—the UK's largest archaeological dig

of Viking-era artifacts. When the archaeologists were finished, the dig site was converted into this attraction. Innovative in 1984, the commercial success of Jorvik inspired copycat rides/museums all over England. Some love Jorvik, while others call it gimmicky and overpriced. If you think of it as Disneyland with a splash of history, Jorvik's fun. To me, Jorvik is a commercial venture designed for kids, with too much emphasis on its gift shop. But it's also undeniably entertaining, and—if you take the time to peruse its exhibits—it can be quite informative.

Rick's Tip: *The popular* **Jorvik Viking Centre** *can come with* **long lines.** *At the busiest times (roughly 11:00-15:00), plan to wait an hour or more—especially on school holidays. Come early or late in the day, when you'll more likely wait just 10-15 minutes. For £1 extra, you can* **book a slot in advance,** *either over the phone or on their website.*

**Cost and Hours:** £10.25, daily April-Oct 10:00-17:00, Nov-March until 16:00, these are last-entry times, tel. 01904/615-505, www.jorvik-viking-centre.co.uk.

**Visiting Jorvik:** First you'll walk down stairs (marked with the layers of history you're passing) and explore a small **museum.** Under the glass floor is a re-creation of the archaeological dig that took place right here. Surrounding that are a few actual artifacts (such as a knife, comb, shoe, and cup) and engaging videos

*Jorvik Viking Centre*

detailing the Viking invasions, longships, and explorers and the history of the excavations. Next to where you board your people-mover is the largest Viking timber found in the UK (from a wooden building on Coppergate). Don't rush through this area: These exhibits offer historical context to your upcoming journey back in time. Viking-costumed docents are happy to explain what you're seeing.

When ready, board a theme-park-esque **people-mover** for a 12-minute trip through the re-created Viking street of Coppergate. It's the year 975, and you're in the village of Jorvik. You'll glide past reconstructed houses and streets that sit atop the actual excavation site, while the recorded commentary tells you about everyday life in Viking times. Animatronic characters jabber at you in Old Norse, as you experience the sights, sounds, and smells of yore. Everything is true to the original dig—the face of one of the mannequins was computer-modeled from a skull dug up here.

Finally, you'll disembark at the **hands-on area,** where you can actually touch original Viking artifacts. You'll see several skeletons, carefully laid out and labeled to point out diseases and injuries, along with a big gob of coprolite (fossilized feces that offer archaeologists invaluable clues about long-gone lifestyles). Next, a gallery of everyday items (metal, glass, leather, wood, and so on) provides intimate glimpses into that redheaded culture. Take advantage of the informative touchscreens. The final section is devoted to swords, spears, axes, and shields. You'll also see bashed-in skulls (with injuries possibly sustained in battle) and a replica of the famous Coppergate Helmet (the original is in the Yorkshire Museum).

### ▲FAIRFAX HOUSE

This well-furnished home, supposedly the "first Georgian townhouse in England," is perfectly Neoclassical inside. Each room is staffed by wonderfully pleasant docents eager to talk with you. They'll explain how the circa-1760 home was built as the dowry for an aristocrat's daughter. The house is compact and bursting with stunning period furniture (the personal collection of a local chocolate magnate), gorgeously restored woodwork, and lavish stucco ceilings that offer clues as to each room's purpose. For example, stuccoed philosophers look down on the library, while the goddess of friendship presides over the drawing room. Taken together, this house provides fine insights into aristocratic life in 18th-century England.

**Cost and Hours:** £6, Tue-Sat 10:00-16:30, Sun 11:00-15:30, Mon by guided tour only at 11:00 and 14:00—these one-hour tours are worthwhile, closed Jan-mid-Feb, near Jorvik Viking Centre at 29 Castlegate, tel. 01904/655-543, www.fairfaxhouse.co.uk.

### ▲▲YORK CASTLE MUSEUM

This fascinating social-history museum is a Victorian home show, possibly the closest thing to a time-tunnel experience England has to offer. The one-way plan ensures that you'll see everything, including remakes of rooms from the 17th to

*Reconstructed Victorian-era street at the Castle Museum*

20th century, a re-creation of a Victorian street, a heartfelt WWI exhibit, and some eerie prison cells.

**Cost and Hours:** £10, kids under 16 free with paying adult, £13 combo-ticket with Yorkshire Museum, daily 9:30-17:00, cafeteria at entrance, tel. 01904/687-687, www.yorkcastlemuseum.org.uk. It's at the bottom of the hop-on, hop-off bus route. The museum can call a taxi for you (worthwhile if you're hurrying to the National Railway Museum, across town).

**Information:** The museum's £4 guide-book isn't necessary, but it makes a fine souvenir. The museum proudly offers no audioguides, as its roaming guides are enthusiastic about talking—engage them.

**Visiting the Museum:** The exhibits are divided between two wings: the North Building (to the left as you enter) and the South Building (to the right).

Follow the one-way route through the complex, starting in the **North Building.** You'll first visit the Period Rooms, illuminating Yorkshire lifestyles during different time periods (1600s-1950s) and among various walks of life, and Toy Story—an enchanting review of toys through the ages from dollhouses to Transformers. Next is the "Shaping the Body" exhibit, detailing diet and fashion trends over the last 400 years. Check out the codpieces, bustles, and corsets that used to "enhance" the human form, and ponder some of the odd diet fads that make today's diet crazes seem normal. Foodies

and chefs savor the exhibit showcasing kitchens and fireplaces from the 1600s to the 1980s.

Next, stroll down the museum's re-created Kirkgate, a street from the Victorian era, when Britain was at the peak of its power. It features old-time shops and storefronts, including a pharmacist, sweet shop, school, and grocer for the working class, along with roaming live guides in period dress. Around the back is a slum area depicting how the poor lived in those times.

Circle back to the entry and cross over to the **South Building.** In the WWI exhibit, erected to mark the war's centennial, you can follow the lives of five York citizens as they experience the horrors and triumphs of the war years. One room plunges you into the gruesome world of trench warfare, where the average life expectancy was six weeks (and if you fell asleep during sentry duty, you'd be shot). A display about the home front notes that York suffered from Zeppelin attacks in which six died. At the end you're encouraged to share your thoughts in a room lined with chalkboards.

Exit outside and cross through the castle yard. A detour to the left leads to a flour mill (open sporadically). Otherwise, your tour continues through the door on the right, where you'll find another reconstructed historical street, this one capturing the spirit of the swinging 1960s—"a time when the cultural changes were massive but the cars and skirts were mini." Slathered with DayGlo colors, this street scene examines fashion, music, and television (including clips of beloved kids' shows and period news reports).

Finally, head into the York Castle Prison, which recounts the experiences of actual people who were thrown into the clink here. Videos, eerily projected onto the walls of individual cells, show actors telling tragic stories about the cells' one-time inhabitants.

*Period room*

# Across the River

## ▲▲NATIONAL RAILWAY MUSEUM

If you like model railways, this is train-car heaven. The thunderous museum shows 200 illustrious years of British railroad history. The biggest and best railroad museum anywhere is interesting even to people who think "Pullman" means "don't push."

**Cost and Hours:** Free but £3 suggested donation, daily 10:00-18:00, café, restaurant, tel. 0844-815-3139, www.nrm.org.uk.

**Getting There:** It's about a 15-minute walk from the Minster (southwest of town, up the hill behind the train station). From the train station itself, the fastest approach is to go all the way to the back of the station (using the overpass to cross the tracks), exit out the back door, and turn right up the hill. To skip the walk, a cute little "road train" shuttles you more quickly between the Minster and the Railway Museum (£2 one-way, £3 round-trip, runs daily Easter-Oct, leaves museum every 30 minutes 11:00-16:00 at :00 and :30 past each hour; leaves town—from Duncombe Place, 100 yards in front of the Minster—at :15 and :45 past each hour).

**Visiting the Museum:** Pick up the floor plan to locate the various exhibits, which sprawl through several gigantic buildings on both sides of the street. Throughout the complex, red-shirted "explainers" are eager to talk trains.

The museum's most impressive room is the **Great Hall** (head right from the entrance area and take the stairs to the underground passage). Fanning out from this grand roundhouse is an array of historic cars and engines, starting with the first "stagecoaches on rails," with a crude steam engine from 1830. You'll trace the evolution of steam-powered transportation, from a replica of the Rocket (one of the first successful steam locomotives), to the Flying Scotsman (the first London-Edinburgh express rail service), to the era of the aerodynamic Mallard (famous as the first train to travel at a startling two miles per minute—a marvel back in 1938) and the striking Art Deco-style Duchess of Hamilton. (The Flying Scotsman and other trains may not be on display, as they are sometimes on loan or under maintenance—ask an explainer if you can't find something.) The collection spans to the present day, with a replica of the Eurostar (Chunnel) train and the Shinkansen Japanese bullet train. Other exhibits include a steam engine that's been sliced open to show its cylinders, driving wheels, and smoke box, as well as a working turntable that's put into action twice a day. The Mallard Experience simulates a ride on the Mallard.

**The Works** is an actual workshop where engineers scurry about, fixing old trains. Live train switchboards show real-time rail traffic on the East Coast Main Line. Next to the diagrammed screens, you can look out to see the actual trains moving up and down the line. **The Warehouse** is loaded with more than 10,000 items relating to train travel (including dinnerware, signage, and actual trains).

*National Railway Museum*

*York Brewery*

Exhibits feature dining cars, post cars, sleeping cars, train posters, and more info on the Flying Scotsman.

Crossing back to the entrance side, continue to the **Station Hall,** with a collection of older trains, including ones that the royals have used to ride the rails (such as Queen Victoria's lavish royal car and a WWII royal carriage reinforced with armor). Behind that are the South Yard and the Depot, with actual working trains in storage.

### ▲YORK BREWERY

This intimate, tactile, and informative 45-minute-long tour gives an enjoyable look at how this charming little microbrewery produces 5,500 pints per batch. Their award-winning Ghost Ale is strong, dark, and chocolaty. You can drink their beer throughout town, but to get it as fresh as possible, drink it where it's birthed, in their cozy Tap Room.

**Cost and Hours:** £8, includes four tasters of the best beer—ale not lager—in town; tours Mon-Sat at 12:30, 14:00, 15:30, and 17:00—just show up; cross the river on Lendal Bridge and walk 5 minutes to Toft Green just below Micklegate, tel. 01904/621-162, www.york-brewery.co.uk.

# EXPERIENCES

## Shopping

With medieval lanes lined with a mix of classy and tacky little shops, York is a hit with shoppers. I find the following two experiences particularly interesting.

**Antique Malls** are filled with stalls and cases owned by dealers from the Yorkshire countryside (all open daily). Each mall is a warren of rooms with cafés buried deep inside. These three are within a few blocks of one another: the **Antiques Centre York** (41 Stonegate, www. theantiquescentreyork.co.uk), the **Red House Antiques Centre** (a block from the Minster at Duncombe Place, www. redhouseyork.co.uk), and **Cavendish Antiques and Jewellers** (44 Stonegate, www.cavendishjewellers.co.uk).

**Charity thrift shops,** run by the British Heart Foundation, Save the Children, Mind, and Oxfam, among others, are located on Goodramgate (stretching a block or so in from the town wall). Your bargain purchases of clothing, accessories, toys, books, and more will help those in need (stores generally open between 9:00 and 10:00 and close between 16:00 and 17:00, with shorter hours on Sun).

## Nightlife

York's atmospheric pubs make for convivial eating and drinking. Many serve inexpensive lunches and/or early dinners, then focus on beer in the evening.

**The York Brewery Tap Room** is a private club, but you can be an honorary guest. It has five beloved varieties on tap (14 Toft Green, just below Micklegate, tel. 01904/621-162, www.york-brewery.co.uk).

**The Maltings,** just over Lendal Bridge, has classic pub ambience and serves good lunches. Local beer purists swear by it (£6-7 pub lunches, open for drinks nightly, cross the bridge and look down and left to Tanners Moat, tel. 01904/655-387).

**The Blue Bell** is is the smallest pub in York, with an old-school vibe and an Edwardian interior (limited food served at lunch only, east end of town at 53 Fossgate, tel. 01904/654-904).

**The House of the Trembling Madness** sits cozily above a "bottle shop" that sells a stunning variety of beers to go (£3-6 snacks, £8-10 meals, daily 10:30-24:00, 48

Stonegate, tel. 01904/640-009).

**Evil Eye Lounge,** is a funky space famous for its strong cocktails and edgy ambience. There are even beds to drink in (£8 meals, food served Mon-Fri 12:00-21:00, Sat-Sun 12:00-18:00, 42 Stonegate, tel. 01904/640-002).

**The Golden Fleece** is considered the oldest and most haunted coaching inn in York. Its wooden frame has survived without foundations for 500 years and the tilty floors make you feel drunk even if you aren't (16 Pavement, across the street from the southern end of The Shambles, tel. 01904/625-171).

**The Last Drop** is a basic pub—no music, no game machines, no children—owned by the York Brewery, with all their ales on tap (27 Colliergate facing King's Square, tel. 01904/621-951).

## Entertainment

**Theatre Royal** offers a full variety of dramas, comedies, and works by Shakespeare. The locals are proud of the high-tech main theater and little 100-seat theater-in-the-round (£10-22 tickets, £8-10 tickets for those under 25 and students of any age, shows usually Tue-Sun at 19:30, tickets easy to get, on St. Leonard's Place near Bootham Bar, booking tel. 01904/623-568, www.yorktheatreroyal.co.uk).

The **City Screen Cinema,** right on the river, plays both art-house and mainstream flicks. They also have an enticing café/bar overlooking the river that serves good food (13 Coney Street, tel. 0871-902-5726).

## Riverside Walk or Bike Ride

The New Walk is a mile-long, tree-lined riverside lane created in the 1730s as a promenade for York's dandy class to stroll, see, and be seen—and is a fine place for today's visitors to walk or bike (Cycle Heaven rents bikes at train station).

This hour-long walk is a delightful way to enjoy a dose of countryside away from York. It's paved, illuminated in the evening, and a popular jogging route any time of day.

Start from the riverside under Skeldergate Bridge (near the York Castle Museum), and walk south away from town about a mile to the striking, modern **Millennium Bridge.** Cross the bridge and head back towards York, passing **Rowntree Park** (you can enter the park through its fine old gate, stroll along the duck-filled pond near the Rowntree Park Café, and return to the riverside lane). Continue into York.

# EATING

The York high-tech industry and university—along with the tourists—build a demand that sustains creative and fun eateries and a wide range of ethnic food. While decent pub grub is served in the bars, there are no great gastropubs. Picnic and to-go options abound, and it's easy to find a bench where you can munch cheaply. On a sunny day, perhaps the best picnic spot in town is under the evocative 12th-century ruins of St. Mary's Abbey in the Museum Gardens (near Bootham Bar).

**Upscale Bistros**—trendy, pricey eateries—are a York forte. I've listed five of my favorites: Café No. 8, Café Concerto, The Blue Bicycle, The Star Inn the City, and Bistro Guy. These places are each romantic, laid-back, and popular with locals (so reservations are wise for dinner). They also have good-quality, creative vegetarian options. Most offer economical lunch specials and early dinners. After 19:00 or so, main courses cost £15-25 and fixed-price meals (two or three courses) go for around £25. On Friday and Saturday evenings, many offer special, more expensive menus.

# City Center
## Cheap Eats Around King's Square

King's Square has several fine quick-and-cheap options for lunch and takeout. Picnic on the square to enjoy the street entertainers, or more peacefully in the Holy Trinity Church yard on Goodramgate (half a block to the right of York Roast Company).

**York Roast Company,** a local fixture, serves tasty and hearty £4-6 pork sandwiches with applesauce, stuffing, and "crackling" (roasted bits of fat and skin). You can even oversee the stuffing of your own Yorkshire pudding (£7-8). If Henry VIII wanted fast food, he'd eat here. Order at counter then dine upstairs or take away (daily 10:00-23:00 except open later Fri-Sat, 74 Low Petergate, corner of Low Petergate and Goodramgate, tel. 01904/629-197).

**Drakes Fish-and-Chips,** across the street from York Roast Company, is a popular chippy (daily 11:00-22:30, 97 Low Petergate, tel. 01904/624-788).

**The Cornish Bakery,** facing King's Square, cooks up £3 pasties to eat in or take away (30 Colliergate, tel. 01904/671-177).

**The Newgate Market,** just past The Shambles, has several stalls offering fun and nutritious light meals. On The Shambles, **Mr. Sandwich** is famous for its £1 sandwiches.

**St. Crux Parish Hall** is used by a medley of charities that sell tea, homemade cakes, and light meals (usually open Tue-Sat 10:00-16:00, closed Sun-Mon, at bottom of The Shambles at its intersection with Pavement, tel. 01904/621-756).

The **Harlequin Café** is a charming place with good coffee and homemade cakes, as well as light meals. It's up a creaky staircase overlooking the square (Mon-Sat 10:00-16:00, Sun 11:00-15:00, 2 King's Square, tel. 01904/630-631).

## On or near Stonegate

**The House of the Trembling Madness,** considered the best pub in town, is easy to miss. Enter through The Bottle, a ground-floor shop selling an astonishing number of different takeaway beers. Climb the stairs to find a small but cozy pub beneath a high, airy, timbered ceiling. The food is more creative than standard pub grub. Come early since seating can be tight (£3-6 snacks, £8-10 meals, daily 10:30-24:00, 48 Stonegate, tel. 01904/640-009).

**Evil Eye Lounge** serves delicious, authentic Southeast Asian cuisine. Some may find the hipster space too much; it's best to avoid the Saturday afternoon party scene (£8 meals, food served Mon-Fri 12:00-21:00, Sat-Sun 12:00-18:00, 42 Stonegate, tel. 01904/640-002).

**Ask Restaurant** is a cheap and cheery Italian chain. In York, it's inside the Neoclassical Grand Assembly Rooms, lined with Corinthian marble columns. The food may be pedestrian, but the atmosphere is 18th-century deluxe (£9-12 pizza, pastas, and salads; daily 11:00-22:00, weekends until 23:00; Blake Street, tel. 01904/637-254).

# Near Bootham Bar and Recommended B&Bs

**Café Concerto,** a casual and cozy bistro with wholesome food and a charming musical theme, has a loyal following. The fun menu features updated English favorites with some international options (£4-8 starters; £9-12 soups, sandwiches, and salads; £12-17 main dishes; vegetarian and gluten-free options; daily 9:00-21:00, weekends until 22:00, smart to reserve for dinner—try for a window seat, also offers takeaway, facing the Minster at 21 High Petergate, tel. 01904/610-478, http://cafeconcerto.biz).

**Café No. 8** is romantic, with jazz and modern art. Grab one of the tables in front or in the sunroom, or enjoy a shaded little garden out back if the weather's good. The food—mod cuisine with veggie options—is simple, elegant, and creative (£6-10 lunches, £13-16 main dishes; daily 12:00-22:00 except opens at 9:00 Sat-Sun, 8 Gillygate, tel. 01904/653-074, www. cafeno8.co.uk).

**Bistro Guy** serves modern English and international dishes with seven cute tables in front and a delightful garden under the town wall out back. Breakfast and lunch are offered daily, with a fancier "bistro" menu for dinner three nights a week (£5-9 breakfast and lunch plates, Tue-Sun 9:00-17:00, closed Mon; £21 two-course and £25 three-course dinners, less if you come before 19:00, dinner served Thu-Sat only 18:00-21:00—deposit required for dinner reservation; 40 Gillygate, tel. 01904/652-500, www. bistroguy.co.uk).

**The Star Inn the City** is an offshoot of Chef Andrew Pern's Michelin-rated restaurant in the Yorkshire countryside, The Star Inn. Local meats and produce are used in memorable combinations. Dine outside along the river or in the mod eatery looking out on the Museum Gardens (£8-12 starters, £16-24 main dishes, breakfast and lunch specials, kids menu, daily 8:30-22:00, reservations smart, next to the river in Lendal Engine House, Museum Street, tel. 01904/619-208, www. starinnthecity.co.uk).

**The Exhibition Hotel pub** has a classic pub interior, as well as a glassed-in conservatory and beer garden out back that's great for kids (£9-12 pub grub, food served daily 12:00-21:00, bar open late, facing Bootham Bar at 19 Bootham Street, tel. 01904/641-105).

**Mamma Mia** is a popular choice for functional, affordable Italian. The casual eating area features a tempting gelato bar. In nice weather the back patio is *molto bello* (£8-10 pizza and pasta, daily 11:30-14:00 & 17:30-23:00, 20 Gillygate, tel. 01904/622-020).

**Sainsbury's Local grocery store** is handy and open late (long hours daily, 50 yards outside Bootham Bar, on Bootham).

# At the East End of Town

This neighborhood is across town from my recommended B&Bs, but still central (and a short walk from the York Castle Museum). Reservations are smart.

**Rustique French Bistro** has good prices and is straight French—right down to the welcome. The big room has tight tables and walls decorated with simple posters (£6 starters, £15 main dishes, £15 two-course and £17 three-course meals available except after 19:00 Fri-Sat, daily 12:00-22:00, across from Fairfax House at 28 Castlegate, tel. 01904/612-744, www. rustiqueyork.co.uk).

**The Blue Bicycle** is passionate about fish. Its charming canalside setting and its tasty Anglo-French cuisine make it worth the splurge. The basement, while *très romantique*, may be hot and stuffy (£6-12 starters, £16-24 main dishes, vegetarian and meat options, daily 18:00-21:30, also open for lunch Thu-Sun 12:00-14:30, 34 Fossgate, tel. 01904/673-990, www. thebluebicycle.com).

**Mumbai Lounge** is the best place in town for Indian food. The space is big and high-energy. Reserve a table on the ground floor; avoid the basement (£11 plates, £7 lunch special, daily 12:00-14:00 & 17:30-23:30, 47 Fossgate, tel. 01904/654-155, www.mumbailoungeyork.co.uk).

**Walmgate Ale House**—casual, homey, and youthful—serves elegantly simple traditional and international meals. The seating sprawls across a ground-floor pub, upstairs bistro, and top-floor loft (£7 lunches, £11-15 dinners, £13.50 two-course and £15.50 three-course meals; Mon-Fri 12:00-22:30, Sat-Sun 9:30-22:30, just past Fossgate at 25 Walmgate, tel. 01904/629-222).

**Il Paradiso del Cibo Ristorante**

**Pizzeria** has tight seating, no tourists, and a fun bustle, overseen by a Sardinian with attitude (£7 pastas and pizzas, £15-19 main dishes, £8.50 lunch/early dinner special Mon-Fri only, cash only, daily 12:00-15:00 & 18:00-22:00, 40 Walmgate, tel. 01904/611-444). A few steps away, you'll find **Khao San Thai Bistro** (52 Walmgate, tel. 01904/635-599) and **The Barbakan Polish Restaurant** (58 Walmgate, tel. 01904/672-474).

## Tearooms

York is famous for its elegant teahouses. These two places serve traditional afternoon tea as well as light meals in memorable settings. In both cases, the food is pricey and comes in small portions—come here at 16:00 for tea and cakes, but dine elsewhere. It's permissible for travel partners on a budget to enjoy the experience for about half the price by having one person order "full tea" (with enough little sandwiches and sweets for two to share) and the other a simple cup of tea.

**Bettys Café Tea Rooms** is a destination restaurant. Pay £10 for a Yorkshire Cream Tea (tea and scones with clotted Yorkshire cream and strawberry jam) or £19 for full afternoon tea (tea, delicate sandwiches, scones, and sweets). Your table is so full of doily niceties that the food is served on a three-tray tower.

While you'll pay a little extra here (and the food's nothing special), the ambience and people-watching are hard to beat. They'll offer to seat you quickly in the bigger, less atmospheric basement, but wait for a place upstairs—ideally by the window, with a fine view of the street scene. Just want a pastry to go? It's OK to skip the line and go directly to the bakery counter. Near the WC downstairs is a mirror signed by WWII bomber pilots—read the story (daily 9:00-21:00, "afternoon tea" served all day; on weekends the special £33 afternoon tea includes fresh-from-the-oven scones served 12:30-17:00 in the upstairs room with a pianist—smart to reserve ahead; piano music nightly 18:00-21:00 and Sun 10:00-13:00, St. Helen's Square, tel. 01904/659-142, www.bettys.co.uk).

**Grays Court,** tucked away behind the Minster, holds court over its own delightful garden just inside the town wall. For centuries, this was the residence of the Norman Treasurers of York Minster. Today, it's home to a pleasant tearoom, small hotel, and bar. Sit outside, at tables scattered in the pleasant garden, or inside, in the classy dining room or Jacobean gallery (£37 for 2-person "afternoon tea" served all day, £6 sandwiches, £6-11 light meals, also serves dinner, daily 11:00-21:00, Chapter House Street, tel. 01904/612-613, www.grayscourtyork.com).

# York Restaurants

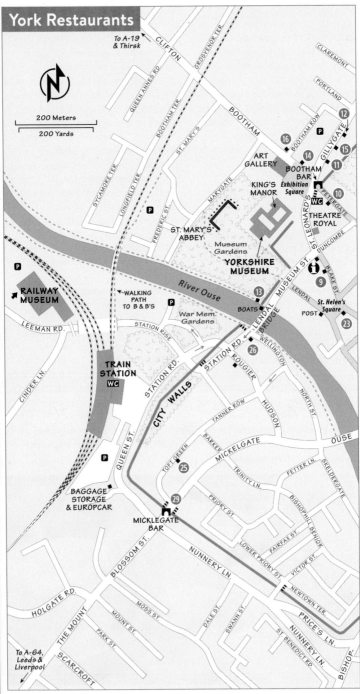

To A-19
& Thirsk

CLIFTON

CLAREMONT

PORTLAND

GROSVENOR TER.

QUEEN ANNE'S RD.

BOOTHAM TER.

ST. MARY'S

BOOTHAM

BOOTHAM ROW

GILLYGATE

12

P

16

14

15

11

200 Meters

200 Yards

ART
GALLERY

BOOTHAM
BAR

10

SYCAMORE TER.

LONGFIELD TER.

FREDERICK ST.

MARYGATE

KING'S
MANOR

Exhibition
Square

WC

PETERGATE

ST. LEONARD'S

THEATRE
ROYAL

P

ST. MARY'S
ABBEY

Museum
Gardens

YORKSHIRE
MUSEUM

MUSEUM ST.

DUNCOMBE

i

9

BLAKE ST.

P

RAILWAY
MUSEUM

River Ouse

WALKING
PATH
TO B & B'S

P

13

LENDAL
BRIDGE

LENDAL

St. Helen's
Square

23

BOATS

POST

LEEMAN RD.

War Mem.
Gardens

STATION RISE

STATION RD.

STATION RD.

26

WELLINGTON

CINDER LN.

TRAIN
STATION

WC

ROUGIER

NORTH ST.

OUSE

CITY WALLS

STATION RD.

TANNER ROW

HUDSON

QUEEN ST.

TOFT GREEN

BARKER

MICKLEGATE

FETTER LN.

SKELDERGATE

P

25

TRINITY LN.

BISHOPHILL SENIOR

BAGGAGE
STORAGE
& EUROPCAR

29

PRIORY ST.

MICKLEGATE
BAR

LOWER PRIORY ST.

FAIRFAX ST.

VICTOR ST.

CINDER LN.

HOLGATE RD.

BLOSSOM ST.

NUNNERY LN.

NEWTOWN TER.

PRICE'S LN.

NUNNERY LN.

BISHOP-

THE MOUNT

MOUNT ST.

PARK ST.

MOSS ST.

DALE ST.

SWAIN ST.

ST BENEDICT RD.

To A-64,
Leeds &
Liverpool

SCARCROFT

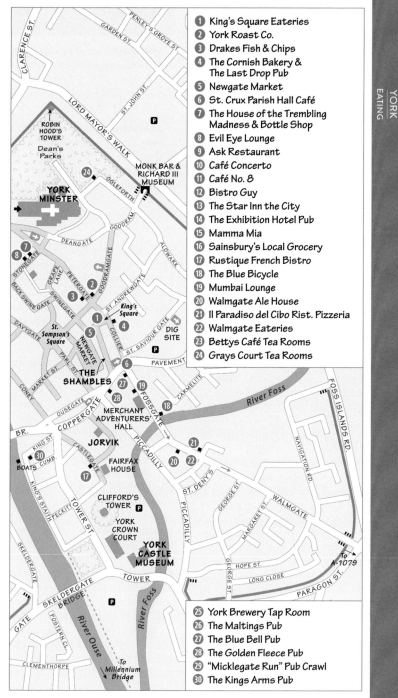

1 King's Square Eateries
2 York Roast Co.
3 Drakes Fish & Chips
4 The Cornish Bakery & The Last Drop Pub
5 Newgate Market
6 St. Crux Parish Hall Café
7 The House of the Trembling Madness & Bottle Shop
8 Evil Eye Lounge
9 Ask Restaurant
10 Café Concerto
11 Café No. 8
12 Bistro Guy
13 The Star Inn the City
14 The Exhibition Hotel Pub
15 Mamma Mia
16 Sainsbury's Local Grocery
17 Rustique French Bistro
18 The Blue Bicycle
19 Mumbai Lounge
20 Walmgate Ale House
21 Il Paradiso del Cibo Rist. Pizzeria
22 Walmgate Eateries
23 Bettys Café Tea Rooms
24 Grays Court Tea Rooms

25 York Brewery Tap Room
26 The Maltings Pub
27 The Blue Bell Pub
28 The Golden Fleece Pub
29 "Micklegate Run" Pub Crawl
30 The Kings Arms Pub

# SLEEPING

I've listed peak-season, book-direct prices; July through October are the busiest (and usually most expensive) months. B&Bs often charge more for weekends and sometimes turn away one-night bookings, particularly for peak-season Saturdays. Prices may spike for Bank Holidays and horse races (about 20 nights a season).

Rick's Tip: **Book a room well in advance** *during* **festival times** *and on weekends any time of year. For a list of festivals, see www. yorkfestivals.com.*

## B&Bs and Small Hotels

These B&Bs are all small and family-run. They come with plenty of steep stairs (and no elevators) but no traffic noise. Rooms can be tight; if maneuverability is important to you, say so when booking. For a good selection, reserve well in advance. B&B owners will generally hold a room with a credit-card number even if they want payment in cash. They work hard to help their guests sightsee and eat smartly. Most have permits to lend for street parking. Please honor your bookings—the B&B proprietors will have to charge you even if you don't show up.

The handiest B&B neighborhood is the quiet residential area just outside the old town wall's Bootham gate, along the road called Bootham. All of these are within a 10-minute walk of the Minster and TI, and a 5- to 15-minute walk or £6-8 taxi ride from the station. If driving, head for the cathedral and follow the medieval wall to the gate called Bootham Bar. The street called Bootham leads away from Bootham Bar.

**Getting There:** Here's the most direct way to walk to this B&B area from the train station: Head to the north end of the station, to the area between platforms 2 and 4. Shoot through the gap between the men's WC and the York Tap pub, past some racks of bicycles, and into the short-stay parking lot. Walk to the end of the lot to a pedestrian ramp, and zigzag your way down. At the bottom, head left, following the sign for the riverside route. When you reach the river, cross over on the footbridge—you'll have to carry your bags up and down some steps. At the far end of the bridge, the Abbey Guest House is a few yards to your right, facing the river. To reach The Hazelwood (closer to the town wall), walk from the bridge along the river until just before the short ruined tower, then turn inland up onto Marygate. For other B&Bs, at the bottom of the footbridge, turn left immediately onto a path that skirts the big parking lot (parallel to the train tracks). At the end of the parking lot, you'll turn depending on your B&B: for the places on or near Bootham Terrace, turn left and go under the tracks; for B&Bs on St. Mary's Street, take the short stairway on your right.

### On or near Bootham Terrace

$$$ **Hedley House Hotel,** well run by a wonderful family, has 30 clean and spacious rooms. The outdoor hot tub/sauna is a fine way to end your day (standard Db-£90-135, larger Db-£90-165, ask for a deal with stay of 3 or more nights, family rooms, good two-course evening meals from £18, in-house massage and beauty

services, free parking, 3 Bootham Terrace, tel. 01904/637-404, www.hedleyhouse. com, greg@hedleyhouse.com). They also have nine luxury studio apartments—see their website for details.

**$$ Abbeyfields Guest House** has eight comfortable, bright rooms up lots of stairs. This doily-free place has been designed with care (Db-£84 Sun-Thu, £89 Fri-Sat, mention this book when reserving; homemade bread, free parking, 19 Bootham Terrace, tel. 01904/636-471, www.abbeyfields. co.uk, enquire@abbeyfields.co.uk).

**$$ St. Raphael Guesthouse** has seven cozy rooms, each themed after a different York street and lovingly accented with a fresh rose (Db-£82 Sun-Thu, £94 Fri-Sat, mention this book when reserving, free drinks and ice in their guests' fridge, family rooms, 44 Queen Annes Road, tel. 01904/645-028, www. straphaelguesthouse.co.uk, info@ straphaelguesthouse.co.uk).

**$$ Arnot House** is old-fashioned, homey, and lushly decorated with Victorian memorabilia. The three well-furnished rooms even have little libraries (Db-£83, 2-night minimum stay unless it's last-minute, no children, huge DVD library, 17 Grosvenor Terrace, tel. 01904/641-966, www.arnothouseyork. co.uk, kim.robbins@virgin.net).

**$ The Bronte Guesthouse,** in a 19th-century townhouse, has five pleasant rooms, newly remodeled bathrooms, a bright breakfast room, and patio (Db£80, family room, 22 Grosvenor Terrace, tel. 0904/621-066, www.bronte-guesthouse. com, enquiries@bronte-guesthouse.com).

**$ Bootham Guest House** features creamy walls and contemporary furniture. Of the eight rooms, six are en-suite, while two share a bath (D-£50-60, Db-£60-70, higher in July-Aug, mention this book when reserving, 56 Bootham Crescent, tel. 01904/672-123, www.boothamguesthouse.co.uk, boothamguesthouse1@hotmail.com).

**$ Number 34** has five simple, light, and airy rooms at fair prices. It's clean and uncluttered, with modern decor (Db-£60-66, 5-person apartment available next door, mention this book when reserving, ground-floor room, 34 Bootham Crescent, tel. 01904/645-818, www.number34york.co.uk, enquiries@ number34york.co.uk).

**$$ Queen Anne's Guest House** has nine basic rooms in two adjacent houses. While it doesn't have the plushest beds or richest decor, it's clean and respectable (Db-£80, family room, mention this book when reserving, lounge, 24 and 26 Queen Annes Road, tel. 01904/629-389, www. queen-annes-guesthouse.co.uk, info@ queen-annes-guesthouse.co.uk).

## On the River
**$$ Abbey Guest House** is a peaceful refuge overlooking the River Ouse, with five cheery, contemporary-style rooms and a cute little garden. The riverview rooms will ramp up your romance with York (Db-£80-90, mention this book when reserving, free parking, laundry service for a fee, 13 Earlsborough Terrace, tel. 01904/627-782, www.abbeyghyork.co.uk, info@ abbeyghyork.co.uk, welcoming couple Jane and Kingley).

## On St. Mary's Street
**$$ Number 23 St. Mary's B&B** is extravagantly decorated, with nine spacious and tastefully comfy rooms and a classy lounge (Db-£80-100 depending on room size and season, discount for longer stays, family room, honesty box for drinks and snacks, lots of stairs, 23 St. Mary's, tel. 01904/622-738, www.23stmarys.co.uk, stmarys23@hotmail.com).

**$$ Crook Lodge B&B,** with seven tight but charming rooms, serves breakfast in an old Victorian kitchen. The 21st-century style somehow fits this old house (Db-£75-85, check for online specials, one ground-floor room, quiet, free parking, 26 St. Mary's, tel. 01904/655-614, www.crooklodgeguesthouseyork.co.uk,

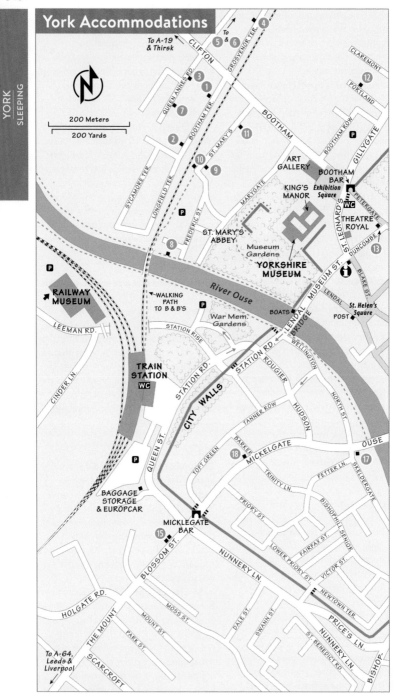

# York Accommodations

To A-19
& Thirsk

To &

CLIFTON

GROSVENOR TER.

4

5 6

CLAREMONT

QUEEN ANNE'S RD.

3 1

12

PORTLAND

200 Meters

200 Yards

7

BOOTHAM TER.

BOOTHAM

BOOTHAM ROW

GILLYGATE

P

ST. MARY'S

11

2

10 9

MARYGATE

ART
GALLERY

KING'S
MANOR

Exhibition
Square

BOOTHAM
BAR

PETERGATE

WC

SYCAMORE TER.

LONGFIELD TER.

FREDERIC ST.

P

ST. MARY'S
ABBEY

Museum
Gardens

YORKSHIRE
MUSEUM

ST. LEONARD'S

DUNCOMBE

THEATRE
ROYAL

13

8

River Ouse

MUSEUM ST.

LENDAL

BLAKE ST.

i

WALKING
PATH
TO B & B'S

War Mem.
Gardens

BOATS

LENDAL
BRIDGE

POST

St. Helen's
Square

RAILWAY
MUSEUM

P

LEEMAN RD.

STATION RISE

STATION RD.

WELLINGTON

CINDER LN.

TRAIN
STATION

WC

STATION RD.

ROUGIER

HUDSON

NORTH ST.

OUSE

CITY WALLS

TANNER ROW

17

P

QUEEN ST.

TOFT GREEN

BARKER

18

MICKELGATE

TRINITY LN.

FETTER LN.

SKELDERGATE

BAGGAGE
STORAGE
& EUROPCAR

PRIORY ST.

BISHOPHILL SENIOR

MICKLEGATE
BAR

15

BLOSSOM ST.

LOWER PRIORY ST.

FAIRFAX ST.

VICTOR ST.

NUNNERY LN.

HOLGATE RD.

THE MOUNT

MOSS ST.

MOUNT ST.

PARK ST.

DALE ST.

SWANN ST.

NEWTOWN TER.

PRICE'S LN.

NUNNERY LN.

ST. BENEDICT RD.

BISHOP

To A-64,
Leeds &
Liverpool

SCARCROFT

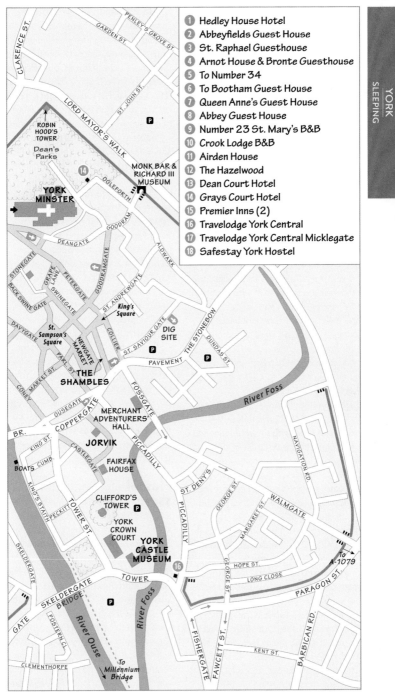

1. Hedley House Hotel
2. Abbeyfields Guest House
3. St. Raphael Guesthouse
4. Arnot House & Bronte Guesthouse
5. To Number 34
6. To Bootham Guest House
7. Queen Anne's Guest House
8. Abbey Guest House
9. Number 23 St. Mary's B&B
10. Crook Lodge B&B
11. Airden House
12. The Hazelwood
13. Dean Court Hotel
14. Grays Court Hotel
15. Premier Inns (2)
16. Travelodge York Central
17. Travelodge York Central Micklegate
18. Safestay York Hostel

crooklodge@hotmail.com, Brian and Louise Aiken).

**$$ Airden House** rents 10 nice, mostly traditional rooms, though the two basement-level rooms are more mod (standard Db-£76-80, traditional Db-£80-90, hot tub Db-£100, mention this book when reserving, lounge, free parking, 1 St. Mary's, tel. 01904/638-915, www.airdenhouse.co.uk, info@airdenhouse.co.uk).

### Closer to the Town Wall

**$$$ The Hazelwood,** more formal than a B&B, rents 14 bright, cheery rooms. The "standard" rooms have small bathrooms, while the "superior" rooms are bigger (standard Db-£80-100, superior Db-£100-130, top-floor apartment good for families, homemade biscuits on arrival, free laundry service for Rick Steves readers if you book direct with the hotel, free parking, garden patio; fridge, ice, and travel library in pleasant basement lounge; 24 Portland Street, tel. 01904/626-548, www.thehazelwoodyork.com, reservations@thehazelwoodyork.com).

## Large Hotels

**$$$ Dean Court Hotel,** a Best Western facing the Minster, is a stately business-class hotel with classy lounges and 37 comfortable rooms. A few rooms have views for no extra charge (small Db-£150, standard Db-£180, superior Db-£210, spacious deluxe Db-£230; best rates midweek, off-season, and on Sun—check specific rates online; elevator, bistro, restaurant, Duncombe Place, tel. 01904/625-082, www.deancourt-york.co.uk, sales@deancourt-york.co.uk).

**$$$ Grays Court Hotel** is a historic mansion—the home of dukes and archbishops since 1091—that now rents nine rooms. While its public spaces and gardens are lavish, the rooms are modest yet elegant. If it's too pricey for lodging, visit its recommended tearoom (Db-£165-280, Chapter House Street, tel. 01904/612-613, www.grayscourtyork.com).

**$$$ Premier Inn** offers 200 rooms in two side-by-side hotels—a workable option if York's B&Bs have filled up, or if you can score a deep advance discount. They have little character, but offer industrial-strength efficiency (Db-£80-95 Sun-Thu, £90-145 Fri-Sat; check for specials online; up to 2 kids stay free, breakfast extra, elevator in one building, pay guest computer, pay Wi-Fi, pay parking, 5-minute walk to train station, 20 and 28 Blossom Street, tel. 0871-527-9194 and 0871-527-9196, www.premierinn.com).

**$$ Travelodge York Central** offers 93 rooms near the York Castle Museum. If you book early enough on their website, rooms can be amazingly cheap. River views make some rooms slightly less boring—after booking online, call the front desk to request a river view (rates vary wildly depending on demand—as cheap as £30 for a fully prepaid "saver rate" 21 days ahead; for best rates, book online; cheapest rates are first-come, first-served; breakfast extra, elevator, pay Wi-Fi, pay parking a 5-minute walk away, 90 Piccadilly, central reservations tel. 0871-984-8484, front desk tel. 0203-195-4978, www.travelodge.co.uk). A second location, **Travelodge York Central Micklegate,** has 104 rooms at the train-station end of the Ouse Bridge (Micklegate, tel. 0203-195-4976).

## Hostel

**$ Safestay York** is a boutique hostel in a big, old Georgian house on a rowdy street (noisy late at night on Fridays and Saturdays). It has some hotel-quality doubles, though most beds are in dorm rooms, with great views and private prefab "pod" bathrooms (dorm bed-£18-32, twin Db-£90-100, king Db-£120, family room for up to four-£192, includes sheets, continental breakfast extra, 4 floors, no elevator, air-con, free Wi-Fi in public areas only, self-service laundry, TV lounge, game room, bar, lockers, no curfew, 5-minute walk from train station at 88 Micklegate,

tel. 01904/627-720, www.safestay.com/
ss-york-micklegate.html, bookings@
safestay.com).

# TRANSPORTATION

## Arriving and Departing
### By Train

The train station is a 10-minute walk from town. Day-trippers can store baggage at the small hut next to the Europcar office just off Queen Street—as you exit the station, turn right and walk along a bridge to the first intersection, then turn right (£6/24 hours, cash only, daily until 20:00).

Recommended B&Bs are a 5- to 15-minute walk away (depending on where you're staying). For specific directions, see page 344.

**Taxis** can zip you to your B&B for £6-8. Queue up at the taxi stand, or call 01904/638-833 or 01904/659-659; cabbies don't start the meter until you get in.

To **walk downtown** from the station, turn left down Station Road, veer through the gap in the wall and then left across the river, and follow the crowd toward the Gothic towers of the Minster. After the bridge, a block before the Minster, you'll see the TI on your right.

**Train Connections to: Durham** (3-4/hour, 45 minutes), **London**'s King's Cross Station (2/hour, 2 hours), **Bath** (hourly with change in Bristol, 4.5 hours), **Oxford** (1/hour direct, 3.5 hours), **Cambridge** (hourly, 2.5 hours, transfer in Peterborough), **Keswick/Lake District** (train to Penrith: 2/hour, 3.5 hours, 1-2 transfers; then 45-minute bus to Keswick), **Edinburgh** (2/hour, 2.5 hours). Train info: Tel. 0345-748-4950, www.nationalrail.co.uk.

**Connections from London's Airports:** Allow three hours minimum to reach York from either Heathrow or Gatwick. From **Heathrow,** take the train (either the Heathrow Express or cheaper Heathrow Connect) to London's Paddington Station, transfer by Tube to King's Cross, then take the train to York. From **Gatwick**

**South,** catch the First Capital Connect train to London's St. Pancras International Station; from there, walk to neighboring King's Cross Station and catch the train to York.

### By Car

Driving and parking in York is maddening. Those day-tripping here should follow signs to one of several park-and-ride lots ringing the perimeter. At these lots, parking is free, and shuttle buses go every 10 minutes into the center.

If you're sleeping in York, park your car where your B&B advises and walk. As you near York (and your B&B), you'll hit the A-1237 ring road. Follow this to the A-19/Thirsk roundabout (next to river on northeast side of town). From the roundabout, follow signs for *York,* traveling through Clifton into Bootham. All recommended B&Bs are located four or five blocks before you hit the medieval city gate.

If approaching York from the south, take the M-1 until it becomes the A-1M, exit at junction 45 onto the A-64, and follow it for 10 miles until you reach York's ring road (A-1237), which allows you to avoid driving through the city center.

---

Rick's Tip: *If you're nearing the end of your trip,* **drop off your rental car upon arrival in York.** *The money you saved by turning it in early just about pays for the* **train ticket that whisks you effortlessly to London.**

---

**Car Rental:** In York, you'll find these agencies: **Avis** (3 Layerthorpe, tel. 0844-544-6117), **Hertz** (at train station, tel. 0843-309-3082), **Budget** (near National Railway Museum behind train station at 75 Leeman Road, tel. 01904/644-919), and **Europcar** (off Queen Street near train station, tel. 0844-846-4003). Beware: Car-rental agencies close early on Saturday afternoons and all day Sunday—when dropping off it's OK, but picking up is only possible by prior arrangement (and for an extra fee).

# BEST OF THE REST

# NORTHEAST ENGLAND

Northeast England harbors some of the country's best historical sights. Marvel at England's greatest Norman church—Durham's cathedral—and enjoy an evensong service there. At the excellent Beamish Museum, travel back in time to the 19th and early 20th centuries. Go even further back in time for a Roman ramble at Hadrian's Wall, a reminder that Britain was an important Roman colony 2,000 years ago.

With a car, you can spend a night in Durham and a night near Hadrian's Wall. For train travelers, Durham is a convenient overnight stop, but it's problematic to see en route to another destination since there's no baggage storage at the station. Either stay overnight, or do Durham as a day trip from York.

## Durham

Without its cathedral, Durham would hardly be noticed. But this magnificently situated structure is hard to miss (even if you're zooming by on the train). The hilly, cobbled town sits along the tight curve of its river, snug below its castle and famous church. Durham is home to England's third-oldest university, with a student vibe jostling against its lingering working-class, mining-town feel.

### Orientation

**Day Plan:** For the best quick visit, arrive by midafternoon, in time to tour the cathedral and enjoy the evensong service (Tue-Sat at 17:15, Sun at 15:30; limited access during June graduation ceremonies). Sleep in Durham, then continue on to your next destination.

**Getting There:** Frequent trains run from York (3-4/hour, 45 minutes); from London, there's one direct train per hour (3 hours). Durham, near the A-1/M-1

motorway, is an easy stop for drivers.

**Arrival in Durham:** From the train station, the simplest way to reach the cathedral is to hop on the **Cathedral Bus. Drivers** should surrender to the 400-space Prince Bishops Shopping Centre parking lot (at the roundabout at the base of the old town, a short block from Market Place—must use cash or card with chip).

---

Rick's Tip: *If you don't feel like walking Durham's hills, hop on the convenient* **Cathedral Bus.** *It links the train station with the city center, Market Place, and Durham's cathedral and castle (£1 all-day ticket, no Sun service, www.durham.gov.uk).*

---

**Tourist Information:** There's no physical TI, but the town maintains a call center and website (tel. 03000-262-626, www.thisisdurham.com). In summer, volunteers staff the **Durham Pointers** information cart in Market Place (late May-early Oct, www.durhampointers.co.uk).

The **Durham World Heritage Site Visitor Centre,** near the Palace Green, offers some guidance and sells castle tour tickets (open daily, 7 Owengate, tel. 0191/334-3805, www.durhamworldheritagesite.com).

**Tours: Blue Badge guides** offer 1.5-hour city walking tours on Saturdays at 14:00 in peak season (£4, meet at Durham World Heritage Site Visitor Centre, contact TI call center to confirm schedule, tel. 03000-262-626).

**Private Guide: David Butler,** the town historian, gives excellent private tours (tel. 0191/386-1500, www.dhent.co.uk).

### Sights

▲▲▲DURHAM'S CATHEDRAL
Built to house the much-venerated bones of St. Cuthbert, Durham's cathedral

offers the best look at Norman architecture in England. ("Norman" is British for "Romanesque.") In addition to touring the cathedral, try to fit in an evensong service.

**Cost and Hours:** Free, donation requested, £5 for tower climb, fee for special exhibits; Mon-Sat 9:30-18:00, Sun 12:30-18:00, daily until 20:00 mid-July-Aug, sometimes closes for special services, opens daily at 7:15 for worship and prayer; tel. 0191/386-4266, www.durhamcathedral.co.uk. Access to the cathedral is limited for a few days in June, when it is used for graduation ceremonies (check schedule online).

**Tours:** Regular tours (£5) run Mon-Sat, usually at 11:00 and 14:00, plus a 10:30 tour in summer—call or check website to confirm times.

**Evensong:** To fully experience the cathedral, attend an evensong service. Arrive early and ask to be seated in the choir (Tue-Sat at 17:15, Sun at 15:30, 1 hour, sometimes sung on Mon; visiting choirs nearly always fill in when choir is off on school break mid-July-Aug).

**Organ Recitals:** The organ plays most Wednesday evenings in July and August (£8, 19:30).

## ⊙ SELF-GUIDED TOUR

Begin your visit at the cathedral **door.** Check out the big, bronze, lion-faced knocker (a replica of the 12th-century original), which medieval criminals sounded to gain temporary sanctuary in the church.

Inside, a handy ❶ **information desk** is at the back (right) end of the nave. Notice the ❷ **modern window** with the novel depiction of the Last Supper (above and left of the entry door), given to the church by the local Marks & Spencer department store in 1984.

Spanning the nave, the ❸ **black marble strip** on the floor was as close to the altar as women were allowed in the days when this was a Benedictine church (until 1540). Take a seat and admire the fine proportions, rounded arches, and zigzag-carved decorations of England's best Norman nave. It is particularly harmonious because it was built in a mere 40 years (1093-1133). The church was built by well-traveled French masons and

*Durham Cathedral*          *Cathedral nave*

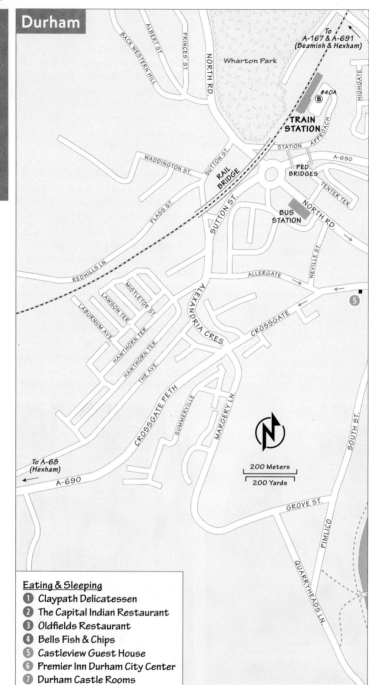

# Durham

To
A-167 & A-691
(Beamish & Hexham)

BACK WESTERN HILL

ALBERT ST.

PRINCES' ST.

NORTH RD.

Wharton Park

HIGHGATE

#40A
**B**

**TRAIN STATION**

STATION APPROACH

A-690

WADDINGTON ST.

SUTTON ST.

**RAIL BRIDGE**

**PED. BRIDGES**

TENTER TER.

FLASS ST.

SUTTON ST.

**BUS STATION**

NORTH RD.

NEVILLE ST.

REDHILLS LN.

ALLERGATE

**5**

LABURNUM AVE.

LAWSON TER.

MISTLETOE ST.

HAWTHORN TER.

HAWTHORN TER.

ALEXANDRIA CRES.

CROSSGATE

THE AVE.

CROSSGATE PETH

SUMMERVILLE

MARGERY LN.

SOUTH ST.

To A-68
(Hexham)

A-690

GROVE ST.

PIMLICO

QUARRYHEADS LN.

200 Meters
200 Yards

## Eating & Sleeping

1. Claypath Delicatessen
2. The Capital Indian Restaurant
3. Oldfields Restaurant
4. Bells Fish & Chips
5. Castleview Guest House
6. Premier Inn Durham City Center
7. Durham Castle Rooms

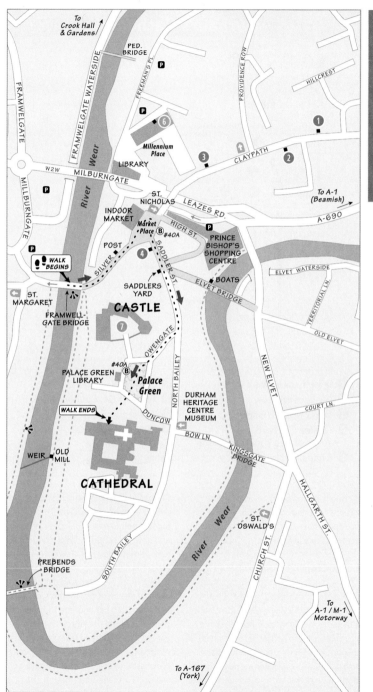

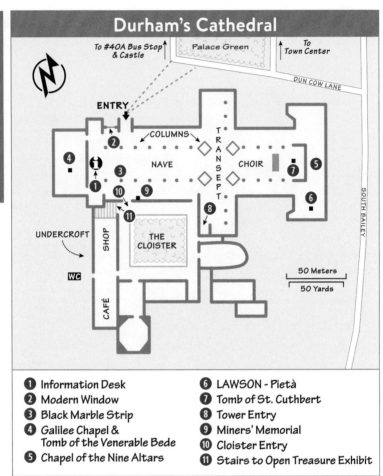

# Durham's Cathedral

To #40A Bus Stop & Castle

Palace Green

To Town Center

DUN COW LANE

ENTRY

COLUMNS

TRANSEPT

NAVE

CHOIR

SOUTH BAILEY

UNDERCROFT

SHOP

THE CLOISTER

WC

CAFÉ

50 Meters

50 Yards

❶ Information Desk
❷ Modern Window
❸ Black Marble Strip
❹ Galilee Chapel &
   Tomb of the Venerable Bede
❺ Chapel of the Nine Altars

❻ LAWSON - Pietà
❼ Tomb of St. Cuthbert
❽ Tower Entry
❾ Miners' Memorial
❿ Cloister Entry
⓫ Stairs to Open Treasure Exhibit

architects who knew the latest innovations from Europe. Its ribbed vault, pointed arches, and flying buttresses were revolutionary in England.

At the back of the nave, enter the ❹ **Galilee Chapel** (late Norman, from 1175). The paintings of St. Cuthbert and St. Oswald (seventh-century king of Northumbria) on the side walls of the smaller altar are rare examples of Romanesque paintings. On the right side of the chapel, the upraised tomb topped with a black slab contains the remains of the **Venerable Bede,** an eighth-century Christian scholar who wrote the first history of England.

Back in the main church, stroll down the nave to the center (you'll be under the highest **bell tower** in Europe—218 feet), and enter the **choir.** Monks worshipped many times a day, and the choir in the center of the church provided a cozy place to gather. Mass has been said daily here in the heart of the cathedral for 900 years. The fancy wooden benches are from the 17th century. Behind the altar is the delicately carved Neville Screen from 1380 (made of Normandy stone in London, shipped to Newcastle by sea, then brought here by wagon). Until the Reformation, the niches contained statues of 107 saints.

Step down behind the high altar into the east end of the church, which contains the 13th-century ❺ **Chapel of the Nine Altars.** Built later than the rest of the church, this is Gothic—taller, lighter, and relatively more extravagant than the Norman nave. On the right, see the modern ❻ pietà made of driftwood by local sculptor Fenwick Lawson.

Climb a few steps to the ❼ **tomb of St. Cuthbert.** An inspirational leader of the early Christian Church in north England, St. Cuthbert lived in the Lindisfarne monastery (100 miles north of Durham, today called Holy Island). Eleven years after his death (687), his body was exhumed and found to be miraculously preserved, stoking his popularity with pilgrims. When Vikings raided Lindisfarne in 875, the monks fled with his body (and the famous illuminated Lindisfarne Gospels, now in the British Library in London). In 995, after 120 years of roaming, the monks settled in Durham, and Cuthbert was re-interred here.

In the **south transept** is the ❽ **tower entry,** as well as an astronomical clock and the Chapel of the Durham Light Infantry, a regiment of the British Army. The old flags and banners hanging above were actually carried into battle.

Find your way toward the cloister (opposite the entry door). Near there, notice the ❾ **memorial honoring coal miners.** The last pit of the Durham coalfields closed in the 1980s, but the mining legacy here is still strong.

It's worth making a circuit of the Gothic ❿ **cloister** for a fine view back up to the church towers. From the cloister, you'll find stairs up to the ⓫ **Open Treasure exhibit,** which holds artifacts from the cathedral treasury and the monks' library—including a copy of the Magna Carta from 1216.

## PALACE GREEN

The Palace Green, which lies between the cathedral and castle, was the site of the original 11th-century Saxon town. Later, the town made way for 12th-century Durham's defenses, which now enclose the green.

## DURHAM CASTLE

The castle still stands—as it has for a thousand years—on its motte (man-made mound), and now houses Durham University. Look into the old courtyard from the castle gate. It traces the very first and smallest bailey (protected area). As future bishops expanded the castle, they left their coats of arms as a way of "signing" the wing they built. Because the Norman kings appointed prince-bishops to rule this part of their realm, Durham was the seat of power for much of northern England. The bishops had their own army and even minted their own coins. The castle is accessible only with a 45-minute guided tour, which includes the courtyard, kitchens, great hall, and chapel.

**Cost and Hours:** Tour-£5, open most days when school is in session—but schedule varies so call ahead, buy tickets at Durham World Heritage Site Visitor Centre or Palace Green Library (near the cathedral), tel. 0191/334-2932, www.dur.ac.uk/durham.castle.

## Eating and Sleeping

**Claypath Delicatessen** is worth the five-minute uphill walk for tasty sandwiches and salads (closed Sun-Mon; from Market Place, cross the bridge and walk up Claypath to #57). Across the street is **The Capital,** with good Indian food (69 Claypath). **Oldfields** serves pricey, updated British classics (18 Claypath).

**Bells,** just off Market Place, is a standby for carryout fish-and-chips. You can **picnic** on Market Place, or on the benches and grass outside the cathedral entrance (but not on the Palace Green).

If you overnight in Durham, consider the restful **$$$ Castleview Guest House** (4 Crossgate, www.castle-view.co.uk); the conveniently located **$$ Premier Inn Durham City Center** (Freemans Place, www.premierinn.com); or the student residence at **$$$ Durham Castle** (generally July-Sept only, Palace Green, www.dur.ac.uk/university.college).

## Beamish Museum

This huge, 300-acre open-air museum, which re-creates life in northeast England during the 1820s, 1900s, and 1940s, is England's best museum of its type.

### *Orientation*

**Day Plan:** It takes at least three hours to explore Beamish's four sections. If you're short on time, skip the Home Farm. Take advantage of the double-decker buses and vintage trams that connect farther-flung sections.

Drivers could visit Beamish en route between Durham and Hadrian's Wall; this is easier for those overnighting near the wall (allowing time for seeing the Roman sights without feeling rushed).

**Getting There:** By **car,** the museum is five minutes off the A-1/M-1 motorway (one exit north of Durham, well-signposted).

Day-tripping from Durham to Beamish by **bus** is a snap on peak-season Saturdays via direct bus #128 (8/day, 30 minutes, runs April-Oct only, stops at Durham train and bus stations, www.simplygo.com). Otherwise, catch bus #21, #X21, or #50 from the Durham bus station (3/hour, 25 minutes) and transfer at Chester-le-Street to bus #8 or #8A, which takes you right to the museum (2/hour Mon-Sat, hourly Sun, 15 minutes, leaves from central bus kiosk a half-block away). Show your bus ticket for a 25 percent museum discount.

**Cost and Hours:** £18.50, children 5-16-£10.50, under 5-free; open Easter-Oct daily 10:00-17:00; off-season until 16:00, weekends only Dec-mid-Feb; check events schedule as you enter, tel. 0191/370-4000, www.beamish.org.uk.

**Eating:** Several eateries are scattered around Beamish (pub, tearooms, fish-and-chips stand). Or bring a picnic.

### ⊙ *Self-Guided Tour*

Attendants at each stop happily explain everything. You'll likely see the sections in this order:

**1900s Pit Village:** This is a company town built around a coal mine, with a schoolhouse, Methodist chapel, and row of miners' homes with long, skinny pea-patch gardens out front.

At the adjacent **Colliery** (coal mine), you can take a 20-minute tour into the drift mine (check in at the "lamp camp"—tours depart when enough people gather, generally every 5-10 minutes).

• *Take the path leading through the woods to...*

**1820s Pockerley:** The Georgian-era home is in two parts. The **Waggonway,** a big barn filled with steam engines, includes a re-created, first-ever passenger train from 1825. Climb the hill to **Pockerley Old Hall,** the manor house of a gentleman farmer and his family, where costumed docents often bake delicious cookies from old recipes...and hand out samples.

*A vintage building at the Beamish Museum*

*• From the manor house, hop on a tram or bus to reach the...*

**1900s Town:** The Edwardian-era Town is a bustling street featuring working shops, homes, and offices that are a delight to explore. In the Masonic Hall, ogle the grand high-ceilinged meeting room, or poke into the stables, which are full of carriages. The heavenly-smelling candy store sells old-timey sweets, and at the newsagent's, you can buy stationery, cards, and old toys.

*• From here, walk or ride a tram or bus to the...*

**1940s Home Farm:** Along with the petting zoo, you'll see a "horse gin" (a.k.a. "gin gan")—where a horse walking in a circle turned a crank on a gear to amplify its "horsepower," helping to replace human labor.

## Hadrian's Wall

This Roman wall is the most impressive Roman ruin in England. Stretching 73 miles coast to coast across the narrowest stretch of northern England, it was built in about A.D. 122, during the reign of Emperor Hadrian, and defended by some 20,000 troops. Not just a wall, it was a military complex that included forts, ditches, settlements, and roads. At every mile of the wall, a "milecastle" guarded a gate, and two turrets stood between each castle.

Marking the Roman Empire's northernmost border, the wall was likely built to keep out troublesome Pict tribes in the north (now Scotland). Originally towering 20 feet tall, the wall is only about 3 to 6 feet high today.

Today, several restored chunks of the wall, ruined forts, and museums thrill history buffs. Three top sights are worth visiting: Housesteads Roman Fort shows you where the Romans lived; Vindolanda's museum shows you how they lived; and the Roman Army Museum explains the empire-wide military organization that brought them here. The wall is easiest to visit by car, though a handy bus links these main sights in peak season (Easter-late Sept).

Hadrian's Wall is not only popular with Rome-aniacs, but also serious hikers, who follow the route from coast to coast,

*Hadrian's Wall is the finest Roman relic in Britain.*

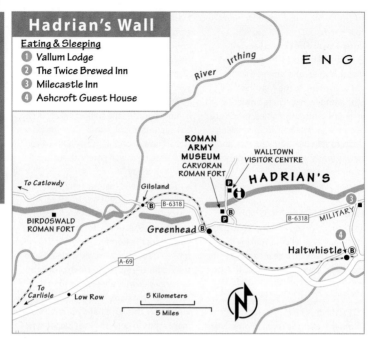

# Hadrian's Wall

### Eating & Sleeping
1 Vallum Lodge
2 The Twice Brewed Inn
3 Milecastle Inn
4 Ashcroft Guest House

taking 4 to 10 days to complete it (Hadrian's Wall National Trail, www.nationaltrail.co.uk/HadriansWall).

## Orientation

The sights described here lie roughly between the midsize towns of Bardon Mill and Haltwhistle, along the busy A-69 highway. To get right up close to the wall, you'll need to head a couple of miles north to the adjacent villages of Once Brewed and Twice Brewed (along the B-6318 road).

**Day Plan:** If you have time for only one stop, choose Housesteads Roman Fort. Drivers with time to do it all could start at the Roman Army Museum (good orientation to Roman soldiers' everyday life), then go to the Walltown Visitor Centre (pick up info on wall walks), then Steel Rigg (hike partway along the wall to Sycamore Gap and return, or hike farther to Housesteads and bus back to your car), Vindolanda, and end with Housesteads Roman Fort.

Nondrivers can take a bus that stops at

Housesteads, Vindolanda, and Walltown (Roman Army Museum and Visitor Centre).

**Tourist Information:** Essential resources for navigating the wall include the *Hadrian's Wall Country Map,* the Hadrian's Wall bus #AD122 schedule, and a local train timetable for Northern Line #4—all available at local visitors centers and train stations.

For an overview website, see www.hadrianswallcountry.co.uk.

The **Walltown Visitor Centre,** which lies along the bus #AD122 route, has info on walks (daily Easter-Oct 9:30-17:00, closed Nov-Easter, just off B-6318 next to Roman Army Museum, follow signs to *Walltown Quarry,* tel. 01697/747-151, www.northumberlandnationalpark.org.uk).

A helpful **TI** is in Haltwhistle, a block from the train station inside the library (Westgate, tel. 01434/322-002).

**Baggage Storage:** It's a challenge, but you have several options: Day-trip from Durham (leaving baggage at your B&B);

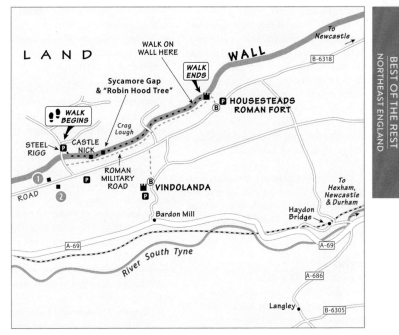

store baggage at Newcastle (at Eldon Square Shopping Center, a 5-minute walk north of train station; tel. 01912/611-891, www.intu.co.uk/eldonsquare); haul your bag along (Housesteads Roman Fort and Vinolanda will likely let you store it temporarily at their entrance); or use a baggage-courier service to send your baggage ahead to your next B&B in the region (about £5 per bag; try Hadrian's Haul, mobile 07967-564-823, www.hadrianshaul.com, or Walkers', tel. 0871-423-8803, www.walkersbags.co.uk).

## Getting Around

Hadrian's Wall is anchored by the big cities of Newcastle to the east and Carlisle to the west. Driving is the most convenient way to see Hadrian's Wall. If you're coming by train, consider renting a car for the day at either Newcastle or Carlisle; otherwise, you'll need to rely on trains and a bus to connect the sights, or hire a private guide with a car.

**By Car:** Zip to this "best of Hadrian's Wall" zone on the speedy A-69; when you get close, head a few miles north and follow the B-6318, which parallels the wall. Official Hadrian's Wall parking lots (including at the Walltown Visitor Centre, Housesteads Roman Fort, and the trailhead at Steel Rigg) are covered by a single one-day parking pass (coin-op pay-and-display machines at all lots).

**By Bus:** Take the made-for-tourists Hadrian's Wall **bus #AD122** (runs from Easter through late Sept). It connects the Roman sights with train stations in **Haltwhistle** and **Hexham** (from £2/ride, £12 unlimited Day Rover ticket, buy tickets on board, 8-9/day in each direction, tel. 01434/322-002, confirm schedule and see route at www.hadrianswallcountry.co.uk).

**By Train:** Northern Line's train route #4 runs parallel to and a few miles south of the wall more frequently than the bus. It doesn't take you near the actual Roman sights, but from the Hexham and Haltwhistle stations, you can catch bus #AD122 to get you there (train runs daily

1/hour, www.northernrail.org).

**By Taxi:** These Haltwhistle-based taxi companies can help you connect the dots: Sprouls (tel. 01434/321-064, mobile 07712-321-064) or Diamond (mobile 07597/641-222). It costs about £11 one-way from Haltwhistle to Housesteads Roman Fort.

**By Private Tour:** Peter Carney, a former history teacher, offers tours with his car and also leads guided walks around the wall (£125/day for up to 5 people, £70/half-day, www.hadrianswall-walk.com).

**Off-Season Options:** Off-season, you can only get as far as the train will take you (i.e., Haltwhistle)—from there, you'll have to take a taxi or hire a local guide to reach the sights.

## Sights

### ▲▲HIKING THE WALL

For a good, craggy, three-mile, one-way, up-and-down walk along the wall, hike between Steel Rigg and Housesteads Roman Fort. For a shorter stretch, begin at Steel Rigg (where there's a handy parking lot) and walk a mile to Sycamore Gap, then back again. These hikes are moderately strenuous and are best for those in good shape. You'll need sturdy shoes and a windbreaker. It's smart to stop at the Walltown Visitor Centre for a free sheet outlining this walk.

To reach the trailhead, take the little road off B-6318 near the Twice Brewed Inn and park in the pay-and-display parking lot at the crest of the hill. Walk through the gate to the shoulder-high stretch of wall, go left, and follow the wall, climbing up-and-down multiple dips and gaps. In the second one is the best-preserved milecastle (at #39, called Castle Nick).

Soon after, you'll reach Sycamore Gap, named for the large symmetrical tree in the middle. You can either hike back the way you came or cut down toward the main road to find the less strenuous Roman Military Way path, which leads back to the base of the Steel Rigg hill, where you can huff back up to your car.

If you continue on to Housesteads, you'll pass a traditional Northumbrian sheep farm, windswept lakes, and more ups and downs. From Housesteads Roman Fort, bus #AD122 can get you back to Steel Rigg.

### ▲▲HOUSESTEADS ROMAN FORT

With its respectable museum, powerful scenery, and a well-preserved segment of the wall, this is your best single stop at Hadrian's Wall. It requires a steep hike up from the parking lot; but once there, it's just you, the bleating sheep, and memories of ancient Rome.

**Cost and Hours:** £6.60 for site and museum; daily April-Sept 10:00-18:00, Oct 10:00-17:00, Nov-March 10:00-16:00; last entry 45 minutes before closing, visitors center with snack bar, bus #AD122 stops here, info tel. 0870-333-1181, www.english-heritage.org.uk/housesteads.

**Visiting the Museum and Fort:** Hike about a half-mile uphill to the fort, and tour the **museum** there. You'll see the giant Victory statue that once adorned the fort's East Gate, cooking pots, spoons, and other artifacts.

Then head out to the sprawling ruins of the **fort.** All Roman forts had the same rectangular shape and design, containing a commander's headquarters, barracks, and latrines (Housesteads has the best-preserved Roman toilets found anywhere). This fort even had a hospital. The fort was built right up to the wall, which runs along its upper end. This is the one place where it's permissible to walk on top of the wall for a photo op.

### ▲▲VINDOLANDA

This large Roman fort, which predates the wall by 40 years, is not as intact as that at Housesteads. But Vindolanda's worthwhile museum is packed with artifacts that reveal intimate details of Roman life. The site is an active dig: From Easter through September, you'll see excavation work in progress.

**Cost and Hours:** £6.75, £10.50

combo-ticket includes Roman Army Museum, daily April-Sept 10:00-18:00, closes earlier off-season, may be open on weekends Dec-mid-Feb, last entry 45 minutes before closing, call first during bad weather, free parking with entry, bus #AD122 stops here, café, tel. 01434/344-277, www.vindolanda.com.

**Tours:** Guided tours run twice daily on weekends only (typically at 10:45 and 14:00); in high season, archaeological talks and tours may be offered on weekdays as well. Both are included in your ticket.

**Visiting the Site and Museum:** Head out to the **site,** walking through 500 yards of grassy parkland decorated by the foundation stones of the Roman fort and a full-size replica chunk of the wall. Over the course of 400 years, at least nine forts were built on this spot. The Romans, by lazily sealing the foundations from each successive fort, left modern-day archaeologists with a 20-foot-deep treasure trove of remarkably well-preserved artifacts.

These excavated objects are displayed well in the **museum.** You'll see the world's largest collection of Roman leather; tools used for building and expanding the fort; locks and keys; a large coin collection; items imported here from the far corners of the vast empire (French pottery and amphora jugs from the Mediterranean); combs and hairpins; and religious pillars and steles.

But the museum's main attraction is its collection of writing tablets. These impressively well-preserved examples of early Roman cursive were discovered here in 1973. Finally, you'll pass through an exhibit about the history of the excavations and the latest discoveries.

## ▲▲ROMAN ARMY MUSEUM

Exhibits at this museum, a few miles farther west at Greenhead (near the site of the Carvoran Roman fort), illustrate the structure of the Roman Army that built and monitored this wall, with a focus on the everyday lives of the Roman soldiers stationed here. Bombastic displays, life-size figures, and several different films—but few actual artifacts—make this entertaining museum a good complement to the archaeological emphasis of Vindolanda. If you're visiting all three Roman sights, this is a good one to start at, as it sets the stage for what you're about to see.

**Cost and Hours:** £5.50, £10.50 combo-ticket includes Vindolanda, daily April-Sept 10:00-18:00, mid-Feb-March and Oct-mid-Nov 10:00-17:00, may be open on weekends mid-Nov-mid-Feb, free parking with entry, bus #AD122 stops here, tel. 01697/747-485, www.vindolanda.com.

## Eating and Sleeping

Near the neighboring villages of Once Brewed and Twice Brewed, you'll find the cushy **$$ Vallum Lodge** (Military Road, www.vallum-lodge.co.uk) and **$$ The Twice Brewed Inn,** with basic rooms and a friendly **pub** (Military Road, www.twicebrewedinn.co.uk). Two miles to the west, **Milecastle Inn** offers the best dinner around—reserve ahead in summer (North Road, www.milecastle-inn.co.uk).

Near Haltwhistle, **$$ Ashcroft Guest House** has luxurious rooms (Lanty's Lonnen, www.ashcroftguesthouse.co.uk).

# England: Past and Present

## Origins
### (2000 B.C.-A.D. 500)

When Julius Caesar landed on the misty and mysterious isle of Britain in 55 B.C., England entered the history books. He was met by primitive Celtic tribes whose druid priests made human sacrifices and worshipped trees. (Those Celts were themselves immigrants, who had earlier conquered the even more mysterious people who built Stonehenge.) The Romans eventually settled in England (A.D. 43) and set about building towns and roads and establishing their capital at Londinium (today's London).

But the Celtic natives—consisting of Gaels, Picts, and Scots—were not easily subdued. Around A.D. 60, Boadicea, a queen of the Isle's indigenous people, defied the Romans and burned Londinium before the revolt was squelched. Some decades later, the Romans built Hadrian's Wall near the Scottish border as protection against their troublesome northern neighbors.

## Dark Ages
### (500-1000)

As Rome fell, so fell Roman Britain—a victim of invaders and internal troubles. Barbarian tribes from Germany, Denmark, and northern Holland, called Angles, Saxons, and Jutes, swept through the southern part of the island, establishing Angle-land. These were the days of the real King Arthur, possibly a Christianized Roman general who fought valiantly—but in vain—against invading barbarians.

In 793, England was hit with the first of two centuries of savage invasions by barbarians from Norway, called the Vikings or Norsemen. King Alfred the Great (849-899) liberated London from Danish Vikings, reunited England, reestablished Christianity, and fostered learning. Nevertheless, for most of this 500-year period, the island was plunged into a dark age.

## Norman Britain and the Middle Ages
### (1000-1500)

In 1066, William the Conqueror and his Norman troops crossed the English Chan-

## Royal Families: Past and Present

**802-1066:** Saxon and Danish kings
**1066-1154:** Norman invasion (William the Conqueror), Norman kings
**1154-1399:** Plantagenet (kings with French roots)
**1399-1461:** Lancaster
**1462-1485:** York
**1485-1603:** Tudor (Henry VIII, Elizabeth I)
**1603-1649:** Stuart (civil war and beheading of Charles I)
**1649-1653:** Commonwealth, no royal head of state
**1653-1659:** Protectorate, with Cromwell as Lord Protector
**1660-1714:** Restoration of Stuart dynasty
**1714-1901:** Hanover (four Georges, William IV, Victoria)
**1901-1910:** Saxe-Coburg (Edward VII)
**1910-now:** Windsor (George V, Edward VIII, George VI, Elizabeth II)

nel from France. William crowned himself king in Westminster Abbey (where all subsequent coronations would take place). He began building the Tower of London, as well as Windsor Castle, which would become the residence of many monarchs to come.

Over the succeeding centuries, French-speaking kings would rule England, and English-speaking kings invaded France as the two budding nations defined their modern borders. Richard the Lionheart (1157-1199) ruled as a French-speaking king who spent most of his energy on distant Crusades. In 1215, King John (Richard's brother), under pressure from England's barons, was forced to sign the Magna Carta, establishing the principle that even kings must follow the rule of law.

London asserted itself as England's trade center. London Bridge—the famous stone version, topped with houses—was built (1209), and Old St. Paul's Cathedral was finished (1314).

Then followed two centuries of wars, chiefly the Hundred Years' War with France (1337-1443). In 1348, the Black Death (bubonic plague) killed half of London's population.

In the 1400s, the noble York and Lancaster families duked it out for the crown in a series of dynastic civil wars.

## The Tudor Renaissance
### (1500s)

England was finally united by the "third-party" Tudor family. Henry VIII, a Tudor, was England's Renaissance king. He went through six wives in 40 years, divorcing, imprisoning, or executing them when they no longer suited his needs. When the Pope refused to grant Henry a divorce so he could marry Anne Boleyn, Henry "divorced" England from the Catholic Church. He established the Protestant Church of England (the Anglican Church), thus setting in motion a century of bitter Protestant/Catholic squabbles. Henry's own daughter, "Bloody" Mary, was a staunch Catholic who presided over the burning of hundreds of prominent Protestants.

After Mary came another of Henry's daughters (by Anne Boleyn)—Queen Elizabeth I. She reigned for 45 years, making England a great trading and naval power (defeating the Spanish Armada) and treading diplomatically over the Protestant/Catholic divide. Elizabeth presided over a cultural renaissance known as the "Elizabethan Age." Playwright William Shakespeare moved from Stratford-upon-Avon to London, beginning a remarkable career as the earth's greatest playwright. Sir Francis Drake circumnavigated the globe. Sir Walter Raleigh explored the Americas, and Sir Francis Bacon pioneered the scientific method.

But Elizabeth—the "Virgin Queen"—never married or produced an heir. So the English Parliament invited Scotland's King James (Elizabeth's first cousin twice removed) to inherit the English throne.

## Kings vs. Parliament
### (1600s)

The enduring quarrel between England's kings and Parliament's nobles finally erupted into the 1642 Civil War. The war pitted the Protestant Puritan Parliament against the Catholic aristocracy. Parliament forces under Oliver Cromwell defeated—and beheaded—King Charles I. After Cromwell died, Parliament invited Charles' son to take the throne—the "restoration of the monarchy."

This turbulent era was followed by back-to-back disasters—the Great Plague of 1665 (which killed 100,000) and the Great Fire of 1666 (which incinerated London). London was completely rebuilt in stone, centered on the new St. Paul's Cathedral, built by Christopher Wren.

In the war between kings and Parliament, Parliament finally got the last word when it deposed Catholic James II and imported the Dutch monarchs William and Mary in 1688, guaranteeing a Protestant succession.

## Colonial Expansion
### (1700s)

Britain grew as a naval superpower, colonizing and trading with all parts of the globe. Eventually, Britannia ruled the waves, exploiting the wealth of India, Africa, Australia, and America...at least until those ungrateful Yanks revolted in

1776. Throughout the century, the country was ruled by the German Hanover family, including four kings named George.

The "Georgian Era" was one of great wealth. London's population was now a half-million, and one in seven Brits lived in London. The nation's first daily newspapers hit the streets. The cultural scene was refined: painters (like William Hogarth, Joshua Reynolds, and Thomas Gainsborough), theater (with actors like David Garrick), music (Handel's *Messiah*), and literature (Samuel Johnson's dictionary). Scientist James Watt's steam engines laid the groundwork for a coming Industrial Revolution.

In 1789, the French Revolution erupted, sparking decades of war between France and Britain. Britain finally prevailed in the early 1800s, when Admiral Horatio Nelson defeated Napoleon's fleet at the Battle of Trafalgar and the Duke of Wellington stomped Napoleon at Waterloo. By war's end, Britain had emerged as Europe's top power.

## Victorian Britain
### (1800s)

Britain reigned supreme, steaming into the Industrial Age with her mills, factories, coal mines, gas lights, and trains.

Eighteen-year-old Victoria became queen in 1837. She ruled for 64 years, presiding over an era of unprecedented wealth, peace, and middle-class ("Victorian") values. Britain was at its zenith of power, with a colonial empire that covered one-fifth of the world.

Meanwhile, there was another side to Britain's era of superiority and industrial might. A generation of Romantic poets (William Wordsworth, John Keats, Percy Shelley, and Lord Byron) longed for the innocence of nature. Jane Austen and the Brontë sisters wrote romantic tales about the landed gentry. Painters like J. M. W. Turner and William Constable immersed themselves in nature to paint moody landscapes.

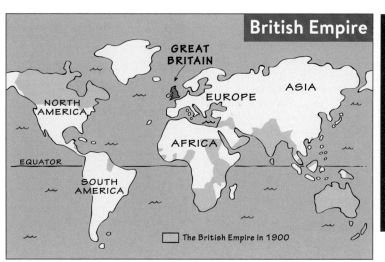

**British Empire**

GREAT BRITAIN

NORTH AMERICA

EUROPE

ASIA

AFRICA

EQUATOR

SOUTH AMERICA

☐ The British Empire in 1900

The gritty modern world was emerging. Popular novelist Charles Dickens brought literature to the masses, educating them about Britain's harsh social and economic realities. Rudyard Kipling critiqued the colonial system. Charles Darwin questioned the very nature of humanity when he articulated the principles of natural selection and evolution.

## World Wars and Recovery
### (20th CENTURY)

The 20th century was not kind to Britain. Two world wars and economic struggles whittled Britain down from a world empire to an island chain struggling to compete in a global economy.

In World War I, Britain joined France and other allies to battle Germany in trench warfare. A million British men died.

In the 1920s, London was home to a flourishing literary scene, including T. S. Eliot, Virginia Woolf, and E. M. Forster. In 1936, the country was rocked and scandalized when King Edward VIII abdicated to marry a divorced American commoner, Wallis Simpson.

In World War II, the Nazi Blitz reduced much of London to rubble, sending residents into Tube stations for shelter and

the government into a fortified bunker (now the Churchill War Rooms). Britain was rallied through its darkest hour by two leaders: Prime Minister Winston Churchill, a remarkable orator, and King George VI. Amid the chaos of war, the colonial empire began to dwindle to almost nothing, and Britain emerged from the war as a shell of its former superpower self.

Culturally, Britain remained world-class. Oxford professor J. R. R. Tolkien wrote *The Lord of the Rings* and his friend C. S. Lewis wrote *The Chronicles of Narnia*. In the 1960s, "Swinging London" became a center for rock music, film, theater, youth culture, and Austin Powers-style joie de vivre. America was conquered by a "British Invasion" of rock bands.

The 1970s brought massive unemployment, labor strikes, and recession. A conservative reaction followed in the 1980s and '90s, led by Prime Minister Margaret Thatcher—the "Iron Lady." As proponents of traditional, Victorian values—community, family, hard work, thrift, and trickle-down economics—the Conservatives took a Reaganesque approach to Britain's serious social and economic problems. They cut government subsidies to old-fashioned industries (closing many factories, earning working-class ire) as they tried to nudge Britain toward a more modern economy.

In 1981, the world was captivated by the spectacle of Prince Charles marrying Lady Diana in St. Paul's Cathedral. Their children, Princes William and Harry, grew up in the media spotlight, and when Diana died in a car crash (1997), the nation—and the world—mourned.

The 1990s saw Britain finally emerging from decades of economic stagnation and social turmoil. An energized nation prepared for the new millennium.

## England Today

After two decades of Conservative politics, Britain entered the new millennium ruled by a Labour (left-of-center) government under Prime Minister Tony Blair. Labour began shoring up a social-service system (health care, education, minimum wage) undercut by years of Conservative rule. But Blair's popularity was undermined when he joined the US invasion of Iraq.

On the morning of July 7 ("7/7") in 2005, London's commuters were rocked by four terrorist bombs that killed dozens across the city. In subsequent years, Britain has had numerous terrorist plots that either caused destruction or were foiled by police.

The question remains how to balance security with privacy concerns. The British have surveillance cameras everywhere—you'll frequently see signs warning you that you're being recorded.

The terrorist threats have highlighted issues relating to Britain's large immigrant population (nearly 4 million). Brits are stunned that many terrorists (like the notorious "Jihadi John" of ISIS) speak the king's English and are born and raised in Britain. And some radical Islamic clerics seem to be preaching jihad in the mosque down the street. It raises the bigger question: How well is the nation assimilating its many immigrants? On the other hand,

### Get It Right

Americans tend to use "England," "Britain," and "United Kingdom" (or "UK") interchangeably, but they're not quite the same.

**England** is the country occupying the center and southeast part of the island.

**Britain** is the name of the island.

**Great Britain** is the political union of the island's three countries: England, Scotland, and Wales.

**The United Kingdom** (UK) adds a fourth country, Northern Ireland.

**The British Isles** (not a political entity) also includes the independent Republic of Ireland.

**The British Commonwealth** is a loose association of possessions and former colonies (including Canada, Australia, and India) that profess at least symbolic loyalty to the Crown.

consider that in 2016, Londoners elected a second-generation Muslim—human-rights lawyer Sadiq Khan—as their mayor.

The large Muslim population is just one thread in the tapestry of today's Britain. While 9 out of 10 Brits are white, the country has large minority groups, mainly from Britain's former colonies: India, Pakistan, Bangladesh, Africa, the Caribbean, and many other places. Despite the tension between some groups, for the most part Britain is relatively integrated, with minorities represented in most (if not all) walks of life.

Then there's the eternal question of the royals. Is having a monarch (who's politically irrelevant) and a royal family (who fill the tabloids with their scandals and foibles) worth it? In decades past, many Brits wanted to toss the whole lot of them. But the recent marriage of the popular William and Kate and the birth of their cute kids have boosted royal esteem.

According to pollsters, four out of five Brits want to keep their Queen and let the tradition live on.

But the single biggest issue facing Britain today is dealing with the repercussions of "Brexit"—the 2016 referendum in which 52 percent of Brits voted to leave the European Union. The Brexit vote stunned Britain, throwing it into uncharted territory with no clear path forward. It also raises questions about Britain's role in the wider, global culture.

The Brexit voite demands a split with the European Union, but it remains to be seen exactly what that will mean. No country has ever left the EU, and the process could take years.

# Practicalities

# TOURIST INFORMATION

**Before your trip**, start with the TI's official website, www.visitbritain.com (www.visitlondon.com for London). The Visit Britain website contains a wealth of knowledge on destinations, activities, accommodations, and transport in Great Britain. Families will especially appreciate the "Britain for Kids & Families" travel suggestions. Maps, airport transfers, sightseeing tours, and theater tickets can be purchased online (www.visitbritainshop.com/usa).

   **In England,** a good first stop in any town is generally the tourist information office (abbreviated **TI** in this book).

Be aware that TIs are in business to help you enjoy spending money in their town. But even if TIs can be overly commercial, they're good places to get a city map and information on public transit (including bus and train schedules), walking tours, special events, and nightlife.

# TRAVEL TIPS

**Time Zones:** England, which is one hour earlier than most of continental Europe, is five/eight hours ahead of the East/West Coasts of the US. The exceptions are the beginning and end of Daylight Saving Time: England and Europe "spring forward" the last Sunday in March (two weeks after most of North America), and "fall back" the last Sunday in October (one week before North America). For a handy online time converter, see www. timeanddate.com/worldclock.

**Business Hours:** Most stores are open Monday through Saturday (roughly 9:00 or 10:00 until 17:00 or 18:00). In cities, some stores stay open later on Wednesday or Thursday (until 19:00 or 20:00). Some big-city department stores are open later throughout the week (until about 21:00 Mon-Sat). On Sunday, when stores are closed or have shorter hours, bigger cities often host street markets lively with shoppers. London has street markets running every day of the week.

**Discounts:** Discounts (called "concessions" or "concs" in England) for sights are generally not listed in this book. However, many sights, buses, and trains offer discounts to youths (up to age 18), students (with proper identification cards, www. isic.org), families, and seniors (loosely defined as retirees or those willing to call themselves seniors. Always ask—though some discounts are available only for European citizens.

# HELP!

## Emergency and Medical Help

In England, dial 999 for police help or a medical emergency. If you get a minor ailment, do as the locals do and go to a pharmacy and see a "chemist" (pharmacist) for advice.

## Theft or Loss

To replace a passport, you'll need to go in person to a US embassy (see next page). If your credit and debit cards disappear, cancel and replace them. If your things are lost or stolen, file a police report, either on the spot or within a day or two; you'll need it to submit an insurance claim for lost or stolen rail passes or travel gear, and it can help with replacing your passport or credit and debit cards. For more information, see www.ricksteves.com/help.

## *Avoiding Theft*

Pickpockets are common in crowded, touristy places, but fortunately, violent crime is rare. Thieves don't want to hurt you; they just want your money and gadgets.

My recommendations: Stay alert and wear a money belt (tucked under your clothes) to keep your cash, debit card, credit card, and passport secure; carry only the money you need for the day in your front pocket.

Treat any disturbance (e.g., a stranger bumping into you, spilling something on you, or trying to get your attention for an odd reason) as a smoke screen for theft. Be on guard waiting in line at sights, at train stations, and while boarding and leaving crowded buses and subways. Thieves target tourists overloaded with bags or distracted with smartphones.

When paying for something, be aware of how much cash you're handing over (state the denomination of the bill when paying a cabbie) and count your change. For tips on using cash machines smartly, read "Security Tips" under "Cash" on page 370.

There's no need to stress; just be smart and prepared.

## Damage Control for Lost Cards

If you lose your credit or debit card, you can stop people from using your card by reporting the loss immediately to your card company. Call these 24-hour US numbers collect: Visa (tel. 303/967-1096), MasterCard (tel. 636/722-7111), and American Express (tel. 336/393-1111).

In England, to make a collect call to the US, dial 0-800-89-0011 and press zero or stay on the line for an operator. Visa's and MasterCard's websites list European toll-free numbers by country.

If you report your loss within two days, you typically won't be responsible for any unauthorized transactions on your account, although many banks charge a liability fee of $50. You can generally receive a temporary replacement card within two or three business days in Europe.

## Embassies and Consulates

**US Consulate and Embassy in London:** Tel. 020/7499-9000 (all services), 24 Grosvenor Square, Tube: Bond Street, http://london.usembassy.gov

**Canadian High Commission in London:** Tel. 020/7004-6000, Canada House, Trafalgar Square, Tube: Charing Cross, www.unitedkingdom.gc.ca

# MONEY

This section offers advice on how to pay for purchases on your trip (including getting cash from ATMs and paying with plastic), dealing with lost or stolen cards, VAT (sales tax) refunds, and tipping.

## What to Bring

Bring both a credit card and a debit card. You'll use the debit card at cash machines (ATMs) to withdraw local cash for most purchases, and the credit card to pay for larger items. Some travelers carry a third card as a backup, in case one gets demagnetized by a rogue machine.

For an emergency stash, bring $100-200 in hard cash. Although banks in some countries don't exchange dollars, in a pinch you can always find exchange desks at major train stations or airports—convenient but with crummy rates.

## Exchange Rate

**1 British pound (£1) = about $1.50**
While the euro (€) is now the currency of most of Europe, England is sticking with its pound sterling. The British pound (£), also called a "quid," is broken into 100 pence (p). Pence means "cents." You'll find coins ranging from 1p to £2 and bills from £5 to £50.

To convert prices from pounds to dollars, add about 50 percent: £20 = about $30, £50 = about $75. (Check www.oanda.com for the latest exchange rates.)

## Cash

Although credit cards are widely accepted in Europe, day-to-day spending is generally more cash-based. I find cash is the easiest—and sometimes only—way to pay for cheap food, taxis, and local guides. Some vendors will charge you extra for using a credit card, some won't accept foreign credit cards, and some won't take any credit cards at all. Having cash on hand can help you avoid a stressful predicament if you find yourself in a place that won't accept your card.

Throughout England, ATMs are the easiest and smartest way for travelers to get cash. They work just like they do at home. To withdraw money from an ATM (known as a "cashpoint" in England), you'll need a debit card (ideally with a Visa

or MasterCard logo), plus a four-digit PIN code. Although you can use a credit card to withdraw cash at an ATM, this comes with high bank fees and only makes sense in an emergency.

**Security Tips:** Shield the keypad when entering your PIN code. When possible, use ATMs located outside banks—a thief is less likely to target a cash machine near surveillance cameras, and if your card is munched by a machine during banking hours, you can go inside for help.

Don't use an ATM if anything on the front of the machine looks loose or damaged (a sign that someone may have attached a "skimming" device to capture account information). Try to withdraw large sums of money to reduce the number of per-transaction bank fees you'll pay.

Stay away from "independent" ATMs such as Travelex, Euronet, YourCash, Cardpoint, and Cashzone, which charge huge commissions and have terrible exchange rates.

While traveling, if you want to access your accounts online, be sure to use a secure connection (see page 386).

## Credit and Debit Cards

For purchases, Visa and MasterCard are more commonly accepted than American Express. Just like at home, credit or debit cards work easily at larger hotels, restaurants, and shops. I typically use my debit card to withdraw cash to pay for most purchases.

I use my credit card sparingly: to book hotel reservations, to buy advance tickets for events or sights, to cover major expenses (such as car rentals or plane tickets), and to pay for things online or near the end of my trip (to avoid another visit to the ATM). While you could instead use a debit card for these purchases, a credit card offers a greater degree of fraud protection.

**Ask Your Credit- or Debit-Card Company:** Before your trip, contact the company that issued your debit or credit cards.

Confirm that your **card will work overseas,** and alert them that you'll be using it in Europe; otherwise, they may deny transactions if they perceive unusual spending patterns.

Ask for the specifics on transaction **fees.** When you use your credit or debit card, you'll typically be charged additional "international transaction" fees of up to 3 percent. If your card's fees seem high, consider getting a different card just for your trip: Capital One (www.capitalone.com) and most credit unions have low-to-no international fees.

Verify your daily ATM **withdrawal limit,** and if necessary, ask your bank to adjust it. I prefer a high limit that allows me to take out more cash at each ATM stop and save on bank fees; some travelers prefer to set a lower limit in case their card is stolen. Note that foreign banks also set maximum withdrawal limits for their ATMs.

Get your bank's emergency **phone number** in the US (but not its 800 number, which isn't accessible from overseas) to call collect if you have a problem.

Ask for your credit card's **PIN** in case you need to make an emergency cash withdrawal or encounter payment machines using the chip-and-PIN system; the bank won't divulge your PIN over the phone, so allow time for it to be mailed.

**Chip-and-PIN Credit Cards:** Europeans use chip-and-PIN credit cards (embedded with an electronic security chip and requiring a four-digit PIN). Most of the chip cards now being offered by major US banks are not true chip-and-PIN cards, but instead are chip-and-signature cards, for which your signature verifies your identity. These cards work in Europe for live transactions and at most payment machines, but won't work for offline transactions such as at unattended gas pumps.

Older American cards with just a magnetic stripe also may not work at unattended payment machines, such as those at train and subway stations, toll plazas, parking garages, bike-rental kiosks, and gas pumps. If you have problems with either type of American card, try entering your card's PIN, look for a machine that takes cash, or find a clerk who can process the transaction manually.

If you're concerned, ask if your bank offers a true chip-and-PIN card. Andrews Federal Credit Union (www.andrewsfcu.org) and the State Department Federal Credit Union (www.sdfcu.org) offer these cards and are open to all US residents.

No matter what kind of card you have, it pays to carry pounds; you can always use an ATM to withdraw cash with your magnetic-stripe debit card.

**Dynamic Currency Conversion:** If merchants or hoteliers offer to convert your purchase price into dollars (called dynamic currency conversion, or DCC), refuse this "service." You'll pay even more in fees for the expensive convenience of seeing your transaction in dollars.

# Tipping

Tipping in England isn't as automatic and generous as it is in the US. For special service, tips are appreciated, but not expected. As in the US, the right amount depends on your resources, tipping philosophy, and the circumstances, but some general guidelines apply.

**Restaurants:** If a service charge is included in the bill, it's not necessary to tip. Otherwise, it's appropriate to tip about 10-12.5 percent. (For more information, see page 374.)

**Taxis:** Round up your fare a bit (for instance, if the fare is £4.50, pay £5). If the cabbie hauls your bags and zips you to the airport to help you catch your flight, you might want to toss in a little more. But if you feel like you're being driven in circles or otherwise ripped off, skip the tip.

**Services:** In general, if someone in the service industry does a super job for you, a small tip of a pound or so is appropriate...but not required. If you're not sure

whether (or how much) to tip, ask a local for advice.

# Getting a VAT Refund

Wrapped into the purchase price of your British souvenirs is a Value-Added Tax (VAT) of about 20 percent. You're entitled to get most of that tax back if you purchase more than £30 worth of goods at a store that participates in the VAT-refund scheme. Typically, you must ring up the minimum at a single retailer—you can't add up your purchases from various shops to reach the required amount.

If the merchant ships the goods to your home, the tax will be subtracted from your purchase price. Otherwise, you'll need to:

**Get the paperwork.** Have the merchant completely fill out the necessary refund document (either an official VAT customs form, or the shop or refund company's own version of it). You'll have to present your passport at the store. Get the paperwork done before you leave the shop to ensure you'll have everything you need (including your original sales receipt).

**Get your stamp at the border or airport.** Process your VAT document at your last stop in the European Union (the airport or border) with the customs agent who deals with VAT refunds. Arrive early enough to allow time to find the customs office—and to wait in line. It's best to keep your purchases in your carry-on. If they're too large or not permitted as carry-on (such as knives), pack them in your checked bags and alert the check-in agent. You'll be sent (with your tagged bag) to a customs desk outside security; someone will examine your bag, stamp your paperwork, and put your bag on the belt. You're not supposed to use your purchased goods before you leave. If you show up at customs wearing your new Wellingtons, officials might look the other way—or deny you a refund.

**Collect your refund.** You'll need to return your stamped document to the retailer or its representative. Many merchants work with a service that has offices at major airports, ports, or border crossings (at Heathrow, Travelex counters and customs desks are located before and after security in terminals 2-5). These services, which extract their own fee (usually around 4 percent), can refund your money immediately in cash or credit your card (within two billing cycles). Other refund services may require you to mail the documents from home, or more quickly, from your point of departure. You'll then have to wait—it can take months.

## Customs for American Shoppers

You are allowed to take home $800 worth of items per person duty-free, once every 31 days. As for food, you can take home many processed and packaged foods: vacuum-packed cheeses, dried herbs, jams, baked goods, candy, chocolate, oil, vinegar, mustard, and honey. Fresh fruits and vegetables and most meats are not allowed, with exceptions for some canned items.

You can bring home one liter of alcohol duty-free. It can be packed securely in your checked luggage. If you want to carry alcohol (or liquid-packed foods) in your carry-on bag for your flight home, buy it at a duty-free shop at the airport.

For details on allowable goods, customs rules, and duty rates, visit www.cbp.gov.

# SIGHTSEEING

Sightseeing can be hard work. Use these tips to make your visits to England's finest sights meaningful, fun, efficient, and painless.

## Plan Ahead

Set up an itinerary that allows you to fit in all your must-see sights. Most sights keep stable hours, but you can easily confirm the latest at TIs or by checking museum websites.

Many museums are closed or have reduced hours at least a few days a year, especially on major holidays. In summer, some sights stay open late. Off-season, many museums have shorter hours. Whenever you go, don't put off visiting a must-see sight—you never know when a place will close unexpectedly for a holiday, strike, or royal audience.

Study up. To get the most out of the self-guided tours and sight descriptions in this book, read them before you visit. The British Museum rocks if you understand the significance of the Rosetta Stone.

## At Sights

Here's what you can typically expect:

**Entering:** Be warned that you may not be allowed to enter if you arrive less than 30 to 60 minutes before closing time. And guards start ushering people out well before the actual closing time, so don't save the best for last.

Some important sights have a security check, where you must open your bag or send it through a metal detector; you can't skip this line even if you have a museum pass.

**Photography:** If the museum's photo policy isn't clearly posted, ask a guard. Generally, taking photos without a flash or tripod is allowed.

**Special Exhibits:** Museums may show special exhibits in addition to their permanent collection. An extra fee (sometimes required) might be assessed for these shows.

**Expect Changes:** Artwork can be on

tour, on loan, out sick, or shifted at the whim of the curator. Pick up a floor plan as you enter, and ask museum staff if you can't find a particular item.

**Audioguides and Apps:** Many sights have audioguides, which generally offer good recorded descriptions. Bring your own earbuds to enjoy better sound. Museums and sights often offer free apps that you can download to your mobile device (check their websites). I've produced free, downloadable audio tours for some sights; look for the 🎧 symbol in this book. For more on my audio tours, see page 27.

**Before Leaving:** At the gift shop, scan the postcard rack or thumb through a guidebook to be sure that you haven't overlooked something that you'd like to see.

## Sightseeing Memberships

Many sights in England are managed by either English Heritage or the National Trust.

Membership in **English Heritage** includes free entry to more than 400 sights in England. For most travelers, the **Overseas Visitor Pass** is a better choice than the pricier one-year membership (Visitor Pass: £30/9 days, £35/16 days; Membership: £50 for one person, £88 for two; tel. 0370-333-1181, www.english-heritage.org.uk).

Membership in the **National Trust** is best suited for garden-and-estate enthusiasts, ideally those traveling by car. It covers more than 350 historic houses, manors, and gardens throughout Great Britain. From the US, it's easy to join online through the Royal Oak Foundation, the National Trust's American affiliate (one-year membership: $65 for one person, $95 for two, www.royal-oak.org). For more on National Trust properties, see www.nationaltrust.org.uk.

# EATING

These days, the stereotype of "bad food in England" is woefully dated. British cooking has embraced international influences and good-quality ingredients, making "modern British" food quite delicious. I find it's easy to eat very well here.

**Tipping:** At pubs and places where you order at the counter, you don't have to tip. At restaurants and fancy pubs with waitstaff, tip about 10-12.5 percent. Most restaurants in London now add a 12.5 percent "optional" tip onto the bill. Tip only what you think the service warrants (if it isn't already added to your bill), and be careful not to tip double.

## Breakfast (Fry-Up)

The traditional fry-up or full English breakfast—generally included in the cost of your room—is famous as a hearty way to start the day. Also known as a "heart attack on a plate," your standard fry-up consists of eggs, Canadian-style bacon and/or sausage, a grilled tomato, sautéed mushrooms, baked beans, toast, and sometimes potatoes or kippers (herring), topped off with tea or coffee.

These days many hotels serve a healthier continental breakfast—with a buffet of everything you'd expect, such as yogurt, cereal, scrambled eggs, fruit, and veggies.

## Lunch and Dinner on a Budget

Even in pricey cities, plenty of inexpensive choices are available.

I've found that portions are huge, and **sharing plates** is generally just fine. Ordering two drinks, a soup or side salad, and splitting a £10 meat pie can make a good, filling meal. If you're on a limited budget, share a main course in a more expensive place for a nicer eating experience.

**Pub grub** is the most atmospheric budget option. You'll usually get reasonably priced, hearty lunches and dinners under ancient timbers (see "Pubs," later).

**Classier restaurants** have some affordable deals. Lunch is usually cheaper than dinner; a top-end, £25-for-dinner-type restaurant often serves the same quality two-course lunch deals for about half the price.

Many restaurants have **early-bird** or **pre-theater specials** of two or three courses, often for a significant savings. Some places offer these on weekdays only; others have them every day. They are usually available only before 18:30 or 19:00.

**Ethnic restaurants** add spice to England's cuisine. Eating Indian, Bangladeshi, Chinese, or Thai is cheap. Middle Eastern stands sell gyro sandwiches, falafel, and *shwarmas* (grilled meat in pita bread). You'll find all-you-can-eat Chinese and Thai places serving £6 meals and offering even cheaper takeaway boxes.

**Fish-and-chips** are a tasty British classic. Every town has at least one "chippy" selling a takeaway box of fish-and-chips in a cardboard box or (more traditionally) wrapped in paper for about £4-7.

Most large **museums** (and many historic **churches**) have handy, moderately priced cafeterias with forgettably decent food.

**Picnicking** saves time and money. Fine park benches and polite pigeons abound in most neighborhoods.

## Pubs

Pubs are a fundamental part of the British social scene, and whether you're a tee-

totaler or a beer guzzler, they should be a part of your travel here. Smart travelers use pubs to eat, drink, get out of the rain, watch sporting events, and make new friends.

Though hours vary, pubs generally serve beer daily from 11:00 to 23:00, though many are open later, particularly on Friday and Saturday. As it nears closing time, you'll hear shouts of "Last orders." Then comes the 10-minute warning bell. Finally, they'll call "Time!" to pick up your glass, finished or not, when the pub closes.

A cup of darts is free for the asking. People go to a pub to be social. They want to talk. Get vocal with a local. The pub is the next best thing to having relatives in town.

**Pub Grub:** For £8-12, you'll get a basic budget hot lunch or dinner in friendly surroundings. In high-priced London, this is your best indoor eating value. For something more refined, try a gastropub, which serves higher-quality meals for £12-18. The *Good Pub Guide* is an excellent resource (www.thegoodpubguide.co.uk).

Pubs generally serve traditional dishes, such as fish-and-chips, roast beef with Yorkshire pudding (batter-baked in the oven), and assorted meat pies. Side dishes include salads, vegetables, and—invariably—"chips" (French fries). "Crisps" are potato chips. A "jacket potato" (baked potato stuffed with fillings of your choice) can almost be a meal in itself. A "ploughman's lunch" is a "traditional English meal" of bread, cheese, and sweet pickles that nearly every tourist tries...once. These

days, you'll likely find more pasta, curried dishes, and quiche on the menu than traditional fare.

Meals are usually served 12:00-14:00 and 18:00-20:00—with a break in the middle. Many pubs stop serving meals early in the evening—especially on weekends. There's generally no table service. Order at the bar, then take a seat. Either they'll bring the food when it's ready or you'll pick it up at the bar. Pay at the bar (sometimes when you order, sometimes after you eat). Don't tip unless it's a place with full table service. Servings are hearty, and service is quick. If you're on a tight budget, it's OK to share a meal. Free tap water is always available. For details on ordering beer and other drinks, see the "Beverages" section, later.

## Good Chain Restaurants

Several excellent chains with branches across the UK can be a nice break from pub grub.

**Pret** (a.k.a. Pret à Manger) is perhaps the most pervasive of these modern convenience eateries. The service is fast, the price is great, and the food is healthy and fresh.

**Côte Brasserie** is a contemporary French chain serving good-value French cuisine (including early-dinner specials) in a reliably pleasant setting.

**Le Pain Quotidien** is a Belgian chain offering hearty meals and fresh-baked bread in a modern-rustic atmosphere.

**Byron Hamburgers,** an upscale-hamburger chain with hip interiors, is worth seeking out if you need a burger fix.

**Wagamama Noodle Bar,** serving pan-Asian cuisine (udon noodles, fried rice, and curry dishes), is a noisy, organic slurp-athon. Portions are huge and splittable.

**Loch Fyne Fish Restaurant** is a Scottish chain that raises its own oysters and mussels. Its branches offer an inviting, lively atmosphere with a fine fishy energy and no pretense.

**Marks & Spencer department stores** have inviting deli sections with cheery sit-down eating (along with their popular sandwiches-to-go section).

**Busaba Eathai** is a hit with Londoners for its good, inexpensive Thai cuisine, boisterous ambience, and snappy (sometimes rushed) service.

**Thai Square** is a dependable Thai option with a nice atmosphere (salads, noodle dishes, curries, meat dishes, and daily lunch box specials).

**Masala Zone** is a London chain providing a good, predictable alternative to the many one-off, hole-in-the-wall Indian joints around town. Try a curry-and-rice dish, a *thali* (platter with several small dishes), or their street food specials.

**Ask** and **Pizza Express** serve quality pasta and pizza in a pleasant, sit-down atmosphere that's family-friendly. **Jamie's Italian** (from celebrity chef Jamie Oliver) is hipper and pricier.

**Japanese:** Three popular chains serve fresh and inexpensive Japanese food; look for **Itsu, Wasabi,** or **Yo! Sushi** (the last lets you pick your dish off a conveyor belt and pay according to the color of your plates).

**Carry-Out Chains:** Major supermarket chains have offshoot branches that specialize in sandwiches, salads, and other prepared foods to go. These can be a picnicker's dream come true. The most prevalent—and best—is **M&S Simply Food** (there's one in every major train station). **Sainsbury's Local** grocery stores also offer decent prepared food; **Tesco Express** and **Tesco Metro** run a distant third.

## Indian Cuisine

Take the opportunity to sample food from Britain's former colony.

For a simple meal that costs about £10-12, order one dish with rice and naan (Indian flatbread). Generally one order is plenty for two people to share. A serving of rice costs £2-3 extra. Many Indian restaurants offer a fixed-price combination that offers more variety, and is simpler and cheaper than ordering à la carte. For about £20, you can make a mix-and-match platter out of several shareable dishes. An easy way to taste a variety of dishes is to order a *thali*—a sampler plate, generally served on a metal tray, with small servings of various specialties. Indian cuisine is very vegetarian-friendly, offering many meatless dishes to choose from on any given menu.

## Afternoon Tea

Once the sole province of genteel ladies in fancy hats, afternoon tea has become more democratic in the 21st century. These days, people of leisure punctuate their day with an afternoon tea at a tearoom. You'll get a pot of tea, small finger foods (like sandwiches with the crusts cut off), homemade scones, jam, and thick clotted cream. Tearooms, which often serve appealing light meals, are usually open for lunch and close at about 17:00, just before dinner.

The cheapest "tea" on the menu is generally a "cream tea"; the most expensive is the "champagne tea." **Cream tea** is simply a pot of tea and a homemade scone or two with jam and thick clotted cream. **Afternoon tea**—what many Americans call "high tea"—is generally a cream tea plus a tier of three plates holding small finger foods (such as cucumber sandwiches) and an assortment of small pastries. **Champagne tea** includes all the goodies, plus a glass of bubbly. **High tea** to the English usually means a more substantial late-afternoon or early evening

meal, often served with meat or eggs.

To cut down on costs and calories, two people can order different teas (such as one cream tea and one afternoon tea) and share the treats.

## Desserts (Sweets)

To the British, the traditional word for dessert is "pudding," although it's also referred to as "sweets" these days. Sponge cake, cream, fruitcake, and meringue are key players.

Trifle is the best-known British concoction, consisting of sponge cake soaked in brandy or sherry, then covered with jam and/or fruit and custard cream. Whipped cream can sometimes put the final touch on this "light" treat.

The English version of custard is a smooth, yellow liquid. Cream tops most everything that custard does not. There's single cream for coffee. Double cream is really thick. Whipped cream is familiar, and clotted cream is the consistency of whipped butter.

Fool is a dessert with sweetened pureed fruit (such as rhubarb, gooseberries, or black currants) mixed with cream or custard and chilled. Elderflower is a popular flavoring for sorbet.

Flapjacks here aren't pancakes, but are dense, sweet oatmeal cakes (a little like a cross between a granola bar and a brownie). They come with toppings such as toffee and chocolate.

## Beverages

**Beer:** The British take great pride in their beer. Many locals think that drinking beer cold and carbonated, as Americans do, ruins the taste. Most pubs will have **lagers** (cold, refreshing, American-style beer), **ales** (amber-colored, cellar-temperature beer), **bitters** (hop-flavored ale, perhaps the most typical British beer), and **stouts** (dark and somewhat bitter, like Guinness).

At pubs, long-handled pulls (or taps) are used to draw the traditional, rich-flavored "real ales" up from the cellar.

These are the connoisseur's favorites and often come with fun names. Served straight from the brewer's cask at cellar temperature, real ales finish fermenting naturally and are not pasteurized or filtered, so they must be consumed within two or three days after the cask is tapped.

Short-handled pulls mean colder, fizzier, mass-produced, and less interesting keg beers. Mild beers are sweeter, with a creamy malt flavoring. Irish cream ale is a smooth, sweet experience. Try the draft cider (sweet or dry)...carefully.

Order your beer at the bar and pay as you go, with no need to tip. An average beer costs about £4. Part of the experience is standing before a line of hand pulls, and wondering which beer to choose.

As dictated by British law, draft beer and cider are served by the pint (20-ounce imperial size) or the half-pint (9.6 ounces). It's considered almost feminine for a man to order just a half, so I order mine with quiche. Several years ago, the government sanctioned an in-between serving size—the schooner, or two-thirds pint—hoping that more choice will woo more beer drinkers (a steady decline in beer consumption, which is taxed, has had a negative effect on tax revenues). For a refreshing light beer, try a **shandy** (half beer and half 7-Up).

**Other Alcoholic Drinks:** Besides beer, many pubs have a good selection of wines by the glass, a fully stocked bar for the gentleman's "G and T" (gin and tonic), and the increasingly popular bottles of alcohol-plus-sugar (such as Bacardi Breezers) for the younger working-class set. **Pimm's** is a refreshing and fruity summer liqueur, popular during Wimbledon.

**Nonalcoholic Drinks:** Teetotalers can order predictable American sodas and other more interesting bottled drinks, such as ginger beer (similar to ginger ale but with more bite), root beers, or other flavors (Fentimans brews some unusual options that are stocked in many English pubs). Note that in England, "lemonade" is lemon-lime soda (like 7-Up). Children are served food and soft drinks in pubs, but you must be 18 to order a beer.

# SLEEPING

I favor accommodations and restaurants that are handy to your sightseeing activities or in my favorite neighborhoods. In many towns, bed-and-breakfast places (B&Bs) provide the best value, though I also include bigger hotels.

Wherever you're staying, be ready for crowds during holiday periods (see page 399 for a list of major holidays and festivals). For tips on making reservations, see page 381.

## Rates and Deals

I've described my recommended accommodations using a Sleep Code (see sidebar). The prices I list are for one-night stays in peak season, and assume you're booking directly with the hotel, not through a hotel-booking website or TI. Booking services extract a commission from the hotel, which logically closes the door on special deals. Book direct.

My recommended hotels each have a website (often with a built-in booking form) and an email address; you can expect a response within a day and often sooner.

If you're on a budget, it's smart to email several hotels to ask for their best price. Comparison-shop and make your choice. In general, prices can soften if you do any of the following: offer to pay cash, stay at least three nights, or mention this book.

## Types of Accommodations
### B&Bs and Small Hotels

B&Bs and small hotels are generally family-run places with fewer amenities but more character than a conventional hotel. They range from large inns with 15 to 20 rooms to small homes renting out a spare bedroom. Places named "guesthouse"

## Sleep Code

### Price Rankings

To help you sort easily through my listings, I've divided the accommodations into three categories based on the highest price for a basic double room with bath during peak season:

**$$$** Higher Priced

**$$** Moderately Priced

**$** Lower Priced

Prices change without notice; verify the hotel's current rates online or by email. For the best prices, always book direct with the hotel.

### Abbreviations

Prices listed in this book are per room, not per person. If a price range is given for a room (such as £80-120), it means the price fluctuates with the season, day of week, size of room, or length of stay; expect to pay the upper end for peak-season stays.

**Db** = Double with private (en suite) bathroom

**D** = Double with bathroom down the hall

According to this code, a couple staying at a "Db-£90" hotel would pay a total of £90 per night for a double room with a private bathroom.

Most hotels also offer single rooms (which can be double rooms they charge less for) and triples (which can be an extra bed added to a double room). Some offer larger rooms for four or more people (I call these "family rooms" in the listings).

Unless otherwise noted, breakfast is included, credit cards are accepted, and hotels have Wi-Fi and/or a guest computer.

or "B&B" typically have eight or fewer rooms. The philosophy of the management determines the character of a place more than its size and facilities offered. I avoid places run as a business by absentee owners. My top listings are run by people who enjoy welcoming the world to their breakfast table. For the best selection, book well in advance.

Many B&Bs take credit cards, but may add the card service fee to your bill (about 3 percent). If you do need to pay cash for your room, plan ahead to have enough on hand when you check out.

B&Bs and small hotels come with their own etiquette and quirks. Keep in mind that owners are at the whim of their guests—if you're getting up early, so are

they; and if you check in late, they'll wait up for you. Most B&Bs either have set check-in times (usually twice a day, in the morning and late afternoon), or will want to know when to expect you (call or email ahead to let them know).

B&B proprietors are selective about the guests they invite in for the night. Many do not welcome children. If you'll be staying for more than one night, you are a "desirable." In popular weekend-getaway spots, you're unlikely to find a place to take you for Saturday night only. If my listings are full, ask for guidance. Mentioning this book can help. Owners usually work together and can call up an ally to land you a bed.

Many B&B owners are also pet owners. If you're allergic, ask about resident pets when you reserve.

Small places usually serve a hearty breakfast of eggs and much more. It's an unwritten rule that guests shouldn't show up at the very end of the breakfast period and expect a full cooked breakfast. If you do arrive late (or if you need to leave before breakfast is served), most establishments are happy to let you help yourself to cereal, fruit or juice, and coffee.

B&Bs and small hotels often come with thin walls and doors, and sometimes creaky floorboards, which can make for a noisy night. If you're a light sleeper, bring earplugs. And please be quiet in the halls and in your rooms at night...those of us getting up early will thank you for it.

**In the Room:** Every B&B offers "tea service" in the room—an electric kettle, cups, tea bags, coffee packets, and a pack of biscuits.

Your bedroom probably won't include a phone, but nearly every B&B has free Wi-Fi (if they don't, I'll generally note it in the listing).

Electrical outlets have switches that turn the current on or off; if your appliance isn't working, flip the switch at the outlet.

You're also likely to encounter unusual bathroom fixtures. The "pump toilet" has a flushing handle or button that doesn't kick in unless you push it just right: too hard or too soft, and it won't go. (Be decisive but not ruthless.)

Most B&B baths have an instant water heater. This looks like an electronic box under the shower head with dials and buttons: One control adjusts the heat, while another turns the flow off and on (let the water run for a bit to moderate the temperature before you hop in). If the hot water doesn't work, you may need to flip a red switch (often located just outside the bathroom). If the shower looks mysterious, ask your B&B host for help...before you take your clothes off.

## Hotels

Many of my recommended hotels have three or more floors of rooms and steep stairs. Older properties often do not have elevators. If stairs are an issue, ask for a ground-floor room or choose a hotel with a lift (elevator). Air-conditioning isn't a given (I've noted which of my listings have it), but most places have fans. On hot summer nights, you'll want your window open—and in a big city, street noise is a fact of life. Bring earplugs or request a room on the back side or on an upper floor.

A "twin" room has two single beds; a "double" has one double bed. If you'll take either, let the hotel know, or you might be needlessly turned away. Most hotels offer family deals, which means that parents with young children can get a room with an extra child's bed or a discount for larger rooms. Teenagers are generally charged as adults.

An "en suite" room has a bathroom (toilet and shower/tub) attached to the room; a room with a "private bathroom" can mean that the bathroom is all yours, but it's across the hall. If you want your own bathroom inside the room, request "en suite."

If money's tight, ask for a room with a

# *Making Hotel Reservations*

Reserve your rooms several months in advance—or as soon as you've pinned down your travel dates. Note that some national holidays merit your making reservations far in advance (see page 399).

**Requesting a Reservation:** It's easiest to book your room through the hotel's website. (For the best rates, always use the hotel's official site and not a booking agency's site.) If there's no reservation form, or for complicated requests, send an email.

The hotelier wants to know:
• the number and type of rooms you need
• the number of nights you'll stay
• your date of arrival (use the European style for writing dates: day/month/year)
• your date of departure
• any special needs (such as bathroom in the room or down the hall, cheapest room, twin beds vs. double bed)

Mention any discounts—for Rick Steves readers or otherwise—when you make the reservation.

**Confirming a Reservation:** Most places will request a credit-card number to hold your room. If they don't have a secure online reservation form—look for the *https*—you can email it (I do), but it's safer to share that confidential info via a phone call or two emails (splitting your number between them)

**Canceling a Reservation:** If you must cancel, it's courteous—and smart—to do so with as much notice as possible, especially for smaller family-run places. Be warned that cancellation policies can be strict; read the fine print or ask about these before you book. Internet deals may require prepayment, with no refunds for cancellations.

**Reconfirming a Reservation:** Always call or email to reconfirm your room reservation a few days in advance. For smaller hotels, I call again on my day of arrival to tell my host what time I expect to get there (especially important if arriving late—after 17:00).

**Phoning:** For tips on how to call hotels overseas, see page 384.

| From: | rick@ricksteves.com |
|---|---|
| Sent: | Today |
| To: | info@hotelcentral.com |
| Subject: | Reservation request for 19-22 July |

Dear Hotel Central,
I would like to reserve a room for 2 people for 3 nights, arriving 19 July and departing 22 July. If possible, I would like a quiet room with a double bed and private bathroom inside the room.

Please let me know if you have a room available and the price.

Thank you!
Rick Steves

shared bathroom. You'll almost always have a sink in your room, and as more rooms go "en suite," the hallway bathroom is shared with fewer guests.

All of England's accommodations are now nonsmoking.

**Modern Hotel Chains:** Chain hotels—common in bigger cities all over Great Britain—can be a great value (£60-100, depending on location; more expensive in London). These hotels are about as cozy as a Motel 6, but they come with private showers/WCs, elevators, good security, and often an attached restaurant. The chain hotel option is worth considering, especially for families, as kids often stay for free.

Room rates change from day to day with volume and can vary depending on how far ahead you book. The best deals generally must be prepaid a few weeks ahead and may not be refundable—read the fine print carefully.

The biggest chains are **Premier Inn** (www.premierinn.com, toll reservations tel. 0871-527-9222) and **Travelodge** (www.travelodge.co.uk, toll reservations tel. 0871-984-8484). Both have attractive deals for prepaid or advance bookings. Other chains operating in Britain include the Irish **Jurys Inn** (www.jurysinns. com) and the French-owned **Ibis** (www. ibishotel.com). Couples can consider **Holiday Inn Express,** which generally allows only two people per room (www. hiexpress.co.uk).

**At the Hotel:** If you're arriving in the morning, your room probably won't be ready. Drop your bag safely at the hotel and dive right into sightseeing.

Hoteliers can be a great help and source of advice. Most know their city well, and can assist you with everything from public transit and airport connections to finding a good restaurant, the nearest launderette, or a late-night pharmacy.

Even at the best places, mechanical breakdowns occur: Air-conditioning malfunctions, sinks leak, hot water turns cold, toilets may gurgle or smell, the Wi-Fi goes out, or the air-conditioning dies when you need it most. Report your concerns clearly and calmly at the front desk. For more complicated problems, don't expect instant results.

To guard against theft in your room, keep valuables out of sight. Some rooms come with a safe, and other hotels have safes at the front desk. I've never bothered using one.

While it's customary to pay for your room upon departure, it can be a good idea to settle your bill the day before, when you're not in a hurry and while the manager's in. That way you'll have time to discuss and address any points of contention.

Above all, keep a positive attitude. Remember, you're on vacation. If your hotel is a disappointment, spend more time out enjoying the city you came to see.

## Hostels

A hostel provides cheap dorm beds and sometimes has a few double rooms and family rooms. Travelers of any age are welcome. Most hostels offer kitchen facilities, guest computers, Wi-Fi, and a self-service laundry.

There are two kinds of hostels: **Independent hostels** tend to be easygoing, colorful, and informal (no membership required); try www.hostelworld.com, www.hostelz.com, or www.hostels.com. **Official hostels** are part of Hostelling International (HI), share an online

## The Good and Bad of Online Reviews

User-generated travel review websites—such as TripAdvisor, Booking.com, and Yelp—give you access to actual reports—good and bad—from travelers who have experienced the hotel, restaurant, tour, or attraction.

While these sites try hard to weed out bogus users, I've seen hotels "bribe" guests (for example, offer a free breakfast) in exchange for a positive review. Nor can you always give credence to negative reviews: Different people have different expectations.

A user-generated review is based on the experience of one person, who likely stayed at one hotel and ate at a few restaurants, and doesn't have much of a basis for comparison. A guidebook is the work of a trained researcher who visited many alternatives to assess their relative value. When I've checked out top-rated TripAdvisor listings in various towns, I've found that some are gems but just as many are duds.

Guidebooks and review websites both have their place, and in many ways, they're complementary. If a hotel or restaurant is well-reviewed in a guidebook, and also gets good ratings on one of these sites, it's likely a winner.

booking site (www.hihostels.com), and typically require that you either have a membership card or pay extra per night. In England, these official hostels are run by the YHA (www.yha.org.uk).

### Other Accommodation Options

Renting an apartment, house, or villa can be a fun and cost-effective way to go local. Websites such as Booking.com, Airbnb, VRBO, and FlipKey let you browse properties and correspond directly with European property owners or managers. Airbnb and Roomorama also list rooms in private homes. Beds range from air-mattress-in-living-room basic to plush-B&B-suite posh. If you want a free place to sleep, try Couchsurfing.com.

# STAYING CONNECTED

Staying connected in Europe gets easier and cheaper every year. The simplest solution is to bring your own device—mobile phone, tablet, or laptop—and use it just as you would at home (following the tips below, such as connecting to free Wi-Fi whenever possible). Another option is to buy a European SIM card for your mobile phone—either your US phone or one you buy in Europe. Or you can travel without a mobile device and use European landlines and computers to connect. Each of these options is described next, and you'll find even more details at www.ricksteves.com/phoning.

## Using Your Mobile Device in Europe

Roaming with your mobile device in Europe doesn't have to be expensive. These budget tips and options will keep your costs in check.

**Use free Wi-Fi whenever possible.** Unless you have an unlimited-data plan, you're best off saving most of your online tasks for Wi-Fi.

Many cafés—including Starbucks and McDonald's—have free hotspots for customers; look for signs offering it and ask for the Wi-Fi password when you buy something. You'll often find Wi-Fi at TIs, city squares, major museums, public-transit hubs, airports, and aboard trains and buses.

**Sign up for an international plan.** Most providers offer a global calling plan

# *Phoning Cheat Sheet*

Here are instructions for dialing, along with examples of how to call one of my recommended hotels in London (tel. 020/7730-8191).

**Calling from the US to Europe:** Dial 011 (US access code), country code (44 for Britain), and phone number.* To call my recommended hotel in London, I dial 011-44-20/7730-8191.

**Calling from Europe to the US:** Dial 00 (Europe access code), country code (1 for US), area code, and phone number. To call my office in Edmonds, Washington, I dial 00-1-425-771-8303.

**Calling country to country within Europe:** Dial 00, country code, and phone number.* To call the London hotel from Spain, I dial 00-44-20/7730-8191.

**Calling within England:** Dial the entire phone number. To call the London hotel from York, I dial 020/7730-8191.

**Calling with a mobile phone:** The "+" sign on your mobile phone automatically selects the access code you need (for a "+" sign, press and hold "0").* To call the London hotel from the US or Europe, I dial +44-20/7730-8191.

*If the European phone number starts with zero, drop it when calling from another country (except Italian numbers, which retain the zero).*

| Country | Country Code | Country | Country Code |
|---------|:---:|---------|:---:|
| Austria | 43 | Hungary | 36 |
| Belgium | 32 | Ireland/N Ireland | 353/44 |
| Croatia | 385 | Italy | 39 |
| Czech Republic | 420 | Netherlands | 31 |
| Denmark | 45 | Norway | 47 |
| England | 44 | Portugal | 351 |
| France | 33 | Scotland | 44 |
| Germany | 49 | Spain | 34 |
| Greece | 30 | Switzerland | 41 |

that cuts the per-minute cost of phone calls and texts, and a flat-fee data plan. Your normal plan may already include international coverage (T-Mobile's does).

Before your trip, call your provider or check online to confirm that your phone will work in Europe, and research your provider's international rates. Activate the plan a day or two before you leave, then remember to cancel it when your trip's over.

**Minimize the use of your cellular network.** When you can't find Wi-Fi, you can use your cellular network to connect to the Internet, text, or make voice calls. When you're done, avoid further charges by manually switching off "data roaming" or "cellular data" (in your device's Settings menu; for help, ask your service provider or Google it). Another way to make sure you're not accidentally using data roaming is to put your device in "airplane" or "flight" mode (which also disables phone calls and texts), and then turn on Wi-Fi as needed.

Don't use your cellular network for bandwidth-gobbling tasks, such as Skyping, downloading apps, and watching YouTube: Save these for when you're on Wi-Fi. Using a navigation app such as Google Maps over a cellular network can take lots of data, so do this sparingly or use it offline.

Limit automatic updates. By default, your device constantly checks for a data connection and updates apps. It's smart to disable these features so your apps will only update when you're on Wi-Fi, and to change your device's email settings from "auto-retrieve" to "manual" (or from "push" to "fetch").

It's also a good idea to keep track of your data usage. On your device's menu, look for "cellular data usage" or "mobile data" and reset the counter at the start of your trip.

**Use Skype or other calling/messaging apps for cheaper calls and texts.** Certain apps let you make voice or video calls or send texts over the Internet for free or cheap. If you're bringing a tablet or laptop, you can also use them for voice calls and texts. All you have to do is log on to a Wi-Fi network, then contact any of your friends or family members who are also online and signed into the same service.

You can make voice and video calls using Skype, Viber, FaceTime, and Google+ Hangouts. If the connection is bad, try making an audio-only call. You can also make voice calls from your device to telephones worldwide for just a few cents per minute using Skype, Viber, or Hangouts if you buy credit first.

To text for free over Wi-Fi, try apps like Google+ Hangouts, Whats App, Viber, Facebook Messenger, and iMessage. Make sure you're on Wi-Fi to avoid data charges.

## The English Accent

In the olden days, an English person's accent indicated his or her social standing. Eliza Doolittle had the right idea—elocution could make or break you. Wealthier families would send their kids to fancy private schools to learn proper pronunciation. But these days, in a sort of reverse snobbery that has gripped the nation, accents are back. Politicians, newscasters, and movie stars are favoring deep accents over the Queen's English. While it's hard for American ears to pick out all of the variations, most English people can determine where a person is from based on their accent...not just the region, but often the village, and even the part of town.

## Using a European SIM Card

This option works well if you want to make a lot of voice calls at cheap local rates or need a faster connection speed than your US carrier provides. Either buy a basic cell phone in Europe (as little as $40 from mobile-phone shops anywhere), or bring an "unlocked" US phone. With an unlocked phone, you can replace the original SIM card (the microchip that stores info about the phone) with one that will work with a European provider.

In Europe, buy a European SIM card. Inserted into your phone, this card gives you a European phone number—and European rates. SIM cards are sold at mobile-phone shops, department-store electronics counters, newsstands, and vending machines. Costing about $5-10, they usually include about that much prepaid calling credit, with no contract and no commitment. A SIM card that also

## *Tips on Internet Security*

Using the Internet while traveling brings added security risks, whether you're getting online with your own device or at a public terminal using a shared network. Here are some tips for securing your data:

First, make sure that your device is running the latest version of its operating system and security software, and that your apps are up-to-date. Next, ensure that your device is password- or passcode-protected so thieves can't access information if your device is stolen. For extra security, set passwords on apps that access key info (such as email or Facebook).

On the road, use only legitimate Wi-Fi hotspots. Ask the hotel or café staff for the specific name of their Wi-Fi network, and make sure you log on to that exact one. Hackers sometimes create a bogus hotspot with a similar or vague name (such as "Hotel Europa Free Wi-Fi"). The best Wi-Fi networks require a password. If you're not actively using a hotspot, turn off your device's Wi-Fi connection so it's not visible to others.

Be especially cautious when accessing financial information online. Experts say it's best to use a banking app rather than sign in to your bank's website via a browser (the app is less likely to get hacked). Refrain from logging in to any personal finance sites on a public computer. Even if you're using your own mobile device at a password-protected hotspot, there's a remote chance that a hacker who's logged on to the same network could see what you're doing.

Never share your credit-card number (or any other sensitive information) online unless you know that the site is secure. A secure site displays a little padlock icon, and the URL begins with *https* (instead of the usual *http*).

includes data costs (including roaming) will cost $20-40 more for one month of data within the country in which it was purchased. The extra expense may be worthwhile because it's typically faster than data roaming through your home provider. To get the best rates, buy a new SIM card whenever you arrive in a new country.

I like to buy SIM cards at a mobile-phone shop where there's a clerk to help explain the options and brands. Certain brands—including Lebara and Lycamobile, both of which operate in multiple European countries—are reliable and economical. Ask the clerk to help you insert your SIM card, set it up, and show you how to use it. In some countries, you'll be required to register the SIM card with your passport as an antiterrorism measure

(which may mean you can't use the phone for the first hour or two).

Find out how to check your credit balance. When you run out of credit, you can top it up at newsstands, mini-marts, mobile-phone stores, or many other businesses (look for your SIM card's logo in the window), or online.

## Public Phones and Computers

You can stay connected in Europe without a mobile device: Check email or browse websites using public computers and Internet cafés, and make calls from your hotel room and/or public phones.

Phones in your **hotel room** generally have a fee for placing local and "toll-free" calls, as well as long-distance or international calls—ask for the rates before you dial. Since you're never charged for receiving calls, it's better to have someone from the US call you in your room.

If these fees are low, hotel phones can be used inexpensively for calls made with cheap international phone cards (sold at newsstands, street kiosks, and train stations). You'll either get a prepaid card with a toll-free number and a scratch-to-reveal PIN code, or a code printed on a receipt.

Phones are rare in **B&Bs,** but if your room has one, the advice above applies. If there's no phone in your B&B room, and you have an important, brief call to make, politely ask your hosts if you can use their personal phone. Ideally use a cheap international phone card with a toll-free access number, or offer to pay your host for the call.

**Public pay phones** are getting harder to find in England, and they're expensive. To use one, you'll pay with a major credit card (which you insert into the phone—minimum charge for a credit-card call is £1.20) or coins (have a bunch handy; minimum fee is £0.60). Only unused coins will be returned, so put in biggies with caution.

**Public computers** are easy to find.

Many hotels have one in their lobby for guests to use; otherwise you can find them at Internet cafés and public libraries.

## Mail

You can mail one package per day to yourself worth up to $200 duty-free from Europe to the US (mark it "personal purchases"). If you're sending a gift to someone, mark it "unsolicited gift." For details, visit www.cbp.gov, select "Travel," and search for "Know Before You Go."

The British postal service works fine, but for quick transatlantic delivery (in either direction), consider services such as DHL (www.dhl.com). For postcards, get stamps at the neighborhood post office, newsstands within fancy hotels, and some mini-marts and card shops.

# TRANSPORTATION

This section covers the basics on trains, buses, rental cars, and flights.

Britain's trains are reliable, efficient, and pricey (I discuss deals later). Buses are an alternative to trains—and may be your only option for reaching some smaller towns—but they are generally slower, and frequency drops on Sundays. Renting a car is great for touring rural areas such as the Cotswolds and the Lake District. You could rent a car for your entire trip, or just for a day or two.

## Trains

Regular tickets on Britain's great train system (15,000 departures from 2,400 stations daily) are the most expensive per mile in all of Europe. For the greatest savings, book online in advance, leave after rush hour (after 9:30), or get a Britrail England pass (if you're using trains for three or more days).

Since Britain's railways have been privatized, it can be tricky to track down all your options; a single train route can be operated by multiple companies. However, one British website covers all train lines (www.nationalrail.co.uk), and another covers all bus and train routes (www.traveline.org.uk—for information, not ticket sales). Another good resource, which also has schedules for trains throughout Europe, is German Rail's timetable (www.bahn.com).

As with airline tickets, British train tickets can come at many different prices for the same journey. A clerk at any station can figure out the cheapest fare for your trip.

**Buying Train Tickets in Advance:** To book ahead, go in person to any station, book online at www.nationalrail.co.uk, or call 0345-748-4950 (from the US, dial 011-44-20-7278-5240, phone answered 24 hours) to find out the schedule and best fare for your journey; you'll then be referred to the appropriate vendor—depending on the particular rail company—to book your ticket. You'll pick up your ticket at the station, or you may be able to print it at home.

**Buying Train Tickets as You Travel:** If you want the flexibility of booking tickets as you go, you can save a little money if you do any of these things: buy before 18:00 the day before you depart; travel after the morning rush hour (this usually means after 9:30 Mon-Fri); or go standard class instead of first class. Also, if you're day-tripping, buy a "day return" (a same-day round-trip); these are particularly cheap. Preview your options at www.nationalrail.co.uk.

**Senior, Youth, Partner, and Family Cards:** If you qualify, these cards allow you to buy most point-to-point rail tickets at a third off the regular fare. Seniors buy a Senior Railcard (ages 60 and up), younger travelers can buy a 16-25 Railcard (ages 16-25, or full-time students 26 and older), and two people traveling together can buy a Two Together Railcard (ages 16 and over). A Family and Friends Railcard gives adults about 33 percent off for most trips and 60 percent off for their kids ages 5 to 15 (maximum 4 adults and 4 kids). You can use the card to buy discounted tickets as you travel; no advance booking is required.

Each Railcard costs £30; see www.railcard.co.uk. To get a card, fill out an application at a train station (see brochures on racks in info center). You'll need to show your passport; a passport-type photo is needed to get a 16-25 Railcard. These cards are valid for a year on almost all trains, including special runs such as the Heathrow Express, but are not valid on the Eurostar to Paris or Brussels.

**Rail Passes:** For train travel outside London, consider getting a BritRail England pass. It covers three or more days of travel, gives you the flexibility to travel on any day you choose, doesn't require advance booking for specific trips, and includes getting (optional) free seat assignments at the station. BritRail passes, as well as Eurail passes, give you a discount on the Eurostar train that zips you to continental Europe under the English Channel. These passes are sold outside of Europe only. For specifics, see www.ricksteves.com/rail.

# Buses

Most domestic buses are operated by **National Express** (tel. 0871-781-8181, www.nationalexpress.com); their international departures are called **Eurolines** (www.eurolines.co.uk).

A smaller company called **Megabus** undersells National Express with deeply

# Public Transportation Routes in Britain

## Rail Passes

Prices listed are subject to change. For the latest prices, details, and train schedules (and easy online ordering), see my comprehensive Guide to Eurail Passes at www.ricksteves.com/rail.

"Standard" is the polite British term for "second" class. "Senior" refers to those age 60 and up. No senior discounts for standard class. "Youth" means under age 26. For each adult or senior BritRail or BritRail England pass you buy, one child (5–15) can travel free with you (ask for the "Family Pass," not available with all passes). Additional kids pay the normal half-adult rate. Kids under 5 travel free.

### BRITRAIL ENGLAND CONSECUTIVE PASS

|  | Adult 1st Class | Adult Standard | Senior 1st Class | Youth 1st Class | Youth Standard |
|---|---|---|---|---|---|
| 3 consec. days | $263 | $185 | $223 | $210 | $148 |
| 4 consec. days | 333 | 220 | 283 | 266 | 176 |
| 8 consec. days | 467 | 315 | 397 | 373 | 252 |
| 15 consec. days | 702 | 467 | 597 | 562 | 373 |
| 22 consec. days | 889 | 590 | 755 | 711 | 472 |
| 1 month | 1047 | 702 | 890 | 838 | 562 |

Covers travel only in England, not Scotland, Wales, or Ireland.

### BRITRAIL ENGLAND FLEXIPASS

| Type of Pass | Adult 1st Class | Adult Standard | Senior 1st Class | Youth 1st Class | Youth Standard |
|---|---|---|---|---|---|
| 3 days in 2 months | $333 | $227 | $283 | $266 | $182 |
| 4 days in 2 months | 414 | 280 | 352 | 331 | 224 |
| 8 days in 2 months | 597 | 403 | 507 | 477 | 323 |
| 15 days in 2 months | 896 | 607 | 761 | 717 | 486 |

Covers travel only in England, not Scotland, Wales, or Ireland.

### Map key:

Approximate point-to-point one-way standard-class fares in US dollars by rail (solid line) and bus (dashed line). First class costs 50 percent more. Add up fares for your itinerary to see whether a railpass will save you money.

discounted promotional fares—the farther ahead you buy, the less you pay (toll tel. 0900-160-0900, www.megabus.com). Try to avoid bus travel on Friday and Sunday evenings, when weekend travelers are more likely to make buses sell out.

To ensure getting a ticket—and to save money with special promotions—book your ticket in advance online or over the phone. The cheapest prepurchased tickets can usually be changed (for a £5 fee), but not refunded. Check if the ticket is only "amendable" or also "refundable" when you buy. If you have a mobile phone, you can order online and have a "text ticket" sent right to your phone for a small fee.

## Renting a Car

If you're renting a car in England, bring your driver's license. Rental companies require you to be at least 21 years old. Drivers under the age of 25 may incur a young-driver surcharge (depending on the class of car rented), and some rental companies will not rent to anyone 75 or older. If you're considered too young or old, look into leasing (see next page), which has less-stringent age restrictions.

Research car rentals before you go. It's cheaper to arrange most car rentals from the US. Consider several companies to compare rates. Most of the major US rental agencies (including Avis, Budget, Enterprise, Hertz, and Thrifty) have offices throughout Europe. Also consider the two major Europe-based agencies, Europcar and Sixt. It can be cheaper to use a consolidator, such as Auto Europe/Kemwel (www.autoeurope.com—or the often cheaper www.autoeurope.eu) or Europe by Car (www.europebycar.com).

Always read the fine print carefully for add-on charges—such as one-way drop-off fees, airport surcharges, or mandatory insurance policies—that aren't included in the "total price."

For the best deal, rent by the week with unlimited mileage. I normally rent the smallest, least expensive model with a stick shift (generally cheaper than automatic). If you need an automatic, request one in advance. An automatic makes sense for most American drivers: With a manual transmission in England, you'll be sitting on the right side of the car and shifting with your left hand...while driving on the left side of the road. When selecting a car, don't be tempted by a larger model, as it won't be as maneuverable on narrow, winding roads.

Figure on paying roughly $250 for a one-week rental. Allow extra for supplemental insurance, fuel, tolls, and parking. For trips of three weeks or more, leasing can save you money on insurance and taxes.

If you want to rent a car for only a day or two (for example, for the Cotswolds or the Lake District), it's easy to do locally, especially if you reserve in advance by email or phone (figure £30-60/day, requires driver's license, a major credit card, and sometimes a second form of ID). I list car-rental agencies in the Bath, Cotswolds, Lake District, and York chapters.

**Picking Up Your Car:** Big companies have offices in most cities, but small local rental companies can be cheaper. If you pick up the car in a smaller city or at an airport (rather than downtown), you'll more likely survive your first day on the road. Be aware that Brits call it "hiring a car," and directional signs at airports and train stations will read *Car Hire*.

Compare pickup costs (downtown can be less expensive than the airport) and explore drop-off options. Always check the hours of the location you choose: Many rental offices close from midday Saturday until Monday morning and, in smaller towns, at lunchtime.

When selecting a location, don't trust the agency's description of "downtown" or "city center." In some cases, a "downtown" branch can be on the outskirts of the city—a long, costly taxi ride from the center. Before choosing, plug the addresses into a mapping website. You may find that the "train station" location is handier. But returning a car at a big-city train station or downtown agency can be tricky; get precise details on the car drop-off location and hours, and allow ample time to find it.

When you pick up your rental car, check it thoroughly and make sure any damage is noted on your rental agree-ment. Rental agencies in Europe are very strict when it comes to charging for even minor damage, so be sure to mark every-thing. Before driving off, find out how your car's gearshift, lights, turn signals, wipers, radio, and fuel cap function, and know what kind of fuel the car takes (diesel vs. unleaded). When you return the car, make sure the agent verifies its condition with you. Some drivers take pictures of the returned vehicle as proof of its condition.

**The AA:** The services of Britain's Automobile Association are included with most rentals (www.theaa.com), but check for this when booking to be sure you understand its towing and emergency road-service benefits.

## Car Insurance Options

When you rent a car, you are liable for a very high deductible, sometimes equal to the entire value of the car. Limit your financial risk with one of these three options:

• Buy Collision Damage Waiver (CDW) coverage with a low or zero deductible from the car-rental company. Basic CDW reduces your liability, but does not elim-inate it. When you pick up the car, you'll be offered the chance to "buy down" the deductible to zero (for an additional $10-30/day; this is sometimes called "super CDW" or "zero-deductible coverage").

• Get coverage through your credit card, which is free if your card automati-cally includes zero-deductible coverage. If you opt for this coverage, you'll technically have to decline all coverage offered by the car-rental company, which means they can place a hold on your card for up to the full value of the car. In case of damage, it can be time-consuming to resolve the charges with your credit-card company. Before you decide on this option, quiz your credit-card company about how it works.

• Get collision insurance as part of a larger travel-insurance policy. If you're already purchasing a travel-insurance policy for your trip, adding collision cov-erage can be economical. For example, Travel Guard (www.travelguard.com) sells affordable renter's collision insurance as an add-on to its other policies.

For **more on car-rental insurance,** see www.ricksteves.com/cdw.

## Leasing

For trips of three weeks or more, consider leasing, which automatically includes zero-deductible collision and theft insurance. Leasing provides you a new car with unlimited mileage and a 24-hour emer-gency assistance program. You can lease for as little as 21 days to as long as 5.5 months. Car leases must be arranged from the US. One of many companies offering affordable lease packages is Europe by Car (www.europebycar.com/lease).

## Navigation Options

If you'll be navigating using your phone or a GPS unit from home, remember to bring a car charger and device mount.

**Your Mobile Device:** The mapping app on your mobile phone works fine for nav-igation in Europe, but for real-time turn-by-turn directions and traffic updates, you'll generally need access to a cellular network. A helpful exception is Google Maps, which provides turn-by-turn driv-ing directions and recalibrates even when it's offline.

To use Google Maps offline, you must have a Google account and download your map while you have a data connec-tion. Later—even when offline—you can call up that map, enter your destination,

# Driving in Great Britain

m = miles
h = hours

Note: Your times may vary based on traffic, sheep, construction & road conditions.

To Durness · 70m · 2.25h
To John o'Groats

**SCOTLAND**

Ullapool
60m · 1.25h
Portree
Skye
35m · 1h
Kyle of Lochalsh
85m · 2h
85m · 2h
120m · 2.5h
20m · .5h
Inverness
105m · 2.75h
Aberdeen
90m · 1.75h
Loch Ness (Urquhart Castle)
65m · 1.5h
90m · 2.5h
Glencoe
90m · 2.75h
Pitlochry
Mull
35m · 1h
Oban
80m · 1.75h
70m · 1.5h
60m · 1.5h
80m · 2h
Fionn-port
Craig-nure
85m · 1.75h
Stirling
50m · 1.5h
St. Andrews
100m · 2.5h
25m · .5h
40m · 1h
Glasgow
50m · 1h
Edinburgh
75m · 2h
Holy Island
90m · 2.25h
1.35m · 2.5h
130m · 3h
125m · 2.75h
80m · 1.75h
Cairnryan
145m · 3h
100m · 2.5h
**Hadrian's Wall** (Housesteads Fort)
Keswick (N. Lake Dist.)
65m · 1.5h
50m · 1h
Durham
85m · 2h
20m · .5h
Windermere (S. Lake Dist.)
120m · 3h
75m · 1.5h
Whitby
50m · 1h
35m · 1h
20m · .5h
100m · 2h
York
Blackpool
Preston
40m · 1h
130m · 3.5h
40m · .75h
60m · 1.25h
Holyhead
25m · .5h
Conwy
Liverpool
30m · .5h
140m · 2.5h
160m · 3h
220m · 4h
Caernarfon
25m · .75h
Ruthin
30m · 1h
75m · 2h
**ENGLAND**
Betws-y-Coed
60m · 1.5h
150m · 3.5h
170m · 4h
Iron-bridge
10m · .25h
Coventry
70m · 1.5h
70m · 1.75h
10m · .5h
Warwick
10m · .25h
35m · 1.0h
Stratford
110m · 2h
Cambridge
**WALES**
Cotswolds (Stow)
70m · 2h
30m
75m
90m · 2h
60m · 1.25h
Tintern
65m · 1.75h
Oxford
Cardiff
65m · 1.5h
60m · 1.5h
**London**
55m · 1.25h
20m · .75h
Bath
50m
Avebury
Wells
50m · 1.25h
30m · 1h
85m · 1.75h
60m · 1.5h
Canter-bury
75m · 1.5h
Glastonbury
10m · .25h
100m · 2h
Salisbury
55m · 1.75h
85m · 3h
Dover
To Land's End
80m · 2h
120m · 2.5h
45m · 1h
50m · 1.5h
Brighton
100m · 2h
Dartmoor Nat'l Park
50m · 1.5h
Corfe Castle
Portsmouth

and get directions.

**GPS Devices:** If you prefer the convenience of a dedicated GPS unit, consider renting one with your car ($10-30/day). These units (called a "satnav" in England) offer real-time turn-by-turn directions and traffic without the data requirements of an app. Note that the unit may only come loaded with maps for its home country; if you need additional maps, ask.

A less-expensive option is to bring a GPS device from home. Be aware that you'll need to buy and download European maps before your trip.

**Maps and Atlases:** Even when navigating primarily with a mobile app or GPS, I always make it a point to have a paper map. The free maps you get from your car-rental company usually don't have enough detail. It's smart to buy a better map before you go (Ordnance Survey, Collins, AA, and Bartholomew editions are all good), or pick one up at a European gas station, bookshop, newsstand, or tourist shop.

## Driving in England

Driving can be wonderful—once you remember to stay on the left and after you've mastered the roundabouts. Every year, however, I get a few notes from traveling readers advising me that, for them, trying to drive in Britain was a headache. Many Yankee drivers find the hardest part isn't driving on the left, but steering from the right. Your instinct is to put yourself on the left side of your lane, which means you may spend your first day or two constantly drifting into the left shoulder. It can help to remember that the driver always stays close to the center line.

**Road Rules:** Be aware of typical European road rules; for example, many countries require headlights to be turned on at all times, and it's generally illegal to drive while using your mobile phone without a hands-free device. In England, you're not allowed to turn left on a red light unless a sign or signal specifically

authorizes it, and on motorways it's illegal to pass drivers on the left. Ask your car-rental company about these rules, read the Department for Transport's *Highway Code* (www.gov.uk/highway-code), or check the US State Department website (www.travel.state.gov, search for your country in the "Learn about your destination" box, then click on "Travel and Transportation").

**Speed Limits:** Speed limits are in miles per hour: 30 mph in town, 70 mph on the motorways, and 50 or 60 mph elsewhere). The national sign for 60 mph is a white circle with a black slash. Motorways have electronic speed limit signs; posted speeds can change depending on traffic or the weather. Follow them accordingly.

Road-surveillance cameras strictly enforce speed limits. Any driver (including foreigners renting cars) photographed speeding will get a nasty bill in the mail.

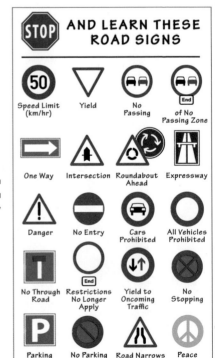

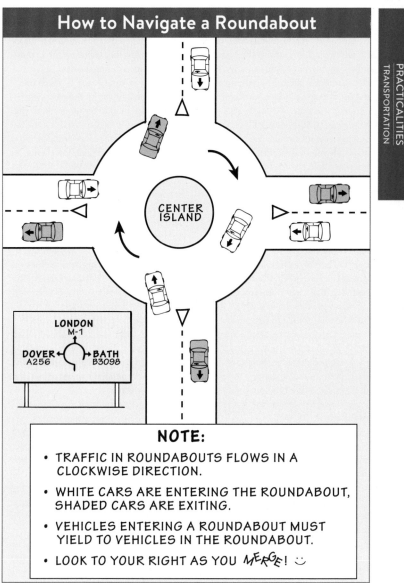

# How to Navigate a Roundabout

CENTER ISLAND

LONDON
M-1

DOVER←
A256

→BATH
B3098

## NOTE:

- TRAFFIC IN ROUNDABOUTS FLOWS IN A CLOCKWISE DIRECTION.
- WHITE CARS ARE ENTERING THE ROUNDABOUT, SHADED CARS ARE EXITING.
- VEHICLES ENTERING A ROUNDABOUT MUST YIELD TO VEHICLES IN THE ROUNDABOUT.
- LOOK TO YOUR RIGHT AS YOU MERGE! ☺

Signs depicting an old-fashioned camera alert you when you're entering a zone that may be monitored by these "camera cops." Heed them.

**Roundabouts:** Don't let a roundabout spook you. After all, you routinely merge into much faster traffic on American high-

ways back home. Traffic flows clockwise, and cars already in the roundabout have the right-of-way; entering traffic yields (look to your right as you merge). You'll probably encounter "double-round-abouts"—figure-eights where you'll slingshot from one roundabout directly into another. Just go with the flow and track signs carefully. When approaching an especially complex roundabout, you'll first pass a diagram showing the layout and the various exits. And in many cases, the pavement is painted to indicate the lane you should be in for a particular road or town.

**Freeways (Motorways):** The shortest distance between any two points is usually the motorway (what we'd call a "freeway"). In England, the smaller the number, the bigger the road. For example, the M-4 is a freeway, while the B-4494 is a country road.

Motorway road signs can be confusing, too few, and too late. Miss a motorway exit and you can lose 30 minutes. Study your map before taking off. British road signs are never marked with compass directions (e.g., A-30 West); instead, you need to know what major town or city you're heading for (A-30 Penzance).

Unless you're passing, always drive in the "slow" lane on motorways (the lane farthest to the left). The British are very disciplined about this; ignoring this rule could get you a ticket (or into a road-rage incident). Remember to pass on the right, not the left.

Rest areas are called "services" and often have a number of useful amenities, such as restaurants, cafeterias, gas stations, shops, and motels.

**Fuel:** Gas (petrol) costs about $10 per gallon and is self-serve. Pump first and then pay. Diesel rental cars are common; make sure you know what kind of fuel your car takes before you fill up. Unleaded pumps are usually green. Note that self-service gas pumps often accept only cash or a chip-and-PIN credit card (see page 371).

**Driving in Cities:** Whenever possible, avoid driving in cities. Be warned that London assesses a congestion charge (see page 125). Most cities have modern ring roads to skirt the center. Follow signs to the parking lots outside the city core—most are a 5- to 10-minute walk to the center—and avoid what can be an unpleasant grid of one-way streets (as in Bath) or roads that are restricted to public transportation during the day.

**Driving in Rural Areas:** Outside the big cities and except for the motorways, British roads tend to be narrow. In towns, you may have to cross over the center line just to get past parked cars. Adjust your perceptions of personal space: It's not "my side of the road" or "your side of the road," it's just "the road"—and it's shared as a cooperative adventure.

Narrow country lanes are often lined with stone walls or woody hedges—and no shoulders. Some are barely wide enough for one car. Go slowly, and if you encounter an oncoming car, look for the nearest pullout (or "passing place")—the driver who's closest to one is expected to use it, even if it means backing up to reach it. If another car pulls over and blinks its headlights, that means, "Go ahead; I'll wait to let you pass." British drivers—arguably the most courteous on the planet—are quick to offer a friendly wave to thank you for letting them pass.

**Parking:** Pay attention to pavement markings to figure out where to park. One yellow line marked on the pavement means no parking Monday through Saturday during work hours. Double yellow lines mean no parking at any time. Broken yellow lines mean short stops are OK, but you should always look for explicit signs or ask a passerby. White lines mean you're free to park.

In some towns, drivers will see signs for "disc zone" parking. This is free, time-limited parking. But to use it, you must obtain a clock parking disc from a shop and display it on the dashboard (set the clock to show your time of arrival). Return within the signed time limit to avoid being ticketed.

Rather than look for street parking, I generally pull into the most central and handy pay-and-display parking lot I can

# Resources from Rick Steves

## Begin Your Trip at www.RickSteves.com

My mobile-friendly **website** is *the* place to explore Europe. You'll find thousands of fun articles, videos, photos, and radio interviews; a wealth of money-saving tips for planning your dream trip; my travel talks and blog; and guidebook updates (www.ricksteves.com/update).

Our **Travel Forum** is an immense collection of message boards, where our travel-savvy community answers questions and shares personal travel experiences—and our well-traveled staff chimes in when they can help.

Our **online Travel Store** offers bags and accessories designed to help you travel smarter and lighter. These include my popular bags (which I live out of four months a year), money belts, totes, toiletries kits, adapters, guidebooks, planning maps, and more.

Choosing the right **rail pass** for your trip can drive you nutty. Our website will help you find the perfect fit for your itinerary and your budget: We offer easy, one-stop shopping for rail passes, seat reservations, and point-to-point tickets.

## Guidebooks, Video, Audio Europe, and Tours

**Books:** *Rick Steves Best of England* is just one of many books in my series on European travel, which includes country and city guidebooks, Snapshot guides (excerpted chapters from my country guides), Pocket Guides (full-color little books on big cities), and my budget-travel skills handbook, *Rick Steves Europe Through the Back Door*. My phrase books are practical and budget-oriented. A more complete list of my titles appears near the end of this book.

**Video:** My public television series, *Rick Steves' Europe,* covers Europe from top to bottom with over 100 half-hour episodes. To watch full episodes online for free, see www.ricksteves.com/tv. Or to raise your travel I.Q. with video versions of our popular classes (including my talks on travel skills, packing smart, most European countries, and European art), see www.ricksteves.com/travel-talks.

**Audio:** My weekly public radio show, *Travel with Rick Steves,* features interviews with travel experts from around the world. A complete archive is available at www.ricksteves.com/radio, and much of this audio content is available for free, along with my audio tours of Europe's (and England's) top sights, through my **Rick Steves Audio Europe** app (see page 27).

**Tours:** Want to travel with greater efficiency and less stress? We organize tours with more than three dozen itineraries reaching the best destinations in this book...and beyond. You'll enjoy great guides and a fun but small group of travel partners. For all the details, and to get our tour catalog and a free Rick Steves Tour Experience DVD, visit www.ricksteves.com or call us at 425/608-4217.

find. To pay and display, feed change into a machine, receive a timed ticket, and display it on the dashboard or stick it to the driver's-side window.

Some parking garages (a.k.a. "car parks") are totally automated and record your car's license plate with a camera when you enter. You'll need to enter the first few letters or digits of your license plate number (which the Brits call a "number plate" or just "vehicle registration") at the payment machine when you pay before exiting.

Most parking payment machines in larger towns accept credit cards with a chip, but it's smart to keep coins handy for machines and parking meters that don't.

# Flights

The best comparison search engine for both international and intra-European flights is www.kayak.com. For inexpensive flights within Europe, try www.skyscanner.com.

**Flying to Europe:** Start looking for international flights at least 4 to 6 months before your trip, especially for peak-season travel. Off-season tickets can usually be purchased a month or so in advance. Depending on your itinerary, it can be effi-cient to fly into one city and out of another.

**Flying Within Europe:** If you're considering a train ride that's more than five hours long, a flight may save you both time and money. When comparing your options, factor in the time it takes to get to the airport and how early you'll need to arrive to check in.

These days you can fly within Europe on major airlines affordably for around $100 a flight. Or you go with a budget airline such as EasyJet, Ryanair, or CityJet. But be aware of the potential drawbacks and restrictions with budget carriers: non-refundable and nonchangeable tickets, minimal or nonexistent customer service, pricey and time-consuming treks to secondary airports, and stingy baggage allowances with steep overage fees. If you're traveling with lots of luggage, a cheap flight can quickly become a bad deal. Read the small print before you book.

**Flying to the US and Canada:** Because security is extra tight for flights to the US, be sure to give yourself plenty of time at the airport. It's also important to charge your electronic devices before you board because security checks may require you to turn them on (see www.tsa.gov for the latest rules).

# HOLIDAYS AND FESTIVALS

This list includes selected festivals in major cities, plus national holidays observed throughout England. Many sights and banks close on national holidays—keep this in mind when planning your itinerary. Before planning a trip around a festival, make sure you verify the dates by checking the festival's website or the British national tourist office (www.visitbritain.com).

| | |
|---|---|
| Mid-Feb | Jorvik Viking Festival, York (www.jorvik-viking-festival.co.uk) |
| Early March | Literature Festival, Bath (www.bathlitfest.org.uk) |
| March/April | Easter Sunday and Monday |
| Early May | Bank Holiday |
| Early-mid-May | Jazz Festival, Keswick (www.keswickjazzfestival.co.uk) |
| Late May | Chelsea Flower Show, London (www.rhs.org.uk/chelsea) |
| Late May | Bank Holiday |
| Late May-early June | International Music Festival, Bath (www.bathmusicfest.org.uk) |
| Late May-early June | Fringe Festival, Bath (www.bathfringe.co.uk) |
| Early June | Beer Festival, Keswick (www.keswickbeerfestival.co.uk) |
| Early-mid-June | Trooping the Colour, London (Queen's birthday parade; www.trooping-the-colour.co.uk) |
| Late June | Royal Ascot Horse Race, Ascot (www.ascot.co.uk) |
| Late June-early July | Wimbledon Tennis Championship, London (www.wimbledon.org) |
| Mid-July | Early Music Festival, York (www.ncem.co.uk) |
| Late July-early Aug | Cambridge Folk Festival (www.cambridgefolkfestival.co.uk) |
| Late Aug | Notting Hill Carnival, London (www.thenottinghillcarnival.com) |
| Late Aug | Bank Holiday |
| Mid-Sept | London Fashion Week (www.londonfashionweek.co.uk) |
| Late Sept | Jane Austen Festival, Bath (www.janeausten.co.uk) |
| Late Sept | York Food and Drink Festival (www.yorkfoodfestival.com) |
| Nov 5 | Bonfire Night, or Guy Fawkes Night |
| Dec 24-26 | Christmas holidays |

# CONVERSIONS AND CLIMATE

## Numbers and Stumblers

• Europeans write a few of their numbers differently than we do: 1 = $1$, 4 = $4$, 7 = $7$.

• In Europe, dates appear as day/month/year; Christmas is 25/12.

• Commas are decimal points and decimals are commas. A dollar and a half is $1,50, one thousand is 1.000.

• When counting with fingers, start with your thumb. If you hold up your first finger to request one item, you'll probably get two.

- What Americans call the second floor of a building is the first floor in Europe.
- On escalators and moving sidewalks, Europeans keep the left "lane" open for passing. Keep to the right.

## Clothing and Shoe Sizes

Shoppers can use these US-to-European comparisons as general guidelines, but note that no conversion is perfect. For info on VAT refunds, see page 372.

**Women:** For clothing or shoe sizes, add 30 (US shirt size 10 = European size 40; US shoe size 8 = European size 38-39).

**Men:** For shirts, multiply by 2 and add about 8 (US size 15 = European size 38). For jackets and suits, add 10. For shoes, add 32-34.

**Children:** For clothing, subtract 1-2 sizes for small children and subtract 4 for juniors. For shoes up to size 13, add 16-18, and for sizes 1 and up, add 30-32.

## Metric Conversions

A **kilogram** equals 1,000 grams and about 2.2 pounds. One hundred **grams** (a common unit of sale at markets) is about a quarter-pound.

One **liter** is about a quart, or almost four to a gallon.

A **kilometer** is six-tenths of a mile. To convert kilometers to miles, cut the kilometers in half and add back 10 percent of the original (120 km: 60 + 12 = 72 miles). One **meter** is 39 inches.

Using the **Celsius** scale, 0°C equals 32°F. To roughly convert Celsius to Fahrenheit, double the number and add 30. For weather, 28°C is 82°F—perfect. For health, 37°C is just right. At a launderette, 30°C is cold, 40°C is warm (default setting), and 60°C is hot.

## Imperial Weights and Measures

England hasn't completely gone metric. Driving distances and speed limits are measured in miles. Beer is sold as pints, and a person's weight is measured in stone.

1 stone = 14 pounds
1 British pint = 1.2 US pints
1 imperial gallon = 1.2 US gallons (about 4.5 liters)

## England's Climate

The first line is the average daily high; second line, average daily low; third line, average days without rain. For more detailed weather statistics for destinations in this book (as well as the rest of the world), check www.worldclimate.com.

### London

| J | F | M | A | M | J | J | A | S | O | N | D |
|---|---|---|---|---|---|---|---|---|---|---|---|
| 43° | 44° | 50° | 56° | 62° | 69° | 71° | 71° | 65° | 58° | 50° | 45° |
| 36° | 36° | 38° | 42° | 47° | 53° | 56° | 56° | 52° | 46° | 42° | 38° |
| 16 | 15 | 20 | 18 | 19 | 19 | 19 | 20 | 17 | 18 | 15 | 16 |

### York

| J | F | M | A | M | J | J | A | S | O | N | D |
|---|---|---|---|---|---|---|---|---|---|---|---|
| 43° | 44° | 49° | 55° | 61° | 67° | 70° | 69° | 64° | 57° | 49° | 45° |
| 33° | 34° | 36° | 40° | 44° | 50° | 54° | 53° | 50° | 44° | 39° | 36° |
| 14 | 13 | 18 | 17 | 18 | 16 | 16 | 17 | 16 | 16 | 13 | 14 |

# Packing Checklist

## Clothing

- ❑ 5 shirts: long- & short-sleeve
- ❑ 2 pairs pants or skirt
- ❑ 1 pair shorts or capris
- ❑ 5 pairs underwear & socks
- ❑ 1 pair walking shoes
- ❑ Sweater or fleece top
- ❑ Rainproof jacket with hood
- ❑ Tie or scarf
- ❑ Swimsuit
- ❑ Sleepwear

## Money

- ❑ Debit card
- ❑ Credit card(s)
- ❑ Hard cash ($20 bills)
- ❑ Money belt or neck wallet

## Documents & Travel Info

- ❑ Passport
- ❑ Airline reservations
- ❑ Rail pass/train reservations
- ❑ Car-rental voucher
- ❑ Driver's license
- ❑ Student ID, hostel card, etc.
- ❑ Photocopies of all the above
- ❑ Hotel confirmations
- ❑ Insurance details
- ❑ Guidebooks & maps
- ❑ Notepad & pen
- ❑ Journal

## Toiletries Kit

- ❑ Toiletries
- ❑ Medicines & vitamins
- ❑ First-aid kit
- ❑ Glasses/contacts/sunglasses
  (with prescriptions)
- ❑ Earplugs
- ❑ Packet of tissues (for WC)

## Miscellaneous

- ❑ Daypack
- ❑ Sealable plastic baggies
- ❑ Laundry soap
- ❑ Clothesline
- ❑ Sewing kit
- ❑ Travel alarm/watch

## Electronics

- ❑ Smartphone or mobile phone
- ❑ Camera & related gear
- ❑ Tablet/ereader/media player
- ❑ Laptop & flash drive
- ❑ Earbuds or headphones
- ❑ Chargers
- ❑ Plug adapters

## Optional Extras

- ❑ Flipflops or slippers
- ❑ Mini-umbrella or poncho
- ❑ Travel hairdryer
- ❑ Belt
- ❑ Hat (for sun or cold)
- ❑ Picnic supplies
- ❑ Water bottle
- ❑ Fold-up tote bag
- ❑ Small flashlight
- ❑ Small binoculars
- ❑ Small towel or washcloth
- ❑ Inflatable pillow
- ❑ Tiny lock
- ❑ Address list (to mail postcards)
- ❑ Postcards/photos from home
- ❑ Extra passport photos
- ❑ Good book

# INDEX

# MAP INDEX

# Start your trip at

*Our website enhances this book and turns*

### Explore Europe

At ricksteves.com you can browse through thousands of articles, videos, photos and radio interviews, plus find a wealth of money-saving travel tips for planning your dream trip. And with our mobile-friendly website, you can easily access all this great travel information anywhere you go.

### TV Shows

Preview the places you'll visit by watching entire half-hour episodes of Rick Steves' Europe (choose from all 100 shows) on-demand, for free.

# ricksteves.com

*your travel dreams into affordable reality*

## Radio Interviews

Enjoy ready access to Rick's vast library of radio interviews covering travel tips and cultural insights that relate specifically to your Europe travel plans.

## Travel Forums

Learn, ask, share! Our online community of savvy travelers is a great resource for first-time travelers to Europe, as well as seasoned pros. You'll find forums on each country, plus travel tips and restaurant/hotel reviews. You can even ask one of our well-traveled staff to chime in with an opinion.

## Travel News

Subscribe to our free Travel News e-newsletter, and get monthly updates from Rick on what's happening in Europe.

# Audio Europe™

## Rick's Free Travel App

Get your FREE Rick Steves Audio Europe™ app to enjoy…

- Dozens of self-guided tours of Europe's top museums, sights and historic walks
- Hundreds of tracks filled with cultural insights and sightseeing tips from Rick's radio interviews
- All organized into handy geographic playlists
- For Apple and Android

With Rick whispering in your ear, Europe gets even better.

## Find out more at ricksteves.com

# Pack Light and Right

*Gear up for your next adventure at ricksteves.com*

### Light Luggage

Pack light and right with Rick Steves' affordable, custom-designed rolling carry-on bags, backpacks, day packs and shoulder bags.

### Accessories

From packing cubes to moneybelts and beyond, Rick has personally selected the travel goodies that will help your trip go smoother.

# Rick Steves has

# great tours, too!

## *with minimum stress*

interesting places with great guides and small groups of 28 or less. We follow Rick's favorite itineraries, ride in comfy buses, stay in family-run hotels, and bring you intimately close to the Europe you've traveled so far to see. Most importantly, we take away the logistical headaches so you can focus on the fun.

nearly half of them repeat customers—along with us on four dozen different itineraries, from Ireland to Italy to Istanbul. Is a Rick Steves tour the right fit for your travel dreams? Find out at ricksteves.com, where you can also get Rick's latest tour catalog and free Tour Experience DVD.

Europe is best experienced with happy travel partners. We hope you can join us.

### Join the fun

This year we'll take 25,000 free-spirited travelers—

## See our itineraries at ricksteves.com

## BEST OF GUIDES

Best of France
Best of Germany
Best of Ireland
Best of Italy
Best of Spain

## EUROPE GUIDES

Best of Europe
Eastern Europe
Europe Through the Back Door
Mediterranean Cruise Ports
Northern European Cruise Ports

## COUNTRY GUIDES

Croatia & Slovenia
England
France
Germany
Great Britain
Ireland
Italy
Portugal
Scandinavia
Scotland
Spain
Switzerland

## CITY & REGIONAL GUIDES

Amsterdam & the Netherlands
Belgium: Bruges, Brussels, Antwerp & Ghent
Barcelona
Budapest
Florence & Tuscany
Greece: Athens & the Peloponnese
Istanbul
London
Paris
Prague & the Czech Republic
Provence & the French Riviera
Rome
Venice
Vienna, Salzburg & Tirol

## SNAPSHOT GUIDES

Basque Country: Spain & France
Berlin
Copenhagen & the Best of Denmark
Dublin
Dubrovnik
Edinburgh
Hill Towns of Central Italy
Italy's Cinque Terre
Krakow, Warsaw & Gdansk
Lisbon

Nearly all Rick Steves guides are available as ebooks. Check with your favorite bookseller. Rick Steves guidebooks are published by Avalon Travel, an imprint of Perseus Books, a Hachette Book Group company.

# Maximize your travel skills with a good guidebook.

Loire Valley
Madrid & Toledo
Milan & the Italian Lakes District
Naples & the Amalfi Coast
Northern Ireland
Norway
Sevilla, Granada & Southern Spain
St. Petersburg, Helsinki & Tallinn
Stockholm

## POCKET GUIDES
Amsterdam
Athens
Barcelona
Florence
London
Munich & Salzburg
Paris
Prague
Rome
Venice
Vienna

## TRAVEL CULTURE
Europe 101
European Christmas
European Easter
Postcards from Europe
Travel as a Political Act

## *RICK STEVES' EUROPE* DVDs
12 New Shows 2015–2016
Austria & the Alps

The Complete Collection 2000-2016
Eastern Europe
England & Wales
European Christmas
European Travel Skills & Specials
France
Germany, BeNeLux & More
Greece, Turkey & Portugal
The Holy Land: Israelis & Palestinians Today
Iran
Ireland & Scotland
Italy's Cities
Italy's Countryside
Scandinavia
Spain
Travel Extras

## PHRASE BOOKS & DICTIONARIES
French
French, Italian & German
German
Italian
Portuguese
Spanish

## PLANNING MAPS
Britain, Ireland & London
Europe
France & Paris
Germany, Austria & Switzerland
Ireland
Italy
Spain & Portugal

**RickSteves.com**  **@RickSteves**

Rick Steves books are available at bookstores
and through online booksellers.

# PHOTO CREDITS

Avalon Travel
An imprint of Perseus Books
A Hachette Book Group company
1700 Fourth Street
Berkeley, CA 94710

Printed in Canada by Friesens

First printing November 2016

ISBN 978-1-63121-321-2
ISSN 2473-3849

For the latest on Rick's lectures, guidebooks, tours, public radio show, and public television series, contact Rick Steves' Europe, 130 Fourth Avenue North, Edmonds, WA 98020, 425/771-8303, www.ricksteves.com, rick@ricksteves.com.

## RICK STEVES' EUROPE
**Special Publications Manager:** Risa Laib
**Managing Editor:** Jennifer Madison Davis
**Project Editor:** Suzanne Kotz
**Editorial & Production Assistant:** Jessica Shaw
**Graphic Content Director:** Sandra Hundacker
**Maps & Graphics:** David C. Hoerlein, Mary Rostad

## AVALON TRAVEL
**Editorial Director:** Kevin McLain
**Senior Editor and Series Manager:** Madhu Prasher
**Editor:** Jamie Andrade
**Associate Editor:** Sierra Machado
**Copy Editor:** Naomi Adler Dancis
**Proofreader:** Kelly Lydick
**Indexer:** Stephen Callahan
**Interior Design & Layout:** McGuire Barber Design
**Cover Design:** Kimberly Glyder Design
**Maps & Graphics:** Kat Bennett